NEW THOUGHT
or
A MODERN RELIGIOUS
APPROACH

*The Philosophy of Health, Happiness, and
Prosperity*

Other Books by the Same Author

Milton and Servetus
The Theory of Logical Expression
The Modernity of Milton
The Plaster Saint
The Religion of the Occident
Wanton Sinner
Church Wealth and Business Income
The Essene Heritage
The Great Tax Fraud
The Churches: Their Riches, Revenues, and Immunities
Praise the Lord for Tax Exemption
When Parochial Schools Close
Tax Revolt: U.S.A.!
The Federal Reserve and Our Manipulated Dollar
The Religious Empire
The Story of Christian Origins
How to Defend Yourself against the Internal Revenue Service
The Essence of Jefferson
How to Establish a Trust and Reduce Taxation
The Essene-Christian Faith
How You Can Save Money on Taxes This Year
The Continuing Tax Rebellion
The Best of Martin A. Larson
The IRS vs. The Middle Class
Jefferson: Magnificent Populist

NEW THOUGHT
or
A MODERN RELIGIOUS APPROACH

The Philosophy of Health, Happiness, and
Prosperity

by

Martin A. Larson

Philosophical Library
New York

Library of Congress Cataloging in Publication Data

Larson, Martin Alfred, 1897-
  New thought.
  Bibliography: p.
  1. New Thought.   I. Title.
BF639.L384   1984   289.9'8   84-7637
ISBN 0-8022-2464-4

Manufactured in the United States of America.

This work is dedicated to all those seeking truth in a religion that meets the needs of modern life. We pay special tribute to the memory of such forerunners as Michael Servetus, Emanuel Swedenborg, Phineas Quimby, Warren Felt Evans, Horatio W. Dresser, Ralph Waldo Trine, Emma Curtis Hopkins, Charles Fillmore, Ernest S. Holmes, Thomas Troward, Joseph Murphy and a host of others who have contributed their ideas and talents to the movement known as New Thought, a philosophy of health, happiness, and prosperity.

Contents

INTRODUCTION

The reader must understand that New Thought is basically a revolt against the old and conventional dogmas of the historic religion of the Western World. As my old friend, Charles S. Braden, indicated in his book *Spirits in Rebellion*, published in 1963, its spokesmen are in rebellion, although many of them regard themselves rather as the true proponents of original Christianity. And there certainly have been conflicts and persecution; Michael Servetus, who, so far as I know, was the first to proclaim the theology and Christology which is at the core of New Thought and actually constitutes its foundation, was burned at the stake in Geneva, Switzerland, in 1553, under the dictatorship of John Calvin. When Swedenborg adopted a similar ideology shortly after 1745, he did not dare make himself known as the author of his books on religion, all of which were written anonymously in Latin and published in foreign countries. When his authorship of these finally became known, this man, then about eighty years of age, was forced to leave Sweden under the threat of prosecution; an attempt was even made to commit him to an insane asylum. Almost 150 years elapsed before his greatness was recognized and he was given a state funeral in the cathedral at Upsala; but even then the honor accorded him was because of his contributions to science and philosophy, and not in the least for his religious innovations.

However, in the United States, a more congenial and a freer religious climate was established by our Founding Fathers; under the concepts of church-state separation and freedom of conscience, dissidents could no longer be prosecuted after 1790 for deviations from generally accepted dogmas. The situation developed, not because of religious tolerance, but because a great variety of religious groups came to this country in search of liberty and the freedom to worship according to conscience. Had any one of these been numerous or powerful enough to establish itself as a state church, there is no doubt that the bigotry and persecution so prevalent in Europe would have been transferred to these shores; and in some places, especially in Virginia (Episcopalian), Massachusetts (Presbyterian), and Maryland (Roman Catholic), attempts were made to enforce religious uniformity under the coercive power of government. However, reluctantly enough, since all were national minorities, the members of these diverse groups agreed that it would be better for themselves, as well as all concerned, to be free of control from others or the state, even if the condition of such liberty had to be based on a surrender of judicial power or any expectation of support from the public purse. Thus, the First Amendment to the Constitution declares that "Congress shall make no law respecting an establishment of religion or prohibiting the free exercise thereof." In short, every denomination would have complete freedom to worship as it pleased, but must be completely private, self-dependent, and without coercive power over others.

However, we must realize that whereas the various sects differed distinctly among themselves on certain points, none denied such basic doctrines or dogmas of Christianity as the Trinity, the Virgin Birth of Jesus, his bodily resurrection and ascent into heaven, his death as an atonement and sacrifice for humanity otherwise lost by reason of original sin, the existence of a physical heaven and hell, the necessity of holy communion, and the belief that Jesus Christ would one day return to earth to conduct the Last Judgment and inaugurate the Kingdom of Heaven, or, as an alternative, that he would awaken those who had died in the faith and transport them into the celestial realms. There were also other historic dogmas which were generally accepted among the otherwise warring sects.

Nevertheless, even though they could not, either singly or in combination, send dissidents to prison or the stake, they could and did exercise great influence upon public opinion. Even such men as Thomas Jefferson strictly forbade private correspondents to divulge the contents of personal letters which discussed religion; and this was true even during a time when only a minority of the people professed any religious commitment at all—as was the case at the beginning of the 19th century. So fierce and powerful were the clerics that they could publicly condemn Jefferson as The Antichrist in the White House.

Furthermore, very nearly all the schools, and especially the institutions of higher learning, were established and controlled by religious denominations well into the 1800s. The University of Virginia, which opened its doors to students about 1824, was, I believe, the first to declare itself a secular institution which would regard religion as an historic phenomenon to be studied objectively rather than a dogma to be inculcated into the minds of students as infallible truth.

When the deist-rationalist Thomas Paine published *The Age of Reason* about 1795—which rejected the entire Bible as a human document filled with error—this was read avidly and widely by many who had no religious affiliation; however, the condemnation to which he was subjected was so effective that even children followed him in the streets and threw stones at him; and when he died, his enemies dug up his bones and scattered the remnants to the four winds.

When New Thought emerged on these shores, first with the Shakers and then with such proponents as Phineas Parkhurst Quimby, its followers did not lay themselves open to such assaults. Like Swedenborg, they accepted the Scriptures and proclaimed them to be divine revelations; but they denied their literal meanings by a method called Spiritual Interpretation, by which they discovered new and different connotations in countless passages; and by this technique, they abolished the entire doctrinal structure of historical or orthodox religion and supplanted it with a totally new and differing body of faith and belief. All this is the subject of this book; and we wish merely to say at this point that this has been the prevailing method of New Thought. The Bible is accepted as the Truth, but with meanings at such variance from those held by the orthodox as to constitute a complete repudiation. New Thought has, therefore, in a sense and in its own way, accomplished an objective somewhat similar to that of the rationalists.

It should also be noted that a number of famous men not specifically identified with religion as such adopted and proclaimed a Swedenborgian-New Thought ideology: among these in America were Theodore Parker, the Brook Farm group, Ralph Waldo Emerson, and Henry James, Senior. Such individuals as Samuel Taylor Coleridge and the Brownings were also Swedenborgians.

At first the Shakers were condemned, persecuted, and ridiculed; but as their numbers and affluence increased, such enmity gradually subsided. Quimby was called a charlatan; but he returned at least as good as he received, and his success placed him on a pedestal from which he could not be removed. The same was true of the Swedenborgian minister, philosopher, and author Warren Felt Evans.

When Christian Science began achieving its extraordinary success, it was attacked bitterly, not only by the clergy and the medical profession, but also by objective scholars who sought only facts; it was also exposed by disillusioned ex-members. It was also torn by internal dissensions, partly because of its authoritative structure and by its suppression of free inquiry by its members.

However, it was not long before a number of very gifted individuals began publishing books proclaiming the principles of New Thought in an atmosphere of complete freedom. Although their writings were extremely popular—Ralph Waldo Trine's *In Tune with the Infinite* sold millions of copies—and exercised enormous influence, they made no attempt to establish any church or permanent organization. Such teachers as Emma Curtis Hopkins conducted two-week classes attended by a thousand students in various cities—each of whom paid $50—but she never tried to create a church-congregation. Nevertheless, she was extremely influential upon the Fillmores, Nona Brooks, and Ernest Holmes, all of whom *did* create the bases for churches. But even these people did not originally intend to do this; when churches finally came into existence as a result of their efforts, this was almost by accident or by spontaneous and popular demand.

Although one could collect a small library of books which criticize or condemn Christian Science, I know of none which attacks the modern New Thought movement or any of its proponents. These people welcome debate and discussion and stand ready at any time to meet any adverse opinions head on in public or in private; they utilize skillfully many passages in Scripture which are in agreement with their teachings; and, probably most important of all, those who are in basic disagreement find it advantageous to ignore the movement as if it did not exist; and today it is obvious that thousands of ministers who belong, for example, to churches which are members of National and World Council of Churches have accepted as their own—perhaps in private—some of the New Thought theses; thus they cannot, in good conscience, attack them; and even though they do not publicly endorse them, they do not condemn what they have accepted in their own hearts. How many Lutheran, Episcopal, or Presbyterian clerics today really believe in all of the Thirty-Nine Articles or in a doctrine according to which the great bulk of the human race is condemned to everlasting torture in hell simply because that is their predestined fate? Thus, the principles of New Thought have penetrated all religious communions and have ameliorated their teachings and humanized their theology.

We should note that the influence of New Thought extends far beyond the membership of its churches. Unity, for example, sends out 85,000,000 pieces of mail annually, only a very small portion of which goes to its 409 churches, which have perhaps 50,000 members. Such popular writers and preachers as Norman Vincent Peale and Robert Schuller belong distinctly to the New Thought cycle. Secular writers like Dale Carnegie who explain how to make friends and influence people should be classified in the same or a similar category, as should, for example, the writings of Maxwell Maltz, whose *Psycho-Cybernetics* is very popular in New Thought circles and elsewhere.

Nor is this by any means all. A great many other writers, many of them popular in New Thought, continue to write one book after another, some of which have sales running into the hundreds of thousands.

It was my hope some years ago that Charles Braden would one day cooperate with me in a joint authorship of this volume; however, he was stricken with cancer and this lovable, self-sacrificing man gradually lost his strength, subsided at last into a coma, and died several years ago.

I would note also that his classic *Spirits in Rebellion*, found everywhere in New Thought churches, published in 1963, has precisely the same attitude and purpose which I have striven to maintain in this study: that is, complete objectivity, without bias or prejudice of any kind, for or against anyone or anything. However, there are some differences between his work and this one—his was written more than twenty years ago, and tremendous developments have occurred since then. He did not include Christian Science in his book, since he had written another dealing with this; he did not go back as far as I do in the treatment of sources; but he covered many facets of the movement which I do not. Furthermore, he focussed largely upon the historical events and the personalities involved, whereas my principal attention is given to the teachings of New Thought theorists, teachers, and organizations.

Nor have I attempted to summarize most of the existing New Thought literature or authors. The special collection of such works in the Unity Library contains more than 6,000 volumes; obviously an entire lifetime would not suffice to complete a study and analysis of all these; nor would an encyclopedia be large enough to contain the results. We believe, however, that we have presented a cross-section of what is most important and representative in New Thought. I know of no other work which has attempted to accomplish a similar objective.

It is my hope, therefore, that this treatise will prove an acceptable and updated addition to the research done by Dr. Braden. I would not hope for anything more rewarding than that.

Martin A. Larson

NEW THOUGHT
or
A MODERN RELIGIOUS APPROACH

The Philosophy of Health, Happiness, and Prosperity

Chapter 1

SWEDENBORG: THE FOUNTAINHEAD

I. AN AMAZING PERSONALITY

Among most people, even the educated, the name of Emanuel Swedenborg evokes only a curious smile, or no response at all; for he is generally unknown or regarded simply as a self-deluded dreamer, or, perhaps, a literal madman, who could not possibly have left any serious or permanent imprint upon the sands of time.

The fact is, nevertheless, that this man has exercised enormous influence, direct and indirect, upon the moral, religious, and intellectual development of the Western world. More than anyone else, he was the catalyst who shattered the age-old creeds and dogmas of Medieval and Reformation Christianity and thereby ushered into being, not only the potent ideology known as New Thought, but also many of the elements which have become increasingly conspicuous in various large and powerful denominations.

Emanuel Swedenborg is surely without parallel in the modern world; for more than thirty years he was a civil servant who performed all the duties of his office faithfully, meanwhile producing scientific and philosophical treatises vast in scope and astonishingly creative in content. He was an indefatigable worker who labored without fanfare and little public notice. He lived a long and, for the most part, a seemingly unruffled existence. Approaching the age of sixty, already with immortalizing accomplishments behind him, he

1

embarked upon what was to be his overwhelming mission in life, in which he continued for more than twenty-five years: the revelation of the unseen, resulting from his constant companionship with the denizens of the spirit-world, all of which he describes in detail, especially in his *Spiritual Diary*.

In all outward aspects, the benign old gentleman could have passed for an orthodox and well-educated member of conventional upper-class society; but a dinner companion might well have been astonished, during a discussion dealing with some abstruse subject, to hear him say quite casually: "Oh, yes, just the other day I had a long conversation on this very point with Aristotle [or some other ancient] and he agrees with me...." In due course, his friends and acquaintances accepted such remarks without comment or surprise. In the meantime, the seer moved in the best circles: he was often the guest of nobility and royalty, including Queen Ulrica Eleonora, by whom his family was ennobled; early in life, he was the confidant of that wild, unbridled ruler, King Charles XII; and during his travels abroad, he became the friend and correspondent of various famous scientists and savants.

Little could the ordinary observer suspect what was going on in the mind of this cultivated scholar, an inveterate bachelor, whose white wig was sometimes awry, who lived frugally and labored incessantly, composing tome after tome, which were published anonymously and in Latin, either in Holland or in England. Under this protective covering, he wrote down his sweeping condemnations and denunciations of scores of individuals, and particularly their religious beliefs and ethical practices and motivations. It was many years before the contents of his lucubrations were identified as his, and secretiveness was indeed important; for when his teachings began to circulate and to gain disciples in Sweden, he barely escaped commitment to an insane asylum, in spite of his extraordinary accomplishments in government, science, and philosophy and in spite of his noble family and venerable age. When death came to him in 1772 at the age of eighty-four, it was in obscurity and in a foreign land. It required his countrymen almost 140 years to recognize his achievements; and the homage they paid him even then, when his remains were restored to his native land and enshrined among the great, was a tribute neither to the theologian nor to the religious reformer, but only to the philosopher and the scientist.

It is impossible accurately to estimate the intensity or the extent of Swedenborgian influence upon individuals, churches, movements, or general thinking. *The World Almanac* of 1964 lists only 58 Swedenborgian congregations with 5,705 members in the United States; but this measures only a minute fraction of its total impact. It is certain that the number, quality, and variety of major minds which have been fascinated by the Swedish seer are indeed impressive and extraordinary. Some may be surprised to learn that Helen Keller, whose book *My Religion* has enjoyed a wide popularity, was for many years a devout and fervent communicant of the New Church. Thomas Carlyle was deeply impressed by Swedenborg's philosophy and his *Sartor Resartus* is drenched in it. Henry James, father of the novelist of the same name and of the famous philosopher William, was a devoted Swedenborgian theologian who transmitted much of his thinking to both of his renowned sons; the celebrated *Varieties of Religious Experience*, which is an attempt to establish a more rational theology, teems with it. In a private letter, now in the library of the Swedenborg Society of London, Coleridge conferred the highest encomiums upon the Swedish theologian and declared that he devoted all the time he could spare to the study of his works. Such men as Tennyson, Patmore, Ruskin, Drummond, O.W. Holmes, Thoreau, Goethe, Heine, and others of comparable stature absorbed in large measure the Swedenborgian teachings and served as the means of transmission by which these have become an integral element in Western culture and ideology. Mark Twain's *Captain Stormfield's Visit to Heaven* is a fantasy based on Swedenborgian sources. The Brownings, especially Elizabeth Barrett, referred to themselves as "we Swedenborgians." Balzac, a devoted student, wrote concerning Swedenborg: "His theology is sublime; and his religion is the only one a superior mind can accept."[1]

Swedenborg's ideas made deep inroads into American culture through the medium of the socialist-liberal-Unitarian coalition which established the communal experiment known as Brook Farm, near West Roxbury, Massachusetts, in 1841. Dr. William Ellery Channing, who was the prime mover in this enterprise, was supported by his son, William Francis Channing, and even more by his nephew, William N. Channing. After the death of the elder Channing in 1842, this nephew, who was also a famous Unitarian minister, became the leading spokesman for the community, especially after it became a Fourierist phalanx at the beginning of 1844, when *The Dial* ceased publication and was successively replaced by *The Present*, *The Phalanx*, and finally *The Harbinger*—in which a socialist society was equated with the Second Coming of Christ on earth. In April 1844, several of the Brook Farm men took part in the national Fourierist convention, of which William H. Channing was the Corresponding Secretary. Among the leaders, in addition to the three Channings, were Albert Brisbane, Horace Greeley, Charles Dana, Margaret Fuller, Adin Ballou, George Ripley, Parke Godwin, James Russell Lowell, John S. Dwight, John Greenleaf Whittier, and Henry James.

Between 1845 and 1849, *The Harbinger*, from the precincts of Brook Farm, proclaimed the social, economic, and theological doctrines espoused by the "Brahmins," who used these as a rostrum from which, in the words of William H. Channing, "to indoctrinate the whole people of the United States with the principles of associative unity,"[2] an expression used by the Fourierists to describe their philosophy.

As Fourierism began to subside after 1845 amidst its multiple failures, a new development occurred at Brook Farm; its leaders, especially Charles Dana and William H. Channing, became ardent Swedenborgians. If they could have created an American state religion, it would have been Swedenborgianism. Strangely enough, they—like the Shakers—considered the teachings of the rugged Swedish exponent of free enterprise in practical harmony with socialist collectivism. Even in *The Present*, Channing had propagated the doctrines of the New Church; in *The Phalanx*, he became more and more insistent in advancing its ideas; and *The Harbinger* contains between thirty and forty articles devoted entirely to the promulgation of its ideology. It was about this time also that Ralph Waldo Emerson—who was at least a semi-Swedenborgian—composed his famous essay entitled "Swedenborg: or The Mystic."

The penetration of his theology into Unitarian thought is further illustrated in the case of Theodore Parker, upon whom the mantle of William E. Channing fell after 1842. Parker repeatedly addresses his impersonal deity in terms which could have no source other than the theological cosmology of Swedenborg. "Thou Central Fire, the Radiant Light of All," he exclaims in passages which equate the Great Sun with God. In another, after setting forth the doctrine of universal influx, he declares: "Thus it is that human souls communicate with the great central Fire and Light of all the world, the Loadstone of the Universe, and thus recruit their powers, grow young again, and so are blessed and strong."[3] The sermons and "prayers" of Parker are studded with Swedenborgian concepts, which have thus and through the writings of William H. Channing and Emerson become an integral element in all Unitarian thinking, and, to a lesser extent, that of all educated Americans.

The penetration of the Swedish sage into modern thought, culture, and religion is succinctly summarized by Emerson: "This man, who appeared to his contemporaries as a visionary...begins to spread himself into the minds of thousands...A colossal soul, he lies vast abroad on his times, uncomprehended." And again: "The most remarkable step in the religious history of recent ages is that made by the genius of Swedenborg.... These truths, passing out of his system into general circulation, are now met with every day, qualifying the views and creeds of all churches and of men of no church."[4]

And this is the simple truth: for Swedenborg's ethics and metaphysics have permeated and profoundly modified the thinking of millions who have never even heard his name. We may say that, as a revealer, he surpassed Zoroaster; as the innovator of a reconstructed religion, only Pythagoras is his rival; as a creative and scientific philosopher, he ranks with Aristotle; as an original theologian, his name belongs with those of Origen and Augustine; as a practical inventor and scientist, he is not at all inferior to Leonardo da Vinci.

Taken as a whole, his mind was more capacious and universal than that possessed by any of these.

A number of years ago, A Believe-It-Or-Not Ripley cartoon[5] summarized Swedenborg's activities and achievements as inventor, botanist, zoologist, chemist, assayer, machinist, cabinet maker, bookbinder, lens grinder, musician, organist, legislator, psychist, clockmaker, linguist, hydrographer, editor, poet, publisher, mining engineer. He was an authority on blast furnaces, glass manufacture, and termite control; the author of the first Swedish textbook in Algebra, and a practical innovator in educational theory. He devised the first threshing machine; and he made detailed sketches of innumerable inventions, many of which have long since come into common use. Early in life, he calculated an elaborate method for determining the earth's longitude by the lunar orbit. He was a diplomat, a financier, a political economist, a practical statesman of the highest order, and a member of the Swedish Riksdag. He was a mathematician, astronomer, metaphysician, and neurophysiologist. He could easily qualify as a medical expert. His acute and voluminous studies in anatomy were so advanced—especially those on the brain—as to be incomprehensible to his contemporaries; among other things, he discovered the function of the ductless glands and the fact that the brain animates synchronously with the lungs; and he made important discoveries concerning the circulation of the blood. He was the first to explain the nature of the Milky Way and to promulgate the Nebular Hypothesis, later expounded by Immanuel Kant and elaborated by Laplace. In geology, cosmology, physics, metallurgy, minerology, and smelting technology his contributions were immense and practical. He added substantially to knowledge concerning atomic theory and the science of radioactivity. He was the first to investigate the meanings of dream symbolisms and to describe the three levels upon which the human psyche operates, later elaborated by Warren Felt Evans and eventually called the Id, the Ego, and the Super-Ego by Sigmund Freud. He produced an ear-trumpet and an airtight, hot-air stove; and he is the father of the decimal system of coinage and of crystallography. He advocated the industrialization of Sweden (which has taken place during the last century) as the means of economic and political independence and domestic prosperity. He did everything possible to advance intellectual, political, and religious libertarianism, as well as a completely republican form of government; and all this two generations before the American and French revolutions. He did not merely touch upon all these things: he wrestled with the problems involved and offered workable solutions, many of which have since been accepted and implemented.

But most of all he was a religious reformer and innovator, the most extraordinary revealer in all History; and it is this phase of his activity which concerns us here. He is the grand fountainhead of a variety of deviationist religious movements; and specifically, the grandfather of New Thought. In the vast expanse of his writings, single details have proved so pregnant with creative force as to become the source of cults and sects; each can take what it chooses, and ignore the remainder. Swedenborg—like Whitman—is large— he contains multitudes: and his epigones and disciples, knowing or unknowing, are as the stars of the heavens or the sands on the seashore.

Every widespread modern movement or philosophy has originated with some great and independent thinker. This does not mean that all its elements derive from one towering intellect; but it does imply that he has organized existing materials, added certain elements of his own, and given the whole a distinctive formulation. What Pythagoras did for ancient religion in the Western world, Marx for socialism, Darwin for the theory of evolution, and Freud for psychoanalysis, Emanuel Swedenborg did for various modern religious movements, but especially for the metaphysical system known as New Thought, the religion of health, happiness, and prosperity, which purports to be as factual and demonstrable as a laboratory experiment. By combining accepted doctrine with his science and philosophy, Swedenborg accomplished a revolution in Christian doctrine, which had been the aim of the martyred Servetus Villanovanus, who had been burned at the stake.

II. HIS OUTWARD LIFE

1. *A Prodigious Scholar.* Swedenborg's complete works consist of something like a hundred tomes dealing with scientific, philosophical, and theological subjects. Hyde's *Bibliography* of 760 pages, with 3,500 entries, conveys some conception of their magnitude; and *The Swedenborg Concordance*, compiled during twenty-seven years by the Reverend John Faulkner Potts, itself consists of 5,500 pages and fills six quarto volumes.[6] Emerson calls him one of the "mastodons of literature.... not to be measured by whole colleges of ordinary scholars."[7]

2. *The Swedbergs.* Emanuel was born in Stockholm, January 29, 1688. Most of those who have founded religious cults have been persons of little or no education: some have been totally illiterate. Quite different, however, was this extraordinary innovator, for his education was the most elaborate possible in his day. His father, Jesper Swedberg, born in 1653, became a professor at Upsala University in 1692, Dean there in 1694, and Bishop of Skara in 1702, in which capacity he continued until his death in 1738. In 1719, the family was ennobled and given the name *Swedenborg.* The elder Swedberg was a fervent and tireless worker, a zealous reformer in the Lutheran Church; he attempted to modernize the parochial schools, popularize the current forms of worship,

and correlate the religious with the truly ethical life; and he declared that a worship consisting primarily of rituals, doctrines, and observances was simply a "devil-faith" and the cause of the lax morality so prevalent among both clergy and nobility. Creatures of the spiritworld, both angelic and devilish, were to him intensely real; and it is recorded that he healed cases of hysteria and other ailments, both physical and mental, by the power of his personal magnetism.[8] He was a man of fierce sincerity, subject to vivid dreams and visions.

Both of Emanuel's grandfathers had engaged in successful mining operations, and from them he received substantial bequests. And so we see that the families of the avid young student combined affluence with the best current learning and the most respectable ancestry.

3. *The Youth.* Emanuel, like his father, was often engrossed in preternatural exaltation. In a letter of a later period, he wrote: "From my fourth to my tenth year, I was constantly engaged in thought upon God, salvation, and the spiritual diseases of men; and several times I revealed things at which my father and my mother wondered...."[9]

At the age of eleven, the precocious child matriculated at Upsala, where René Descartes had lit the torch of freedom shortly before he died of pneumonia in 1650. Emanuel entered as a student of philosophy, which at that time included the physical sciences. After ten years, he graduated in 1709, having mastered a classical education in which the Graeco-Roman authors became his mentors and Latin as familiar as his mother tongue.

In 1710, he set out on his Grand Tour of Europe, during which he visited England, Holland, France, Germany, and Italy, where he studied much, observed widely, absorbed multifariously.[10] In 1714, he sent home a list of fourteen inventions, accompanied by detailed descriptions and drawings.[11] Among these were sketches of a "flying carriage," a "universal musical instrument," a "method of ascertaining the desires and affections of the mind by analysis," and a "ship which, with its men, can go under the surface of the sea, wherever it chooses, and do great damage to the fleet of the enemy."[12]

4. *Publisher and Lover.* Soon after returning, he founded, edited, and published a scientific journal called *Daedalus Hyporboreus,*[13] which marked the inception of the Society of Sciences at Upsala.[14] This brought him to the attention of the renowned scientist, mathematician, and inventor Christopher Polhem, with whose young daughter, Emerentia, he fell in love. His affection, however, was not requited.

5. *Assessor, Scientist, and Philosopher.* Through the good offices of Polhem, King Charles in 1716 gave the 28-year-old Swedenborg an appointment as Assessor in the Board of Mines, a position in which he continued until June 17, 1747, when he retired to devote the remainder of his life to his mandate as revealer-extraordinary.

We can here only glance at the massive literary productions of the assessorship-years. He published his *Motion and Position of the Earth and the Planets*, a treatise on astronomy and cosmology, and his *Height of Water*, a study of geological formations, in 1719. Two years later came the *Prodromus of a Work on the Principles of Natural Philosophy*, an attempt to explain the phenomena of chemistry and physics by means of geometry; this was followed, after more than ten years of laborious research, in 1734, by the great opus in three parts dealing with philosophy and minerology, called *Principia*, *On Iron*, and *On Copper*. The first of these is Swedenborg's basic contribution to cosmology, in which the Nebular Hypothesis is for the first time clearly stated,[15] and in which he advances the theory that the universe is a mechanism governed throughout by mathematical law.[16] He declared that atoms are actually entities of energy and activity; and so anticipated the modern concepts of electrons, protons, and neutrons. In the second and third parts of this monumental work, he performed a signal service in the field of smelting and metallurgy. He gathered from innumerable sources existing knowledge concerning these industries and published it for all to read.

The year 1734 marks the culmination of one phase of his development: for at this point his overriding interest in science, as such, came to a close and he sought wider horizons in the realm of metaphysics. With the publication in that year of his treatise *The Infinite*,[17] he began an intensive search for the human soul, which was to dominate his interest for ten years. In the hope of discovering this elusive entity, he became an authority in anatomy. His first major work in this field was the ponderous *Cerebrum*, written in 1738-40, and finally published in Philadelphia in 1940. This was followed by a number of other extensive works: *The Economy of the Animal Kingdom*, 1740-41, and *The Fibre*, 1741, published in 1918; *The Rational Psychology*, 1742, published in 1950; *The Brain*, 1743-44, published in 1882, and *The Animal Kingdom*, 1743—of which Part I and II were published at The Hague in 1744; Part III at London, 1745, and Part IV and V at Philadelphia in 1912.

Swedenborg was so far in advance of his age in the knowledge of anatomy that a century had to elapse before the scientific world could understand his contributions. Then, at last, it was realized that here was the man who had cleared the way for future research, not only in this field, but also in metallurgy, psychology, cosmology, physics, chemistry, and various other scientific disciplines.[18]

6. *Philosophy Abandoned*. The small volume *The Worship and the Love of God*, 1745, signaled Swedenborg's transition from philosophy to theologian and revealer. Between 1747 and 1772, he labored most of the time in Stockholm, where he had acquired a comfortable home, complete with garden and study, in which he did most of his writing. However, he made journeys to, and

spent considerable time in, The Hague and London, where his treatises were published. Outwardly, he continued as a comfortable middle-class citizen; but his esoteric life was a phenomenon without parallel. One bulky manuscript after another grew under his industrious hand; these were written in classical Latin and published secretly, and of course anonymously, at his own expense.

7. *Heresy, Conflict, and Persecution*. Bishop Swedenborg had been accused of heresy; and an edition of his hymnal was destroyed because he had addressed the Savior as the Son of Man rather than as the Son of God.[19] The publication of any religiously unconventional literature in Sweden, even in Latin, was proscribed in 1750. Not before 1766 did Swedenborg openly divulge his responsibility for his writings by affixing his name and humbly describing himself as the Servant of the Lord Jesus Christ. His first Swedish disciples, obtained in 1765, were the teacher-journalist Dr. Johann Rosén and Dr. Gabriel Beyer, professor of theology in the parochial college at Gothenburg; both were subjected to the severest strictures.[20] Another convert, the Reverend Sven Schmidt, was defrocked, declared insane, and sent to prison.[21]

The most bitter experience of Swedenborg's life was his persecution, at the age of eighty-two, for heresy, of which he had been warned by friends in England in 1769. The storm first broke in Gothenburg, where Dr. Rosén had just written a highly favorable review of *The Apocalypse Revealed*; and where Dr. Beyer had published a volume of *Household Sermons*, surcharged with Swedenborgianism, because of which his students had rioted in his classes.[22]

Once this new doctrine began competing for popular support, it engendered the fiercest hostility among the established clergy. Olaf Ekebom, Dean of the Consistory of the Lutheran Synod and an archenemy of the New Church, declared that Swedenborg's teachings were "corrupting, heretical...diametrically opposed to God's Word...full of the most intolerable errors..."[23] When he added that the Christology was Socinian, Swedenborg retorted that such a statement constituted "a cursed blasphemy" and that "the Dean's opinion may be taken for the flood which the Dragon cast out of his mouth after the Woman, to drown her in the wilderness."[24]

A shipment of books from England for distribution among members of the Diet was confiscated by the customs agents. Bishop Filenius, a nephew-in-law of the author, who had caressed his old relative upon his return, led the movement to proscribe his writings; and the enraged revealer called the cleric a modern Judas Iscariot.[25]

In December 1769, Bishop Lambert charged that Swedenborg's writings were "plentifully tinged with Mohammedanism," because of his lush descriptions of connubial bliss in heaven.[26] A movement was instigated to put him away as a lunatic. On January 2, 1770, the Royal Council forbade all circulation, reviews, or translations of his writings; and it called upon the Consistory to make an exact and detailed report of all errors and heresies lurking in them. It would seem, however, that this was too great an undertaking, for this body never complied with the behest.[27]

Drs. Beyer and Rosén wrote astute and spirited defenses in which they maintained that Swedenborg's teachings were based entirely upon authentic interpretations of Scripture, but to little avail. When the report reached him that his two foremost disciples were not only to be deprived of office and livelihood but also to be banished, he issued an eloquent and denunciatory letter to the Royal Council. This at least had the effect of bringing an informal decision that the sage himself was to remain inviolable. Furthermore, his heresies were formulated so subtly and often so much in conformity with emerging philosophy and morality that it was difficult to make out a decisive case against him. Actually, those who accepted the Bible *literally* had been much reduced in number and influence, and few were prepared to defend the true implications of many of its precepts.

8. *Condemnation and Departure.* Nevertheless, on April 26, 1770, the Royal Council "totally condemned, rejected," and forbade the dissemination of Swedenborgian literature or doctrines.[28] The argument that they were in agreement with Scripture was brushed aside with the declaration that no individual could repudiate the Augsburg Confession.[29] Dr. Beyer was prohibited from teaching theology and Dr. Rosén was warned not to intermix any novelties in the study of Terence and Cicero.[30]

Swedenborg complained bitterly in a letter to the King, May 25, 1770, that he had "been treated as no one has ever been treated before in Sweden since the introduction of Christianity...."[31] On July 23, he declared that his "trial had been the most important and the most solemn...during the last 1700 years, since it concerned the New Church which is predicted by the Lord..." in the Scriptures.[32]

Since the authorities could not lay their hands on the person of the venerable seer, it was their devout hope that he would not embarrass them by his presence. In this, at the age of eighty-two, he accommodated them; for he soon left for Holland and England, never to see his home again.

On December 7, 1771, the Royal Council referred the prosecution of Swedenborg's doctrines to the Gothic Court of Appeals, which, after three years, shuttled it to Upsala University for a study of his writings. However, this proved too great a task for them also; and no report was ever submitted.[33]

9. *After Death, Triumph!* Soon after Swedenborg's death on March 29, 1772, an organization consisting of substantial individuals was formed in England to translate and publish his theological works and to promulgate his teachings. It was, however, many years before his own countrymen began to comprehend the saintly iconoclast with the giant intellect. As a result of steps taken by the Royal Academy of Sciences, the Swedish Government dis-

patched a cruiser to retrieve his mortal remains. The ship left London on April 7, 1908; and on May 13, amidst resplendent ceremonies, the bones of Swedenborg found a final resting place among the immortals in the Cathedral of Upsala. The city was decked with flags and memorials; there was a long procession, led by his family descendants, and followed by representatives of many Swedish and foreign scientific organizations. The students of Upsala University proceeded up the long aisle singing, and dipped their banners as they passed the coffin of the incomparable heretic. It was an hour of majestic solemnity, unparalleled in the annals of the nation; and every eye offered its generous tribute of tears.

III. HIS INTELLECTUAL LIFE

1. *Practical Undertakings.* Although for thirty-one years, as Assessor of Mines, it was Swedenborg's duty to listen patiently to countless minor disputes, his activities ranged far beyond the confines of his bureau. In July, 1718, he devised a practical means by which Charles XII was able to transport five brigantines fifteen miles overland in a single day.[34] On another occasion, we find the young inventor laboring with Polhem, attempting to build a canal from Stockholm to Gothenburg; even though this was not accomplished at that time, their work served as the basis for the great Göta Canal, still in operation, complete with locks, constructed a generation later.[35]

2. *The Political Economist.* When Charles XII died of a bullet in the back of his head before Frederickshall, December 11, 1718, an era in Swedish history came to an end. The cost of this monarch's spectacular military adventures had been staggering in life and treasure. A ruinous inflation had developed and Sweden was bankrupt. Vast quantities of rapidly deteriorating currency had been issued, and no end was in sight. At this juncture, the young Swedenborg memorialized the Riksdag in a closely reasoned essay in which he declared that a sound currency was essential to the economic and political stability of the nation and its position in the international market. He was the first who advocated the financial policies which his country pursued thereafter.[36]

In 1725, the young man, now ennobled, entered the politico-economic lists once more, this time by memorializing the Riksdag with an essay which he called *The Balance of Trade.* Sweden, he declared, should industrialize, establish its own metallurgical and manufacturing plants. Instead of purchasing inferior products abroad, the Swedes should manufacture superior ones and offer them on the competitive market with a quality and at a price which would conquer all competition.[37]

3. *The Statesman.* In 1734, a political crisis arose because one faction

wished to make an alliance with France for the purpose of waging war on Russia to recover some territories lost after the death of the late king. Swedenborg argued convincingly that his country had everything to lose and nothing to gain by war; that it should husband its resources and encourage mining, metallurgy, and manufacture, thus embarking upon the ways of peace in a solid, industrialized economy. He declared that Sweden should never engage in any conflict except in the event of an overt military attack upon her mainland;[38] and this also became her policy during the ensuing generations.

4. *The Nebular Hypothesis.* Immanuel Kant in 1765 advanced in part the Nebular Hypothesis, which was perfected by Laplace in 1796 and which offers an explanation for the origin of the solar system. However, Swedenborg had already clearly set forth this cosmological theory in his *Principia* in 1734 and again in his *Worship and the Love of God* in 1745.[39] According to this theory our solar system—together with the planets—came into existence when, by the force of gravity, the central nebula threw off masses which, by centrifugal force, separated in the form of rings and gave birth to the orbiting lesser suns with their satellites. This scientific theory is crucial in Swedenborgianism, for without it his theology, his theory of influx, and various other distinctive religious doctrines could never have been developed.

5. *Revelatory Claims.* Swedenborg is now best known as seer and revealer; and we must note that never before or after him have comparable claims to divine authority been advanced. Those of Ann Lee, Joseph Smith, Mary Baker Eddy, and Charles Taze Russell are comparatively modest. Mohammed declared that he was a mere passive instrument who received divine communications in a trance-like state. Of all the historic prophets, only Zoroaster and Pythagoras emerge as rivals to Swedenborg. The Persian declared that he was transported to the throne of Ahura Mazda seven times, where all the secrets of religion, which he wrote down as dictated to him, were made known. Pythagoras declared that he received direct revelations from the God of the Universe; and once, after an absence of seven years, he appeared worn and haggard before his followers, declaring that all this time he had lived in the spirit-world. Zoroaster was a prophet, but not a scientist; only Pythagoras and Swedenborg were at once scientists, philosophers, cosmologists, metaphysicians, political economists, prophets, great religious innovators, and creators of new religious movements. These two men, therefore, separated by twenty-three centuries, are remarkably similar. Pythagoras, who died in 502 B.C., formulated the religious synthesis which became the forerunner of Christianity; Swedenborg reconstituted that religion in terms of modern culture, philosophy, science, and morality.

Zoroaster and Pythagoras lived at a time when the human race was just emerging into introspective consciousness; the critical faculty had not yet emerged. Swedenborg appears as an anachronism, because he was the product of the same age which saw the birth of Higher Criticism and which produced Voltaire, Diderot, Kant, Locke, Hume, Hobbes, and Edward Gibbon. Yet it was, strangely enough, also an age of religious bigotry which made outlaws of countless heretics.

6. *Traumatic Illumination.* "It has pleased the Lord," wrote Swedenborg, "to prepare me from my earliest youth to perceive the Word...."[40] During much of his life he had indeed been given to introspection and religious meditation. Often he alternated between fits of extreme depression and indescribable exaltation,[41] or suicidal impulses and a sense of preternatural ecstasy. This development reached its supreme culmination in an overwhelmingly traumatic experience at Delft, Holland, on Easter Day, April 5, 1744, and on the succeeding night at The Hague, all of which is recorded in detail in the *Journal of Dreams,* covering April through October 1744 and never intended for any eyes other than his own. After being lost for about 200 years, this document was purchased and printed by the Royal Library in Stockholm, but there restricted to private use. Finally, it was translated into English at Bryn Athyn, Pennsylvania in 1918, where it was printed but never published; however, it has been made available to scholars by special permission in the library of the Academy of the New Church.

When he wrote the description of his illumination, Swedenborg was in a state of superinduced fantasy: "I had in my mind and body the feeling of indescribable delight, so that had it been in any higher degree, my whole body would have been, as it were, dissolved in pure joy.... I was in heaven and heard speech which no human tongue can utter...."[42]

It is clear that we have here a psychological condition in which the subject could easily hear strange voices and see extraordinary visions; and this is certainly what happened. Half an hour after he went to bed at ten o'clock on the evening of April 6, he heard a great roar as of a mighty hurricane, was seized with a powerful trembling, and sensed a holy presence, which caused him to fall upon his face. "It was," he wrote, "a countenance of a holy mien" such as Jesus had "while He lived on earth.... I awoke with trembling." And he continued: "...and so I said, 'It was Jesus Himself.... Our Lord has been willing to show such grace to so unworthy a sinner.' "[43] Note the word *grace*, later deleted from his theology and his vocabulary.

7. *Prophet and Revelator.* The *Journal* establishes beyond all question that these experiences were dreams only; but the psychological effect was permanent and supreme. From this time forward, Swedenborg was a different man; for he had received his divine mandate. "If you only knew what grace I am enjoying..!"[44] he exclaimed rapturously. In 1771, at the age of 83, he wrote to the Landgrave of Hesse-Darmstadt: "The Lord our Savior foretold that He would come...and institute a New Church.... But as He cannot come again into the world in Person, it was necessary that He should do it by means of a

man, who should not only receive the doctrine of that church by his understanding, but also publish it by means of the press; and as the Lord had prepared me for this from my childhood, He manifested Himself in Person before me, His servant, and sent me to do his work. This took place in 1745; and afterwards He opened the sight of my spirit, and thus introduced me to the spiritual world, granting me to see the heavens and many of the wonderful things there, and also the hells, and to speak with angels and spirits, and this continuously for twenty-seven years. I declare in truth that this is so."[45] (We note that here, as elsewhere in Swedenborg's writings, the date of the divine appearance is incorrect; and, what is more important, that what was in reality a dream has here become objective reality.)

8. *The Dream-Life of a Seer.* In the weeks following the Illumination, the visions became progressively more frequent and distinct. On September 21, he records the first instance in which he is addressed directly by a supernatural being (note this particularly), who told him: "Hold your tongue or I will strike you!"[46] He took this to mean that he must not write anything as if it were his own or of human origin. He began to think of himself as a passive agency of the divine power; and he exclaimed: "I wish I could become the instrument for slaying the Dragon!"[47] which, to him, was the Reformed Lutheran and Calvinist churches.

He dreamed of a lovely woman who owned a beautiful estate and whom he was to marry; she signified piety and wisdom.[48] In one passage, he noted an abatement of his sexual desires,[49] which would indicate that he was undergoing sublimation. The *Journal* closes with a description of a fantasy in which a lovely girl approaches him, but falls into the arms of a companion.[50]

9. *The Vision Grows.* The only authentic description of his illumination is that written by Swedenborg himself in the *Journal of Dreams.* How this was elaborated and how his theology evolved, becomes apparent as we read his own later versions of that event. Years later, he told his friend Robsom that after eating at a restaurant in April 1745 (note the altered date), he returned to his room, where "that night the same man revealed himself again..." who "said that he was the Lord God, the Creator and Redeemer of the world, and that he had chosen me to declare to men the spiritual contents of Scripture...."[51] The description of the same event as given to, and repeated by, Dr. Beyer shows not only that the vision grew more gorgeous with time, but also that the prophet added various things unrecorded in the *Journal.* "The information respecting the Lord's personal appearance...in imperial purple and majestic light, seated near his bed while He gave Assessor Swedenborg his commission, I had from his own lips at a dinner party in the home of Dr. Rosén, when I saw the old gentleman for the first time."[52]

At all events, by 1748, Swedenborg was irrevocably committed as the Great

Seer, the Unique Revealer, the man appointed by the Lord to establish the New Church.

10. *The Second Coming.* In 1845, Swedenborg, still orthodox, believed that the physical Parousia was then imminent. "Jesus Christ, our Savior," he wrote, "is the Messiah about to come...and judge the world; the time is now at hand."[53] In November 1846, he continued: "Now is the holy day to be expected when the Messiah will return with His Bride to the Land of Canaan."[54]

11. *The Preparation.* Swedenborg now spent three years compiling his own cross-indexed concordance of the Bible, so that he could find instantly any desired passage.[55] He also composed a spiritual interpretation of the Lord's Prayer, phrase by phrase,[56] for the purpose of showing that it was really a prophecy of the coming kingdom of the Lord, just as Mary Baker Eddy was to do in the following century. He also prepared another document, *The Hieroglyphic Key*,[57] in which he explained precisely how the Scripture should be understood in its spiritual sense, a method universally applied throughout the New Thought movement.

12. *No Sign or Miracle.* After 1759, when Count Bonde learned that Swedenborg was the author of his works, many were they who demanded some confirmation of his daily companionship with the departed. To all such requests, he replied that no one believed Jesus when he was on earth and that no sign would be given now. The gift of conversing with spirits and of traveling into their realms "cannot," he declared, "be transferred from one person to another" or be received by anyone unless "the Lord Himself—as has been the case with me—opens the sight of the spirit of that person."[58]

13. *Spiritualism and Clairvoyance.* We should note, briefly, Swedenborg's unparalleled reputation for clairvoyance. There was, he said, nothing miraculous concerning the information he was constantly receiving from the spirit-realm: it was merely that he conversed daily with the inhabitants there as if they were still in the world. He declared that he "conversed with Paul for an entire year.... Three times I spoke with John, once with Moses, a hundred times with Luther...."[59] He said that he had explored various scientific questions with Paul and Luther;[60] once, when the Finnish scholar Henrick Porthan visited Swedenborg at his home, he overheard an animated conversation, all in the same voice, going on in the study. Finally, the seer emerged and, with much bowing and polite ceremonial, seemed to be ushering someone out, who, according to him, was none other than the poet Virgil.[61]

A great many tales with intriguing designations were related and widely accepted: even Immanuel Kant at one time gave them credence,[62] although later he repudiated this.[63] It may be significant that none of these stories are related by Swedenborg himself; they were perhaps created, or at least embellished, by the myth-making propensity of the popular imagination. Of these, we mention only two of those considered best established. According to one, he became aware of a fire in Stockholm near his own home while he was in Gothenburg, three hundred miles away.[64] The other dealt with the alleged treasonous conduct of Queen Lovisa Ulrica.[65]

How, then, shall we regard this extraordinary reputation for clairvoyance? In 1768, the German Professor H.W. Clemm published a book titled *A Complete Introduction to Religion and Theology*,[66] which offered three explanations of the phenomena accredited to Swedenborg, namely:[67] (1) that they are sheer fantasies; (2) that they are delusions of the spirit; or (3) that they are the truth. However, Dr. Ernesti, editor of the *New Theological Library*,[68] called Swedenborg's teachings the ravings of a demented heretic.[69]

In spite of rationalistic explanations, the intensity of Swedenborg's emotional experiences can neither be questioned nor overestimated. The *Journal* establishes beyond doubt that his visions of 1744 were often accompanied by violent tremors and prostrations. On a later occasion, he remained in a trance-like state for more than three days, which he describes in *The Apocalypse Revealed*.[70] On another, this condition continued for more than three weeks, during which he took practically no nourishment.[71] Once in 1748, he went through the experience of dying and being resurrected, which he describes in detail in *The Spiritual Diary*.[72] Sometimes he believed himself assailed by demons.[73]

14. *The Inner Dynamic.* History is studded with men who created revolutionary ideas or techniques even at the price of poverty, ridicule, persecution, personal destruction, or even death at the stake. We can only say that such personalities are driven by an overwhelming compulsion which forces them to continue their work, against all odds. The fact, therefore, that usual motives are absent by no means proves that Swedenborg's claims were based upon objective reality. His purpose was nothing less than to transform and recreate the ethics, philosophy, and religion of the Western world; and such a motive can be sufficient to drive a man of great genius into the most unconventional persuasions and activities.

We can only conclude that during most of his life Swedenborg had been intensely preoccupied with what he considered the deficiencies, contradictions, and irrational dogmas of the Christianity he knew; that his dream-experience of 1744 constituted for him a climactic call to personal dedication; that, once embarked on this course, it became a supreme obsession; that he found in this activity an emotional and intellectual outlet so overwhelming that nothing beyond it mattered to him; and that his spirit-world, even if self-created, was, nevertheless, for him, endowed with supreme reality. It is by no means unreasonable to assume or conclude that he could project himself at will into a world of his imagination. We believe that his reputation for clairvoyance was largely the result of the myth-making propensity of the popular imagination, for this is a common historical phenomenon.

We believe that Swedenborg elaborated his revelations for the purpose of mounting his assault upon the bastions of orthodoxy; and that their reality or unreality is relatively immaterial in the system itself or to the convictions of the devout Swedenborgian communicant; for much of what is essential to the faith is quite independent of the prophet's revelatory claims.

15. *Rejections.* Most of those who reject Swedenborg do so probably because of convictions or persuasions to which they are already committed. Those who accept an existing or orthodox faith will with no effort at all dismiss him as deranged. The skeptic will brush him aside as Omar Khayyam did other prophets, along with the devout and learned, who told their dreams to comrades and then to sleep returned. The rationalist and the naturalistic Humanist will say that, since there is no prima facie evidence to verify his revelations, they must be rejected out of hand.

16. *Whence Came These Novel Doctrines?* Much that we find in Swedenborg was quite original, for we search in vain for definite predecessors. However, we note also that he often refers to the diabolical heresies of Arius and Socinus, from whose Christology his differs sharply; but he never refers to Servetus or Sabellius, whom he must have understood thoroughly, and with whom he had much in common.

17. *The Corpus of Theological Literature.* Of the thirty volumes of basic theological works containing some 20,000 pages, twelve are known as the *Arcana Coelestia*, written between 1748 and 1756; six as *The Apocalypse Explained*, 1758-59; and two as *The Apocalypse Revealed*, 1766. These twenty volumes, which constitute his Key to the Scriptures, are line-by-line commentaries or spiritual interpretations of Genesis, Exodus, and Revelation, covering every phase of theology and religious doctrine and practice. His principal remaining works, some of them much more widely read than the preceding, are: *Heaven and Its Wonders, and Hell*, 1758; *Divine Love and Wisdom*, 1763; *Divine Providence*, 1764; *Conjugal Love*, 1768, and his final summary of doctrine, *The True Christian Religion*, 1771. Various shorter disquisitions are now available in *The Four Doctrines*, 1763, and the *Miscellaneous Posthumous Theological Works*.

18. *A One and Only.* Whatever else one may say about Swedenborg, we must admit that he is unique. From beginning to end, his thought is a vast, strikingly original, and generally consistent system of ethics, philosophy, metaphysics, cosmology, Christology, theology, anthropology, eschatology, regeneration, redemption, practical conduct, sexual morality, health, happiness, temporal success, and eternal well-being, which, to say the least, was novel in the extreme. We may also add that his theological synthesis consti-

tuted a fully rounded structure which, presented as a spiritual interpretation of Scripture, mounts a devastating assault upon the old and accepted mansions of orthodoxy and, if accepted, reduces them into one stupendous ruin.

IV. THE SWEDENBORGIAN SYSTEM AND SYNTHESIS

A. *The Spiritual Revelation*

1. *The Word Divine.* Swedenborg's vast system of doctrine purports to rest solely upon the Christian Scriptures: "It is impossible," he declares, "to derive a single theological truth from any other source...."[74] And "man has no knowledge of...the other world except from revelation...."[75] The Word, however, has an internal or mystical meaning, an arcanum[76] which "lies hidden in every detail" thereof.[77] In its literal meaning, the Word is often trivial, immoral, illogical, and even repulsive: this could not be unless it concealed divine mysteries.[78]

Despite various passages in the Bible, Swedenborg says that God is never angry, never repents, never leads anyone into temptation, never tortures the damned in hell, and never predestines the innocent, or even the wicked, to eternal damnation.

The spiritual interpretation of Scripture often yields surprising meanings. When, for example, Genesis speaks of the Great Flood, this simply signifies an influx of evil spirits which suffocated the people.[79] Genealogical names symbolize heresies, following the first, which was called Cain.[80] Noah signifies a new church and his three sons are simply three doctrines.[81] When we read in Revelation of those "who are not defiled with women," this designates those who have not falsified the truths of the Word.[82] When Jesus speaks of treading on scorpions, he refers to "murderous persuasions."[83] All proper names have spiritual meanings: for example Isaacher means reward[84] and Zebulon cohabitation.[85] Several of Swedenborg's works conclude with long indexes of words, which are spiritual interpretations of Biblical terms, later imitated in the glossaries of all editions of *Science and Health* after its author fell under Swedenborg's direct influence; and Charles Fillmore's *Metaphysical Bible Dictionary* is written strictly in the Swedenborgian tradition.

Although some of these examples may seem unimportant or even humorous, we discover that such free treatment can easily lead to very significant results. For example, Swedenborg tells us that adultery means the corruption and falsification of Scriptural truth,[86] an interpretation adopted by Mary Baker Eddy in her controversies with opponents. He was also moved to revise Matthew 5:28 to make it read: "Whosoever looketh on *the woman of another* to lust after her, hath committed adultery with her already in his heart."[87] The ultimate use of the *Key* finds its expression in the explanation of the Second

Coming, the Last Judgment, and the City Foursquare: for all these signify nothing more or less than the revelations he was himself commissioned to proclaim. Since the Pauline writings, as well as certain other New Testament documents, were wholly contrary to Swedenborg's beliefs and purposes, he declared that they lack internal meaning.[88] Swedenborg never tires of repeating that Paul himself had become a nefarious spirit;[89] and it is because the Reformed Church had accepted his teachings that it had departed from the paths of charity.[90] He ranked all the books of the Bible on this basis.[91] When, however, the literal meaning agreed with his exegesis, he was quite willing to accept it; for example, when the Fourth Gospel states that the Son and the Father are one, this proves conclusively that a trinity of persons is anti-Scriptural.[92]

2. *A Cult Is Born.* And so Swedenborg declared that the Scriptures "down to the smallest jot, are Divine" and "dictated by the Lord...."[93] But since no new cult can come to birth except on the basis of a new or at least a supplementary revelation, it became mandatory for him to supply such an authority. And so, with what seemed to his contemporaries a staggering effrontery, he proclaimed, first, that he had personally witnessed everything that exists in the world of spirits, as well as in heaven and hell in particular; and, second, that it had been given to him alone to understand the ancient revelations in their true, internal, and spiritual sense.

B. *Dismantling the Old*

1. *Everything Condemned.* Before the ground could be cleared for the establishment of the New Church, the old structures had to be demolished. Swedenborg, outwardly so calm and gentle, was filled with a fierce animosity in opposition to almost everything and everyone around him—especially in the religious realm. At least he was impartial: almost nothing escaped his vitriolic pen. The intensity of this spirit in rebellion against prevailing doctrine and practice is to be measured by the extent and bitterness of his condemnations; and this spirit has been the hallmark of those whom he has influenced. He gazed with loathing and contempt upon the various churches, creeds, dogmas, rituals, and disciplines which filled the world. And it is interesting to note that in his world of spirits the Christians fare worse than the heathens.[94] Because the Gentiles have not been falsely indoctrinated, he declares, they are more easily redeemed in the after-life.[95] There is no bar against regeneration and redemption of moral pagans;[96] they are never condemned because they lack the Christian Scriptures or sacraments.[97] It is not his creed, doctrine, or belief, but rather his moral propensities that enable the newcomer in the world of spirits to achieve salvation.

2. *The Jews.* Since they believe that they are a chosen people "and that all the rest of mankind are relatively slaves to them...and confirm this belief from the sense of the letter of the Word," this prevents "any conscience from ever being formed" among them.[98] They are the most avaricious of all people.[99] All they pray for is to become rich.[100] Those Christians are most deluded who "believe that the Messiah...will bring them [the Jews] back into the land of Canaan...."[101] Even in the world of spirits, they go on deluding themselves that they will one day rule over all the Gentiles, while they attempt to sell fake jewelry.[102]

3. *The Protestants.* Swedenborg had nothing but contempt and condemnation for the Protestant sects in general. However, his animosity toward the Lutherans and others whom he called the Reformed intensified as he suffered persecution. He conceded, however, that "if the papal dominion had not been broken at the time of the Reformation," the Catholic Church "would have raked together the possessions and the wealth of all the kingdoms of the whole of Europe;"[103] yet he never forgave the "leading Reformers, Luther, Melanchthon, and Calvin," because they "retained all the dogmas concerning the Trinity of persons...the origin of sin from Adam, the imputation of the merit of Christ, and justification by faith alone, as they had been held by Roman Catholics...."[104] The "Great Red Dragon" of the Apocalypse, we are told, "signifies those in the church of the Reformed who make God three and the Lord two, and who separate charity from faith...."[105] The Reformed have all taken the mark of the beast[106] (mentioned in Revelation) and worship it.[107] The only virtues of the Reformation consisted in hating the Harlot, which obviously was the Roman Catholic Church;[108] in making the Word available to the people; and in rejecting altogether "the dogmas that have proceeded from the Papal Consistory...."[109]

In attempting to suppress the Church of the New Jerusalem, the Lutherans were guilty of an atrocious crime.[110] "They who are about to attack this doctrine," Swedenborg assures us, "are meant by the 'Great Red Dragon, the old serpent,' " and those "who constitute the head of the Dragon."[111]

4. *The Roman Catholics.* Swedenborg's denunciations of the Vatican were even more fierce; for it not only taught every vicious and erroneous dogma retained by the Protestants, it was also an unspeakable economic exploiter and, even worse, the ultimate among all the political and intellectual tyrannies ever devised by man. The Catholic Church, according to Swedenborg, was the Scarlet Woman of Revelation, the Whore that Sitteth upon the Seven Hills.[112]

During his first journey through France, he was outraged by the social conditions and by the common practice of the Hierarchy. "Everywhere," he wrote, "the convents, churches, and monks are wealthiest and possess most land. The monks are fat, puffed up, and prosperous...lead a lazy life...I am told besides that the ecclesiastical order possesses one-fifth of all the property in the state and that the country will be ruined if this goes on much longer."[113] He was filled with contempt at such frauds as the bones of the Three Wise Men at the Cathedral of Cologne[114] and the "relics near the altar" in St. John Lateran represented as being "the heads of Peter and Paul, under a rich tabernacle or shrine."[115]

Roman Catholicism, declared Swedenborg, is only a Christianized "paganism, where the images of sanctified men are exhibited for adoration,.."[116] which "is simply and foully idolatrous..."[117] They have committed a sacrilege in exalting "Mary...a goddess or queen over all their saints."[118] Another of their infernal heresies consists in teaching that they have "the power to let into heaven and shut out from heaven whomsoever" they will;[119] the power to do this was never given even to Peter,[120] and for this reason they must be considered demented.[121]

In this world, the popes demand veneration, and plot to rule tyrannically over all men;[122] the papists call the pope "the Lord's Vicar and thus they make him god upon earth...."[123] Dominion, not salvation, is the purpose of their decrees.[124] They have profaned "the Lord's Divine authority by transferring it to themselves."[125] They have adulterated "every truth of the Word and thence of every holy thing in the church";[126] papal bulls have displaced the holy Scriptures;[127] they entombed the Word of God for many centuries,[128] and they have no regard whatever for its authority.[129] In fact, they must reject any belief in life after this, for they seek only their own advantage in this world.[130] "Purgatory...is purely a Babylonish fiction for the sake of gain...."[131] The dominant objective of the Roman Catholic priesthood is to become the supreme lords of the whole world and to reduce all others to the most abject slavery.[132] In order to accomplish this purpose, they have "kept all in the densest ignorance, thus blocking the way to light, thus to heaven...."[133]

These merchants of Babylon, mentioned in the Apocalypse, are "the greater and the lesser in rank in that hierarchy, who through dominion over the holy things of the church strive for Divine majesty and super-regal glory...."[134] The Catholic Church has grown rich and mighty "by threats and terrors, especially in regard to purgatory, into which everyone is to come...."[135]

That Church is guilty of every venality, fraud, and corruption in its pursuit of wealth and temporal power: it sells matrimonial dispensations and divorces; for a price, it permits criminal enormities or gives exemptions from temporal punishments. It "promises heavenly joys to those who enrich monasteries and augment their treasuries, calling the gifts good works..."; and it "takes advantage of the rich when they are sick," and thus obtains great legacies in return for the offer of a gradual delivery from purgatory.[136] The victims of these priests do not understand the snares devised by them "for arrogating to themselves Divine worship, and for possessing all the property in the world...,"[137] and their dupes actually believe that their religion to be "supereminent over every other in the world."[138]

He warms to his thesis: "They make and multiply saints..." but "those who dare to speak against the Papal throne and their dominion, they shut up in a horrible prison, which is called the Inquisition. All these things they do for the sole end that they may possess the world and its treasures and live in luxury and be the greatest, while the rest are slaves."[139]

Is it any wonder, after all this and much more, that Swedenborg should have nightmares in which enemies assailed him screaming: "Drag him forth, crucify him, crucify him; go, go all of you see the great heretic, and amuse yourselves with him."[140]

C. *Historic Christianity*

1. *The Original and the Hellenic Reconstruction.* The Synoptic Gospels proclaim a forthright synthesis of communal ethics based on personal renunciation; a Christianity which delared that Jesus was the god-man who died for the sins of humanity in order to accomplish the salvation of those elect men and women chosen from eternity for this glorious destiny; an eschatology which declared that Jesus would one day return in power to conduct the Last Judgment and establish the Kingdom of Saints, and a soteriology which involved worldly renunciation.

When however, these pristine teachings appeared in the Gentile world, they underwent a profound Hellenization in the Pauline literature and the Fourth Gospel. Here the Christology becomes mystical, an elaborate theological concept, in which Jesus is the Word, a pre-existing deity; everlasting torture in hell is no longer proclaimed; saintly poverty is replaced by private enterprise and charity, and there is no ethical imperative for renunciation; there is no Last Judgment or Kingdom of Saints. Only the doctrine of redemption by vicarious atonement remained intact.

2. *Catholicism.* Pauline Hellenization constituted indeed a basic revision, but Catholicism went far beyond this. For it drew heavily upon Monachism, Manichaeism, and Mithraism, as well as the cults of Isis, Adonis, Orpheus, and Eleusis in order to become the universal, or catholic, communion.

3. *The Reformation.* The paramount purpose of the Reformation was to break the stranglehold of the feudal Catholic hierarchy upon a northern economy struggling for freedom to develop into free enterprise and competitive production. It stripped from Catholicism many of its excrescences; but it returned, not to pristine Christianity, but rather to the Hellenized form found in Paul and the Fourth Gospel. However, it retained the dogmas of the

Trinity, Original Sin, the two natures of Christ-Jesus, the creation of the world out of nothing, and indeterminate but sometime-expected literal Parousia, as well as several other tenets not clearly enunciated in the original Gospels.

D. *The Cosmological System*

1. *The Central Sun.* Swedenborg's theological cosmology is precisely that of the *Principia*, written many years before his Illumination. At the center of the universe is a great sun, or primary substance, the parent of all the other celestial bodies, which are derivative from this original source and move about it in orbital circuits. There are thousands, perhaps millions, of these secondary suns, of which ours is one, each of which has its own primary and secondary satellites. The primary sun is the ultimate source of light, heat, vitality, life, and existence in the universe; the derivative suns are pure fire and their function is simply to relay the life-giving force proceeding from the original center to the lesser bodies and to any creatures who may live upon them.

2. *Other Inhabited Earths.* Swedenborg was the first spaceman, if only in imagination or in his spiritual body. "There are many inhabited earths in the universe,"[141] he declared; and he estimated their number at "some hundreds of thousands."[142] He delineates the habits, appearance, beliefs, ethics, and religious practices of the people living on the planets of our solar system;[143] not content with this, he tells us how he visited "while in a state of wakefulness" the first earth of the starry heavens...where there appeared many who "are actually men."[144]

E. *The Theological System*

1. *God and the Central Sun.* God, or the Lord, is equated with the central sun of the universe;[145] he is, therefore, not only the fountainhead of all that lives or exists, but is also identical with all substance or existence. "There is only one substance," he states, "from which all things are, and the sun of the spiritual world is that substance."[146] "Creation must...be wholly ascribed to the sun of the spiritual world...a living force...."[147] "The Lord from eternity... created the universe and all things thereof from himself and not from nothing."[148] Since "God is omnipresent,"[149] we read, his absence "from man is no more possible than the absence of the sun from the earth through its heat and light."[150] "There is only one fountain of life, and all life is therefrom.... Creation is the continuous operation of this vital force."[151] "There is one only life, and whatever things live, live from that life...the Lord is that Life itself...."[152]

2. *No Providence*. God, then, is the source of light, heat, life, vitality, and generative power, which are omnipresent and flow into every object which exists. This was the central thesis of Michael Servetus, and the basis of his unitarian theology. The Swedenborgian God, like that of Epicurus and modern deists, can never be appeased, won over, or persuaded to grant any special favors:[153] for he is not a personality; he is the creative force, the cosmic law, the universal substance. We find no vestige of an orthodox Providence in Swedenborg, or one as known to historical Christianity; not one word concerning supplication to the deity or its efficacy as a solution for the ills or the problems of humanity.

3. *Historic Theology*. The original Synoptic Gospels knew little of theology or metaphysics. Following Paul and the Fourth Gospel, however, theological and Christological theories (heresies) proliferated apace in the ancient world and subdivided Christianity into innumerable cults. The theology which finally prevailed, known as Trinitarianism, declares that God the Father, God the Word or Son, and God the Holy Spirit are three distinct persons, existing nevertheless from eternity as a single godhead, indivisible and consubstantial (homoousian); and this concept was frozen into dogmas which declared that Christ-Jesus was a single person with two natures indivisibly and harmoniously conjoined.

4. *Heresies*. But before these dogmas were established, Christianity had been torn by fierce controversies and bloody wars for centuries, in which literally tens of millions perished and Graeco-Roman culture was destroyed. One of the more virulent of the early heresies, brought to its culmination by Sabellius, was known as Monarchianism, which sought to establish the unity of God through a trinity of succession: as Creator, God existed as the Father; as Redeemer, in human form, he was the Son or Word; after the resurrection, God exists timelessly as the Holy Spirit. This heresy was known also as Patripassionism, because according to it God the Father suffered on the cross.

With the suppression of Monarchianism, another persistent heresy arose, known as Adoptionism, of which the principal exponent was Paul of Samosata, Bishop of Antioch, in 260; this declared that Jesus was born as are other men; but that, by a special divine dispensation, he was able to continue in a totally sinless state and could therefore be adopted by God as his Son and become by this process divine and thus capable of removing human iniquity through his sacrificial death and atonement.

Adoptionism culminated in what is known as Arianism, which involves the very core and essence of Christianity—the efficacy of the atonement. The crux of Arianism consisted in its separation of the Son from the Word, which was accorded eternal existence; but the Son, even though he came into being before the world, was said to have been created in time and was therefore mutable and not a member of the godhead. The cornerstone of both Catholic and Protestant theology and Christology is officially to this day the Nicene Trinitarianism, in which the Word and the Son are identical.

Not until the Reformation did any new or distinctive theological or Christological doctrines appear. The principal exponents of the heresies which then arose were Servetus, born in 1511 or 1509 and executed by Calvin at Geneva in 1553; Faustus Socinus, born at Sienna in 1539, and Laelius Socinus, uncle of Faustus, born in 1525. The younger Socinus preached an uncompromising Unitarianism; and his Christology was a total Adoptionism. Servetus, to whom modern Unitarians usually trace their origin, taught various concepts also found among the Socinians; but his distinctive contribution consisted of a theology which proclaimed a divine triunity, not of succession, as the Sabellians did, but of eternal manifestations, dispositions, attributes, or modality.[154] According to his metaphysics, God the Father is the substance of the universe; God the Word is its active or creative agency; and God the Holy Spirit is its vital, generative, and sustaining force. It is obvious that Swedenborg was much closer to Servetus and the Sabellians, whom he never mentions, than to the Arians and Socinians, whom he often condemns.

We should perhaps at this point note that during the early and formative period of the Christian movement, three principal Christologies were prevalent. The first of these—and the original—was simply that Jesus was a man born, like all others, in the ordinary course of nature, but that he was endowed with the Christ-Spirit at his baptism, which enabled him to perform his great mission and the sacrificial atonement. The second was embraced by a great variety of Gnostic communions, which proliferated throughout the Graeco-Roman Empire and which proclaimed that Jesus the Christ was not a human being at all, but a phantasm or emanation sent by the supreme God of the Universe (a Zoroastrian concept) to reveal his plan of salvation to mankind. In this Christology, the Christ is a power rather than a person or a personality; and it is obvious that Swedenborg and New Thought in general are much closer to some form of Gnosticism than to any other historical ideology. The third, the conventional and orthodox, was closely patterned upon that held by many pagan cults centuries before the establishment of Christianity: namely that Christ-Jesus, like various pagan savior-gods, was born of a virgin as a result of divine impregnation and therefore at once both god and man. In order to establish this dogma as the foundation of Christianity, Matthew 3:17 was corrupted; the original proclamation of the heavenly voice heard during the baptismal rite—"This is my beloved Son; This day have I begotten Thee"—was altered to read: "This is my beloved son in whom I am well pleased." Without this alteration of the original gospel, it may be doubted that Christianity could have converted the Greek and Roman masses, of whom millions had already accepted one or another of the various savior-cults so widespread throughout the Mediterranean area.

5. *Theological Rationalism.* "A Trinity of Persons from eternity," says Swedenborg, "is not only above reason, but opposed to it."[155] "How can the divine essence," he asks, "which is one, the same, and indivisible, fall into number, hence be either divided or multiplied?"[156] "The Athanasian Faith is such as to be incomprehensible, and thence incredible, and likewise contradictory."[157] "The heresies, from the first ages to the present day, have sprung up from no other source than from the doctrine founded in the idea of three gods."[158]

6. *A Triune Unitarian.* Instead of a trinity of persons, says Swedenborg, there is one of operations or attributes: "These Three, Father, Son, and Holy Spirit, are Three Essentials of One God, since they are One, as soul, body, and operation with man are one."[159] Jehovah God is also the redeeming Christ: "By the Lord, the Redeemer, we mean Jehovah in the Human" who "Himself descended and assumed a Human in order that He might effect redemption."[160] "The Divine Itself," we read, "is the Trine...This Trine itself, and the one Divine, is the Lord."[161] And again: "By three persons I understand three Divine attributes going forth, Creation, Redemption, and Regeneration, and that these are attributes of one God..."[162] manifested in three successional operations. The Lord "is both Father and Son."[163] Concerning the Holy Spirit, Swedenborg states that it "is the same as the Lord."[164]

7. *The Impersonal God.* Swedenborg ridicules those who think of God as someone who can be seen or on whose right hand the Son might be seated.[165] He is certainly not "an old man, holy, with a gray beard."[166] We note that during Swedenborg's twenty-seven years in the spirit world, during which he conversed with a hundred thousand of the departed, including Moses, the twelve disciples, and the Virgin Mary, he never mentions seeing the Lord, or Jesus Christ, much less the Father, except as the Central Sun. The Christ is a power, not a person or a personality.

8. *In Summary.* God, then, is the uncreated, impersonal, and basic substance of the universe, which is revealed successively as Creator, Redeemer, and Regenerator, which are the triune attributes or operations of the unitarian God. It is perhaps pertinent to note that the Monarchians were not the only ancients who believed the Savior to be literally God, appearing as a man among men; for there is an ancient document known as *The Testaments of the Twelve Patriarchs*, probably written in its entirety by the Essenes, which teaches precisely the same doctrine. There was, therefore, nothing wholly new in Swedenborg's theology; but it was certainly constructed and reformulated upon a unique hypothesis and assumes, therefore, the nature of a startling originality.

However, if there were predecessors who proclaimed theological concepts similar to Swedenborg's, there were none who had ever formulated anything comparable to his cosmological theology, which is related integrally, as we have already noted, to the Nebular Hypothesis, and therefore unique.

F. *The Major Derivative Doctrines*

1. *Divine Penetration or Influx*. According to the Doctrine of Influx, a vitalizing power flows constantly and universally from the central life-giving force into everything that exists. Without this, there could be no health, moral or physical, in any living creature. "God alone is life," says Swedenborg; and, employing almost the very language of Servetus in his *De Erroribus Trinitatis*, continues: "It follows without question that from His life He gives life to every man...as...the sun of the world with its whole essence, which is heat and light, flows into every tree, every shrub and flower, every stone...each object draws its own portion from the common influx...he gives it all, and to man the ability to take either little or much."[167] Birds and beasts derive their skills[168] and bees their wisdom[169] from this influx. Without it, man "would instantly fall down dead."[170] Were it not for this cosmic vitality, the whole universe would become, as it were, an infinite corpse.

2. *Departure into New Thought*. The doctrine of Influx marks the point of departure into New Thought, the metaphysical system of philosophy and religion in which the ancient creeds and dogmas are no longer valid; for, in this, God, made manifest in Christ, becomes the life-force which animates the cosmos. Every living being in it, and especially the apex of creation, Man, needs only open the sluice-gates of his mind-soul to allow this natural force to flow in and possess him. All this is declared a universal and scientific reality; it is neither mystical nor mysterious; it is all around us, and presses upon us for admission. A religion built on such premises therefore purports to be as completely demonstrable in discipline and as certain in its assumptions, operations, and results as any empirical science, verifiable by repeated experiment.

3. *Dualism*. However, in the Swedenborgian metaphysics, there is a certain dualism:[171] each human being is a moral receptacle, seeking to absorb whatever fosters his own basic love. Good as well as evil can exist in man; there is freedom and moral responsibility because everyone has the capacity "of perceiving whether a thing is so or not so"; he has this power because of the "influx from the spiritual world."[172] But if men were not protected by divine power from infernal evils and temptations, these "would rush in like a vast ocean, one hell after another,"[173] and overwhelm him utterly.

4. *Spiritual Balance*. Because of this duality, man stands poised between

two profound influences;[174] he is in a state of perpetual "equilibrium between heaven and hell...."[175]

5. *Freedom of Choice*. Since this equality is so perfectly adjusted, man, endowed with perceptional cognition, has the power to choose either; and, by so doing, determines his everlasting fate. "Man is placed in the middle between heaven and hell...and he has the freedom to think what is good or...what is evil. This freedom the Lord never takes from anyone, for it belongs to his life and is the means of his reformation."[176]

6. *The World a Replica by Correspondence*. The Doctrine of Correspondences was first developed in *The Animal Kingdom*, 1740; it means that our world is a copy of the eternal and spiritual, which is a concept foreshadowed in Platonism. "The natural world," says Swedenborg, "could not exist except from the spiritual."[177] "There is a correspondence of all things in the world with all things in heaven; also there is a correspondence of all things of the body with all things in the mind of man...."[178]

7. *The Ethical Imperative*. The Doctrine of Correspondences extends also into the realm of ethics. "A man," we read, "who is in correspondence, that is, who is in love to the Lord and charity toward his neighbor...is also a little heaven in human form...."[179] Again: "Man is so created as to be an image of heaven and an image of the world, for he is a microcosm."[180] And so we have countless millions of immortal but finite creatures in the world, everyone of which is a replica of the cosmos, which is God or the Grand Man.

8. *The Origin of Evil*. "Hereditary evil did not come from Adam and his wife Eve by their eating of the tree of knowledge...."[181] But "everyone who commits actual sin" develops an evil nature which is never dissipated "except in those who are being regenerated by the Lord."[182]

9. *Eradicable Wickedness*. This anthropology was anathema to the theologians of the Reformation because of two basic deviations. The first is that the evil in men here emphasized is not the ineradicable Original Sin which lies at the center of Pauline and Reformation doctrine; it is only an acquired propensity, for which "no man ever suffers punishment in the other life";[183] and which can be eliminated by the aid of the divine influx available to everyone. The second was even more fundamental: for it postulated a regenerative process which results from voluntary conduct wholly independent of the Vicarious Atonement. In Swedenborgianism, there are no elect and no reprobates; God has predestined no one to heaven or to hell. "He loves the universal human race and desires eternally to save every member of it..." and "no one has ever been predestined to hell...."[184] The God of Swedenborg is one of universal love.

G. The Redemptive System

1. *The Atonement.* All orthodox Christian denominations agree that Jesus was the divine God-man, who died as an atonement for the sins of humanity and whose sacrament must be consumed for redemption. By rejecting this, the Unitarians, the Swedenborgians, and all New Thought communicants have placed themselves outside the periphery of historic Christianity. However, when Swedenborg wrote *The Worship and the Love of God*, he still accepted the historic doctrine of the atonement; and this was a full year after his Illumination![185]

2. *All This Rejected.* This Christology, however, soon underwent a drastic reconstruction, in which the Christ-Lord became the Supreme God Himself, appearing on earth in the form of a man. "Redemption could not have been effected," declares Swedenborg, "except by God Incarnate."[186] How the Lord came into the world, put on and then deified his humanity, and so became the savior of mankind is "the Second Arcanum" of religion.[187] The doctrine that salvation is accomplished through faith or a vicarious atonement is "no religion" at all, but mere "emptiness and vacuity"[188] because it would be a "reformation and regeneration without means...."[189] "Be it known that no one is purified by the Lord's passion on the cross, thus by his blood...."[190] The "Lord did not come into the world to propitiate the Father and to move Him to mercy, nor to bear our iniquities and thus to take them away, nor that we might be saved by the imputation of His merit...."[191]

And here lies the very heart and core of all New Thought and of the Swedenborgian heresy and doctrine.

3. *The Apotheosis of the Human.* "Jehovah, who is the Lord," says Swedenborg, "descended and took upon Himself a Human, by conception ...from a virgin, such as is that of another man; but this he expelled, and ...made the Human that was born" a divine essence. By this process, he became "the Lord."[192] Before the Incarnation there was no Son or Lord, but only Jehovah God, the cosmic essence; this creative power appeared in human form as Christ-Jesus, and constituted his soul; yet in his body, derived from his mother, human evil and weakness still existed,[193] just as it does with all mankind. He was, however, able (necessarily by his own effort since there was at that time no divine influx) to conquer and overcome all temptations. In so doing, he underwent a process by which the human element became divine. The passion on the cross was merely his last temptation. In his resurrection, therefore, he emerged with a spiritualized body.[194]

4. *Why the Incarnation?* "The Lord Himself came into the world and became Man...to...the end that...He might" teach and instruct mankind in the principles of salvation,[195] as the ancient Gnostics declared.

5. *The Integrity of the Will.* The Catholic and Reformation councils, says Swedenborg, hatched "one after another direful heresies based upon...man's impotence in spiritual things, and also that most pernicious heresy, predestination...all of which imply that God is the cause of evil, or that he created both good and evil."[196] He emphasizes "that it would be impossible for any good to be rooted in man except in his freedom,"[197] which enables "every man...to desist from evil, because He [the Lord] gives him to will and to understand.... By this, the Lord brings man into a state of conjunction with Himself, and in this...reforms, regenerates, saves him."[198] This is accomplished by the divine influx, available to all humanity.

"Every man is born into two diabolical loves, the love of self and the love of the world...."[199] For this reason, everyone should struggle against his own evil propensities. In spite of this, however, the Lord enables man, through cooperation with the divine influx, to withdraw himself entirely from the natural state; and "thus man becomes, as it were, created anew, and this is what was called reformation and regeneration..."[200] Without freedom, "nothing could be given to him, and he would be like an inanimate body."[201]

6. *No Compulsion.* Should God, however, manifest his power by miracles in order to persuade, these would "close the internal man, and deprive him of all that free will, through which" he "is regenerated."[202] God could by fiat decree that all should be saved; but this would be an ethical perversion comparable to universal damnation without guilt. Since compulsion does not reconstitute the will, signs, miracles, visions, threats of future punishment, and conversation with the dead cannot regenerate.[203] "If man," continues Swedenborg, "could have been reformed by compulsion, there would not be any man in the universe who would not be saved; for nothing could be easier for the Lord than to compel men to fear him, to worship him...." But worship under compulsion has no value whatever.[204]

7. *Conventional Doctrine of Redemption.* Swedenborg thus summarizes Pauline, Augustinian, Lutheran, and Calvinist teaching, according to which "man is so utterly corrupt and dead to good that.... there does not abide in his nature...even a spark of spiritual strength by which...to understand...or do anything toward his own conversion...in the smallest measure."[205] All this, concludes Swedenborg, "is at this day a fiery flying serpent in the church, and by it religion is abolished, security reduced, and damnation imputed to the Lord...."[206]

8. *True Basis for Redemption.* How, then, *does* regeneration take place? We read that it is only necessary to live a truly ethical life, obey the Commandments, observe the civil law, and live a life of charity and neighborly love; but we must do this because it is in accord with our internal will and *not because of expediency or external pressure of any kind.* In short, good ethics, practiced from internal choice, constitutes the highest religion. We must love

our neighbor as ourselves, and do to others as we would have them do unto us, *because we can tolerate no other way of life.* "Everyone who makes these commandments the principles of his religion," we read, "becomes a citizen and an inhabitant of heaven...."[207]

9. *What Is One's Own?* "Most in the Christian World," he declares, "do not make" true love of God and charity toward the neighbor "the principles of their religion"; they refrain from various external evil acts, not "because they are sins against God, but because they have fears for their life, their reputation, their office, their business, their possessions, their honor and gain, and their pleasure...Because, therefore, such form for themselves no communication with heaven....they cannot be saved."[208] Furthermore, any opinion received from others is worthless, for "if a man's faith is to remain with him after death it must be his own faith; and it becomes his own when he sees, wills, and does what he believes...from interior affection...."[209]

10. *Ethical Road to Heaven.* It is quite possible for anyone who sincerely desires regeneration to abhor what is prohibited by the law.[210] Actually, "it is not so difficult to live the life of heaven as some believe," for, as "a man accustoms himself" to think ethically, "he is gradually conjoined to heaven...."[211] By making his desire for righteousness paramount, man begins the slow and arduous process of regeneration:[212] "in the measure in which the spiritual internal and heaven are opened to man, the natural internal is purified from the hell that is there. This is not done at once, but successively, by degrees...."[213] "Every man may be regenerated..." If he is not saved, it is "because he does not cooperate."[214]

11. *Innovations.* Regeneration, salvation, and eternal redemption, then, can result only from life actuated by a love of God and charity for one's neighbor.[215] But the question arises: how is love for God to be expressed? And what constitutes a life of charity toward one's neighbor? And finally: who *is* my neighbor?

Brushing aside the precepts of the theologians and of various popular religions, Swedenborg declares that the moral regeneration and eternal redemption offered by the Christ-religion are quite compatible with the enjoyment of material and intellectual pleasures and well-being; the health, prosperity, and ultimate happiness of the individual, therefore, emerge as wholly permissible objectives. This revolutionary transformation was accomplished largely through a system of ethics which glorified science, self-reliance, free enterprise, private property, personal integrity, and individual responsibility; and which requires of each and every one that he care for himself, practice the Golden Rule, and contribute to society at least as much as he receives.

If charity to the neighbor is paramount, who, then, *is* my neighbor? "The collective man, that is, a community smaller or greater, and composite man formed of communities, that is, one's country, is the neighbor that is to be loved," says Swedenborg.[216] And again: "The objects of charity are the individual man, a society, one's own country, and the human race; and all men are the neighbor...."[217] True religion consists in activity useful "to the neighbor, from affection and delight."[218] The ethical religion of Swedenborg may be summed up in these words: "All religion is of the life, and the life of religion is to do that which is good."[219]

"The charity that comes from a selfish or worldly end...is not charity," but only that which "regards as its end the neighbor" and "the general good...."[220] "In common belief, charity is nothing else than giving to the poor, relieving the needy, caring for widows and orphans, contributing to the building of hospitals, infirmaries, asylums, orphans' homes, and especially of churches...."[221] "Some think that if good works must be done for the sake of eternal life, they must give to the poor all they possess, as was done in the primitive church, and as 'the Lord commanded the rich man'...."[222] In Swedenborg's ethical system, however, no error could be greater than this.

"The poor," he says, "come into heaven, not account of their poverty, but because of their life...Moreover, poverty leads and draws man away from heaven just as much as wealth does."[223] Many of the poor are not content with their lot, but believe riches to be blessings and when they do not get them "harbor ill thoughts about Divine providence...."[224]

True charity requires that all be socially productive: "No man is wise or lives for himself alone, but for others also...Living for others is being useful. Uses are the bonds of society; these bonds are as many as there are good uses, and in number uses are infinite."[225] And further: "Every man must make provision for himself so as to have the necessaries of life, as food, clothing, a place to dwell in, and other things...and this not only for himself, but also for his family; and not only for the present time, but also for the future. Unless each person procures for himself the necessaries of life, he cannot be in a state to exercise charity toward the neighbor, for he is himself in need of all things."[226]

We live a life of true charity when we deal justly and honestly with every man, contribute more to society than we take in return, do useful and productive work constantly and competently, and live self-reliantly without aggression toward anyone.[227] "Magistrates and officers" practice charity "if they discharge their respective functions from zeal for the common good...."[228] Conducting a business honestly is a life of charity;[229] as is fighting a defensive war.[230] Making a fortune in the production and distribution of honest merchandise may well be the highest form of charity.[231]

12. *New Meanings for the Gospel.* Swedenborg declares that "'to renounce all possessions" is to attribute nothing of intelligence and wisdom to one-

self...."[232] When the Lord told the rich young man to sell all that he had and give it to the poor, this meant only that "he should remove his heart from riches"; and the command to take the cross "meant that he should fight against concupiscences...."[233]

13. *The Riches of Holiness.* Wealth, prosperity, honors, material well-being, beauty, and pleasure in this life are, then, not merely permissible: they are in the highest degree laudable—the proper objectives of the truly religious life. In Swedenborg's heaven, there are parks, palaces, libraries, and enjoyments of every kind, including the most exquisite sexual and dietary delights; and all these things are equally praiseworthy on earth, when rightly acquired and utilized. We read that those who "have lived in luxury, splendor, and elegance, provided they have lived at the same time in faith in the Lord and charity to the neighbor, are among the happy in the other life."[234]

It is precisely this ethical concept which separates Swedenborg and New Thought as a whole from the historical Christian disciplines. He informs us that he had learned "from conversations with the angels" that it is not necessary to discard "riches and honors" in order to "live the life that leads to heaven."[235] "Truth is falsified," he continues, "when it is said that no man can enter heaven except one who has...reduced himself to miseries."[236] Not only are rich men and women, if virtuous, welcome in heaven;[237] what is more,[238] they continue there in eternal opulence. "Riches and wealth are hurtful" only when used for evil purposes.[239]

Swedenborg warns, however, that there are wicked people who persuade themselves that their own personal advantage and aggrandizement constitute the common good.[240] Anyone who desires power and wealth so that he can reduce his fellows to servitude "murders them in his heart,"[241] and can never breathe the pure atmosphere of heaven.

H. *The New Church*

Swedenborg declared over and over that he had been commissioned by the Lord to reveal the doctrine of the New Church "which is" that "foretold by Daniel...."[242] Some have adopted the erroneous belief that at "the Last Judgment all things on earth are then to perish, and that a new heaven and a new earth will exist in their place...." But "the day of the Last Judgment does not mean the destruction of the world...."[243] In fact, "The state of the world" will continue as "it has been.... divided churches will exist among the Gentiles. But henceforth" men will be more free in their thinking about matters of faith.[244] And the Church of the New Jerusalem will be available to all the inhabitants of the earth.

I. *Eschatology*

1. *The Final Last Judgment.* Never before had any professed Christian publicly denied that there would one day be a great Parousia in which Christ-Jesus, surrounded by myriads of angels, would appear in the earthly sky, descend to earth, and there conduct the Last Judgment and receive his saints. But, according to Swedenborg, all this was a purely spiritual event, to be followed by the institution of the Church of the New Jerusalem on earth. There would never be another judgment.

2. *Life in the Spirit-World.* A substantial portion of Swedenborg's revelation deals with existence in the Spirit-World. This consists of three great realms, heaven, hell, and the world of spirits, the last of which is an interspace between the other two,[245] into which good influx descends from which heaven and evil influx rises from hell.[246] The term *Spirit-World* designates the three realms collectively.

Imagine a being who is pure spirit, yet identical in every essential respect to what he was on earth: this is the Swedenborgian Man, the immortal. Emotionally, intellectually, morally, and anatomically, he is a replica of his former self.[247] "A spirit or an angel...has a similar face, similar body...in a word, he is a man in external form altogether like a man of the world.... interior viscera of the body are similar.... conjugal love is also similar with all its effects...."[248]

3. *New Thought Metaphysics.* We find here not only the probable source of the metaphysics of Christian Science and New Thought in general, but also the basis for their theory of sin, sickness, disease, healing, and well-being. Since the mind is the true essence of man and the only aspect which is real or permanent, it follows that the body is only a temporary integument, the portion of man which, at death, as it is called, fades as a dream, leaving the reality. Although Swedenborg never taught the unreality or non-existence of matter or of the physical body, we can understand how one who failed to understand him fully might leap to this conclusion by studying him cursorily; and conclude that the body has no actual existence and that, therefore, all sickness and disease are pure delusions, errors of mortal mind.

All who inhabit the other world were once men, women, or children in some inhabited earth; there are no other beings in the spiritual world or the world of spirits. We learn that "hell did not originate in any devil created an angel of light and cast down from heaven, but both heaven and hell are from the human race...."[249] The earth is simply the seminary in which human beings are born for their eternal destiny in the World of Spirits.

4. *The Heavens and Life in the Spirit-World.* According to Swedenborg, the transition to immortal life is rapid, easy, and without shock; he declared that he had conversed with at least "an hundred thousand" in the other world who had been dead for differing periods, "of whom many were in the heavens

and many in the hells." Many had been spirits for centuries; but he had "also spoken with some two days after their decease...."[250]

"Every man after death becomes a spirit...and all spirits, before they are cast down to hell or raised up into heaven, are first in the world of spirits...."[251] "From the things seen during so many years, I am enabled to relate...that in the spiritual world...there are hills and mountains, plains and valleys and also fountains and rivers, lakes, and seas; there are paradises and gardens, groves and woods, palaces and houses...writings and books, offices and trades.... in a word...all things that exist in the natural world...."[252]

When a man "comes into the spiritual world, which for the most part takes place the third day after he has expired, he appears to himself in a life similar to that to which he had been in the world.... This happens...that death may not appear as death, but as a continuation of life...."[253] He "does not know that he has died."[254] For "he is equally a man after death.... he walks, runs, and sits as in the former world; he eats and drinks, enjoys connubial delight.... From which it is plain that death is but a continuation of life and is only transition."[255] This is a word usually used in New Thought to describe death.

When a man becomes a spirit, every virtuous or immoral act committed in his former state will have contributed to the formation of his present character.[256] His ethical constitution has been formed for eternity; and he must live according to his dominating love or desire. Whatever he had become on earth is taken with him into the other world: this is emphasized again and again.[257] When he enters the spiritual world, every basic passion is intensified; and, since no hypocrisy is possible there, and since there are no artificial restraints, the wicked translate into overt action all their most detestable and repulsive qualities and passions.[258]

In this realm where all spirits from every earth gather, come millions of new arrivals in never-ending streams. They are of every race, color, moral nature, and indoctrination. They are given a course in the truths of religion, ethical and metaphysical; if they have already confirmed themselves in moral wickedness or in false and vicious doctrine, they cannot be reformed; but if they are of basically ethical character, only misled by false teachers, they prove amenable to instruction, are regenerated, and so redeemed. The wicked deteriorate progressively and are cast down into the hells; the good improve and in time become more beautiful, entirely fit for life in heaven,[259] while the wicked together with their habitations become more ugly and repulsive, until each kind reaches the zenith or the nadir of their development.[260] We should note that all those who have been confirmed in, and will not renounce, the erroneous dogmas concerning the Trinity, the Lord, predestination, etc. "are cast down into hell."[261]

The angels are delightful creatures who never grow old. In fact, as in the paradise of Zoroaster, "all who come into heaven return into the springtime of their youth, and into the vigor of that age and remain so to eternity."[262] And not only do the old grow young: for good "women who have died worn out with age" can "advance...into the flower of youth and early womanhood, and attain to a beauty that transcends every conception of such beauty seen on the earth."[263] And so the Swedenborgian old ladies, bent and withered, even spinsters who had always been rejected, blossom and become queens of beauty and of love!

Those who were subjected by priests in the spiritual world to endless prayer, preaching, and worship were often driven to rebel against this regimen.[264] Those who envisioned heaven as a place of everlasting feasting, games, and other diversions were equally mistaken,[265] as were those who thought it would be a place of everlasting rest. The angels had long since discovered that happiness consists in useful activity, in service to others, which takes an infinity of forms.[266] In heaven, idleness is as unknown as it is intolerable:[267] the angels engage in scientific pursuits;[268] they carry on athletic contests, games of ball, tennis, etc.; they produce spectacular stage entertainments.[269] They have libraries of all kinds[270] and museums, gymnasiums, and colleges, where their literary sports are held.[271] All children, whether born of pious or impious parents, whether born in the church or outside it are received by the Lord when they die and are brought up to heaven.[272]

5. *Sex, Love, and Marriage in Heaven.* Swedenborg declares that Man as Male and Man as Female are drawn together by a "disposition to conjunction" and by congenital forces which seek to make them one. And while such unions are too often frustrated because of conditions in the natural world, no such barriers exist among the spirits.[273]

Matrimonial arrangements are elaborate in heaven, where the yearning for sexual consummation not only continues, but is much intensified. Those who are married to each other in the world "most commonly meet after death, recognize each other, consociate again...." But "as they put off things external...they perceive...whether they can live together or not." If each finds in the other his eternal soul-mate, they remain married; otherwise, they separate and seek new affinities, in which partners "enjoy similar intercourse with each other as in the world, only more delightful and blessed, but without proliferation."[274]

Those who condemned marriage in the world on the ground that it is immoral or inferior to celibacy are excluded from heaven; and we learn that chastity does not consist in sexual abstinence[275] but in faithful conjugal love.[276] The beautiful maidens and the even more lovely wives[277] in the spirit-world are adorned only by their own personal beauty.[278]

We read that "those who have lived in a chaste love of marriage...continue unceasingly in the flower of youth. The delights of their love are ineffable, and increase to eternity...."[279] "Angels have perpetual potency, because they are in perpetual love."[280] One angel told Swedenborg exultingly: "I...have lived with my wife now a thousand years...and I can assure you that the faculty with me has been and is perpetual."[281] Angels "are in continued potency.... after the sex acts, there is never any weariness.... the married pair pass the night in each other's bosoms as if they were created into one.... their delights...cannot be described...in any language in the natural world...."[282]

6. *The Fate of the Wicked.* "No one is tormented in hell by angels of the Lord"[283] and the misery of the devils arises not from remorse "but from their not being able to do evil, which is the delight of their life...."[284] When, however, they are able to inflict it, other devils are instantly at hand to chastise and requite them in kind.[285] For "the greatest delight of their life consists in being able to punish, torture, and torment one another...whereby they know how to induce exquisite suffering...."[286] "By the Law of Correspondences, the inmates of hell become creatures wholly repulsive, monstrous, and malodorous,"[287] so frightful that it is impossible to give an adequate description of them.

J. Spiritualism

1. *Another Cult.* We can say with a fair degree of certainty that Swedenborg was also the primary source and father of the modern, widespread spiritualist movement, which became one of the more important American cults which flourished in the 19th century, but which has now declined to the point of being little more than a fad. "Spiritualism is Swedenborgianism Americanized," wrote John Humphrey Noyes in his *History of American Socialisms.*[288]

2. *The Potent Invisibles.* The various activities of spirits, beneficent and malignant, constitute a basic element in Swedenborgianism, as they did in ancient Essenism and its offspring, Ebionism, an early form of Jewish Christianity. Not only do these invisible beings range far and wide and come into contact with those still in the natural world; every human being has an associate spirit which can travel into space at all times. The natural man, according to Swedenborg's teachings, has a great propensity toward evil and is therefore a prime receptacle for the noxious beings of the spirit-world.

Swedenborg's later life, like that of Mary Baker Eddy, was a bitter struggle against the hostile spirits who sought to infest and destroy him. In one passage, he describes in detail the machination of one who could kill "by a certain magical art...without the use of any knife, sword, or dagger, or other instrument...."[289] This was a power identical to the Malicious Animal Magnetism of Mary Baker Eddy.

Swedenborg's servant of many years, Maria, testified that he often wept bitterly at night and cried out in a loud voice, "Oh, Lord, my God, do not forsake me!" Sometimes he would not even rise from his bed for days on end, and his friends thought he would expire.[290] *The Apocalypse Revealed* contains a long description of one of these anguished experiences, in which he lay as dead for three days.[291] Only the beneficent influx kept him from total destruction.[292]

K. *Disease and Health*

1. *The Temporary Integument.* Swedenborg's assumptions concerning the ever-present spiritual beings and of man as a substantive mind-essence lead directly to his theories concerning health and disease. Since the body is only the temporary abode of the real self, which is mind or spirit, it follows that nothing of serious consequence can attack or injure this exterior. It exists, yes; but in the metaphysical sense *the body does not possess essential reality.* Sickness is simply a malady which, because of sin or error or a failure of understanding, attacks the temporary or unreal man; the spiritual man can have no cognizance of disease.[293] It is true that while man remains in this world, his "faculty of sensation" is manifested in the body; but even then it was only "the spirit that sensated."[294] However, it is only if we permit them to enter and inflict themselves upon us that evils or devils have the power to infest us; and with them come sin, concupiscence, hatred, error, heresy, sickness, diseases, and every manner of personal devastation, including, at last, death itself.

2. *The Metaphysics of Health.* Elaborating an ancient doctrine set forth by the Ebionite Peter in *The Clementine Homilies,* Swedenborg declared that, wherever possible, malignant spirits "diffuse themselves.... like poisons.... upon the nerves and fibers, from which break forth the most grievous and fatal diseases."[295] The "infernals," he declared, "induce diseases and death."[296] Swedenborg refused any remedy for a toothache, saying that it was caused by a certain hypocritical spirit who would soon depart.[297] He was certain that all apparently physical ailments are but the concomitants of the sins we permit to infest our minds. He declared that "diseases also have correspondence with the spiritual world" and "correspond to the cupidities and passions of the lower mind...for the origins of diseases are, in general, intemperance, luxury of various kinds, mere bodily pleasures, as also feelings of hatred, revenge, lewdness, and the like, which destroy men's interiors; and when these are destroyed, the exteriors suffer, and drag man into disease, and so into death. It is known...that the death of man is from evils or on account of sin; and it is the same with diseases, for these belong to death."[298] "All diseases" result "from excessive indulgences of various vices...from lascivious practices and from anxiety about the future.... These things vitiate the blood; and when this

is vitiated, they obstruct and choke up the very small vessels...wherefore diseases break out."[299]

For this reason, every sickness may be cured by spiritual means, "because the power of the Lord is infinite."[300]

3. *Disease is Sin and Error.* And so Swedenborg was the first modern to proclaim that all maladies result from evils, errors, or devils, which infest the mind. When we open our emotional and intellectual sluice-gates (the will and the understanding) for the divine influx to enter, we experience a healing regeneration which makes sin and sickness alike impossible. Since the divine influx is universal, no one can possibly refuse its benefits except through perversity or error, which thus becomes synonymous with sin. And since this truth can be demonstrated as in a laboratory, it becomes a scientific instead of a mystical process; we have, therefore, at last an empirical religion, in short, a scientific Christianity.

4. *Sickness and Death.* Swedenborg sometimes utilized his anatomical knowledge to illustrate the nature of physical maladies: "As death is from no other source than sin, and sin is all that which is contrary to Divine Order, therefore evil closes the very smallest most invisible vessels.... Hence come the first and inmost obstructions...into the blood. When this vitiation increases, it causes disease, and finally death. If, however, man had lived a life of good, his interiors would be open to heaven, and through heaven to the Lord; and so too would the very least and most invisible little vessels.... In consequence, man would be without disease, and would merely decline to extreme old age.... when the body could no longer minister to his internal man or spirit, he would pass without disease out of his earthly body into a body such as the angels have, thus out of the world directly into heaven."[301]

The Christ-Power, then, or the Lord, when permitted to enter, drives away every sin and disease. Sickness is caused by physical indulgence, lustful desire, or ethical and doctrinal error carried into the human viscera by evil agencies, which thus debilitate the whole human organism.

L. *The Church of the New Jerusalem*

1. *The Great Mission.* This brings us to the crowning achievement of Swedenborg: his proclamation of the Second Coming, the Parousia too long awaited by the Christian churches. This constitutes his interpretation of Revelation, and particularly of certain passages in chapters 12 and 21 relating to the woman crowned with the twelve stars and the holy city Jerusalem descending out of heaven. It was because of this that his communion is known as the Church of the New Jerusalem.

His mission, expanding that of Servetus in his monumental *Christianismi*

Restitutio, was nothing less than the complete restoration and restitution of true religion in both the natural and the spiritual worlds. In 1769, he published *A Brief Exposition of the Doctrine of the New Church*, in one extant copy of which these words are inscribed in his own hand: "This book is the advent of the Lord, written by command."[302] In his final work, *The True Christian Religion*, 1771, he informs us solemnly that "some months ago the Lord called together His twelve disciples, not angels, and sent them forth throughout the spiritual world, with the command to preach the Gospel there anew, since the Church that was established by the Lord through them has at this day become so far consummated that scarcely a remnant survives...."[303] The long-awaited Parousia is therefore nothing more or less than Swedenborg's proclamation of the New Church.

He was fully aware that "many who read" his descriptions of the other world "will believe that they are fictions of the imagination; but I declare they are...things actually done and seen...in a state of full wakefulness. For it has pleased the Lord to manifest Himself to me, and to send me to teach the things that will belong to the New Church, which is meant by the New Jerusalem in the Apocalypse."[304] And he reassures us: "I have not received anything whatever pertaining to the doctrines of that church from any angel, but from the Lord alone...."[305]

2. *What Is the New Jerusalem?* "The prevailing opinion in the churches...is that, when the Lord shall come for the Last Judgment, He will appear in the clouds of heaven with angels and the sound of trumpets; will gather together all who have died; will separate the wicked from the good...cast the wicked into hell, and...raise the good...into heaven; and...will create a new visible heaven and a new habitable earth, and...send down upon the earth the city called the New Jerusalem, built according to the description of it in the Apocalypse...."[306] Ann Lee, foundress of Shakerism, and that other prophetess, Mary Baker Eddy, each declared or at least implied that she was herself the Woman of Revelation, "clothed with the sun, and the moon at her feet, and upon her head a crown of twelve stars."[307] Fertile, however, as were the brains of these ladies, this idea did not originate with them. "By the Woman, the New Church is meant," says Swedenborg; and by the child she brought forth, its doctrine. "And behold, a great red dragon signifies those of the church of the Reformed."[308] And further: " 'A woman clothed with the sun and the moon under her feet' signifies the Lord's New Church in the heavens ...and the Lord's New Church which is about to be on earth, which is the New Jerusalem";[309] "by the crown of twelve stars upon the head of the Woman, the wisdom and intelligence of the New Church is signified";[310] and "the doctrine concerning the Lord is meant by the little book...."[311]

3. *The Red Dragon.* "That this 'woman' signifies the New Church, which is to be established by the Lord after the end of the church now existing" was

obvious to Swedenborg, since she brought forth a male child which the dragon wished to devour even after she fled into the wilderness.[312] "From this," he declares, "it is clear that 'the dragon persecuting the woman'...signifies" those who "reject and revile the Church which is the New Jerusalem, because it has the doctrine of life."[313] When we read that the serpent cast out a river of water after the Woman, this "signifies crafty reasonings in abundance respecting justification by faith alone..."[314] When Ann Lee fled from Great Britain to the forests of New England for safety, this was *her* Wilderness.

4. *The Church Everlasting.* And so the mandate had fallen upon Swedenborg to reveal the doctrine of the New Jerusalem, and thus to establish the New Church,[315] without which no "flesh can be preserved."[316]

This church is "to endure for ages of ages, and is thus to be the crown of all the churches that have preceded...."[317] It "will endure to eternity";[318] it "succeeds" all previous ones, and "will never undergo consummation."[319]

And so Swedenborg extends "an invitation to the whole Christian world to enter this church...."[320] However, only those who practice its ethics and accept its doctrines can qualify. "No others are received," he says, because "those who do not believe them and live thus are not in accord with the life of heaven."[321] And so the new saints will for the time being be few in number, because "the former church is become a wilderness...."[322] In his 18th letter to Dr. Beyer, April 30, 1771, Swedenborg discussed his forthcoming *True Christian Religion*: "I am certain," he stated, "that after the appearance" of this book, "the Lord our Saviour will operate both mediately and immediately towards the establishment throughout the whole of Christendom of a New Church based upon this 'Theology.' "[323]

M. *No Mass Communion*

1. *The Conservative Prophet.* Swedenborg's message was beamed primarily toward the members of that emerging class of men and women able to achieve success ethically, according to the prevailing codes; it is not intended for the lazy, the unambitious, the stupid, the starving, the poverty-stricken, the social failures, or those who refuse to prepare themselves by study and otherwise for success in life.

Swedenborg lauded comfort and wealth and condemned every kind of charity which takes the form of gifts, handouts, or maintainence for any human being who will not strive to support himself. Every person must be socially useful and productive or he has no right to enjoy life in an organized community. Society is not in debt to the individual: it is the reverse. And here Swedenborg establishes the philosophic basis for the ethical standards which have dominated the New Thought movement.

2. *The Price of Redemption.* When Swedenborg declared that the complete observation of the prevailing morality and civil law could lead to spiritual regeneration, he laid the basis for a communion founded in ethical-temporal imperatives. Furthermore, his rejection of the atoning, sacrificing savior, which is the core and essence of historical Christianity, creates a deep, wide chasm between his followers and the orthodox. And since his religion requires in practice that man regenerate himself with the aid of an influx equally available to everyone, it places upon the communicant the definite requisite of personal responsibility.

3. *The Wrath of the Orthodox.* To the established clergy, the far-reaching innovations of Swedenborgian proclamations were like ghastly specters charging upon them from the darkness. No wonder that their reaction became violent when these new doctrines were offered as the basis for a competing popular communion and when they heard themselves denounced as the Red Dragon of the Apocalypse. They accused Swedenborg of twisting the Scriptures to suit his whim in what he called a spiritual interpretation, of being personally dishonest or actually insane because of his revelatory claims, of having no standards beyond his personal opinions, of adducing no proof for his fantastic "revelations," of offering bait that smacked of Mohammedanism and unbridled licentiousness.

4. *Assailed or Ignored.* However, Swedenborg smote his opponents in many a vulnerable spot; in the course of time, they absorbed far more of him than they would ever admit. While his Latin tomes lay unread, they ignored them and him; but they unleashed a hurricane of frenzied assault when his first followers preached his doctrines in the vernacular. Finally, when it became clear that his permanent cult would be limited to a small number (mostly intellectual and therefore harmless persons), they could again regard this last great and original Christian theologian with benign toleration and dismiss him with a sneer.

N. *The Dénouement*

1. *Health, Happiness, and Prosperity.* We know that Swedenborg and some of his disciples hoped that the existing communions would accept his reconstitution of Christianity as a definitive revelation the purpose of which was (1) to declare God's will and explain the destiny of mankind; (2) reveal the true nature of the life eternal; (3) disclose the truth concerning the Last Judgment, the Second Coming, the Parousia, the nature of the deity, the true regenerative process, etc.; and (4) most important of all, accomplish a more complete reconstitution of the Christian religion.

2. *The Rare Mutation.* Basic changes in human thinking are as rare and

difficult as are physical mutations in any animal species. But once a great idea is born which meets a general need, it spreads with extreme rapidity and ease. It runs like quicksilver wherever the slightest opportunity is offered; and it finds reception in the most remarkable and unexpected places. There is no barrier to the penetration of new ideas; and there is no power comparable to one of these when its hour has come.

And so it was with Swedenborgianism, the indirect influence of which has been incalculable. And who could have foreseen that his doctrine would find a lodging in the mind of the illiterate Ann Lee and so furnish the impetus for the Shaker movement? Who could have believed that an intense and creative but unlearned New Englander by the name of Quimby would fall under the influence of Swedenborg and so be weaned from his mesmerism into a totally new philosophy, which gave birth to a revolutionary religious cult? Who could have foreseen that the Swedenborgian Warren Felt Evans would become the first to proclaim New Thought as a systematized religion, or that Julius and Horatio Dresser, also disciples of Quimby, would continue that work? And who could have thought it possible that fifteen years after leaving Quimby, Mary Baker Eddy would herself become an ardent student of Swedenborg and thereafter permeate her works with her own reinterpretations of his ideology? And who could have predicted that New Thought, in the space of a few decades, would erect thousands of dedicated temples, produce an enormous literature, and draw within its orbit many millions of people? These communicants are, for the most part, successful, well able to defend themselves, and beyond the reach of any sanctions or retaliation; they are eminently respectable and constitute a mighty movement, with innumerable subdivisions, which collectively have swept over the face of the earth.

3. *A Difficult Problem.* After everything else has been said concerning Swedenborg, the researcher is faced with a knotty question: was he totally sincere, or were his pretensions to revelation, conversations with the dead, journeys to the world of spirits, etc. wholly or partially a mere technique to accomplish certain practical objectives? This is no academic matter, nor one to which a ready or conclusive answer is readily available. And, should we admit his sincerity, what can be offered in the way of explanation that will satisfy unbelievers?

Let us note that his 1744 Illumination, as explained in his unpublished *Journal*, was definitely only a dream, but that in subsequent years it became an objective reality. Is it impossible or even unlikely that intensive thought and brooding over this experience persuaded him in due course to accept this as an actual fact?

It would seem that an acceptable hypothesis can be offered from the whole Swedenborgian syndrome: we believe it possible that the trances into which he entered from time to time (one of which was said to have lasted three weeks) were really states of self-hypnosis, now an officially recognized condition. The mind is a mysterious entity: we know that hypnotized individuals can talk, walk, answer questions with lucidity, reveal their most secret thought, travel to distant places, perform astonishing physical feats, and, upon awakening, retain no memory of this. Perhaps Swedenborg's self-hypnosis was of a somewhat different character and his experiences were so deeply etched into his consciousness that he remembered vividly everything he had imagined.

If we accept this or a similar hypothesis, an entirely new light illuminates the entire Swedenborgian complex. We know that since early childhood he had been subject to extraordinary emotional and psychological experiences. We know also that these became more intense, culminating in the 1744 Illumination. From that time forward, such experiences may have become routine with him and constituted a continuous state of mind which enabled him, with complete sincerity and total commitment, to pursue the monumental revelatory labors which filled the last twenty-seven years of his life.

4. *The Originality of Swedenborg.* There may be those who will say that the theology and other teachings of Swedenborg had been part and parcel of the intellectual heritage of the Western world long before his day. But we must reply that such persons are quite mistaken. For his entire system is not only homogeneous and interdependent in its parts, it is also inseparably bound up with the Nebular Hypothesis (which belongs to him alone) and it could have originated only in the mind of one who applied this to Christian dogma and tradition. His theology stems from his physical, cosmological, and anatomical science; his religious doctrines came into existence only when conventional Christianity was melded in the alembic of his metaphysics.

O. *The Specific Contributions*

What, then, were the creative Swedenborgian concepts which have exercised a wide influence upon Western religious ideology and which are now central in several major American cults or denominations?

Among the more important, we may list the following:

(1) that God is impersonal and unitarian, the life-giving force which exists in the universe and which is shared by every creature that inhabits it; God, in fact, is the substance of the cosmos;

(2) that no one is redeemed by the vicarious atonement of a Godman, but that every human being may create in himself, by ethical conduct, which he is free to embrace or reject, a character which will fit him for blessed immortality;

(3) that the Bible is throughout the Word of God, but that it possesses a spiritual sense which cannot rightly be understood except through an inspired

interpretation which reveals its true significance, often quite at variance with its literal meaning;

(4) that whatever we become on earth we continue to be after death—in short, we *will* take it with us;

(5) that if we practice the best ethical code of our own society, there need be no fear of punishment hereafter;

(6) that productive activity, both intellectual and material, is the highest ideal of the ethical man;

(7) that the neighbor is all mankind and that we best express our love for him in performing useful and reciprocal services;

(8) that the highest charity consists in dealing honestly with our fellow men and in doing our work well at all times; and that the comforts of life may be enjoyed and wealth obtained by methods completely just and virtuous;

(9) that the pursuit, possession, and temporal enjoyment of material comforts and even luxuries are highly laudable, so long as these are obtained through honest service to our fellows or the creation of social wealth, and so long as the money so gained is not the sole or the principal objective;

(10) that the Second Coming consists simply in the proclamation of reconstituted Christianity; and that the New Jerusalem, of which we read in Revelation, is that reconstituted church;

(11) that the Last Judgment and the Parousia are purely spiritual events, consummated without the cognizance of the people on earth;

(12) that there is a universal, vitalizing, and beneficent influx or emanation from God—the central sun of the universe—which, if we allow it to flow into ourselves, fills us with vigor, health, and moral virtue;

(13) that the failure or refusal to accept this divine influx is simply a failure on the part of our understanding or a misuse of our free will; thus, sin is really only a form of error or ignorance;

(14) that sickness and disease, whether mental or physical, are caused by lustful thoughts, evil desires, or corrosive hatred, which destroy a person's peace of mind and, transferred to the bodily functions, bring on every form of malady and illness;

(15) that sickness may be cured and eliminated from the body by permitting the divine influx to permeate our beings entirely;

(16) that both heaven and hell exist within us as subjective states, which are simply transferred to the next life at the transition called death;

(17) that the punishments which ultimately overtake the wicked are self-inflicted; and

(18) all this being true, that a scientific religion is demonstrably possible which has, as its objective, the well-being, health, happiness, success, and prosperity of its communicants in this life and an immortality of joyous activity and pleasure for eternity. We may call the Swedenborgians the

modern Gnostics, somewhat reminiscent of various ancient cults known by that name.

In succeeding chapters, we shall see to what extent these concepts and teachings, all so antithetical to the teachings of historical Christianity, have dominated a number of cults and movements which have arisen on American soil; this, of course, in addition to the permeation of the Swedish seer's ideology into the thinking and the doctrines of churches in general.

Since this study necessarily focuses upon Swedenborg's religious work and contributions, we have merely, without specific documentation, mentioned some of his scientific and philosophical achievements. Nor have we discussed his remarkable grasp of psychology; but the fact is that he was the first who understood that the human psyche operates on three levels which, in due course, his disciple Warren Felt Evans delineated and which Sigmund Freud finally called the Id, the Ego, and the Superego.

Swedenborg was indeed an all embracing scientist, genius, and revelator.

Chapter 2

THE SHAKERS

I. THE BIRTH OF A CULT

1. *A Variant Form of Swedenborgianism.* Since Shakerism was surcharged with Swedenborgianism; since it sought by a different practical route to achieve health, success, happiness, and prosperity in this life through religion; and even though it rejected the Swedish seer's reliance on free enterprise, individual effort, and personal responsibility in favor of celibacy and communal property, it was nevertheless substantially Swedenborgian and therefore belongs in the general movement known as New Thought.

2. *Health, Happiness, and Prosperity Cults.* During the century following 1770, a number of groups, some secular but most of them religious, attempted to establish communal societies on American soil, all of which had as their aim health, happiness, success, and prosperity. Among these were Brook Farm, the Fourierist phalanxes, Robert Owen's New Harmony, the Amanas, the German sect known as the Ephratas, the Zoarites known also as the Separatists or Come-Outers, the Rappites or Economists, the free-lovers known as Perfectionists, the Icarians known also as Free Socialists, and a Swedish group which settled at Bishop Hill, Illinois, in 1848. Most of these were short-lived; others, like the Amanas, in due course, abandoned communism in favor of free enterprise, prospered, and became permanent. Of all these, the Shaker communes were by all odds the most interesting and important. They

47

were the most determined attempt ever undertaken to re-establish Christianity in its pristine form with Essenism as its model, but also with an overwhelming infusion of Swedenborgian ideology.

3. *The Shaking Quakers.* Within the anti-clericalist organization calling itself the Society of Friends, sporadic phenomena reminiscent of its original afflatus sometimes erupted; and such an event occurred in 1747, when the Quaker tailor, James Wardley, and his wife formed a small group known as Shaking Quakers. Mrs. Wardley, known as Mother Jane, became the hierophant of these enthusiasts.

4. *The Prophetess.* Ann Lee (as she was later known), born February 29, 1736, was the eldest daughter of John Lees, a blacksmith. Devoid of schooling, she remained an illiterate throughout her life; nevertheless, she was endowed with a personality so powerful that she could dominate everyone with whom she came into contact.

Like Swedenborg, she "was the early subject of religious impressions, and was often favored with heavenly visions."[1] In 1758, at the age of twenty-two, she fell under the spell of Mother Jane and became a member of the Wardley group. On January 5, 1762, she was married; but the evidence indicates that she soon developed an extreme horror of the sexual relationship;[2] she groaned and shook at night with such violence that her husband was glad to desert her bed.[3] "In my travail and tribulation," she said later, describing this period, "my sufferings were so great that my flesh consumed upon my bones...."[4]

Ann's influence in the Wardley group increased rapidly after 1766; and several significant converts joined, including her father and brother William. As Ann gradually assumed leadership, the discipline became more strict, and her diatribes against the flesh and lusts of concupiscence became progressively more tempestuous. In due course, the Shaking Quakers were charged with heresy, witchcraft, and the disturbance of the peace.

The hostility against Ann herself took many forms; and finally, when she was haled before the authorities in Manchester, they threatened to brand her cheek with a red-hot iron and bore a hole in her tongue.[5] It was said that the jailors tried to starve her to death.[6]

We read that in the year 1770 Ann received a special manifestation of the Divine Light; and that, "from that time forward, was acknowledged as *Mother in Christ* and...called *Mother Ann.*"[7]

5. *Violence and Prison.* On July 14, 1772, Ann, with several of her followers, including her father, was arrested for disturbing the peace and destroying property; daughter and father were sentenced to serve one month in prison. On October 5 following, a mob attacked the house of a recent convert, John Townley; and two weeks later, the constable broke into the Lees home and arrested Ann's brother James. In July, 1773, Ann, with a band of zealots, invaded Christ Church, Manchester, during the "time of divine ser-

vice, disturbing the congregation then assembled at morning prayers...."[8]
They were, we are told, "severally fined 20 pounds each."[9]

Unable to pay such sums, they were sentenced to indeterminate incarceration; and during this period Ann experienced what we may call her Great Illumination. Like Swedenborg some twenty-nine years earlier, she had a vision of Jesus Christ, with whom she conversed and who commissioned her to preach the gospel of the virgin life; and he suffused her with such spiritual power that she became, not only the special instrument of revelation, but nothing less than the vehicle of Christ in the Second Appearing. As a result of this vision, Ann became the sanctified Bride of Christ. She declared that she felt his blood coursing through her soul and body; and when she emerged from the dungeon, she declared herself to be "Ann, the Word, the Woman Clothed with the Sun."[10] When she faced her small group of enthusiasts again, she had become the Mother in Christ, or Ann Christ, the Mother of the New Creation; meanwhile she honored Jane Wardley as her John the Baptist in the Female Line,[11] as she was in due course to acknowledge Swedenborg as her John the Baptist in the Order of the Male.

6. *Christ in the Superior Female.* Henry Blinn, a devout follower, declared later that she, like Swedenborg, was clairvoyant, had visions all her life, and had healed the sick, apparently by a miraculous Christ-Power.[12] To the faithful, she was the mediatrix for sinners, the Second and Supreme Christ in the Superior Female, the Queen of Heaven, the Holy Mother Wisdom, co-equal and co-eternal with the creator of the universe.

7. *To America!* As the group was assailed by troubles on every side, one member, the energetic James Whittaker, experienced a vision of Christ's kingdom in America, which was accepted as a mandate. Ann became the Woman of Revelation Who Fled into the Wilderness, and whose opponents, like those of Swedenborg, were the Red Dragon of Revelation 12:1 who Spewed Out a Flood to Drown Her and Her Child, that is, the Gospel of Christ in His Second Appearing. The Shaking Quakers came to port in New York on August 6, 1774.

One historian describes the hejira thus: "Ann Lee...with her eight companions...fled to the wilderness of America, from the face of the 'fiery flying serpent'...the Protestant Episcopal Church of England—she, being the eldest daughter of the great 'Mother of Harlots,' who love to commit adultery with the State, and to exercise all the power of the beast by religious persecution in the name of the State."[13]

II. THE BUILDING OF ZION

1. *In the Wilderness.* Immediately after landing, the little band marched up

Broad Way; and, turning into Queen Street, Ann boldly addressed the mistress of a rooming house: "I am commissioned of the Almighty God to preach the everlasting Gospel in America, and an angel commanded me to come to this house, to make a home for me and my people."[14]

Hocknell, William Lee, and James Whittaker went up the Hudson and bought a tract of land at a place near Albany called Niskeyuna, where the first "church" was established.

A study of Scripture and pristine Christianity soon convinced them that celibacy and community property constitute the twin pillars of practical Christianity. Economic egalitarianism thus emerged gradually as the prerequisites for Christ-like love; it was certainly well established Shaker doctrine before the "gathering" of 1781-82.

In 1779, great religious revivals occurred in New Lebanon, New York; Hancock, Massachusetts, and other nearby towns: a lay preacher, Joseph Meacham, was one of the prime movers in this Great Awakening. Meetings were held in barns and in the open fields, where emotion erupted nightly with signs, visions, agitations, shouting, screaming, prophetic trances, and the falling of men and women as if struck dead. "Some had visions and prophecies," says Evans, "that the day of judgment and redemption was at hand, and that the second coming of Christ was nigh...."[15] It was believed that all existing churches would shortly be abolished. The hysteria continued for months; but by autumn, the people were seized with a kind of lethargic despair and exhaustion because the expected Second Coming had not occurred.

2. *An Important Convert*. The following March, two of the disillusioned visionaries happened to pass through the Shaker community, where they were told that the Second Coming had already occurred, that the Last Judgment of the Apocalypse (à la Swedenborg) was now in progress in the Spirit World, and that the real resurrection occurs only whenever a convert enters the life of the spirit. The two returned posthaste with these glad tidings to Meacham, who sent his first lieutenant, Calvin Harlow, to investigate further; falling under the magnetic spell of the prophetess, he soon came back with an enthusiastic report. Now Meacham himself, accompanied by two others, journeyed to Niskeyuna, where, after a soul-searching confrontation, he gave himself as an irrevocable disciple of the Second Christ. Nurtured in the doctrines of St. Paul and St. Augustine, Meacham had long been an ascetic; and when, now vividly recalling the various key texts in the Christian Gospels, he heard the prophetess declare that "you must forsake the marriage of the flesh, or you cannot be married to the Lamb, nor have any share in the resurrection of Christ,"[16] he was convinced. Ann pronounced him her first-born son, who would gather the faithful into the fold.

Meacham became the driving force of the cult, and he carried its message into the highways and byways. On May 10, 1780, the sun seemed weirdly darkened, and many thought the Day of Judgment was upon them. As they wrung their hands in despair, strange tales concerning the Prophetess of Niskeyuna flew like wildfire over the countryside; and filled with stories of miracles, healing, mysterious signs, and singular rituals, many took the road to gaze upon her countenance.

3. *Ann's Gospel.* Ann denounced the filthy gratifications of the flesh and the carnal, indwelling devil, the Mystery of Iniquity, which has dragged the human race, created in perfection, into the depths of misery, corruption, and the prospect of everlasting torture in hell. She declared that if the fleshly passions are not conquered in this world, they would become more devastating in the World of Spirits, and bring certain doom upon sinners there.[17] "Blessed are those not defiled with women,"[18] she cried. Her "testimony was like flames of fire...She exposed with keen and cutting severity the deceitful craftiness of young men to tempt and seduce young women; and the alluring acts of young women to ensnare young men...."[19] "The marriage of the flesh," she proclaimed, "is a covenant with death.... If you want to marry, you may marry the Lord Jesus Christ."[20]

Many tales of spiritual healing, done by exorcism, were bruited abroad. Concerning these, Ann's reputed power grew progressively, as time and distance increased. Whether these stories originated with the Shakers or were elaborated by the myth-making propensity of the people, it is certain that Mother Ann was credited with the power of healing diseases by casting out devils through the same Christ-Power that enabled Jesus to achieve the same results.

4. *A Skeptic.* We are fortunate in possessing a pamphlet, the oldest dealing with the Shakers, dated 1781, and written by Valentine Rathbun, a Baptist minister who went to Niskeyuna, who saw and heard but did *not* believe. "The whole number," he wrote, "consists of five males and seven females."[21] "When any visitor arrives, they are all smiles and say that they knew yesterday he was coming,"[22] "that they know all his thoughts,"[23] and "that not one soul has gone to heaven during the past 1200 years."[24]

Rathbun continues: "When he comes again, they meet him with great joy, clasp him in their arms, and tell him...that he must confess his sins to them, from his childhood...that he may be born again."[25] Furthermore, "they tell him that they are angels and converse with them and hear them sing...."[26] And "they further tell him the song that they sing is the song of the hundred and forty-four thousand, which no man can learn, but they who are redeemed from the earth. Then they tell him they have a Mother, pointing to a woman...and say that she speaks seventy-two tongues" which "the living people cannot understand...yet the dead understand her, for she talks to them."[27] (Like Swedenborg!)

They say, continues Rathbun, "that the judgment is now going on, and that they are the judges; that there are many hells... where people suffer according to their sins; and when they are refined, they come to stand before us, where they are judged."[28] They declare also that while the body he had occupied hung on the cross, Christ preached "to the spirits in prison" so that some of them might be redeemed by living according to the will of God. They say that the aforementioned woman is the one of Chapter 12 of Revelation "who was clothed with the sun, having the moon under her feet, and on her head a crown of twelve stars; and that she has travailed and brought forth the man child. Further, that she is the Mother of all the elect... and that no blessing can come to any person but only through her; and that" redemption comes "by confessing their sins to them, and repenting of the same, one by one, according to her direction."[29] And "some say that this woman called the Mother has the fullness of the Godhead, bodily dwelling in her, and that she is the Queen of Heaven, Christ's wife."[30]

At their meetings, said Rathbun, they shake their heads, go through terrific contortions, bark, groan, scream, and roll.[31] "Presently, a strange power begins to come on and takes place in the body—which sets the person a-gaping and a-stretching; and soon sets him a-twitching, as though his nerves were in convulsion. I can compare it to nothing" but "an electrifying machine..."[32] Thereupon, they go into a great variety of convulsions, which they call the work of the spirit.[33] Meanwhile, "others will be shooing and hissing evil spirits out of the house, till the...dancing, drumming, laughing, talking, and fluttering, shouting, and hissing make a perfect bedlam; and this they call the worship of God."[34]

They teach pacifism;[35] and they denounce the works of generation more than any other sin,[36] declaring that "carnal copulation" has "ruined the world."[37] "They tell the man to abstain from his wife and the wife from the husband; and say that if the wife does not agree to it, to put her away."[38] "They tell young men and young women, if they marry and have anything to do with the works or the lusts of the flesh, they can never be born again."[39] They tell anyone who comes to them that "if he turns back, there is no forgiveness, neither in this world, nor in that which is to come"; that "he must come often to them to be instructed, or he will be in danger of being taken by evil spirits and led astray; and that he must not think that he can understand the Bible..."[40] by his own light.

Rathbun wrote that the Shakers burned all the conventional books on theology they could find, and predicted that Albany would be destroyed by fire within four weeks.[41]

Warm receptions were prepared for any skeptic or opponent: "They get around him, threaten him with damnation, storm and stamp at him, stare at him with wide-open eyes, pucker up their mouths, and cry oh! oh! oh! at him...enough to scare Hercules out of his wits."[42]

5. *The Cult Takes Root.* With the ministry of Joseph Meacham, Calvin Harlow, and others in 1780, the real history of Shakerism in America begins. But, since the war with England was then raging and since most of the Shakers were English pacifists, it is not surprising that they were charged with treason and imprisoned.[43] However, with Ann's release in December, missionary activity increased. In May 1781, a band of determined emissaries invaded Massachusetts, where their agitation produced a harvest of converts. In various districts, Baptists, Congregationalists, Come-Outers, New-Lighters, and others came over singly or in groups. Furthermore, a number of substantial farmers made their decisions for Ann-Christ and took up their crosses against flesh and devil; and, by throwing their property into the common pool, gave the societies a solid economic base.[44]

The wonderful news of Christ's Second Appearing transported many of the hard-handed sons of the soil with visions of magnificent mansions awaiting them in the Swedenborgian World of Spirits. Converts were overwhelmed with ineffable exaltation: it was said that some of them were propelled through the air in spiraling gyrations; they whirled among stones and stumps, and sometimes into nearby lakes, whence they were returned, as if by magic, to the very spot where the seizure had begun.[45]

So successful were the missionaries in that emotionally surcharged climate that the cult spread all over eastern Massachusetts and into southern Maine. The Free-Will Baptists became so concerned that they appointed a day of fasting and prayer to curb the new madness.[46] Others took more direct action: a mob attacked the house where Ann and her cohorts were kneeling in prayer, broke open the doors, dragged men and women into the street, forced them to walk several miles while being beaten and abused in almost every conceivable manner.

Such violence was frequent during the early years. Ann herself was repeatedly beaten and whipped, as were other members of her cult. This was called "the war between Michael and the Dragon and the final assault of a dying Anti-Christ."[47]

Valentine Rathbun and his son Daniel continued to pour oil on the flaming sea by publishing one diatribe after another against the cult; the Shakers called their tormenters boogers, devils, and Sodomites, who retorted that the cultists pushed, bit, struck, and pulled the hair and spat in the faces of all who dared to oppose them.[48]

6. *The Cities of Zion Are Organized.* Before her death on September 8, 1784, Ann had developed her communal doctrine fully as an integral element in her gospel. Like the ancient Essenes, they created separate communities for themselves; and these operated by pooling all possessions and income.

In July 1785, there were already hundreds of converts, scattered over five states. The practical task, therefore, was how to organize permanent societies before their members could slide back into "the World." This undertaking fell largely upon Joseph Meacham, whom Mother Ann had anointed as the First Apostle of Her Ministry, the Chosen One, greatest man born of woman in 600 years.[49] Indeed, had it not been for him, the cult might well have dissolved after Ann's death.

The first period of Shaker expansion continued for ten years. Communes were established in New York, Massachusetts, Connecticut, New Hampshire, and Maine.[50] The membership was approaching 1,000.

By 1779, mercantile shops were already in operation, manufacturing a variety of goods which were sold in "the world." There were no parasites— everyone did productive work, even the bishops and the Ministry. Women enjoyed equality with men in every way.

7. *The Declining Enthusiasm*. When Ann, who had been expected to live a thousand years, died at the age of forty-eight, a number of stalwarts defected; and, as the younger members, who had been brought into the Order as small children, grew up, most of them became restive and refused the Cross of Christ. An exodus of these, therefore, took place in 1795. The enormous labors necessary to establish eleven widely separated communities, ten of which endured into the 20th century, had sapped the strength of Joseph Meacham; and the apostates, with their condemnations, were more than he could bear.[51]

This man was an introvert; he had frequent visions of heavenly angels and received constant messages from Mother Ann, now Queen of Heaven. He described and instituted the seraphic dances which he said he had witnessed and which, when adopted by the Shakers, served as a means of sublimating the suppressed and frustrated sexual energies of the cultists.[52] Worn out by labor and disappointment, he was laid to rest in the summer of 1796. He had, however, composed his *Concise Statement of the Principles of the Only True Church* in 1790, which was the first authentic declaration of Shaker doctrine and practice and served as the basis for all subsequent cultic "Bibles."

The conciliatory and peaceful policies of Whittaker and Meacham had done much to ameliorate the attitude of the "World" toward the Eastern Shaker communities; not only was there outward peace in 1800, but an extensive trade had been established for their products outside. However, since the original exaltation had subsided, a general spiritual lethargy had set in, and there was very little expansion in the East after 1794.

8. *Religious Madness in the West!* Shortly after 1800 came the electrifying news of great religious revivals in Kentucky and Ohio, which, strangely enough, seem to have been a reaction against the rapid spread of deism and rationalism. The Ministry decided to dispatch three Witnesses, who left January 1, 1805, and who, after a 1200-mile journey of eighty-three days, arrived in Turtle Creek in southern Ohio.

The great revival had then spent its force; and many of the exhausted seekers after salvation, in despair because Jesus had not appeared on the clouds of heaven, were ready to hear the joyful tidings that Christ had already come and that the resurrection was to be achieved solely by joining the Church of the New Jerusalem.

One of the first converts was Richard McNemar, a Presbyterian minister who had mastered Latin, Greek, and Hebrew. The celibate-communist doctrine of the Synoptics, as presented by the Shaker missionaries, soon convinced this tall, gaunt cleric that theirs was indeed the only true gospel of Christ. He never wavered in the faith; and his *Kentucky Revival*, published in 1808, which described in detail the excitement which preceded the coming of the Shakers, remains a classic. It began, he wrote, "in individuals who had been under deep conviction of sin, and in great trouble in their souls...."[53] "At first, they were taken with an inward throbbing of heart, then with weeping and trembling; from that to crying out in apparent agony of soul; falling down and swooning away, till every appearance of animal life was suspended...."[54]

Children were as fearfully taken as their parents,[55] and their convictions of their lost state were "quick as a lightning's flash...."[56]

The mania soon seized entire populations; and camp-meetings or encampments were established in the open fields.[57] "To these...people flocked in...thousands, on foot, on horseback, and in waggons...."[58]

"The first" encampment "began on the 22nd of May, 1801, and continued four days and three nights. The scene was awful beyond description; the falling, crying out, praying, exhorting, swaying, shouting, etc. exhibited such new and striking evidence of a supernatural power that few, if any, could escape..." and "great numbers fell on the third night...and they were collected together and laid out in order...like so many corpses...."[59] "No sex, color, class, nor description were exempt from the prevailing influence of the spirit; even from the age of eight months to sixty years...."[60]

In one conclave, the attendance totalled 20,000, of whom 3,000 "fell."[61] Even those who came to mock, oppose, deride, and persecute were often unable to withstand the power, and "were struck down like men in battle...."[62]

McNemar describes "the rolling exercise," which "consisted of being cast down in a violent manner...with the head and feet together, and rolled over and over like à wheel.... Still more mortifying and demeaning were the jerks," which "commonly began in the head, which would fly backward and forward, and from side to side with a quick jolt...." The one afflicted went "as he was stimulated, whether with a violent dash on the ground and borne from place to place like a football, or...with head, limbs, and trunk twitching and jolting in every direction, as if they must inevitably fly asunder...." "Some imitated a canine beast" and were forced to "move about on all fours, growl, snap the teeth, and bark in so personating a manner as to set the eyes and ears of the spectator at variance."[63]

McNemar states that the Shakers had adopted their dances as a practical means of escaping the jerks and barks.[64] John Woods adds that they were "designed to mortify the flesh and keep down the lustful propensities of our nature."[65]

9. *A New Empire in the West.* And so the ground was cleared for the harvest: one Shaker commune after another was established. The process in all cases was similar: following revivals predicting the imminent return of Christ which had run their course, many disappointed converts threw in their lot with the Shakers, consecrated themselves and their possessions to the Community. Like the Essenes of old, they gave everything to the poor, who were themselves, communally, in order that all might be right; and they took up their celibate crosses in the service of Christ, where they could find a hundredfold of sisters and brothers.

10. *An Estimate of Shaker Wealth.* The period from 1784 to about 1837 was one of almost constant growth, construction, and expansion. Every commune had its separate apartment buildings, usually multi-storied, for men and for women, and, where necessary, for male and female children. In some of the larger communes, there were more than a hundred well-built structures, always plain but highly functional, endowed with a severe, Socratic beauty. There were community facilities, such as schools, churches, and meeting houses; and there were shops, granaries, store-houses, barns, sheds, mills, and a variety of manufactories. There were rolling acres of grain and every other kind of crop; there were berries, gardens, and vegetables to meet every need; and there were orchards with fruits of many kinds.

We cannot know the precise value of Shaker property at its height, about 1840-1850; but we would say that, in terms of dollars current in 1983, the nineteen Shaker communes must have owned land and improvements with a total value of perhaps $400 million, all debt-free. This represented the capital contributions and savings of about 3,000 workers who gave their surplus over a period of fifty years, or about 150,000 labor years—an average of about $2,600 for each year. And since there were 5,000 Shakers in 1845 (including children) the pro-rated share of each would have been about $80,000—no mean corpus of wealth. The ultimate failure of Shakerism, therefore, was not economic; and the cause of its decline and dissolution must be sought in non-material imperatives.

11. *The Decline of the Order.* After 1805, there was only one more pheno-menon comparable to the great revivals of 1779 and 1801-5. About the year 1831, William Miller—who established the Seventh-Day Adventist Church—began preaching the imminent Second Advent of Christ in Massachusetts; and, basing his chronology on Daniel 8:14, argued that, since the 2,300 days must mean that number of years following 457 B.C., Christ would appear in 1843. He obtained a large following, many of whom sold their lands and houses in preparation for the Advent, and who went forth clad in white

ascension robes on the day predicted to welcome the Lord. When nothing happened, the prophet found that he had made a slight mathematical error and that the Parousia would certainly occur on October 22, 1844. Again, the faithful trooped forth from Boston to welcome Christ at midnight; and when again nothing happened, many were deeply distressed and a considerable number, learning that Christ had already come, that the judgment was in progress, and that great and magnificent cities awaited them in the Spirit-World, came over to the Shakers. Two hundred Millerites joined the Western communities in 1846, and others were enrolled in the Harvard, Canterbury, and Enfield communes in the East.[66]

There were 1,632 Shaker Believers in 1803;[67] 3,899 in 1823 and 4,369 between 1835 and 1845;[68] 2,750 in 1858,[69] and 2,415 in 1874.[70] There were fifteen communities with 1,728 members in 1891,[71] who were reduced to 1,000 by 1903.[72] According to the almost complete enumeration of the Western Reserve Historical Society in Cleveland, 16,828 individuals had at some time been members of the Order;[73] and in 1874, eighteen societies owned 49,335 acres of land.[74]

Some of the communes had already been dissolved before 1900, and after 1905 this process was accelerated. In 1972, only two remained—one at Sabbath Day Lake, Maine, and another at Canterbury, New Hampshire—with a membership consisting of fourteen elderly women. No new members were admitted after 1964. In 1981, there were only nine Shakers left.

III. THE ASSAULT FROM OUTSIDE

1. *The Clergy on the Warpath.* With the first success of the new cult in the West, an orthodox minister at Turtle Creek centered his attack upon the key Shaker doctrine that Christ had already appeared a second time; and he ordered Isaachar Bates "back to hell."[75] The forests rang with fiery denunciations; the Shakers were called false prophets, seducers, liars, deceivers, wolves in sheep's clothing. But the fiercest outcry was that they were destroying the churches and breaking up families—the twin mainstays of order and civilization.

Ministers who had lost members or feared the defection of their entire congregations circulated the wildest and most scurrilous tales; not only were the Shakers destroying the family: they were also accused of plotting the theft of land and other property; inciting the Indians to massacre the whites; running their own communities under an iron autocracy; extirpating all natural affection; castrating some of their own males; dancing naked and thereafter engaging in the most depraved sex-orgies; murdering the illegitimate children of this criminal intercourse, and much more.

Hostility reached such a frenzy that attacks upon the Believers and their property became frequent and progressively more violent. On the 27th of August, 1810, a mob of 500 armed men, followed by a huge rabble, marched on Union Village and demanded (1) that children held against their wishes be released, (2) that the Shakers abandon their form of organization and worship, and (3) that they leave the country at once. They replied that the children were all contented and that none were held against the will of anyone, that they had purchased their land and had every right to occupy it, that the American Constitution guarantees full freedom of worship. Delegates were invited to inspect the premises and question anyone. When nothing amiss was found, the mob left reluctantly. However, for years there was recurring violence, which probably only strengthened the communes, both in numbers and resolution; for during this period they grew rapidly and, by 1823, the seven Western societies embraced 1,649 members.[76]

2. *Legal Problems.* During the early years, the Shakers operated without any written covenant; and they made it a general policy to repay defecters and apostates upon withdrawal whatever contributions they had made. However, in 1795, a written contract consisting of five articles was established, which all members were required to accept and which provided that no one could ever demand compensation or restitution for any services rendered or for any property consecrated to the Order.[77]

No monetary suit was ever prosecuted successfully against the Shakers; however, when only one parent joined, the children of that family involved a more delicate problem. In 1818, Eunice Chapman brought an action in which she detailed her harrowing experiences after her husband became a Shaker and took their children and all their property into the Order. As a result of this litigation, she was granted a divorce by act of the New Hampshire legislature; and it was made a felony for the Shakers to take children away from their parents or their mothers[78] or "to retain, conceal, or remove from the state any children of a woman who wished to see and have custody of them."[79]

With this, the Shakers became exceedingly circumspect in all their dealings with children and with the property of members who abandoned their mates. They also made provision for the care and education of minors which would meet the minimum requirements of the educational authorities.

3. *Enemies Attack.* During the early period of Shaker organization, a variety of enemies, among whom were apostates, published the most inflammatory charges against the Order, its foundress, and its subsequent leaders. Since these are too extensive and well documented to be ignored, they are entitled to some credence.

Thomas Brown, who was a member for six years beginning in 1803, published a large volume in which he stated that male and female Shakers danced naked together,[80] that it was common knowledge that Ann drank heavily,[81] that the elders also imbibed and sometimes fought violently,[82] and that Mother Ann and her brother Father William once almost killed each other in a furious quarrel[83]—a story confirmed, or at least repeated, by others.[84]

Since the cultic leaders could not ignore all these charges, they sought, in their first "Bible," to render them ridiculous by exaggeration. Their detractors are quoted as follows: "The first founder of this wild sect was one Jane Lees; she lived in the town of Manchester, in England; was of low parentage and procured her living at the expense of her chastity...which character she supported in America until her death."[85] In view of Ann's sexual revulsion, the Shakers could afford such calumnies. Other charges, however, were not so easily refuted; and it was admitted that "the crime of drunkenness, in particular, has often been charged upon Mother and her companions with a degree of assurance that seems to defy contradiction."[86] Actually, no one had ever accused Ann of being a prostitute.

There were many tales of Shaker cruelty to children. Mrs. Chapman, whose husband deserted her in favor of the Order, declared that a small girl was locked in a barrel, rolled around violently, and then told that the devil had punished her for disobedience.[87] It seems that such harsh discipline was general for, according to testimony at an 1849 legislative investigation, various witnesses stated that children were whipped mercilessly.[88]

The redoubtable Mary Dyer, who, together with her children, was carried into the Order by her husband, was a reluctant member for fifteen years after 1800. She published a large book in 1822, which attained wide circulation and in which she charged that Ann Lee was an habitual drunkard,[89] that recalcitrant female members were stripped naked because of "their thoughts,"[90] and that Shaker elders and eldresses lived in whoredom or bigamy under the name of spiritual marriage.[91] The elders, she said, had recently produced a book called *Mother Ann's Sayings*, which was used in the instruction of children and which told of the awful torments awaiting those in the next life who deserted the Order; and Mary Dyer reproduced a long list of affidavits from other Shaker apostates confirming her charges in minute detail.[92]

John Woods, who was converted in Kentucky in 1805, and who defected after a few years, declared that the missionaries said that Mother Ann had performed innumerable miracles;[93] and that Shaker men, at the sight of an attractive female, would exclaim, "God damn the flesh!" and use many other similar imprecations, even in meeting, to mortify and defuse their indwelling evils or devils of concupiscence.[94]

When legislative sanctions against the Shakers were threatened in 1818, they issued *A Remonstrance*,[95] which listed the charges frequently made against them.[96] Hervey Elkins, who was inducted into the order at the age of fourteen, renounced it at the age of twenty-nine and published a well-written account of his experiences. He declared that many members were filled with mutual rancour and reckless libertinism,[97] that they were taught and compelled to perjure themselves when called to testify in the courts,[98] and that they lied, even under oath, in any confrontation with "the world."[99]

Whether the leaders, who were not subject to supervision, practiced liberties denied the common members, we cannot say; but the Ministry was certainly less than honest when it stated that "we believe in one true God, who is a spirit, the fountain of all good—and we believe also in Jesus Christ as the only savior of mankind."[100] On their face, these statements were outright lies.

IV. THE SPIRITUALIST REVIVAL

1. *Ennui Sets In.* After the last commune was organized in 1826, the Order continued to increase for two or three decades; nevertheless, it is certain that the movement had passed its apogée in fervor, missionary zeal, and capacity to penetrate into the outside world. Even before that date, in the words of John Woods, Shakers at work "would sometimes be attacked by those twin mighty champions of the devil, namely reason and common sense,"[101] of which the elders stood in such mortal dread.

2. *Incredible Infestation.* This situation culminated in an unbelievable spiritualist revival: Evans states that "in 1837 to 1844 there was a great influx from the spiritual world...making media by the dozen."[102] Hundreds fell into trances and experienced visions. "Through this wonderful influence," declares Elder Henry C. Blinn, "the sick were healed, the dead were restored to life, and persons carried bodily from the earth into the heavens."[103] "On the 16th of August, 1837," he continues, "a new era commenced in the society.... At first some little children, who were learning to sing and to read, were suddenly entranced...and began to shake and whirl.... Under the direction of spirit-guides, they were conducted from place to place..." and witnessed all the marvels of the Spirit World.[104]

The afflatus was contagious, for "an older class were soon passing away into visions and trances...."[105] Early in 1838 "not less than eight persons entered the trance state," and sometimes as many as eighteen simultaneously.[106] "Messages were received by the mediums...for the encouragement and admonition of all...."[107] More and more, the wonder grew: "During the year ending November 30, 1838, five visionists visited the spirit-land some two hundred and eighty-nine times.... One of the visionists was entranced eighteen times."[108]

"While on these visionary journeys," we are told, "no food of any kind was administered, as there seemed to be no action of the bodily functions."[109] "More than a score of new dances," declares Elkins, "were performed with an attitude of grace and with the precision of a machine, by about twenty female clairvoyants. They *said* they learned them from the seraphs before the throne of God."[110] They beheld wonderful sights, such as cities and palaces,[111] which adorn the Spirit World;[112] "they were taken into the mansions of the saints, and were shown the terrors of the abodes of the wicked, the sight of which would seem unbearable."[113] Blinn states that one visionary saw former white slave-masters serving their former Negro slaves.[114]

3. *Rebellion in Paradise.* While the orthodox Shaker writers barely mention that the spiritualist revival began as a desperate revolt among the youth, one or two of them hint at this fact; and Hervey Elkins gives us a full and dramatic picture of what really happened in this so-called devil-infestation.[115] Even the devout Blinn declares that "their very breath was hatred, their language vile and profane. No respect was shown either to age or official position...."[116] Apparently unaware of what they had said during their trances, the young mediums would then become sober and return to their duties.

One night, according to Elkins, as the hysteria developed, a girl of thirteen, previously known as a clairvoyant, emitted the most terrible shrieks. Then "two or three more girls were soon taken in the same manner and became uncontrollable. They were all instruments for reprobated spirits, and breathed nothing but hatred and blasphemy to God. They rolled, they cursed, they swore, they heaped the vilest epithets upon the heads of the leaders and most faithful of the members; they pulled each other's and their own hair, threw knives, forks, and the most dangerous of missiles."

In time, however, the elders discovered an effective treatment: when girls were placed in straightjackets and confined to a place where they could proclaim their blasphemies only to each other, their infestations miraculously came to an end.

Whenever these phenomena were "afterward spoken about," says Elkins, "they were designated...'The Devil's Visitation'...."[117]

4. *The Authorities Seize the Initiative.* On April 22, 1838, the spiritualist manifestation was taken over by the official medium, Philemon Stewart, through whom Mother Ann began sending messages, explaining how the Order had deteriorated and departed from its original principles.[118] Thus the movement was snatched from the rebels, and the result was the final revision in 1845 of the authoritative *Millennial Laws.*

Elkins bore eloquent testimony to the magnetic force of these spiritual excesses: "I have myself seen males, but more frequently females, in superinduced condition, apparently unconscious of earthly things and declaring in the name of the departed spirits important and convincing revelations."[119] When he was told that the Holy Mother Wisdom was among them, "I sometimes thought that I could actually see that ethereal, holy, and omniscient principle which created, and dwells in, the universe and man; and which we call God."[120]

A pamphlet entitled *A Revelation of the Extraordinary Visitation of Departed Spirits...Through the Living Bodies of the Shakers*[121] throws further light on these strange phenomena. "As soon as" an elder "had terminated his address, one of the brethren was seized with violent agitation of the body...." At one time, "a young woman of singular beauty of face and figure commenced whirling around with great rapidity. Her gyrations were so rapid that her face for the time became indistinguishable. She continued for an incredible length of time, and such a performance this writer never witnessed upon the theatrical stage or anywhere else."[122]

Thereupon, many began "speaking in tongues"; and about sixty of the members were filled with the spirits of people long dead and prophesied in their names,[123] speaking in the persons and presumably in the voices of many residents from the Spirit World,[124] including those lost in a ship in 1841.[125] These were followed by such worthies as Cicero, Julius Caesar, Alexander, Washington, Lafayette, Robespierre, Benjamin Franklin, Napoleon, Shakespeare, and all the signers of the Declaration of Independence.[126]

5. *The Final Revelations.* Henry Blinn states that "in 1840, another phase of inspiration was brought forward."[127] The first resultant literary production was *The Holy, Sacred, and Divine Roll, and Book: From the Lord God of Heaven, to the Inhabitants of Earth,* compiled by Philemon Stewart and published in 1843. This was announced by trumpets resounding throughout the Shaker communes and was deposited "in the heart of Zion on earth..."[128] (which was New Lebanon) "for they are the sentences of your Eternal God and Creator."[129]

Here Shaker theology is reaffirmed: "Through a female was Christ made known, as a Spiritual Mother, to complete the order of the kingdom which was begun in its first appearing."[130] And "it may truly be said of the Daughter of Zion, that...in her the Spirit of Christ appeared, with full and complete salvation...."[131] Yet we are told that the Age of Miracles was at last terminated.[132] Shaker doctrine is fully reviewed and established;[133] and the tome closes with the testimony of sixty-eight mediums, who had experienced angelic visions and who delivered communications from the Spirit World.[134]

Ambitious as was the work of Stewart, it was overshadowed by the subsequent revelations of Paulina Bates, which, she assures us, she wrote down as a passive instrument.[135] Again, the Lord God addresses the nations of the earth. The apostles Peter, James, Paul, Jude, Matthew, Mark, Luke, and the Virgin Mary all display perfection in the niceties of Shaker dogma; Ananias and Sapphira deliver constructive homilies on the wickedness of retaining personal property that should be consecrated to the Church.[136] The Holy Mother Wisdom herself explains her history, nature, power, and deification, together with a Swedenborgian description of heaven and hell.[137] Finally, there is a long oration from King David, who also was obviously well instructed in all the finer points of Shaker doctrine, to which he had been converted in the Spirit World.[138]

V. A SHAKER SCHOLAR

1. *The Making of a Shaker Theorist*. Among the Shaker leaders after Mother Ann, the most outstanding was the erudite Frederick William Evans, who, in his *Autobiography*, delineates his background and intellectual experiences. In his youth, he was a rationalist and possibly an atheist;[139] and he states that after reading the Koran and all the other "bibles" he could obtain, he studied Locke's *Human Understanding* and *The Being of God*,[140] after which he became a devotee of Paine and Voltaire—in short, a deistic freethinker. In 1820, he and his brother George published a paper called *Young American*, which called for many dramatic and liberal reforms; he boasted later that he lived to see nine of his twelve demands enacted into law.[141] In 1825, he helped to organize the Locofoco Party and supported Andrew Jackson for the Presidency. Shortly, he became a fervent socialist-communist, and attempted to set up a community along the lines of Robert Owen's New Harmony.[142]

Evans declared that his Great Illumination came after a group of Quakers had prayed for him: he heard, as it were, flights of birds rushing at him as he lay in bed.[143] He had already imbibed heavily of the Swedenborgian lore, which became thenceforth the lodestar of his life; and now he was "persuaded at last that intelligences not clothed in what I had called matter were present with me, remaining with me more...logically...than any mere world man or woman has ever done since. This first visitation of angels to me continued until about one o'clock in the morning, having lasted several hours...."[144] With this experience, his materialism, skepticism, and agnosticism vanished.[145]

Evans now entered into the same relationship with the spirit-world as had his illustrious Swedish predecessor. And he states that "it was by these spiritual manifestations that I, in 1830, was converted to Shakerism."[146] No longer, then, was religion a mystical or authoritarian creed; it was, instead, "science by Divine Revelation...as in the case of Swedenborg—one of the most learnedly scientific men of his time—by whom it evolved into Spiritualism...which is the last and the highest of the sciences, inasmuch as it teaches the geography of the Spirit World...."[147]

2. *The Swedenborgian Scientist*. Evans, then, embraced a belief in a scientific religion intended to create universal health and well-being; he became a Shaker because, in its metaphysics, this cult was already Swedenborgian. And he gave the organization its mature coloring, its final historical image.

After more than forty years of constant labor in the Order, he was still its chief propagandist, its intellectual coryphaeus. His writings constitute a small library; some of his books are distinguished by the widest and most acute scholarship. He was, we believe, the first who declared that Jesus must have been an Essene and that the first Christian congregation consisted of members of that Order and was based entirely on Essene principles and organization. When Evans became a Shaker, the cult was young, virile, expansive; when he died, it was long past its zenith and, assailed by irresistible forces, was slowly declining toward its sunset.

VI. SHAKER THEOLOGY AND OTHER DOCTRINES

1. *Rejection of Orthodoxy.* Like the Swedenborgians, the Shakers rejected the Trinity, predestination, salvation by faith, the vicarious atonement, the divinity of Jesus, the personality of Christ, the resurrection of the body, the efficacy of baptism or the eucharist, and the necessity of prayer. Their repudiation of the leading churches and their doctrines—Catholic and Protestant alike—was, if anything, even more fierce than Swedenborg's and finds typical expression in the seventy-sixth hymn of *The Millennial Praises:*

> "The monstrous beast, the bloody whore
> Reigned 1300 years or more;
> And under foot the truth was trod,
> By their mysterious three-fold god..."

But then

> "The Holy Ghost at length did bear
> The 'Anointed One,' the Second Heir,
> A virgin soul, a holy child,
> A Mother pure and undefil'd."

2. *The Mother-Father God.* According to Shaker theology, the deity is a dual entity, a Mother-Father God, a concept found among the ancient Gnostics and the German Ephratas, and in due course appropriated by the Mormons and Theodore Parker, for which the Scriptural authority is Genesis 1:27: "God created man in his own image; male and female created he them." This idea runs like a red thread through all Shaker thought, and is the message of countless hymns:

"The Father's high eternal throne
Was never filled by one alone;
There Wisdom holds the Mother's seat,
And is the Father's helper meet.
This vast creation was not made
Without the fruitful Mother's aid...."[148]

And again:

"From Father and Mother, the fountain of love,
The spirit descends like a heavenly dove."[149]

William Leonard published a philosophical treatise in which, rejecting the trinity of three male persons,[150] he declares: "The great book—the universe—teaches in language not to be misinterpreted...that the Fountain whence all things originally flowed is dual—Male and Female—God."[151] Both sexes, he states, are clearly manifested in all creation and exist throughout the vegetable kingdom.[152] Since this is a fact, Woman can no longer be denied her just and equal rights.[153] The new Believers therefore proclaim "the gospel of Christ's Second Appearing, which is based upon the recognition of the true order of the Godhead, as Male and Female—an Eternal Heavenly Father and an Eternal Heavenly Mother."[154]

Frederic Evans summarizes the dogma: "An all-important, sublime, and foundational doctrine...is the existence of an Eternal Father and an Eternal Mother in Deity—the Heavenly Parents of all angels and human beings..."[155] "the male and female in man...is peculiarly the 'image of God.' "[156]

3. *Christology.* Directly or indirectly, Ann Lee had probably absorbed the concepts of the dual deity and the docetic Christ from various sources; but she developed a related doctrine which was entirely her own and which makes Shaker Christology unique: the dogma that the Second Appearing of the Christ-Power must be made manifest in the Order of the Female and that she herself was the vehicle of that Power.

We learn that Jesus, son of a carpenter, and Ann, the daughter of a blacksmith, both simple and unlearned persons, were alike the tabernacles of the Christ-Power, the supreme attribute of the Mother-Father God, which entered Jesus at his baptism and Ann when she lay in prison. In Jesus, God became manifest in the Order of the Male; in Ann, he did so in the Order of the Female. The ministry of Ann constitutes therefore the Second Appearing of Christ on earth; and, since the revelation of God is progressive, the Christ-Power in Ann is greater than that in Jesus; in her, God's revelation is completed. Further, since Christ is the judge of the human race, Ann now sits in judgment on all souls entering the World of Spirits.

Mary Dyer, whose statements are amply confirmed in the official docu-ments of the Order, declares: "After Mother Ann was acknowledged as spiritual Mother," she announced that she was also "the Word,"[157] and maintained "that the divine nature as much dwelt in her, as it did in" Jesus; and, as the second coming of Christ was to be more glorious than the first, "she was seven times more glorious than Jesus."[158] Furthermore, "Ann...declared that she had the power to judge the world, and that she was now daily judging the dead of all nations...."[159] Pursuant to this power, she required all sinners to confess to her or to her representatives.[160] The Shakers "believe there is a probationary state, or purgatory, out of which sinners may be released, by the intercession of the Mother, and that regeneration or salvation is by the Mother...that being born again is a progressive work."[161]

The Shakers, continues Mary Dyer, "represent Ann Lee as being co-equal and co-eternal with God...."[162] They say, in the character of the Holy Ghost, " 'She is unchangeably one with the Father, in union and essence, and is everlastingly with the Father, before the world was or ages were set in order.' " They also "represent her as being the Mother of the Son of God."[163] In this, as in other doctrinal concepts, we find a striking similarity to Roman Catholic dogma.

Mary Dyer states further that the Shakers deny the personality of Christ, the vicarious atonement, and the resurrection of the body; and hold that not Christ, but only the mortal Jesus, was crucified.[164]

Thomas Brown declared that, according to Shaker doctrine, "Mother Ann suffered in spirit like unto Christ, and bore the different states of the peo-ple..."[165] This tribulation, however, must not be confused with a vicarious atonement, but constitutes rather a necessary purification preparatory to receiving the Christ Spirit.

John Dunlavy, the assistant of Richard McNemar at Union Village, Ohio, published a long theological treatise in which he argues that since "Christ is a Spirit" and since his "coming again" in "the second revelation should...*be* a woman—consequently all reasonable objections against Mother Ann as the Anointed of God for that purpose are obviated."[166]

In his biography of Ann Lee, Evans declares that the dual Christ "is a supermundane being, and was the agent of the new revelation in Jesus," who first taught the immortality and the resurrection of the soul.[167] He continues that Jesus predicted the ruin of his Church and that "another appearing on earth of the same Christ (or second Adam and Eve) as had been manifested in him (Jesus) would take place, t , establish a second and more perfect Christian Church..."[168] In this "second appearing," the "Christ should be manifested in the order of *Mother*, through a Female, as he had been in the order of *Father* through Jesus...."[169]

All created things, he continues, are dual; and "Jesus, being a male, could only reveal and manifest the Father in Christ and God. But when the *second* Adam appeared in Ann, and became her spiritual Parents, she, being a female, revealed and manifested the Mother Spirit in Christ and deity."[170] Because the second appearing of Christ is the only key by which to unlock the mysteries of the Bible, this book is regarded as being only "more or less perfect,"[171] and far inferior to the direct revelations of Ann-Christ herself.

It was established through the prophecies of Daniel and John, declares Evans, that the reign of the Beast, the Catholic and Protestant Churches, was to continue for 1,260 years, and would therefore end in the year 1792, "when our order was founded."[172] "When Jesus...the first Messiah, as Ann Lee is the second," he continues, "was ascending up out of the river, the Christ Spirit... descended upon him, in the form of a dove...."[173] This was actually an "angel from the fourth heaven..."[174] and "the only individual...begotten of the...resurrection heaven...until the second appearing of Christ; which of necessity must be...of a female...."

"This female the earth produced under the action and guidance of the same creative angels that brought forth Jesus..." who, with "his apostles stood superior to Moses...." No wonder, then, that "Mother Ann has wrought works—facts—beyond what Jesus attained...."[175]

An elaborate and tightly reasoned work by Calvin Green and Seth Y. Wells, published in 1823, expounds Shaker Christology further: "Christ, the Anointed of God, was first revealed in Jesus of Nazareth";[176] and it is an error to believe "that Christ is to come in the clouds of heaven and that all shall see him."[177] Since God created man in his own image, male and female, "it must appear obvious that, in the spiritual creation, man and woman, when raised to a spiritual state, must still be male and female...."[178] Therefore the Christ-Spirit can never be complete until it has appeared in a woman also.[179]

"Ann Lee was the distinguished female who was chosen for that purpose...to manifest the spirit of Christ in the female line. Hence the likeness and image of the Eternal Mother was found in her, as the firstborn daughter, as well as the image and likeness of the Eternal Father was formed in the Lord Jesus, the firstborn Son. Thus was she constituted the second heir in the covenant of promise, and was placed in a correspondent connection with Jesus Christ, as the second pillar of the church of God in the new creation." Although the "human tabernacle of Ann Lee...was but flesh and blood...it was a chosen vessel, occupied as an instrument, by the Spirit of Christ, the Lord of Heaven, in which the second appearance of the Divine Spirit was ushered into the world."[180] She is "the divine Spirit of Wisdom...in the new creation of God."[181] In Philemon Stewart's *Holy, Sacred, and Divine Roll* a heavenly voice proclaims that "through a female was Christ made known.... And I declare to all nations the spirit of the chosen female to be the Bride, the Lamb's Wife, the Queen of Zion, and Mother of the new and spiritual creation, which shall never be destroyed."[182] Through Paulina Bates, the Lord makes similar declarations;[183] and she states: "The wilderness of America was discovered by the providence of God to be the field for the manifestation of Christ in the female..."[184] and even though "the dragon did cast forth floods out of its mouth, to swallow up her testimony,"[185] it shall be triumphant.

Harvey L. Eads published an intricate *Expression of Faith* in 1873 which reflects the Gnostic nature of Shaker Christology and which holds that the God of the Jews is an inferior divinity,[186] that the man Jesus was not the Christ,[187] that the Christ was simply an agency imported from another sphere who took up temporary residence in the body of Jesus.[188]

"Mother Ann," declares Evans, "received an independent revelation from a Christ-Spirit, as did Jesus."[189] And the clouds on which Jesus declared he would return "are the eighteen societies of Believers,"[190] already established and now operating as the Swedenborgian Church of the New Jerusalem.

Shaker hymns are surcharged with this Christology:

"Once again hath Christ descended,
To be born upon this earth;
Once again the world's offended,
At the meanness of the birth."[191]

And again:

"Let me be united to good Mother Ann,
Her favor is heavenly bliss;
No riches that God has bestowed upon man,
No comfort, no blessing, like this...."[192]

"We're in the New Creation
With all our dear relation,
We're joinèd heart and hand....
This lovely way to Zion
Through Mother was revealed;
The final dispensation
Which long had been concealed."[193]

Sometimes Jesus qualifies as a parent also:

"To our parents eternal, be honor and glory,
To Jesus our Lord and our good Mother Ann."[194]

4. *The Fall, Depravity, and Redemption.* Many cults have taught that the sex-relationship is the very essence of evil. It was in her prison-illumination

that Ann Lee came to understand the nature of the Fall, explained in *The Summary View of the Millennial Church*. "She saw the Lord Jesus Christ in his glory, who...fully satisfied all the desires of her soul. In these extraordinary manifestations, she had a full and clear view of the Mystery of Iniquity, of the root of human depravity, and of the very act of transgression committed by the first man and woman in the Garden of Eden. Here she saw whence and wherein all mankind were lost from God, realized the only possible way of recovery."[195] Since a man who looks upon any woman to lust after her has committed adultery with her in his heart (Matt. 5:28), the Christ-Spirit could not have dwelt in either Jesus or Ann had they been defiled by sexual contamination.

"Through the insinuations of her deceitful spirit," we read in *The Summary*, the serpent "infused into the...woman the lust of concupiscence, which she communicated to the man, and by which they were both overshadowed with darkness" and "led into the act of sexual coition...." "Thus they partook of the forbidden fruit. Hence, the curse which followed...can never be taken off without a full and final cross against the indulgence of that same fleshly lust, and the final destruction of that nature which leads to it."[196]

The nature of the Fall is explained in one of the *Hymns and Poems for the Use of Believers*, published in Watervliet, Ohio in 1833. Here we find that Adam was created upright, sinless, a perfect bisexual Man, so that he could have reproduced himself without copulation. Because of his loneliness, God gave him Eve; and one day, as he paused "to view the beauties of my wife," his soul was replaced by the wicked serpent:

"An idle beast of highest rank....
Showed to Eve a curious prank,
    Affirming that it was no crime....

"All this was pleasant to the eye,
    And Eve affirmed the fruit was good;
So I gave up to gratify
    The meanest passion in my blood.
O horrid guilt! I was afraid:
I was condemned, yea, I was dead.

"Here ends the life of the first man,
    Your father, and his spotless bride;
God will be true, his word must stand—
    The day I sinned, that day I died:
This was my sin, this was my fall!
This your condition, one and all."

And so, when Adam indulged in sexual intercourse, he died; and the vile serpent, who had deceived his wife, took over his physical tabernacle and became the second, the fallen Adam, who thus transmitted his own depraved nature to the entire human race.

> "Now in my name this beast can plead
> How God commanded him at first
> To multiply his wretched seed
> Through the base medium of his lust.
> O horrid cheat! O subtle plan!
> A hellish beast assumes the man!
>
> "This is your father in my name:
> Your pedigree ye now may know:
> He early to perdition came,
> And to perdition he must go.
> And all his race with him shall share
> Eternal darkness and despair....
>
> "Now his lost state continues still,
> In all who do their fleshly will,
> And of their lust do take their fill...."

Regeneration and salvation are therefore possible only by conquering this congenital lust; in this victory, we take up our crosses and follow Christ:

> "But this prize can not be gained,
> Neither is salvation found,
> Till the Man of Sin is chained,
> And the old deceiver bound.
> All mankind he has deceived,
> And still binds them one and all,
> Save a few who have believed,
> And obeyed the Gospel's call.
>
> "By a life of self-denial,
> True obedience to the cross,
> We may pass the fiery trial,
> Which does separate the dross.
> If we bear our crosses boldly,
> Watch, and ev'ry evil shun,
> We shall find a body holy,
> And the tempter overcome."

The following from the *Sacred Hymns* strikes the same note:

"Depart from me, all worldly lust!
'Twas you that God in Eden curs'd,
When from the Garden you were thrust,
And sentenc'd to perdition...."[197]

5. *Marriage and Family Rejected.* We note again and again that even though the Shakers, by and large, followed the free Swedenborgian spiritual interpretation of Scripture, they were the strictest literalists whenever its texts agreed with their own teachings. Whereas all the conventional denominations found other meanings in the declarations of Jesus concerning sex and the family, to the Shakers they meant precisely what they said. And while almost all other churches found comforting interpretations to explain the command of Jesus to the rich young man or the story of Lazarus who was destined for Abraham's bosom, the Shakers knew very well that to become a disciple for Jesus it was first necessary to renounce family and property.

It is not surprising, therefore, that Shaker doctrine concerning the Fall of Man is combined with the Gospel commandment: "If any man come unto me, and hate not his father, and mother and wife, and children, and brethren, and sisters, yea and his own life also, he cannot be my disciple."[198]

Mary Dyer declares that, under intensive indoctrination, she "strove to hate my family, believing natural affection would carry me to hell—I believed the more work I did for the Shakers, the more treasure I should lay up in heaven...."[199] The common members, she said, were forced to work like slaves, even when they were sick.[200] "Every impulse of the mind," she continued, "must be condemned," as though it were an "evil spirit...."[201] "We were commanded to hate our natural relations, and give up our children."[202] "The Elders say that the marriage covenant is a covenant unto death...."[203]

Another apostate, John Woods, declared: "We were taught to hate the flesh and to despise the relation of father, mother, wife, children, etc. with all our mind and spirit...."[204] "When a man and woman, not in office in the church, happened to meet, the order of custom was to pass without speaking. For...the woman who looked a man full in the face was in danger of being censured as a base woman."[205]

However, the devil could not always be denied; for, in spite of every precaution and the fiercest indoctrination and discipline, strong attachments sometimes grew up between the sexes. When these occurred, one or both offenders were suddenly transported elsewhere, sometimes with tragic consequences.[206] Hervey Elkins relates the heart rending story of Urban and Ellena; the girl was spirited away to a distant commune, where she pined away and died; the young man abandoned the society in revulsion and disgust.[207]

Eunice Chapman declares that her husband, after deserting her, "often spit in my face...saying that 'it was the filthiest place he could find,' " since her desire for connubial love was reflected there.[208] Nor is this statement incredible; for the devout James Whittaker wrote to Thomas Brown, when seeking the latter's conversion: "I hate your fleshly loves and your fleshly generation, as I hate the smoke of the bottomless pit...."[209]

The fact is, of course, that Shaker celibacy seemed irrefragably anchored in the Gospel; for in various passages marriage and family are denounced in the most explicit terms, as in Matthew 19:29 and Luke 20:34-35. In their Order, the Shakers "found the words of Jesus verified to the very letter...."[210] The children of this world, continues Leonard, heathen and Christian alike, marry, have father and mother, houses and lands, and are therefore excluded from the kingdom of God.[211]

Evans declares that the "lust of generation" and the craving for personal possessions are the twin evils which have destroyed all previous churches;[212] and he reiterates that marriage and private property are inseparably combined.[213] "All 'who marry and are given in marriage,' " he notes, "or who support that order, the Shakers term 'the children of this world'; thus, on this ground, throwing heathens, Turks, Catholics, Protestants, infidels, etc. all into one general class, or company."[214]

Evans asserts that the Gospel of Jesus was overthrown and destroyed when "the Gentile Christian Church...introduced marriage and private property."[215] Adultery is defined as cohabitation of husband and wife.[216] "Thus, the same spirit that creates souls 'anew in Christ Jesus,' causes them to 'forsake and to hate father and mother, wife and children, brothers and sisters, houses and lands, and their own [generative] life also.' "[217] And so the saints sang loud and clear:

"Of all my relations that ever I see,
My own fleshly kindred are furthest from me;
How ugly they look; how distant they feel;
To hate them—despise them—increases my zeal."[218]

6. *The Communal Philosophy*. William Leonard declared that "community is the outward expression of that love of God, and that love to our neighbor, which marks the true Christians before...the World, who marry and are given in marriage, and buy and sell their property. Marriage and private property God and nature have joined together."[219] The original Christians practiced the Essene-Shaker communism and renunciation.[220]

"The true doctrine of the Gospel," declares Paulina Bates, "cannot be mistaken: all must be forsaken and given up for Christ," especially "the carnal life of sin" and the possession of private wealth.[221] Mother Ann explains that the saints must gather "where hundreds of souls can dwell together in brotherly love, as brethren and sisters of one family...daily crucifying the flesh, with its affections and lusts...."[222]

Evans declares that only the pristine Christian church was truly communal; that the Gentile organization which succeeded was a corruption of the original; and that "unless this distinction between" those "be observed, the various writings of the New Testament cannot be understood...."[223] And he continues: "The five most prominent practical principles of the Pentecost Church were, first, common property; second, a life of celibacy; third, non-resistance; forth, a separate and distinct government; and, fifth, power over physical diseases."[224]

With amazing perspicacity, Evans declared that "Jesus was an Essene, and the Essenians...were communists, holding property in common. 2. They were celibate, neither marrying nor giving in marriage.... 3. They were hygienic spiritualists" who "practiced the gift of healing diseases, and exorcising evil spirits.... 6. they...dwelt alone....

"The Essenians were, many of them, converted on the day of Pentecost, and formed the body of the Jerusalem Church...."[225] Thus, the members of the first Christian Church "were Essenes. They loved one another so that they sold their possessions and had all things in common. They forsook the generative life, with its wives and husbands, its fathers and mothers, brothers and sisters, sons and daughters, for Christ's sake and the Gospel's...."[226] "This new Church—the 'Shakers'—much resembles the Essenes of Philo's time."[227] And Evans continues: "Shakerism only is successful communism; and it is the only religious system that teaches science by divine revelation...."[228] Finally, it is the only truly Gentile Christian communion in all history—the "Second Pentecostal Church."[229]

When the Gospel was Hellenized in the Fourth Gospel, it was subverted: "Thus the Gentile system of generation and selfish individual possessions, or 'dividing the land for gain,' is to this day the order in Babylon of all nations professing the Christian name, and of all their constitutions."[230] And "this radical doctrine establishes beyond all dispute that private selfish property, to any account, is incompatible with original Christianity, and is also a sure test of the quality, standing, and truthfulness of all spirits and of their communications."[231]

When a person is converted to Shakerism, "he becomes a virgin character— a spiritual man...a religious communist—a Christian...."[232] There can be no relative sainthood: if we are to follow Jesus in the regeneration, we may not retain so much as five dollars of private property, for this will exclude us from the holy communion as completely as would five million.[233]

Again we hear the voice of the saints in ecstatic song:

> "And when we hear the solemn call,
> Let's be prepared to give up all;

That when on earth our work is done,
We may receive the prize we've won;
For if to God we daily live,
This nat'ral life we freely give;
And leave all earthly things below
To live and reign where mercies flow."[234]

Again and again we note the obvious contradiction: on the one hand, the Shaker was required to give up everything and to take upon himself the cross of Christ in order to obtain eternal glory; but, on the other, he would obtain in this world a hundredfold, or a thousandfold, in return for this renunciation.

7. *Spiritualism and the Spirit-World.* Of all the Swedenborgian elements in Shakerism, the concepts concerning the spiritual body, the celestial spiritual world, and earthly intercommunication with it are perhaps the most distinctive and all-pervasive; and caused Evans to write this lilting song:

"My heart is in the Spirit-World,
My soul is soaring there;
I dwell amid the denizens
Of that bright world so fair...."[235]

That direct and continuing revelation is mandatory for true religion was a basic Shaker doctrine; and this means that current personal communications from the celestial realms supersede all written documents delivered in the past. "Without revelations from the Spirit-World," writes Evans, "man is ever liable to mistake the Divine Agency, by which all the operations of the visible world are effected.... there is a...spirit-world, which to the natural man is the prototype and transcript of this; and in all ages, there have been intelligent communications, from one to the other...."[236]

"All revelations," he continues, "from evil spirits—false religions— terminate in the violation of the law, and the abuse of the functions of reproduction."[237] Again following Swedenborg, he describes the three churches or eras, of which that in which Christ-Jesus appeared was the third, and in which he enabled the dead to rise, the blind to see, the lame to walk, and the dumb to speak. "Love was its soul or life; and community of property, its body, or outward form."[238]

"When the first Christian Church...fell," continues Evans, "and the anti-Christian kingdom of the Beast was fully set up under Constantine, then every great principle and doctrine...was entirely abrogated, denied, and denounced by the Nicene and other subsequent councils."[239] By declaring through its leaders that revelation had ceased, the "Church cut itself off from a living communion with the spirit-world and thereby consummated the 'falling away'; and therefore the 'man of sin' sat in the temple of the Church of God, who typifies the present Christian leadership, and particularly the pope."[240] Leonard stated that "there is a natural and a spiritual world and a natural and a spiritual body...."[241]

8. *The Historical Churches.* There have, declares Evans, been four epochs, within which smaller cycles appear:[242] "By dividing the spiritual history of the human race into four great eras—the Patriarchal, the Mosaic, and the First and Second Christian—we can thus more easily trace the creation, the fall, and the rise of man."[243] The First Era "commenced in Adam; the Second in Abraham; the Third, in Jesus, and the Fourth with Ann Lee."[244]

The First Era enjoyed easy intercommunication with the spiritual world,[245] because man then used his sexual organs only for generation, and never for lust.[246] This period ended with the so-called flood, which was simply an inundation of evil spirits.[247] The Second Era ended with the destruction of Jerusalem.[248] The Third Church, of course, was that established by Jesus,[249] who "continually referred to the next, or the Fourth and last, great cycle as the time for 'the restitution of all things, which God hath spoken by the mouths of all his prophets since the world began.' "[250]

The wicked prophets who now infest the so-called Christian churches are simply another infestation of devils.[251] When Constantine "was converted, he founded and became the heathen head of the Roman Catholic Church,"[252] which is the " 'beast' that John saw" in the Apocalypse.[253]

"That was the falling away and degeneration of the Gentile Christian Church.... and the union of Church and State...by which it trod down all liberty of conscience...."[254] Thus, the Roman Church is the beast of the Apocalypse with the seven heads and ten horns; and the second beast, which rose thereafter and which spoke like a dragon and exercised the power of the first,[255] represents the Protestant Reformation; and its twin horns are Luther and Calvin.[256] "The faithful...who compose the" Shaker Church "are the 'very elect' who cannot be deceived,"[257] because they espouse the true law of the Gospel, which consists of community property and celibacy.

"The lust of generation," explains Evans, "is the one great evil that marred all the designs and works of God in the first three Eras.... The practical fruit of" the Fourth "Church is the entire banishment of poverty and want, and sin and misery; and a full supply of physical and spiritual necessities for the body and soul, of every one of its members."[258] And so "the Fourth Era has commenced, and the Church thereof is now established upon earth...."[259]

9. *Catholic and Reformation Christianity.* An early Shaker Bible—*The Testimony of Christ's Second Appearance*[260]—states that the early Catholic Church incorporated all pagan cults into the Christian Church[261] in order to make it universal and thus to destroy it as a Christian institution.[262] Once established by the Roman emperors,[263] it became the reign of Antichrist.[264]

" 'And upon her forehead was a name written, MYSTERY, BABYLON THE GREAT, THE MOTHER OF HARLOTS AND ABOMINATIONS OF THE EARTH.' "[265]

The Reformation was simply a "grand division in the Kingdom of Antichrist,"[266] which did nothing to accomplish a restitution of Christianity.[267] The Protestants have simply erected the Scriptures as another Pope, thus substituting one Antichrist for another.[268] Luther is denounced;[269] Calvin is utterly condemned, but Servetus is highly commended.[270]

10. *The Theory of Diseases.* The Shaker doctrine concerning physical and mental health is also constructed upon Swedenborgian premises. Thus all forms of sickness and even untimely death were caused by demonic infestation. Mary Dyer declared that "among the Shakers, sickness was called a devil" which "we must fight and overcome..."[271] Ann was credited with miraculous healings;[272] when Shaker missionaries arrived in Kentucky, they told of countless miracles performed by her,[273] somewhat similar to those later claimed by Mary Baker Eddy. The maladies which disappeared under the ministrations of Ann Lee included infected teeth, broken ribs, limbs thrown out of joint, mouth-cancer, canker-rash, high fever, issues of running sores, wounds from an axe, etc., etc.[274]

The Swedenborgian doctrine of Influx, as we learn from James Whittaker, was also an integral part of Shaker metaphysics.[275]

The more sophisticated Evans, writing after God had announced through an inspired medium that miracles were no longer to be performed openly, provided a somewhat more naturalistic explanation for Shaker health and longevity: "All physical diseases," he declares, "are the result of violated natural laws in agriculture and diet."[276]

Whatever we may think of these theories, it is certain, first, that no medical doctors were tolerated in the Shaker communes; and, second, that life expectancy there was at least fifty per cent greater than in "the world." Many Shakers continued to work full time well into their eighties.

11. *The Progressive Judgment.* Mary Dyer states that "Ann claimed the power...to judge the world, and that she was now daily judging the dead of all nations...."[277] The Shakers taught that they had special societies in the Spirit World and their missionaries were busily engaged in the instruction of all those arriving in the celestial realms. The Shaker "Bible" of 1823 states that the Shaker saints are the judges there even as they are on earth.[278] And "This glorious judgment will never cease until the work of God shall be fully accomplished.... It will effect the final decision and termination of the probationary state of all souls....

"It will be gradual and progressive, but certain and effectual; and it will continue till a full and final separation shall be made between good and evil. Then shall Antichrist no longer beguile mankind with the mere name of religion in which there is no reality...and all flesh shall be judged according to the deeds done in the body...."[279]

And so we have a probationary state in the World of Spirits, even as on earth, from which sinners may be released by the intercession of Ann Christ; and the regeneration and salvation to be achieved by the individual himself is a progressive operation.[280] And this process of instruction, during which they improve or regress, continues in the spiritual world, until their departure takes place into their eternal destiny in heaven or hell.[281]

12. *The Soul and the Resurrection.* All Shaker concepts of immortality, the soul, the spiritual body, the resurrection, and life in the Spirit World are in complete harmony with the teachings or Swedenborg. The Shaker "Bible" of 1823 describes in detail the celestial bodies after death,[282] when the fleshly integument is simply shuffled off, as the butterfly abandons its chrysalis.[283] There is the natural body, and the spiritual body in which we are immortalized.[284] In the language of Evans, "Death is the disengagement of the spiritual from the fleshly—the severance of the sympathetic partnership between the spiritual and the earthly bodies.... Soul and spiritual body, often confounded with spirit, are synonymous. We employ the terms soul and spiritual body reciprocally: and, as constituting the man, use this formula—Physical body, Spiritual body, Spirit; or body, soul, and spirit."[285] Evans had even adopted the Swedenborgian doctrine of associate spirits;[286] and he adds that "all men, if worthy, have guardian angels, and sometimes ministering spirits...."[287]

That the body itself is of little consequence is reflected in various Shaker funeral hymns:

"Our mortal bodies will decay,
The silent grave receives the clay...."[288]

"How happy the soul, when the spirit shall say,
Come enter the courts of a bright endless day;
The faithful and blessed and owned of the Lord,
Come enter, O enter, receive thy reward."[289]

13. *The Will.* The Swedenborgian Evans states, among many other things, that man has free will, given him by God; and though fallen, he can rise again.[290] The Shaker "Bible" declares that "there is nothing to be found in the sacred volume, that affords the smallest proof of that gloomy and soul-darkening doctrine of eternal and unconditional decrees, which so unjustly fixes the final salvation or damnation of souls without a special regard to works...."[291]

Since the daily life of the Shakers constituted the conditioning process by which lust was overcome and the love of mankind was established, the doctrines of eternal election and salvation by faith alone must have been particularly repugnant to them.

14. *Revelation and Scriptural Authority*. We have noted that although the Shakers invested with supreme authority the literal meaning of certain passages of Scripture, they condemned the Protestants for elevating the Bible into a second pope. Mary Dyer accused the cult of teaching that it was of no use; that "their Mother and her Elders were perfect, and stand on the sea of glass, could speak with tongues...."[292] And again: "They forbid our reading the Scriptures, said they were a back dispensation, we were in a new one, where God's will was manifested by the elders, and that was Gospel enough to carry us to heaven."[293] Furthermore, "the Shakers taught all their subjects, not to think of Christ, but to pray rather to Mother and the Elders."[294] And finally, "the Elders say that they have the keys of heaven and hell and can save and damn souls."[295]

Official Shaker documents confirm all this. We have noted that the Bible was officially regarded as only partially reliable; the necessity of continuing or permanent revelation from spirit-world is often stressed, especially in the Shaker "Bibles."[296] Leonard states explicitly that no religious truth can be known except in this manner.[297] Elkins declares that among the Shakers "Infidelity" consisted in "unbelief in the revelations of their mediums."[298] Various hymns declared:

> "I love the blessed Gospel,
>   Reveal'd by Mother Ann...."[299]
> "So let us all be thankful
>   For Mother's Gospel's come...."[300]
>
> "How has Christ to us appeared?...
>   First in our beloved Mother—
> In her followers next he's found....
> Through this channel we received him....
> Zion is the holy temple
> Where the Savior does repose...."[301]
>
> "How blessed—O how blest are we!
> How very thankful we should be,
> That we have Elders, O so true!
> A Father and a Mother, too."[302]

Yes, indeed, authentic Shaker doctrine could be received only through channels which delivered truth from the Spirit World to the Believers in this day of Christ's Second Appearing!

VII. SHAKER DISCIPLINE AND GOVERNMENT

1. *Purgation and Confession.* The Shakers enforced one important ritual and practice reminiscent of Roman Catholicism: auricular confession to their elders and eldresses. This was instituted by Ann herself and no one could join the Order until he had been thoroughly cleansed of every sinful thought and fleshly impulse. Lying on his knees, the penitent would be urged to conjure up from his entire past, even into his childhood, every selfish or lustful thought that had ever entered his mind.

> "Had we not grovelled in our loss,
> Had we never known the cross,
> For to take away the dross—
> Oh! what grief and sadness!"[303]

This confessional purgation was a perpetual necessity to maintain mind and body as a fit tabernacle for the saintly spirit:

> "If from the way one step I've trod,
> And knowingly transgressed,
> I'm not accepted of my God,
> Till that I have confessed:
> Then hastily I must repent,
> And keep in watchful labor;
> My mind for righteousness be bent,
> Then I may know His favor."[304]

According to Mary Dyer, all Shakers were required to confess their sins in public;[305] her own husband foreswore wife and family on his knees.[306] Woods was told that, since "the Devil is very tough, and not willing to die, therefore you must cast him out and purge yourselves by confessing your faults to one another."[307] Evans emphasizes that "a radical and most important principle in the Shaker...Church is the oral confession of sins...in the presence of...witnesses."[308] And Paulina Bates adds: "The heart of man must be subdued by confession and repentance, before the seed of the Gospel can be planted and profitably cultivated in it."[309]

It should be obvious that all this was an effective means of discipline, of maintaining the authority of the elders, who, in their respective communes, were scarcely less than absolute rulers. It is almost impossible to conceive any kind of brain-washing or sensitivity training more effective or self-abasing; any common member who would not submit to it was in a state of total rebellion against dictatorship and subject to extreme censure. Humility and useful labor were constantly inculcated by precept, doctrine, authority, group pressure, and communal song:

> "And here the meek may always find
> A fountain clear, a living spring,
> Which happifies the humble mind,
> And makes the soul rejoice and sing....

> "To be in my duty, by night and by day,
> And feel satisfied therein,
> I find is a sure and infallible way
> To keep out of actual sin:
> For while I am faithful to do what is right
> And have not a moment to spare,
> I'm guarded around by the angels of light,
> And Satan can never come there."[310]

Poignantly descriptive and informative is the hymn called "Mother's Rod":

> "What solid peace, what joy and Heaven
> I feel when I can be forgiven;
> I kiss my blessed Mother's rod,
> That makes my soul cry out to God.

> "Kind Elders, help me on, I pray,
> Within this pure and holy way;
> O do not spare the chastening rod,
> Pray help, O help my soul to God."[311]

The following blasphemy, composed by the irreverent Industrial Workers of the World, might be considered a parody on the above:

> "Work and pray,
> Live on hay—
> You'll get pie in the sky when you die!"

2. *The Duties of Man.* Even as the Buddhists had their seven-fold path, so the Shakers had their Seven Duties of Man, which constituted their Great Moral Principles: the Duty to God,[312] the Duty to Man,[313] Separation from the World,[314] Practical Peace (or pacifism),[315] Simplicity of Life and Language,[316] the Right Use of Property (communism),[317] and the Virgin Life.[318] To these in the sphere of specific action, should be added Obedience to Authority[319] and Confession of Sin.[320]

The implementation of these duties and principles in practice constituted the day-to-day life in the Shaker communes.

3. *The Communal Hierarchy and Government*. Charges by such apostates as Hervey Elkins that the Shaker ministry and hierarchy were a dictatorship similar to the military and exercising an extreme form of thought-control are amply confirmed in the documents of the Order.[321] A favorite hymn began: "To God and our elders we'll always be subject...."[322] Evans points out the similarity of Shaker organization to that of the Essenes: only after many examinations, a period of probation, and the complete consecration of himself and his possessions could the candidate become a full-fledged member; and all "the consecrated property of the Society is held in trust by trustees belonging to each community."[323]

Evans explains the orders of membership: the first, or novitiate class, accept the faith of the Society, but live in their own families and manage their own temporal concerns.[324] (The Essenes, as well as *their* precursors, the Pythagoreans, had identical peripheral memberships.) The second or junior class, undertake the communal life on a trial basis; they may place their property in escrow with the Order and recover it at any time. (The Essenes had an identical arrangement.) The third, or Senior Class, consisted of those who were prepared to enter freely and fully into the life of the Society and who agreed to devote themselves and their possessions forever to the service of God, and promised solemnly never to bring any claim or demand against the Society or any member thereof for any property or service thus devoted to the purposes of the institution.

So well were these covenants drawn that no suit for payment of services or return of property was ever upheld; and Evans states in 1858 that during the preceding twenty years not a single legal claim against it had been entered in any other court.[325]

Evans insisted that the Shaker communion was the only authentic representative of Christianity since the first Jerusalem church; and he added that "the history of the world does not furnish a single instance of any other religious institution having stood seventy years without any visible declension of its principles and order.... The members," he continues, "are all entitled to equal benefits and privileges, and no difference is ever made on account of the property any individual may have contributed."[326] Evans emphasizes that the Ministry, or government, up and down the hierarchy, consisted always of paired males and females, who were equal in status; and this, he adds, should satisfy the most zealous advocates of " 'Women's Rights,' " which "here find a practical realization of their ideal."[327]

The first Shaker agreement, known as the *First Covenant of the Church of Christ*, was committed to writing in 1795 by Joseph Meacham; this was finally printed at Albany in 1835. It consisted of five articles, of which the last three provide that all members may consecrate their possessions as a joint interest of the community; that all have equal privileges and duties in the Church; and that none of the signatories will ever bring Debt or blame against the Church, or each other, for any interest or Services we should bestow to the joint interest of the Church...."[328]

4. *A General Constitution.* The Union Office issued a document in 1833 known as *The General Rules of the United Society and Summary Articles of Mutual Agreement and Release* which consisted of seven articles, the first of which placed the supreme authority in the Ministry, one man and one woman, located in New Lebanon, New York, to appoint, control, and remove all other officers throughout the communes. It also established three kinds of officials in every family: Elders "appointed to the spiritual duties"; Deacons "appointed to the care and management of the temporal concerns of the Church"; and Trustees "appointed to receive, hold, use, improve, and appropriate all gifts, grants, and donations which are or may be bestowed and surrendered to the consecrated use, benefit, and support of the institution."[329]

Articles II and III provide that each family—which generally consisted of from forty to eighty persons—within a commune, be a separate legal entity, owning its property in the name of the trustees. Article IV provides that members shall be "of sufficient knowledge and experience, of good moral character, free from debt, or any legal involvement.... That no one can be admitted who holds any personal property or private interest; that no property can be received...which is subject to any private or personal claim or demand...."[330]

Article V deals with the property of probationary members, which may be returned upon demand, but without interest, "within sixty days after it shall be demanded."[331] Article VI provides that no member shall be charged for food, clothing, and other services; but "that no person can be admitted...with any expectation or upon the condition of receiving any wages or hire...or return of a...gift, present, grant, or donation, voluntarily bestowed to the uses of the institution...."[332]

5. *The Shaker Manual of Discipline.* Like the ancient Essenes, the Shakers had an elaborate manual of discipline, known as the *Millennial Laws* (reprinted by Andrews in *The People Called Shakers*), consisting of four parts and thiry-three sections, which was never printed or published by the Shakers. There can be no doubt that the hundreds of provisions in this elaborate code of conduct were the result of a gradual development, during which the absolute control over the Society by the central theocracy became more and more fully intrenched; and they reflect the necessity of control by a central authority in any egalitarian society.

Part I, which deals with organization, provides that the different orders and families may communicate with each other only by "liberty" from the Elders; and that no person may enter the Senior Order unless he utterly renounces all relatives and private property. Supreme authority is vested in the Holy Anointed at New Lebanon; they are "the called and the chosen," "the first and leading Ministry," to whom all other officers and members are accountable; they are also entrusted with the keys of the Heavenly Kingdom, the gates of which they have power to open and shut. The Elders must look to the Ministry for strength, and must maintain complete control of the members under their direction. The members must confess their sins to their Elders, who stand as mediators between themselves and the throne of God. Members may never judge, or even reason with, their Elders; they may only listen and obey.

Like the Essenes, Believers were severely restricted in all their contacts with the world; only those in authority could buy or sell; and complete reports were required concerning all transactions with the outside. All argument or discussion with the Children of Perdition was prohibited; and any conversation with apostates, for whom the Shakers entertained a preternatural abhorrence, was strictly forbidden.

Whenever Believers emerged into the World, they were required to stay so close together that even a small dog could not pass between them.

The common members never received any accounting from their officers; the Deacons and Trustees, however, were required to make a full financial disclosure to the Elders.

Since sickness or disease was regarded as a demonic infestation, little sympathy was ever given one who complained of illness; and the malady could be treated only by the Elders or Eldresses. No medical practitioner from the world was ever tolerated within the communes, except, perhaps, in the case of a child whose parents were unbelievers, and then only by the decision of the Ministry or Elders.

Part II provides for full confession by the common members to the Elders, and commands the former to report all sins and transgressions observed to the rulers. If any member was heard to complain about his trials, sisters, brethren, Elders, Deacons, or Trustees, such disaffection must be disclosed to the authorities. When anyone was reprimanded by the Elders, he was forbidden to seek the identity of the informer. If any member offended or injured another, he was barred from his place in the Society until he had been purged and cleansed by full confession.

Again, the similarity to Essenism is obvious.

The regulations governing the relationships between the sexes were necessarily elaborate and strict, since these controlled the lives of all adults, many of whom were undivorced wives or husbands living in proximity and celibacy. Since the Essenes had no female adepts, this problem did not exist in their communes.

No common brother or sister, we read, could ever be together alone, touch each other unnecessarily, exchange presents, lend articles, or whisper to each other, communicate in any private manner, pass on a stairway, or shake hands. They could work together only if they were officers, or under certain conditions by special liberty from the Elders. The members of each sex were strictly forbidden to approach the quarters of the other, except the sisters— when they made up the rooms of the brethren in their absence.

The seats occupied by brethren and sisters at any meeting had to be at least five feet apart. No perfumes were permitted. No sister could leave a building unless accompanied by another female.

It was an offense of the highest magnitude for any common member to criticize the Order, or to speak of leaving it. Stories heard in the World must never be repeated. Gossiping, tattling, backbiting, jesting, joking, worldly conversation, or any discussion of politics was strictly forbidden. No one could carry news to other members, or mention sins or errors which had been confessed and forgiven.

Upon a given signal, every member arose from his bed *quickly*, at a very early hour; fifteen minutes later, all the brethren vacated their apartments, and five minutes after that the sisters entered them to do their daily chores. All were required to go to bed at a given moment; none could keep a light burning, or sit up in bed after the signal to retire. As if these regulations were not sufficient, we learn that all talking or laughing after bedtime was forbidden; and *all must lie straight in bed*.

Before and after each meal, all were required to kneel, close their eyes, and devote their spirits to silent prayer and thanksgiving.

Small mirrors were permitted in the rooms, and only such maps, almanacs, or newspapers as might be permitted by the Elders; and these had to remain in the office of the outer court. No hymns, anthems, or songs of any kind could be carried out of or into the commune without permission from the Elders. One or two approved spiritual journals could be kept in each family.

Members could neither purchase nor borrow books outside the commune, or even from the families of other Believers. When out of their own enclaves, Shakers were forbidden to look at any literature of any kind. Any member receiving a letter was required to submit it to his Elder before reading it, and could read it only in his presence. Whenever a common member wrote a letter, it had to be approved by the authorities and a copy filed in the office before it could be mailed. Modern prisons are, in comparison, havens of riotous freedom. Deacons and Trustees, however, were exempt from such restrictions.

Visiting with anyone from another family, but particularly with acquaintances or with natural parents or children from the world, could be done only at the office, and even there only by special liberty from, and in the presence of, the Elders. No one could go there to meet any visitor, except by special permission. The common members, like the Essenes, were strictly forbidden to make known the rules or regulations of their communes to any one.

When away from the farm, members were forbidden to go into stores, inquire the price of merchandise, loiter around, or enter museums, theaters, steamboats, or other public facilities.

If unavoidable contact was made with an apostate, this had to be reported at once in minute detail to the Elders.

Provision was made for the education of children; and, it should be noted, this was more liberal and extensive than might have been expected.

When a Shaker, like an ancient Essene, hired out, he could not retain a penny of his wages for his own use.

Part III and IV deal with the temporal economy and the minutiae of everyday life; they contain endless provisions for the care and protection of the communal property. Common members could not keep any private possessions under lock and key in any box or container—this was a privilege reserved for the Elders. No one was permitted to frolic with pets or keep them in shops or dwellings.

6. *The Iron Discipline that Leads to Death.* As we contemplate this Draconic regimen, we can understand why the human spirit must, under such restrictions—except among the most fanatical illuminates—at least rebel or grow cold in frustration; in the long run, in spite of an incomparable religious commitment and even with a high standard of material comfort, together with complete economic security, there would be a vast seething sea of discontent. That this never found expression in any overt rebellion, or in any actual schism, is a tribute to the remarkable discipline and indoctrination which held the Order together; for it never splintered, nor did cracks ever appear in its monolithic body. It simply died by attrition. But the fact that the Ministry could place so little trust in their members was also the measure of their weakness and the ultimate cause of Shaker dissolution.

Shaker life was certainly no bed of roses; and many Shaker hymns bear eloquent testimony to their heavy burdens, calculated not only to provide the material comforts of life, but dedicated also to the spiritual objective of crucifying the flesh and conquering the indwelling devil.

> "How hard I work,
> How does it look?
> Just for my clothes and victuals!"[333]

the Shaker sang in mock lamentation, because

> "...good soldiers now endure the cross,
> And heaven will reward your toil...."[334]

And finally:

"Come look at the true living order,
And see the foundation of peace,
O Zion, how lovely thy borders!
They show forth the long increase.
Their subjects are ever employed
In works of both virtue and love;
The evil must all be destroyed,
To lay up our treasures above."[335]

VIII. SHAKER STRENGTH AND WEAKNESS

1. *Cultic Longevity.* Josephus states that the Essenes[336] attained extraordinary longevity, and that some surpassed the century mark. Charles Nordhoff, after visiting the South Union commune about 1875, declared that the Shakers "are long-lived. A man was pointed out to me, now eighty-seven years of age, who plowed and sowed last summer; two revolutionary soldiers died in the society, aged ninety-three and ninety-four; and they now have people aged eighty-seven, eighty-five, eighty-two, eighty, and so on."[337]

The observations of Nordhoff are fully confirmed by the research of Edward D. Andrews, who reproduces statistics showing that Shaker life-expectancy averaged at least twenty years more than in the general population. Many lived to be well over eighty in all Shaker communities, and a considerable number even beyond the ninetieth year.[338] Between 1784 and 1889, there were 301 deaths in the Harvard commune, and the average age was 59.73 years.[339] In Massachusetts, the average age at death was 39.5 in 1850.[340] During the decade 1881-89, the average age at death for Shakers was 71.3, when the State as a whole reported one of 42.5 years.

These statistics were used by the Shakers to prove that the celibate-communal way of life was far superior to that of lust, generation, and private greed; however, one might suggest that this longevity was due, at least in large part, to a careful selection of members and the economic security enjoyed by them, which was in such contrast to the tensions and uncertainties inherent in the early American struggle for wealth, power, or survival.

2. *Security vs. Freedom.* Whether democratic socialism is possible, or whether communism can ever be maintained except at the point of a bayonet, are questions that only the future can resolve. Three of the most powerful human drives are those which seek sex-consummation, the possession of property, and personal economic, political, and intellectual freedom; on the other hand, the desire for security and the urge to escape responsibility are

perhaps equally powerful. But since it seems that these are mutually exclusive, humanity must ultimately choose between these two ways of life. The active and self-reliant will opt for freedom; the unsuccessful and those who wish to regiment others will prefer security.

Shakerism offered an island of autocracy and security in the midst of an ocean of free enterprise and individualism. The battle which ensued reflects on a microcosmic stage the whole struggle for the mind of man.

3. *Wherein Lay the Shaker Strength?* There is no doubt that had their gospel been economic only, the Shaker communities would have perished as quickly as did the democratic and anti-religious Owenite experiment at New Harmony, which, though completely financed and without debt, destroyed itself in two years. The Swedish commune in Illinois foundered as quickly on the rock of free enterprise.

Would the Shaker communities have been more successful had they not been celibate or fanatically religious? On the contrary, we believe that this was precisely the secret of their strength. The waverer in Luke 14:20, who had just married a wife, excused himself from the wedding feast; and Jesus comments, *ibid.* 26, that only those who hate father, mother, sister, wife, and children may enter his kingdom. Had the Shakers continued in the married and generative state, they would have been concerned primarily, as almost all of us are, with individual success; and the Shaker communes would have been wrecked on the Scylla of individualism and the Charybdis of personal ambition, as were all others that permitted conventional marriage.

Could the Shaker societies have survived longer or more successfully with a more democratic constitution? Certainly not: for even the smallest degree of freedom would have led to the formation of factions, to fierce disputes, and the inevitable splintering of the communes.

The Shaker experiment is the most important and instructive lesson in voluntary communism in modern history. It enjoyed many advantages; once organized, it was never injured by outside forces; it was highly productive and successful materially; it had almost no overhead; it never suffered an internal rebellion; it was rich, secure, and comfortable. Yet, as soon as the period of wild revivals in the general community came to an end, it was doomed to slow extinction.

The history of this and other cults seems to prove conclusively that voluntary communism cannot succeed without abolishing the family; that it must be based upon an extreme and fanatical religious conviction; that it cannot control its members except through an iron dictatorship; and that its mandatory repressions lead inevitably to ultimate dissolution. The vitality of the Shaker Order stemmed from its religious fervency; and when this cooled and when qualified members from the outside were no longer available, the Order began its decline. We may say with equal assurance that the similar forces which gave birth to the ancient Essene and Pythagorean communities operated in the same manner.

Since the Shakers received large gifts of land, money, and other forms of wealth from their members, they were free from debt on their capital investments. They could choose their members, accepting only the most capable, thrifty, consecrated, and ascetic. Like the Essenes, they tolerated no parasites; even their trustees, deacons, and elders were required to perform useful labor. They were incomparably industrious and creative; their significant inventions, such as the circular saw, were so numerous that almost half a page is required merely to list them by name.[341] They were very successful agronomists; they also operated a great many shops and manufacturing enterprises and carried on a thriving commerce with "the World," where they were highly respected because of the quality and the prices of their merchandise.

Since they had no criminals, parasites, welfare recipients, or serious disciplinary problems, their societies were almost without overhead and almost every hour of labor contributed directly to their living standard or capital increment. The Shakers paid no taxes; although they had no medical services as such, they enjoyed remarkably good health and longevity. There were no pensions to pay and all members worked as long as they were physically able, some beyond the eightieth year. The cult attracted scores of outstanding men and women whose compensation consisted of positions of influence, never in the consumption of more goods and services than common members. In due course, the Order accumulated large tracts of prime land, built hundreds of solid structures, and operated countless mills, canneries, dairies, etc., in nineteen communes with approximately seventy-five families; the cult developed a complete panoply of religious, economic, and political theory, bolstered by a vast literature.

Consider the contrast with our own society: if there were no crime, war, government, or taxes; if there were no unproductive functionaries or occupations, and no wealthy people who escape labor; if there were no people on welfare or receiving expensive educations; if there were no jails, prisons, or insane asylums to maintain, what could then be our living standards and accumulation of wealth? We are spending about $6,000 annually for every human being in the United States (more than $1.4 trillion) for public education, wars, government, crime, and churches alone; if this expense, together with other vast sums expended for entertainment, liquor, insurance, interest, private education, automobiles, casualties, medical care, etc., etc., were to be eliminated, we could drastically reduce our necessary hours of labor and yet double, triple, or even quadruple our per-capita consumption of goods and services.

IX. THE FAILURE OF SHAKERISM

We believe the decline and ultimate extinction of the Order stemmed from four basic causes:

1. *The Decline of Religious Traumas.* It is doubtful that anyone ever became a good Shaker unless he had previously undergone a fearful emotional experience which caused him to renounce the world and all its works; and this was an emotion which could never be transmitted from one person to another. In general, only individuals like Frederick William Evans, who had already undergone his illumination, or who had experienced the terrible shock incidental to the periodic and hysterical revivals which continued until the Civil War, could fully embrace the Shaker way of life. Less than one-tenth of those who applied for membership ever qualified for full consecration in the cult. Even more disappointing was the fact that, after spending years indoctrinating children who had been adopted at an early age or who were inducted with their parents and who were strictly insulated from the outside world, more than ninety per cent of these abandoned the Order. During its majority, the Society simply refused couples otherwise qualified if they had children. It must have been disheartening in the extreme for the leaders of the cult to realize that almost no one could be educated or indoctrinated into the faith, even from infancy.

As the religious traumas became more rare, the cult could no longer find large numbers of recruits.

2. *The Renunciation that Failed.* Since the most important drives in American life were and continue to be the need for sexual consummation, the yearning for political freedom, and the desire to accumulate private property, any system which denies these utterly faces overwhelming odds. The Shakers offered security and economic equality. We know, however, that in the social order known as civilization, man abhors *equality*. One reason why religious or secular bureaucracies have been able to rule so much of the time is that they offer groups or classes of aggressive persons the lure of controlling their fellow-men without the necessity of first achieving economic success in a competitive society.

The Shaker Ministry could rule only by religious persuasion. It had no police, no jails, no penal system; it utilized no outwardly coercive force. Members could escape into the world outside simply by walking away. When, therefore, the Ministry demanded ceaseless labor and complete subordination, its power gradually waned. As the old soldiers faded away, new recruits could rarely be found who would barter freedom, individualism, a normal sex-life, private property, and their total possessions for equality, security, and the hope of mansions in heaven.

3. *The Intellectual Suppression.* For the assertive individual, the intellectual repression must have been more galling even than the renunciation. Since a free-enterprise economy offers freedom in business competition, it demands and also creates freedom in the realm of ideas. In a communist or socialist system, all determinations are made by authority; and this was peculiarly true of the Shakers, who were ruled by revelation, which involved the ultimate death or stagnation of the intellect.

4. *The Failure to Convince.* Herein lay the supreme weakness of Shakerism; despite its security, prosperity, fanaticism, elaborate doctrines, and unique revelations, its common members could not be trusted to mingle with "the world."

The eventual decline of the Order probably stemmed from the fact that, in spite of all its songs, dances, discipline, indoctrination, threats, emotional excesses, and extensive literature, it simply could not convince many of its own people, and especially the youth trained in its teachings from childhood. Nor could it supply members with ammunition to meet the arguments of skeptics or unbelievers. Those who are happy do not sing songs which proclaim their delight but are composed by tyrants whom they serve; those who really wish to crucify the lusts of the flesh do not proclaim their joy in so doing. All this was an artificial means of concealing an underlying and profound resentment; and that widespread disillusionment existed became evident as early as 1794—1797, when the young people abandoned the Order almost en masse; and again with the frustrated juveniles who started the spiritualist revival in 1837 and who, in their trance-like state, heaped the vilest and most profane, even obscene, abuse upon the faithful brothers and sisters and, most of all, upon the trustees, deacons, elders, and Ministry.

The fact is that Shaker doctrine claimed too much; by what authority could it demand belief in Ann as the Second Christ, the Holy Mother Wisdom, the Queen of Heaven, the Co-Creator of the Universe? By what authority was it said that revelation could be complete only when Christ had appeared in the Order of the Superior Female? We, who are not Shakers, reject these doctrines as puerile or ridiculous; and the fatal weakness of the Order was that they could never be thoroughly established by argument even among the faithful. And as the Shaker strength was also its Achilles heel, the secret of its endurance was also the source of its doom.

The handwriting on the wall became visible long before the end. As time went on (1) there were not enough workers to operate the farms and the shops; (2) of those remaining, the women outnumbered the men by a ratio of two or even three to one; (3) since desirable young recruits, especially males, could not be obtained, more and more of the labor had to be done by hired hands. This development completely altered the nature of the societies; instead of being communes, they were in fact transformed into the very antithesis: they became capitalist corporations.

In one Shaker family after another, as also happened with other communist groups which had accumulated property, the older workers remained until they were so few that the organization could no longer operate. The surviving members then sold the assets and divided the proceeds among themselves; and this was assuredly the ultimate irony, the very fiend's arch-mock, the last supreme sarcasm of Satan: those who had consecrated their lives and their possessions to the service of God and the common welfare, finally alienated the communal property for their own private enrichment.

> Thus fleet the works of men back to earth again;
> Ancient and holy things fade like a dream.

Chapter 3

PHINEAS PARKHURST QUIMBY

I. A FORERUNNER: FRANZ A. MESMER

1. *Early Education*. Franz Anton Mesmer (1735-1815), an Austrian born at Weil, near Lake Constance, sought new pathways to knowledge through the study of divinity, philosophy, and law. After earning two doctorates, he turned to medicine, in which he obtained a third degree in 1766. In his last thesis, he advanced the theory that there is a cosmic fluid which originates in, and is controlled by, the bodies of the solar system; and that the emanation penetrates and affects every living organism with a magnetic, curative force which can heal all disease.

Mesmer was avidly interested in the latest discoveries in geology, physics, chemistry, mathematics, and abstract philosophy; on the lighter side, he cultivated the musical arts and became an adept with the piano-forte, violincello, and glass harmonica. In 1786, he married a wealthy widow ten years older than himself, moved into her large home, and began enjoying an elaborate social life. His garden parties became famous in Vienna, where he entertained such friends as Mozart, Haydn, and Gluck.

2. *The Searcher*. But Mesmer was no dilettante. He continued his search for a new and more scientific explanation of health, disease, and the invisible forces of the universe. Even in his dissertation, he showed the influence of the half-legendary Swiss Paracelsus (1493-1541), who had declared that magnet-

ized metal possessed extraordinary powers to dissipate and destroy disease and who, without formal training in medicine, had struck out into untrodden ways and attacked the medical faculties with ferocity. In 1774, two years after Swedenborg's death and the very year in which Ann Lee crossed the ocean, a case came to the attention of Mesmer in Vienna in which a piece of magnetic iron was said to have cured a patient of stomach disorders. He thereupon obtained several such instruments and applied them to the throat, the heart, and other infected portions of the anatomy, in some instances achieving remarkable results. However, since he had not been able objectively to establish a causal relationship between the method and the effect, he continued his experiments.

3. *The Cosmic Fluid.* In his far-flung research, Mesmer must have encountered the ideas of Swedenborg; at all events, his 1766 lucubration contains elements reminiscent of the Swedenborgian Influx. The cosmic fluid, said Mesmer, is a great life force which saturates the universe and constitutes its sustaining power. It is a kind of impalpable gas in which all things are immersed.

At this point, however, Mesmer took a long leap into obscurity: by proclaiming that magnetism was the creative ardor or ether of the cosmos, he made an error which led to others and which ultimately rendered his work, per se, of little permanent value.

4. *Magnetism.* Persuaded that the metallic magnet had the power to heal, Mesmer set up a large facility in 1774, where he magnetized trees, dishes, clothing, beds, mirrors, etc. He had his patients join hands, while they bathed in water magnetized by steel rods; and he hired musicians to play musical instruments so that their melodies might exercise or at least neutralize a horde of diseases with dulcet harmony.

Mesmer's fame and practice grew by leaps and bounds: hundreds of wealthy patients, who came from far and near, testified that they had been cured.

To his credit it must be emphasized that Mesmer claimed power to heal "nervous diseases" only; whenever patients with organic ailments came, he refused them, recommending that they seek help from the conventional medical faculty.

Then, quite suddenly and by accident, he discovered that his magnetized objects, which he had thought transmitted the healing fluid to the patient, were without force, and therefore unnecessary: for he found that his cures could be accomplished quite as well without these props. He thereupon discarded this entire paraphernalia; persuaded that the power to transmit the cosmic fluid lay in himself, he renamed this *animal magnetism*, an expression destined to have a remarkable history. In order to facilitate the transfer of healing power to the patient, he utilized manipulation: like the first Apostles, he cured by the "laying on of hands." His touch effected the same results as had previously been achieved by the use of the magnet: and he declared that the cosmic fluid, flowing through and emanating from himself, streamed into the patient, and restored his health.

5. *The New Transmission.* The next step in Mesmer's progress was his discovery of "distant treatment." He found that he could exert influence upon patients separated from him by a thick wall or even by a considerable distance. And so he gradually abandoned the tactile treatment also; but he was still persuaded that in some mysterious way his healings resulted from the emission of the magnetic fluid.

6. *Driven from Vienna.* Mesmer's "health factory" now became greater than ever; but, as might have been expected, the medical profession, which at first had been skeptical, now became extremely hostile. The opportunity to inflict punishment came with the case of Maria Theresa Paradies, a young woman who had become blind at the age of four but who, as a royal ward, had developed into a famous concert pianist. Mesmer undertook the restoration of her sight, and was on the road to success when her guardians were pressured into withdrawing their consent to further treatment, after which she relapsed not only into total blindness but also into depression. The result was that Mesmer was discredited, and forbidden by the authorities to practice. He fled his native land and took refuge among the French.

7. *Success Again!* During the years following his arrival in Paris in 1778, Mesmer once again became popular and famous: Madame de Pompadour and Marie Antoinette were among his clients. The great and the rich flocked to his salon, where all the trappings of mystery were utilized to attract and overawe. He was, indeed, an unparalleled success, for streams of patients came to his parlors, many in magnificent carriages. Simpler treatments were available for the less affluent, and even for those who could pay nothing at all. He established a great hospital in the Montmartre, where, for five years, patients from all walks of life were received.

It must be pointed out that Mesmer still did not understand what he was doing, for the trance-like state into which he placed his patients was actually *hypnotic*; in the emotional purgation which accompanied this condition, many experienced relief from nervous and even organic maladies. The patients sat in a circle, touching hands; the great healer would then enter dramatically, dressed in a magnificent lilac robe, like a Zoroastrian or Hindu magician, bearing his wand; and, when he communicated his will to his clients by a deft touch, an extraordinary phenomenon ensued, similar to what happened at the fantastic camp-meetings in Kentucky, in which people "fell" into cataleptic trances. As the music began, someone in the company would tremble, then twitch convulsively; others would groan, scream, choke, laugh hysterically, break out in profuse perspiration, or dance like dervishes. A chain reaction followed around the mesmeric "baquet." This culminated in what was called "the crisis," during which, one by one, the subjects subsided into a hypnotic trance, from which, when awakened, many declared themselves healed.

The result was that Mesmer was almost deified by his devotees; he was beset by duchesses and princesses who pleaded for the privilege of touching the hem of his garments. He became a chief topic of conversation, and much of France partook of an hysteria which we may call Mesmeromania.

8. *A Branded Exile.* But there were skeptics and powerful enemies. King Louis XVI, who hated turmoil, set his face against the new therapy; and in March, 1784, he commanded that a commission be set up to investigate the nature of this "animal magnetism." The members of this body were chosen from the Academy of Medicine and of Sciences and included such names as Dr. Guillotin, Benjamin Franklin, the astronomer Bailly, the chemist Lavoisier, and others of imposing stature. After exhaustive inquiry, in which a number of the savants were personally "magnetized," the Commission concluded that the fluid or animal magnetism had no objective existence; and that, therefore, it could not possibly serve any useful purpose. It also declared that any effect which might be observed resulted from a stimulus of the imagination and operated through the mind alone. Mesmer's treatment was therefore officially branded a complete fraud.

Shortly after this report was made public, the French nation had something more serious than animal magnetism on its hands, for in 1789 the great revolution swept away the whole fabric of the old society; and Mesmer and his therapies were almost forgotten. In 1794, friendless and penniless, he fled to Vienna, whence, because of old prejudices and reputed sympathy for the French revolutionaries, he was driven into exile once more. He took refuge in Frauenfeld, Switzerland, near Zurich, where, in comparative obscurity, he continued to practice for more than twenty years, until his death at eighty-two, at Lake Constance, where he was born. During these years, he was not even aware of the controversies raging over the therapies of his disciples and epigones.

II. THE DISCOVERIES OF THE MESMERIZERS

1. *A Truth Is Born.* Time had been when a decree of the Academy would have annihilated "Mesmerism" forever; but after the Revolution, ex-cathedra authority was no longer final. Even before Mesmer abandoned Paris, many sprang to his defense; his disciples multiplied; in fact, they became nothing less than a cult. The eminent botanist Jussieu, who refused to set his name to the bull of Mesmer's excommunication, expressed open dissent from the findings of the Commission. He had put his finger on the weakness in the reasoning of

his learned colleagues: for obviously there was present in the mesmeric therapy some kind of active force, even if this could not be detected by the senses or weighed in a mechanical balance. It was, he said, not one whit less potent whether it operated through the mind or through the imaginative faculty.

2. *The Count de Puységur.* It must be admitted, however, that, if the Commission failed to comprehend what went on during the mesmeric therapy, Mesmer did also. It is therefore ironic that his name is still attached to a psychic phenomenon which a disciple of his, the Count Maxime de Puységur, was the first to understand or control. Quite by accident, like so many great discoveries, while practicing the mesmeric therapy, he discovered that one of his entranced patients, a simple, healthy, young peasant, could perform extraordinary feats while sleepwalking. The practitioner's amazement became still greater when he found that this subject could answer questions with complete lucidity while entranced, but had no memory of such conversations upon awakening. The Count's conquest of psychic phenomena was still further advanced when he found that he could, at will, plunge his subject into, or awaken him from, this strange sleep; and that he could accomplish identical results with others.

Nor was this all: the Count concluded that while his medium was magnetized the latter could read the thoughts of the people about him, travel in spirit to distant places, diagnose the symptoms of the sick and the diseased, place his hands on the parts where pain existed, and, finally, prescribe drugs and other remedies for every malady. He still believed, however, that the trance was induced by the transference of the mesmeric fluid.

This new therapy became known as Mesmerism, although Mesmer had nothing to do with it. However, the discovery of Puységar let loose in Europe, and later in America, a horde of practitioners using this new technique, which was a form of mental healing.

Mesmer planted the seed, but others reaped the harvest. As usual, the academic world, donning its black spectacles of ignorance, saw no more reality in the controlled trance of Puységur than it had in the cosmic fluid of Franz Mesmer.

3. *Hypnotic Healing.* It remained for James Braid (1795-1860), a Scottish surgeon who practiced in Manchester, to demonstrate in his book *Neurohypnology* (1843) that there is no such thing as a cosmic fluid and that Mesmerism is a purely subjective force, which he called *neurohypnotism*, and later simply *hypnotism*. He maintained at first that the subject was not put to sleep by the hypnotist, but rather by the use of some mechanical object, like a glass ball or a shiny piece of metal. He failed to comprehend the power of suggestion exercised by the hypnotist over his subject. Gradually, however, this truth also dawned upon him; and, at about the same time that Quimby was making the same discovery in America, Dr. Braid became aware that a

subconscious mental level exists, which he called "double consciousness," an understanding of which finally led to the Freudian analyses of the *id* and the *superego*.

Mesmerism cut a wide swath long before the advent of Freud; a whole cult of healing sprang up, with many practitioners and thousands of clients in Europe. The standard technique was simple enough: the mesmerizer travelled about with a colleague, one who could easily be entranced. In this state, it was proclaimed that the medium was clairvoyant, could read the thoughts of people near or far away, travel in spirit to distant places and describe minutely what was there (as Swedenborg had done), diagnose the diseases of all who submitted themselves for analysis, and prescribe cures for every malady.

4. *The Swedenborgian Healer.* In the very year that Mesmer died, 1818, the Swedenborgian Society in Sweden conducted elaborate spiritualist thera-peutic experiments based upon a subjectivist therapy, quite similar to the technique used by Quimby toward the close of his mesmeric period. After 1850, the American spiritualist cult under the leadership of the Swedenbor-gian Andrew Jackson Davis replaced the mesmeric healers. Spiritualism became so popular that at one time it had hundreds of congregations; in the 1850s, there were more than a hundred clairvoyants practicing in New York City alone. In Europe and America, they were numbered in the thousands and counted among their adherents many famous people, including Sir Arthur Conan Doyle.

Thus, the "fad" of mesmeric healing passed away and was replaced by Swedenborgian spiritualism. The result was that not only Mesmer's work but that also of his disciples vanished. Nevertheless, the mesmeric movement furnished the original foundation and the connecting link by which an extraordinary American created the foundation for the superstructure of New Thought.

III. QUIMBY: OUTWARD LIFE AND CAREER

1. *Who and What Was He?* Quimby was born in Lebanon, New Hamp-shire on February 16, 1802; two years later, his family moved to Belfast, Maine, where he spent an uneventful boyhood. In due course, he became a clockmaker; and it was said that his products were so excellent that some of them were in good working order a century later.

Among therapeutic practitioners, he is probably unique. He had undergone little intellectual discipline and had no scientific training, but was a sincere and determined man with an extraordinary bent for originality. For authority in general, he had only supreme contempt; and, since he was burdened neither with erudition nor with tradition, he played fierce havoc with the conventional judgments and beliefs of the past. Perhaps his outstanding characteristics consisted in a constant search for truth, an all-pervasive skepticism concerning accepted doctrines; a relentless rejection of popular conceptions, a capacity to turn all things into something resembling their opposites, and an intransigent enmity toward vested interests and respectabilities. He declared that ninety per cent of all beliefs are erroneous.[1]

He was a plain, simple, humble man; but his dark, piercing eyes could penetrate and transfix, and his convictions were contagious. He was utterly selfless; he so gave himself to the service of his patients that he sacrificed his own life for them; and, what was more serious, this left him no time to organize his philosophy, or to prepare others to practice his technique.

2. *Quimby's Own Healing*. Quimby's first great experience came in 1833, when he was thirty-one, which he described in an article written in 1863, first published by Julius A. Dresser in 1887 as part of a lecture called *The True History of Mental Science*.[2] "I was very sick," he wrote, "and was considered fast wasting away with consumption. At that time, I became so low that it was with difficulty that I could walk...My symptoms were those of any consumptive, and I had been told that my liver was affected, and my kidneys were diseased, and that my lungs were nearly consumed. I believed all this, from the fact that I had all the symptoms, and could not resist the opinions of the physician while having the proof with me. In this state, I was compelled to abandon my business, and, losing all hope, I gave up to die."[3]

However, when told that riding horseback might cure him, he took a ride in a carriage, after which all the symptoms vanished; and he was convinced that the disease had no reality except in his belief.

Physical maladies, however, or at least a belief in them, continued to plague Quimby: he had pains in his back, supposedly caused by his partially consumed kidneys. He was also told he had ulcers on his lungs. "Under this belief," he wrote, "I was miserable enough to be of no account in this world. This was the state I was in when I commenced to mesmerize. On one occasion, when I had my subject asleep, he described the pains I felt in my back...and he placed his hand on the spot where I felt the pain. He then told me that my kidneys were in a very bad state; that one was half consumed.... This was what I believed to be true, for it agreed with what the doctors told me, and with what I suffered.... I asked him if there was any remedy. He replied, 'Yes...and you will get well...' He immediately placed his hands upon me...and from that day I never have experienced the least pain....

"Now what is the secret of the cure? I had not the least doubt but that I was as he described; and if he had said, as I expected...that nothing could be done, I should have died in a year or so. But when he said that he could cure me...I discovered that I had been deceived into a belief that made me sick. The absurdity of his remedies made me doubt the fact that my kidneys were diseased...."[4]

3. *French Mesmerists in America.* Mr. Du Commun, a pupil of Puységur, first introduced the mesmeric therapy into the United States in 1829. He was followed in 1836 by the renowned Charles Poyen, who, accompanied by his medium, lectured and practiced in New England, where his entranced colleague diagnosed the diseases and maladies of those who applied for treatment and prescribed drugs to alleviate and cure their diseases. Fascinated by this "science," Quimby became a mesmeric healer.

4. *The Progressing Doctor.* Beginning with 1836, Quimby's life divides into three periods: (1) the mesmeric (1836-1847), when, as an itinerant hypnotist, he travelled from place to place; (2) the intermediate phase of experimentation and discovery (1847-1859), during which he set up what might be called temporary clinics in various towns; and (3) the period of maturity (1859-1865), with an office in Portland, Maine, where he committed his ideas to writing and began to obtain disciples and commmand serious attention.

The following excerpt from the *Bangor Democrat*, April 1843, is the first public discussion of Quimby's work which has come to our attention: "Mr. Quimby of Belfast has visited here by invitation.... He has with him two young men, brothers, one twenty-three and the other seventeen. They are clairvoyant subjects.... The young man was magnetized by Mr. Quimby, when one of our citizens was put in communication with him. In *imagination*, he took the boy to St. John, New Brunswick, before the New Custom House....

"The gentleman says no one knew where he proposed to take the boy: the boy had never seen the building, and yet he described it...accurately.... This gentleman's word is not to be questioned...."[5]

Since we hear no more of these two brothers, Quimby must shortly have replaced them with the nineteen-year-old Lucius Burkmar, the medium who continued as his colleague until 1847, and who, while "magnetized," possessed, according to Quimby's own testimony, not only clairvoyant power, but also the ability to read the thoughts of any person in proximity, see through solid matter, travel in spirit to distant places, be in two locations at the same time, detect and diagnose diseases, and, finally, prescribe cures for every malady.[6]

The fame of Quimby and Lucius grew apace; and, although ministers and medical practitioners called him a charlatan, his popularity increased and many credited him with extraordinary cures. Lucius himself kept a journal, beginning in December 1843, in which he wrote that some of Dr. Quimby's cures, performed through magnetism, were actually miraculous.[7]

Toward the end of the mesmeric period, however, Quimby began to suspect that his success depended very little either upon the diagnosis of Lucius or the drugs he prescribed. We must point out that the mesmeric therapy was not intended as any form of mind-healing, but only as the most reliable diagnosis possible of ordinary diseases. The discovery which Quimby was now about to make was therefore momentous: he was the first to proclaim a system of healing dependent entirely upon mental processes.

"When I mesmerized my subject," he wrote later, "he would prescribe some simple herb that would do no harm or good of itself. In some cases this would cure the patient. I also found that any medicine would cure if he ordered it. This led me to investigate the matter, and arrive at the stand I now take: that the cure is not in the medicine, but in the confidence" of the patient in "the doctor or medium."[8]

This belief ripened into conviction when Lucius ordered drugs costing twenty dollars, which was more than the patient could afford. However, when a simple herb was substituted, the patient "got well."[9] From this experience Quimby finally concluded—as had no other mesmerizer—that his cure depended, not on the diagnosis, the clairvoyance, or the prescriptions of his medium, but upon the force, power, or dominance exercised by the practitioner, which filled the patient with confidence in the healer and the expectation of recovery. The whole process thus became subjective; and Quimby leaped to the conclusion that sickness and disease have no reality except as they are created by the mind.

With no further need for Lucius, mesmerism, or placebos, Quimby discovered that he was himself as clairvoyant in the waking state as Lucius had been when "magnetized";[10] he could read the thoughts of his patients, be in two places at the same time, perceive phenomena without the use of the bodily senses,[11] and take upon himself the physical symptoms of his patients.[12]

5. *Experimentation and Writings.* And so Quimby set forth upon the second phase of his career, which continued for twelve years, during which he experimented ceaselessly until he was convinced that he had indeed discovered an infallible scientific method by which to achieve universal health and happiness.

When Horatio W. Dresser published *The Quimby Manuscripts* in 1921, a vast lode of knowledge concerning the origin of New Thought was at last made public, even though only 101 of the 311 articles written by Quimby were included. Some valuable material, however, had already been given the world in 1895 when Annetta Gertrude Dresser published *The Philosophy of P.P. Quimby.*

6. *The Impact of Swedenborg.* We know that Quimby studied Berkeley between 1843 and 1847,[13] and probably encountered the works of other idealist philosophers. We know also that he discovered Swedenborg,[14] who left a pervasive influence upon his thinking. It is also possible that Quimby came into contact with Brook Farm, after its leaders became Swedenborgians; and we believe that this philosophy was the catalyst which transformed Quimby from a mesmeric practitioner into a self-proclaimed mind- and faith-healer, utilizing a technique and vocabulary essentially taken from this

source. It must not be supposed, however, that he was a mere copyist; every element reproduced by him from preceding sources was always stamped with a peculiar originality when it re-emerged from the Quimby alembic.

8. *The Advertising Therapist.* From 1847 to 1859, then, the tireless, searching Quimby went from town to town offering mental therapy through the power of faith. He distributed a brochure in 1855 which repudiated the mesmeric technique and which read in part: "Dr. P.P. Quimby would respectfully announce...that...he will attend to those wishing to consult him in regard to their health, and, as his practice is unlike all other medical practice, it is necessary to say that *he gives no medicine and makes no outward applications,* but simply sits down by the patients, tells them their feelings and what they think is their disease. If the patients admit that he tells them their feelings, etc., then his explanation is the cure; and if he succeeds in correcting their error, he changes the fluids of the system and establishes the truth or health. *The truth is the cure.*"

When people consult a regular physician, the flyer continues, "Five or ten dollars is then paid, for the cure of some disease they never had, nor ever would have had but for the wrong impression received from these quacks or robbers...." The doctors have in mind only their "own selfish objects—to sell their medicines. Herein consists their shrewdness!—to impress patients with a wrong idea, namely—that they have some disease. This makes them nervous and creates in their minds a disease that otherwise would never have been thought of. Wherefore he [Quimby] says to such, never consult a quack: you not only lose your money, but your health.

"He gives no opinion, therefore you lose nothing. If patients feel pain, they know it, and if he describes their pain he feels it and in his explanation lies the cure....

"There are many who pretend to practice as he does, but when a person, while in 'a trance,' claims any power from the spirits or the departed, and recommends any kind of medicine to be taken internally or applied externally, beware! Believe them not, 'for by their fruits ye shall know them.' "[15]

9. *A Settled Practice.* In 1859, Quimby set up a permanent office in Portland, Maine, to which came those who were sick in body and tortured in mind. He sat down by them, and took upon himself the sins, the errors, and the maladies of his patients, all of which, by some mysterious process or principle, passed from their bodies into his. He did not ask them to describe their pains or their symptoms; and when he succeeded in explaining theirs in terms they could not gainsay, *this was the cure.*

Quimby states that during his ministry, as it should be called, he treated 12,000 patients;[16] and he declared that during the Portland period he administered to 500 every year.[17] Few indeed sought him out except as a last resort; only when all else had failed, and then often amidst the hoots and sneers of enemies and skeptics, did many of his clients drag their weary feet over his threshold. Some had been ill for years, their maladies beyond all aid or diagnosis. Yet by the dozens and the hundreds they were restored to health, and went their way rejoicing, proclaiming the wonderous powers of Phineas Parkhurst Quimby to cure as no man had cured since Jesus of Nazareth had healed the halt, the blind, the scrofulous, and those bedridden with ailments unknown.

At the close of 1865, he returned to Belfast to recuperate from exhaustion; but he was completely worn out and died in January 1866.

IV. QUIMBY'S RELIGIO-PHILOSOPHICAL SYSTEM

1. *The Simple and Central Problem.* It must be recognized that Quimby's system was limited in scope; beyond a few convictions basic to his therapeutic system, his metaphysical concepts were blurred and sometimes inconsistent. He was no Swedenborg; and he never came to grips with many questions which lie close to his principal thesis. It is difficult to discover just what he *did* believe in regard to matter, the human soul, or what takes place after death. Concerning all this, we have hints only.

Quimby's conviction focussed upon a single point: that the science of health is also the science of life and happiness. Although the question of health was significant to Jesus, Swedenborg, and the Shakers, for all of them this was only one among various facets in the life-complex. To Quimby, health was the *ne plus ultra*: ninety per cent of all people, he maintained, suffer from some kind of malady; and if we could only rid the world of this suffering, a human paradise would ensue. His indictment against the clergy is not so much that they teach false doctrine as that they fill the world with sickness and disease.

Quimby's efforts are therefore directed to the achievement of perfect happiness through the science of health, which is identical with the Science of Christ, or Christian Science.

Theology and Christology. Quimby's references to deity are often negations or abstractions. "God," he says, "is a spirit and not a man";[18] and there is no personal god.[19] Again, God is a principle,[20] without form or sex,[21] which has never spoken;[22] God is the only reality,[23] and everlasting essence, existing without matter.[24] God is Science,[25] the principle which Jesus taught as the Christ.[26] The reality which is Man is also God,[27] and all men and women are part and parcel of deity.[28] The gods of all existing creeds and religions have been created by men;[29] the Christian God, in particular, is a terrible tyrant,[30] worthy only of being cursed.[31] On the contrary, the true God is benevolent, and could, therefore, never have created disease.[32]

"I must," says Quimby, "make the reader detach his senses from a god of man's belief and attach them to this invisible Wisdom which fills all space, and whose attributes are all light, all wisdom, all goodness and love, which is free from all selfishness and hypocrisy, which makes or breaks no laws, but lets man work out his own salvation; which has no laws and restrictions and sanctions men's acts according to their belief, and holds them responsible for their belief, right or wrong, without respect to persons."[33]

Quimby's Christ-Science, inseparable from his Christology, is more elaborate and distinct than his theology. This Science of Life and Happiness was, he says, founded by Jesus Christ[34] and is the only true religion.[35] When this is established, it will take the place of all other sciences;[36] it is eternal life in Christ;[37] it is Divine Wisdom reduced to self-evident propositions,[38] and it is therefore universally demonstrable, like a mathematical equation. Jesus put intelligence, not in matter, but in Christ, or Science;[39] all those subversions of his doctrine which now pass as religion must one day give way to Truth,[40] which is the Christ-Science,[41] and which anyone can learn.[42] Finally, it is the only Key to Heaven.[43]

3. *The Healing Christ-Science.* The core of Quimby's system is, then, that all diseases may be cured by an exact science, which was that of Jesus Christ. We know, says Quimby, that Christ healed scientifically because "there can be no such thing as accident with God; and if Christ was God, He knew what He was doing." When he was accused of curing disease through the aid of the Evil One, "He said, 'If I cast out devils or disease through Beelzebub or ignorance, my kingdom or science cannot stand; but if I cast' " them out " 'through a science of law, then my kingdom or law will stand, for it is not of this world.' " When others cast out disease, they cured by ignorance or Beelzebub, and there was no science in their cures, although an effect was produced; but not knowing the cause, the world was none the wiser for their cures."[44]

Quimby proclaimed that he practiced this Christ-Science and healed as Jesus healed;[45] and in so doing, was simply emulating the original disciples, whom Jesus commissioned to do the same.[46] Jesus certainly had a science which could be taught, and thus practiced by others;[47] and Quimby's truth was the Truth of Christ.[48]

This Christ-Science, first taught 1800 years before,[49] was the same that enabled Quimby to heal the sick.[50] Believing in Jesus Christ,[51] he practiced the same science, which is simply the Wisdom of God,[52] and the practical religion of Jesus.[53] This "Christ," says Quimby, "whom you think is Jesus, is the same Christ that stands at the door of your dwelling or belief, knocking to come in and sit down with the child of Science that has been led astray by blind guides into the wilderness.... To be born again is to unlearn your errors and embrace the truth of Christ; this is the new birth, and it cannot be unlearned except by a desire for the truth, that Wisdom that can say to the winds of error and superstition, 'Be still!' "[54]

Although Quimby declared that he had "no belief in religion of any kind..." he stated that Jesus was the only true prophet that ever lived on this earth;[55] that he is the bread of life and happiness, which we should eat; that Christ of Science is the body of that Christ of which we may partake;[56] that the Christ in Jesus is eternal life, or Science;[57] and that Man, when reborn in Christ, is himself this Science, which is also the Wisdom of God.[58] The Christ of Jesus, who was crucified by the priests and the doctors of his day, is still being crucified by the priests and doctors who mislead and delude the blind.[59] This Christ-Science or Science of Life, as Quimby calls it again and again, "is shown in the progress of Christian Science...."[60] and is the most precious thing on earth; for those who find it will be resurrected into eternal life, which is Christ, or Science.[61]

4. *The Gnostic Christ.* Quimby's Christology is basically the same Gnostic concept which we find in Shaker doctrine, in Swedenborg, and in many ancient cults. Christ was simply a spirit which, for a time, occupied the flesh-and-blood body known as Jesus. At the crucifixion, Christ remained what he had been before and, when he appeared to his disciples, this apparition was simply clothed in a condensation of spiritual body.[62] Jesus and Christ are, therefore, different identities;[63] Jesus was a man, just as we are; he had a natural body of flesh and blood like ours.[64] Christ is God, the unseen principle in Man.[65] Christ is a power which has appeared intermittently in all ages.[66] Jesus was therefore only the oracle, but Christ was the Wisdom of God.[67]

Understanding the difference between Jesus and Christ, says Quimby, is the key to the understanding of all religion. The construction given their relationship by the Church makes our life one thing and our religion another. Jesus created a Science which "separates us from the world of sin and death and brings life and immortality...Ignorance of Christ or Science put 'Jesus' and 'Christ' together and said 'Jesus Christ...' "[68]

The power of Jesus was the Christ within him,[69] which is health, as Health is Heaven;[70] again, Christ is the heavenly man of Science,[71] who is in each and every one of us.[72] He is the Science of Health;[73] to accept him is to have Christ within us,[74] which is the Christ-Truth available to all; and which, for example, when exhibited through the man Franklin, was called electricity.[75]

5. *Creeds, Priests, and Medicine Men.* The great absurdity in the Christian churches, says Quimby, is the requirement that its communicants believe, on pain of everlasting damnation, that the man Jesus was Christ and a member of the tripersonal Trinity, that he died on the cross, that he rose from the dead, and that he went to Heaven to sit at the right hand of God. And so man's salvation is made to depend upon accepting such a false and ridiculous creed.[76]

Those who teach that Jesus came to save mankind from damnation after death are teaching a grievous error;[77] in fact, he never taught any doctrine concerning another world;[78] and he certainly never believed that his natural body would rise from the dead.[79] He came to destroy death and the devil[80]— that is, disease and error; he was opposed to all forms and ceremonies;[81] he had no "religious" opinions, as such;[82] and he cured simply by changing the minds of those afflicted with maladies.[83]

Quimby's condemnations of the clergy are the most ferocious found in his writings. It would not be amiss to say that his healing mission consisted primarily in freeing his patients from the diseases created in them as a result of the fears resulting from priestly threats of eternal torture. In his essay "The Senses and Language," he explains that since, in primitive society, it was necessary that someone interpret the phenomena of nature, certain persons were appointed for that purpose; and so priests and prophets arose who had to be supported by taxation. As the tribes grew into nations and kingdoms, the priests seized political power also; and since the priesthood was founded on superstition, inventions of all kinds were devised to keep the people in ignorance. As scientific truths were discovered, these were kept in concealment so that any chemical or mechanical advance might be passed off as a gift through the priests from heaven. When astronomy was developed, they kept it as their own, and all their calculations were made, not as a science for the benefit of the people, but as a divine revelation.[84]

Priests, said Quimby, are "fake-guides" who have subverted the Scriptures;[85] they have stolen the teachings of Jesus and engrafted them upon a system of their own. After these deceivers arrogated to themselves the role of revelators, "another swarm of hungry dogs, called doctors, who invent diseases..." came along to devour an additional portion of what the people produce.[86] Superstition, religion, and slavery have always gone hand in hand;[87] they have conspired to rule and ruin;[88] and have filled the earth with error, ignorance, and disease.[89] Religion, law, and medicine are the actual Christian Trinity: "I will introduce a priest, a doctor, and the law as the Godhead, for these three are equal in power. Religion is the father, medicine is the son, and law is the Holy Ghost...."[90] Every creed serves only as an instrument by which one set of liars, charlatans, and imposters seeks to replace another.[91] Priests have created a fictitious world in the hereafter filled with torment and despair, in order to terrify their victims and fill their own pockets.[92] Priests and religion crucified Christ;[93] and priests have always made violent and bloody persecution the highest virtue.[94] They have twisted the teachings in the Book of Revelation for their own ulterior purposes; they want people to have creeds, but never understanding.[95] To the priest, an infidel is simply anyone who will not accept his peculiar interpretation of the Bible.[96] Religion is literally a disease, invented by humbugs.[97]

Many are driven insane or are afflicted with all manner of disease because of the deceptions and terrors of religion;[98] countless persons are sick because of this all their lives.[99] Religious sects fight like maniacs to establish their own false and degenerating opinions;[100] and when they obtain proselytes, these victims are filled with torments.[101] Thus religion, which should be a source of consolation, brings sickness and despair.

Prayers offered in Christian churches are a travesty: for they are pleas for what is not deserved, or for what can only be harmful to others, as in the North and the South during the Civil War.[102]

The great exploiters of mankind, says Quimby, are the priests, the doctors, and the politicians. The people have given their souls to the priests and their bodies to the medicine men;[103] and these two professions have destroyed both body and soul.[104] Like the robbers from the beginning,[105] condemned by Jesus, these have gained domination over the masses;[106] by working together,[107] they have become the worst enemies of humanity.[108] In their hands men are mere pawns[109] who have become impoverished through their machinations.[110] There are now more diseases than ever before[111] because the opinions and teachings of the priests and doctors create ninety per cent of the miseries and maladies which infest the human race.[112] Priests invent fears and doctors invent sickness;[113] "disease was conceived in priestcraft and brought forth in the iniquity of the medical faculty."[114] Together, they cause "more misery than all other evils" combined.[115]

Priests and doctors, of course, had nothing but contempt and condemnation for a man like Quimby.[116] "I am hated by some," he wrote, "laughed at by others, spit upon by the doctors, and sneered at by the priests, but received into the arms of the sick who know me."[117] He declared that he could restore more people to health during a lecture than all the clergymen and doctors in the whole state of Maine.[118]

In all ages, continues Quimby, deceivers exploit the people beyond endurance; and this is why periodic revolutions are inevitable.[119] After the priests and the medicine men have taken their pounds of flesh, the politicians, who always pretend to love the people and the poor, seize what is left.[120]

"The religious belief," says Quimby, "prepares the mind for the medical belief, one based on old superstitions; this gets the mind worked up like mortar, and then the doctor or potter moulds the mind into disease."[121] Since the doctors would have no income or occupation if health were universal, it is to their interest to create ninety per cent of all diseases.[122] When a man or woman is freed from the terrors inculcated by priests and doctors, the victim, in a real sense, is resurrected from the dead.[123]

Quimby and the genesis of New Thought can be understood only in the context of mid-19th century religious dogma. The official doctrine in various large denominations, especially the Reformed, Lutheran, Calvinist, and Congregational-Presbyterian, declared that the ninety-nine percent of the human race which had not been chosen by God before the foundation of the world to constitute the community of Elect Saints would be tortured eternally in hell fire. Hapless men and women cowered and trembled in terror before the face of an angry God who, without the slightest compunction or compassion, and in the course of simple justice, would plunge into everlasting perdition those upon whom he had not conferred a full measure of prevenient grace. Countless individuals spent much of their lives brooding over this frightful destiny.

The first thing Quimby wanted to know, therefore, was the religious belief and background of his patient. The awful thing about religion, he said, was its absorption with creeds, rewards, and punishment,[124] because of which society was submerged in poisons and diseases which cause even the mother to transmit these to her chidren.[125]

"I went to see a young lady during the Miller excitement [1843-1844]," he wrote. "She was confined to her bed, would not converse with any person, lay in a sort of trance with her eyes rolled up in her head, took no notice of any person; the only thing she would say was that she was confined in a pit, held there by a large man...and she said to me, 'I shall never die, nor ever get well.' She had been in this condition for one year, refused all nourishment, and was a mere skeleton at the time I went to see her.... in about an hour I saw the man she had created, and described him to her, and told her that I would drive him away. This seemed to frighten her, for she feared for my safety. But when I assured her that I could drive the man away, she kept quiet. In three hours, she walked to the door, and she recovered her health. I could name hundreds of such cases, showing the effect of the mind upon the body."[126] Here Quimby definitely recognizes the psychosomatic nature of his therapy.

We see, therefore, that in addition to the conscious practice of psychosomatic healing, Quimby believed he could read the thoughts and visualize the idea-images of his patients. He believed also that his curative powers were intimately related to the empathy he felt with his patients.[127] A constant stream of sufferers came to him who were sick of worry[128] since they were persuaded that God had predestined them irrevocably to everlasting torture.[129] One was so ensnared by her beliefs that, rather than surrender them, she wished to die of her disease; some were satisfied that they had committed the unpardonable sin.[130] Some suffered actual paralysis as a result of the religious doctrines preached to them.[131] Getting religion, he declared, is the prelude to misery; and he delineated the process by which an innocent and happy young woman is converted, gets religion, becomes miserable, and, in due course, is filled with weird diseases.[132]

6. *Quimby's Technique.* Whenever, therefore, these sufferers came to Quimby, he began by explaining that God is benevolent, that he loves all members of the human race, that he has condemned no one to hell, and, most of all, that he never created any disease.[133] His method was essentially psy-

choanalytic, that used by Freud and his successors, by which they removed neuroses through the discovery and explanation of their origin. Horatio W. Dresser explains that "what Quimby taught was that false ideas and mental imagery causing the disease were directly impressed on the plastic substance of the mind, which included what we now call the sub-conscious."[134]

Quimby offered himself simply as "a teacher of Christ, or Science...."[135] Jesus was to Christ precisely what Quimby was to Christ-Science.[136] Jesus and Quimby both taught the wisdom that destroys death and the devil;[137] and since God, as the Wisdom of Science, is in Quimby, he and God are one, even as the Son Jesus was one with the Father.[138]

Quimby was accused of making himself equal to Jesus;[139] but this was a misconception due to the fact that people think of Jesus the Christ as a single entity, when, as a matter of fact, Jesus was simply a human being who, like Quimby, was filled with the Science of God, or the Christ-Spirit. Quimby was also accused of interfering with the religion of his patients,[140] a charge he readily accepted, since religion was the basic cause of their maladies. And he asserted: "It is necessary to say that I have no religious belief"[141]—only a God-Wisdom properly called the Science of Christ. Since correct or scientific beliefs lead to heaven, and false or "religious" beliefs create the hells of mankind,[142] it was his principal objective to eradicate from the minds of his patients every vestige of orthodox dogma, especially that which requires suffering on earth to merit the joys of heaven.[143]

8. *The Superior Feminine.* In his evaluation of Woman—the Female Principle—Quimby served as a transmission belt between the Shakers and Mary Baker Eddy. Of the two elements which constitute Man,[144] the female has always been the higher; spiritual wisdom has always been transmitted through her. Man as male, or Adam, was of the earth, earthy; yet there was in the man also "this Science in the form of a rib, of this higher power," known as "Woman."[145] Women are more elevated and scientific than men;[146] they would, if they had the power, soon rid the world of priests and doctors,[147] and in the future, Woman will be the teacher of health and happiness.

V. THE QUIMBY THERAPY

1. *Treatment and Cure.* If Quimby's therapeutic technique was basically psychoanalytical,[148] his cure, in the majority of cases, was a para-religious experience.[149] "The question is often asked," he notes, "why I talk about religion and quote Scripture while I cure the sick. My answer is that, sickness being what follows a belief, the belief contains the evil which I must correct. As I do this, a chemical change takes place. Disease is an error the only remedy for which is the truth. The fear of what will happen after death is the beginning

of man's troubles, for he tries to get evidence that he will be happy, and the fear that he will never arrive at happiness makes him miserable."[150] In short, the fear of hell is the basic cause of sickness and disease.

When a woman unable to walk was brought to him, he made the following typical analysis: "Your belief is the sepulchre in which your wisdom is confined.... Your opinions and ideas are your garments and the truth is the Holy Ghost or angel which will roll away the stone and heal your grief. The God in you will burst the bonds of your creed and you will rise from the dead or your belief into the truth. You will then walk into the sitting room, and the friends will start as though you were a spirit...You will leave the body of belief and take that of Science and rise into health. This is the resurrection from the dead."[151]

Quimby said that he was not superior to other men, except as he had learned to use the wisdom of God, or the Christ-Science.[152] When called a harmless humbug,[153] who relieved the nervousness of a few patients,[154] Quimby replied that he had enabled hundreds of those long bedridden to rise again into excellent health,[155] that he had enabled the lame to walk—a fact to which the canes and crutches left in his office bore eloquent testimony.[156] He had not only caused the dumb to speak,[157] he could also teach others to cure by his method.[158] Some there were who said that he cured by the aid of the devil; to which, like Jesus, he replied that a house divided against itself cannot stand.[159]

2. *Mind and Matter.* At the base of Quimby's metaphysics was his belief that mind is Spiritual Matter.[160] He found, he says, that "*if I really believed in anything, the effect would follow whether I was thinking of it or not.... I found it could be condensed into a solid and receive a name called 'tumor,' and by the same power under a different direction it might be dissolved and made to disappear.*"[161] In another passage, he elaborates: "After I found that mind was spiritual matter, I found that ideas were matter, condensed into a solid called disease...."[162] He emphasized, however, that there is neither wisdom nor intelligence in matter.[163]

We read that the human body or "natural man" is merely a diseased shadow of reality or substance, condensed into matter.[164] The body is a house for the mind;[165] but it is error to postulate a duality of body and soul,[166] for Man is an indivisible entity. When the body grows old, it withers away, and, like a tree, simply decomposes,[167] and mingles again with the visible condensation of mind which is the universe.

Quimby was certain that one human mind could directly affect and influence another. "It is an undisputed fact," he declared, "that persons affect each other when neither are conscious of it. According to the principle by which I cure the sick, such instances can be accounted for, and it can be proved beyond a doubt that man is perfectly ignorant of the influences that act upon him, and being ignorant of the cause is constantly liable to the effect."[168] There are therefore, constant, even though unconscious, mental intercommunications;[169] and for this reason diseases which afflict children are actually the result of the unconscious influence of community opinion.[170]

The Natural Man, or the body,[171] says Quimby, is simply the tenement occupied temporarily by the real man, which is the invisible, spiritual reality.[172] Man, therefore, has an identity entirely independent of matter.[173] The senses are independent of the body;[174] and, together with all the faculties of man, they will continue intact when the body is laid aside.[175] This spiritual body, which has an identity separate from the natural,[176] was something that Quimby could see[177] and with which he could converse.[178]

3. *Disease: the Self-Created.* Diseases, says Quimby, are lies which make us ill—smallpox and kine-pox are such lies.[179] Water will poison us, no matter how pure, if we believe it to be toxic.[180] Disease is a self-imposed prison, which makes of the victim, as it were, a helpless stranger in an alien land.[181]

"Disease," continues Quimby, "is the natural result of ignorance and error governed by discords of the mind." Bronchitis is like a belief in witchcraft;[182] and the belief in witches at Salem was no more of a superstition[183] than a belief in the efficacy of vaccination.[184] A disease is comparable to the misery caused by the loss of $10,000, the recovery of which is the cure.[185]

To illustrate how error creates disease, Quimby describes the onset of bronchitis and the subsequent pneumonia. It comes like a cloud which presages rain or storm. "So in your belief you...are shaken, the earth is lit up by the fire of your error, the heart rises, the heaven or mind grows dark...At last the winds or chills strike the earth or surface of the body; a cold clammy sensation passes over you."[186] And so the bronchitis develops into pneumonia and consumption, and the victim dies. In the same way, fear creates the malignant tumor called cancer.[187]

4. *Exorcising the Devil.* Unfortunately, most people accept as truth what is nothing but error and this is "the evil that dwelleth in us" which "comes from the knowledge of this world...To separate us from the error...is to explain the false idea away and then all sorrow will pass away...like a dream or a nightmare...."[188] Since sickness is an evil infestation,[189] diseases are cured when devil-error is cast out.[190]

5. *Chemicalization of the Body-Fluids.* Quimby's theory of disease and its cure involves his teaching concerning changes in body-fluids which take place as disease originates, grows, or disappears. "The mind is the name of the fluids of which your body is composed, and your thoughts represent the change of the fluids or mind...."[191]

In one essay, Quimby explains how the patient, under the influence of the medical profession, creates his disease and destroys his own happiness. "A chemical change in the fluids of the system takes place," we read, "and you condense them into a phenomenon corresponding with your plan." In order to "destroy the disease, I convince you that what the doctor said was an idea gotten up by error, not knowing how to account for some little disturbance...you were led astray into the darkness of heathen superstition where all kinds of evil spirits and diseases dwell in the brain of man."[192]

"Disease," repeats Quimby, "is what follows the disturbance of the mind or spiritual matter."[193] And "mind," we note, is the body-fluid or "a spiritual matter which, being agitated, disturbs the spirit. This disturbance contains no knowledge of itself, but produces a chemical change in the fluids of the system."[194] Every phenomenon observed in the natural or temporary man is only a reflection of his spiritual entity; and when "death" occurs, nothing happens except that the essential man, retaining all the senses, faculties, and qualities of its earthly manifestation, sheds its material chrysalis and begins its permanent existence.[195]

As disease injures the mind or the body-fluids, "chemicalization" takes place, a process which is simply reversed when healing follows; when an impression is made upon the mind, "I found that by the power of my own mind I could change the mind of my patient and produce a chemical change in the body, like dissolving a tumor."[196] Again: "All effects produced in the human frame are the result of a chemical change of the fluids with or without knowledge...."[197] Matter exists, says Quimby, "only as it is spoken into existence...." And as a man's belief changes, "the matter or opinion will change, and when a chemical change takes place, the mind or opinion will be destroyed and truth or Science takes its place.... When man arrives at that, then death will be swallowed up in Science."[198]

The "word consumption," he says, "is of itself nothing to the person who has never heard of it. To make it is to create the opinion or building and then reduce it to an idea. So matter in the form of words is so arranged as to make the idea in the opinion. While the opinion is forming in the mind, a chemical change is going on, and the matter is held in solution till it is condensed into a form according to the pattern given by the direction of the mind...."[199]

6. *The Power of Faith.* Following his mesmeric period, Quimby came to understand fully a therapeutic element which perhaps no one had ever explained before: the importance of suggestion and the confidence of the patient in his healer. "Your faith is what you receive from me..."[200] he wrote to one patient. He emphasized that the afflicted person must wish to recover, believe healing to be possible, have implicit faith in the physician, and be ready to abandon old religious terrors and beliefs. Even as Jesus told the sick that their faith had made them whole, so Quimby told his patients that what he gave them was the moral certainty that they could and would be healed. For beliefs, he said, act upon the mind, and can produce a salubrious chemical change;[201] and he was sure that the doctor, by talk alone, can accomplish this transformation in the mind, the fluids, or the spiritual matter of the patient.

7. *The Mystery of the Sub-Conscious.* After studying Berkeley, Sweden-borg, and others, Quimby gradually concluded that nothing of a mesmeric nature passes from one body to another.[202] Nevertheless, the hypnotic trance continued to fascinate him for a time: "I once put many persons into this state," he wrote later. "A mesmerized subject is all that any person can be in a waking state; at the same time, he is another person, separate from his earthly identity. He can feel, fly, walk, and pass into the sea and describe things lost. He can find things that he knows not of in another state.

"Now where and what was this invisible something that could pass in and out of matter? What is this clairvoyance? It is the mystery or power that has troubled the wisdom of the world to solve...To understand the phenomenon is to go back to the First Cause and see what man was."[203] What was this but the Swedenborgian separate spiritual self or body?

VI. THE SWEDENBORGIAN INFLUENCE

1. *How Quimby Used His Sources.* After Quimby repudiated mesmerism as well as Berkeley's idealism, he began an intensive study of the healing technique described in the Synoptics and he utilized the Swedenborgian interpretation of Scripture. Capitalizing on the universal acceptance of Jesus as the savior, he transformed the Christ of the Gospels into a most unconventional redeemer.

He took from his sources—particularly the Bible—only what he wanted and then he interpreted it according to his needs. It is certainly true that ideas may be original in a second appearance; however, the similarities between Quimby and Swedenborg are too many, pervasive, striking, exclusive, and characteristic to be written off as mere coincidence, especially since we know that he had "discovered" Swedenborg, who was in great vogue at the time. We do not mean that Quimby was a mere disciple of the Swedish revelator; but we must note that when he formulated his belief or "creed," he did so almost in the very words of Swedenborg. "My religion," he declared, "is my life, and my life is the light of any wisdom I have."[204]

2. *The Psyche and Absent Healing.* The mesmerizers had no explanation for the mysteries of the psyche; but Swedenborg had solved the problem for Quimby by equating mind with spiritual matter, the essential man; this reality, now obscured by the body, has powers and qualities as yet uncomprehended. The spiritual man can leave the natural body, converse with unseen persons, and read the thoughts of others. Clairvoyance, then, is a natural function of the spiritual man. Conquest over disease becomes possible for those who master this science, and then it ceases to be a mystery.

Since the Swedenborgian Spiritual Man is not restricted by place or time,

Quimby found he could practice "Absent Healing," which has always been standard procedure with the Christian Scientists. Quimby tells us that, when Jesus cured the centurion's servant, he became clairvoyant and utilized this technique. Julius Dresser, who, we are told, was cured by Quimby of "typhoid pneumonia,"[205] declared that he healed many patients whom he had never seen and who lived far away.[206] Quimby wrote patients that he would visit them *in spirit* at specified times, when they would experience relief from their maladies, and finally achieve complete recovery.[207]

To one patient he wrote: "When you receive this letter...I think you will feel better. Sit up straight. I am now rubbing the back part of your head...I am in this letter, so remember and look at me...."[208]

To another he wrote: "Perhaps you cannot see how I can be sitting by you in your house, and at the same time be in Portland.... If you understood, you would not doubt that I am now talking to you.... So I shall try to convince you that, although I may be absent in the idea or body, yet I am present with you in mind...."[209] To still another he wrote that because he had thirty patients on his hands, he could not leave "in person," but would nevertheless give a treatment for a stomach ailment; for remember, "I am in this letter and as often as you read this and listen to it you listen to me."[210] On a certain Sunday, between eleven and twelve, he visited in spirit one woman patient who had been bedridden for nine months; and at that hour, she arose, walked into the dining room, and, in short, recovered her health completely.[211]

3. *The Spiritual Man.* The "natural man," says Quimby, "never can understand the things of the Spirit; for all these are governed or created in the heavens or spiritual world...."[212] Although its exact locality is a "mystery,"[213] there is no doubt that he accepted its factual existence. He explains that "in the spiritual world there are things as they are in the natural world that affect us as much, but these are not known by the natural senses...."[214] Ideas, he says, have a *real* existence in the spiritual world as well as in the natural.[215] And again: "As the degrees from total darkness or ignorance are progressive, they embrace all kinds of talent, like teachers from the lowest classes of this world to the highest of the spiritual world. All science to the natural world is looked upon as mystery, witchcraft, sorcery, etc., because the natural world cannot use anything beyond itself."[216] Near the close of his career, he wrote: "I think now that I have succeeded so that any person of ordinary talent can see" that his teaching "is the key to unlock the mysteries of the spiritual world."[217]

4. *Death and the Resurrection.* Quimby's son, George W., wrote concerning his father: "Although not belonging to any church or sect," he had "a deeply religious nature, holding firmly to God as a first cause, and fully believing in immortality and progression after death.... An hour before he breathed his last, he said to the writer: 'I am more than ever convinced of the truth of my theory. I am perfectly willing for the change myself, but I know

you will feel badly; but *I* know that I shall be right with you, just the same as I have always been. I do not dread the change any more than if I were going on a trip to Philadelphia.' "[218]

Quimby believed, he said, in another world, but not as the clergy do;[219] but when we try to determine his exact meaning, we have no definite answer. Rising from the dead means simply *"a resurrection from an error into truth.* '[220] Jesus never meant that his body would live again;[221] what appeared to his disciples was only a condensation of his spiritual entity;[222] and all "He meant was that His senses should rise from the dead or the error of the people who believed that the senses are a part of the idea called body."[223] At the transition called death, "life rises to that happy state where death, hell, disease, and the torments of existence find no place, from whence no traveller ever returns, but where man knows himself."[224]

Nowhere is Quimby more Swedenborgian than in his concept of death, which, he says, "does not change us at all. We are just what we were before. If we have any ideas which make us unhappy, we still have them."[225] Death is a painless and even unconscious transition or transferral in which all that was before continues.[226]

"Christ," says Quimby, "lost nothing by the change" called death. "Every person rises from the dead with their own belief; so to themselves, they are not risen and know no change, and the dead, as they are called, have no idea of themselves as dead."[227] When Jesus appeared to his disciples after the crucifixion, "they thought he was a spirit, for they believed in spirits, but Christ Himself was the same Jesus as before.... when you *think a person dead he is dead to you, but to himself there is no change, he retains all the senses of the natural man,* as though no change to the world had taken place. This was what Jesus wanted to prove."[228]

5. *The Spiritual Interpretation of Scripture.* The fact that a man who previously had shown no interest in religion or the teachings of Jesus should suddenly, upon contact with Swedenborg, become so intensely absorbed in these, adopt many concepts strongly reminiscent of the Swedish seer, and embrace that savant's method of interpreting the ancient texts points, persuasively to direct influence. Quimby declares that the "Bible is spiritual truth illustrated by literal things but religious people follow the shadow or literal explanation and know nothing of the true meaning."[229]

As with Swedenborg, and later with Mary Baker Eddy, almost every page of Quimby is studded with restatements of Scripture which illustrate the method. Nothing means what the words say; in fact, many of them are given interpretations which seem to have little relevance.

When Jesus told the rich young man that he must sell his possessions and distribute them among the poor, he meant that the questioner should repudiate his Judaic doctrines and accept those of Jesus.[230] According to another passage, he meant that he should "go and give your ideas away and follow the Science, or Me."[231] When he said that he would rise from the dead, he meant only that even if his flesh and blood were destroyed, the knowledge of them would remain, and this knowledge would create another body.[232] When the rich farmer said he would build larger barns to store his grain, he meant that he would "dress up and go into more educated society, among the literary, and enjoy himself."[233] The Kingdom of which Jesus spoke and which came down to the natural man was the stone or Science which the builders of error rejected and which had become the head of the foundation in the new Science of Life.[234] The new heaven and the new earth of Revelation will be the new world, free from error, which will exist when the fire of Science has destroyed all bigotry, disease, and superstition.[235]

Science is "the New Jerusalem that came down from heaven," which may also be "called the kingdom of heaven."[236] When Jesus said that the Scribes and Pharisees placed burdens upon the people, he was speaking of diseases and false opinions.[237] When he spoke of his Kingdom, he meant his Christ-Science.[238] When the Samaritan woman said that she had had several husbands, this signified that she had embraced different religious creeds in the past "and as each was destroyed by her wisdom, she became a widow."[239] When Jesus told the fishermen who became his disciples to throw away their nets, he meant that they should discard their old creeds.[240]

6. *Summary.* We find, therefore, that Quimby's concepts of death, the natural and spiritual man, the moral progression which continues before and after "the change," the nature of the body and its relation to disease and health are definitely Swedenborgian, as was his belief that he could travel to distant places with his spirit. Quimby's impersonal theology, his libertarianism, and his pursuit of temporal health and happiness as supremely laudable objectives are thoroughly Swedenborgian; and we should certainly realize that, except for the Swedenborgian concept of spiritual matter and the spiritual man, which constitutes the core of Quimby's metaphysics and the basis for his therapy, his whole system would have been without foundation and his great contribution to New Thought would have been impossible. Finally, his antagonism toward orthodox Christianity is distinctly Swedenborgian.

VII. THE EVALUATION OF QUIMBY

1. *Quimby's Discovery of Psychic Levels.* Quimby definitely comprehended the psychological factors which operate through the emotions and which the Freudian school was one day to lay bare. He discovered that man has two levels of mind or consciousness; his "reason" is active on the upper level, but his beliefs are active on the lower, or the sub-conscious.[241] "This

shows," he declares, "that every man has two selves, one acknowledged by the natural man, the other by the spiritual man."[242] Elsewhere, he says that "the mind is the medium of a higher power independent of the natural man.... As our bodies are the machine to be moved like the locomotive, and our mind is the steam, the whole must be kept in action by a power independent of itself.... These two powers govern the mind and body as the engineer governs the steam-engine."[243]

Whatever Quimby may have meant by Science, Spiritual Body, the Real Man, etc., it is certain that he grasped clearly the fact that the Mind of Man, even though a unity, exists and operates on different psychic levels which have their own peculiar functions and nature. Like the later psychoanalysts, he had a deep sympathy with his patients: he did not judge—he sought only to understand and heal, first the mind, and then the shadow, the mortal coil. With him, sin in the theological sense was abolished; and there remained only the error which separates Man from Science, which is perfection of life and happiness.

2. *His Limitations.* We should, however, recognize Quimby's limitations. Although he discovered important verities, the world has not accepted them as the whole truth. He was mistaken in his belief that the primary mission of Jesus consisted in healing the sick. With Swedenborg, whose encyclopedic mind embraced virtually all knowledge, the problem of physical health played an even smaller, although a significant, role. In assuming, as Quimby did, that health encompasses all success and happiness, he was certainly in error; for a multitude of other facts are involved in the complex business of a successful life. Finally, when he declared that all sickness and disease exist only because they are previously created by an error of the mind, either in the victim or in the doctor, or in the community as a whole, his diagnosis was certainly incorrect. Had he followed Mesmer by stating that only those burdened by emotional maladjustments could be treated successfully under his therapy, he might now be recognized as a great creative genius; but then he would not have inspired the founder of Christian Science to scale the heights of incredible achievement.

3. *Quimby's Patients.* His success was due, in large part, to the failure of others; for there is little doubt that the patients who came to him did so only as a last resort.[244] This meant that only those who had undergone the standard medical treatments without benefit but who had still managed to survive were likely to become his clients; and these were precisely the ones he could help. For had these victims suffered from organic or physical illness, they would either, in most cases, have died or recovered; but the hypochondriacs, those trapped by strange neuroses, or sick to distraction from religious fears or psychotic disturbances, were (1) beyond the aid of conventional medicine; (2) in little danger of imminent death, no matter how crippled, miserable, or laden

with the symptoms of physical illness; and (3) highly susceptible to mental suggestion and physical improvement when peace of mind had been restored or an emotional catharsis achieved. It was as simple as that.

There were, a hundred years ago, and there are today, countless sufferers who cannot be healed or cured by drugs or surgery and who, without help, face a lifetime of infinite misery; and to many of these, Quimby was an angel of hope and mercy.

4. *Saving the Terrified.* New England teemed with the victims of Calvinist terror; actually, the old, wild, religious revivals had served a profound therapeutic purpose for thousands who otherwise might have gone quite mad. Quimby parted company with Lucius Burkmar at the very moment when the last great revival (the Millerite) was in its climacteric; such relief was therefore no longer available to the distressed victims of phantasmagoric fear. Quimby offered such people—and to the lame, the halt, the speechless, the broken, the hopeless, the frustrated, the bedridden, and those awaiting death in quivering terror—a new hope, the assurance that God is beneficent, that all disease exists only as an error of the mind. He proclaimed that the ministers who had threatened them with eternal hell-fire were liars, charlatans, and impostors; that the doctors, who had taken their precious money while accentuating their maladies, were the original creators of the diseases which cursed them. To all these, whose sufferings actually originated in their minds or emotions, Quimby's gospel was one of joy and deliverance.

If Quimby had discarded his religious terminology, if he had recognized the fact that his patients almost exclusively suffered from emotional rather than physical ailments, and had he understood that his treatment constituted a therapy specifically aimed at the solution of their psychic maladies, it is possible that he, instead of Freud or Adler, would now be regarded as the founder of modern psychiatry.

5. *The Architect of New Thought.* Innocent of formal learning, without medical or anatomical training, without any broad grasp of human problems as a whole, Quimby nevertheless looms large on the horizon; he made an original and significant contribution, religious, psychological, and therapeutic. It is possible that even without him there might have been a New Thought movement, but it assuredly would not have taken the course it did, nor could it have become what it is today; and it is incontrovertible that no Warren Felt Evans, Julius Dresser, or Mary Baker Eddy could have followed.

Quimby was the principal creator on American soil of what we may call the Religion of Health, Success, Prosperity, and Happiness.

Chapter 4

WARREN FELT EVANS

I. THE MAN HIMSELF

1. *His Unique Position.* Warren Felt Evans (1817-1889), less original than Quimby, was a widely read scholar, a tireless investigator, and a gifted writer who made all forms of psychotherapy his province, which he practiced throughout his mature life. He was the first who reduced this system of healing into an intellectual discipline, preached it to the world, and described it in a series of books—which sold widely—expounding his wide-ranging principles. He also sought to prepare others to practice his therapies.

2. *Cure in Portland.* He was ordained a Methodist minister about 1838; shortly thereafter, however, he fell under the fascination of Swedenborg, whose lifelong devotee he became. An important factor in his life was a mysterious malady because of which he sought help from Quimby in 1863, along with Mary Baker Patterson, Annetta Seabury, and her soon-to-be husband, Julius A. Dresser. Evans experienced personal relief, and when he witnessed the recovery of others without benefit of material medication, he discovered his own new career.

3. *Writings.* Even before meeting with Quimby, however, Evans was already a psychotherapist; but thereafter he became a pioneer and prophet. Years before Mary Baker Eddy was able to present her ideas to students, Warren F. Evans was lecturing, writing, and healing at his own clinic. In 1869, only three years after the death of Quimby and six years before *Science and*

Health appeared, Evans published *The Mental Cure, Illustrating the Influence of the Mind upon the Body.* His second mature work, *Mental Medicine:
A Theoretical and Practical Treatise on Medical Psychology,* was printed in
1872; his third, *Soul and Body: or the Spiritual Science of Health and Disease,*
in 1876; his fourth, *The Divine Law of Cure,* in 1881; his fifth, *The Primitive
Mind-Cure, the Nature and Power of Faith,* in 1884, and his last, *Esoteric
Christianity and Mental Therapeutics,* in 1886.

4. *The Swedenborgian.* As Julius Dresser declares, Evans had already
found in Swedenborg the principles "which directly lead to the practical
method for which Dr. Quimby stood"; and it was only necessary for him "to
find a man who was actually proving what he had theoretically anticipated in
order to accept the entire therapeutic doctrine."[1]

The Swedenborgianism absorbed by Evans before 1863 was already his
dominating influence. It is possible that he could have entered upon what
became his life-ministry without Quimby; but it is more likely that the meeting
with the Portland doctor was the catalyst which enabled him to formulate his
own philosophy and make the decision to become a therapeutic healer. Had
he not become ill, had he not met or been helped by Quimby, it is likely that he
would have remained a minister in the Church of the New Jerusalem, engaging, the while, in part-time therapy, as before; instead, he blazed a new trail for
the religion of science, health, success, happiness, and prosperity.

Evans, however, seems to have considered Quimby of minor importance in
his own development; for, although he often echoes or reproduces the very
ideas proclaimed by Quimby, he refers to him only once in all his books, and
then, not as an authority, but simply as one of many successful mental healers
who had flourished from time to time.* In 1864, the year following his
encounter with Quimby, Evans published *The New Age and Its Messenger.*
The messenger, of course, was Swedenborg.

Previous to his meeting with Quimby, Evans had already published two
books summarizing and popularizing the teachings of his master.[2] We know
that he had already practiced mental healing, because he wrote in 1884 that he
had at that time been engaged in this pursuit for twenty-five years.[3] "The
writings of Swedenborg," says Evans in 1864, "have taken a deep hold upon
my mind, and affected my inner life." And he continues: "A new Jerusalem,
then, can mean nothing but a new church, for a new and a better dispensation."[4] And he added, "...that Emanuel Swedenborg, servant of the Lord Jesus

---

* Evans wrote in 1872: "The late Dr. Quimby, of Portland, one of the most successful
healers of this or any age, embraced this view of the nature of disease, and by a long
succession of most remarkable cures, effected by psychopathic remedies, at the same
time proved the truth of the theory and the efficiency of that mode of treatment...He
seemed to reproduce the wonders of the Gospel history." (*Mental Medicine,* p. 210.) Of
course, none of Quimby's writings were available at that time.

Christ, was the instrument of Providence for ushering in a new and a better age...."[5]

Although Evans cites a vast number of other authors, Swedenborg continued from first to last as the overriding influence. In his six mature works, he names the Swedish seer as his source and authority no less than 160 times; and definitely Swedenborgian concepts appear in more than 250 other passages. In 1876, he calls his master "the pioneer and John the Baptist of the new age..."[6] and declares that his own "doctrine of health and disease will be readily accepted by the disciples of Emanuel Swedenborg, and all those who are acquainted with his doctrine of correspondence between soul and body...."[7]

In 1881, Evans wrote: "In Emanuel Swedenborg, we see a man in whom science and religion were so wedded as to render even a temporary divorce an impossibility. His intellect was always and everywhere religious, and his religion was at all times intellectual.... The system of spiritual science which is unfolded in his voluminous writings, and exemplified in his remarkable experiences, is having a silent but powerful influence in moulding and modifying the religious beliefs and changing the thoughts of men, throughout Christendom...."[8]

Evans remained always a devout Swedenborgian; in his last work, he declares: "He who carefully studies that development of Christianity which we have in the writings of Swedenborg will find there all the truth that exists in the various schools of mental cure."[9]

5. *Popularity*. We do not know how many copies of Evans' works were sold between 1864 and 1900; but at a time when *Science and Health* was yet in the future or had made little impact upon the general public, the works of Evans were in wide demand. For example, *Mental Medicine*, 1872, had sold 15,000 copies by 1855,[10] and was in its fifteenth edition in 1897; other, even more popular titles were reprinted in quantity again and again, distributed all over the country, sold without an organization to promote them, and exercised direct and indirect influence upon all New Thought writers and organizations.

II. EVANS' PHILOSOPHICAL SYSTEM

1. *The Developing Technique*. A complex of philosophical and theological concepts, drawn substantially from Swedenborg, continued unaltered in all of Evans' writings; and even though his therapeutic technique evolved over the years in the direction of a purely psychological method, the influence of Swedenborg continued undiminished. Since, therefore, we have a philosophical superstructure in addition to a technical therapy, it is necessary that we treat them separately.

2. *Theology*. At the center of Evans' system stands precisely the same theological concept that we find in Swedenborg: God is an impersonal, universal power by which all nature, and every living creature, lives, and moves, and has its being. God is the Central Sun, the Primal Force, the source of light, heat, and vitality, without which the cosmos would be totally dark and devoid of life. This concept, which runs like a red thread through all his works, is the very essence of his religion and, of New Thought. "God," he says, "is the First and the Last.... Everything, from the insect to the angel, exists by virtue of a life proceeding from him. We live because he lives, our life being the stream of which he is the fountain, or it is a ray of which he is the central sun...It is the inmost essence of all created things."[11] "The Central Sun of our system," he explains, "is what Jesus calls the Father, because from Him everything springs."[12] God is "the ever-present ever-acting, and indivisible life of the world."[13] He "emanates from this living center, and is communicated to all, constituting the ground of all finite existence."[14] This Central Life "is the life of God in nature which perpetually creates and unerringly governs the world and all it contains."[15] God is the "universal life-principle," the "primal matter and cosmic substance...."[16] And, finally, "this only saving, healing principle in the universe is identical with the *sun* of the spiritual world as described by Swedenborg, and which he defines as the proximate emanation from the 'invisible God.' "[17]

From all this stems the metaphysical thesis which constitutes the core of New Thought therapy. Since God is "the verimost essential in the universe," and because all souls find "their *immediate* principle, beginning, or ground of existence in" him, they "are *consubstantial* with Him and also with one another."[18] All of us are therefore sons of God, bound indivisibly by a divine unity which Swedenborg describes as the "deific point, where God and man meet within the soul..."[19] and where man is brought into "vivifying conjunction with the Central Life."[20] "Each immortal spirit," says Evans, "is...a direct emanation of the universal spirit...and is possessed of all the attributes of its parent source...."[21] Evans rejects the three-headed god of the creeds with scorn and contempt in favor of a unitary Mother-Father Deity.[22]

3. *Christology*. The Holy Spirit, or the "Christ within," declares Evans, is "the immortal and incorruptible self, which is forever exempt from disease and death."[23] In Jesus, "God was *manifested* in the flesh...." He was "the God-Man and the Man-God. In his personality there was a humanization of the Divine and a deification of the human."[24] The Christ or the Christ-Power is a phenomenon which has appeared "many times and in various parts of the world..."[25] and sometimes, as in Jesus, with such intensity as to transform the recipients into prophets or revelators. All men and women partake of this illumination to a greater or lesser degree in a "grand unity of spirit...just as a drop of the ocean possesses all the qualities...of the great deep...."[26]

Evans, like Swedenborg, repudiates totally all the dogmas of orthodox

Christianity. He condemns the doctrine "of the infinite God begetting *Himself*" through the medium of a woman as a monstrous, even a blasphemous absurdity.[27] He declares that "the incredible dogma of a literal resurrection" refers only "to a state of emancipation from material and corporeal thralldom...."[28] He denounces the doctrine of "vicarious atonement"[29] and the orthodox concept of redemption as a "total inversion of the divine order..." and he assures us that the fall of man did not occur as "the result of...eating some forbidden fruit..." but was, in contrast, a gradual and individual process by which the natural man gains dominion over the spiritual. "By redemption," he continues, "we mean a deliverance from the controlling influence of the body...and it is only because" men have fallen "under the dominion of the... animal senses," that they need salvation at all.[30] Furthermore, to believe that the sacramental bread and wine "represent the presence of God" is sheer nonsense or ignorance, or the evidence of a feeble mind.[31] "Our redemption or liberation from corporeal bondage is not effected by the passion of the cross, nor by anything external, but always comes from *within*. It is a development of the inmost and real Self." Redemption through Christ Jesus is possible because, by making "his life and his righteousness our own," we can live as he lived and so rise into a similar state of perfection.[32]

The life of Jesus exhibits the triumph of faith "over disease, misery, and death. It was in him a living power that united him to God, the Central Life."[33] When it is said that Jesus gave his life as "a ransom for many," we are to understand that by the "impartation of sanative virtue and vital force, he delivered multitudes from diseased states of mind and body. Thus men were saved by him, not by his death...."[34] Jesus, or Joshua, means "savior, or health-giver, and he was sent into the world" to redeem humanity from "the spiritual seeds of disease."[35]

Thus, with a few bold strokes, Evans, like Swedenborg, abolished the creeds of Christendom. Just what, then, *was* Jesus and why is he called the *Christ*? Here Evans, like his master and the Shakers, embraces the Adoptionist doctrine taught in the third century by Paul of Samosata: "Jesus, the son of Mary and 'the son of man,' became the Christ...by his receptivity of the Logos, or the Word...."[36] Jesus was a human being, "the son of Joseph and Mary. The Christ," however, "is Jesus.... with the immense addition of an open communication with the Divine Intellect and Life."[37] He "was not born the Christ any more than Abraham Lincoln was born President of the United States."[38]

It was through his "unexampled spiritual evolution" that the man Jesus "became merged and blended into a unity with...the Universal Christ."[39] This marvelous development or unfoldment made of this "*man* Christ Jesus more of a Savior, Restorer, and Redeemer than all the church creeds have ever done.... If this is a heresy, may it rapidly spread over the entire globe...."[40] Ours, he continues, is not "the Christ of the popular theology, where the idea shrinks and dwindles down to an isolated personality...." He is, instead, "a larger, fuller, diviner... eternal, an all-prevailing, all-containing, and universal Christ. This is the universal spirit, first emanation from the Father, whom no man knoweth, and who is beyond the reach of thought."[41]

Evans, like his Shaker namesake, was certain that Jesus, as well as Luke, had been members of the Essene order who had transmitted the esoteric wisdom of their brotherhoods to the first Christian community.[42]

The true objective of Jesus was quite otherwise than is taught in the orthodox churches. It is true, Evans concedes, that the Christ-Power was manifested for the purpose of redeeming mankind; but we must understand that the sin he came to eradicate is simply "the cause of disease" resulting from "an error, a wrong way of thinking, feeling, and acting."[43] The overwhelming and omnipresent sin under which mankind, in its manifold misery, now staggers toward its untimely grave, is the persuasion that disease exists in the body, or that it is anything other than an erroneous opinion. And the true function of the Christian ministry is to achieve redemption for others by healing them after the manner of Jesus—by casting out these demons of false belief. The paramount "error of the world" is the fact that men do not yet understand that "sin and disease are no part of the immortal and real man...."[44]

May there soon, says Evans hopefully, be raised up "thousands of such followers of Jesus the Christ" that they may, "in a world of sickness and sorrow, pain and death, be qualified by the perception of his spirit to perform this sublime and sacred function..." of healing as he healed.[45] "To follow Christ," we read, "is to reproduce his life and experience," which was made by him "the essential condition of discipleship."[46] In his "spiritual philoso-phy...religion and health" are always identical. The power to obtain or confer these is latent in every human being; for we are all part and parcel of the universal Christ, and draw our powers from the same source which gave him dominion over the devils of madness and disease.

4. *The Doctrine of Influx.* The concept of Influx is described or discussed more than a hundred times in Evans' mature works. "The word influx," we read, "signifies" what "constitutes our essential life" and "is momentarily received from its central source..."[47] simply by *"breathing we are connected with the Universal-Life-Principle* [48].... all life is continual influx from the Deity, the only fountain of being...the Central Life."[49] "Creation has gone forth from this, and the life that thrills in the universe owes its origin to this primal source...it goes out in endless and perpetual undulations, and all live by virtue of life transmitted from him."[50]

"If we open our hearts to receive the influx of the divine and heavenly life" we become "finite receptacles of the divine good and truth."[51] "This primary and exhaustless source of life and spiritual energy we have in the sun of the spiritual world, as described by Swedenborg..."[52] from whom we also know that this "spiritual something that answers to an umbilical attachment and forever binds us to God, the Primal and Central Life, has never been severed."[53]

Influx from this source enables the recipient (who may thus become a Christ-Healer), not only to enjoy life abundantly himself, but also to impart this beneficence to others, so that they too may be placed "in contact with the Universal Life, where they may buy for themselves, and thus become divinely self-reliant."[54]

5. *The Spiritual World.* Angels, says Evans, are only "the spirits of men who have graduated to the inner world, and passed into the heavens."[55] "The world of spirit," he continues, "is as real in itself, and to the sensations of its inhabitants, as this outside range of created things."[56] Our relationship with the "universal and ever-present spiritual world is a vital one, as Swedenborg taught"; and, as the inhabitants of that other realm come into greater communication with us, they "bring down to mankind a higher and happier physical and mental existence...."[57] In fact, "the truly spiritual man" has already "found the ever-present kingdom of the heavens. He dwells on the border-land between the two worlds...." To him, therefore, death is but "an empty name..." for such as he already "live and move in the antechamber of the celestial habitations."[58]

6. *Matter and Spirit.* Evans' beliefs concerning the nature of men are, in general, an expression of historic idealism, but based specifically on Swedenborgian soures. Here again we have a fundamental metaphysical element, without which his therapeutic principles would not have been possible. The natural man, the body, the outward and visible apparition, indeed exists: but it is only a projection into space of the spirit, the real and essential man. Whatever is present in the soul is reflected in its integument; and the latter appears or vanishes as it is created or abolished by the eternal reality of which the body is the shadow. All material manifestations, in fact, are simply outward forms assumed by the underlying spiritual *esse.* "For it is an established law of the divine order that a man must inevitably become outwardly what he is inwardly, and in this life physically what he is mentally."[59] "The relation between body and soul is that of correspondence...." in which each adjusts itself into harmony with the other,[60] a fact which is of the greatest importance in psychotherapy. When the inner man sheds "its fleshly envelope, there remains the same consciousness of a body as before."[61] As Swedenborg reveals, "the body is perpetually derived from the soul"; it is only "the *form* or external boundary" by "which the soul enters into time and space."[62]

Evans means that what we call matter is only phenomenal manifestation. "*There is not,*" he elaborates, "*one single quality, attribute, or property of the body of which we can form any conception that is not in the mind....* The soul, the mind, the spirit...is the only *substance*. Without it, nothing material could exist.... the soul perpetually creates its body out of itself, just as God creates the universe, not from nothing, but from Himself.... This destroys the dualistic conception of man as being made up of soul *and* body, and reduces the two departments of nature to an indivisible and inseparable unity."[63] He adds, however, that it is not necessary to deny the existence of matter, but only to affirm *"that its essential reality* is spiritual."[64] "In its reality and inmost essence,"[65] matter "is divine—the second emanative principle from God."[66] "The idealists," continues Evans, "do not deny the *reality* of external things. They only deny that they have any reality independent of mind...."[67]

7. *Man, the Immortal.* When death occurs, says Evans, all the properties of our bodies survive and are "transferred with the soul to a spiritual realm of life."[68] It is "only transition to a higher life,"[69] in which nothing is lost.[70] What is called death is simply a new phase of the life we already have; and in this we will progress until we stand in the very presence of the "Central Life."[71] When the connection between the mind and the natural man is sundered, "the bodily envelope comes at once under the operation of certain chemical laws or forces which were before held in check by the animating soul, and is decomposed into its original material constituents."[72] And so the lower aspect of man is resolved into its cosmic elements; but his higher essence enters upon its eternal career as a conscious entity in the spiritual world.

8. *The Body vs. Reality.* "*Thought and existence,*" says Evans, "*are absolutely identical and inseparable.*" Nothing else has real existence; mind is the only actual substance.[73] This is a great truth which most people have yet to learn; and it is therefore not strange that the material-external often leads us astray. Thus deceived, men pursue the unreal and the evanescent, the illusions and phantoms of the lower senses; we seek as the objective "of supreme quest, that which is of no worth and even hurtful. In this dense ignorance, the body is viewed as the man. The shadow is taken for substance."[74]

"The body," continues Evans, "is no more myself than the clothes I wear..." A wart or a tumor will disappear if I disown it. Concealed beneath this visible integument lives the immortal and substantial reality, "the soul" or "the real man...."[75] The "curious and wonderful structure and mechanism" of the body "only render it a form in the lower degree of created things receptive of an animating principle from a higher range of being."[76]

9. *The Resurrection.* When we discover the essence which constitutes our real selves, we also "begin to exercise supernatural faculties.... We can go where we please, see without the eye, and hear with the inner ear the sounds of the unseen world, as distinctly as you hear my voice in the phenomenal world. We have begun to live eternal life. We rise out of that region of delusion where disease is possible into that higher realm where it is impossible."[77] This discovery and consequent activity on the spiritual plane is, in truth, the

"resurrection" itself, "attainable in the present life. It is the liberation of our spiritual powers and faculties from their material thralldom." "That Heaven and eternal life," declares Evans, are "states of the soul to be unfolded here and now, and not to be reached by locomotion through space to some distant stellar orb in the material universe, at some indefinite future time, is one of the plainest teachings of Jesus, the Christ."[78]

The resurrection is not something that occurs only *after* what is called death, but is rather the result of a regeneration in the present, by which "the inner senses" of men "will be opened, and they will become conscious inhabitants of a higher world."[79] The spiritual mind or body, continues Evans, enables each of us "to become inhabitants of two worlds at the same time...."[80]

10. *The Curse of Orthodox Religion.* That Evans belonged among the *Spirits in Rebellion*, as they are so aptly named by Dr. Charles S. Braden in a book so entitled, is obvious enough. Almost in the very words of Quimby, Evans describes the "unhappy patient" who "imagines that the theological scarecrows, hung up by the pulpit, are, in his case at least, living realities, that he is the most wicked of men, has blasphemed the Holy Ghost, committed the sin unto death...and is guilty of all manner of imaginary evil. Such persons suffer untold misery...overwhelmed with a sense of guilt...."[81]

Those who attend the established churches ask "for bread and get a stone"; when they seek the truth, they "are turned off with a scorpion." They "go through their round of outward ceremonies" and "rehearse an unintelligible creed," dreaming they have been fed; but, behold, they "are empty!"[82] As used in these communions, prayer is little less than blasphemy, since it is devoted to selfish and even hurtful ends; unless its purpose is to obtain a larger portion of sanative influx, it is a "solemn mockery...."[83] The "unhappy soul would be brought nearer to heaven by a judicious application of soap and water...."[84]

Jesus came to cast out demons and heal the sick—that is, to "save the world from error and disease."[85] Nine-tenths of the public life of Christ was spent in curing diseases of the mind and body. "To truly follow Christ is to do the same.... He who cannot do it is only half a Christian minister...though he has been ordained by the pope or even St. Peter himself."[86] Evans cites the mandate of Mark 16:17-18, that those who cannot cast out demons and cause the sick to recover are no messengers of Christ; and if this power has departed from the church, it is because it is dead or moribund.[87]

Evans declares that "the apostles and primitive believers" knew nothing of "the incomprehensible...jargon of the Athanasian Creed..."[88] The historical church, he continues, "took away the keys of the kingdom of heaven and neither entered themselves nor suffered those who would to enter in. The dark and bloody history of the Church has been the result...an *inhuman* religion, a relentless and persecuting bigotry."[89]

11. *The Realm of Psychoanalysis.* Basing his theories on Swedenborg,

Evans developed psychoanalytical formulations leading directly to Freud. According to a book published in 1872, he declared that there are "two distinct departments of the mind," in the first of which "the intellectual predominates, in the other the affectional or emotional."[90] He adds that our rational thought is under "the control of our volitions, but the feelings and emotions are not so."[91] There is, therefore, a twofold psychic life "which manifests itself in the two forms of conscious and unconscious mental actions."[92] However, each of these spheres exists "in three degrees or planes of mental life...imaged in the cerebral system." These consist, first, of "the *cerebrum*, the large brain... then we have the *cerebellum*, or little brain, about one-eighth of the former in size...Next we have the primitive brain, or *medulla oblongata*...which would weigh but little more than the Koinoor...the celebrated diamond of Queen Victoria, much smaller than the *cerebellum*, but a myriad times more sensitive and vital. These three distinct brains are correspondences and organs of the three degrees of mind...In our normal state and our waking hours, we use the cerebrum as the instrument of our thoughts and volitions. This, in sleep, becomes quiescent.... Its vital force has retreated downward and backward to the *cerebellum*. On the dividing line between sleeping and waking, the mysterious dreamland, the mental powers become greatly exalted and quickened, so that the experiences and perceptions of hours, and even weeks and months, are crowded into moments. Thus the mind breaks loose from its material limitations of time, place, and sense, and asserts its innate freedom. It sees without the external eye, and to distances almost unlimited. It perceives distant objects, persons, and things...."[93]

By 1876, Evans, having developed his formulations further, wrote that of the three levels of human consciousness, the "outermost, which lies next to the body and the external world, is what we call sensation; the interior is intelligence; and the inmost is love" (a term denoting passion and emotion). He adds that "there is a spiritual principle of sensation, one of intellect or intelligence, and one of love, manifesting itself, or coming to consciousness, in affections, desires, and emotions."[94] Although the terms and applications diverge somewhat, it is clear that Evans is here describing the three planes of psychic activity which Freud was one day to call the *Id*, the *Ego*, and the *Superego*.

In his latest works, published in 1884 and 1886, Evans delineates the human psyche in a pattern which makes its lowest level identical to the Freudian *Id*: "The lowest degree of our immortal nature is called the animal soul...the basement story of our immaterial intellectual nature. It is the region in us of the evil and the false, of sin and disease....

"The next degree or region of the mind is where it rises above the darkness and fallacies of the senses, and thinks and acts on the plane of pure intellect.... It has been called also the rational soul...as reason belongs to the psychical man.... In it also is found conscience of which animals are destitute....

"The *pneuma* or spirit is the supreme degree of the mind or thinking principle, the dome of the temple of God in man...denominated by Pythagoras, the *Nous*, pure intelligence.... It is the Christ-principle within; [in] its divine and immortal nature, it is never diseased or unhappy."[95]

Evans prepared a diagram which may well have been used by the Freudian analysts. Here we find depicted the triune man, consisting of four circles of diminishing size. In the highest aspect, he is *Nous*, Pure Intelligence, the Inward Voice or Conscience, Intuition, the Indwelling Christ, or the Real Self. In the next lower level, Man's psyche embraces Justice, Ideas, Reality, the Intellectual, or Human Mind. In the lowest or Animal Soul, we have Instinct, External Sense, Opinion, Appetites, Passion, Evil, Sin, Disease. At the extreme bottom, is Matter, Maia, Shadow, Body, Soma, the Unreal Man.[96]

12. *The Spiritual Sense of the Word.* Another Swedenborgian teaching, without which New Thought could not have based itself on the Christian Scriptures, was the conviction that these contain arcane meanings, wholly obscured by the external sense. "That the deepest mysteries lie concealed in the internal sense of the word," says Evans, is manifest, as "Swedenborg plainly teaches,"[97] whose profound ability to interpret the Scriptures spiritually enabled him to proclaim a reconstituted form of Christianity. Evans declares that "this living light" remains today the highest achievement of Christianity;[98] and he utilizes the method throughout his mature writings, one which also became standard procedure in New Thought everywhere and is found particularly in such works as *Science and Health.*

13. *The Anatomist.* Like Swedenborg, Evans was deeply fascinated by anatomy. In a passage written in 1869, he discusses the marvelous composition of the skin, with its millions of pores;[99] and in another, the heart and the lungs, with their "six million of blood cells," the complicated intestinal tract, and the stomach, with all its varied functions.[100] In 1867, we find him describing the functions of the liver, the bile, the lungs, the gall bladder, and the epigastrium.[101] By 1872, he had embarked upon research in the nature of the brain, the nervous system, and the spinal column,[102] which led to his extraordinary formulations concerning the triune nature of the human psyche.

14. *The Doctrine of Correspondence.* According to this, everything is created by the spirit, and all things on earth are replicas of others in the spiritual world. "The objects of nature are God's mysterious manuscript," we read, "and by Swedenborg's science of correspondence the soul can learn to read this arcane, Divine language."[103] The universe of nature "is the outside boundary of an interior spiritual realm, the point where the wave of creative influx proceeding from the Central Life terminates...every object in nature corresponds...to something in the spiritual world.... Matter in all its forms is only spirit made visible.... All material things are the counterparts of spiritual entities...."[104] And again: "In the spiritual philosophy of Swedenborg, it is

taught that...the whole visible universe...is only spirit manifested and made visible and tangible. If we could suppose the world of spiritual realities to be withdrawn or annihilated, the whole visible universe would disappear...."[105] "Without this correspondence and connection, the human body would...be motionless, powerless, and without animal vitality."[106]

III. THE THEORY OF HEALING

1. *The Instructor.* Evans declares that a study of his book *Mental Medicine* would "qualify every person of ordinary intelligence to be his own family physician."[107] *Primitive Mind-Cure*, says the author, was written "in the interest of self-healing, and contains the essential features of the instruction...given to numerous persons during the last twenty years."[108] However, Evans sought also to prepare others to practice the phrenopathic method; and his works are intended as texts "which should elevate the subject into the dignity of a science."[109] He declares in *Mental Medicine*, 1872, that at that date, long before the appearance of *Science and Health*, many were already "successfully practicing this apostolic mode of healing the sick without fee or reward...."[110] And in his final work he states that it had been his "aim to educate men and women up to that degree of spiritual development" which would enable them to become "successful practitioners."[111]

2. *Disease and the Spirit-World.* Evans, like Swedenborg, asserted that human ailments have their source in the spiritual realm: casting "out demons" and releasing "the patient from a disorderly psychological influence and control are in the Gospels equivalent expressions." All our "mental and spiritual" conditions are governed by "the intelligences, good or evil," which exist in "the other sphere of life."[112] Man, in his present fallen condition, is subject "to all evil influx from the lower region of the world of spirits," which "intensifies the tendency of any morbid condition of the mind and body...."[113] Every diseased condition in man places him in direct communication "with disordered and unhappy minds in the other world."[114] The destructive "influences of the ever-present world of spirits intensify" the sufferings of patients and retard their recovery. Sometimes the results amount "to an almost positive insanity...."[115] On the other hand, however, says Evans, we know from the revelations of Swedenborg "that there are associations of spirits in the other world whose use and happiness are found in ministering to minds diseased."[116]

3. *The Healing Sun.* Basic in Evans' therapeutic system is the Swedenborgian doctrine that when we open the sluice-gates of our egos for the reception of the divine influx, we place ourselves in direct communication with the healing power of the Central Sun. "Any remedial agency that places the sick in body or mind in vital communication with the Central Life is a holy sacrament and means of grace."[117]

4. *Whence Comes Disease?* What we call disease is an apparent disorder of the body, which reflects an error existing in the mind; since it stems from spiritual sources alone, it can be eliminated only by eradicating from the soul, or the real man, the causes of the affliction. "The real body of man," says Evans, "is never diseased, for in its essence it is a divine, an indestructible, and immortal substance."[118] When we disavow and renounce "the *idea* of the malady as being any part of our real self, it will fade away from thought and existence, because we have cut the root from which it derives all its life."[119] Since "the universal spirit," which is God, "is free from disease and evil...we may affirm the same of our true self, which is included in it."[120] When we free ourselves from bondage to the senses, we also emancipate ourselves from sickness.[121] "Disease, then, as was affirmed by Swedenborg...is always an *impure* state" of mind. "It is the echo in the body of some form of spiritual disorder."[122]

5. *The Power of Suggestion.* Disease and healing are alike psychosomatic: there was, for example, the case of food poisoned by the grief occasioned by a funeral.[123] It has been found that "bread pills, water drops, and homeopathic pellets have been attended with marked beneficial results." Such relief or cure stems from "the influence of a physician's psychic force over the medicine he prescribes and prepares, and his power of suggestion.... Charms and amulets possess power whenever people think they do."[124] A letter written to a patient is highly charged "with psychological force."[125] "Persons have been shot dead with blank cartridges."[126] It is known that a criminal, hearing the dripping of water and believing it to be blood from his own severed artery, died because he believed that he was bleeding to death.[127] Conversely, a diseased organ can be healed by thought.[128]

6. *Ministers of Health.* "To save a man from bodily disease, without an effort of the soul, is to act like the fireman who should rush into a burning building to rescue a sleeping inmate, and should seize only his clothes...."[129] Those "who would cure diseases of mind and body by psychic and spiritual force, must have faith," which unites them "with the Central Life" and which "augments the power of every faculty of the human mind," since it places "the soul in vital conjunction with the divine omnipotence."[130] Unless the psychic practitioner "himself be in sympathy with the fountain of life and light..."[131] he can never heal as Jesus healed. "In the cure of disease by the psychopathic treatment," declares Evans, "we should have a boundless confidence in spiritual aid, and an undoubting faith in the power of mind over matter."[132] Did Jesus, asks Evans, "deal in pills and potions?"[133] Every malady will yield to the Christ-Healer, whose function it is to reunite his patient in a harmonious relationship "with the...living universe...."[134]

Evans sent forth a clarion-call for men and women to minister to the minds and bodies of those diseased. The new missionaries would be "the mediators, the intercessors, and the true priests of humanity...the Messiahs, the Christs of the World."[135] The power to heal "was an essential element of Christianity, and was bequeathed by Jesus, the Christ, to his followers in all ages. The works that he did, they were to do, and even greater marvels of healing.... Where" now, exclaims Evans, "is the lineal priesthood of this great restoration? Where are the claimants for this substantial apostolic successorship?... Where is the clergy to whom sickness makes its last appeal for health, when doctors have pronounced the death-words, No hope?"[136]

In contrast to the impotent parrots of a moribund creed, the new healer "comes into conjunction with the Central Life and Power of the Universe...." As a result, "a Divine energy will burst forth from him, and exhibit itself in works of healing the souls and bodies of men."[137] The professions of ministry and medicine should never have been divided; for "the priest, as in the older civilizations, should" still continue to be "the physician of both soul and body."[138] The power of healing will be revived one day when Christianity is restored as a religion of abundant life and well-being.[139]

7. *Scientific Psychotherapy.* The cures effected by Jesus were in no sense "miraculous"; they were entirely scientific, since they were in accord with universal law,[140] through which the power of God may be intensified by the minister as he expels madness and disease. Evans declared that "the teaching of Jesus Christ is Christian Science, and *scientifically religious...*"[141] and the true metaphysics.[142] The authority under which Evans operated was a "*Gnosis*, or absolute interior knowledge and certitude of truth...."[143] The "umbilical attachment" which forever "binds us to God, the Primal and Central Life, has never been severed."[144] Anyone who masters the teachings and principles set forth by Evans, "has won the key that unlocks the spiritual mystery of health and disease...."[145]

As practitioners of the psychopathic art, says Evans, "we should so consecrate ourselves...that we may become an organ of communication between the Universal Divine Life and the diseased and unhappy one to whom we are called to minister."[146] Successful mental healers must be of "high mental and moral character.... A bad man may administer drugs...but cannot cure diseases by the divine method."[147] When the healer opens his own soul to receive the inexhaustible store from the spiritual realm, he can convey the sanative force to his patient.[148] If we expel the morbid idea "from its throne,... convalescence will commence."[149] Although we do not "deny the *fact* of the disease, as a state of consciousness," continues Evans, we declare "that the immortal Ego, the spiritual entity and real man, is neither diseased nor unhappy."[150]

8. *The Microcosm and the Macrocosm.* "After we have thoroughly mastered the doctrine of the triune nature of man," says Evans, "and have learned that the spirit is a personal limitation of the Supreme Spirit, it ought not to be difficult to form a true idea of a patient."[151] "The man that I am in Christ...is

the God of the microcosmic man, as the Universal Christ is the God of the macrocosm.... When the spirit penetrates and pervades" even our "corporeal organism, then the Christ comes in the flesh, and the man is an incarnation of God. This is the divine ideal becoming the actual.... This is full salvation, and perfect health."[152]

9. *Limitations*. It is certainly to Evans' credit that he did not claim absolute jurisdiction for psychotherapy. He maintains, however, that mental diseases were in his day heavily on the increase;[153] and he had no doubt that all "nervous disorders," which are often reflected in the physical organism, "are wholly mental."[154] He was also certain that psychopathic cures could be achieved in many cases after the best medical science had pronounced the sentence of death.[155] Yet Evans never denounced the regular medical fraternity in such sweeping terms as we find in Quimby or Mary Baker Eddy. Even Jesus, we read, could cure only "the receptive few, and left the unreceptive many as they were."[156] "I do not affirm, or believe," says Evans, "that this system of medical psychology will cure every form of disease...."[157] He was too astute to deny that poisons can kill, regardless of belief; and, after explaining that their effects are influenced by opinion, he states frankly in 1884 that if anyone should ask him "to swallow stricnia or Prussic acid," he would tell his tempter: " 'Get thee behind me. Satan...' "[158] Elsewhere he admits that medical science has real value;[159] and in his last book he pays a glowing tribute "to the modern science of surgery, which is accomplishing such marvels in saving life."[160] He never maintained that a bone could be set or the flow of blood from an open wound stanched by psychotherapy. But he emphasized again and again that his system of phrenopathy was identical to that of Jesus and, in its field, infinitely superior to all others.[161]

IV. THE DEBT TO QUIMBY

With Quimby, Evans believed that physical diseases are created by the victims in their own minds. "The very fact," he says, "that a man imagines himself sick is a proof that he is so; for the disease is only the effect of an abnormal action of this *creative* power."[162] If we tell a person "that he looks sick," this will produce "a morbid condition in the body.... In proportion as the ideas suggested by a physician are accepted by the patient, they will have their influence in modifying the bodily state. They will tend to kill or make alive. On his work hangs life or death, health or disease."[163] "Many a person has been doctored into the graveyard by treating him for diseases he never had...."[164] Since every malady exists in the mind alone, "it should be the aim of the physician to banish it from the thought of the patient, and exile it into the region of forgetfulness."[165]

In all his earlier works, Evans, like Quimby, condemns any reliance upon "senseless formulas and deleterious drugs."[166] Healing never results from the use of these, but from the belief of the patient that he will recover, as illustrated in the case of the "paralytic" who "no sooner felt the thermometer between his teeth, than he...declared he felt its healing power throughout his whole body."[167] There is no such thing as a real headache or toothache.[168] Paralysis is not in the body,[169] as has been proved by cripples who have leaped from their wheel chairs and run away from a fire.[170] The potency of a poison is increased or reduced by our belief concerning it;[171] neither the toe nor the corn on it "is any part of the real Ego or self. Both could be removed by surgery, and the inner man not be mutilated or touched."[172]

Like Quimby, Evans elaborates on the psychic auto-genesis of disease: "If a person by some means forms the idea that a harmless tumor is a cancer, and the thought becomes fixed, nature, in order to maintain the unity of body and soul, actually changes the character of the tumor and transforms it into a cancer." In the same way a cold develops into consumption.[173]

V. EXTRA-SENSORY PERCEPTION AND DISTANT HEALING

1. *The Psychical Influence.* Since, according to Evans, there is a psychical interdependence among all humanity, "by the law of sympathy, certain diseased states both of mind and body become contagious. The convulsions of hysteria are often propagated among young women in this way.... We insensibly imbibe the tastes, manners, habits, and even the bodily conditions of others."[174] "There is," he continues, "a numerous class of invalids whose nervous system is so delicately and abnormally sensitive, that they are unduly affected by...those in whose presence they may happen to be. The diseased condition of others is transferred to them...."[175] Furthermore, under stress of fear and error, all diseases are "both contagious and infectious."[176]

2. *Psychical Perceptions.* Neither the mind nor the spiritual essence, says Evans, is "subject to the limitations of time and space."[177] The soul "can transport itself, *with all its senses*, to any part of the world...for it is where it *thinks* to be." Meanwhile, the life of the body "and all its vital processes are carried on by the Universal Soul, of which the individual soul is a part."[178] We can travel to any spot on earth, yet never "be missed by our friends in the same room."[179] Mind acts upon mind whether near or far away,[180] an influence without any "communication through the five senses...." This fact "constitutes the foundation of a practical...system of Phrenopathy or Mental Therapeutics," a principle promulgated by Swedenborg.[181]

"We must learn to see through the all-seeing eye, and hear through the everywhere-present ear..." and "*whatever any person in any part of the world sees, or hears, or feels, we may perceive.*" This great mystery is a demonstrable fact: for "time and space are not external entities, but exist in us as modes of thought...." Disease "exists in the animal soul as a false way of *thinking*. It may," therefore, "come to us from the general current of the world's life, an established wrong belief in the collective soul from which we are not disconnected."[182]

3. *Distant Healing and Interactive Sympathy.* Mental telepathy, thought-speaking, and idea-transference are of great value in psychotherapy; for "it is by no means incredible or unreasonable that, in treating a patient near or far off in space, our spiritual thought, directed to him, should affect his spirit."[183] Such "transmission of thought," continues Evans, "has been practiced by many persons in various countries...our spirit may enter into the soul of...another...as readily as the sun enters a skylight...."[184] Evans therefore, like other New Thought healers, practiced the art of distant healing. For them, space was dissolved in the power of mind over disease, no matter where it may exist.[185]

Thought-communication and distant treatment, Evans assures us, are "perfectly natural and easy to the spiritual man."[186] "Thoughts," he continues, are "substantial realities" and *"transmissible entities."*[187] "A quarter of a century ago," he wrote in 1886, "we instituted a series of experiments...some of them when the subject was removed from us several hundreds of miles...." The fact was established that " 'every time we *think* of an absent person, we affect him for good or evil.' " Therefore, "through this telepathic influence.-..they may be cheered and strengthened.... The mental state of the one who is the most positive will predominate and take possession of the other.... In this way, a morbid mental condition of a" far-distant "patient may be loosened or removed...."[188] This Power of Positive Thinking "is the cardinal principle on which the whole system of mental healing is based."[189]

Evans declares with Quimby that there is an interdependent relationship between patient and healer, whether near or far, and that the practitioner takes the symptoms of the sick upon himself.[190] "When examining a patient hundreds of miles away, we have sometimes been sensibly affected with their diseased state of mind and body."[191] There must be a profound and interacting sympathy between patient and healer, who is often "affected in return with the diseased condition of the patient. Sometimes he finds it difficult to throw off the sympathetic influence for days." The therapist, however, will be successful "just in proportion as he is affected by the diseased symptoms of the patient.... In this way Jesus...'Himself took our infirmities and bore our sicknesses.' "[192]

VI. THE EVOLUTION OF EVANS' THERAPEUTIC TECHNIQUE

1. *The First Phase.* In *Mental-Cure*, 1869, Evans, although still a mesmeric

healer, based his metaphysical system entirely on Swedenborg. There are twenty-two direct references to him, fifteen citations of specific Swedenborgian concepts, seventeen discussions concerning the spiritual world, and twenty-eight descriptions of influx. Some fifty-five other authors (mostly German, French, and English doctors, scientists, or philosophers) are mentioned, some of them two or three times, but the majority only once, and then only to reinforce some distinctively Swedenborgian idea or doctrine.

At that time, Evans was still using the "magnetic treatment," which he considered most successful.[193] He was, in fact, a follower of Mesmer himself, rather than of his disciples, except that he was hypnotizing his patients by conscious design.

"In the trance," he declares, "both the cerebrum and the cerebellum are quiescent...and their vital force has passed into the primitive brain, the *medulla oblongata*.... Usually, but not *necessarily*, there is a loss of consciousness...and the soul is transported...to the perception of" the spiritual world.[194]

As control over the patient's psyche is surrendered, says Evans, first by the cerebrum and then by the cerebellum, the real or celestial man places the subject in direct communication with the Central Force and enables him to receive the divine and redemptive influx. A conviction of his spirituality thus established, the subject understands that sin, error, and disease are only illusions of his inner nature; health and well-being are the result. Furthermore, the practitioner is able to speak directly to the celestial aspect of his subject and compel the departure of every disease.[195]

2. *The Second Phase.* In *Mental Medicine*, 1872, Evans has become the mesmeric healer, using the technique of Charles Poyen, under whose domination Quimby fell in 1838. This fact itself indicates how little practical influence Quimby ever exercised over Evans; for here, twenty-five years after the former had wholly abandoned the magnetic method, we find the latter proclaiming and practicing it to the hilt.

In this book, the name and the distinctive ideas of Swedenborg occur fifty times; but the "science of magnetism" is lauded twenty-eight times, the mesmeric theory or practice sixteen times, and other hypnotic healers, such as Deleutze, Cahagnet, Townsend, Fahnestock, D'Eslon, Gregory, Richenbach, and Braid,[196] are cited over and over. It is obvious that Evans had greatly extended his studies, which he continued to pursue voraciously, for he cites sixty authors, of whom the majority are medical theorists or practitioners. He was searching for supporting evidence to buttress his commitment to the healing art substantially as practiced by the mesmerists.

By this time, however, Evans had rejected the principal technique of the conventional mesmerizers; he never uses a medium nor does he hypnotize his subjects; he declares that "it is only necessary that the patient be thrown into the *impressible conscious state*."[197] This can be done by the operator, who can achieve this effect with everyone.[198] Evans had established "by hundreds of successful experiments" that in this condition it is possible to "increase or diminish the action of the heart, change the character of the respiration, affect, in any desirable way, the functional movements of the stomach, the liver, the kidneys, and the intestinal canal.... You can control the vital action of any organ of the body, render any part insensible to pain, and calm the excited nerves, and, in a word, produce the specific effects of any medicine that was ever administered...." When the impressible state is fully established, "*the silent suggestion of the operator, or his simple will, without any vocal expression, will act with equal force....*"[199]

Evans explains that although he could place his subjects or patients in the impressible, magnetized, or hypnotized condition without passes and even at a distance, he found manipulation effective in communicating the sanative force,[200] especially when performed on the head.[201] And since the brain and the spinal column are most susceptible to suggestion, he achieved the most salubrious results by rubbing the back of the head. He found also that magnetizing the spinal column was very helpful.[202] By this method, the practitioner propels a large portion of the nerve-force from the cerebrum to the cerebellum, where the involuntary mind will obey the practitioner when told to expel disease.[203]

"Only a few minutes," he explains, "will be necessary to produce the impressible state, in which...*suggestion* will act as a controlling power." When you rub the "back of the head and the neck," the vital force will retreat from the cerebrum to the cerebellum. You will then "find that your control of the patient is fully established. What you say to him is the law of his being. You hold the key to his very life. You can render him insensible to pain in any part by a simple suggestion.... In an instant, it can create disease...and create health.... It becomes an image of the eternal Logos, the Word that was in the beginning with God, and was God, by which all things were created."[204] In this state, the patient can be made to forget his disease, which, once banished from the memory, is completely abolished.[205]

In this manner, spiritual cures are accomplished by placing the patient in direct communication with the Central Power of the universe,[206] from which we naturally imbibe the living soul of all things. The subject is restored "to harmony and sympathy with external nature..." so that all his "organic movements shall keep step with the grand symphony of the universe."[207]

3. *The Third Phase.* By 1876, when the slender volume *Soul and Body* was published, Evans had undergone a profound change: mesmerism, the magnetic treatment, the transferral of vital force from practitioner to subject, the efficacy of manipulation, and the necessity of inducing the somnambulistic state had been abandoned. Though some sixty-five authors, mostly physicians and scientists, are cited, they are not considered authorities. However, as in his previous work, Evans was still absorbed in Swedenborg, who is

quoted directly or cited specifically at least sixty-five times. In this book, health and happiness are achieved by the patient in proportion as he understands his own nature and his relationship to the Central Sun and as his mind, soul, or spirit establishes complete control over his body, which has now passed from operator or physician to patient.

We may regard *Soul and Body* as a midway station between the author's mesmeric period and his maturity, in which he reaches the height of his powers in a more mystical interpretation of psychotherapy as well as of man and the universe.

4. *The Fourth Phase. The Divine Law of Cure*, 1881, was Evans' most successful and influential work; in this his Swedenborgianism is intact. However, the last vestige of mesmerism has vanished, and he has become an even more voracious scholar and investigator than ever. His research now attempts to encompass the historic background of all human thought and thus he made an indelible imprint upon later New Thought writers, many of whom proclaim that its foundations are to be found in countless thinkers and prophets. In this work, he cites 185 writers, among whom appear for the first time a wide galaxy of idealist and mystical authors. In addition to some 500 Biblical references, there are something like 550 other citations, of which 50 are to Swedenborg, 25 each to Berkeley and Fichte, 20 to Hegel and Sir William Hamilton, 12 to Kant and Plato, 10 to Schelling, Spinoza, and J.S. Mill, 7 to Schleiermacher, Leibnitz, Jacobi, Morrell, and the Buddha, 6 to Boehme, Descartes, Confucius, Zoroaster, Theodore Parker, Jonathan Edwards, Herbert Spencer, and Thomas Brown. There are more than 150 others, most of whom are cited only 2 or 3 times. This is the most learned and elaborate attempt ever made to establish the Swedenborgian metaphysics by diversified, supporting testimony.

Rejecting Mesmer's cosmic fluid,[208] Evans declares that "the secret of the influence of what is called magnetism is the influence of the thought and will of the operator over the mind and through the mind, over the body of another."[209] This statement, which constitutes a total repudiation of the therapy proclaimed in *Mental Medicine*, means simply that the real curative power resides within the patient himself or is absorbed by him directly through influx from the Central Sun; *it does not come from or through the physician*, who has now become simply an instructor or way-shower who points the way by which the sick may heal themselves.

Every prophet in history, says Evans, has shared the same inner light:[210] "God," we read, never intended that only a few should have "a monopoly of inspiration," which "is the privilege of all..." and which is "an impartation of life, health, and peace to the whole man...an influx of life from God, seen everywhere through the three kingdoms of nature."[211] Actually, it is "the Divine incarnation" which "can be predicated in a degree of all humanity," all of which "embodies more of God" collectively "than any one individual..." ever has had.[212]

We see, then, that in 1881, Evans had virtually ceased being a practicing physician: he had, like his master, become a seer and prophet, the supreme instructor, pointing the way that can lead to universal health and happiness.

5. *The Fifth Phase.* In *The Primitive Mind-Cure*, 1884, we find that Evans had progressed even further. Swedenborg still remains the supreme lode-star, but now we find our author delving deeper into sources of purely mystical lore. While the Swedish seer appears in sixty passages, the Kabala, Hindu, or Buddhist sources are cited forty times; while Fichte and Berkeley are mentioned only six times each, Pythagoras appears ten times, and Plotinus and the Neo-Platonists twenty times each. In addition to several hundred Scriptural references, there are about 400 to some 100 other sources.

His transcendental therapy had now resolved itself into a single grand objective: that of teaching mankind to accomplish its own spiritualization. A "change of thought," says Evans, "adjusts the form of the intellectual soul into its representative image, and this latter moulds" the spiritual body "into its expression, and through this it passes outward to the physical organism." And so by the "law of correspondence...the outward body" is transfigured into an expression of the mind "on a material plane."[213]

6. *The Sixth Phase.* When Evans wrote *Esoteric Christianity* in 1886, his system had already been completed; and the value of this work consists in the lucidity with which he restates its mature principles. The very title indicates its mystical premises; yet Swedenborg, whose name and doctrines are cited some fifty times, continues to the end as the overriding authority. In a much-reduced field of other sources, Plato and the Kabala alone are prominent.

He now declares that "the magnetic sleep is not necessary or even desirable..." and only so much of the magnetic force is to be used as is necessary to place the patient in complete rapport with his physician.[214]

VII. SUMMARY AND CONCLUSIONS

1. *Prophet and Formulator.* We would say, then, (1) that Warren Felt Evans drew almost all of his basic religious, metaphysical, and therapeutic concepts from Emanuel Swedenborg; (2) that he made Swedenborgianism the living force in a world-wide religious movement, now embracing millions of communicants and sympathizers; (3) that he was the most important New Thought theorist who had yet appeared; (4) that, in spelling out the ideology of the movement, he placed it upon a firm philosophical foundation; (5) that by gathering a great number of various authorities together, he gave the movement a much broader historical base than it could otherwise have had;

and (6) that almost every thought, practice, or technique found in New Thought were fully enunciated in his writings.

2. *The Swedenborgian Parallels.* Among the Swedenborgian doctrines reproduced by Evans, the following are obvious:

(1) ...that God is the impersonal Central Sun or Creative Force, the vital power of the universe, the source of life, health, and existence.

(2) ...that from this Central Point a stream of vitality or beneficent influx flows constantly throughout the cosmos, and may be received by every human being, in whom it naturally creates health and well-being.

(3) ...that the Christ-Power, which is an aspect of deity, is the active, energizing, life-giving, and redemptive force in the universe, of which all men may share, but which possessed Jesus so completely that he was able to perform the task of human redemption through an adoptionist process, during which this Christ-Power assumed entire control of his psyche.

(4) ...that every practitioner of the same healing art is actually another Christ, carrying on the work of the Master.

(5) ...that the orthodox doctrines concerning the Trinity, the Virgin Birth, the divinity and the resurrection of Jesus, the Vicarious Atonement, the orthodox teaching concerning the Fall of Man, the metaphysical corruption of human nature, the necessity of such sacraments as baptism and the eucharist—in fact, the entire complex of both Catholic and Protestant dogmas—are totally false and should be rejected summarily.

(6) ...that matter, being only the shadow of mind or soul, has no real, that is, essential or eternal existence.

(7) ...that man is an immortal and celestial spirit, which is his permanent reality.

(8) ...that at death nothing happens except that the body, the shadow, the integument, is laid aside, while the Real Man goes on as before.

(9) ...that, since the human body is only the temporary shadow without real existence and since nothing appears in this shadow except what already exists in the mind, therefore disease can be eradicated by spiritual action, or influence.

(10) ...that sin and error are synonymous and may be eradicated by replacing them with spiritual truth.

(11) ...that a world of spirits does exist, in which we are to spend eternity and of which we are already actually a part.

(12) ...that the good or evil which we permit to occupy our minds is an emanation from the other sphere; and that when we achieve health, we literally cast out devils; but that, if we do not cast them out here, they will follow us into the spirit-world after "death."

(13) ...that the Christian Scriptures possess an interior or spiritual meaning,

which alone has validity and which may be understood only through revelation.

(14) ...that, since man is a spirit, he has the power to rise above his temporal integument and can communicate without the use of the senses with others, far or near, and can travel anywhere, unlimited by space or time.

(15) ...that, since the Real Man is not subject to material limitations, mental therapy can be administered to patients who are far removed, as well as those who are face-to-face with the healers.

(16) ...that the search for health and happiness is the highest and most laudable objective taught in the religion of Jesus and Christ.

(17) ...that the revelations of Swedenborg, which are supported by hundreds of other prophets and scientists, constitute the ultimate interpretation of Christianity and religion, and may or certainly should, in due course, restore that religion to its pristine purity.

(18) ...that the doctrine and therapy taught by Evans are as demonstrable as a mathematical theorem or as an experiment in a laboratory; that his religion is, in fact, a scientific Christianity, a Christian Science.

3. *Evans, the Transmission Belt.* It should be noted that by adopting and adapting the religious doctrines of Swedenborg, Evans bequeathed to the New Thought movement a theology and a Christology so altered from the orthodox as to constitute a totally new system; yet this gave its communicants the firm conviction not only that they were the truest of all Christians and so in continuity with the past, but also that their metaphysical concepts were believable, rational, and scientific. This new religion was therefore intellectual and convincing to all its adherents; it transformed an incredible creed with a bloodstained historical record into a satisfying and acceptable philosophy. In short, while rejecting conventional orthodox Christianity *in toto*, this was transfigured into a modern faith and practice that enlightened men and women could embrace with fervor and by which they might live happily and joyously in the natural world, and even look forward—without fear or perturbation—to everlasting pleasurable activities in a higher sphere of life.

4. *An Appraisal.* We must understand that the founder of a cult or a new religion has no room for compromise: absolutes are necessary. True believers in mystical psychotherapy will not embrace a gospel with modest claims: it must be all or nothing. Had Evans declared that his science was effective for many but not *all* diseases, he might have made a substantial contribution to modern psychoanalysis, but he would not have created the basis for a great religious movement.

It is easy to say that he went too far and claimed too much. Few may now agree that matter is without real existence, that spirit creates its external integument, that every disease which appears in the body is first created in the mind, and that its annihilation will follow the denial of its existence. Nevertheless, the most conservative medical science today admits the reality of psycho-somatic maladies and that body and mind interact in many strange and potent ways. Had Evans candidly admitted that colds are caused by a virus, that cancer kills regardless of belief, and that contagious diseases infect their victims without mental influence, he might now be recognized as one of the pioneers in scientific psychical research. As it is, he was certainly one of the most important forerunners of present-day psychoanalysis, and did, without question, give ultimate formulations to the doctrines of New Thought. And we will find that later spokesmen for the movement, while no longer embracing the extreme positions of this scholar, still base their teachings concerning religion, health, and happiness upon the general principles laid down by Warren Felt Evans.

Furthermore, we believe that if people would observe a few simple rules relating to diet, rest, and exercise; if they would cease poisoning themselves with nicotine, alcohol, and narcotics; if they would avoid sweets and fattening foods; if they would live so as to avoid the economic worries and personal conflicts which now plague them almost day and night; if they could enjoy intellectual pleasures during maturity by developing their minds during their earlier years; if they would develop their knowledge and understanding so that they would not fall victims to economic, religious, and other kinds of crooks and charlatans; if they would protect themselves against the hazards of heat, cold, loss of sleep, self-abuse, over-exertion, etc., and if they would cease worrying about every little physical disturbance which soon passes away of itself, we believe that those seeking relief from the medical profession could be reduced by more than seventy-five per cent.

Few will now deny that physical diseases and maladies *do* exist in the body, that many of these can be cured or alleviated by the medical profession, and that, in spite of the healthiest mind, they often kill. However, it is no less certain that the mind does influence the body in manifold ways. Men have been struck blind on a battlefield and have recovered their sight when the danger was over; a shock of black hair has turned snow white in a few hours because of terror. Entire bodies have been covered with rash because of sudden panic. Similar instances without number have been officially recorded.

I have known several persons—mostly women—who were ill for years or decades; most of them developed their maladies because of some deep-seated neuroses to which the illness offered a species of emotional relief. I have known them to complain of diseases which were confirmed by expert diagnosticians but which disappeared when the sufferers had no further psychiatric need for them. Such victims may be bedridden for years, without organic affliction; and I have known at least one who, like Mary Baker Eddy, arose from her sick-bed and became a dynamo of achievement and energy when she discovered an activity which satisfied her neurotic needs.

We believe there were thousands of such cases in Evans' day; now that religious terror is less prevalent, the proportion of persons so afflicted may be less, but other causes continually operate to augment the number of emotional invalids.

If the therapy of Warren F. Evans served to alleviate the tortures of one such victim, it was not in vain; we believe that it has aided thousands, and that millions could profit from something similar.

Evans recognized the extraordinary capacity of nature for self-healing. "In consequence of this indwelling of God," he declares, "which is the common life of the Universe, in us, recuperation is natural to the human body and to all living things. There is a Divine energy inherent in the system that immediately and with omniscient skill reacts against every disorder of mind or body, and exhibits itself in a physical and physiological effort to restore harmony."[215] If left alone and simply ignored, "at least four-fifths" of all diseases "come to an end by their own accord by the principle of self-limitation."[216]

We have known a number of people of both sexes who have become parents, raised families, and continued in sound mental and physical health and activity until the age of ninety or more without ever, even once, calling for any ministration by a physician, except in the case of a broken bone or some similar exigency. If the Shakers could enjoy far better health than the rest of the American community, continue to work well into their eighties and outlive their neighbors by fifty percent, while outlawing completely the whole medical profession, why cannot all of us do far better than we do? Are millions of us to survive only by the use of drugs, tranquilizers, and barbiturates? Are the medical expenses of our people to become so onerous as to make us the slaves of the medical profession and our multitudinous maladies?

We consider it an incontrovertible fact that, even though Evans is no longer in popular vogue, New Thought owes him an enormous debt, which is too often forgotten, but which should now be fully acknowledged. Emanuel Swedenborg was the fountainhead and Warren Felt Evans the supreme American prophet of the New Christianity, the faith which sought health, happiness, success, and prosperity as its *summum bonum*, its highest goal, the *sine qua non* of life, both temporal and eternal.

VIII. THE TEMPLE NOT BUILT WITH HANDS

Why, in view of all this, did not Evans found a denomination, or at least one permanent church? The answer is that the great originators seldom do: witness the Buddha, Jesus, Swedenborg, Quimby, and many others. Men such as they are so deeply intent on the content of their message, so engrossed in the giving of themselves, that they cannot, or simply will not, construct the temporal organism which is to institutionalize and proclaim their gospel.

Furthermore, Evans, like Quimby, was so involved in the service he was giving his patients, that he could not mold a visible tabernacle for his ideas; and, like Swedenborg, he was so utterly absorbed in his studies that he had little time for outward organization. We might add that he, like Quimby, was so little concerned over money that he could never obtain the economic base necessary to create an apparatus which might become self-perpetuating by maintaining a bureaucracy with a vested interest. "He who desires to make money out of spiritual science," he declared, "is like the man who vainly sighs for the wings of a dove that he might use them in wading in the mud."[217] In this, as in much else, he was the complete antithesis of Mary Baker Eddy.

And so, like other creative individuals, Warren F. Evans remains the prophet who built for the human spirit a temple not made with hands; following him, others, many others, lesser mortals, constructing less-enduring monuments, built churches and cathedrals of steel, glass, and granite.

Chapter 5

CHRISTIAN SCIENCE

Part One—History and Analysis

I. COMMUNICANTS AND CHURCH SERVICES

Christian Scientists are, by and large, thrifty, successful, well-groomed, reliable, and substantial individuals, endowed with a full complement of social graces. Most of them have comfortable homes and enjoy the material amenities. They practice good ethical standards and tend toward conservatism. They believe in church-state separation. They avoid debate concerning their tenets; but no other group is more determined that no one shall denigrate their faith publicly or cast aspersions upon their church or its founder.

While Christian Science was expanding rapidly between 1890 and 1936, a plethora of sermons, pamphlets, and books appeared which denounced this new religion in the most vitriolic terms; the counterattack was no less colorful and emotional. Since then, however, as the denomination appears to be losing membership and influence, doctors and ministers, no longer fearing serious defections among clients or communicants, rarely attack Christian Science in public.

Lest anyone conclude, however, that the Mother Church has suffered any serious diminution of wealth, we suggest that he visit Boston and survey the magnificent complex which comprises the national headquarters and which has recently been enhanced by a splendid high-rise office building costing $82 million. Some exceedingly opulent and many fine sanctuaries were constructed during the period of its most rapid expansion, when nearly a hundred new congregations were added annually.

Each Sunday morning, every Christian Science church conducts an identical service prepared by the Boston headquarters. There are two readers, a man and a woman. There are three congregational songs from the Christian Science hymnal, of which one is always a composition by Mary Baker Eddy. There is also an aria sung by a male or female soloist. There is no interpretation, and not a word is spoken except what is authorized and prepared by the Mother Church. Preceding the "Lesson," there is a responsive reading of the Lord's Prayer, in which the congregation repeats the words from Matthew 6:9-13 and the readers, in unison, respond with Mrs. Eddy's spiritual interpretation of each portion, as follows:

Our Father which art in heaven,
Our Father-Mother God, all-harmonious,
Hallowed be Thy name.
Adorable One.
Thy kingdom come.
Thy kingdom come; Thou art ever-present.
Thy will be done on earth, as it is in heaven.
Enable us to know—as in heaven, so on earth—God is omnipotent, supreme.
Give us this day our daily bread;
Give us grace for today; feed the famished affections;
And forgive us our debts, as we forgive our debtors.
And Love is reflected in love;
And lead us not into temptation, but deliver us from evil;
And God leadeth us not into temptation, but delivereth us from sin, disease, and death.
For Thine is the kingdom, and the power, and the glory, forever.
For God is infinite, all-power, all Life, Truth, Love, over all, and All.

The principal portion of the service consists of the rendition of Bible texts by the female reader and of "correlative" passages from *Science and Health* by the man. The ritual then closes with a recitation by the male reader of Mrs. Eddy's Scientific Statement of Being: "There is no life, truth, intelligence, nor substance in matter. All is infinite Mind and its infinite manifestation, for God is All-in-All. Spirit is immortal truth; matter is mortal error. Spirit is the real and eternal; matter is the unreal and temporal. Spirit is God, and Man is His image and likeness. Therefore man is not material; he is spiritual."

One who has not winged his way from Sense to Soul may regard a Christian Science service as trite, stilted, and even ridiculous. But for the True Believer, it can be an experience that transcends anything else that life can offer. As the devotee who has been healed of some deadly malady (or is at least persuaded that such is the case) attends the Sunday service, he or she gazes with spiritual eyes and, uplifted in spirit, sees a vision that never was on sea or land. As the pulpits fade, the walls recede; and, instead of one or two hundred upturned faces, a vast throng appears on an ethereal plain; and high above rises a majestic figure in resplendent robes, crowned with twelve stars; they see her as a presence holy or even divine.

II. A PORTRAIT OF MARY BAKER EDDY

1. *By Mark Twain.* He called her "easily the most interesting person on the planet, and, in several ways, as easily the most extraordinary woman ever born upon it" (*CS* 355).* He adds, however, that "she is by a large percentage the most erratic and contradictory and untrustworthy witness that has occupied the stand since the days of the lamented Ananias" (357).

2. *An Incredible Personage.* She was indeed a strange complex. Even if her early writings are crude, chaotic, florid, turgid, illogical, ungrammatical, and replete with contradictions, they burn with an insistent message. Even if many of her ideas were absorbed from others, we must recognize that no other woman in the history of religion has equaled her accomplishments. Repeatedly, her following rebelled and rejected her; but she rose triumphant over every obstacle. Her proud spirit, which informed her fragile tenement of clay, never accepted defeat. Most of those who turned against her (but not all) sank into obscurity; she had the vision and determination which could lead to ultimate victory. Even if her methods were sometimes ruthless, she conquered because she saw herself as the great hierophant; and, in due course, she gained a following who accepted her at her own valuation. As she transformed herself into a veritable divinity, she clothed her proclamations with the aura of Holy Writ. She used her servants to advance her gospel and to glorify herself; she covered with blandishments those who served her, but discarded those who did not. Rich or poor, rejected or invested with power, she was always a personage of regal mien and bearing; if others did not recognize her greatness, she never doubted it herself.

3. *Health and Sickness.* Although Mrs. Eddy's healers have given aid and comfort to the distressed, they have certainly failed to cure or give relief to many of their most famous and devoted members. Edward A. Kimball, who proclaimed that he had been snatched from the jaws of death by Science and

---

*In this chapter, citations are given in the text, instead of at the end.

who held vast audiences spellbound, died in 1909 at the height of his career. Five years after he conferred his name on Mary Patterson, Asa G. Eddy died at the age of fifty of a disease, the existence of which his wife denied. Many other leading Scientists died at comparatively early ages of diseases which they declared did not exist; and we should note that some of these earned large incomes from a practice which may have hastened their exit from this world.

III. CHRISTIAN SCIENCE CENSORSHIP

As the assaults upon Mrs. Eddy became more virulent late in her life, she established the Committee on Publication, which was followed by the Committee on Business. The former, centered in Boston, has full-time representatives in every state and in various foreign countries. According to Sec. 2, Art. XXXIII of the *Church Manual*, its purpose is "to correct in a Christian manner impositions on the public in regard to Christian Science..." which may appear in the public press. As a result of pressure upon editors, publishers, and booksellers, anything the Mother Church considers inimical to itself rarely appears in print. We might add that books dealing with Christian Science but not approved by the Church have had an odd habit of disappearing from libraries.

IV. THE LITERATURE

1. *Various Categories*. Several types of literature must be studied to obtain a comprehensive understanding of Christian Science: (1) works offered by its Publishing Society which consist largely of Mrs. Eddy's works and her authorized biographies; (2) studies by objective scholars, such as Georgine Milmine, Edwin Franden Dakin, and Charles S. Braden; (3) critiques or denunciations which may be described as exposés, such as Mark Twain's book, Peabody's *Religio-Medical Masquerade*, and Powell's first biography of Mrs. Eddy, called *Christain Science—The Faith and Its Founder*; (4) books by Scientists who remained loyal to Mrs. Eddy but parted company with the Church, such as Augusta Stetson, Herbert Eustace, Alice Orgain, and Studdert-Kennedy; (5) treatises by ex-Scientists who turned in fury upon the Church *and* its founder, such as Josephine Woodbury, Annie Bill, and John V. Dittemore; (6) expositions by mental healers who embraced the general principles of Mrs. Eddy's gospel but rejected certain of its elements: among these are Ursula Gestefeld, Emma Curtis Hopkins, Margaret Laird, Frances Lord, Julius Dresser, George Quimby, Jr., Horatio W. Dresser, and many others, all of whom are regarded by Christian Scientists as adulterers of Divine Science, and (7) certain writings which were produced by the most reverential protago-

nists of the Church but which it wishes to suppress above all others: this classification includes the early editions of *Science and Health*, early files of the *Journal of Christian Science*; Calvin Frye's *Diaries*, Samuel Putnam Bancroft's *Mrs. Eddy As I Knew Her in 1870*, and, most of all, the *Memoirs of Mary Baker Eddy* by Adam H. Dickey.

2. *Eliminating Obnoxious Literature.* The campaign to remove from libraries all critical, objective, or simply unauthorized literature dealing with Christian Science has gone on constantly. Although the Mother Church failed to prevent the publication or impede the distribution of Dakin's *Mary Baker Eddy: the Biography of a Virginal Mind*, it purchased the copyright to the books by Milmine, Bancroft, Dickey, and Dittemore; and then collected and destroyed every copy it could obtain. When the *Quimby Manuscripts* with Mrs. Eddy's letters to Quimby appeared in 1921, the Church threatened suit; these have, therefore, been omitted from subsequent reprints. This means that Milmine became public property in 1965, Bancroft in 1977, Dickey in 1983, and that Dittemore's book will do so in 1988.

3. *The Antithetical Versions.* Because of partisanship and hostility two portraits of Mrs. Eddy have emerged: in the words of Mark Twain, written in 1903, she was, according to her detractors, "grasping, sordid, penurious, famishing for everything she sees—money, power, glory—vain, untruthful, jealous, despotic, arrogant, insolent, pitiless.... illiterate, shallow, incapable of reasoning outside commercial lines, immeasurably selfish...." But, according to her followers, she was "patient, gentle, loving, compassionate, noble-hearted, unselfish, sinless, widely cultured, splendidly equipped mentally, a profound thinker, an able writer, a divine personage, an inspired messenger whose acts are dictated from the Throne and whose every utterance is the Voice of God" (*CS* 285-6).

4. *Science and Health.* The first edition of this work was published in 1875, the second in 1878, and the third in 1881; almost all copies of these were in due course gathered and destroyed so that, until re-issued by the Rare Book Company, they had become extremely scarce. The fourth and the fifth were reprints of the third; but the sixth through the fifteenth, now also rare, contained a number of significant changes. The sixteenth through the forty-ninth editions, 1886-1891, as well as all later ones, embody the skillful and progressive handiwork of the Reverend James Henry Wiggin, whose employment was terminated in 1891. In 1906, the book attained its definitive form.*

---

*Wiggin wrote on Dec. 14, 1889 (Mil. 338) that Mrs. Eddy was "getting out an entirely new edition, with which I had nothing to do..." However, the version of 1891 surely embodies the labors of Wiggin; we know that he was working on *Science and Health* late in 1890 because, in a letter Mrs. Eddy wrote to William G. Nixon on Aug. 28 of that year (335-336), she complained that Wiggin was the cause of repeated delays in

Under incredible pressure from Christian Scientists, Congress hastily passed an act in 1972 which granted the Mother Church a seventy-five-year extension of copyright for all editions of *Science and Health*—which means that in this study we can quote only brief excerpts from any of these, must paraphrase passages, or refer to them simply by citation.

The Christian Science Publishing Society distributes also Mrs. Eddy's *Prose Works*, a compilation consisting of more than 1,300 pages; this ranks in importance and authority just below the *Church Manual* and *Science and Health* itself.

5. *A Portrait. Mrs. Eddy As I Knew Her in 1870*, published in 1921, was written by one of her most loyal students, S.P. Bancroft. Since it provides an intimate description of the prophetess during the formative stages of her career, it is under the official ban.

6. *Biting Satire*. Mark Twain's book is an incisive analysis of Mary Baker Eddy and her doctrines; it gives her extravagant credit for accomplishment, but only as a crafty charlatan. Official writers, particularly Kimball (*Lectures* 361-378), had a field-day quoting and deriding the author for saying that the ideas in her book were not her own and that Mrs. Eddy did not write it (*CS* 291-292);* that by 1930, there would be nearly forty million Scientists in the United States and Great Britain alone (72); that the cult would assume political control of this country by 1940; that, before long, the Mother Church would be collecting untold revenues from 300 million members (73); and that it would conquer one-half of Christendom within a century (82), for the simple reason that more than four-fifths of all ailments have no physical reality.

7. *A Monumental Work*. Georgine Milmine's *Life of Mary Baker Eddy and the History of Christian Science* is a vast mine of original source-material deeply detested by the Church. About 1905, *McClure's Magazine* commissioned the author to write a series of articles on the subject. With a team of co-workers, including Willa Cather, Miss Milmine, following the trail of Mrs. Eddy from her earliest childhood, obtained affidavits from a great many persons who had known her personally; and she transcribed a mass of documents and records which throws a sharp light on her activities over a period of more than 70 years.

8. *A Book for the Faithful*. Following the series in *McClure's*, the obscure periodical *Human Life* began the publication of very different material, intended as an antidote for the Milmine revelations. This *Life Story of Mary*

---

preparing manuscript for the printer. This reference must be to the fiftieth edition, released in 1891, which became virtually the definitive textbook of the Christian Science Church. Thereafter the principal changes consisted merely in a different sequence of material.

*Which was correct in a sense, since it had been completely revised by Wiggin.

Baker Eddy by Mrs. Sibyl Wilbur, published in 1907, has been awarded canonical status by the Church.

9. *The Rector Who About-Faced.* Lyman P. Powell, an Episcopal clergyman, is distinguished as the author of *Christian Science, the Faith and Its Founder*, published in 1908, after he had traveled 2,500 miles to check the results of Milmine's investigations, all of which he described as of "singular accuracy" (v). He declared that Christian Science is "nothing less than philosophical anarchy..." (130) and a "fatuous folly, which seems to have a weird affinity for crude intellects and undisciplined emotions" (218). Since George Quimby had made his father's manuscripts and Mrs. Patterson's letters to Quimby available to Powell, the latter declared tersely that Mrs. Eddy's "claim in later years that the Quimby manuscripts were her own...which she had left with Quimby years before can be established only by discrediting all the other witnesses and by denying the facts themselves" (62).

In 1930, however, Powell published *Mary Baker Eddy, a Life-Size Portrait*, a Church commission, in which she emerged as an incomparably unselfish, gentle, angelic, generous, beneficent, and self-sacrificing saint who had merely overrated Quimby (103).

10. *An Exposé. The Faith, the Falsity, and the Failure of Christian Science*, written by three scholars, declares that Christian Science "is an assassin of humanity...the advance agent of scourge and pestilence, the ally of smallpox and consumption, the confederate of appendicitis and typhoid fever, and the executioner for cancer and intestinal obstruction" (403). Such was the evaluation of the medical profession at the time.

11. *The Devastating Disciple.* Adam H. Dickey was Mrs. Eddy's closest confidant and advisor during the last three years of her life. Her last official act made him a director of the Mother Church; and in due course, he became Chairman of the Board. His naive and sincere *Memoirs of Mary Baker Eddy*, written as her last request and published in 1927 by his widow, two years after *his* death, became a dreadful embarrassment to the Church Directors; and rare copies of the book have commanded fabulous prices from unbelievers.

12. *A Battle over a Book.* The publication by Scribners in 1930 of *Mary Baker Eddy: the Biography of a Virginal Mind* was a romance in itself. Buttressed by massive documentation, this book by Edwin Franden Dakin has been impregnable. It popularizes and complements the research of Milmine. The Church tried desperately to suppress the work; heavy pressure was exerted upon booksellers and the title soon disappeared from department stores; a great many newspapers refused paid advertising for it. However, it soon went through several printings and into the hands of thousands of avid readers.

13. *The Time Bomb.* In 1932, Alfred Knopf published the blockbuster, *Mary Baker Eddy, the Truth and the Tradition*, by John Valentine Dittemore

and Ernest Sutherland Bates, who collaborated in giving the world another treasure-trove of source-material which the Church has tried to suppress.

During his years as Director of the Mother Church, Dittemore had gathered huge quantities of top-secret material, including many unpublished letters, manuscripts, and intimate documents. Perhaps the most significant and shocking of these consisted of the Frye Diaries, which, in addition to many other similar entries, included one recorded on May 9, 1910 which noted that on the previous evening Adam Dickey had told Mrs. Eddy that she could have no more morphine since she had very recently been given two injections. Dickey believed that it was her old morphine habit reasserting itself which made her crave the unnecessary dosage (445).

14. *One Who Defected.* The case of Arthur Corey, a highly successful practitioner who resigned from the Church at the peak of his career in 1945, is even more intriguing. His book, *Christian Science Class Instruction*, first published in 1945, was in its twenty-third printing in 1967. He operated the Farallon Foundation, which, under his editorship, brought out a number of other significant titles. Since his own book reveals what goes on during the indoctrination of Christian Science practitioners, it is officially banned. However, its enormous sale indicates that it was widely read by Church healers, as well by many other Scientists.

Mr. Corey read this manuscript years ago, and offered a number of constructive suggestions; but, while he criticized Church members severely, he still held its founder in reverence. Before leaving for Central America, where he died in 1978, he presented his great collection of Christian Science books to the Bridwell Library of Southern Methodist University in Dallas, Texas.

15. *A Kindly Critic and Scholar.* In 1958, Charles S. Braden published his *Christian Science Today: Power, Policy, and Practice*, which is now generally accepted outside the Christian Science denomination as a definitive work the documentation of which is completely unassailable.

16. *The Final Word.* Shortly after Braden's book appeared, Robert Peel, a Church functionary, published the inevitable rejoinder, *Christian Science: Its Encounter with American Culture*, in a format so similar to Braden's as to be at first glance almost indistinguishable. In 1966, Peel published a sequel called *Mary Baker Eddy: the Year of Discovery*, which simply continues and elaborates the work of Wilbur, Powell, Beasley, and others commissioned by the Church to write the kind of books they desire.

V. MARY BAKER EDDY HERSELF

1. *Forbears and Relatives.* Mary Morse Baker-Glover-Patterson-Eddy was born July 16, 1821, in Bow Township, near Concord, New Hampshire.

Her father, the dominating Mark Baker, was a strict Congregationalist. She had three brothers and two sisters, all of whom became respected and conventional citizens.

2. *The Dominating Child.* While other members of her family performed their tasks dutifully, Mary not only refused to do any work, but reduced her entire family to servitude (Mil. 21-22). The little girl who could defeat her iron-willed father and compel her whole family to do her will displayed the same qualities as the woman who later induced thousands to worship at her feet. The slightest opposition to her will brought on hysterical, catatonic seizures. "At times the attacks," we read, "resembled convulsions" (21). We do not know just when Mary first became addicted to morphine, a curse which dogged her to the grave, but it is certain that the habit began when she was very young. Given her during early convulsions (Ditt. 41-42), it became a medical necessity.

3. *One Separate and Apart.* "At church, too, Mary made a vivid impression.... she took pains with her costume, and the timing of her arrival.... She always made a ceremonious entrance, coming up the aisle after the rest of the congregation were seated, and attracting general attention by her pretty clothes and ostentatious manner. No trace of early piety can be found in the first-hand study of Mrs. Eddy's life..." (Mil. 18-19).

4. *The Wedded Child and Her Infant.* And so Mary became a full-grown child, whose illiteracy is reflected in various letters published by Dittemore (10-20). However, when it pleased her, she could exhibit a charming personality; and so it was that George Glover, a bluff young contractor, became so enamored that he married her on December 12, 1843, when she was twenty-two. She accompanied him to the South, where he died a few months later of yellow fever. The Masons, to whom he belonged, conducted the funeral and helped Mary return to her father's house, where her son George was born the following September.

And thus began what may be called the first phase of Mary's adulthood. Since no one now took her seizures seriously, she escaped responsibility by becoming a confirmed invalid. "At her sister's house," where she stayed a part of the time, "they tiptoed about the rooms" and at her parental home "she was rocked to sleep like a child in the arms of her father or sister..." (Mil. 27).

5. *Mythology.* When she was eighty-six years old, Mrs. Eddy told *The Boston Globe* that during this period she earned $3,000 a year by writing for *The Oddfellows Covenant* (Ditt. 44). She declared elsewhere that at this time "my income from literary sources was ample..." ('02 15). In her reply to *McClure's* (*My.* 312), she stated that during this period "my salary for writing gave me ample support." In 1903, she declared in the Boston *Journal*: "At sixteen years of age, I began writing for the leading newspapers, and for many years I wrote for the best magazines in the South and the North" (*My.* 304).

6. *The Spiritualist.* Shortly before this time, the Shakers had practiced

Spiritualism and it had been given popular vogue by the Fox sisters of Rochester, New York. It should, therefore, not be surprising that the volatile Mary Glover "developed the habit of falling into trances. Often, in the course of a social call, she would close her eyes and sink into a state of apparent unconsciousness, during which she would describe scenes and events. The curious and superstitious began to seek her advice.... Once she tried to locate a drowned body.... she heard mysterious rappings at night; she saw 'spirits' of the departed standing at her bedside; and she received messages in writing from the dead" (Mil. 29-30). Frequent seances were held in Mark Baker's house.

7. *Little George and a Second Marriage.* When her mother died in 1849, Mary was nearly thirty. When her father remarried, George was about seven years old; two years later (32), when Mahala Sanborn married Russell Cheney, the boy became a permanent member of their household. In spite of later denials by Mrs. Eddy, it is certain that Mary Glover implored the Cheneys to take her child (Ditt. 67) two years before she married Dr. Daniel Patterson on June 21, 1853. At the age of thirteen, in 1857, George accompanied his foster parents to the West. Mary's aversion to her son had increased over the years, as "her invalidism, hitherto intermittent, soon became a settled condition" (Mil. 33). She never lost contact with him, however, for the Cheneys sent back news concerning him from Enterprise, Minnesota, at frequent intervals and she wrote many letters to him over the years.

Married to Dr. Patterson, Mary faced the normal duties of housekeeping; but if he dreamed that she, who was destined to dwell among the stars, would scrub floors or wash dishes, he was much mistaken. He had, however, been forewarned; for her conscientious father had told him of her nervous afflictions, and, at the wedding, he "was obliged to carry his bride downstairs from her room for the ceremony and back again when it was over" (33).

The illnesses, hysteria, high temper, and hypersensitivity of Mrs. Patterson became the gossip of North Groton. "She required" her husband "to keep the wooden bridge over the creek covered with sawdust to deaden the sound of footsteps or vehicles, and...he spent many evenings killing discordant frogs, whose noise disturbed her" (34).

8. *From Pillar to Post.* In March 1860, Dr. Patterson failed to meet the mortgage payment on the house (Dak. 33-34) and eviction followed. Residing at a boarding house, and propped up amidst her pillows, Mary pontificated that she was suffering from a spinal affliction (Mil. 38) and demanded constant service from her husband and her host. From this excruciating situation, the tortured dentist escaped to the arena of the Civil War, where he hoped to gain Federal employment; however, captured by the Confederates early in 1862, he was confined in a prison camp (39-41). Penniless, Mary fell back on her long-suffering sister, Abigail, who was living in Tilton, New Hampshire.

9. *Enter the Great Doctor!* In the meantime, the fame of Phineas Park-

hurst Quimby had been growing. On Oct. 14, 1861, Dr. Patterson had written him that his wife had "been an invalid for a number of years; and is not able to sit up but a little." (*QMSS* 146). On May 29, 1862, Mary wrote to Quimby herself (147) saying that she must die unless he could save her; and added that her sister was anxious that he should attend her.

Actually, Abigail was bitterly opposed to Quimby, and, instead, sent Mary to Dr. Vail's Hydropathic Institute at Hill, N.H., whence she wrote Quimby the following August. By hoarding small sums, she saved enough to travel to Portland (Mil. 43-44), where she arrived at the Doctor's office in the International Hotel in October. Assisted up the stairway to the waiting room, she was introduced to Quimby by Julius A. Dresser (56).

10. *Resurrection in Portland.* And now the supreme experience of Mrs. Patterson-Eddy's life began, for it was not health, but power, that she was compulsively seeking. It seems that Quimby developed a distinct interest in this "devilish bright woman..." (58). And she was not only cured of her ailments: visions of new fields, green and lush, opened up before her, far more attractive than Spiritualism. On Nov. 7, 1862, she published a long article in the Portland *Courier*, in which she compared the healings of her benefactor to those of Christ. "The belief of my recovery had died..." she declared. "With this mental and physical depression I first visited P.P. Quimby; and in less than one week from that time I ascended by a stairway of one hundred and eighty-two steps to the dome of the City Hall, and am improving *ad infinitum*" (58-59). She explained that Quimby used neither Spiritualism nor animal magnetism; and "now I can see dimly at first, and only as trees walking, the great principle which underlies Dr. Quimby's faith and works.... This truth which he opposes to the error of giving intelligence to matter.... changes the currents of the system to their normal action; and the mechanism of the body goes on undisturbed. That this is a science capable of demonstration becomes clear..." (59).

In reply, the rival *Advertiser* ridiculed Quimby and his fervent disciples, which spurred her to an even more explicit declaration: "P.P. Quimby stands upon the plane of wisdom with his truth..."; and he "heals...as never man healed since Christ.... is not this the Christ which is in him...?" (60). And she continued, "P.P. Quimby rolls away the stone from the sepulchre of error, and health is the resurrection" (*ibid.*). She promised to supply some quotations from her mentor's theory of Christ (Ditt. 91). Shortly thereafter, the *Courier* printed a sonnet which Mary offered as a tribute to Quimby:

> "Mid light of science sits the sage profound
> Awing with classics and his starry lore,
> Climbing to Venus, chasing Saturn round,
> Turning his mystic pages o'er and o'er..." (92).

11. *A Prophetess Is Come!* Mrs. Patterson returned to Sanbornton Bridge in November 1862. Since her husband had escaped from the Confederate prison, Sister Abigail fed and housed them both. But Mary was no longer the whining invalid; instead, she was filled with a burning mission to convert the world to Quimbyism. If the hypochondriac had been a perpetual burden, the flaming evangelist was even more intolerable to her sister. Anyone who doubts Mrs. Patterson's attitude toward Quimby during this period should read her letters—all fourteen of them—which, as a result of legal action by the Christian Science Church, are to be found only in the first edition of the *Quimby Manuscripts* (147-158).

12. *At the Feet of the Master.* Evidently, Mary's presence at Sanbornton Bridge soon became unbearable; for late in 1863, we find the Pattersons at Saco, Maine (Mil. 61), where Mary's symptoms became so acute that she returned to Portland early in 1864 (62). There she spent ten or twelve weeks, studying Quimby's methods with avidity. Mrs. Crosby reported that Quimby, now more interested than ever in this receptive and enthusiastic pupil, sometimes spent entire afternoons with her, after which she would return to her boarding house and write down what she had learned (62).

Instead of returning to her husband, Mary went to the home of Miss Jarvis in Warren, Maine, who had also been one of Dr. Quimby's patients (63-64). While there, she wrote to the Doctor effusively on March 31; and on April 5, she related how the former editor of the *Banner of Light*, a Spiritualist periodical, had learned the truth from her about Quimby. During the following weeks, she wrote several more letters in which she stated that she had given a thinly attended lecture, that she would speak on Quimby's spiritual Science of healing, and that she was now up and about, by the aid of the Lord Quimby (*QMSS* 150-157). Shortly thereafter, she moved to Albion, where she stayed for a while with Mrs. Sarah G. Crosby and talked incessantly about Quimby (Mil. 64-68).

13. *A Victim Escapes.* In June, 1864, Mary returned to her husband in Lynn, Massachusetts, where on July 8 she wrote Quimby, imploring help for her mate. Patterson, however, only laughed at this proposal, and it seems that he had at last come to the end of his matrimonial journey. In August, he called on Mrs. Tilton and Mark Baker and arranged to pay his estranged wife $200 annually—which he did for a number of years (Ditt. 116-117).

From August 1864 to the fall of 1865, Mary lived again with her sister; but now there could be no peace unless all and sundry accepted her new gospel of health and happiness as expounded by Dr. P.P. Quimby. However, after a violent scene, Abigail slammed the door in Mary's face and left orders that she must never again be admitted to the house (Dak. 57-58, Ditt. 123). When Mark Baker died shortly thereafter, he left not one penny of his considerable estate to his disowned daughter (Mil. 108, Ditt. 105).

14. *The Death of the Teacher.* Dr. Quimby died January 16, 1866, and Mary published a poem in the Lynn newspaper which concluded thus:

"Rest should reward him who hath made us
whole,
Seeking, though tremblers, where his footsteps trod" (Mil. 70).

15. *The Great Fall.* Two weeks later, an event occurred which had no significance at the time, but which in due course was to be invested with epochal importance. On February 1, Mrs. Patterson fell on the ice, was taken to a nearby house, treated by Dr. Cushing, and removed the next day to her own rooms. According to the official version, her case was beyond the reach of medical science (*Ret.* 24), but she suddenly recovered completely on the third day while reading Matt. 9:2-7. "In that hour," we are told, she "received a revelation for which she had been preparing her heart in every event of her life" (Wilbur 127). Rising from her bed, says Beasley (5), she astonished the people of the household who had already sent for a minister to console her in her final hour. Years later, the attending physician, who still retained his clinical notes, signed an affidavit declaring that the accident was not serious (Mil. 84-86).

16. *Nowhere to Lay Her Head.* In June 1866 began a period of tragic wandering. "I then withdrew from society about three years," she wrote much later, "to ponder my mission, to search the Scriptures, to find the Science of Mind..." (*Ret.* 24).

Her first refuge was with Mrs. George S. Clark, in Lynn, who was a fellow-spiritualist. Perhaps to pay for her keep, she attempted to heal the crippled Mr. Clark; and this was one specific cure that she still claimed to the end of her career, even though he denied that it had ever occurred. Forced to leave the Clarks, she found sanctuary with Mrs. James Wheeler of Swampscott, where she made herself so obnoxious that she was ordered to leave. Refusing to pay any board, she declared that her treatment of Mr. Wheeler's sore finger was ample equivalent for value received (Mil. 109-110). In the fall of 1867, Mrs. Glover found shelter with Mrs. Mary Webster at Amesbury, Massachusetts, who conducted frequent seances in which Mary played the part of a medium, meanwhile also promoting the Quimby Science. However, the budding prophetess soon became *persona non grata* to the husband, Captain Nathaniel Webster, and even more so to the son-in-law, William Ellis. When she refused to move, Mr. Ellis threw her trunk out the front door in the middle of the night, pitched the owner into the driving rain, and locked the door in her face (Mil. 114-117, Ditt. 123-125).

17. *A Practicing Student at Last!* The resourceful Mary, however, sought

out another fellow-spiritualist, a seamstress, Mrs. Sarah Bagley, and from her obtained food, lodging, and personal services in return for instruction in the Quimby Science. Mrs. Bagley shortly renounced her needles in favor of mental healing; and this gave her mentor such confidence that on June 20, 1868 she placed an ad in the *Banner of Light* offering unparalleled success via the new Science. "No pay is required," she promised, "unless this skill is obtained" (Mil. 118).

18. *The Imperious Parasite*. Let no one suppose that Mary's harsh experiences had subdued her proud spirit; on the contrary, "wherever she went, she took her place as the guest of honor..." (119). She always dominated any house in which she stayed; even while extorting precarious charity, she invested her person with ritual and ceremony, and she had an infinite capacity for gracious condescension. She was, indeed, a penniless nomad of forty-seven; her clothes were few and shabby; her growing Quimby manuscript was her only treasure; she was the butt of crude and brutal wit; nevertheless, she acted her role as though she were a queen on a throne.

In the fall of 1868, Mrs. Glover returned to Stoughton and found a home with still another spiritualist, Mrs. Sally Wentworth, whom she agreed to instruct in the Quimby Science for $300, to be paid her in form of board and lodging, which extended into two years. The teaching was based on a document, copied by Mrs. Wentworth and almost identical to the chapter in the *Quimby Manuscripts* called "Questions and Answers."*

However, Mr. Wentworth grew so hostile to Mrs. Glover when she tried to persuade his wife to mortgage the homestead to finance the publication of her Great Work that she was forced to seek shelter elsewhere—after attempting to set fire to the house (Mil. 132).

VI. THE GENESIS OF THE CHRISTIAN SCIENCE MOVEMENT

1. *Science Established*. After this unconventional departure, Mrs. Glover returned to Miss Sarah Bagley in Amesbury (134), where she had met a bright and interesting youth, Richard Kennedy, then 18, who had shown such a lively interest in the new science that he had become a potential partner. Since Mrs. Glover's forte did not, apparently, consist in healing, it was imperative that

---

*Cf. Powell, 71; Peabody, 82-83; Mil. 125-131; Dak. 75-78. For twenty pages, the Wentworth MS., called the *Science of Man* and said on its title page to consist of extracts from Doctor P.P. Quimby's writings, is almost word for word the same as Chapter 13 of the *QMSS* 165-178. The Wentworth MS., in the handwriting of Mrs. Wentworth, contains a number of notations in the handwriting of Mrs. Patterson. This document, printed in *The New York Times* on July 10, 1904, is an earlier version of the *Science of Man* published in 1876 by Mrs. Eddy.

she find a colleague to perform this all-important function. In 1870, these two rented quarters from a Miss Magoun in Lynn, and the Science of Mental Healing became a going concern (135-137).

Since Mary had conferred a degree on the boy, the sign Dr. Kennedy appeared at the front of the house; and he received patients in his office, while Mrs. Glover met her classes and worked on her manuscript on the second floor. It was agreed that Kennedy do the healing, send likely candidates to her for instruction, give her half of his gross income, and pay *all* expenses from his share. On the other hand, she was personally to retain all income derived from teaching (Ditt. 138).

Kennedy soon channeled several applicants into Mrs. Glover's three-week course: each paid $100 for twelve lessons; agreed to pay her 10% *for life* of all professional earnings, and, in case they did not practice, forfeit $1,000. Each student was placed under a $3,000 bond not to show the manuscript, *The Science of Man*, to anyone (Mil. 140-141).

Mrs. Glover then raised her tuition to $300 (146). In two years, her bank account swelled from almost nothing to $6,000 (Mil. 153). As students flowered into practitioners, they went forth to spread the gospel of health and happiness, and Mary Glover became a personage, having already accomplished something that neither Quimby nor Evans ever achieved.

2. *The Boastful Teacher.* As Mrs. Glover gained confidence, her declarations became more sweeping. However, after practicing briefly, one of her students, Wallace Wright, repudiated his teacher as a mesmerist and attacked her in the Lynn *Transcript* (150). On February 10, 1872, he publicly challenged her to demonstrate that she could raise the dead, walk on water in her bare feet, heal broken bones without artificial means, live twenty-four hours without air, and abstain from food for twenty-four days without ill effects (150-151, Ditt. 143-144).*

In a letter published December 16, 1898, in the New York *Sun*, Mrs. Eddy declares: "I challenge the world to disprove" that "I healed consumption in its last stages, that the M.D.s, by verdict of the stethoscope and the schools, declared incurable, the lungs being mostly consumed. I healed malignant tubercular diptheria and carious bones that could be dented by the finger, saving them when the surgeon's instruments were lying on the table ready for their amputation. I have healed at one visit a cancer that had so eaten the flesh

---

*She told Tomlinson (*Twelve Years*) that she performed so many cures in Lynn that the city resounded with them (47); that she cured a violent maniac (49-50); that she healed a man's broken bones in Quimby's office (54); that she resurrected a dead child (57); that she healed one of the reporters who came to Concord by talking to him on the telephone (64); that people were healed by watching her drive past in her carriage (51-52), and that she never accepted any fees for her cures.

of the neck as to expose the jugular vein so that it stood out like a cord."* This declaration is still published in the *Prose Works*, where the author adds: "I have physically restored sight to the blind, hearing to the deaf, speech to the dumb, and have made the lame to walk" (*My.* 105).

3. *Exit Kennedy*. Friction had gradually developed in the Glover-Kennedy operation because of the lady's fantastic claims and their inequitable contract. After a quarrel on Thanksgiving Day, 1871, he threw his contract into the fire; Mrs. Glover begged and threatened, but from that moment, he was through with her. He set up his own practice, in which he was quite successful (*Mil.* 152-153).

4. *Battling upward Again*. Since recruits to Mrs. Glover's classes no longer were available from Kennedy's labors, she was forced to give up the accommodations at Miss Magoun's. Nevertheless, as she moved from one boarding house to another, she gradually made new contacts; and on March 31, 1875, she bought the house, now a Christian Science shrine, at 8 Broad Street, Lynn, for $5,650, assuming a mortgage of $2,800. She rented out the first floor, conducted classes on the second, and used a small cubicle on the third as a study; here she read proof for the first edition of *Science and Health* and prepared the second and third (153-154).

At last the great opus was ready for publication, only money was lacking, and the author had no intention of using her own. She therefore induced two of her students, George W. Barry and Elizabeth Newhall, to advance $1,500; but, because of the many changes after the plates were cast, the cost increased by $700, which the same students provided (176-177). As Mrs. Eddy tasted the first fruits of success, power, and adulation, Quimby gradually faded from her consciousness, and her book contains only a single, patronizing reference to him (I *S&H* 373-374). At that time, Mrs. Eddy made no claims to revelation or divine authority; nevertheless, her sentences reverberate with the echoes of a Yahweh prophet.

Mrs. Glover's brainchild, published in 1875, was stillborn; it was not her book, but her students and practitioners who made Christian Science successful. Spofford, who had helped in the preparation of the book, finally achieved some success by spending $500 of his own money for publicity and forsaking

---

*Peabody 106. She made the same claims in her own publications (*My.* 105), that she had cured the poet James G. Whittier at a single visit (*Pul.* 54); that many of her students were healed in her classrooms (*Rud.* 14); that Christian Scientists heal functional, organic, chronic, and acute diseases which the M.D.s have failed to heal (*Pan.* 10). While turning down an offer of $2,000 to demonstrate her curative powers under scrutiny, she declared, about 1885, that fifteen years earlier she had healed every kind of disease, including severe cases of morphine addiction in three days, but that now "there would be no sign given" (*Mis.* 242).

his own lucrative practice (Mil. 176-178, 232-235) to give full time to this effort without personal compensation.

5. *A Church!* In the first edition of *Science and Health*, church organization is roundly denounced (166-167). However, on July 4, 1876, the students reorganized as the Association of Christian Scientists; and on May 26, 1878, these disciples arranged that Mary Baker Glover would preach to them (Ditt. 163-164). Eight of these, including Elizabeth Newhall, George Barry, Daniel Spofford, Amanda Rice, and Samuel P. Bancroft, signed the resolution, and pledged various sums for one year, ranging from fifty cents to two dollars weekly and totalling ten dollars for the support of their instructor. The first meeting was attended by about sixty (164).

On August 6, 1879, the Church of Christ (Scientist) applied for a charter, which was issued on August 23. During the first sixteen months, Sunday services, sometimes attended by only four or five persons, were held at the homes of members. Meanwhile, the Boston circle, which met at the home of Clara Choates, was about the same size (Mil. 269-270).

VII. WARFARE, REBELLION, AND M.A.M.

1. *Enter Eros.* And now a strange development occurred. Mrs. Glover either wished to marry Spofford or at least wanted him free from other marital bonds; he therefore brought suit to divorce his wife, which was denied (Ditt. 163). Thereupon Mary, quite suddenly, informed one of her students, Asa Gilbert Eddy, whom Spofford had introduced to her, that she would marry him, and this obedient, unassuming individual became her husband on January 1, 1877 (177-178, Mil. 174-175).

2. *At War with Spofford.* Even before the first edition of *Science and Health* was sold out, Spofford began collaborating on a second. In a letter of April 19, 1877, Mary demanded that he underwrite the cost, advertise, promote, and distribute the book for three years, and then pay her a royalty of twenty-five per cent of all sales. Spofford replied that he could not, in view of the losses already sustained, assume such obligations (Mil. 215-217). A complete rupture followed; and Mrs. Eddy had him expelled (Dak. 127-129). As a result, he soon became a supreme mesmeric diabolist.

When the abortive second edition, consisting of 500 copies with 167 pages, was completed in 1878, Mrs. Glover was unable to obtain the money to pay for it from her students; and since she refused to use her own, the printer simply destroyed the entire stock rather than let her have it without the required payment.

As complete failure now stared her in the face, she became convinced that her enemies were projecting into the atmosphere streams of evil which ruined the work of her students and caused general devastation. In April 1878, she sued Spofford for payment of the ten per cent of his total income from his successful practice due her under their contract (Mil. 247). This was dismissed on a technicality and never refiled.

In May, an incredible event occurred (234-244), reminiscent of the trials and executions for witchcraft which had taken place in the same town two centuries before. One of Mrs. Eddy's graduates, Miss Dorcas Rawson, had a patient named Lucretia Brown, who suffered a relapse shortly after the defection of Spofford. He was thereupon accused of spewing forth the deadly M.A.M., Malicious Animal Magnetism.

Mrs. Eddy had a lawyer draw up a Bill of Complaint, which was signed by Lucretia L.S. Brown of Ipswich, setting forth that Daniel S. Spofford was causing her terrible pains, maladies, and irreparable injury by the practice of mesmerism. It was alleged that he could destroy and blight homes and project his baleful influence throughout the whole universe (Mil. 240-241, Ditt. 192). Since the attorney declined to take the case into court, Mrs. Eddy had herself and one of her disciples, Edward Arens, appointed attorneys-in-fact. Leading a bevy of some twenty students, she marched into the Supreme Judicial Court of Salem on May 14, 1878 to place Spofford forever under legal interdict. When his attorney filed a demurrer, the judge dismissed the case, while the newspapers had a field-day (Mil. 240-242).

3. *Sedition in Lynn*. In 1881, the third edition of *Science and Health* saw the light; the publisher was Asa G. Eddy, of 8 Broad Street, Lynn. It consisted of two volumes, 484 pages; it bristles with demonology, the name given Chapter VI, in which Kennedy and Spofford are bitterly excoriated. And by this time, Arens had also become equally anathema.

However, after eleven years, Mrs. Eddy's M.A.M. and the notoriety attending her court cases had created such disillusionment among her students that eight of the most prominent, including Dorcas Brown and Miranda Rice, resigned on October 22, 1881, declaring that Mrs. Eddy was guilty of "frequent ebullitions of temper, love of money, and the appearance of hypocrisy...." We "*cannot*," they continued, "longer submit to such leadership...." And they added that they "could no longer entertain the subject of Mesmerism which had lately been made uppermost in the meetings and in Mrs. Eddy's talks" (Mil 276, 277-278).

4. *In the Hub*. Before this debacle, however, Mrs. Eddy's practitioners had struck root in New York, Cincinnati, Philadelphia, and especially in Boston, where Mrs. Clara Choate had established a steadily paying clientele. The Massachusetts Metaphysical College, empowered to grant medical degrees, was chartered on January 31, 1881 while the Eddys were still in Lynn (Mil. 281). In April, 1882, they removed to Boston, and leased for $1,000 a year a

building at 569 Columbus Avenue, which housed the Metaphysical College until its dissolution (281-283, Ditt. 217-218).

5. *Spiritual Terror*. The horrors of malicious magnetism continued to increase: Mrs. Eddy was sometimes thrown into catatonic or hysterical seizures which required the attention of her students at any hour of the day or night; at times, she seemed almost insane, denounced her friends with ferocity; and sometimes she would remain unconscious for hours (Mil. 159). She was persuaded that her mail was intercepted or subject to mesmeric influence; and when she wrote letters, she had students drop them in distant boxes. She kept the pictures of the great diabolists on her desk, marked with crosses: those of Spofford and Arens were red, but Kennedy's was black, since he was the "Lucifer of mesmerism...." Whenever she spoke of them, her body shook spasmodically (266-267).

As Mr. Eddy declined in health, his wife was persuaded that Arens exercised a "mesmeric influence" upon him, which she called "arsenical poison, mentally administered" (285). She called Dr. Rufus Noyes, who declared that Mr. Eddy was suffering from a severe heart ailment and might die at any moment, which he did on June 3, 1882. Certain that he had been mentally murdered by Arens, Mrs. Eddy had Dr. Noyes perform an autopsy, which revealed a calcareous heart. Nevertheless, she declared in newspaper interviews that her "husband's death was caused by malicious mesmerism.... I know it was poison that killed him, not material poison, but mesmeric poison" (286-288, Ditt. 218-222). For years, this was Christian Science dogma.

6. *The Permanent Servant*. Mrs. Eddy soon found a replacement for her docile husband in Calvin Frye, who served her in various capacities with a certain proud but loyal canine servility until her death nearly thirty years later.

VIII. THE CONSOLIDATION OF CHRISTIAN SCIENCE

1. *A Feminist Success*. Christian Science became a success when it was able to reach isolated individuals scattered across the country, as it could with a publication and a central headquarters. Settling in Boston was, therefore, the great turning point in Mrs. Eddy's career; as faithful practitioners sent her students who graduated from her College after brief courses, the cult began to expand. In addition to Mrs. Choate, other leaders of ability emerged, including Arthur Buswell, Julia Bartlett, Hanover P. Smith, Emma Curtis Hopkins, Josephine Woodbury, and Augusta Stetson.

Whatever else Christian Science may have been, it was also a definite part of the feminist movement then sweeping the country.* Ann Lee and Dr. Quimby had proclaimed the superiority of woman; and Christian Science declared her rights and priority in the most emphatic terms. "Woman," announced Mrs. Eddy, "is the Spiritual Idea..." (*Mis.* 175), and "the highest species of man..." (*Un.* 51). Christian Science is a revolt by women (*Pul.* 80), millions of whom are now "singing most for their own sex" (82).

Every city, town, and hamlet had its quota of frustrated spinsters many of whom were hypochondriacs with little income or property, who ate the bitter bread of charity and who were infested by countless pains and mysterious maladies. Exploiting this bonanza, Christian Science grew by leaps and bounds.**

2. *The Great College.* The Massachusetts Metaphysical College began its operations in 1882. Mrs. Eddy declared that she taught more than 4,000 students there (*S&H* F xii).*** In 1932, however, Dittemore published the complete roster (463-473); a total of 532 had taken the primary course, of whom 370 were women. The number of students increased from twenty-nine in three classes in 1882 to sixty-eight in a single class in 1889, which was also the last. Among the 162 men, more than half of whom received free tuition, most were doctors, ministers, or husbands of paying registrants. Some of these, including Edward A. Kimball, Ira O. Knapp, Joseph Armstrong, Erastus N. Bates, Alfred Farlow, William Nixon, and James Henry Wiggin, were destined for important roles; and all of them testified to the magnetic personality of the teacher. The normal course, which began August 8, 1884 and ended with the class of January 3, 1888 had a total of 138 enrollees; and there were 31 in the obstetrics course taught only in 1887. Since the primary course was a prerequisite and since some registrations were repeated, the total number of students ranged somewhere between 525 and 550, in addition to those taught in Lynn, who may have totalled 60 or 70; and, allowing for free tuitions, the total income was probably about $200,000 in seven years. This undoubtedly made Mrs. Eddy the best-paid teacher who had ever lived on this planet.

The Massachusetts Metaphysical College was chartered under an act of

---

*Of 85,717 communicants listed for 1906, 62,979 are female; of 202,298 in 1926, 168,598 or 83% are women (*Census of Religious Bodies*, 1906 I 200 and 1926 II 348). Actual counts of Christian Science practitioners show that about 90% are women, according to rosters printed in the *Christian Science Journal.*

**Mrs. Eddy wrote, "Among my thousands of students, few were wealthy. Now" they "are not indigent; and their comfortable fortunes are acquired by healing mankind morally, physically, spiritually" (*Mis.* ix).

***In another passage, Mrs. Eddy placed the number of her students at "about five thousand..." (*Mis.* 29).

1874 so loosely drawn that questionable institutions sprang up on every hand. In 1883, medical schools thus chartered were prohibited from granting degrees (Mil. 281-282). And before the decade was over, Mrs. Eddy had good reason to fear that the Attorney-General was about to outlaw her college (Ditt. 299-300).

Fear of legal restrictions, however, was probably not the principal reason for closing this highly lucrative undertaking, for Mrs. Eddy had an uncanny sense of timing. Her strength was waning and it was becoming necessary to conceal her physical ailments from her disciples and the public. She must also have sensed that her power was greatest over those who did not long continue in personal contact. Since she now had two or three hundred successful practitioners—many conducting their own classes or institutes—an ample number of new healers were being prepared; and she knew that the time had come for her to become a mysterious, inaccessible divinity, mounted on a distant throne. Finally, the golden stream, now accruing from her publications and other holy commerce, so wittily described by Mark Twain, reduced to insignificance the $10,000 or even more she could obtain by giving seven lectures in a few days. Thus it was that, after 1889, she ruled her kingdom with a rod of iron *by remote control.*

3. *The Instructor Turns Editor.* After establishing her College, Mrs. Eddy's second stroke of genius consisted in the creation of her bi-monthly eight-page *Journal of Christian Science*, the first issue of which was dated April 14, 1883. It carried the cards of her practitioners and included testimonials of remarkable healings. At first, the circulation was very small, but soon "copies found their way to remote villages...where people had much time for reflection, little excitement, and a great need to believe in miracles.... Mrs. Eddy and Christian Science began to be talked of far away.... Lonely and discouraged people brooded over these editorials which promised happiness to sorrow and success to failure. The desperately ill had no quarrel with the artificial rhetoric of these testimonials in which people declared that they had been snatched from the brink of the grave" (Mil. 313-314).

4. *Another Defector.* On December 27, 1883, Emma Curtis Hopkins had enrolled in Mrs. Eddy's primary course. Residing among the elite at 569 Columbus Avenue, she became editor of the *Journal* in June 1884. Under her direction, it was greatly enlarged, vastly improved, made into a monthly, and, in April 1885, renamed the *Christian Science Journal.* After two years, however, she turned her back on Mrs. Eddy and became a part of the larger movement known as New Thought; for this, she was charged with mesmerism and took her place among the anathematized (Ditt. 252, 264-265), together with Choate and many others. It seems that those who performed the greatest services were the first to go.

Other editors followed, but the *Journal* remained Mrs. Eddy's personal organ until her death; and, although it was supplemented by the *Sentinel*, the *Quarterly*, and the *Monitor*, as well as by foreign periodicals, it remains to this day the basic publication of the Church.

5. *A Faithful but Cynical Servant.* Since Mrs. Eddy's vocabulary, grammer, diction, repetitiousness, and artificial style were the butt of widespread ridicule, her acumen was demonstrated in 1885 when she engaged the services of a sybaritic dramatic critic, the Reverend James H. Wiggin, a Unitarian minister-turned-literary-entrepreneur, whose belief was a species of agnostic skepticism which, among much else, denied the historicity of Jesus. He laughed inwardly at Mrs. Eddy's bizarre metaphysics and cryptic prose, but he had a profound respect for her financial astuteness; and he performed faithfully the literary tasks for which she paid him a reported $40,000. He declared that it was his purpose to keep her from making herself completely ridiculous; she insisted only that, in rewriting her prose, he leave the thought intact. The world was not to learn of this collaboration until 1906.

In a letter dated December 14, 1889, and published years later, Wiggin wrote a friend: "Christian Science, on its theological side, is an ignorant revival of one form of ancient Gnosticism, that Jesus is to be distinguished from the Christ, and that his earthly appearance was phantasmal....

"As for the High Priestess of it...she is—well I could *tell* you, but not write. An awfully (I use the word advisedly) smart woman, acute, shrewd, but not well read, nor in anyway learned. What she has, as documents clearly show, she got from Quimby...animal magnetism...is *her* devil. No church can long get on without a devil, you know....

"As for the book, if you have any edition since Dec. 1885, it had my supervision.... As for clearness, many Christian Science people thought her early editions much better, because they sounded *like* Mrs. Eddy. The truth is, she does not care to have her paragraphs clear.... You know sibyls have always been thus oracular....

"...in her book, and in her class (which I went through) she says, 'Call a surgeon in surgical cases'....

"You see, Mrs. Eddy is nobody's fool" (Mil. 337-339).

Beginning in 1886, with its Wigginite polish, *Science and Health* became a best-seller. Before that date, only some 15,000 copies had been printed; but by 1895, the total was 95,000 and by 1901, 211,000; by 1904, 300,000; and by 1906 "over four hundred thousand..." (*My.* v). Practitioners and loyal Scientists were urged to purchase copies of every new edition, each of which consisted of 1,000 copies.

6. *The Boston Church.* As early as 1878, Mrs. Eddy appeared in Boston, where she addressed small audiences on Sunday afternoons in the Baptist Tabernacle on Shawmut Avenue (Ditt. 205). In 1879, the services were moved to the Parker Fraternity Building on Appleton Street (206). In December

1880, the congregation moved to Hawthorne Hall on Park Street (209). By June 1884, there were sixty-one members in addition to a periphery of interested people (Mil. 307). As the audience increased, even the Tremont Temple became too small. In order to meet future needs, a site was purchased on Falmouth Street in the Back Bay area in'1885: a cash payment of $2,000 left a mortgage of $8,763.50 (341), which, by December 1888, had been reduced to $4,963.50 (399). The financial transactions by which Mrs. Eddy obtained personal title to this property reflect her canny foresight (400-404).

IX. REVOLT, HERESY, AND AUTOCRACY

1. *Rebellion in Boston.* However, Mrs. Eddy's iron rule, her claims to divinity, her reputation for greed and self-glorification, and her contradictory teachings soon became intolerable to many of her students. Worse than all this was the everlasting M.A.M. which exerted its pervasive and "sinister influence...Morning, noon, and night the thing had to be reckoned with" as if it were "a dangerous maniac or some horrible monstrosity which was always breaking from confinement and stealing about the chambers and hallways..." (301).

On June 6, 1888, there was a stormy congregational meeting in which Mrs. Eddy was denounced. But, since the convention of the National Association was to convene in Chicago on June 13, where she achieved the greatest triumph of her career, she could not deal with the sedition until her return. Even though there was talk of expelling Mrs. Eddy, most of the insurgents wished only to be done with her forever. But, since the by-laws provided that anyone who withdrew broke his oath and was guilty of immorality, this was not easy. By a stratagem, however, thirty-five of the dissenters obtained possession of the Church records. Upon her return, Mrs. Eddy cajoled, threatened, and pleaded in order to retrieve them; but they were returned only when the defectors received honorable letters of dismissal (357-360). When the loyal Boston following was thus reduced from 200 to 14 (Beasley 185), Mrs. Eddy made elaborate plans to prevent the recurrence of such a disaster.

2. *The War on Heresy.* At this time, Mrs. Eddy began her attack against deviationist literature emanating from a group of extremely capable healers and writers who had developed around the Evans-Dresser school and who included several of Mrs. Eddy's most gifted former students, such as Kennedy, Ursula Gestefeld, Frances Lord, and Emma C. Hopkins, whose *Scientific Christian Mental Practice* is still a New Thought classic. All of these were teaching and healing, and publishing pamphlets, books, and periodicals precisely as if Mrs. Eddy did not exist. All repudiated autocracy, rejected M.A.M., and denied all claim to unique revelation or divine authority.

Frances Lord's *Christian Science Healing* may still be found in second-hand bookstores. Mrs. Gestefeld had been a student in the class of 1884; in 1888, she published *A Statement of Christian Science*, a lucid presentation of Mrs. Eddy's basic theories; but, since it deleted M.A.M. and omitted all reference to her as the Second Christ, Mrs. Gestefeld was expelled from the Chicago church as a mesmerist. When she countered with her *Jesuitism in Christian Science*, she became, not only another diabolist, but also another influential worker in New Thought (Ditt. 291-293).

Mrs. Eddy lived in constant terror that her followers might draw inspiration from sources other than herself; she therefore decreed in the 22nd *Manual* that her students must not "buy, sell, nor circulate Christian Science literature which is not thoroughly correct..." (now Sec. 11, Art. VIII).

The proscription of unauthorized literature is one of the principal elements in Christian Science, whose communicants must never read so-called scientific works antagonistic to their faith (*Ret.* 78). Therefore they need no books or other publications except the Bible and those offered by the Publishing Society; the *Monitor* even eliminates the need for a local daily newspaper. "Burn every scrap of Christian Science literature," she declared in the *Journal* of October, 1890, "except Science and Health, and the publications bearing the imprint of the Christian Science Publishing Society." All other schools of mental healing are false and evil (*Rud.* 16-17).

3. *The Affluent Autocrat.* As we have seen, Mrs. Eddy purchased her first property—in Lynn—in 1878 for $5,600. At the end of 1887, she moved into a $40,000 residence at 385 Commonwealth Avenue, Boston (Mil. 342). In 1889, she moved to Concord and purchased and renovated an estate called Pleasant View, where she concentrated on the consolidation and perpetuation of her empire. After abolishing her College in 1889, she retired also from the personal editorship of the *Christian Science Journal*, which published the "Seven Fixed Rules" by which she effected her total inaccessibility (398).

4. *The Mother Church.* On September 23, 1892, the First Church of Christ, Scientist, reorganized with twelve First Members and Mary Baker Eddy as Pastor Emeritus; on that date also the Church By-Laws were adopted which made her the supreme ruler (405-406). *After* this was done, she transferred her ownership of the land to the Church, but only under a trust deed which provided that a building costing not less than $50,000 be erected on it; that all services therein conform strictly with the doctrines and practices of Christian Science as taught in *Science and Health*; that these directors constitute a self-perpetuating corporation and be loyal believers; and that any violation of the terms of the trust or the cessation of services would cause the land, *together with all improvements*, to revert to Mary Baker Eddy, or her heirs or assigns (Mil. 400 ff.).

Thus the Mother Church, THE First Church of Christ, Scientist, was founded. It was to be owned and ruled by four (after 1902, five) Directors, who, in turn, were to be ruled by Mrs. Eddy throughout her lifetime, and forever afterward by her *Manual.* A few years later, Mrs. Eddy purchased the Christian Science Publishing Society for $1.00, and, by another deed of trust, dated January 25, 1898, gave it to a corporation ruled by three trustees under provisions similar to those which gave her control of the Mother Church. An article in the *Christian Science Journal* of May 1906 glorified her for making this wonderful gift, then valued at $45,000 (*My.* vi.).

Members of the branch churches were urged to join the Mother Church. By 1893, 1,545 had done so; and the next year, an intensive drive for building funds began. On October 2, 1894, the Mother Church had 2,938 members. On January 6, 1895, the new building, seating more than 1,000, was dedicated. Its cost exceeded $200,000.

X. THE LITTLE BROWN BOOK

1. *The Ultimate Mrs. Eddy.* Since the text of *Science and Health* attained virtual finality with the fiftieth edition of 1891, the principal labors of its author thereafter were devoted to the control of her Church and the completion of her Law as stated in the Church *Manual,* which became her perpetual rod of dominion. "Her government," wrote Mark Twain, "is all there; all in that deceptively innocent-looking little book, that cunning little devilish book, that slumbering little brown volume, with hell in its bowels" (*CS* 344). It established the centralized power-structure of a completely authoritarian institution.

2. *A Personal Theocracy.* Under the original by-laws, the directors could be chosen only by the unanimous approval of the First Members, who also elected the First Reader and their own replacements. This delegation of authority, however, soon became intolerable to Mrs. Eddy; she therefore decreed in the first edition of the *Manual* that the directors, appointed by herself, elect all officers in the Church, including the readers, with her approval. The eighth edition, 1898, provided that all candidates for First Member receive her prior endorsement. In the tenth edition, 1899, Mrs. Eddy gave herself the power to increase the number of First Members to anywhere from 40 to 100; thus, she could always pack this body with enough supporters to override a rebellion. The twentieth edition, 1901, stripped the First Members of all remaining influence: although they were still allowed to meet once a year, they could not even attend business meetings or nominate additions to their own ranks. The twenty-sixth edition, 1902, Sec. 2, Art. XXV, went still further by providing for their easy expulsion. In the twenty-ninth edition,

1903, their name was changed to Executive Members. In the seventy-third, 1908, even these were abolished; thus the last vestige of democracy perished. Articles IV-VIII make ample provision for the discipline and excommunication of any member who evinces disloyalty, heterodoxy, or independence; the twelfth edition, 1899, Sec. 14, Art. VIII, decreed that "it shall be the privilege and duty of every member who can afford it, to subscribe for the periodicals which are the organs of the Church...."

3. *Readers vs. Preachers.* No less important than her control over the Mother Church was Mrs. Eddy's concern over the content of Church services. In the early years, she herself preached and conducted a ritual similar to that found in Protestant communions. In due course, however, such services were abolished, for very important reasons. Not only was Mrs. Eddy intent upon making her own gospel supreme; she lived in constant terror lest powerful personalities, such as Josephine Woodbury or Augusta Stetson, should build great followings of their own and one day reinterpret the message of Christian Science. Furthermore, the kind of pastorate established by Mrs. Eddy kept at an absolute minimum the cost of operating hundreds of small churches and tiny societies. The need of seminaries to train pastors and budgets to maintain competent ministers was therefore eliminated. Sixteen persons may organize a church and a much smaller number a society, and they can conduct services identical to those performed in the largest and most opulent sanctuaries.

The first *Manual* established a First and a Second Reader and provided that "the readers of Science and Health...shall distinctly announce its full title and the author's name" (Sec. 5, Art. III). The tenth edition, 1899, provided that the Second Reader, a woman, open the principal part of the service with texts from the Bible; and that the First Reader (always a man) follow with the correlative passages from *Science and Health* (Sec. 4).

4. *Internal Discipline.* The first *Manual* provided that any Christian Scientist could be excommunicated for "malicious mental malpractice." A revision in the third edition (Sec. 1, Art. XII) provides that readers, teachers, and practitioners may be placed on three years' probation, which means that any prominent member, under suspicion, may be deprived of income and position during this period, though he or she could hope meanwhile for reinstatement. But, though the deviationist might well remain silent, he or she would be gradually discredited; and, when all power to lead others out of the Church has ended, "shall be dropped from the roll of this Church."

5. *The Index.* After Frederick Peabody published his *Complete Exposure of Eddyism or Christian Science* in 1901, and after the *Cosmopolitan* articles by Mark Twain, Mrs. Eddy composed two by-laws for the thirty-ninth *Manual*, 1904, which still remain. "Only the Publishing Society of Mother Church selects, approves, and publishes the books and literature" to be used (now Sec. 8, Art. XXV); and no Christian Scientist shall "patronize a publish-

ing house or bookstore that has for sale obnoxious books" (now Sec. 12, Art. VIII).

6. *Again on the Defensive.* As a result of Mrs. Eddy's radical teachings concerning sex and marriage, a number of her disciples adopted "spiritual children," or, separating from their legal spouses, took "spiritual mates." This scandal rocketed to a climax when Josephine Woodbury announced that her son, the Prince of Peace, was parthenogenetically conceived. Mrs. Eddy therefore decreed in the twenty-sixth edition, Sec. 4, Art. XXVII, 1902, the immediate excommunication of anyone guilty of this offense.

Mrs. Eddy called herself "Reverend" and continued to confer the title of Doctor until the closing of her College; however, since this courted serious legal difficulties, Sec. 12, Art. XXVIII of the twenty-fifth *Manual* provided that no Christian Scientist could use these titles unless conferred under the laws of the state (now Sec. 19, Art. VIII).

While in Lynn, she had incurred onerous expense and public ridicule in her many unsuccessful litigations. She therefore provided in the twenty-sixth edition, Sec. 16, Art. XXVII, that Christian Science practitioners must never sue to collect fees (now Sec. 22, Art. VIII). And because of serious encounters with the law over obstetrics, the twenty-fifth edition forbade all teaching on this subject.

7. *Power and Income.* The eighth *Manual*, 1898, provided that all "net profits" of the Christian Science Publishing Society, established that year, "shall be paid over semi-annually to the Treasurer of the Mother Church...." However, by her deed of trust, Mrs. Eddy pre-empted to herself during her lifetime all the revenues from the *Journal* and all royalties from her own writings. Under the direction of her adopted son, Dr. Ebenezer Foster-Eddy, these payments grew from $11,892.79 in 1893 to $18,481.97 in 1895 (Mil. 420). There was no published accounting during the later years of Mrs. Eddy's life, but her annual income from royalties alone may have reached $100,000 by 1900.* Under Herbert Eustace, the payments of the Publishing Society to the Mother Church exceeded $450,000 during six months of 1918.**

8. *The Intellectual Elite.* The eighth *Manual* established a Board of Lectureship, "subject to the approval of Mary Baker Eddy," the speakers of which, almost always men, constitute the elite expositors of Christian Science. Their fees range upward from $100 plus expenses for each appearance. Every church is expected to sponsor at least one or two lectures annually. Such stars

---

*Cf. Dak. 298. Between 1901 and 1904, approximately 35,000 copies of *S&H* were sold annually at $3.00 or more per copy; the profit on each may have exceeded $2.00. In addition, there were large profits from the *Miscellaneous Writings* and other publications.

**Cf. *Christian Science and Organized Religion*, Studdert-Kennedy, 149.

as Edward A. Kimball and Bicknell Young may have earned in excess of $25,000 a year from this activity when such an income was tantamount to more than twenty times that number of dollars in the 1980s.

9. *Love and Marriage.* The tenth and eleventh editions of the *Manual* included complete wedding rituals to be performed by Christian Science officials in their own churches; however, discovering that such marriages had no legal status, Mrs. Eddy decreed very soon that her communicants could be united in wedlock only by a regular clergyman, a provision spelled out in the twelfth and fourteenth *Manuals.* Previously, the sixty-second edition of *Science and Health*, 1891, had proscribed all sexual activity during pregnancy (271-272); and in 1899, it virtually outlawed cohabitation among the spiritually advanced (274-275).

10. *Only the Leader Can Change It.* The final provision in the *Manual* declares: "No new Tenet or By-Law shall be adopted, nor any Tenet or By-Law amended or annulled without the written consent of Mary Baker Eddy, the Author of the Textbook, *Science and Health.*"

As it became obvious that the end must be approaching, those directors who had access to Mrs. Eddy begged her to add one by-law to clarify the succession and power. But she did nothing; she would neither define the degree of autonomy to be conferred upon the Publishing Society nor make any provision for the operation of the Church when her required consent, or approval in her own handwriting,* could no longer be forthcoming. Perhaps she was persuaded, along with some of her followers, that she would never die!

11. *The Final Struggle.* From the bowels of the Church *Manual*, therefore, inevitably emerged one of the bitterest religious conflicts of the twentieth century: for Mrs. Eddy had set up two virtually independent trusts—one for the Mother Church and another for the Publishing Society. The latter demanded a certain degree of autonomy; the Board of Directors claimed absolute authority. The courts first ruled that the trustees of the Society were legally correct; but later declared that, in the last analysis, the Directors must prevail, for otherwise the Church could not survive, and such a result was certainly not contemplated by the creator of the trusts.

The story of the great Suit in Equity, in which some of the nation's leading legal talent, including Charles Evans Hughes, was employed, is told in detail in Studdert-Kennedy's *Christian Science and Organized Religion.* The conflict divided the membership into hostile factions; and when the battle ended, many of the most brilliant Scientists had abandoned the Church.

---

*Cf. Secs. 2, 3, Art. I; Sec. 4, Art. XXIV; Secs. 3, 4, Art. XXV; Sec. 1, Art. XXXIII; and many others.

XI. THE LADY WHO LOST HER FAITH

One of the most scintillating members of the Boston Church was Mrs. Josephine Woodbury, a convert of 1879, whom her teacher often compared to John the disciple that Jesus loved. One of the fourteen Boston loyalists who remained after the debacle of 1888, she had become the leader of a mystical, romantic group which had premonitions and revelations; saw omens and portents; longed ecstatically for martyrdom; and lived in small, white cells, adorned only by pictures of Jesus Christ, all of which exasperated Mrs. Eddy beyond endurance (Mil. 428-430).

Mrs. Woodbury had taken somewhat too literally her mentor's teachings concerning spiritual generation, the agamogenesis one day to be perfected in Science. In June 1890, she gave birth to an unexpected son, whom she named the Prince of Peace, and whom she and her followers believed to be the result of an "immaculate conception." Mrs. Eddy, however, promptly called him "an imp of Satan" (430-431).

Although Mrs. Woodbury was "forever excommunicated" in 1896, she continued to attend services in the Mother Church, and sent her Prince to the Sunday School, until both were bodily ejected. She then began public services of her own in a rented hall (435).

In 1897, when Mrs. Woodbury published a pamphlet, *War in Heaven*, Mrs. Eddy became convinced that its author was the most potent mesmerizer since Kennedy; for months, the fires flashed back and forth between them; and finally, on May 1, 1899, totally disabused of her mysticism, the rebel published in the *Arena*, a New Thought journal, an extremely incisive, rationalistic attack upon Mrs. Eddy called "Christian Science and Its Prophetess." In it Mrs. Eddy's claim to being the star-crowned Woman of the Apocalypse was ridiculed: and it reproduced her laudatory newspaper contributions concerning Quimby as evidence that she had purloined her "science" from him. Before Mark Twain published his diatribes Mrs. Woodbury made sport of Mrs. Eddy's English and diction; insinuated that she was forced to close her College because its degrees were fraudulent; accused her of insatiable greed; exposed her as a former medium and the victim of demophobia; declared that she had made countless claims to mystical healings, particularly of important people (435-440, Ditt. 368-370), and charged that she taught the possibility of spiritual generation, and that, if the mother of Jesus could conceive by the Holy Ghost, then women today can do likewise. She declared that some of Mrs. Eddy's students were terrified by the fear of demonic impregnation. "Whatever her denials may be," continued Mrs. Woodbury, "such was Mrs. Eddy's teaching while in her college..." The only thing the "Founder of Christian Science" ever discovered, wrote Mrs. Woodbury, "are ways and means of perverting and prostituting the science of healing to her own ecclesiastical aggrandizement, and to the moral and physical depravity of her dupes. As she received this science from Quimby it meant simply the healing of bodily ills through a lively reliance on the wholeness and order of the Infinite Mind... What she has 'founded' is a commercial system, monumental in its proportions, but already tottering to its fall" (Mil. 438-439, Ditt. 367-369).

XII. THE WAR AGAINST CHRISTIAN SCIENCE

1. *The Ironic Wit.* Between 1899 and 1902, Mark Twain published his series of articles in *Cosmopolitan*; and in 1903 another in the *North American Review*. All of these were combined in *Christian Science*, published in 1907. The author's trenchant wit pierced Mrs. Eddy's armor and exposed to ridicule her claims of divine revelation. She therefore renounced the title of Mother in the twenty-ninth edition of the *Manual*; and wrote in the New York *Herald*: "I believe in one Christ, teach one only Christ, know of but one Christ. I believe in but one incarnation, one Mother Mary. I know I am not that one and I have never claimed to be..." (*My.* 303). On the surface, this sounded like a valid renunciation: but it was merely an exercise in semantics, since it states only that she and Jesus are not the same bearers of the Christ-Power. For this reason, she actually renounced nothing.

2. *The Baying Hounds.* After Mrs. Eddy virtually became inaccessible in 1906, Joseph Pulitzer of the New York *World* sent two reporters to investigate her in Concord. Interviewing J. Wesley Plummer, president of the local Christian Science Church, they were astonished to learn that he had never seen her and that he knew nothing of her practice of deeding real estate to others in order to frustrate legal judgments.

3. *Mrs. Eddy and Her Son.* After sending her son West after his visit to Boston in 1879, she wrote in 1887 that she could not receive him; nevertheless, he made a long visit in 1888 (Mil. 454-455). In the following years, he made several visits in search of money, but always returned empty-handed. However, on November 22, 1906, an agent of the *World* left for Lead City and persuaded George that his mother was unable to look after her interest, and that he had a good chance of inheriting millions (Ditt. 403-404). When he wrote his mother that he intended a trip East, this threw her household into consternation; and she wrote in the most emphatic terms that he should stay away, since "I cannot see you for many months..." (404). This confirmed his direst suspicions and he left at once for Washington, armed with his mother's eighty letters (Mil. 456-457). George W. Baker, a nephew of Mrs. Eddy, and her now repudiated foster-son, Ebenezer Foster-Eddy, also became parties to what was called the "Next Friends Suit" (403-410).

When George and his daughter arrived in Washington late in December, one of Mrs. Eddy's most trusted lieutenants, Irving Tomlinson, was waiting for him; he had two missions: (1) to persuade him to come to Pleasant View without talking to anyone else; and (2) to obtain the letters, which were already in a safe-deposit vault. Although Tomlinson got down on his knees (Dak. 422-423), George remained obdurate and incommunicative (Ditt. 404).

On advice of a Senator Chandler, George went unannounced to Pleasant View, where he arrived on January 2; his mother was affable, and obviously anxious to secure his cooperation. However, she was quite feeble, her sight and hearing were badly impaired; and George returned to Washington fully persuaded that his mother lacked the capacity to handle her enormous financial interests (Dak. 423-429).

The knowledge that George was associated with Chandler sent cold chills through the Christian Science high command. A letter from Mrs. Eddy to her son dated January 11 implored him to send *all* the letters she had written him and promised in return to give him and Mary some presents of value (Mil. 456). When this appeal brought no response, she wired a sum of money to the National Bank at Lead City, and sent a telegram to George in Washington to proceed to Dakota at once to claim it. But this bait did not interest George (Dak. 429, Ditt. 405-406).

On March 1, 1907, in the Superior Court of Concord, the Next Friends Suit was filed on behalf of Mrs. Eddy against nine leading men of the Christian Science Church. This demanded that all of Mrs. Eddy's properties be placed in receivership and that a full accounting of all her assets, income, and expenditures be made. Mrs. Eddy then made one last desperate effort to avert the impending battle: she offered to set up a trust fund of $125,000 for George and his children; but it was too little and too late (Dak. 428-431).

Hoping thereby to invalidate the claims of the "Nexters," Mrs. Eddy, on March 6, 1907, conveyed to three trustees, by deed of trust, all her real estate, personal property, copyrights, and liquid assets (Dak. 431, Beasley 618-623). But this had no effect on the proceedings.

When the case came to trial in August, Senator Chandler declared that Mrs. Eddy's paranoia created delusions of such character as to render her mentally incompetent, that is, virtually insane (Dak. 434-441). He cited her fear of M.A.M., which, he declared, amounted to dementia. However, the defense was able to limit all evidence to events following 1890; and the only question which finally faced the court was whether she was competent to execute the recent deed of trust. The court appointed three "Masters" to examine Mrs. Eddy at Pleasant View (Ditt. 412-413), which they did on August 15, 1907 (Dak. 440).

Fortunately for her, she was enjoying one of her best days and had no difficulty showing that she could manage her own affairs (Dak. 440-450, Beasley 440-470). Thereupon, Senator Chandler withdrew the suit.

This, however, did not terminate the danger; and for this reason Mrs. Eddy's counselors advised her to make a settlement with her son, for otherwise the whole future of the Christian Science Church might be imperiled. On November 10, 1909, it was agreed that Ebenezer Foster-Eddy should receive $50,000 and George Glover $250,000. The latter returned his mother's letters; both made irrevocable agreements never to contest Mrs. Eddy's will or make any further demands upon her, her heirs, or assigns (Dak. 460, Ditt. 418). Surely, Mary Glover's son had given her very little joy!

Her will, made years before, provided that her copyrights, and all other property, real or personal, go to the Mother Church and be subject to the same trust by which it obtained title to the land on which its buildings had been erected. The trust deed of March 6, 1907 provided that the trustees should manage her properties during her lifetime and convey them to the Church at her death.

4. *The Heavy Artillery.* By 1907, the attacks upon Christian Science and Mrs. Eddy were coming thick and fast. Peabody followed his pamphlet, *The Complete Exposure of Christian Science*, with a pitiless book, *The Religio-Medical Masquerade*; ministers, seeing their members slip away became alarmed; and medical men, losing patients right and left, took up the cudgels. No one knew how far this new "craze" might go.

As emotional diatribes multiplied, it became obvious that an objective study was indicated; and this was accomplished by Georgine Milmine and a team of investigators in a series of articles in *McClure's Magazine* in 1907-1908, and released in book form by Doubleday in 1909. Month after month the devastating material appeared; and the Woman of the Apocalypse, communing with God at the Mount in Pleasant View, began to appear something less than divine. Seldom has seer or prophet been subjected to such scathing scrutiny. Mrs. Eddy wrote a reply in the *Journal* (*My.* 308-316) to the opening article; but when the massive documentation became irrefutable, she observed her own by-law and retired from the debate.

XIII. THE HIEROPHANT OF CHESTNUT HILL

1. *The Battle with Mesmerism.* For years, the express service, the mail boxes, the roads, the trees, and the large frame house at Pleasant View had been thoroughly infested with M.A.M. In spite of her guards, who stood their shifts day and night, Mrs. Eddy had been attacked from all sides. She was terrified by day, and hysterical by night, when seizures felled her into catatonic states. She must flee, on pain of losing her church and every penny she had in the world!

She therefore ordered her trustees to find her a more suitable retreat. They discovered a magnificent mansion in the Boston suburb of Chestnut Hill, which was purchased for $100,000 and on which an equal sum was spent for repairs, alterations, reconstruction, furnishings, and decorations (Dak. 462-465, Ditt. 420-421).

On Sunday, January 26, 1908, the unannounced removal occurred. Mrs. Eddy's special train was preceded by one locomotive and followed by another to make certain that the machinations of the diabolists would be foiled. Eluding the newsmen, she entered her great new home; the doors were secured from within, and six armed guards took up their watch (465).

2. *The Monitor.* However wracked with pain and tormented by corrosive fear, Mrs. Eddy's restless mind never ceased to direct her empire. On August 8, 1908, she ordered her Publishing Society to establish the *Christian Science Monitor*, which would not carry news dealing with crime, corruption, or scandal, but would meet all the secular needs of Scientists and appeal also to the world at large.

3. *The Relentless Monster.* After twenty-seven months in the mansion on the Hill, Mary Baker Eddy surrendered her restless and troubled spirit on December 3, 1910. For thirty-five years, she had been fleeing from M.A.M.; but it pursued her into the grave. A few weeks later, twenty-five leading *men* of the Church escorted her mortal remnant from Boston's Mt. Auburn cemetery to a final resting place on the shores of Halcyon Lake, where the casket was lowered into a huge grave and covered with eighty tons of concrete reinforced with steel.*

4. *The Revenge of Calvin Frye.* During his many years of faithful service, Frye kept a diary in shorthand, which, upon his death, came into Dittemore's possession (228-232, 445-449, Dak. 525-530). When portions of this were published in 1932, the result was devastating; for it revealed that Mrs. Eddy suffered terribly from renal calculi; that she was under constant dental and optical care; that she was a regular patient of the M.D.s; that she had a fearful and ungovernable temper, which often erupted into violence, and that ever since childhood, she had been subject to cataleptic seizures.

Even more damaging, however, was the revelation that she had, since youth, been a narcotics addict; that Frye had been trained to hold her forcibly while administering hypodermic injections during seizures,* and that such occurrences were a regular part of the routine in the near-madhouse where Mary Baker Eddy reigned as the Second Christ.

Indeed, Mrs. Eddy herself admitted that she used morphine constantly, for she wrote: "Many years ago my regular physician prescribed morphine, which

---

*Cf. article in New York *Sun*, Jan. 26, 1911; and Olston 128-131.

*In one passage quoted from the Frye Diaries, complete directions are given, according to which Mrs. Eddy received her regular injections of morphine (Ditt. 389).

I took, when he could do no more for me." And she added that, to test the malpractice of her enemies and to discover whether the drug would have any effect on her, she took "large doses of morphine" which "had no effect on me whatever," when she was attacked by mesmerists (*Mis.* 248-249), as she was almost every day of her life for nearly forty years.

5. *The Incredible Adam H. Dickey.* Mrs. Eddy's last official act was to make Adam H. Dickey a director of the Mother Church on November 21, 1910. With naive devotion, he had served as a member of her household and had become her closest confidant. When he died in 1925, he was Chairman of the Board. On August 25, 1908, Mrs. Eddy made him take a solemn oath that he would write and publish a history describing how she had been mentally murdered (Dickey xv). Obedient to his vow, he wrote an innocent-looking little volume called *The Memoirs of Mary Baker Eddy*, which his widow published two years after his death and which reveals facts as weird as they are indisputable.

Mr. Dickey explains that when he came into Mrs. Eddy's household, all those serving her were subject to the influence of such malpractice as existed nowhere else on earth (3-4). It was therefore necessary that she have capable guards to protect her, for otherwise she could not continue her great labors for the salvation of mankind (8). Since she was like the general of a great army fighting for survival, she must be protected at all costs; and since she was besieged day and night by demonic forces (11), it was mandatory that she have the best possible bodyguards (10). Dickey relates sadly that on the very day of his arrival, the coachman died of believed heart failure because he had not realized the terrible power of mesmerism (35).

The guards, who numbered from twelve to eighteen, were charged with the duty of turning aside the streams of mental malpractice constantly assailing Mrs. Eddy (43); for otherwise she could not perform her God-given, sacred task of redeeming humanity from sin, sickness, and death (44). Since she could always discern what course evil was pursuing, she was able to tell the guards exactly what their mental work would be (45). When she went to bed at 9, the watchers, one after another, took up their positions outside her door, where each stood a two-hour shift (107). It was an everlasting battle to preserve the Leader's life so that she could devote her energies entirely to the redemption of mankind. Sometimes, however, the evil forces became so preponderant that she would fall victim to another seizure (108).

Mrs. Eddy explained that since her church-government was divine, it incurred universal hostility (114). Every institution must, she declared, to be successful, have a responsible head; and that was the reason she had made herself the supreme authority in her Church. She abolished the First and the Executive Members because, since they were vulnerable to the attacks of malicious mesmerism, they could never be entrusted with power. She declared with pathos that if she could find one individual worthy of confidence, she would place him at the head of her church. But, since she could not alter the divine commandments, she must rule alone; and the duty of her members was only to obey (116).

She often expatiated upon her divine nature and mission (131-132). Even before she was born, her mother, like the Virgin Mary, had presentiments that the child would be holy. When only eight years old, she was already a devoted student of the Bible (132-133). When she was yet a child, God indicated her future role by levitating her from her bed, and then gently replacing her. She told no one about this at the time; but remembered it when God called her to demonstrate the nothingness of matter (140-141).

Dickey states that on one occasion Frye actually died, and that Mother resurrected him, thus again demonstrating her power over death and the grave (107-112).

XIV. MRS. EDDY'S PERSONAL ACCUMULATIONS

In spite of the $300,000 she was forced to pay her sons, the large sums she spent in litigation, and the expense of maintaining her large establishment, it has been estimated that her personal accumulations reached $3 million (Dak. 512). Her gross income must, therefore, have approximated $4 million between 1880 and 1910. *The Religio-Medical Masquerade* devotes a chapter called "Immeasurable Greed" to Mrs. Eddy's commercial undertakings (Pea. 121-146), such as the spoons which sold for $3.00 to $5.00 each, and which " 'each scientist *shall* purchase...and those who can afford it, one dozen...' " (144). She even decreed in 1897 that all practitioners must abandon their incomes from teaching for one year to sell and distribute her *Miscellaneous Writings* (*CSJ* March 1897). Since she always placed her cash in good investments, we can be sure that these doubled every ten or twelve years.

In addition to her cash, bonds, real estate, etc., Mrs. Eddy gave her Church her copyrights, which, in terms of current and future income, were of far greater value than her accumulations. As Mark Twain pointed out (*CS* 201-203), she craved this wealth so that with it she could perpetuate her power and glory by establishing eternal control over her church through deeds of trust.

XV. QUIMBY AND MARY BAKER EDDY

1. *The Genesis of New Thought.* The thirty-five prominent students who left the Boston Church in 1888 all believed with Mrs. Eddy in certain metaphysical principles, but they rejected her M.A.M. and her claims to revelation

and divinity. They joined forces in the general New Thought movement; all were individualists who traced their ultimate antecedents to Swedenborg and to techniques established by Quimby.

2. *The Divided Stream.* Christian Science and New Thought had, therefore, even before 1900, split into two streams, both of which believed in the supremacy of mind over matter. However, those loyal to Mrs. Eddy taught and the others denied that a revelation had come to her with the fall in Lynn; that the Bible and *Science and Health* constitute cognate sacred Scriptures; that matter has no objective reality or existence; that sin, disease, and death are mythical and that all belief in them will ultimately disappear; that M.A.M. is the cause of these "errors"; that Mrs. Eddy was the manifestation of Christ in the feminine, as was Jesus in the masculine, and that her own revelation as the Motherhood Idea of God is superior to the orthodox Christian. Particularly revolting to New Thought was the doctrine, freely taught in Christian Science circles, that, even as Jesus was the offspring of an immaculate conception resulting from his mother's communion with the Holy Spirit, so was Mrs. Eddy's book and ideology the result of a similar process.

3. *The Godlike Quimby.* It is indeed intriguing to pursue Mrs. Eddy's successive versions concerning the Portland healer. Modern Christian Science places the beginning of its era on February 1, 1866, when Mrs. Patterson fell on the ice in Lynn; but just a few days before, as we have noted, on January 22, she had sent a poem commemorating the death of Quimby to the Lynn *Reporter*, which it published on February 14, and in which she rhapsodized concerning her mentor:

> "Growing in stature to the throne of God;
> Rest should reward him who hath made us
> whole,
> Seeking, though tremblers, where his footsteps
> trod" (Ditt. 107).

On the very day these verses appeared, she wrote a supplication to Julius Dresser, urging that he take up the mantle of Quimby and come to her aid. This letter, written two weeks after the Fall, contains no hint that she was any worse than she had been during previous years; she *did* mention the accident, but declared (*QMSS* 163) that in two days she rose from her bed and walked. There was no mention of the divine healing or the Scriptural reading which much later was said to have occurred; and Dr. Cushing, who attended her, in due course furnished an affidavit, based on his clinical notes, in which he declared that Mrs. Patterson's injuries were of little consequence (Mil. 84-86).

4. *The First Revelation.* In her *Science of Man*, copyrighted in 1870, but revised before publication in 1876, Mrs. Eddy declared (6-7): "In early

youth...I was given up to die. At that period God revealed to me the *science* of being, and it healed me, and my higher creed today is SCIENCE, CHRISTIANITY, AND GOD." Accordingly, she received her Great Illumination while still a young girl and was, presumably, permanently healed at that time.

However, in the first edition of *Science and Health* there is an entirely different statement, according to which she recovered her health by refusing to continue the Graham starvation diet prescribed by a physician during her childhood (189-190).

In the first and second editions of *Science and Health*, the fall in Lynn is simply cited as one of the hundreds of cures beyond the reach of *materia medica*, but accomplished by divine science (I 343, II 104). However, by 1881, the Accident had begun to assume greater proportions, for she declared that her case was pronounced fatal by the physician who attended her and who declared that she would not survive more than three days. On the third, however, she read from the third chapter of Mark, where Jesus healed the withered hand. She declared that instantly a change came over her, and that she arose from her bed, completely healed (III *S&H* I 156). (Note that previously the reading was from Matthew.)

In the sixteenth edition, 1886, a new version of the Great Accident and Year of Discovery had been formulated in Wigginite phraseology: she declared that in 1866 she discovered metaphysical healing and called it Christian Science (11). In the fiftieth edition (1) she added that God had for many years been fitting her to receive a final revelation concerning absolute, scientific Mind-Healing. So now the revelation of Christian Science became complete and final in 1866. Actually, she had called her therapy by various other names, such as the Science of Man, for twenty years after that date.

5. *The Great Controversy*. After Arens charged Mrs. Eddy with plagiarizing her ideas from Quimby, her attitude toward her once-revered master became one of hostile condescension; she wrote that about the year 1862, after hearing of a certain mesmerist in Portland, she went to see him and that he helped for a while. After his death and her accident, she discovered that the only principle of healing is God, and thus she regained her health. She admitted that the "old gentleman" had some advanced views about healing, but was neither religious nor scholarly. She said that she had interchanged some thoughts with him on the subject of healing and that she cured some of his patients that he failed to heal. She also left with him, she said, some of her writings, which corrected his and which have now gone to one of his patients living in Scotland. When he died in 1865, he had published nothing. The only writing of his that she ever saw—and that only to correct it—was perhaps of twelve pages, most of which she had composed. Since he used manipulation, his method was physical and not mental. And she added that she had increased his public esteem by her writings (VI *S&H* I 3-4).

In 1882, Julius A. Dresser and his wife Annetta returned to Boston, where they established their own practice. Through George Quimby, they had access to his father's manuscripts. Dresser was outraged by finding that Mrs. Eddy was teaching her version of the Quimby science but giving no credit to her mentor. Dresser therefore published a letter signed A.O., which appeared in the Boston *Post* on February 8, 1883, declaring that Dr. Quimby had written a great deal "on the subject of mental healing, or his theory, which he termed the 'Science of Health.' " And he continued: "Some parties healing through a mental method, which they claim to have discovered, did, in reality, obtain their first thoughts of this truth from Dr. Quimby, and have added their own opinions to the grain of wisdom thus obtained, presenting to the people a small amount of wheat mixed with a great quantity of chaff..." (Ditt. 234).

Under date of February 19, and under the alias E.G., Mrs. Eddy replied in the same publication that "Dr. Quimby's method of treating the sick was manipulation.... He never called his practice a mental method.... We asked him several times if he had any system aside from manipulation and mesmerism...and he always evaded the subject. We were his patients, but he never gave us any further information relating to his practice, but always said it is a secret of [his] own.... His scribblings were fragmentary, but sometimes very interesting. He requested us to transform them frequently and give them different meanings, which we did.... He called his scribblings essays, but never the 'Science of Health.' 'Science and Health' is a work of Mrs. Mary B.G. Eddy, issued in 1875. She...finally sealed her proof by a severe casuality, from which she recovered through her exercise of mental power over the body, after the regular physicians had pronounced her case incurable..." (235).

To this, Dresser made a sharp retort on February 24 over his own signature. E.G.'s statements are "false from beginning to end.... Mrs. Patterson-Eddy knows positively," he stated, "that the late Dr. P.P. Quimby of Portland, Maine, was actually and solely originator and founder of a mental method of treating diseases...." Furthermore, she knew "that Dr. Quimby was a mesmerist in his young days, but that...at the time she knew him he never used mesmerism at all...." Dresser then quoted Mrs. Eddy's despairing letter to himself (236-237).

To this, Mrs. Eddy composed a rambling reply, which appeared March 7 in the *Post*: "We had laid the foundation of mental healing before we ever saw Quimby.... We made our first experiments in mental healing in 1853, when we were convinced that mind had a science which, if understood, would heal all diseases; we...never saw Dr. Quimby until 1862.... He was somewhat of a remarkable healer, and at the time we knew him he was known as a mesmerist.... We knew him about twenty years ago, and aimed to help him. We saw he was looking in our direction and asked him to write his thoughts out. He did so, and then we would take that copy to correct, and, sometimes...wrote his name on the back of it....

"But lo! after we had founded mental healing and nearly twenty years have

elapsed, during which we taught some 600 students,*...the aforesaid gentleman announces to the public, Dr. Quimby [is] the founder of Mental healing"
(238-240).

On February 6, 1887, Julius Dresser delivered a lecture entitled *The True
History of Mental Science*, later published in pamphlet form. Mrs. Eddy, he
declared, knew nothing concerning mental healing when she first came to
Portland; he included quotations from Quimby's writings and reprinted several of Mrs. Patterson's effusive declarations, such as the following: "P.P.
Quimby stands upon the plane of wisdom with this truth." Since he "speaks as
never man before spake, and heals as man never healed since Christ, is he not
identified with truth, and is not this the Christ which is in him?... P.P. Quimby
rolls away the stone from the sepulchre of error, and health is the resurrection." And then Dresser fired this parting shot: "It is now easy to see just *when*
and *where*" Mrs. Eddy " 'discovered Christian Science' " (25).

Confronted with this evidence, she turned to Wiggin; but when she admitted writing the quoted material, he told her tersely that there was nothing
more to be said (Mil. 102). Nevertheless, she wrote in the *CS Journal* for June
1887: "Did I write these articles purporting to be mine? I might have written
them twenty or thirty years ago, for I was under the mesmeric treatment of Dr.
Quimby from 1862 until his death in 1865. He was illiterate and I knew
nothing then of the Science of Mind-Healing.... Mind-science was unknown
to me; and my head was so turned by Animal Magnetism and will-power,
under his treatment, that I might have written something as hopelessly incorrect as the articles now published..." (Ditt. 243-244, Mil. 102).

Completely contradicting herself again, however, she wrote in the same
article: "As long ago as 1844, I was convinced that mortal mind produced all
diseases, and that the various medical systems were in no proper sense
Scientific. In 1862, when I first visited Dr. Quimby, I was proclaiming—to
druggists, spiritualists, and mesmerists—that Science must govern all healing." And she concluded: "He never intimated to me that he healed mentally
or by the aid of Mind.... His healing was never considered anything but
mesmerism" (*My.* 306-307).

6. *The First Important Quimby Publications.* In March 1888, George
Quimby published an article concerning his father in the *New England Magazine*; and in 1895, the widow of Julius Dresser, Annetta, published the
114-page *Philosophy of P.P. Quimby*, which, for the first time, reproduced
extensive and representative selections from his essays, together with an
historical sketch of his life and an analysis of his theories. It included news-

*Actually, the total was somewhere between 60 and 100 in February, 1883, of whom 32
had enrolled in the Massachusetts Metaphysical College (Ditt. 463).

paper articles dated from 1857 to 1865 which prove that Quimby did not practice mesmerism at all during this period.

7. *Dr. Quimby as John the Baptist.* In order to counteract these revelations, Mrs. Eddy declared that "quotations have been published, purporting to be Dr. Quimby's own words, which were written while I was his patient.... Some words in these," she proclaimed, "certainly read like words which I said to him, and which I, at his request, had added to his copy when I corrected it." And then she elaborated: "In his conversations with me, and in his scribblings, the word science was not used at all, till one day I declared to him that, back of his magnetic treatment and manipulations of patients, there was a science, and it was the science of mind, which had nothing to do with matter, electricity, or physics" (306-307).

We find, however, that the word *science* occurs 390 times in the *Quimby Manuscripts*, 83 times in the two which we know Mrs. Eddy saw, and 24 times in letters written before Quimby ever met her.

"After this," continues Mrs. Eddy, "I noticed that he used that word, as well as other terms which I employed that seemed at first new to him. He even acknowledged this himself, and startled me by saying what I cannot forget—it was this: 'I see what you mean, that I see that I am John, and that you are Jesus' " (*My.* 307).

After thirty-five years, therefore, Quimby became to Mrs. Eddy what Swedenborg had been to Ann Lee.

8. *The Official Position.* For years, Mrs. Eddy's spokesmen denied the existence of any Quimby manuscripts. In spite of the fact that thirty-six pages of them had appeared in 1895 and that both Peabody and Milmine had quoted from additional essays, Sibyl Wilbur O'Brien proclaimed in 1907, in a passage unaltered to this day, that "veritable Quimby manuscripts are absolutely hypothetical..." (95). The official version concerning Mrs. Patterson's effusive tributes to Quimby, when not completely ignored, has long been, not that she was mesmerized, but that, being overly generous, she gave boundless credit where little or none was due: in the words of Lyman P. Powell, in his second book, she overrated "in a grateful woman's way what she owed to Quimby..." (II 110).

XVI. THE EVOLUTION AND STRENGTH OF CHRISTIAN SCIENCE

1. *Membership.* In 1889 Kimball declared (*Lectures* 50) that "Christian Science" had "in immediate affiliation with it hundreds of thousands..." also that it had healed "nearly 2,000,000 sick" (120); and that multitudes more were in the process of joining (296). Mrs. Eddy stated in 1907 that she was "the

beloved Leader of millions of good men and women in our own and other countries..." (*My.* 315).

The *Manual* (Sec. 28, Art VIII) decrees that no report for publication shall be made of the number of Church members, either in the Mother Church or in the branches. Nevertheless, such statistics were supplied to the Federal Government for the 1906, 1926, and 1936 *Census of Religious Bodies*. From this and other sources, we are able to compile the following totals:

EARLY CHRISTIAN SCIENCE MEMBERSHIP AND ORGANIZATION

Year	1893	1899	1901	1902	1906	1908
Members, Mother Church	1,545[a]	16,000[b]	21,631[c]	24,278[d]	40,011[e]	43,000[f]
Number, Branch Churches					682[g]	
Number, Societies					267[h]	
Members of 614 Churches					41,944[i]	
Estimated Total Members					50,000[j]	

We have also the *Christian Science Journal*, which lists churches, societies, teachers, and practitioners.[k] In 1926, there were 1,206 sanctuaries;[l] in 1936, there were 1,600.[m]

CHRISTIAN SCIENCE MEMBERSHIP IN THE UNITED STATES

1906	Mother Church Members (counted twice)	85,717[n]
	Total of different members (census estimate)	65,717[o]
	The probably correct estimate	50,000[p]
1926		202,298[q]
1936		268,915[r]

[a] *My.* 57
[b] *'00*, 1
[c] *'01*, 2
[d] *'02*, 1
[e] *My.* 57
[f] *Ibid.* 141
[g] *Ibid.* 57
[h] *Ibid.*
[i] *Ibid.*
[j] Since most members of the Mother Church were also members of branches or societies, the latter of which probably did not average more than 10 members, and since 90% of the churches had about 42,000 communicants, we estimate a total 1906 CS membership of about 50,000.
[k] Some practitioners may not be listed in the *CSJ*.

PRACTITIONERS, TEACHERS, CHURCHES, AND SOCIETIES

Year	Pract. & Teachers in World	In World Total	Chs.	Socs.	In United States Total	Chs.	Socs.	Abroad Total	Chs.	Socs.
1906[s]					638					
1906[t]		949	682	267						
1916[u]	5,660	1,565	845	720	1,388	759	629	177	86	91
1927[v]	9,293	1,944	1,372	572	1,665	1,210	459	279	162	117
1936[w]					2,113					
1936[x]	11,165	2,740	1,687	1,053	2,164	1,383	781	576	304	272
1946[y]	11,123	2,744	1,804	940	2,148	1,473	675	596	331	265
1956[z]	9,769	3,112	2,114	998	2,366	1,706	660	746	408	338
1966[aa]	7,919	3,136	2,233	903	2,366	1,809	587	770	424	346
1976[bb]	6,200	2,991	2,441	750	2,252	1,787	465	739	454	285
1980[cc]	5,592	2,876	2,164	712	2,145	1,708	437	731	451	275
1982[dd]	4,664	2,745	2,042	703	2,077	1,627	450	668	415	253
1984[ee]	4,455	2,731	1,993	738	2,020	1,556	454	771	427	284

[l] 1926 *Census of Religious Bodies* II 346

[m] 1936 *Ibid.* II, Part I, 390

[n] 1906 *Ibid.* II 200. Since Christian Scientists in Massachusetts are listed as totalling 43,547, which was nearly 40,000 too many for the state alone, it is obvious that the total number in the U.S. in 1906 would not have exceeded 50,000.

[o] 1936 *Ibid.* II Part I, 391

[p] Cf. TABLE above

[q] 1926 *Ibid.* II 348

[r] 1936 *Ibid.* II Part I, 390. Since foreign groups were quite small, it is unlikely that total 1936 membership could have exceeded 300,000.

[s] 1906 *Ibid.* II 200, Part I 148

[t] *My.* 57

[u] *CSJ* Oct. 1916

[v] *Ibid.* Nov. 1927

[w] *Census of R.B.* II Pt. I 390

[x] *CSJ* April 1936

[y] *Ibid.* Sept. 1946

[z] *Ibid.* Nov. 1956

[aa] *Ibid.* May 1966

[bb] *Ibid.* Oct. 1976

[cc] *Ibid.* May 1980

[dd] *Ibid.* Oct. 1982

[ee] *Ibid.* June 1984

2. *The Peak Is Passed.* It is obvious that, had Christian Science continued to expand at its early rate, it would today have become a tremendous power; but the preceding indicates that this development has not occurred. Between 1906 and 1936, its churches and societies quadrupled; had this continued, there would today be about 20,000 congregations with perhaps four million members. Instead, they have actually declined in number since 1936 in the United States, while the population has doubled.

According to the statistics above, the average Christian Science congregation in 1906 had 53 members; in 1925-1927, 110; in 1936, 125.

Since it is a cult of health, the number of active practitioners is the most reliable index to growth or decline. The total of these grew proportionately with the congregations from 3,280 in 1911 to 11,166 in 1936, but dropped slightly to 11,123 in 1946. Beginning with this date, however, the decline became more rapid; in 1956, it had fallen to 9,769 and in 1976 to 6,200, a loss of almost 45 percent; and in 1984 to 4,455, which was only about 40 percent of the 1936 total. Considering the increase in population, this would indicate that Christian Science today is less than one-third as large a factor in American life as it was in 1936. In the meantime, total church membership in the country increased from about 30,000,000 to 132,000,000.

We have no doubt at all that the strict authoritarian rule of the Christian Science Church is a significant deterrent to growth, since it fosters sterility. However, there are also other factors contributing to stagnation or decline. In this regard, we may mention the scandal which erupted in 1973-1975 and which was described in a brochure distributed by a former prominent member, Reginald Kerry. He charged that the Board of Directors spent $82 million for the new high-rise building in Boston when it could have been completed for about $30 million; and he implied that the Board had failed to account for something like $150 million, which had been in the treasury a few years previously. Furthermore, he strongly urged the membership to withhold contributions to the Mother Church until they received a full and audited financial statement from the Directors. Although statistics concerning Church membership are not available, it is possible that this has declined even more than the ratio of practitioners. Although he professes great devotion to the Foundress, Kerry condemns the Board of Directors of the Mother Church. He states that membership in the great London church had fallen from 1,200 to 20; that almost everywhere, except in retirement communities, attendance has fallen off drastically, and that the total membership may now be no more than 30,000.

3. *One Loses, Another Gains.* We believe that another factor is involved in the gradual Christian Science decline: and this is the enormous growth of other New Thought organizations. The religion of health, happiness, and prosperity has not diminished; it has, on the contrary, increased tremen-

dously, but the expansion has occurred among the freer communions, led by people who hearken back to Swedenborg-Quimby-Evans-Dresser origins and may now embrace at least 250,000 communicants.

XVII. THE SUCCESSIVE EDITIONS OF SCIENCE AND HEALTH

1. *The Eddy Cycle.* Probably no other work in religious history has undergone such a long and constant evolution under the control of a single individual as *Science and Health.* Whatever the shortcomings of its first edition may be, it is certainly closer to Quimby than its successors; nevertheless, it embodies the ultimate Christology, therapeutic theory, and metaphysical concepts of Christian Science. Although the author was yet to discover that her message was a divine revelation, that she was herself the Woman of the Apocalypse, that the Key to the Scriptures devised by Swedenborg was a necessity, or that Christian Science constitutes the completion of Christianity as envisioned by the Revelator on the Island of Patmos, it is a full statement of her religion, an extraordinary accomplishment, and virtually without parallel on the American scene. In successive editions, material was added or deleted, altered or expanded, polished or rewritten, as it underwent continuous change in a labor virtually completed in 1891.

2. *The Third Edition.* The third edition, of which the fourth and fifth are replicas, reflects progress, perhaps the result of Spofford's collaboration. Many sentences are rewritten and, for the most part, read more smoothly. Several of the chapters are renamed and most of them revised. However, except for the chapter called Recapitulation, which is a virtual reprint of the 1876 *Science of Man*, the entire third edition is simply a recension of the first combined with the second. However, The Key to the Scriptures, consisting here only of a Glossary, appears for the first time. Thus we know that Mary Glover had discovered Swedenborg!

3. *The Wiggin Cycle.* Beginning with the sixteenth edition, we have a drastic development: for here, for the first time, God becomes the Mother-Father deity; the entire work is a revelation; and Mrs. Eddy, at least by implication, is the Woman of the Apocalypse. Furthermore, the name Christian Science is found on almost every page; in hundreds of passages it replaces such terms as metaphysical healing, mental science, the science of mind, or science and truth—all of which indicates that, as Quimby receded in time, his influence became actually more prevalent.

This edition is deeply tinged with the handiwork of the skillful agnostic, James Henry Wiggin, who was true to his trust: he did not alter ideas—he merely clothed them in a more felicitous garb. When Mrs. Eddy engaged him, she wanted a crash program for her revision. He wrote that "the misspellings, capitalization, and punctuation" in her manuscript "were dreadful, but these were not the things that fazed me. It was the thought and the general elemental arrangement of the work. There were passages that flatly and absolutely contradicted things that preceded, and scattered all through were incorrect references to historical and philosophical matters." He found it necessary "to begin absolutely at the first page and re-write the whole thing!" And this, as he concluded later, "was the very thing she had intended that I should do in the first place" (Dak. 225-226).

To realize what Dr. Wiggin did, it is only necessary to compare almost any passage in the fifteenth and sixteenth editions of *Science and Health*:

Fifteenth Edition, II 1, 1885	Sixteenth Edition, 234, 1886
Phenomena not understood surround us, every day is a mystery, while we are pecking our shells to learn somewhat of our surroundings and to enter the laboratory of the real.	Mortal life is an enigma. Every day is a mystery. The testimony of the senses cannot inform us what is reality and what is delusion; but the revelations of Science unlock the treasures of truth.

Or note the following, which is the opening sentence of the Preface:

The First and Third Editions

Leaning on the sustaining Infinite with loving trust, the trials of today are brief, and tomorrow is big with blessings.

The Sixteenth Edition

Leaning on the sustaining Infinite, today is big with blessings.

Final Version

To those leaning on the sustaining Infinite, today is big with blessings.

In the sixteenth edition, the word *Wayshower* appears for the first time as the name of Jesus (508). Thereafter it became one of Mrs. Eddy's favorite names for him. It is found several times in the final version of *Science and Health* (e.g. 30, 497); it occurs twelve times in her *Prose Works*; and one of her most popular hymns is called "Shepherd, Show Me How to Go."

Wiggin began his revisions in 1886 and continued to revise until the virtually definitive version appeared in 1891 as the fiftieth edition. Here we find that an all-pervasive internal transformation has occurred. It is no longer possible to follow the text by juxtaposing it with previous editions, for not only has almost every sentence and paragraph been again rewritten, the material itself has been completely rearranged.

By comparing two early passages with the two final recensions by Wiggin, we can follow the evolution of expression in *Science and Health*:

First Edition, I 400, 1875

The time approaches when mind alone will adjust joints, and broken bones, (if such things were possible then), but in the present infancy of this Truth, so new to the world, let us act consistent with its small foothold in the mind.

Third to Fifteenth Editions, I 220, 1881-1885

The time approaches when mortal mind will let go of its personal, structural, and material basis, sufficiently for the immortal Mind and its formations to be apprehended, and no material thought will interfere with the spiritual fact that man is an idea instead of material substance and all form indestructible and eternal.

Sixteenth through Forty-Ninth Editions, 328, 1886-1891

The time approaches when mortal mind will forsake its personal, structural, and material basis, sufficiently for the Immortal Mind and its formations to be apprehended, in a realm where material thought interferes not with the spiritual facts of man, whose form is indestructible and eternal.

Fiftieth Edition, 400, 1891

The time approaches when mortal mind will forsake its corporeal, structural, and material basis, when immortal Mind, and its formations, will be apprehended in Science, and material thought will not interfere with spiritual facts. Man is indestructible and eternal.

In 1891, Mrs. Eddy parted company with the Reverend Mr. Wiggin, charging him with a "most shocking flippancy" (Mil. 335). However, we can be sure that his services were terminated, not because of his alleged irreverance, which he had never attempted to conceal, but because his work had been completed. The final version of *Science and Health* was a reality.

When Mark Twain read the first sentence in an early edition, he believed that it was written by Mrs. Eddy, since it was full of grammatical and other errors. But when he read the book in its final form and studied its polished prose, he declared that she could not have composed this. He even noted an improvement in the third over the first edition; and, since he knew nothing of Spofford's collaboration or the labors of Wiggin, he concluded that some hand other than Mrs. Eddy's had been involved. And he was certainly correct!

CHRISTIAN SCIENCE

Part Two—Doctrine and Practice

I. THEOLOGY AND CHRISTOLOGY

While most of Mrs. Eddy's doctrines remained substantially unchanged, portions of her system underwent a basic evolution as a result of additions. Her Christology and her theories concerning sickness, health, therapy, sex, eschatology, and soteriology belong to the first category; but her persuasion concerning deity, revelation, personal apotheosis, and demonic obsessions belong to the latter. Her preoccupation with M.A.M. began with the second edition of *Science and Health*, 1878; direct Swedenborgian influence, appearing for the first time in the third edition, was much enlarged in later ones, and Shaker concepts, beginning with the sixteenth in 1886, became progressively more evident.

Mrs. Eddy's early concepts of deity were at first based squarely upon Quimby's, as he had absorbed them from Swedenborg. God, therefore, is not a person, but a Principle, a tenet emphasized over and over. Belief in a personal deity is atheism (*S&H* I 20); all theories of a personal God must now yield to science (52); there is neither a personal God nor a personal man (227). God is infinite, the only Life, substance, Spirit, or Soul, the only Intelligence in the universe, including man (F 330). In place of the tripersonal God of orthodox theology, which "suggest polytheism" (256), Christian Science

191

offers a triune Principle, called Life, Truth, and Love (331). Thus "God...is a trinity in unity, not three persons in one, but three statements of one principle" (*Heal.* 3).

This impersonal power constitutes the law, intelligence, vitality, and spiritual substance of the cosmos. Therefore all prayers, supplications, and attempts to placate his wrath or obtain special favors must be absurd. Prayers cannot influence him (*No* 39); they are no better than drugs (I *S&H* 192); they cannot cancel sin (284); they never made a Christian of anyone (286). If prayer should seem to overcome disease, this is only one false belief casting out another (F 12).

The Lord's Prayer with its Spiritual Interpretation is recited responsively at all Christian Science services; but this is not a supplication, but an affirmation of Christian Science faith and doctrine.

About the year 1885, Mrs. Eddy absorbed the ancient Gnostic and the modern Shaker-Evans concept of the Father-Mother God. According to this, the "true man and true woman, the all-harmonious 'male and female,' " are of "spiritual origin, God's reflection," and the "children of one common parent" (*Mis.* 18), who is "all-wise, all-knowing, all-loving..." (*'01*, 7). In Mrs. Eddy's system, as "applied to Deity, Father and Mother are synonymous terms; they signify one God. Father, Son, and Holy Ghost mean God, man, and divine Science" ('00, 5) and constitute "our Father-Mother-God" (*Pan.* 15).

Mrs. Eddy's Christology is similar to an ancient Gnostic belief which held that Jesus was born in the ordinary manner but was endowed with the Christ-Spirit at his baptism. The Great Exampler, Teacher, and Instructor were common appellations applied to him; and most of the Gnostics rejected the concept of vicarious atonement. That "somebody in the flesh is the son of God, or is another Christ," wrote Mrs. Eddy, is a "belief in anti-Christ" (*Mis.* 111). "Jesus was the son of Mary," she declared, "but the Christ-Jesus represented both the divine and the human, God and man." "Christ," she explained, is "a spiritual divine emanation..." (*'01*, 10).

In this reconstruction of Christian doctrine, Christ-Jesus emerges as Our Great Example (F 555), the Great Exemplar (395, 577), and the Wayshower (30, 497) who, having demonstrated by divine science the highway to blessed immortality, enables all those who understand his Gospel to gain, like him, complete victory over sin, disease, and mortality.

A unique element in Mrs. Eddy's Christology is her doctrine that the conception of Jesus was not simply virginal, but that it occurred without an impregnating agency. Since he "was born of the Virgin Mary's spiritual thoughts of Life..." (*My.* 261) he came nearest to the record of Genesis in which man was made by spirit (I *S&H* 311). In the final version of *Science and Health*, however, we discern the astute hand of Wiggin: for although Jesus is here the offspring of Mary's self-conscious communion with God and

endowed with the divine Christ-spirit, he partakes of Mary's earthly condition, which enabled him to become the Wayshower and Mediator between
men and God (29-30).

In healing the sick by divine science, Jesus accomplished his first great
demonstration; rising from the grave with the same body as before (45) was his
second; his ascent into the celestial realms and sending the Comforter, which
has now appeared as divine Science, constitutes his third and supreme demonstration (I *S&H* 143, *My.* 218). Jesus, we read, "was the most scientific man on
record" or "that ever trod the globe" (1883 *SofM* 6, I *S&H* 41, F 313); he was
therefore able to achieve in his own life what will be possible for all humanity
after the complete victory of Christian Science.

Although Jesus declared three days after his burial that his body was still
flesh and bones, this was only because he had not yet relinquished all belief in
matter as substance (I 41). It was only by degrees that even he was able to cast
off all remnants of mortal mind. His spiritual body, or incorporeal idea, came
only with the ascension, after which he entered upon his own "probationary
and progressive state beyond the grave" (F 46). During his three days in the
sepulchre, he mastered the principle of Christian Science, and demonstrated
the power of mind over "medicine, surgery, and hygiene" (44). His victory
enables his communicants to conquer death, for "his resurrection was also
their resurrection" (34).

Jesus therefore embodies the supreme historic victory of divine Science: his
spiritual generation, parthenogenetic birth, resurrection, ascension, and gift
of the Comforter, all demonstrate the Christ-power with which he was
endowed.

II. THE DOCTRINE OF ATONEMENT

Like Quimby, Swedenborg, Evans, and the Shakers, Christian Science
repudiates the central dogma of orthodox Christianity, namely, that by his
death Christ-Jesus accomplished a sacrificial and vicarious atonement for
humanity, otherwise damned in original sin. Worthy only of contempt are
those who believe they can reach perfection and immortality through the
sacrifice and suffering of another (I *S&H* 208). For God to vent his wrath on
his only son is neither humane nor logical and only a man-made belief
(301-302). Jesus never ransomed man by paying the debt which sin incurs; for
whosoever sins must suffer (312). No one may be pardoned from sin by a
substitute (284). Every dereliction must meet its own retribution; and restitution must precede forgiveness (292).

"It was not to appease the wrath of God, but to show the allness of Love and
the nothingness of hate, sin, and death that Jesus suffered. He lived that we

also might live" (*No* 35). "Divine Science," continues Mrs. Eddy, "has rolled away the stone from the sepulchre of our Lord...The at-one-ment with Christ has appeared—not through vicarious suffering, whereby the just obtain pardon from the unjust—but through the eternal law of justice; wherein sinners suffer for their own sins, repent, forsake sin, love God, and keep his commandments, thence to receive the reward of righteousness: salvation from sin, not through the *death* of a man, but through a divine *Life*, which is our Redeemer" (*Mis.* 123).

Beginning with the fiftieth edition of *Science and Health*, the elements of the Mass and the Holy Supper are called cannibal tidbits (F 214). When we obey and follow the precepts of Jesus to heal the sick, cast out evils, and raise the dead, then only do we drink of his cup and partake of his bread (31).

III. MATTER, SUBSTANCE, AND REALITY

1. *The Quimby-Swedenborgian Concept.* We found that the Swedish seer spent much of his life in pursuit of the human soul; and that he finally concluded that it was a spiritual, invisible, and eternal reality of which the body is simply the temporary integument. He did not imply that our physical elements are without existence, but that, when these are sloughed off at death, the celestial entity continues; and that the emotional, ethical, and intellectual complex which is *man* continues as before. The Swedenborgian soul may be compared to the butterfly which emerges from the chrysalis, except that the celestial body is invisible to the eye of the natural man.

The theory of Quimby and Evans concerning disease and healing was based upon this metaphysical concept. Since, in their system, the spiritual body is the primary reality which creates and controls its physical habitation, it is only necessary to cleanse the "soul" of all impurity, contradiction, discord, and false beliefs to accomplish a parallel rejuvenation in its temporary dwelling.

2. *A Study in Semantics.* Mrs. Eddy, who seems never fully to have absorbed this prognosis, concluded instead that matter and even the cosmos have no actual existence. In her early writings, her declarations are categorical, "That all is mind and there is no matter" (1876 *SofM* 5, I *S&H* 267). Substance, she says, is "eternal, and incapable of discord or decay. Truth, Life, and Love are substance.... Spirit is substance, Soul is Substance, and man is shadow. God is substance, and the universe is shadow" (1876 *SofM* 6). Furthermore, "if God is Spirit, and God is all, surely there can be no matter; for the divine All must be Spirit." (*Un.* 31.)

Beginning with the fiftieth edition of *Science and Health*, however, perhaps under the influence of Wiggin, similar declarations are less absolute; nevertheless, the original implications remain. We are told that if matter is substance, then spirit is not the only creator (F 257), and Christian Scientists regard substance as Spirit, while opponents believe that it is matter (349-350).

3. *Confusion.* In its metaphysics, Christian Science departed from Quimby, became involved in contradictions, and created a barrier between itself and all other forms of mental healing. Had Mrs. Eddy embraced the Swedenborgian concepts of matter, soul, reality, spiritual substance, and the celestial body as set forth in Evans and the *Quimby Manuscripts*, Christian Science would have been a quite different system of philosophy, religion, and therapeutics. Not only does it lack a harmonious concept of substance, it never achieved any comprehension of the threefold emotional and intellectual structure of the human psyche.

4. *The Spiritualization of Man.* Since God is All and is Spirit, sin, disease, and death are only a suppositional absence of Life (215); and growth into spiritual immortality "will be rapid, if you love good supremely, and understand and obey the Wayshower, who, going before you, has scaled the steep ascent of Christian Science, stands upon the mount of holiness...and bathes in the baptismal font of eternal love" (*Mis.* 206).

5. *Dualism.* In spite of manifold declarations that Mind or God is All and that matter does not exist, we find that Mortal Mind and the physical ills of the body constitute the most pervasive element in Christian Science. Often, indeed, the language nearly takes on the coloration of absolute dualism, as proclaimed in Zoroastrian or Essene literature, to express the profound gulf separating divine spirit from Satanic matter. Matter and Spirit, we read, are opposites (I *S&H* 224), which never mingle (254). Since God did not create an evil mind, there must exist a sinister power which can and does produce it (F 207).

Here we are confronted with a basic contradiction compounded by statements such as that the body is the substratum of mortal mind (371), but are told elsewhere that the latter is a solecism and therefore without existence (114). Anything material, we learn, is mortal (477); and mortals are no more material than their dreams (397). Yet it is certain that both Soul and body are immortal (I *S&H* 30), inseparable, eternal, and indestructible (399).

However, we read also that mortals are wicked because they think wickedly (F 270). The will is capable of all evil (206). Furthermore, Mortal Mind is the drive behind human motivation and produces in the body discordant action, which is harmonious only if it proceeds from the Divine Mind (239). Christian Scientists "cannot arm too thoroughly against original sin, appearing in its myriad forms: passion, appetites, hatred, revenge, and all the *et cetera* of evil" (*Mis.* 114).

Unless, therefore, language is devoid of meaning, we have here two substantially equal forces poised over against each other in a combat which will determine human destiny.

IV. THE SENSES AND SENSATION

1. *Physical Impressions.* Since spirit is the only reality and matter has no objective existence, it follows that impressions gained through the material media are erroneous. "Sickness, or sensation in matter...is an illusion..." in which "the sick are like the insane..." (1883 *SofM* 11). Since the evils of existence come from the physical senses, neither pain nor pleasure can exist in matter (I *S&H* 14-15). And since sensations come through the mind, they belong to the soul (17-18). The five senses are only beliefs, the source of error and discord (20).

2. *Spiritual Science vs. the Physical Senses.* We shall begin to live and be without sensation when the belief that we inhabit a body is destroyed (46). Once science is understood, the fable that man consists of solids and fluids will be ended (49). The mind creates diseased bones, and alone governs the internal organs, which is the true explanation of disease (154).

Since health is a condition of mind and not of matter, the senses cannot be trusted (F 120). And since matter can neither suffer nor enjoy it has no relationship with pain or pleasure (181). It therefore follows that the nerves cannot feel, the brain think, or the stomach make a man cross; neither can limbs cripple him nor matter kill (I 14). That the body can suffer from heat, cold, or fatigue is only a false belief (337). To transform each of these into its opposite, it is only necessary for any one to change his opinion concerning them (355). The arm of the blacksmith grows strong only because he believes that exercise will make it so (366).

3. *The Fatuity of Food.* Man requires meat and bread only because of his delusions (240-241); when first created, man's life was self-sustaining (244). Food neither helps nor harms (404); there is only false evidence that it is necessary to sustain life (405). Eating never made a man live nor has abstention from it ever caused death (438).

4. *The Myth of Sensation.* A boil cannot be painful, for it merely manifests by inflammation and swelling a belief which is called a boil (F 153). Sound is only a mental impression on mortal belief (213). The true remedy for fatigue is in understanding the power of Mind over physical weariness, for matter cannot be weary or heavy-laden (217). Pain will continue in a tooth that has been extracted or a limb that has been amputated (212). When a bone is broken or a head chopped off, the man remains unchanged (I 398).*

5. *Man, the Celestial.* In Christian Science, Mind is everything, and so-called matter nothing. The human being and (mortal) mind are only myths. Since the body does not exist, it never lives or dies (347); and since man is

---

*The fiftieth edition states simply that "bones have only the substantiality of thought which formed them" (421) and says nothing about decapitation.

immortal, he can never undergo death (355). It necessarily follows, therefore, that mind controls the physical body. Told that he was bleeding to death, a certain man expired, although he never lost a drop of blood (74); another died of cholera because he imagined himself infected with it (F 154). A cold apple can burn the hand if it is believed to be hot (I 89); a mesmerist can cause a blister to rise and then to disappear (102). A woman who became insane at twenty-one never aged anymore thereafter during half a century because she thought she was still young (214, F 245).

V. ESCHATOLOGY

In Christian Science, as in Quimby and Evans, heaven is not a locality (37); it is, instead, a state or condition, "the reign of divine Science...a mental state" (*Mis.* 174). Man does not die when the body becomes lifeless, because life was never in the body (F 207). "Waking from the dream of death, proves to him who thought he had died that it was a dream and that he did not die..." (*Mis.* 58). After the change, man does not lose his identity; his mind remains "still in a conscious state of existence..." (42).

Christian Science deviates from Swedenborgian eschatology only in that it has no hell except in the evil beliefs that originate in mortal mind (F 266). Mrs. Eddy states that there will be no final judgment (F 291). The ultimate fate of each and every man will thus be determined by his or her progress here and in the evolution that will follow; either each individual will rise from sense to soul or degenerate into nothingness. Once the change has occurred, "the departed... progress according to their fitness to partake of...heaven" (*My.* 267). Those who have advanced on earth "awake from a sense of death to a sense of Life in Christ...because their lives have grown so far...that they are ready for a spiritual transfiguration..." (*Un.* 2).

VI. SEX, MARRIAGE, AND GENERATION

"Man and woman," declares Mrs. Eddy, in her early writings, "were created by God and not by a union of the sexes..." (1883 *SofM* 14). Such false beliefs are strongest among those who have the most material natures (I *S&H* 303). Bees and butterflies propagate without a male element (262); various animals multiply without sexual conditions (F 549). Many organisms reproduce by means of eggs, buds, and self-division (I 262). In the beginning, crops grew without seed (336).

There can be little doubt that Christian Science in its attitude toward sex is basically ascetic. Marriage, we read, is *not* better than celibacy (*Mis.* 288); in fact, it is "synonymous with legalized lust..." (*My.* 5). If "the wife esteems not" the privilege of becoming a mother, she may, "by mutual consent," gain more "exalted and increased affections..." (*Mis.* 289). The "words of St. Matthew," she wrote tersely, which say that it is good not to marry, have a "special application for Christian Scientists..." (298). Nevertheless, and again bowing to expediency, she declared: "Until time matures human growth, marriage and progeny will continue unprohibited in Christian Science" (286).

Because of the embarrassment created by some prominent Scientists who took "spiritual mates," Mrs. Eddy couched her later declarations concerning sex and marriage in less explicit terms. "I hereby state," we read, that "a man or woman having voluntarily entered into wedlock...is held in Christian Science as morally bound to fulfill all the claims growing out of this contract..." (297). But, she added significantly, "God will guide" Christian Scientists in their marital conduct (287).

"We look to future generations," she declares, "for ability to comply with absolute Science, when marriage shall be found to be man's oneness with God..." (286); and the day will come when masculine Wisdom and feminine love will generate the race without the necessity of sexual union (I *S&H* 322).

In the definitive *Science and Health*, the chapter on Marriage (56-69) closes with the Scriptural passage (Luke 20:35) upon which ancient Gnostic communions and the modern Shakers based their mandatory celibacy: "The children of this world marry, and are given in marriage: but they which shall be accounted worthy to obtain that world, and the resurrection from the dead, neither marry, nor are given in marriage." This was one passage for which Mrs. Eddy needed no spiritual interpretation, for it states categorically that those who marry are children of perdition and will neither rise from the grave nor inherit the kingdom of heaven.

VII. MORTAL MIND

Quite exclusive with Mrs. Eddy were the term and concept Mortal Mind, which scarcely occurs in the first edition of *Science and Health* but is found 238 times in the 211th edition and 144 times in the *Prose Works*. Whatever this may be, it pervades Christian Science and constitutes the basis for a novel dualism. Since "God is just," we must "admit the total depravity of mortals, *alias* mortal mind..." (*Mis.* 2). Human beings are, then, totally corrupt, for they are identical with *mortal mind*, which, like the Pauline Original Sin (F 239), is the source of human motivation and leads to every disorder in the body.

However, we are told elsewhere that "mortal mind is a myth..." (*Mis.* 82) and has no actual existence (F 114). Yet it is the worst foe of the body (176). Nevertheless, the two are one and the same; neither can exist without the other, and both can be destroyed by Immortal Mind, which creates the superstructure of which the material body is the grosser portion (177). However, we read also that mortal or carnal mind is not Mind at all; and that sin finds a residence there only because an illusion of mind in matter still lingers with us (311). It would seem, then, that mind is not mind and that sin exists, even though evil cannot.

Like Pelion upon Ossa, contradictions are piled upon negations. Although man is incapable of sin, sickness, or death (475), all humanity is descended from the wicked or evil one; for man began in dust as a material embryo, and never knew perfection; from the beginning, he was conceived in sin and brought forth in iniquity (476).

What then *is* Mortal Mind? How can it accomplish such devastation if it does not exist? If God is the only mind in the universe, is not man, who is also immortal, his divine derivative? If man is thus spiritual and immortal, why is he so burdened with the depravity of mortal mind? If all mind and all creation come from God, and he can produce nothing unlike Himself (*Un.* 23), how can man or Mortal Mind be so depraved? If Mortal Mind is nothing and does not exist, how can it produce all the diseases which plague humanity? And if man is immortal, how can he be identical with his body?

VIII. MALICIOUS ANIMAL MAGNETISM

1. *The Great Malevolence.* Pervasive in Mrs. Eddy's system also is her doctrine of demonology, known also as mesmerism, mental malpractice, or simply M.A.M. She created this, her distinctive concept of diabolism, to account for evil, her own defeats, and the failures of her students: as Milmine points out, it added "certain abnormalities" to Quimby's system "which, if universally believed and practiced, would make of Christian Science the revolt of the species against its own physical structure..." (209).

2. *Kennedy, Chief Diabolist.* In the *Science of Man*, 1876, we find Mrs. Eddy's first prognosis of what was to become the "devil" of her Science.* "We regret to say it was the sins of a young student that called our attention to this question for the first time.... By thorough examination and tests, we learned manipulation...established a mesmeric connection between patient and practitioner..." (12-13). When the first edition of *Science and Health* was published, the continued success of Kennedy and her own frustrations had driven Mrs. Eddy frantic. She complained that she had been weakened by this malpractice (194). Since he continued the manipulation she had taught him, even as she had learned it from Quimby, she peremptorily outlawed the

---

*This was written shortly after Kennedy threw his inequitable contract into the fire and set himself up in independent practice.

technique (99), which she now called an inanimate poison, the criminal at large who undertakes even more daring felonies. It would be safer to permit a doctor infected with the small-pox to treat a patient than trust one who manipulates (193), for this method can be more dangerous than addiction to opium (382). The perils of Salem witchcraft are still present (107), she declared; in the future, any one who hates his neighbor will be able, without warning, to enter his house to destroy him by the use of mesmerism alone; and unless this terrible scourge is prevented by Science, nothing sacred will remain (123). Evil thoughts reach farther and do more injury than any other crime, for they fill the minds of individuals with mental poison and contaminate the air itself with malice, evil, and lust (123-124).

Filled with hatred and revenge, continues Mrs. Eddy, the malpractitioner depends on manipulation alone. By this method, he controls his patients, but remains immune to exposure; he can therefore demoralize an entire community without punishment. His victims obey him, trusting his honesty and character (375-376). The falsehoods and prejudices derived from him are nothing less than Satanic; more subtle than any serpent, he attacks innocent people while they sleep (377-378).

Because we rebuked a false student, continues Mrs. Eddy, he separated us from friends of many years, raised himself in their estimation, and concealed his own villainies (382). The mesmeric terror began when a young student reversed our method of metaphysical healing. But he was young only in years; and even though we strove to remove the great evil of his character, we could not destroy it (III *S&H* II 1-3).

3. *Spofford, Malpractitioner Supreme.* When the second edition of *Science and Health* was printed, Spofford had joined Kennedy as an almost equally sinister diabolist; and now, since the latter had never rubbed a head, we find that mesmerism can be practiced with or without manipulation. We have, declared Mrs. Eddy, seen the crime of an additional outlaw, who does not usually manipulate, but who would nevertheless pay for his crimes on the gallows if they were understood (II *S&H* 136-138). Since he has no terror of the bottomless pit into which he is sinking and the tortures he will endure because of his sin against the Holy Ghost, he continues to hold high carnival together with all that is evil and corrupt (138).

In her frenzy, Mrs. Eddy cried that this criminal should be sent to prison or consigned to the hangman (140). Those who believe that our courts should not deal with mental crime do not comprehend the Scriptures, which still declare we must not "suffer a witch to live." (143).

4. *The Third Minion of Darkness.* Just as the third edition of *Science and Health* was going to press in 1881, another student, Edward A. Arens, defected, went into business for himself, and published a pamphlet in which he reproduced material taken from Mrs. Eddy's book without giving it credit. He

stated flatly that there was nothing original in her science and that she had obtained her own theories from Quimby. She lost no time in suing him for plagiarism; and the court decreed that he pay the cost of the litigation and destroy all copies of his pamphlet. Thereupon, Mrs. Eddy declared that her originality had been established in a regular court of law (Mil. 306-307).

5. *The Permanent Mesmerism.* Scattered throughout Mrs. Eddy's *Prose Works*, we find innumerable references to mesmerism, mental malpractice, and the dreaded Malicious Animal Magnetism, which, if permitted, "will end in insanity, dementia, or moral idiocy" (*Mis.* 113). So subtle are "the inventions of animal magnetism," we read, that they "could deceive, if possible, the very elect" (78). "This unseen evil is the sin of sins; it is never forgiven.... The crimes committed under this new-old *regime* of necromancy or diabolism are not easily reckoned," but "the laws of our land will handle its thefts, adulteries, and murders, and will pass sentence on the darkest and deepest of human crimes" (*'01,* 20).

6. *M.A.M. Expunged and Denied.* All reference to specific malpractitioners and almost all discussion of M.A.M. were meticulously expunged from the editions of *Science and Health* following Wiggin's revision; and ever since the turn of the century, the official policy of the Christian Science Church has been to deny that any of this originated with, or was ever proclaimed by, its founder.

IX. THE SPIRITUAL MEANING OF THE SCRIPTURES

Like Quimby, Evans, and Swedenborg, Mrs. Eddy rejected Biblical literalism. The profound truths of Scripture have been overlaid with a vast accretion of fable, inconsistencies, and outright error (I *S&H* 251, 255). The New Testament can scarcely be an accurate rendition of the Gospel as taught by Jesus, since this existed only as an oral tradition for 300 years (255). Since many passages are opposed to Love and Wisdom, we can accept them only as the opinions of pagans who transcribed the inspired texts (251).

The Scriptures have a spiritual import which teaches the science of life (171). Should this be removed, they can no more help humanity than moon beams can melt a frozen river (F 241). They "cannot properly be interpreted in a literal way.... There is a dual meaning to every Biblical passage...and to get at the highest, or metaphysical, it is necessary rightly to read what the inspired writers left for our spiritual instruction. The literal rendering...often is the foundation of unbelief and hopelessness" (*Mis.* 169).

The Glossary (F 579-599), composed in the Swedenborgian tradition, gives the spiritual meaning of Biblical words. Like those of Quimby and Swedenborg, Mrs. Eddy's works are studded with such interpretations. For example,

Christ crucified signifies truth and the cross that attends it (I 124). Adam was a metaphor (255). When Jesus declared that his followers could handle serpents without injury, he meant that they should "put down all subtle falsities and illusions..." (*Mis.* 24). The commandment "Thou shalt have no other gods before me" signifies that we must not believe that life is mortal (F 19). The "evil spirits" cast out by Jesus were simply false beliefs (79). When he said, "He that believeth in me shall not see death," he meant that whoever understands the true idea of Life no longer accepts a belief in death (324-325).

X. ATTITUDE TOWARD THE RELIGIOUS AND MEDICAL ESTABLISHMENTS

On the front cover of *Science and Health*, we find the following inscription: "Heal the Sick, Raise the Dead, Cast out Demons, Cleanse the Lepers." This is the power which has been lost by Christianity for centuries, but which Science now restores to mankind (146, 328). Religion degenerated as soon as it lost its primitive power to heal sickness and cast out evils (*Heal.* 3).

For Mrs. Eddy, as for Quimby and Evans, Christ-Jesus was the great healer who promised health, happiness, prosperity, well-being, and an abundant life. All considered the conventional churches and their hired expositors as hypocrites who had subverted the message of Christ. Even Mrs. Eddy for a long time had no thought of founding a church. There is no record, she declared, that any form of church worship was ever instituted by Jesus (I *S&H* 167). If indeed his disciples ever established any religious organization or church rites, this was a mistake never made by the Master Himself (166).

Even after she established her own congregation, Mrs. Eddy declared it unnecessary "to ordain pastors and to dedicate churches.... If our church is organized, it is only to meet the demand, 'Suffer it to be so now' " (*Mis.* 91). The time will come, she continues, "when the religious element, or Church of Christ, shall...need no organization..." (145). She stated that religion as now practiced draws us away from spiritual Truth (I *S&H* 181-182). Prayers ground out in lofty edifices are worth no more than those for which small coins are paid in the Orient (289).

Again and again, Mrs. Eddy attacked credalized and dogmatic religion: material concepts of God have "overturned empires in demoniacal contests over religion." And "speculative theology" has "made monsters of men.... The eternal roasting amidst noxious vapors, the election of the minority to be saved and the majority to be eternally punished, the wrath of God to be appeased by the sacrifice and torture of His favorite Son—are some of the beliefs that have produced sin, sickness, and death..." (*Peo.* 2-3).

In her early days, Mrs. Eddy bristled with virulence against both doctors and clerics. Even the definitive *Science and Health* is studded with passages which reflect her true feelings. It is recorded, she states, that professional medicine began with the idolatry of pagan priestcraft (F 158) and it is certain that the armies of Aesculapius are filling the world with diseases (150-151). Echoing Quimby and Evans, she continues that they frequently plant diseases in the thoughts of their patients (180), to whom the doctor's diagnosis is like a sentence of death which actually creates the disease that kills (198).*

XI. HEALTH, DISEASE, AND SCIENCE

1. *Personal Hygiene and Public Sanitation.* Since in her system the body is a myth, Mrs. Eddy had nothing but contempt for rules of hygiene and the laws of sanitation. One of her favorite passages, repeated in all editions of *Science and Health*, declares that daily baths for an infant are no more natural or necessary than to take a fish out of water, cover it with dirt, and then wash it (I *S&H* 319, F 413). Statistics prove, she contends, that laws dealing with health have neither reduced sickness nor lengthened life; since man-made theories replaced primitive Christianity, acute diseases have become fatal and death more sudden (I 330).

2. *The Nature of Food.* Mrs. Eddy stated that food affects the body only by the dictates of mortal mind (F 389). However, she herself never failed to eat regularly, nor did she venture to require her unpaid household servants to subsist on pure Science. She even conceded that it would be foolish to stop eating until we reach perfection through an understanding of the spirit (388); but she insisted that we abstain from alcohol, tobacco (*My.* 114), tea, coffee, and opium (*Mis.* 348-349).

3. *Concessions.* Mrs. Eddy conceded that it would not be in obedience to Wisdom for a man to rush into the flames of a burning building or remain in a storm until his body was frozen (I *S&H* 51); in fact, her practical sanity became evident whenever her theories threatened to involve her in serious legal difficulties. She admitted, for example, that for a broken bone or dislocated joint, a surgeon should be called until further advances are made in mental science (400). When seized with a violent pain, even a Christian Scientist may receive a hypodermic injection (F 464). And, until our beliefs change drastically, we should not stop eating entirely (I *S&H* 434-435).

4. *Avoiding Conflict.* Under severe counterattack, Mrs. Eddy made her uneasy peace with the law, public opinion, and the medical profession.

---

*That she did not really believe this is proved by the fact that Mrs. Eddy was constantly under the care of occultists, dentists, and medical doctors, to whom she paid large sums (Ditt. 373, Dak. 367-368). She even paid for operations performed by surgeons on her relatives.

"Rather than quarrel over vaccination," she wrote, "I recommend, if the law demand, that an individual submit to this progress..." (*My.* 219, 344-345).

5. *No Patients.* Beginning with the second and continuing in later editions of *Science and Health*, Mrs. Eddy made it clear that *she* would have nothing to do with patients (5). In the sixteenth, she declared that she had no time for medical consultations (10), a statement dropped after her death.

XII. THE THEORY AND TECHNIQUES OF CHRISTIAN SCIENCE

1. *The Nature of Disease.* The fundamental principles of Christian Science therapy may thus be summarized: (1) since spirit is everything and matter does not exist, sin, sickness, and death are only false beliefs or errors of mortal mind; (2) this being true, it is only necessary for those afflicted with mental or physical disorders to arrive at a correct understanding of truth or Principle in order to abolish sin, sickness, and death itself; (3) when this enlightenment or resurrection occurs, it constitutes the cure, and all devils or evils harbored by mortal mind vanish and the patient becomes virtuous, healthy, happy, and immortal; (4) the process of regeneration is accompanied by a chemicalization which renews mind and body, and restores both to pristine purity, and (5) this system of therapy is effective for every kind of disease, malady, or injury, whether it is called mental, functional, organic, or physical. In Science, cures result, not from faith, but from *knowledge*: the sick are healed because they *know* there is no sickness (F 447).

"Sickness is a belief and illusion...a state of suffering caused by a belief, whether this belief is cancer, consumption, smallpox, or a broken bone..." (1876 *SofM* 21). Maladies are like insanity—simply beliefs or (d)evils to be cast out (1883 *SofM* 11, I *S&H* 13, F 159, *Mis.* 63). Since diseases can be discerned in the patient's mind months before they appear in the body (F 168), any appearance there can be prevented (I *S&H* 398, F 400). We catch fevers only when we believe ourselves liable to have them (408). Since talking about sickness creates it, we should never discuss it (342, 396, 417). Patients should never be told anything about their ailments (417-418). Christian Science teachers never mention anatomy (*Rud.* 11-12). In fact, we should never even think about the body (I *S&H* 432). If you deny that a tooth can ache, it cannot cause pain (*Mis.* 44-45).

2. *Drugs and Man-Made Theories.* Faith in drugs and the rules of health simply beget disease (F 169, 184). Nevertheless, faith in them sometimes does bring a cure, because placebos are just as effective as drugs (I *S&H* 187-188, 341, F 155, 174, 370, *My.* 107), which belong in the same category as whiskey (F 158).

Birds and other wild creatures, says Mrs. Eddy, are never sick (I 186). Even a horse, however, can be miseducated to catch a cold without his blanket (F

179). Savages enjoyed perfect health until missionaries brought them a knowledge of disease (I 437). Our own ancestors lived ruggedly and free from sickness (F 175); their ignorance concerning medicine and laws of health kept them well (197). Climate is unhealthy only when we believe it to be so (377). Only the mind can determine whether or not a wound will cause the discoloration of the flesh (385).

3. *Christ, the Way-Shower.* "In Science,...you cannot eradicate disease if you admit that God sends it or sees it" (*No* 31). Healing the sick and reforming the sinner are one and the same (F 404); it is "a divine largess" through which "the great Way-Shower, invested with glory...illustrates 'the way, the truth, and the life' " (*My.* 349). Every patient is healed when his belief in sickness vanishes (F 377); and this truth applies as fully to organic diseases as it does to hysteria or nervous disorders (176-177).

4. *The Basic Contradictions.* The underlying flaw in Christian Science metaphysics—declare some of its critics—developed from its concept of substance—its denial that the material universe has objective reality. This scientific error bound the cult in a philosophical straightjacket from which it could extricate itself only by repudiating the basic premises of its founder. Had she admitted that emotional conflicts and psychosomatic maladies are the specific field for mental therapy, her cult would certainly have achieved an incomparably higher intellectual level; whether it would have become a powerful religious denomination or have obtained its historic wealth and influence is an altogether different question.

XIII. THE DEIFICATION OF MARY BAKER EDDY

1. *Science Becomes Holy.* In the early versions of *Science and Health*, although couched in the language of authority, there is no implication that the author had received a personal revelation or that she was endowed with an aura of holiness. Her system of therapy was then merely scientific. The revised *Science of Man*, however, published in 1883, declares that "the Holy Ghost is Science, the only revelator of God—the principle of man and the universe—and was the Comforter to come that should lead into all truth" (16). Even this, however, was only a modest prelude to the proclamations which followed.

2. *The Swedenborgian Key.* It was in the sixteenth edition of *Science and Health*, 1886, that The Key to the Scriptures—a Swedenborgian innovation—first became a major division of the book. The Key consists of four chapters, Genesis, Prayer and Atonement, Revelation, and Glossary. The exegesis of the first and last books of the Bible consists of sixty-four pages—designed to accomplish for Christian Scientists what her predecessor had done in twenty large tomes. The method is precisely the same: after each Scriptural text, its

spiritual import is explained. However, little more than the first chapter of Genesis and a few texts from the twelfth of Revelation are analyzed.

In the fiftieth edition of 1891, the Key attains its final stature. The chapter on Prayer and Atonement is now placed under two headings in the main section; the exposition of Genesis is somewhat expanded, and the interpretation of the Apocalypse is increased to twenty pages, in which additional texts from Chapter 10 and 12 are presented as prophecies of Christian Science and its founder.

3. *The Inspired Prophetess.* Many years after they allegedly occurred, Mrs. Eddy remembered remarkable events which presaged her divine calling. Her mother, like the mother of Jesus, had received messages concerning the divine child she was to bear (Dickey). When very young, she, like Samuel, heard voices calling her (*Ret.* 8); from her childhood, she was impelled toward holy things (31); reminiscent of the encounter between the twelve-year-old Jesus and the doctors in the temple, we find her at the same age speaking against predestination to the leaders of her church (13-15); "a still small voice" came to her "in the silence of the night," as it did to Elijah, and told her to call her book *Science and Health* (*'02*, 15-16). She had learned that, according to prophecies in Daniel, the return of the Christ was due in 1866 or 1867—which is now the Christian Science Year of Discovery (*My.* 181); however, the year 1875, when *Science and Health* first saw the light, was also cited as that in which the Second Coming of Christ would occur (*'00*, 6-7). The Mother Church was dedicated on January 6, the date of the Epiphany, for centuries celebrated as that on which both the nativity and the baptism of Christ occurred (*Pul.* 20), and when she summoned the Seventy to Pleasant View in 1898 for final instructions, this was a repetition of an act performed by Jesus in Luke 10:1 (Ditt. 361-363).

4. *The Spiritual Principle.* Mrs. Eddy, like Ann Lee, declared that although "Jesus of Nazareth was a natural and divine Scientist..." the ultimate divine Science must be a discovery and "Woman must give it birth...since none but the pure in heart can see God..." (*Ret.* 26). Only such a woman could give a true explanation of the Bible meanings after she had "read the inspired pages through a higher than mortal sense" (*Mis.* 58). To Jesus, God revealed only the spirit not the absolute letter of Christian Science. He, therefore, could teach only a general outline of divine Principle, and he never prepared any exact rule for its demonstration, now finally revealed in Christian Science (F 147).

Since God had entrusted Mrs. Eddy with this ultimate revelation, she could not "choose but obey" (*'01*, 31). Neither human tongue nor pen, she declared, had imparted this science to her (F 110). While it is a fact that "no person can compass or fulfill the individual mission of Jesus," it is equally true that "no person can take the place of the author of Science and Health, the Discoverer and Founder of Christian Science.... The second appearing of Jesus is, unquestionably, the spiritual advent of the advancing idea of God, as in Christian Science" (*Ret.* 70). Divine Science is the Comforter promised by John (F 55) and is certainly the true Logos (134).

5. *Mother Mary.* Mrs. Eddy's divine revelation was signaled by the fact that the "star of Bethlehem is the star of Boston," which rests over the Mother Church (*Mis.* 320) located there, the "great window" of which "tells its pictorial story of the four Marys—the mother of Jesus, Mary anointing the head of Jesus, Mary washing the feet of Jesus, Mary at the resurrection; and the Woman spoken of in the Apocalypse, chapter 12, God-crowned" (*Pul.* 27).

Mary Baker Eddy was, then, the final interpreter of the Scriptures and the supreme revelator. Even after Mark Twain had pilloried her with such ridicule that she foreswore the title of Mother in the public prints and amended the by-law in which she had first assumed it, she still employed it in her Christmas message to the faithful (*My.* 263). Who else, we might ask, has ever been able to persuade so many to believe so much on her own authority?

And so, by successive escalation, Mrs. Eddy rose (1) from the humble discipleship of Quimby to an authority in mind-healing, and did so by her own efforts and a will of iron; (2) thence to the status of Revelator for an infallible Christ-Science; (3) then, like Ann Lee, to divinity as the Second Christ, manifested in the Superior Female; (4) to recognition as the Woman of the Apocalypse whose little book should transform and rule mankind; and (5) finally to membership in the supreme godhead as the embodiment of the Mother-Principle in deity.

Who else, in all history, has claimed or accomplished so much?

6. *Mrs. Eddy, Star-Crowned.* The advent of Mrs. Eddy as the sun-clothed Woman of Revelation was first proclaimed in 1886, in the sixteenth edition of *Science and Health* (511-524), where we learn in the chapter named The Apocalypse that the Revelator, in his 12th chapter, refers to the 19th century and the establishment of Christian Science in the vision where he foresaw "a great wonder in heaven—a woman clothed with the sun, and the moon under her feet, and upon her head a crown of twelve stars" (511).

On the ceiling of the great Mother Church Extension in Boston, there is an immense painting of the Woman of the Apocalypse, illumined by the light of the sun, with the moon under her feet, and her head crowned with twelve stars.

7. *The Spiritual Idea.* This ineffable personage is, of course, Mrs. Eddy, or at least the divine science she revealed. As long as we entertain a false estimate of her who voices the idea of God, we can never, we are told, comprehend its greatness (512), which had only a short history in the earthly life of Jesus, but which shall one day rule all nations as the immaculate offspring of the Woman and which shall baptize with fire (517). Even as John the Baptist prophesied the coming of the immaculate Jesus, so did the Revelator on Patmos foretell

the appearance of the Woman, who would typify the Motherhood of God (F 561-562). And even as Jesus was the masculine representative of the immaculate idea, so is it now represented at last by Woman, or Christian Science, whose discoverer and founder embodies the spiritual idea of God (565).

In cryptic language, Mrs. Eddy thus elevates herself into the third aspect of a Servetian-Swedenborgian modalistic Trinity. Christian Science recognizes God as a triune principle: Life, which is the Father; Truth, which is the Son, and Love, which is the Mother (568-569). The faithful understand full well that their Leader constitutes in herself the highest attribute of deity.

8. *The Enemy*. But now appears the great Red Dragon, which, to Swedenborg, was the Protestant Reformation and to Ann Lee the bondage to sex, family, and private property. But to Mrs. Eddy, it symbolized the belief that Substance, Life, and Intelligence can be material; it signifies malicious animal power and the belief that organic life can produce sin, sickness, or death (15 *S&H* 514-515). This error seeks to destroy, both morally and physically (515).

When we read that the Dragon persecuted the Woman which brought forth the manchild, the reference, of course, must be to the enemies of divine Science. It is imperative, therefore, that all true believers expose this monster (522). And when "the serpent cast out of his mouth water as a flood, after the Woman..." (F 570 reads Christ-idea), the reference applies to all those who spewed forth torrents of mesmerism intended to overwhelm and destroy Christian Science and its Founder (522-523).

For the fiftieth edition of *Science and Health*, as we have already noted, the original version of the Apocalyptic Woman was rewritten and expanded from fourteen to twenty pages; here the author's claim to Christhood is set forth more explicitly (538-557). The Red Dragon here and in the final version is no longer Animal Magnetism; it becomes, instead, the serpent, who is also (d)evil and the delusion that there is intelligence in matter which can either benefit or injure men (F 567).

9. *Divine Science is the Little Book Open*. We find that also the "mighty angel" of Revelation 10:1-2, who "had in his hand a little book open," is a prefiguration of divine Science (558) and contains its revelation (559). Actually, it is *Science and Health with Key to the Scriptures*, concerning which the voice from heaven commanded, "Go and take the little book.... Take it and eat it...." Mortals should obey this heavenly gospel and accept divine Science. Read, study, and absorb this book (559).

10. *The New Jerusalem*. According to Swedenborg, the New Jerusalem which comes down from heaven and "lieth foursquare" was his reconstitution of Christianity. According to Ann Lee it was fulfilled in the Shaker communes. But, according to Mrs. Eddy it is the proclamation of a City the four sides of which are the Word, Christ, Christianity, and divine Science (575).

11. *The Dilemma*. Mrs. Eddy, torn between a desire to proclaim herself the

ultimate Christ and revelator and the certainty that doing so would provoke an avalanche of ridicule, searched for words and images which would declare this to the faithful and yet leave her free from the onus of such a claim among the unbelievers. Chapter XVI of *Science and Health* stands today as her ultimate effort in semantics.

12. *A Pictorial Apotheosis.* One of her boldest strokes of self-deification is found in the 1895 publication *Christ and Christmas*, to which the reaction was so hostile that she withdrew it from circulation for a time. When attacked by clergymen because of its illustrations, Mrs. Eddy's response was that these only "present the type and shadow of Truth's appearing in the womanhood as well as in the manhood of God, our divine Father and Mother" (*Mis.* 33). However, as the denunciations intensified, she declared: "Notwithstanding the rapid sale...of *Christ and Christmas*,... I have thought best to stop its publication," for it is unwise to cast "pearls before the unprepared thought" (307). In 1897, however, she reissued the work, which has since gone through many printings.

The poem, studded with Gnostic doctrine concerning the Christ that was never crucified, traces, in eleven scenes, the origin, proliferation, and final triumph of Christian Science. The ninth stanza and accompanying painting depict Jesus accepting instruction from a woman teaching from a scroll named Christian Science; and in the tenth, the same personage, carrying the same scroll, is knocking at the door of a fine home filled with merrymakers. The final scene shows a shadowy earth, burdened with a huge, black cross; but, above it, we see another decked with flowers and encircled with birds, and beyond this, a white dove and the Cross of Christian Science soaring aloft into the celestial realms.

13. *Hailed as a Divinity.* Augusta Stetson, the most successful Christian Science organizer, who built the magnificent New York Church, attributed to Mrs. Eddy even greater attributes of divinity. And Alice Orgain, in two books discussing the progressive editions of the Church *Manual* and *Science and Health*, saw in every word uttered or written and in every act performed by Mrs. Eddy portents of universal significance for the destiny of all mankind. The attitude of the faithful Julia Field-King, an educated and cultured woman, later excommunicated, was probably typical. In a letter to Mrs. Eddy, she declared: "I see that a greater than Jesus is here," who is "the divinely chosen of Divine Principle for a present Savior...You," she added, "have been appointed as my Wayshower, and I will follow even to the hour of the Ascension.... Science and Health...is the Absolute Word of God to me" (Ditt. 311).

14. *Tomlinson's Deification.* It remained, however, for that same Irving Tomlinson who, lying on his knees, begged the letters Mrs. Eddy had written to her son to write the definitive apotheosis which Christian Science has

bestowed upon its founder—all denials to the contrary emanating from the Board of Directors notwithstanding. In his *Revelation of St. John an Open Book*, he wrote 257 pages to expound precisely, verse by verse, how every facet of Christian Science was foretold in the Apocalypse.

15. *The Ultimate Christ.* In the Roman Catholic Church, the Virgin Mary is the Intercessor for sinners, the Queen of Heaven, the Patroness of America, and the Mother of the Church; but the founder of Christian Science persuaded her followers to accept her as the Second Christ made manifest in the Superior Female and the dominant aspect of an omnipresent, omnipotent, modalistic Trinity. Edwin Franden Dakin remarks that of all the miracles that exist in this world, there is none to compare with the capacity of humanity TO BELIEVE.

XIV. LATER THEOLOGICAL ABSORPTIONS

1. *From Shakerism.* It should be emphasized that Mrs. Eddy's appropriation of distinctively Shaker doctrine came late in her development; it is apparent for the first time in the sixteenth edition of *Science and Health*, which is distinguished by a chapter on the Apocalypse embodying Mrs. Eddy's Shakerite doctrines concerning herself. But even at that point (1886), she had not yet adopted the Mother-Father theology which, in due course, became central in her system and which is generally considered the most significant contribution of Ann Lee to modern religious ideology.

Only five miles from Sanbornton Bridge, where Abigail Baker went following her marriage, and to which Mary herself moved at the age of fifteen with her family, was the Shaker commune of East Canterbury, to which Mary refers in a letter (Dak. 13) dated the next year. There can be no doubt that she had heard much of these strange people, their heretical tenets, and their unconventional practices.

In her maturity, Mrs. Eddy incorporated into her system a variety of distinctively Shaker doctrines: (1) that God is masculine and feminine, the Father-Mother Deity; (2) that she was herself the bearer of the same Christ-power demonstrated in Jesus, but now manifested in the female; (3) that she embodied the Motherhood of God and was therefore to be called Mother with the connotations of divinity; (4) that she was the Woman of the Apocalypse; (5) that she had been forced to flee into the wilderness (from Lynn, even as Ann Lee was driven from England) because of the vicious attacks of the Great Red Dragon; (6) that she was persecuted by the Serpent, or M.A.M., because of her devotion to the Christ-Gospel; (7) that God created Adam in his own image so that generic man comprised both sexes; (8) that sexual generation is to be abolished or made unnecessary in the higher form of religion or Divine Science about to be established; (9) that, since Woman is more spiritual than man, she must be the bearer of this new and final dispensation of Christianity,* and (10) that Mrs. Eddy, like Ann Lee, holds a position superior to that of Jesus. In addition, Mrs. Eddy, like Ann Lee, called her cult the Church of Christ; and both called their central headquarters the Mother Church.

The manner in which Shaker ideology influenced Mrs. Eddy in her maturity can be seen also in her spiritual interpretation of the Lord's Prayer. In the version found in the sixteenth edition of her text, the deity is addressed as the "Divine Supreme Being, who art in eternal harmony..." (494). In the fiftieth, however, the Shaker concept of God has attained full stature. Here (322, F 16) the spiritual interpretation reads: "Our Father and Mother God, all-harmonious..." Finally, the God of dual sex, unknown in the earlier chapters called Creation and Genesis, becomes an important feature in the Key to the Scriptures (F 516, 529).

Shakerism and Christian Science, of course, have various other doctrines in common, such as their eschatology, Gnostic Christology, impersonal theology, spiritual healing, ethical redemption, and the belief that the purpose of the Christ-Gospel is to achieve the health, happiness, success, and economic well-being in this world.

2. *From Swedenborg.* Although various Swedenborgian elements were transmitted by Quimby to Mrs. Patterson, it is apparent that in later years she began an independent study of the Swedish seer; for, at first gradually, and then in increasing volume, we find specific Swedenborgian elements which are present neither in Quimby nor in her own earlier works. Since we have already noted this, we need now only offer a brief summary.

We know that Mrs. Eddy had become acquainted with the Church of the New Jerusalem before 1878, because, in the second edition of *Science and Health*, she states that the Swedenborgians declare that Life is God (122). However, as she drank more deeply from this source, it is never mentioned again.

Distinctive Swedenborgian expressions began to appear in her works after 1880. For example, she speaks of "the influx of divine interpretation," "spiritual influx," "the divine influx," "the influx of Divine Science," etc. (*My.* 114, 206, 212, and 62 *S&H* 348). Over and over, she used that favorite expression of Swedenborg, *in propria persona* or *personae* (*My.* 5, 25, 143, *Pul.* 1, etc.). In one place she speaks of "the divine Esse" (*My.* 202), a definite Swedenborgianism scarcely to be found anywhere else.

The evidence that Mrs. Eddy came under this direct influence after 1880 is quite conclusive. From the first through the fifteenth edition (1885) of *Science*

*There is an interesting touch which may be significant. Mrs. Eddy uses the word "happify" (1*S&H*315) and it is found in all editions of *Science and Health* (F57). This term was used in a popular Shaker song called "The Gospel Flame," *Sacred Hymns*, Canterbury, N.H., 1845.

and Health, there is a long and rambling chapter called Creation, which deals with Genesis only as if by accident. In the sixteenth, however, this was entirely rewritten and renamed Genesis; even more significant is the fact that it followed precisely the method used by Swedenborg in the *Arcana Coelestia*, a verse-by-verse exegesis in which each text is illumined by its spiritual interpretation. In the sixteenth edition, this material became Chapter XIII; and, in the fiftieth, it became Chapter XV, filled fifty-five pages, and assumed virtually its definitive form.

    3. *The Great Reconstitution.* The mature ideas of Mrs. Eddy concerning herself are, then, definitely Shakerite—those of her amazing forerunner, Ann Lee; but the format and the general coloring in which she presents them were modelled upon originals created by Swedenborg.

    New Thought, including Christian Science, which is a far-reaching reconstitution· and repudiation of historical Christianity, revolutionizes the entire New Testament Gospel, both in its Synoptic and Pauline-Johannine forms. It has as its objective the transformation of the conventional religion into a system of therapy, philosophy, and theology intended to confer health, success, and happiness upon the human race and to make life in the here and now a triumphant experience. Of all this, Emanuel Swedenborg was the supreme hierophant; and Mary Baker Eddy was one of the most remarkable laborers who have ever toiled in this vineyard of renascent faith. She and she alone could and did advance deific claims for herself and pontificate them in language that thousands would accept. This it was that set her apart among the stars in a position which no one else has ever been able to share.

    In this brief study, we have been able only to summarize some important elements of Christian Science and forced to omit others entirely. We should point out, however, that the cult utilized to the full the techniques of every successful new religion: while it purported to accept the historic and canonical Scripture and glorified its deified savior, it offered startlingly new interpretations of the former and an entirely novel concept of the latter. In addition, it offered new revelations, equal in authority to those long established, and thus created a bridge over which converts could march from their previous habitations into their new mansions. By so doing, they could embrace a profession which transformed the recipients into special vessels of enlightenment and superiority.

    By this process, Christian Science also forged its powerful hold upon converts and provided them with a faith that could withstand the shocks of defeat and laugh at every merely rational attempt to undermine or destroy it.

    For such is the nature of FAITH, devout and all-consuming.

Chapter 6

THE GREAT POPULARIZERS

I. INTRODUCTION

In this chapter, we present brief analyses of the teachings and philosophies of fourteen historic individuals who belong definitely in the cycle of New Thought and whose writings have exercised an enormous influence on the religious and therapeutic persuasions and practices, not only among the American people, but also of those in the entire Western world.

Although these differ in various details, they generally agree on a philosophic syndrome, largely Swedenborgian, summarized as follows:

1. That God is a great, central, and impersonal force and energy immanent in the universe as a whole and in every portion thereof. He may be regarded as a trinity in unity of modalistic manifestation.

2. That the universe is governed by immutable law; actually, God is identical with the universe and constitutes all substance.

3. That, since this is true, prayer addressed to the deity is as meaningless as a plea directed at an electric dynamo; that prayer can be nothing more than an expression of personal need and yearning. Affirmative prayer, however, is highly beneficial.

4. That a stream of influx flows into, or is available to, every human being from this source of energy, sometimes referred to as the Central Sun or Fire, which gives heat, light, and life to all that lives.

5. *That there is no such thing as inherited or original sin from which humanity need be redeemed.*

6. *That the orthodox doctrine of salvation or redemption through the sacrifice of Christ on the cross is entirely erroneous and must be rejected.*

7. *That Jesus was neither savior nor redeemer, but simply the Great Exemplar whose life and experience can foreshadow our own.*

8. *That every person is responsible for his own actions; and that personal salvation is the result of right living among our fellow-men.*

9. *That Christ is not a person or an entity, but a universal power of illumination available to every man, woman, and child.*

10. *That, since Christ became manifest so that we might have life and have it more abundantly, the purpose of true religion is realized when we achieve the utmost in health, success, prosperity, happiness, and well-being in every phase of life.*

11. *That death is merely a transition to another similar but more spiritualized life; and that heaven and hell are not places, but simply conditions of the mind and emotions.*

12. *That physical and mental health is and should be one of the prime objectives of religion.*

13. *That the human psyche exists on three levels: the conscious, the subconscious, and the superconscious; and that these are closely intertwined with and interdependent upon the health of the physical body.*

14. *That physical health can be achieved, according to some, in many instances, and, according to others, in all cases, by mental science, which consists in cleansing the mind or psyche of evil, corrosive, destructive, and negative beliefs, errors, or emotions.*

15. *That the Bible, properly interpreted, is a vast storehouse of wisdom and revealed religious truth; neverthless, much of it must never be taken literally, since its spiritual and true import differs radically from the literal meaning of its language.*

16. *That true religion may draw heavily from various, including occult, sources for verifications of Biblical revelation.*

17. *That heavy emphasis should be placed on mental therapy—sometimes almost to the exclusion of other techniques.*

18. *That extrasensory perception is a fact and that distant healing is a valid technique.*

19. *That what is called "supply" is not only a desirable objective, but that the good life in terms of the best housing, food, entertainment, etc. is a proper ingredient in religion.*

20. *That, since institutionalized ecclesiastism as found in the orthodox churches and in Christian Science leads to formalism and loss of freedom, specific organization should be, insofar as possible, rejected.*

21. That, therefore, the gospel of New Thought may best be propagated through books, lectures, classes, and personal contact.

22. That even though churches and denominations should be established in order to minister to those seeking more intimate and permanent fellowship, these should be entirely devoid of creeds, rites, specific doctrines, or centralized authority.

Virtually all of these principles were fully enunciated by Swedenborg, who was the guiding light of the Shaker theoretician Frederick William Evans; the John the Baptist of Ann Lee, foundress of the movement; the mentor of Warren Felt Evans, the great New Thought innovator; a personal guide for both Phineas Quimby and Mrs. Eddy. Horatio Dresser and Henry Drummond were ordained Swedenborgian ministers; and the Unitarians who founded Brook Farm later became full-fledged Swedenborgians, as was the elder Henry James. Almost every New Thought writer or teacher exhibits a direct or indirect, but pervasive, Swedenborgian influence.

We should note again that Swedenborg encompassed a number of elements which few of those who drew upon him, except those belonging to the Church of the New Jerusalem, have accepted in their entirety. Few, for example, in New Thought adopted his teachings concerning infestation by evil spirits; and fewer still his declarations concerning the Last Judgment of 1757 or the vast and cavernous domains of Hell, where the wicked undergo eternal vastation. All this was simply ignored and forgotten by the hosts who eagerly embraced other teachings which we have summarized. Some who accepted his speculative doctrines established communal societies, which would have been anathema to him had he lived to witness them. Thus, it was possible for Ralph Waldo Emerson to reject certain portions of Swedenborg as fantasies and yet confer greater praise upon him than upon any other representative man in all history.

There have, of course, been a host of important New Thought proponents— lecturers, writers, teachers, theoreticians, philosophers. We would like to summarize the messages of others in addition to those discussed in the following pages: however, space does not permit; and we believe that those we present contain the principal and basic ideologies found in the movement.

II. THE UNITARIAN SWEDENBORGIANS

Although the eminent English Unitarian and scientist Joseph Priestley came to the United States in 1794, where he soon established a congregation in Philadelphia, William Ellery Channing is considered the "father" of American Unitarianism. He became the leader of a Unitarian group in 1819 and was the founder and principal organizer of the Unitarian Association in 1825. Having embraced what was virtually the ancient Arian theology, he became the first native American heresiarch. However, once the wall of orthodoxy was breached, others soon went far beyond their precursor.

Among these, Ralph Waldo Emerson (1803-1882) was the most famous; he holds also a unique and honored position in American letters. Since he was an inveterate individualist, it would be inaccurate to describe him as a Swedenborgian or to place any other label upon him; for his was an immense intellect which absorbed various elements from disparate sources. Yet the Swedenborgian influence probably transcended all others of a specifically religious nature. Although he rejected the Swedenborgian revelations in regard to hell, heaven, and the Last Judgment as figments of the imagination that should now be discarded,[1] he discovered a great deal in the Swedish seer that was not only unique, but also truth, impregnable to attack. Emerson declared, therefore, that supreme honor was due this Representative Man.

Emerson's 1838 Divinity School Address at Harvard was a landmark in American religion and philosophy. Paying homage to Swedenborg by name, its total thrust, from beginning to end, is based on the concept that the central sun is the divine power of the universe, the deific power which fills and animates all things, whether they be stars, trees, men, or grains of sand. God is the vital, omnipresent power without which there would be nothing but darkness and death. Emerson's religion deifies Nature and makes each man and woman a divine creature of the cosmos. Here the Swedenborgian ethic becomes also a soteriology: "He who does a good deed is instantly ennobled. He who does a mean deed is by the action itself contracted. He who puts off impurity...so far is he God...Thus of their volition souls proceed into heaven, into hell."[2]

In his theological cosmology, "one mind is everywhere active, in each ray of the star, in each wavelet of the pool...Good is positive. Evil is merely privative... like cold. All things proceed out of the same spirit...The perception of this law of laws awakens in the mind a sentiment which we call the religious.... By it is the universe made safe and habitable...."[3]

Emerson repudiates the superstructure of Christian theology and, in the tradition of Swedenborg, erects in its place a faith based upon the Over-Soul and the Cosmic Natural God. "Yourself," he proclaims, "a new-born bard of the Holy Ghost, cast behind you all conformity, and acquaint men at first hand with Deity."[4] Addressing the seminarians directly, he declared: All men "with you are open to the influx of the all-knowing Spirit, which annihilates before its broad noon the little shades and gradations of intelligence...."[5]

Among Emerson's *Representative Men* (written about 1845-1846), Swedenborg alone appears as seer and prophet. "This man," he declares, "who appeared to his contemporaries as a visionary...no doubt led the most real life of any man then in the world: and...he begins to spread himself into the minds of thousands."[6] "A colossal soul, he lies vast abroad on his times, uncomprehended by them, and requires a long focal distance to be seen...."[7] Emerson pours forth tribute after tribute: "The moral insight of Swedenborg, the correction of popular errors, the announcements of ethical laws take him out of comparison with any modern writer and entitle him to a place, vacant for some ages, among the lawgivers of mankind. That slow but commanding influence which he has acquired...must of course have its tides, before it subsides into a permanent amount. What is real and universal cannot be confined to the circle of those who sympathize strictly with his genius, but will pass forth into the common stock of wise and just thinking. The world...attracts what is excellent in its children, and lets fall the infirmities and limitations of the grandest mind."[8]

And again: "The genius of Swedenborg, largest of all modern souls in the department of thought, wasted itself in an endeavor to reanimate and conserve what had already arrived at its natural term...." Yet "his books have become a monument...in this immolation of genius and fame at the shrine of conscience, [there] is a merit sublime beyond praise. He lived to a purpose; he gave a verdict. He elected goodness as the clue to which the soul must cling.... he observed and published the laws of nature.... he was fired with piety at the harmonies he felt, and abandoned himself to his joy and worship.... If the glory was too bright for his eyes to bear, if he staggered under the trance of delight, the more excellent is the spectacle...of being which beam[s] and blaze[s] through him...."[9]

None of the other Representative Men—Plato, Montaigne, Shakespeare, Napoleon, and Goethe—were deemed worthy of such accolades.

How rapidly and far afield some of the Unitarians moved from the position of William E. Channing is reflected in that extraordinary phenomenon established near West Roxbury, Massachusetts and known as Brook Farm. Channing's nephew, William Henry Channing (1810-1884), afire with zeal for a socialist-communal society to be modeled upon the Christian gospel, became the moving spirit of this experiment conducted on a 200-acre farm where all were to receive equal emoluments, work for the common good, and create the evangelistic force that would transform the whole of society into a universal communal brotherhood. Emerson, the individualist, was skeptical; Hawthorne, the realist, although a Unitarian, was contemptuous. Nevertheless, a band of dedicated idealists set out in 1841 to transform the human race and establish forthwith the Kingdom of Heaven on earth, as set forth in the Christian gospel. In one proclamation after another, the Brook Farmers declared that their movement was literally the Second Coming of Christ.

However, since these men and women were intellectuals, quite emancipated from the imperatives which sustained the Shaker communes, the original experiment was very short-lived. Alas and alack! few indeed were prepared to risk their time and savings in a venture dedicated simply to the good of humanity. The unlettered, thus again, proved far wiser than the learned.

This was precisely the time when the Fourierist societies were spreading in the United States. About the end of 1843 or the beginning of 1844, Brook Farm reconstituted itself as a Fourier phalanx, a quasi-communal corporation in which marriage would be abolished, a complex form of community sex-relationship established, and wages commensurate with production given to everyone, plus interest on money invested in the project. Early in 1845, the Farm dedicated itself to the propagation of this gospel and sent lecturers out to popularize it and create new phalanxes. "We have a solemn and glorious work before us," declared Channing in his *Appeal to Associationists*. "1, To indoctrinate the whole people of the United States with the principles of associative unity; 2, To prepare for the time when the nation, like one man, shall reorganize its townships upon the basis of perfect justice...This is a Christian Nation; and Association shows how human societies may be so organized in devout obedience to the will of God, as to become true brotherhoods, where the command of universal love may be fulfilled indeed."[10]

Financing, as usual, was the principal problem. With land valued at $30,000, the community collected funds for a building program, which included a central structure 50 x 175 feet, begun in 1844 and intended to house many of its residents and supply offices for its activities. On March 31, however, the uninsured building, seventy per cent complete, burned to the ground in ninety minutes; and this was the death-knell of Fourierism at Brook Farm.

Then—no one seems to know precisely how—Brook Farm was transformed into a center for Swedenborgianism; and, by a strange irony, for a second time on American soil, its religious concepts (although dedicated to free enterprise) were absorbed by a group of talented individuals who had at one time been dedicated to the doctrines and practices of Essene-Christian communalism. Among its members were a number of Unitarian leaders, including W.E. Channing, Margaret Fuller, George Ripley, Theodore Parker, Charles A. Dana, John S. Dwight, Parke Godwin, Murat Pratt, and Elizabeth Peabody, who became its American hierophants. Half a dozen periodicals emanating from Brook Farm or under the control of its leaders proclaimed to the world the sublime doctrines of the Swedish seer. In addition, a group of talented and educated men explained them from their pulpits, and in the classrooms of liberal seminaries. They were adopted by philosophers such as the elder Henry James; through many channels, they began to permeate the whole culture and to become a definite element in the American heritage. Those who adopted Swedenborgianism as a total revelation were then and have ever since remained few; but those who accepted certain elements expanded into millions until scarcely anyone remained wholly untouched.

One of the leading personalities in the development of American Unitarianism was Theodore Parker (1810-1860). If we are justified in calling Emerson a fifty percent Swedenborgian, it would be accurate to classify Parker as seventy-five percent of that persuasion. As a leader among the Brook Farm radicals, he was openly identified with, and committed to, this theology; and, as such, represents an extreme Unitarian development. He fought for women's suffrage and against slavery; denounced the war of 1846-1848;[11] conspired with, and aided, John Brown; was condemned and ostracized by the majority of his own church. Instead of proclaiming the mystical Over-Soul of Emerson, his was a rationalist theology. He stated categorically that Jesus was not the son of God,[12] that the Old Testament and most of the Bible stories were nothing but myths and fables,[13] that Nature is our only true religious book,[14] and that creeds and sacraments are worthless.[15] Like various ancient Gnostics and the modern Mormons and Christian Scientists, he postulated a Mother-Father God.[16] Love, he said, is the feminine savior of mankind.[17]

Swedenborgian concepts permeate Parker's thinking, in which God is the Central Sun of the Universe. Among his works, we find a series of so-called Prayers which are actually invocations, since it was inconceivable to him that God would intervene in the individual affairs of men. God is the "Central Fire, and Radiant Light of all," and the "Infinite Spirit who thyself art perpetual presentness, whom the heaven of heavens cannot contain, but who hast thy dwelling place in every little flower that blooms, and in every humble heart...."[18]

And again re-echoing the modalist Trinity of Servetus and Swedenborg: "The stone I sit on is in communion with God, the pencil I write with, the gray field fly reposing in the sunshine at my foot. Let God withdraw from the space occupied by the stone, the pencil, the fly, they cease to be...The mineral, the vegetable, and the animal represent three modes of existence; and hence so many modes and degrees of dependence on God and of communion with him...."[19] "Should God withdraw himself or any of his qualities from my mind, I could not think; from consciousness, I should know nothing of the right; from the heart, there could be no love; from the soul, there could be no holiness, no faith in Him who made it."[20]

The doctrine of influx pervades Parker's thought: "Thus does the man, that will, hold commune with his Father, face to face, and get great income from the Soul of all.... Thus...human souls communicate with the great central Fire and Light of all the world, the loadstone of the universe, and thus grow... blessed and strong."[21]

As Parker discarded the historic doctrines and practices of the old churches, he embraced the Swedenborgian concepts to an ever-increasing degree. "Our Father and our Mother," he cries, "we thank thee for that transcendent world near to the earth of matter and the soul of man, wherein thou dwellest, thou and the blessed spirits thou enclosest, as the sea her multitudinous and her fruitful waves."[22] And again: "We thank thee for the just ones made perfect who have gone from us, and those who in their imperfection have been translated, for we know that thou placest them in the line of advancement, and leadest them ever upwards, and still further on."[23]

Thus it is clear that the Unitarian movement during the middle of the 19th century developed largely on a Swedenborgian base and made significant contributions to what eventually came to be known as New Thought. It was therefore no accident that a considerable number of Unitarian—and sometimes Universalist—clergymen transferred in the course of time to New Thought pulpits before and shortly after the turn of the century.

III. HENRY JAMES, SR.

William James (1778-1832) was an Irish Presbyterian immigrant who arrived in this country in 1793, accumulated a considerable fortune, established himself as a leading, solid citizen of Albany, New York, and reared a large family there, of whom the most outstanding was Henry James, Sr. (1811-1882).

It is a never-ending cause for amazement to observe how the disciples of the Swede differ in their Swedenborgianism. In our first chapter, we summarized his theology and philosophy with, we believe, correct proportional emphasis on each of its elements. Yet Henry James, Sr., who considered himself a Swedenborgian *par excellence*, ignores much that is central in his mentor. In several areas he is actually in basic disagreement. The truth is that he, like so many others, by eclectic absorption, appropriated only those metaphysical concepts that appealed to him.

In his lucubrations, James dealt entirely in speculation concerning matters that have little relevance to practical life. This may have resulted from the freedom conferred upon him by inherited wealth, and from his personal antipathy to the stern theology and the materialistic interests of his father. If so, he was not the last rich man's son who turned to socialism in emotional reaction.

In 1830, Henry graduated from Union College, to which his father had made large contributions; and in 1835 he matriculated at Princeton Theological Seminary, where, at the age of twenty-eight, he first discovered his antipathy to the dogmas of Calvinism and where he abandoned both the school and his father's religion at the same time.

On his first journey to England in 1837, Henry encountered his second great intellectual influence: Sandemanianism, an antinomian cult which had a brief career but which so entranced him—albeit briefly—that he edited and published its principal publication, *Letters on Theron and Aspasio*.

He was married in 1840 and had two sons—both of whom became famous American men of letters—born in 1842 and 1843: William, the psychologist-philosopher; and Henry, Jr., the novelist, who made a career of analyzing and delineating upper-class frustrations.

In 1844, he was again in England, where he was plunged into an emotional and physical depression so devastating that he lost all will to live: overcome by a sense of shame, guilt, and unworthiness, he could find neither meaning nor objective in existence. Then "one day," he explains, " 'fear came upon me, and trembling, which, made all my bones shake.' To all appearances, it was a perfectly insane and abject terror.... I felt myself a complete wreck, that is, reduced from a state of firm, vigorous, joyful manhood to one of almost helpless infancy. The only self-control I was capable of exerting was to keep my seat. I felt the greatest desire to run...for help to my wife—to run to the roadside even, and appeal to the public to protect me.... this ghastly condition of mind continued....for two years...."[1]

Hoping to find revival from this depression, he sought the Water Cure in Devonshire, where he met a Swedenborgian lady who explained that he was merely undergoing "vastation"—an experience prerequisite for the New Birth, the secret of divine creation and providence. He was so impressed that he journeyed to London, where he purchased copies of *The Divine Love and Wisdom* and *The Divine Providence*. As their message flowed through his mind, he experienced his Great Illumination. "Imagine," he wrote many years later, "a fever patient, sufficiently restored of his malady to be able to think of something beside himself, suddenly transported where the free airs of heaven blow upon him and the sound of running waters refreshes his jaded senses, and you have a feeble imagine of my delight in reading. Or, better still, imagine a subject of some petty despotism condemned to die.... lifted by a sudden miracle into felt harmony with universal man, and filled to the brim with sentiment of indestructible life instead, and you will have a true picture of my emancipated condition."[2]

And, he continued: "Swedenborg's writings...[bring] to the aching heart and the void mind...famished upon those gross husks of religious doctrine whether orthodox or Unitarian.... infinite balm and contentment."[2] Elsewhere, he declares: "The incomparable depth and splendor of Swedenborg's genius are shown in this, that he alone of men has ever dared to bring creation within the bounds of consciousness—within the grasp of the soul...."[3]

Here and now, as C. Hartley Grattan observes, "Henry James had found his truth. Henceforth he never travelled without carrying Swedenborg's works along with him."[4] He also became a close friend of James John Garth

Wilkinson, the English Swedenborgian, who gave the world a beautiful translation of his master's works.

During the remainder of his life, James published a dozen books, all of which are Swedenborgian analyses of speculative metaphysics.

Back again in America, James made extensive contacts with the Brook-Farm Fourierists, and was smitten with his own concepts of what he called Spiritual Socialism, which became the fourth element in his metaphysical system. Once again, Swedenborg, the inveterate economic individualist, was pressed into service for Christian collectivism; but it was a strange amalgam which James espoused to the end, long after the Unitarians and Transcendalists had abandoned Fourierism. In 1850, he wrote: "Socialism promises to make God's great life in man possible, promises to make all our relations so just, so beautiful and helpful, that we shall be no longer conscious of finiteness, or imperfection, but only of life and power utterly infinite.... Every one who trusts in a living and therefore active God...behooves to acquaint himself forthwith with the marvelous literature of Socialism, above all with the writings of Charles Fourier."[5]

We believe that Swedenborg provided such an infinite experience because in him James found the instruments with which to demolish not only the claims of the medieval authoritarian church, but also those of Calvinism, Sandemanianism, Protestantism in general, and even the current Arian Unitarianism. Fourierism probably attracted him because it nourished perhaps an unconscious resentment to his father's aggressive materialism. Yet, whenever James discovered a new enlightenment, he superimposed this upon his previous persuasions.[6] Thus, he never discarded completely either the Calvinism or the Antinomianism of his earlier days.

James explains repeatedly that democracy implies the disappearance of both the state and Protestantism and the subsequent disintegration of the Church.[7] Since he was opposed to authoritarianism and ecclesiastical institutionalism, this seemed to him the very essence of progress; and, with Whitman, he was persuaded that humanity is certain to advance.[8] He even condemned the Swedenborgians for establishing The Church of the New Jerusalem;[9] he referred to Mormonism as "downright deviltry."[10] And even though he proclaimed the principles of Fourierism, he made it plain that he was not interested in any specific experiment.

Instead, he envisioned what he called the Christian Church "because all but it are destitute of a philosophic basis, that is, [they] profess no doctrine of God in nature, but only in the private soul. The Christian Church is immortal because its fundamental dogma involves a doctrine of God so ample and clear, as to satisfy every profoundest want of the heart and every most urgent demand of the head towards God forever."[11]

In his beatific visions, James saw a church that would be coextensive with society and based on a Socialist-Fourierist reorganization in which all members would come to a full understanding of God and their correlation with him. He declares that "what attracts me in Socialism" is "the unconscious service it renders to the divine life in me, the complete inauguration and fulfillment it affords to the Christian hope of individual perfection."[12] And he continues: "Socialism alone supplies the science of this great consummation. It reveals the incessant operation of laws by which man's physical and social relations will be brought into the complete subjection of his inward or divine personality. It is the demonstration of a plenary unity between man and nature and man and man."[13]

Although James accepted the ethical principles of Swedenborg, vestiges of Calvinism remained; in one passage he declared that "redemption is an objective work, or an exclusively Divine proceeding which took place centuries before we were born...quite independent for its truth both upon our knowledge and belief."[14] And his concept of evil is semi-Calvinist, for he states that "a man becomes spiritually evil *originally* or from within himself, by resisting 'that great unitary life of God in our nature, which we call society, fraternity, fellowship, equality, and which from the beginning of human history has been struggling to work itself...into final, perfect and objective recognition....' "[15] This is curiously similar to the Essene-Gospel doctrine, which assumes that whoever refuses to join the community of saints thereby rejects redemption and salvation.

In most aspects of his thought, however, James reproduces the Swedenborgian ideology accurately. Like countless other proponents of New Thought, he embraced a Gnostic Christology, in which the second attribute in a Trinity of manifestation becomes the Christ-Power, a deific emanation available to every member of the human race.[16] As Frederic H. Young notes, "James derived the basic structure and much of his philosophical terminology from the Swedish thinker," especially in regard to moral perfection, the spiritual creation, the trinity of operational manifestation, the nature of the Esse or Divine Substance, the Central Sun of the Universe as God, and the nature of the so-called Incarnation.[17] James adopted fully the Swedenborgian concept of influx, which flows into every man and woman from the central sun as well as from the spirits in the spirit-world, in the existence of which he had a childlike faith and where he was certain he would one day rejoin his adorable wife.[18]

The theology of James is certainly Swedenborgian: "God," we read, "is the sole substance or reality of everything embraced in the sensible universe, from its central sun to the planetary earths that encircle it, and from these again to the tiniest mineral, vegetable, and animal forms that enliven their surface."[19]

Since it is a fact that a great and ultimate influence is wielded by those whose thought permeates the great popularizers, there can be little doubt that the philosophy of Henry James, Sr., has affected millions who are not aware of its source. Although his sons were neither Swedenborgians nor protagonists of New Thought, *per se*, various elements of this nature filtered through them into the general stream of culture. The docetic Christology of James; his theology which postulates a deity who is also the central sun, and his concept of Christianity as a spiritual socialism which would one day create the ideal and perfect society, all distinguish him as one of that galaxy of Americans who belong definitely in the New Thought tradition and who contributed to the establishment of a religion of health, happiness, and prosperity.

IV. HENRY DRUMMOND

During his brief life, Henry Drummond (1851-1897), who began his education at the University of Edinburgh, became not only an evangelical in the spirit of Moody and Sankey, but developed also into an outstanding scientific exponent of Swedenborgianism, wherein he made a unique and creative contribution to New Thought. He wrote a number of immensely popular books and tracts, among which *The Greatest Thing in the World*—circulated in millions of copies—is the best known. In 1888, he published *Tropical Africa* and in 1894 *The Ascent of Man*, both of which evince deep sympathy for, and understanding of, animals. Since, like Swedenborg, he was deeply versed in scientific lore, it was no accident that his *Natural Law in the Spiritual World*, which, throughout, bears the imprint of Swedenborg, should be recognized as the foremost attempt of the 19th century to base revealed Christianity upon a scientific foundation. In 1877, he lectured on science at the Free College of Glasgow; and in 1884, he became a minister-professor in the Church of the New Jerusalem.

Drummond declares that since the "difficulty...which men of Science feel about religion is real and inevitable,"[1] it is necessary to show, not merely that there is no contradiction between them, but also that there is, on the contrary, a sublime and universal agreement. No one who "feels the universal need of a Religion, can stand idly by while the intellect of the age is slowly divorcing itself from" religion.[2] What must be done, therefore, is to establish "the naturalness of the supernatural...."[3] And even as Newton and other scientists have demonstrated the reign of law in the Natural World, so must we "see the Reign of Law...in the Spiritual Sphere."[4] If the reign of law were not universal, the cosmos would quickly descend into a state of chaos.[5]

Throughout, the author seeks to equate the two realms: just as science demonstrates the Rule of Law in the natural world, so does revelation give concomitant evidence of Law in the Spiritual. And the first foundation on which this edifice is constructued is the Swedenborgian Law of Correspondence. "Is there not reason to believe," he demands, "that many of the Laws of the Spiritual World...are simply the Laws of the Natural World?"[6] And he continues: did the Creator "divide the world into two, a cosmos and a chaos...?" Since this is impossible, we are told that "the Phenomena of the Spiritual World are in analogy with the Phenomena of the Natural World...."[7] Drummond reproduces a Swedenborgian passage which states his own view: " 'In our doctrine of representations and correspondences, we shall treat of both' " as if " 'the physical world was purely symbolical of the spiritual world.' "[8] Its laws are, therefore, not only "analogous to the Natural Laws, but...they *are the same Laws.*"[9] According to Drummond's Law of Continuity, which is the Law of Laws, the lowest form of matter (the inorganic) proceeds upward through the vegetative, the animal, the human, and finally to the everlasting existence in the world of spirits.[10] This follows from the fact that the precedent spiritual world was the model after which the natural was formed.[11]

Since the reign of law is universal, it must exist also in the spiritual world;[12] otherwise religion and theology would be totally without foundation.[13] The latter have, in the past, depended upon authority; but now "a new basis" in universal law "must be sought and found" for them.[14] We must have a scientific theology, and we must proceed on the basis of a "Positive method of thought."[15] As for proof of life in the spiritual world, this will be discovered in the same manner as in the natural.[16] Thus it is that the latter becomes spiritual; for "Nature is not a mere image or emblem of the Spiritual. It is a working model...."[17]

Science has done much to purify religion;[18] but "with the inspiration of Nature to illuminate what.... Revelation has left obscure, heresy in certain whole departments shall become impossible.... Theology must draw upon...the seen for the further revelation of the unseen."[19] Therefore "the greatest among the theological Laws are the Laws of Nature in disguise."[20] The Creator would "simply project the higher Laws downward so that the Natural World would become an incarnation, a visible representation, a working model of the Spiritual."[21]

In a series of chapters, the author elaborates his position partly by science, partly by revelation. The first of these, called Biogenesis, lays down the thesis that like can spring only from like; matter from pre-existing matter, vegetation from vegetation, etc.; and, finally, the Spiritual Life can come only from the pre-existing and eternal Spiritual Life, which, in Drummond's Swedenborgian system, is God.[22] The proposition is presented in detail; it means in short that "the Spiritual Life is the gift of the Living Spirit."[23] And he declares: "With the elevation of Biogenesis to the rank of scientific fact, all problems concerning the Origin of Life" are solved.[24] Since there is no life in inorganic matter,[25] and since there is "no passage from one Kingdom to another...the intervention of Life is a scientific necessity...."[26]

What, then, is the life that is given to man? It is the "Christ" which "is the source of Life in the Spiritual World";[27] and "a remarkable harmony exists here between the Organic World as arranged by Science and the Spiritual World as arranged by Scripture."[28] And so "the inquiry into the Origin of Life is the fundamental question alike of Biology and Christianity."[29]

This leads directly to Drummond's Swedenborgian explication of soteriology. The difference between the Christian and the non-Christian is neither in intellect nor morality: it is the possession of something here called Life, and is similar to what differentiates the Organic from the Inorganic.[30] "He who lives the Spiritual Life has a distinct kind of Life added to all other phases..." thereof;[31] and this determines "*what he shall be.*"[32] There is life in plants, insects, and animals;[33] but when a man has the Christ within him, he has "an endowment from the Spiritual World...."[34] We are redeemed, not through a vicarious atonement, but by living the Christ-Life, which we achieve by acting unselfishly for the benefit of mankind; and we do this, not because it will eventuate in a final reward, but because our basic nature is so transformed *that we cannot do otherwise.*[35]

The chapter entitled Degeneration[36] notes that unless we work with our limbs, they lose their power and atrophy; likewise, unless we exercise ourselves in virtue, the soul dies.[37] Unless we develop the capacity to escape from the world of sin and selfishness, we can never "escape to heaven"; for "where is the capacity for heaven to come from if it be not developed on earth?"[38] "Escape," says Drummond, "means nothing more than the gradual emergence of the higher from the lower.... It means the gradual putting off of all that cannot enter into the higher state, or heaven, and...the putting on of Christ."[39] The good life "being a germ of the Christ-Life, it must unfold into *a Christ.*"[40] "The regenerate soul is a new creature in...Christ-Jesus."[41]

In the chapter titled Growth, Drummond explains the force which propels this development, and here he comes very close to a new concept of election or predestination.[42] "The Lord God is a Sun,"[43] we read, who "lives and moves and has his being in them" who receives his grace but who, in themselves, neither earn nor manufacture anything.[44] Like the mariner who "puts his sail and rudder in position," the Christian experiences a miracle: even as the wind fills the sails of the ship, "so, holding himself in position before God's Spirit, all the energies of Omnipotence course within his soul."[45] With this influx of divine power, he is gradually transformed into an entity suitable for progression in the Spiritual World.

In the chapter called Death, Drummond emphasizes that this is a law in the Spiritual as well as in the Natural World. Even as atrophy occurs constantly in the organic world, so does it in the spiritual. If men do not rise to communion with the Spiritual, they will descend into dust, and their residue will be resolved into its inorganic elements.[46]

This brings us to Drummond's Swedenborgian concept of God, who or which is that force or power in the universe from which Life emerges and without which the cosmos would be nothing more than inorganic matter. We may call our relation to this a correspondence or a communion without which we would be spiritually dead.[47]

There are those, we are told, who call Nature or the Cosmos God, but this is an error;[48] God is something more than the force and power in nature; he is rather "an ever-living and perfect Mind, supreme over the universe...." To believe in this "is to invest moral distinctions with immensity and eternity...to the imperishable theatre of all being."[49] God is the "Spiritual Environment" without which "there is no thought, no energy, nothing...."[50] Although, in the embryonic state all living creatures are virtually identical, God is the Life and the Artist which makes one embryo into a fish and another into a man.[51]

The chapter on Mortification is an elaboration of Drummond's soteriology. In order to gain the Spiritual Life, we must mortify ourselves to the world; and we find again a Swedenborgian concept: we must not steal, embezzle, deceive, exploit, indulge in evil temper, for, in so doing, we die in sin.[52] "The love of money up to a certain point" is necessary, and therefore good; "beyond that it may become the worst of sins."[53]

In the chapter on Eternal Life we read that organisms enjoy longevity in ratio to their complexity. And since human beings live longer than lower forms and are more complex, they approach more nearly the spiritual level. When "a spiritual organism" is in "perfect correspondence with a spiritual Environment," the "conditions necessary to Eternal Life are satisfied."[54]

It is interesting to note that while the orthodox churches repudiated the theory of evolution, Drummond, the scientist, postulated his entire system upon it: "the condition necessary for the further Evolution" of man "is that the spiritual be released from the natural. That is to say, the condition of the further Evolution is Death...the final sifting of all the correspondences is the indispensable factor of the higher Life.... This is the last and the greatest contribution to mankind. Over the mouth of the grave, the perfect and the imperfect submit to their final separation. Each goes to his own—earth to earth, ashes to ashes, dust to dust, Spirit to Spirit."[55] Here Drummond departs from Swedenborgianism, for in his own system there is no hell—only annihilation for the non-spiritual.

Once the transition to the Spiritual World has taken place, "the subtle influences which form and transform the soul are Heredity and Environment."[56] "Living in the spiritual world, nevertheless, is just as simple as living in the natural" for "there are not two kinds of worlds."[57] However, "in the spiritual world...we are new creatures" and must learn how to live there.[58] And even as one embryo becomes a bird, so is another, through the intervention of the Christ-Life, made into an image of Christ.[59]

The chapter on Semi-Parasitism[60] is a further development of Swedenborgian soteriology. The person who seeks salvation in the Roman Catholic or the Protestant churches is like the hermit crab, which moves into the shell abandoned by another crustacean and therefore loses the use of his limbs and becomes the host for parasites. The members of such churches depend upon an institution or on the atonement of Christ for redemption, rather than upon the exercise of their own capacities. The orthodox churches all preach a parasite-doctrine;[61] there can be no hope in or from a church which declares that "a blackguard from the streets" can, by agreeing to a "plausible formula," become an instantaneous convert. Between the Evangelical and Roman churches there is a deep affinity, and both are utterly false and immoral.[62] Salvation is possible only by achieving a *"likeness to Christ,"*[63] Seeking "a mechanical security that we may cover inertia and find a wholesale salvation in which there is no personal sanctification—this is Parasitism."[64]

If the hermit crab lives a semi-parasitical life, then the organism which receives its food and security from another is a total parasite, examples of which are frequent in nature. In the same manner, that person who accepts his Truth "by imbibation from the Church" soon finds that his "faculties for receiving the truth...become distorted. He who abandons the personal search for truth...abandons truth."[65] This is the condition of all those who accept their beliefs on authority.

This Draconian edict, reminiscent of Milton, is indeed strong medicine; but Drummond demands nothing less, for this only can serve as a passport to the spiritual world. He condemns the great churches in truly Swedenborgian terminology: "The effect of a doctrinal theology is the effect of Infallibility..." and the result "is mere Credulity...Those who framed the Thirty-Nine Articles or the Westminster Confession are responsible."[66] We must not accept the orthodox belief in the Trinity or the Atonement upon authority;[67] rather "we must work, think, separate, dissolve, absorb, digest; and" this we must do for ourselves.[68] "Better a little faith dearly won...than perish on the splendid plenty of the richest creeds."[69]

In the last chapter, Classification, Drummond declares that Christianity is a religion based on biological science;[70] that the Christian is separated from the world in his "uncompromising allegiance to the Kingdom of God;..."[71] that the kingdom which progresses beyond the Organic is the Spiritual, which is the Kingdom of God,[72] and that this is the goal of man's ultimate evolution.[73]

Drummond concludes with a statement stemming from Swedenborgian nebular theory: "Of the...first development of the earth from the nebular matrix of space, Science speaks with reserve. The second, the evolution of each individual from the simple protoplasmic cell to the formed adult, is proved. The still wider evolution...of all individuals...is at least suspected.... But now, at last, we see the Kingdoms themselves evolving. And that supreme law...now begins again directly the evolution of these million-peopled worlds as if they were simple cells or organisms.... This is the final triumph of Continuity, the heart secret of creation, the unspoken prophecy of Christianity. To Science...this mighty process...is simply *Evolution*. To Christianity.... it is *Redemption*."[74]

V. EMMA CURTIS HOPKINS

Emma Curtis Hopkins (1855-1925) was known as The Teacher of Teachers and the Grand Lady of New Thought. She taught classes in various cities which sometimes enrolled as many as 1,000 students, each of whom paid $50 for a two-week course of 12 lessons. For years, she operated the Christian Science Theological Seminary, established in Chicago in 1887. Charles Braden observes that a roster of those who received instruction from her "reads like a *Who's Who* among New Thought leaders. To name only a few, there were Frances Lord; Annie Rix Millitz and Harriet Rix; Malinda E. Cramer, co-founder of Divine Science; Mrs. Bingham, teacher of Nona L. Brooks; Helen Wilmans; Charles and Myrtle Fillmore, founders of the Unity School of Christianity; Charles A. and Josephine Barton, editor of *The Life*, in Kansas City, Missouri; Dr. H. Emilie Cady, writer" of Unity textbooks; "Ella Wheeler Wilcox, New Thought poetess; Elizabeth Towne...and Ernest Holmes, founder of the Church of Religious Science."[1]

Thus we see that, although Mrs. Hopkins did not establish a church of her own, she was instrumental in starting or shaping the careers of those who founded the most important New Thought organizations (not including the Christian Science Church) which exist today in the United States.

Mrs. Hopkins matriculated in Mrs. Eddy's Primary Class of December 1883. Her abilities must have been extraordinary for, instead of continuing with advanced studies or as a private practitioner, she became the editor of the *Christian Science Journal* in September 1884, and so continued for more than a year. However, she found the restrictions imposed upon her quite intolerable, and was dismissed from the post in October 1885 the reason being, according to Bates and Dittemore, that she was absorbing metaphysical material from sources other than Mrs. Eddy.[2] This is undoubtedly true, since her writings are studded with references to, or citations from, Emerson, Swedenborg, Eckhardt, Plato, Plotinus, Zoroaster, *The Book of the Dead*, and the *Bhagavad Gita*.

As a practitioner in Chicago in 1886, Mrs. Hopkins was still intensely loyal to Mrs. Eddy; we believe, in fact, that she would have preferred so to continue. However, her capacious and inquisitive mind led her into pathways which made her excommunication inevitable. In 1887 and again in 1888, Mrs. Eddy condemned her and Julius Dresser by name in the *Journal* as Mind-Quacks who were "spreading abroad patchwork books, false compendiums of my system, crediting some ignoramus or infidel with teachings they have stolen from me. The unweaned suckling whines while spitting out the breast-milk which sustained him...."[3]

By 1890, therefore, Mrs. Hopkins was well launched on her own brilliant career, which spanned several decades. The profound influence she exercised is reflected in a statement, probably written by Charles Fillmore, which appeared in *Modern Thought*, announcing a class to be conducted by her in Kansas City, beginning January 6, 1890. "She is undoubtedly the most successful teacher in the world.... in many instances those who enter her classes confirmed invalids come out at the end of the course perfectly well...her very presence heals and those who listen are filled with new life." He doubted that "ever before on this planet were such words of burning truth so eloquently spoken through woman."[4]

After the death of Mrs. Hopkins in 1925, her sister continued her work from headquarters established at Joy Farm (later High Watch Farm) in Connecticut. The operation was continued as the High Watch Fellowship at Cornwall Bridge. Excerpts from the writings of Mrs. Hopkins, entitled *Understanding the Scriptures*, were published in mimeographed form in 1940, as were the Twelve Lessons used in her classes and called *Scientific Christian Mental Practice*. The latter, published in a handsome printed volume in 1958, is available from the Rare Book Company in New York. This volume, as well as *Bible Interpretations, High Mysticism, Resumé*, and other works, may be obtained from the De Vorss Company in Los Angeles.

The literature of New Thought (1) is characterized by certain general and well-defined metaphysical premises; but (2) is distinguished also by a great variety of individual differences among its exponents. Whereas Christian Science imposed a total uniformity and conformity, many proponents reacted against this authoritarianism by permitting, even encouraging, an infinitude of variation. Thus, while Christian Science enjoys the security of certainty, New Thought luxuriates in freedom—a libertarianism which has fostered many remarkable careers, but has made it difficult to establish powerful sectarian denominations.

These facts are well illustrated in the career and teachings of Emma Curtis Hopkins. Her following was enormous; but, since she did not claim a special revelation or emphasize an authoritarian approach, her direct, personal influence died with her. Had it not been that some of those whom she inspired established organizations with vested property and revenue, she would now be little more than a memory.

Since she began her career as the editor of the *Christian Science Journal* and called her school the Christian Science Theological Seminary, and was, moreover, an ardent admirer of Mary Baker Eddy, it is not surprising that her class instruction comes nearer to orthodox Christian Science than those of most of the other New Thought teachers. In her own writings, as in *Science and Health*, we find a virtual denial of material existence. Since God is All-Good, sin and sickness are false affirmations;[5] in the twelve lessons, her system is often referred to as Christian Science; one of the first things she impressed upon her students was her Statement of Being, which reminds us of Mrs. Eddy's and is the title of Lesson One. She repeats Mrs. Eddy's basic dictum that there is no life, substance, or intelligence in matter;[6] and declares categorically that there is no sin, sickness, or death[7] and that all illness results from false belief.[8] Doctors, we read, think the healing power acts through drugs, but the Scientist knows that the cure comes from the belief in their efficacy.[9]

Mrs. Hopkins, however, not only deleted from her system several elements that are crucial in *Science and Health* such as Malicious Animal Magnetism and the near-deification of Mary Baker Eddy, she also added others, or at least developed them on a new basis. She called the commonly held errors of mankind—who look upon sin, evil, sickness, poverty, and death as inevitable—race beliefs[10] or race iniquities,[11] a concept found also in the ideology of Troward and Holmes. She declared over and over—in fact, it was the basis of her therapy—that sin, sickness, poverty, etc. do not exist at all, and that the cure of those who have false beliefs consists simply in declaring them non-existent.

Even St. Augustine sometimes interpreted Scripture "spiritually"—a technique which Swedenborg and Quimby and New Thought in general elevated into a kind of science. However, nowhere have we found such interesting and radical examples of the method as in Mrs. Hopkins. For example, in the parable of the Lost Sheep, the ninety-and-nine symbolize our herd of thoughts, which must be so kept under control as not to think a false note; and the one thought that must be recovered signifies the everlasting soul.[12] When God ordered the earth to bring forth cattle, these symbolize schools, homes, family, and governments; while the "creeping things" signify "affairs like business, daily tasks, eating, drinking, sleeping."[13]

The faith of Mrs. Hopkins was of the kind that can move mountains. For example, there can be no such thing as stealing; for "is not God the only living being? Can God steal?"[14] Elsewhere, she states that by ordering coffee and tea not to make one nervous, one makes them harmless;[15] since God is everywhere, we have as much intelligence in our feet as in our brains;[16] and we are told that a certain Negress made the kinky hair on her child straight by talking to it.[17]

In the Bible Lesson published in *Inter Ocean*, April 2, 1893, Mrs. Hopkins explained her metaphysical principles, which may have been derived directly from Swedenborg and which may have influenced both Troward and Holmes, since they are reproduced by them. "There is," she declares, "one indestructible substance pervading all things from the remotest star to the nearest dust particle.... It can only be cognized by the mind.... And only the understanding power of the mind can make it useful. He who by any manner...handles this substance and realizes that its nature is his nature soon finds himself experiencing vital renewals throughout body and mind." In the *Inter-Ocean* article we find also a restatement of the Doctrine of Influx, which is often made or implied in her writings. It was the power deriving from this universal substance that constituted the impersonal Christ-power which enabled Jesus to perform his mighty works: "By a process he made clear to His disciples, He made a draught upon the universal principle.... and He healed every blindness by His radiation of the seeing mind with which He had stored Himself. He called it the Father sometimes. He called it God sometimes. He called it Lord and Holy Spirit."

"Jesus Christ by his coming forth unharmed from material injuries brought to light the immortality of all powers of mankind...." And she continued: "The life stuff of which his being inhaled to overflowing was the Christ. All who learn the way of life that he taught...are also Christ."

And further: "The glory of Jesus Christ was that, having all the virtues through drawing rightly upon all the life of the universe, He took each man's estate and explained unto him separately how, through all time, he should proceed to have more abundant life.... The man who molds the vital ethers of omnipotence by right thoughts about its bounty brings forth bountifully."

When the poor hear this gospel, it means resurrection for them: for "the life stuff pervading all things now may be manifested in all things as infinite life, infinite health, infinite strength of any faculty."

Mrs. Hopkins's technique of healing was adopted virtually intact by Ernest Holmes: treatment consisted primarily of positive affirmations. The first six lessons in *Scientific Christian Mental Practice* set forth the general metaphysical principles on which the system is based; the last six propose specific techniques for different patients, and each closes with a formal statement to be made orally or silently by the practitioner. Lesson Twelve, "The Crown of Glory," closes with the following affirmation or exhortation:

"You are a perfect creation of the Living God, spiritual, harmonious, fearless, free. You reflect all the universe of Good.

"From every direction, everywhere, come words of Truth, making you know that you are free, wise, and happy.

"You are satisfied with the world in which you live.

"You show forth to the world health, wisdom, peace.

"You show to me perfect health in every part of your being.

"You are fearless, free, strong, wise, and able to do everything that belongs to you to do each day. God works through you to will and to do that which ought to be done by you.

"You are a living demonstration of the power of Truth to set free into health and strength for living service to the world.

"You acknowledge to the world that you are every whit whole.

"You acknowledge to yourself, and to me that you are well and strong and alive through and through.

"God is your life, health, strength, and support forever.

"In the name of the Father, and of the Son, and of the Holy Ghost, I pronounce you well and strong.

"As God saw the works of His hands Good, so I see you Good. All is Good. Amen."[18]

If this sounds like wholly impractical optimism, let it be recorded that thousands found comfort and healing in this therapy; and let it be noted also that the genius and spirit of Emma Curtis Hopkins has indeed left footsteps in the sands of time.

VI. THOMAS TROWARD

Judge Thomas Troward (1847-1916)—who was for many years a Divisional Judge in the Punjab, India—was well versed in Hindu lore and had devoted much of his leisure to the art of painting. Shortly after returning to retire in England about 1900, he discovered the New Thought movement, in which he carved out a brilliant career for himself. In 1904, he presented *The Edinburgh Lectures on Mental Science* at Queens Gate Hall; these have been published in countless editions comprising hundreds of thousands of copies. Even more famous, the *Doré Lectures*, given at the Doré Art Gallery in London in 1906, have gone through something like thirty printings.

To this day, Troward remains the most influential exponent of the new religion in Great Britain; and he has exercised a profound influence upon many American leaders, especially the Holmes Brothers, whose writings are studded with Trowardian words, phrases, ideas, and healing techniques.* We may say that his system is the most original, brilliant, and compelling elaboration and restatement of the Servetian-Swedenborgian theology and cosmology ever produced. Although his works consist of only a few slender volumes, their influence has reached to the ends of the earth.

In addition to the two volumes of lectures, Troward wrote three other important books: *The Creative Process in the Individual, The Law and the World,* and *The Hidden Power.*

---

*Such terms as "livingness," "the Thing Itself," "the cosmic mind of consciousness," and the use of affirmation as a means of emplacing curative and creative powers in the subconscious of the patient.

In the Edinburgh and The Doré Lectures, we find a religion based primarily on science. The author uses Scriptural quotations and references, sometimes in substantial numbers; but these are offered as corroborative evidence, not authoritarian revelation. As Troward views world history, he finds glimpses of Truth revealed in various ages, among many peoples, and in different religions. There can be little doubt that he would have constructed the same ideological synthesis had there been no Christianity in the Western world. His intellectual debt is not to the Bible—which is regarded like any other book— but to Swedenborg and modern science. Following in the footsteps of Henry Drummond,[1] he offers an explanation of nature and the universe which derives from logic, experiment, metaphysics, and the Swedish seer. Citations from the Scriptures are used to confirm and reinforce his philosophic super- structure. "The Science of Spirit," he declares, "is not one whit less scientific than the Science of Matter;..."[2] and it is the business of the Mental Scientist "to regard even the most exalted spiritual phenomena from a purely scientific standpoint, which is...the working of a universal natural Law."[3]

Since the Doré Lectures set forth the Trowardian theses with supreme clarity, we feel that a summary of them may be helpful.

In order that any object, from a leaf or an insect, to the great universe itself, may possess life, it must be animated by what Troward calls Spirit; and since the cosmos is instinct with Life, there must always have existed an "originating Spirit of Life".[4] This Power is not only Life but Intelligence also, which expresses itself in a scheme of cosmic progression, seeking ever to proliferate into higher forms.[5]

This Creative Spirit is without individual personality; it "can only work cosmically by a generic Law...."[6] Working through untold ages with deathless energy, it seeks a perpetual advance to ever higher degrees of life.[7] In all this, we detect the influence of Henry Drummond.

"The whole problem of life consists in finding the true relation of the individual to the Universal Originating Spirit..."[8] which can act on the plane of the Particular and through expression in the individual.[9] "Man's place in the cosmic order is that of a distributor of the Divine Power...."[10] The Divine Mind, the Central Creative Agency, is like a great dynamo, which transmits vitality to every portion of the universe.[11] Individual man is thus made into "the creative center of his own world."[12] The "All-Originating Power" works in and through him at all times, according to the law that governs the universe.

We have, therefore, a single Universal but an unlimited number of Individ- ual Minds,[13] which "is the individualizing of the Universal Spirit,"[14] the "power which concentrates the primordial ether into forms, and endows these forms with various modes of motion, from the simply mechanical motion of the planets to the volitional motion in man."[15]

The supreme and universal intelligence flows from the Great Center into every existing phenomenon, and adapts all these to their specific purposes.[16] This "Divine operation is always for expansion and fuller expression, and this means the production of something beyond what has gone before...since the Divine cannot change its inherent nature, it must operate in the same manner in me; consequently, in my own special world, of which I am the centre, it will move forward to produce new conditions in advance of any that have gone before."[17]

This leads to what Troward calls the Law of Reciprocity: man receives the influx from the Creative Power; but he becomes himself a finite center, a microcosm, from which power also emanates in all directions.[18] It is thus that we become the differentiated and "differentiating centers of Divine Thought...."[19]

Since we are replicas of the Infinite Central Power, why are not all human beings great, noble, successful? The answer is simple enough: only a few have learned to cooperate with the Spirit—to live in harmony with its immutable laws.[20] The "Divine Ideal can only be externalized in our objective life in proportion as it is first formed in our thought; and it takes form in our thought only to the extent to which we apprehend its existence in the Divine Mind."[21] What people have not learned but must comprehend "is that the human mind forms a new point of departure for the work of the Creative Spirit..." It is only as we realize this truth that we "shall find ourselves entering into the new order of life in which we become less and less subject to the old limitations."[22]

Every earthly "manifestation" is in essence the expression of the "Parent Mind,"[23] which presses forward "through the individual and particular"; and our lives will be great precisely in proportion as we utilize this universally available power and operate according to its laws.[24] Since we are the offspring of this Parent Mind and can always draw upon its power, there is no limit to our potential.[25] We are the "sons and daughters of the Almighty," the children of the All-Originating Divine Mind,[26] which operates in the individual[27] as the Christ-Idea, which is simply a universal principle capable of reproduction in every human personality.[28]

At the base of Troward's cosmic system is the Swedenborgian nebular hypothesis. "The physical history of our planet," he states, "shows us first an incandescent nebula dispersed over vast infinitudes of space; later, this condenses into a central sun surrounded by a family of glowing planets, hardly yet consolidated from the plastic primordial matter...."[29] Animating all this, there is "Pure Spirit," which "is the Life-principle considered apart from the matrix in which it takes...a particular form. In this aspect, it is pure intelligence undifferentiated into individuality."[30] And, as such, it "is the Formless principle of Life...."[31] It may also be called "Atomic intelligence";[32] furthermore, "this primordial, all-generating living spirit must be commensurate with infinitude...."[33] It must also be a unity which "can be neither multiplied nor divided...";[34] and, since this "Originating Life Principle is infinite...the *whole* of it must be present..."[35] in all its parts. Its substantive properties must be life and light, from which power proceeds.[36] For this all-originating spirit we must predicate an eternal existence.[37]

God, then (Troward rarely uses the word), is "the intelligence of undifferentiated spirit."[38] It is identical in all its specific modes.[39] It is, furthermore, wholly devoid of individual personality in its operation as the life-principle which gives rise to all the particular manifestations of nature; this power is a unity in essence which finds multiplicity in expression.[40] Those who attribute personality to the Universal Mind are guilty of the error which has sapped the foundations of religion in all ages.[41] This impersonal power is without specific intention; instead, it works by a law of averages for the advancement of the race as a whole, and is never concerned with the individual.[42]

This originating force is "the primordial substance"; but it is inseparable from spirit for the latter contains the primary substance. There can be no duality, for then we should have to postulate another power in the universe.[43] There is a single intelligence subsisting throughout nature, everywhere inherent in its manifestations, which is the ultimate foundation of every material creation.[44]

Thus it is that we live "in the midst of an ocean of undifferentiated, yet intelligent, Life, above, below, all around, and permeating ourselves both mentally and corporeally...."[45] Underlying and directing this totality of things, there is a great intelligence[46] which is seen throughout the cosmic scheme, where matter adheres because of the cosmic will.[47]

Immutable law is the governing principle of this infinitude, and from this there can never be any departure in any portion of the universe.[48] It applies as well in the invisible as in the material world.[49] The reign of law is the pillar on which the universe is founded.[50] It is also the foundation of all mental science.[51] There can be no exception to law, since the acts of God are never capricious, motivated by favoritism, or influenced by bribes or flattery.[52] If chance were to rule the universe, it would quickly be reduced to chaos.[53]

Although the Creative force is impersonal, it is endowed with what Troward calls "*personalness*," which implies a generalized divine consciousness. We must, however, never impute to it the concept of individuality.[54]

The "Originating Spirit," we read, holds "a boundless potential of Creativeness...."[55] This is a process "inherent in the Universal Mind,"[56] which confers life but, by its own imperative, seeks to create higher forms of evolutionary law.[57] Thus, "the higher the grade of life, the higher the intelligence,..." a truth "clearly demonstrated by the grand natural order of the universe."[58] Nor can we conceive of any limit to evolution.[59] In achieving higher levels, man simply fulfills the creative process.[60]

Troward recognizes several kingdoms, all endowed with differing degrees of intelligence or "livingness": minerals, plants, animals, and man, to which he adds a fifth[61]—man spiritualized after he has "passed over" or become, while still in this world, a "Son of God."[62] The organic world is superimposed upon the inorganic in this march toward higher forms; and the science of embryology foreshadows spiritual prototypes.[63] The creative process necessitates what Troward calls the Law of Progression, ever impelling life to seek higher forms;[64] and there is a universal Law of Continuity which develops ever more perfect individuals and impels life-forms upward from mineral to vegetative to animal to human and finally to spiritual.[65] And, since this creative evolution is inexorable, the Law of Continuity, as in Drummond, is unbreakable.[66] In this way, the cosmic intelligence becomes individualized in infinite diversity based upon a universal unity;[67] and we can, therefore, realize our "own identity of being with the Universal Mind, which is commensurate with the Universal Law."[68]

The universal life "forever unfolds itself in all the infinite evolutionary forces of the cosmic scheme" and, in its onward march evolves "into higher and higher conscious intelligence in the successive races of mankind..."[69] At the apex of this development "every human soul is an individualization of that Universal Being, or All-Spirit, which we call God" and which "can never be shorn of its powers but, like Fire, which is its symbol, must always be fully and perfectly itself...."[70]

This metaphysical substance leads to the Doctrine of Correspondences, which Troward interlocks with the concept of the microcosm and the macrocosm. "You are the world and the universe in miniature,"[71] he declares. "Our own consciousness or personality can only be accounted for by the existence...of a corresponding quality in the Originating Spirit."[72] The first step, he continues, in "the production of any external fact must be the creation of its spiritual prototype..." as "elaborated by...Swedenborg in his doctrine of correspondences...."[73]

Since all human minds are projections of the cosmic mind,[74] the same laws which govern the macrocosm apply equally to the microcosm;[75] and, since this is true, we can, by investigating ourselves, comprehend the corresponding principle which exists throughout the invisible universe.[76]

True religious worship, therefore, consists not in creeds, dogmas, ritual, or any purported written revelations, but in "the study of the Universal Life-Principle, 'the Father,' in its nature and its modes of action..."[77] But we are warned against attributing personality to the Father, since the term is purely symbolic.[78]

The Trowardian theory of healing stems from the Swedenborgian doctrine of Influx, which postulates the "Good" as "a stream flowing from the exhaustless Infinite...."[79] The universal Life or Power is, as it were, the central dynamo from which we draw vitality. Nature, in her "most arcane depths, is one vast storehouse of life and good, entirely devoted to our individual use." And we can draw streams of vital energy from her for the accomplishment of whatever we desire.[80] By opening up a channel in himself, "the individual lives directly from the Originating Life...."[81] We can "find in the boundless ocean of central living Spirit the source from which we can go on taking *ad infinitum*..."[82] This "All-Originating Love and Beauty will thus flow out as peace of mind, health of body, discretion in the management of our affairs, and power in carrying out our undertakings...."[83]

The cosmic mind, which has no individuality, is implanted in every manifestation of life; and in human beings it appears as subjective mind, in contrast to the objective, or conscious.[84] The former reasons only deductively, while the latter can do so inductively as well[85] and therefore controls the former,[86] which, however, is endowed with various extraordinary powers, such as thought-transference, clairvoyance, etc. And beyond all this, it is endowed with a unique capacity for building the body and creating health.[87]

This universal mind is the creative power in nature;[88] and since it is impersonal, the subjective human mind is the same.[89] Health can therefore be induced by suggestion from the objective mind;[90] the solid basis for Mental Science rests upon the fact that health can be externalized in the body by the action of the subjective mind, the creative power lodged within us.[91] The cure itself depends on belief.[92] In every healing process, therefore, the right belief is essential.[93] Wrong beliefs externalize as sickness, for they regard secondary causes as primary.[94] In this area, Troward approaches the doctrines of Quimby and Christian Science. "The only conception you can have of *yourself* in the absolute...is as *purely living spirit*... and therefore not subject to illness; and when this idea is firmly impressed upon the subconscious mind, it will externalize it" and banish disease.[95]

Healers must "understand our relation to the great impersonal power we are using" and operate as its instruments.[96] In thought, healer and patient must ignore the symptoms of disease and recognize only "the purely spiritual individuality...."[97] When the outer mind of the patient is receptive,[98] the healer can address the patient's sub-conscious as though it were his own, for both are identical.[99] The function of the healer is to employ the objective mind as a link between the universal and the patient's subjective.[100]

Again and again, Troward declares that thoughts are potent facts,[101] "one of the great forces in the Universe."[102] In fact, the "Universal Spirit, by Self-contemplation, evolves Universal Substance."[103] "Thoughts are things," he continues, and "therefore, as we *will* our thoughts to be, so" will outward things become.[104] Since mental creations are spiritual realities[105] and positive thought produces positive results,[106] the healer need only transfer the conceptions of the cosmic spirit to the level of the individualized particular...thus to create the conditions which externalize in health.[107] The power of thought is without limit; the individual simply gives direction to a force infinitely greater than his own.[108] The Law of Correspondence guarantees a similar externalization, "and to this law there is no limit."[109]

There is indeed a universally creative and all-permeating intelligence; however, this cannot confer health through mental treatment unless the patient's mind is receptive.[110] When this response is present, "thought-power is able to produce results on the material plane...."[111]

In effecting a cure, "the Law will serve us exactly to the extent that we first observe the Law."[112] Nature will obey us precisely as we first obey her;[113] but every infraction carries a punitive consequence.[114] Except through knowledge, there is no escape from this law; but if we obey and cooperate with Nature, it becomes our unfailing friend and servant.[115] Thus we draw from the cosmic resources virtually unlimited physical, mental, moral, and financial benefits. Since the universal creative power has no mind of its own, it can be placed under the direction of positive thought; and, since it never abrogates its function as creative power, it performs the work assigned to it. Thus it is that "mental action produces a corresponding re-action in the mind of the Spirit...."[116] Thought-power acts upon the cosmic element inherent in all things, from mineral to man; being impersonal, it has "no private purpose of its own with which to oppose the suggestion impressed upon it."[117] It is through the "cosmic element, inherent in all things from mineral to man, that Thought-Power acts...."[118]

As an indispensable condition for healing, the practitioner and patient alike must picture to themselves the fulfillment of their "desires as already accomplished on the spiritual plane...."[119] Through a union of the individual's subconscious with all-creative spirit, "specialized effects can be produced in his body" which "transcend our past experiences...."[120] The power of the word, cosmic or individual, "whether spoken or only dwelt upon in Thought, impresses itself upon the impersonal element around us, whether in persons or things."[121] Since space does not exist for the cosmic mind, absent treatment is equally effective.[122] The word of the healer produces a "corresponding vibration in the soul of the subject," and this communicates similar ones to its body.[123] The creative thought thus externalizes in health. When we realize that we are pure spirit, we can "send forth our Thought to produce any effect we will."[124]

Since there is no duality in the universe and since the creative power is all-good, it can have no opposite except mental negation. If you admit that evil has reality, you create it, together with all its consequences of sorrow, sickness, and death. Since disease and death are negations of life, we know that spirit cannot embody disease or death.[125] By acting negatively, we oppose the spirit.[126] The constant influx of health, happiness, and prosperity from the universal spirit is available to the individual only when there is no inversion in his presentation of himself to the Originating Power.[127] The healer should use the cosmic mind to make suggestions to the subconscious of his patient[128] and thus create in him a nucleus which draws creative power to itself, which, in turn, will externalize in a corresponding form.[129] Our thought is like a magnet attracting to us those conditions which accurately correspond to itself. Since thoughts are things, if we THINK life, illumination, harmony, prosperity, and happiness, all these will be added unto us.[130]

Since the originating spirit operates only according to the Law of Reciprocity,[131] and is altogether good,[132] we cannot establish rapport with the cosmic mind unless our own motives and intentions are pure.[133] And, as we come into a full understanding of Mental Science, we learn that we must guard against all negative or hostile thoughts and words.[134]

Healing is accomplished when the practitioner can "speak to the subconscious mind of the patient as though it were his own for, both being pure spirit, the *thought* of their identity *makes* them identical..."[135] By repeating, "I am—therefore I can—therefore I will," we experience a "projection of our powers, whether interior or external, to the accomplishment of the desired object."[136]

Troward emphasizes the deleterious effects of what he calls negative Race-Thought or Consciousness, that is, inherited false beliefs which are not easily banished[137] and which accept the inevitability of sickness and death.[138] The essence of the New Thought gospel consists in the creation of a new standard in which these will no longer be unavoidable because we will know that they have no existence in the Eternal Essence.[139]

When the Law of Life is applied through total affirmation, nothing remains impossible. The body will not only be kept in perfect health, but it will be renewed and one day be perpetuated. Since the Law of Continuation calls for racial progression,[140] there is no limit to the height which we can achieve, and, since an immortal body is the logical dénouement of evolution, the day will come when we will no longer be tied to a body at all, but will put it on or off at will.[141] The resurrection body will be a new one, as real as the old, but free from its imperfections and disabilities.[142] Troward follows Swedenborg in saying that "we shall continue to go on in the same way, and so on *ad infinitum*, so that our life will become one endless progress...."[143]

Finally, since death is the result of inverted thought,[144] it will one day cease, for the simple reason that life alone is the enduring principle; but, since our evolutionary progress is not yet sufficient,[145] death is still the common lot of humanity.[146]

As in New Thought generally, the old and orthodox dogmas are rejected in the Trowardian system. God is an impersonal power; nothing is said concerning the practice or the efficacy of prayer; sin consists in negations which prevent the beneficent influx[147] and sin punishes itself.[148] The doctrine of atonement means simply "that in the Person of Christ every human being, past, present, and to come, was self-offered for the condemnation of his [own] sin...."[149] The Trowardian Christology expresses the same docetic concept found in Swedenborg and throughout New Thought: "Christ," we are told, "is the Son of God, that is, the Divine Principle of Humanity out of which we originated and subsisting in us all, however unconsciously to ourselves...."[150]

In addition to these abstract principles, there are intensely practical elements in Troward's system. It is not money, but the love of it *for its own sake* that is the root of all evil; the *spirit* of opulence is precisely the thing which is furthest removed from this. If you THINK opulence, you will also realize the means of achieving it, for it "will flow to you from all quarters, whether as money or as a hundred other things not to be reckoned in cash."[151]

New Thought, declares Troward, promises "health to the body, peace of mind, earthly prosperity, prolongation of life, and, finally, even the conquest of death itself...."[152] Although God does not put cash in our pockets by some conjuring trick,[153] the "Law of Supply will...bring us into a new world where the useful employment of all our powers, whether mental or physical, will be...a perpetual source of health and happiness...."[154]

Such, in brief, is the Religion of Health, Happiness, and Prosperity as presented by one of its most acute and influential exponents.

VII. CHARLES BRODIE PATTERSON

1. *Biographical.* Charles B. Patterson (1854-1936), previously editor of *Mind*, became the supervising editor of *Arena* in 1900; since these were then probably the most influential publications in the New Thought movement, there can be no doubt that Patterson exercised great influence in shaping its course. He was president of the International Metaphysical League and secretary of the subsequent New Thought Federation. In addition to the various official positions he occupied and the many lectures he delivered, he wrote a number of books which were widely read and which may still be found in second-hand bookstores. Among these, we may mention *The Will to Be Well, The Measure of a Man, Dominion and Power, A New Heaven and a New Earth, Love's Song of Life*, and, finally, *What Is New Thought?*

A general characteristic among all New Thought leaders of note—and this is particularly true of Patterson—is their general intellectual dependence on Swedenborg*, although with individual variations. Only a few, such as

---

*Patterson declared: "Yes, the dream of the alchemist, the vision of a St. John or a Swedenborg, shall become realized in our daily lives."[1]

Quimby, Evans, Emerson, Drummond, Troward, were sufficiently creative to make their contributions permanent elements in the movement; thereafter, lesser intellects, often far more successful as popularizers, gave manifold expression to the gospel of health, happiness, and success.

2. *Cosmic Theory*. Since cosmic theory is so important in New Thought, we must examine Patterson's metaphysical system. The "enlightened soul," he states, "perceives that God and His creation are all there is; that in spirit we are one with God; that in our bodies we are one with all forms; that the spirit within is God, and the body without His handiwork; that whatever we possess or whatever we are comes from the One giver of every good and perfect gift..."[2] And again: "God is the Father and Mother of all humanity;... all men and women are brothers and sisters...."[3] "We are so related to one another that there is among us in continual operation an alternative outflow and influx— and the latter inevitably partakes of the qualities of the former."[4]

This theology is repeated over and over. "The whole visible creation is the outer, the visible Word of God, and man, as Image and Likeness of God, must become the epitomized universe in physical form...."[5]

Patterson often emphasizes an idea which had permeated New Thought by 1900. "The soul is differentiated *spirit*; that is, each soul contains within itself a picture (or image) of the great, universal soul" which "is the all-comprehensive Soul. Everything that is in God enters into the human soul; thus does God seek expression through the life of man."[6] The human soul is "the differentiated ...individual spirit, the microcosm...."[7] There is a constant influx of life, which flows through the grand organism, which is also the only life and intelligence.[8]

The cosmos is governed by immutable law. "Nothing ever happens....there is no chance."[9] Again, "everything in the universe is subject to the operation of the eternal and unchanging law of God, which regulates every part...."[10]

3. *Healing*. Since human beings share in the nature of God, they must also be immortal.[11] "Life is eternal; health is a natural condition; worries, difficulties, sorrows, cease" as we pass from death into life.[12] Although the planet earth will one day reclaim the body which "it has loaned for a season"[13] in the transition known as death, we know that, since "life is indestructible...the departing tenant lives" on and will "build a new temple,"[14] a celestial body. There can be no such thing as a soul without a body.

Although the mental and spiritual aspects of man take precedence over the physical, we must understand "that life is one, that there is really no separation between the physical, mental, and spiritual planes of being...."[15] "When we all come to the conviction that the causes of disease are mental, then in eliminating one cause we will at the same time have thus wiped out of existence perhaps half a dozen so-called diseases...The Germ of disease is not physical; it is in the mind...."[16] In every sickness, the mind is the first to get well.[17] "It is much easier...to retain health...than it is to regain it..." "Forethought saves us from many mistakes...."[18] "Ignorance, sin, sorrow, pain, disease are nothing in and of themselves—only seeming conditions to be overcome by the light of truth...."[19] When we realize this profound fact, "evil loses its seeming power ...and we can at any moment bring the light of the Central Life to dispel all the outer darkness which we call evil."[20] It is the diseased thought that begets the diseased body.[21] Once man realizes that he is one with Universal Life, sickness and disease will be no more.[22]

All this is the Master Key to Patterson's technique of healing. When it is fully understood that evil and destructive thoughts create disease, "no one will resort to any medicine or to any physician..." and "a diseased body will be literally unknown."[23] Whatever we strongly desire, becomes "the greatest factor in causing the desire to be realized."[24] All thoughts and mental pictures "take form, and express themselves in, one's physical organism...."[25] Again, "whatever we feel and whatever we think, that we become...."[26] Every person "has also a magnet within his own life, that is attracting to him...whatever he is attuned to...."[27] By thinking good, unselfish thoughts, "we attract to ourselves everything necessary to our well-being—happiness, health, strength, friends."[28]

4. *Divergencies.* Despite all this, Patterson differs widely from Christian Science. He rejects "the false or so-called animal magnetism."[29] Disease, he declares, is very real[30] and it would be absurd to deny the existence of sin, sickness, and death.[31] "If you say that there is no sin, sickness, or disease, you have simply succeeded in hypnotizing yourself into an erroneous belief."[32] "I do not believe," he states, that "there is any good reason why anyone should be ill, but good health does not come to an individual without.... effort...."[33] And he continues: "If we breathe and sleep properly, there is no reason why we may not, at the age of a hundred years, be enjoying the full use of every faculty...."[34] Nothing is more destructive than worry.[35] "Fear is at the root of all so-called Evil; all sin, sorrow, disease, and death have their origin in Fear";[36] "fear and doubt not only paralyze mental activity, but dissipate physical vitality. These two false emotions, which mother a brood of kindred spirits, poison the mind and this in turn expresses itself as physical poison in the body...."[37]

Patterson, however, proclaimed supreme potential victories over the flesh. "We are coming," he declared, "into the beautiful springtime of a new age, and with this...will come the changes from sickness and disease and death. I say death, because we shall not all sleep.... The last enemy to be overcome is death, and man will overcome that enemy."[38]

5. *The Subconscious.* Patterson's concepts regarding the psyche are basically Swedenborgian. "All conscious mental action becomes later subconscious, establishing habits of thought and action...."[39] Everything that a man ever does "survives in his subconscious mind.... a whole menagerie of wild animals lurk in the jungle of subconsciousness only awaiting some conscious impulse of anger or hate to become fully awakened and to dominate life as it

was ruled in the past."[40] "We are," he declares, "writing the book of life daily...which will last when this world shall be no more...."[41] Thus it is that "man makes his own fate."[42] "I do not believe that we will ever attain to a heaven where we will play on golden harps...or rest eternally.... I believe we will...always *do* something."[43] "New Thought teaches neither future punishment nor reward other than that the individual rewards or punishes himself as he conforms to or opposes the Laws of Life...."[44]

Although Patterson does not deny the desirability of material things, he stresses the importance of "supply" or prosperity less than many of the New Thought proponents. The pursuit of personal, selfish pleasure breeds satiety;[45] and real "happiness is made up of a continual giving and receiving...."[46] Remember, he warns "that success does not, of necessity, include material riches..."[47] for they are only a golden calf,[48] a shadow worship.[49] However, there is nothing "wrong in using mind and body for the acquisition of material wealth...."[50] Our physical needs should be properly evaluated "for religion must be practical or nothing."[51]

6. *Spiritual Interpretation.* Patterson interprets Scripture in the best tradition of Quimby and Swedenborg. The tares and thistles, for example, that must be consumed in fire and the sheep that shall be divided from the goats are the unreal conditions of life to which humanity has been subjected.[52] Elsewhere, he declares that "the second coming of Christ means the coming of the Universal Christ in the hearts of all people."[53] The shedding of Jesus' blood was the casting off of the old nature, no longer useful.[54]

7. *The Attack against Religious Orthodoxy.* Patterson assailed traditional religions very much in the manner of P.P. Quimby and Swedenborg. "The gentle Nazarene," we read, "whose greatest object in life was to bring peace and good-will to all men, is made to stand, as it were, sponsor for this so-called Christian civilization, which has in it the cruelty of the tiger and the rapacity of the hyena."[55] "Of what use," he asks, "is it to Christianize the people of the world unless you can inculcate the real Christian doctrine of life?" As now practiced, "Christianity is...a religion of hypocrisy, cant, and deceit."[56] For centuries, "we have been trying to enforce on other people, at the point of the sword and the bayonet, Christian doctrines which we ourselves have not practiced."[57]

"What the world needs today," he continues, "is practical, not theoretical, Christianity."[58] The worldly nature of the Church is manifest in the outward trappings it displays. "Costly edifices continue to be erected...but church attendance is steadily falling off."[59] Nevertheless, money continues to flow into the coffers of the churches in great abundance.[60]

This materialistic church is spiritually bankrupt: "viewed from the dogmatic, theological standpoint, it is...a colossal" failure.[61] "The reign of dogmatic, theological Christianity is passing away" for "It has had its day...."[62] And the time has come for "the Church...to make a new statement of the vital truths of the Christian religion; let it burn away the straw and the stubble of the past and build on a new foundation...."[63] "Religious creeds, forms, and symbols are all of man's own making."[64] "How long," he thunders, "shall the self-appointed priesthood or clergy seek to blind the eyes...of their followers in order that they may have temporal power?"[65]

8. *Religious Eclecticism.* As we have noted on a number of occasions, an element often found in New Thought is its readiness to accept revealed truth from various sources. As prophets, Patterson places Krishna, the Buddha, and Christ on an equal footing.[66] And he declares that "Abraham, Isaiah, Confucius, Zoroaster, Socrates, and Plato were alike prophets of God...."[67]

In Patterson's system, the old theology and Christology are swept away. "Some," he says, "would have us fall down and worship the man [Jesus]; they would have us believe that it is through the shedding of his material blood that we are saved."[68] The devil was invented to account for the existence of sickness and death. "Then came the idea that something must be sacrificed to propitiate an angry deity, and perfect things without blemish were offered up by priests...."[69]

9. *Strictures against the Medical Profession.* In the light of the preceding, we are not surprised at his condemnations of the medical profession. "Doctors make strenuous efforts to procure legislation prohibiting the practice of mental and Christian Science," not because they are concerned over the public welfare, but because of interference with their incomes.[70] The medical profession seeks to "overcome the poisons in the system by the introduction of still others...." They are "blind leaders of the blind trying to overcome darkness with darkness...."[71] "If the bodies of people could have been made well and whole through physical remedies, surely by this time the so-called science of medicine should have overcome all kinds of physical diseases; but the fact is that diseases multiply as fast as new remedies multiply, and the science of drug-medication today is really no further advanced than it was in the dark ages."[72]

10. *Anti-Ecclesiasticism.* Like others in New Thought, who were suspicious of all organized religion, Patterson was bitterly opposed to ecclesiasticism in any form and therefore declared that "we have churches enough...."[73] We do not, he said, "desire to build up any sectarian organization or to tear down any that now exists."[74] Perhaps he, like Swedenborg, hoped that the new ideology would penetrate and reconstruct the doctrines of the existing churches: we have "no belief in creed or dogma," he explained, yet we recognize the full rights of those who do. The "New Thought movement has not come to destroy, but to fulfill."[75] It does not seek to supersede the Christian faith, but to implement it;[76] it is, therefore, to be called "applied Christianity."[77]

11. *Social Justice.* Since New Thought had as one of its principal objectives the achievement of human happiness, Patterson was imbued with a strong bent for social justice. All people are entitled to equal rights, whether rich or

poor, whether men or women.[78] He excoriates the practice of jailing men simply because they have no visible means of support.[79] Society will one day understand that it is far better to keep all its members usefully employed. Today, we have wealthy parasites who exert a far more pernicious influence than the poverty-stricken drones. In that better world which is dawning, we will have neither sluggards nor laggards, but all will rejoice in useful work.[80]

If this sounds somewhat socialistic, it is interesting to note that Patterson was a firm believer in self-reliance. "Of late years," he laments, "a most pernicious doctrine has been instilled into the minds of many...: that they can get something for nothing."[81] "In a really civilized community, there should be no drones, no people living at the expense of other people...."[82] And, since all life is an infinite unity, it is an ethical imperative that our lives be spent in the service of mankind.[83] Greatness requires work, work, work.[84]

12. *The Successful Life.* Healing occurs by principles already emphasized by Judge Troward and Emma Curtis Hopkins: "New Thought teaches that health, happiness, and success in life constitute the legitimate birthright of every child of the All-loving Father-Mother God, and that through knowledge of, and conformity with, Divine Law, one enters into his real inheritance."[85] Again, "physical health may be fully and freely realized when we take the one way that is open, and steadily follow in that way. Picture in your mind all that you wish...your body to become.... In this way, each ideal shall be realized...."[86] Since "the spirit is the cleansing power, the flesh is of no profit. The body is not the man...and can never become the man."[87]

Since the power of God is the force that creates health, "the healer then supplies the medium through which that power passes to reach the patient...."[88] The secret of healing lies in positive declaration. "Error is to be overcome, not by the denial that error exists, but by affirming the existence and power of the eternal truths."[89] Every person should say, "It is right that I should be well and strong. God is the Source of my life; in him, I live and move and have my being."[90]

To achieve and retain health, therefore, we must obey the laws of life and recite the New Thought Credo: "I am one with all life. I am one with all Intelligence. I am one with all the Health and Wholeness of Universal Health and Universal Wholeness. I live, I move, and have my being in God. I now have eternal life. I am rich because all things are mine. I am powerful because my will is one with Universal Will. Through heart and mind, I control and direct the full force of my own life. My rightful inheritance as a Child of God brings to me every good and every perfect gift.... The deep within me speaks to the Everlasting Deep, and I know that I am Son of God, joint heir with Christ having dominion and power both in the age that now is and in the age which is to come."[91]

This was Charles Brodie Patterson's Affirmative Prayer.

VIII. THE NEW THOUGHT POETS

A. *Edwin Markham*

Charles Edwin Markham (1850-1940), who reached his apogée following the publication of "The Man with the Hoe" in 1899, continued to pour out volume after volume, including *Eighty Songs at Eighty*, 1932, and *The Star of Araby*, 1937. Although the *Cumulative Book Index* lists five of his titles in 1922, nine in 1929, and seven in 1937, these have not been reprinted and are now quite scarce.

Many of his poems are brief and without special message. Those with titles like "The Goblin Laugh," "In the Storm," "The Hidden Valley," "The Cricket," etc. are rather vignettes of nature or of the lesser emotions. However, those for which the author is best known are surcharged with social passion wedded to the religious aspirations of New Thought. Since it was Markham's destiny to reach the fullness of his powers just as the Socialist and similar movements were approaching a zenith, it may not be surprising that in several of his poems he struck the diapason heralding a better life for toilers through holy emancipation. The opening lines of "The Man with the Hoe" are still entrenched in our language and have become an integral element in the American Heritage:

"Bowed by the weight of centuries he leans
Upon his hoe and gazes on the ground,
The emptiness of ages in his face,
And on his back the burden of the world....
O master, lords, and rulers in all lands,
How will the future reckon with this Man?
How answer his brute question in that hour
When whirlwinds of rebellion shake the world?
How will it be with kingdoms and with kings—
With those who shaped him to the thing he is—
When this dumb terror shall reply to God
After the silence of the centuries?"

After this prophetic denunciation, came others, of which "To High-Born Poets" may be regarded as a cry of desperation rising from the earth:

"There comes a pitiless cry from the oppressed—
A cry from the toilers of Babylon for their rest—
A clear sane cry wherein the God is heard

To speak to men the one redeeming word.
  No peace for thee, no peace,
  Till blind oppression cease;
  The stones cry from the walls,
  Till the gray injustice falls—
Till strong men come to build in freedom-fate
The pillars of the new Fraternal State."

"A Harvest Son" tells of the workers whose labor is done:

"And now the idle reapers lounge against the bolted doors;
Without are hungry harvesters, within enchanted stores....
Now they are strolling beggars, for the harvest work is done."

In the poem called "Brotherhood," the theme is expanded:

"The crest and crowning of all good,
Life's final star, is Brotherhood....
Come, clear the way, then, clear the way:
Blind creeds and kings have had their day.
Break the dead branches from the path:
Our hope is in the aftermath—
Make way for Brotherhood—make way for Man."

The toiler is like the fabled Sisyphus:

"When I see a workingman with mouths to feed....
I see a man doomed to roll a huge stone up an endless steep.
He strains him onward inch by stubborn inch,
Crouched always in the shadow of the rock....
Will the huge stone break his hold,
And crush him as it plunges to the gulf?"

In "Little Brothers of the Ground," we find the full-blown Socialist philosophy:

"Little ants in leafy wood,
Bound by gentle brotherhood,
While we gaily gather spoil,
Men are ground by the wheel of toil;
While ye follow Blessed Fates,
Men are shriveled up with hates....

Ye are fraters in your hall,
Gay and chainless, great and small;
All are toilers in the field,
All are sharers in the yield.
But we mortals plot and plan
How to grind the fellow-man...
And the idlers lord the feast.
Yes, our workers they are bound,
Pallid captives to the ground;
Jeered by traitors, fooled by knaves,
Till they stumble into graves.
How appears to tiny eyes
All the wisdom of the wise?"

In "The Desire of Nations," Markham strikes a specifically religious note heralding the return of Christ:

"He comes to loosen and unbind,
To build the lofty purpose of the mind....
Nor will he come like carnal kings of old,
With pomp of pilfered gold;
Nor like the pharisees with pride of prayer....
In tedious argument of fruitless creed;
But in the passion of the heart-warm deed
Will come the Man Supreme.
Yes, for He comes to lift the Public Care—
To build on earth the Vision hung in air...."

In "Love's Vigil," we discover echoes of Drummond:

"Then all the worlds will know that Love is Fate—
That somehow he is greater even than Heaven—
That in the Cosmic Council he is God."

In "One Life, One Law," we find a distinctly New Thought-Swedenborgian soteriology:

"What do we know—what need we know
Of the great world to which we go?...
That as men sow they surely reap—
That every thought, that every deed,
Is sown into the soul for seed."

In "The Song of the Divine Mother," we find the specific New Thought theology:

"Come, Bride of God, to fill the vacant throne,
Touch the dear Earth again with sacred feet;
Come build the Holy City of white stone,
And let the whole world's gladness be complete."

Even as the genius of Ralph Waldo Trine blended in its later development with rationalism, so we find that Edwin Markham's songs reflect the marriage of New Thought with the economic aspirations of the toilers. However, in "These Songs Will Perish," he had a premonition that his work, if not his aspiration, was ephemeral:

"The singer and the song die out forever;
But star-eyed Truth (greater than song or singer)
Sweeps hurrying on: far off she sees a gleam
Upon a peak. She....
Cries through all the ruins of the world—
Through Karnack, through the stones of Babylon—
Cries for a moment through these fading songs."

B. *Ella Wheeler Wilcox*

Ella Wheeler Wilcox (1850-1919) flashed across the firmament like a comet in the days of her halcyon splendor. For years, she wrote a daily poem for a syndicate of newspapers, and her name, like that of Edgar Guest in later years, became a household word. The *Cumulative Book Index* listed thirty-three of her titles in 1922, seventeen in 1928, but none in 1937. Today her books are rarely found even in good libraries or large second-hand bookstores. De Vorss carries no reprint of them; neither histories nor anthologies of American literature accord her much space, and yet her name has achieved a niche of its own in the lore of this nation.

As a student of Emma Curtis Hopkins in the middle Eighties, she embraced the New Thought gospel with an all-consuming passion that continued throughout her life and is stated most succinctly, perhaps, in a thin but handsome volume of prose entitled *The Heart of New Thought*, published by the Psychic Research Company of Chicago in 1902.

Although Mrs. Wilcox proclaims the general principles and attitudes of New Thought, she is distinguished by certain characteristics of her own. For example, she was sure that proper diet, cleanliness, deep breathing, and exercise are absolutely necessary to good health.[1] She gave ample attention to the practical and the physical. People who eat too much or take unhealthful foods are sure to become obese and have gastric disturbances. No one should eat more than two meals a day; those not engaged in physical labor should take only one.[2] She declared emphatically that old clothes should be discarded, since they are relics of past days; but, at the same time, if given to charity, they should be bestowed only upon the deserving, for otherwise they would perpetuate idleness,[3] which is infinitely worse than poverty. Although child labor, pauperism, and wage-earning mothers are serious evils, unearned wealth is even worse.[4]

Mrs. Wilcox warned against the belief that difficulties or disabilities can be overcome quickly; indeed, in many cases, they are irremediable. Since these are in many instances not attributable to the sufferers, she embraced the Hindu-Buddhist doctrines of karma and reincarnation: for in no other way could they be reconciled with the concept of law and a God of justice. "The three-year-old child who toddles in front of a trolley car," we read, "cannot be blamed for wrong thinking...Neither can the deaf mute or the child born blind or deformed. We must go farther back, to former lives, to find the first cause of such misfortunes."[5]

"Remember," she declares, "you are the maker and molder of your destiny."[6] And again, "every thought word and deed is helping decide your next place in the Creator's magnificent universe. You will be beautiful or ugly, wise or ignorant, fortunate or unfortunate, according to what use you make of yourself here and now.... Even if you escape the immediate results" of your "course of action here, you must face the law of *cause and effect* in the next state. It is inevitable. God, the maker of all things, does not change His laws."[7] And further: "You can destroy the body, but the *You* who suffers in mind and spirit will suffer still, and live still. You will only change your location from one state to another. You did not make yourself among the spiritual tramps who hang about the earth's borders, because they have not prepared themselves for a better place..."[8] Such souls will be like the unburied Greeks and those in Dante's Limbo.

Like many other proponents of New Thought, Mrs. Wilcox proclaims the substantiality of *thoughts* and their decisive influences:

"You never can tell what your thoughts will do
   In bringing you hate and love,
For thoughts are things, and their airy wings
   Are swift as a carrier dove.

They follow the law of the universe—
    Each thing must create its kind,
And they speed o'er the track to bring you back
    Whatever went forth from your mind."[9]

And again:

"Our thoughts are shaping unmade spheres,
    And, like a blessing or a curse,
They thunder down the formless years
    And ring throughout the universe."[10]

Since thoughts are so potent, "if you think peace, hope, and happiness, you are sending a note of harmony and success."[11] Watch your temper—keep it even. "Clear your mind of every gloomy, selfish, angry or revengeful thought. Allow no resentment or grudge toward man or fate to stay in your heart over night."[12]

There are hundreds of thousands of people who believe themselves sick, sorrowful, and poverty stricken, but who "would be well, glad, and prosperous if they only thought themselves so."[13] Many people think only the worst, for example, the millionaire who complained that he had been robbed because he was not permitted to make his own fortune.[14]

Mrs. Wilcox attacked the old creeds and churches with sharp virility. The "orthodox" Christian who declares that all humanity is "vile—selfish—sinful"[15] carries "a moral malaria with him, which poisons the air...and...is *projecting pernicious mind stuff* into space, which is as dangerous to the peace of the community as dynamite bombs" and constitutes a "false, unholy, and blasphemous 'religion.' "[16] She was filled with pity and sorrow when she heard some "orthodox" woman repeat the old cliches that we are born to endure suffering and misery. "Thank God," she exclaims, "that the wave of 'New Thought' is sweeping over the land, and washing away those old blasphemous errors of mistaken creeds."[17]

Man has the power to re-create himself. To this end, he must "think success, prosperity, usefulness."[18] "We are heirs of God's kingdom, and rightful inheritors of happiness, and health, and success."[19] Since *"Man is what he thinks,"* he can free himself "from any chains, whether of poverty, sin, ill health, or unhappiness."[20]

In contrast with Christian Daa Larson, however, Mrs. Wilcox warns against a mere philosophy of optimism. Although the world was full of New Thought literature, it was effective only for those who would undertake the task of remaking themselves from within. Those who have accepted the necessity of sin, ill health, poverty, or unhappiness, "must not expect to batter down the walls you have built" during a lifetime "in a week, or a month, or a year."[21] Victory may require a long time, but it will come. "All that our dearest hopes desire will come to us, if we believe in ourselves as rightful heirs to Divine Opulence, and work and think always on those lines."[22]

Failure or success is not measured by the wealth one accumulates or the fame of success one attains; on the contrary, it consists in the building of character that will confer peace and happiness in this life and guarantee a better destiny for the next.[23] Woe unto him "who cultivates his mental and spiritual powers only" to gain wealth or power.[24] "Into the Great Scheme of existence, as first conceived by the Creator, money did not enter.... There was no millionaire and no pauper soul created by God."[25]

Mrs. Wilcox was acutely aware that since New Thought was a New Idea, it attracted "hysterical women, unbalanced men: the erratic and irresponsible."[26] She denounced the belief that health, wealth, youth, beauty, etc. were to be had in a miraculous way, or that practitioners could become great healers in a brief space of time.[27] None of these things can be attained by reading occult literature,[28] or through an instant illumination.[29]

In the final article in *The Heart of New Thought*, Mrs. Wilcox virtually labels the followers of Mary Baker Eddy as cranks or lunatics. "I once chanced to call on a lady who," she discovered, "considered her illness a mere 'claim' her 'mortal mind' had made...."[30] All such talk "is very ridiculous,"[31] as are the absurd notions that one day we will require neither food nor money.

And this, perhaps, marks the gulf that separated some of Mrs. Hopkins's students from the fountainhead of the Christian Science Church.

IX. RALPH WALDO TRINE

1. *Amazing Popularity.* One of the most famous and effective popularizers of Swedenborgianism was Ralph Waldo Trine (1866-1958), named to bear the illustrious mantle of Emerson, to whom, in due course, he was to accord second place among the sages of mankind.[1] Neither a churchman nor a healer, nor yet an original thinker, he was an author and lecturer whose message influenced millions, especially through his most successful book, *In Tune with the Infinite.* Completed at the age of thirty, it went through more than fifty editions and sold more than 1,500,000 copies in the United States alone; it was translated into more than twenty languages, where it sold another half million. Henry Ford attributed his own success to the inspiration he derived from it. Although Trine attained the age of ninety-two, his most productive period extended from 1895 to 1915, when he still had more than forty years of life remaining.

2. *The Eclectic Amalgam. What All the World's A-Seeking*, published in 1896, reflects an admixture of influences drawn primarily from Emerson, W.F. Evans, and Greek and socialist sources. Here we find no direct Swedenborgian influence. Happiness and greatness, we read, are the byproducts of a life spent in service to others; thoughts are things and exercise influence for good or evil;[2] we must get rid of creeds and dogmas;[3] surplus wealth is useless and destructive;[4] animals may have immortal souls;[5] and sin is the result of ignorance.[6] He then launches into a discussion of the class-struggle,[7] of working people, and the churches from a definitely socialist point of view;[8] and he praises economic cooperation.[9] Christ, we read, is not a sacrificial savior, but an exemplar. The body, we read, is good and beautiful in all its parts,[10] and asceticism should be outlawed. The world is a manifestation of God,[11] and Christ is the divinity existing within. Death is simply "that transition" in which "all material accumulations and possessions are left behind, and the soul takes with it only the unfoldment and growth of the real life" in the Spirit World.[12] The book closes with a denial of original sin and an Emersonian dithyramb to virtue and self-reliance.

3. *Swedenborg Discovered*. About 1890, Trine must have discovered the Swedish seer because his next and most famous book, *In Tune with the Infinite*, 1897, is a symphony vibrating with a new vision based on his revelations. Afire with his newfound gospel, Trine burst into jubilation and, since it was simplistic and practical, it reached the heart of all humanity. Swedenborg, declares Trine, is "the highly illumined seer...pointing out the great laws in connection with what he termed the divine influx, and how we may open ourselves more fully to its operations."[13] The whole book is a philosophic popularization of his new master. "The great central fact of the universe," we read, "is that Spirit of Infinite Life and Power that is back of all, that animates all, that manifests itself in and through all; that self-existent principle of life from which all has come and...is continually coming.... This Infinite Power is creating, working, ruling through an agency of great immutable laws and forces that run through the universe.... God, then, is this Infinite Spirit which fills all the universe with Himself alone, so that all is from Him and in Him and there is nothing that is outside."[14]

The doctine of influx is stated or implied on almost every page; we "can open ourselves so fully to the incoming of the divine inflow, and so to the operation of those higher forces, inspirations and powers, that we can indeed and in truth become what we may well term God-men."[15] Again, "in the degree that we open ourselves to the inflowing of this immanent and transcendent life, do we make ourselves channels through which the Infinite Intelligence and Power can work."[16]

The idea is repeated again and again: "the man of power, Centered in the Infinite...has...connected himself with...the great powerhouse of the universe.... His strong, positive, and hence constructive thought is continually working success for him along all lines.... Silent, unseen forces are at work which will sooner or later be made manifest in the visible."[17]

Another recurring theme deals with health and disease, and is based on Swedenborgian hypotheses. "The moment a person realizes his oneness with the Infinite Spirit, he...no longer makes the mistake of regarding himself as body, subject to ills and diseases, but he realizes the fact that he is spirit, spirit now as much as he will or ever can be...."[18] "In the degree...that you come into...oneness with the Infinite Spirit of Life...you open yourself to the divine inflow" and "set into operation forces that will sooner or later bring even the physical body into a state of abounding health and strength. For...this Infinite Spirit of Life can from its very nature admit of no disease...."[19] "I as spirit...can in my own real nature admit of no disease. I now open my body, in which disease has gotten a foothold...fully to the inflowing tide of this Infinite Life...and the healing process is going on."[20]

Evil emotions and bad mental attitudes (similar to the Swedenborgian infestations) are the causes of physical ailments: "practically all disease, with its consequent suffering, has its origin in perverted mental and emotional states and conditions.... No disease can enter...our bodies unless it find therein something corresponding to itself...."[21]

The theme is reiterated: "The time will come when...the physician will not...attempt to heal the body, but to heal the mind, which in turn will heal the body...and...there will come a time when each will be his own physician.... As a rule, those who think least of their bodies enjoy the best health."[22]

Trine, however, never denies the reality of matter, the physical: "Give the body the nourishment, the exercise, the fresh air, the sunlight it requires, keep it clean, and then think of it as little as possible.... Don't talk of sickness and disease. By talking of these you do yourself harm and you do harm to those who listen to you."[23] Sleep is a great restorer;[24] and we should avoid "the heavier, grosser, less valuable kinds of food and drink, such as the flesh of animals, alcoholic drinks, and all things of the class that stimulate the body and passions rather than build the body and the brain into a strong, clean, well-nourished, enduring, and fibrous condition."[25] "When you allow your thoughts of anger, hatred, malice, jealousy, envy, criticism, or scorn to exercise sway, they have a corroding and poisoning effect upon the organism; they pull it down, and if allowed to continue, will eventually tear it to pieces by externalizing themselves in...particular forms of disease...."[26]

Many who have long been invalids could be restored to health by a "vital realization of...oneness with the Infinite Power" and by opening themselves "completely to the divine inflow...."[27] Trine never tires of exposing the corrosive effects of destructive emotions. "Fear has become with millions a fixed habit.... To live in continual dread, continued cringing, continual fear of anything, be it loss of love, loss of money, loss of position or situation, is to take the readiest means to lose" everything we have.[28] The action "of fear, grief, worry, despondency...upon the various bodily organs and functions seems to be of a slow, corroding, lowering of activity, and slowly poisoning nature...a falling state of mind is always followed by a falling condition of the body."[29]

Like his mentors, Trine repudiated all orthodox dogma. In the spirit of Emerson, he finds one basic principle in all the religions of the world;[30] he even finds greatness in every kind of dissident. Since "God...is the Infinite Spirit of Life and Power...there can be no infidels or atheists...The earnest, sincere heretic is one of the greatest friends true religion can have. Heretics are among God's greatest servants...Christ was one of the greatest heretics the world has ever known."[31]

Trine elaborates the Swedenborgian doctrine of correspondences: "Within and above every physical planet is a corresponding ethereal planet or soul world, as within and above every physical organism is a corresponding ethereal organism, or soul body, of which the physical is but the external counterpart and material expression."[32] The *ipsissima verba* of Scripture poses no difficulty, for it is always susceptible to spiritual interpretation. Thus "blessed are the pure in heart for they shall see God" means simply: "blessed are they who in all the universe recognize only God, for by such God shall be seen."[33]

4. *Happiness and Opulence.* Trine equated the new Christianity not only with mental and physical well-being, but also with happiness and success: "This is the Spirit of Infinite Plenty...continually bringing all things into expression in material form. He who lives in the realization of his oneness with the Infinite Power becomes a magnet to attract to himself a continued supply of whatever he desires.... The old and...prevalent idea of godliness and poverty has absolutely no basis for its existence, and the sooner we get away from it the better.... It had its origin...in the minds of those who had a distorted, one-sided view of life."[34]

"Opulence," we read, "is the law of the universe, an abundant supply for every need...."[35] Furthermore, since "the supply is always equal to the demand..."[36] there is no excuse for want or poverty and no reason for it except our own deficiencies. "Suggest prosperity to yourself. See yourself in a prosperous condition. Affirm that before long you will be in a prosperous condition; affirm it calmly and quietly, but strongly and confidently. Believe it...Expect it...You thus make yourself a magnet to attract the things that you desire."[37] Do this, and you will have health, happiness, success, and prosperity!

Yet (and again following Swedenborg) Trine emphasizes over and over that wealth should not be sought for its own sake. "He who is enslaved with the sole desire for material possessions here will continue to be enslaved even after he no longer retains his body.... Perchance this torture may be increased by his seeing the accumulations he thought were his now being scattered and wasted by spendthrifts."[38] Wealth is good and useful as a trust in the service of humanity. "All about us are persons with lives now stunted and dwarfed who could make them rich and beautiful, filled with a perennial joy, if they would begin wisely to use that which they have spent the greater portion of their lives in accumulating."[39]

5. *The Eschatology.* Trine's eschatology is precisely that which Quimby transmitted from Swedenborg to New Thought: a transition in which "the individual...has gone out of his physical body" but "the life" goes "on the same as before...exactly where it has left off here; for all life is a continuous evolution, step by step...."[40] "The loss of friends by the transition we call death will not cause sorrow to the soul that has come into this higher realization, for he knows that there is no such thing as death...."[41]

6. *The Humanist. In The New Alignment of Life*, written in 1913, we find that Trine, although still a Swedenborgian, has absorbed various new elements and moved decisively in the direction of rationalism and humanism. He is utterly opposed to all forms of ecclesiastism;[42] he declares that Jesus "did not attempt to found any new religion..."[43] or establish a church.[44] The early Christian communions were merely small communal associations.[45] It is evident that Trine had become a student of comparative religion and a devotee of higher criticism. Christianity, he declares, was paganized by the Catholic Church;[46] the old mysteries, their rites and ceremonies, were thus interwoven with the life, death, and worship of Jesus.[47] Paul based his teachings upon a revelation of his own, which was actually a repudiation of the gospel as delivered by Jesus.[48] Worse than that, the Church united with the state and became a great persecutor under Constantine, to accomplish a total destruction of freedom;[49] and, under the Inquisition, it became the most oppressive and destructive force to appear on this planet.[50] With Popes at its head, the Catholic Church has been guilty of shedding seas of blood, as, for example, in the Thirty Years War.[51] "These atrocious acts, that persecution of truth...must ever remain the darkest stain upon the Christian religion, and today they constitute the most valid objection in the minds of educated men to enrolling themselves under Christ's banner."[52] "So through a number of centuries, all initiative and all independence of thought was crushed; whenever any torch-bearer arose, who would...threaten the hold of this Church upon the people, he was thwarted or silenced...all religious leadership was through the dictation of an infallible Pope of Roman origin." But then "an infallible Pope was followed on the part of the Protestant churches by an infallible Bible."[53]

With advancing knowledge, youth is no longer attracted to the churches.[54] We have now reached the point where all the old beliefs and doctrines should be discarded in their entirety.[55] Trine then summarizes the Christian story of creation and the doctrine of redemption in order to ridicule them almost in the tradition of Ingersoll.[56] He hails science and Darwin as the great iconoclasts demolishing the biblical myths.[57]

We must therefore rid ourselves completely of ancient creeds and dogmas[58] which crush the intelligence[59] and render the church suicidal.[60] The doctrine of infant damnation is a monstrous example of what the Church has taught;[61] and we certainly do not need a Virgin Birth[62] or an Athanasian Creed.[63] Trine points out that the delayed and never realized Second Coming of Christ, as expected in the early Church, was and remains a delusion;[64] and he delineates the parallels in the stories told concerning the Buddha and by Christian mythologizers.[65] For material, he draws freely upon Gibbon, Loisy, Frazer, Wrede, and Gilbert Murray. He is no longer even certain of personal immortality;[66] and we find him approaching the humanist position by declaring that many are now "taking their chances rather on the divinity of man."[67]

Trine's proclamations concerning health, happiness, success, plenty, etc., however, are as heavily emphasized as ever. But he is no longer so sure that man, the spiritual, is immune to disease. Instead of declaring that disease is an evil infestation, he advocates "prevention hygiene." Our "National Public Health Service," we read, has made "splendid advances in its knowledge" of disease.[68] The bubonic plague and tuberculosis, which result from unsanitary conditions, are being brought under control.[69] Better physical conditions and surroundings will reduce the danger of disease and death.[70]

7. *Health.* "Body building...is accomplished through the operation of *the Life-Forces within.* They will always build healthily and harmoniously unless interfered with."[71] People become sick because they eat too much or improper food and do not get enough exercise.[72] But always we must remember that the mental and physical intertwine in what we may now call a psychosomatic unity.

The moral and the physical aspects of man are also inseparable. "If a man stops thinking wrongful, immoral, or sinful thoughts, then the wrongful, immoral, or sinful actions will not occur...."[73] Likewise, the number of those "whose bodies have been reduced to a low and sluggish tone...both mentally and physically...is simply enormous.... The number of stomach and digestive disorders" thus created "are simply legion.... Think also of the vast company of those whose nervous breakdown...is primarily, if not entirely, due to this cause," as are "pulmonary troubles...which *always* bring about a lowering of the tone of the system.... The condition of the blood determines.... the condition of the entire physical organism.... Mind and body are continually acting and reacting upon one another."[74]

When Trine's gospel was rationalized in this manner, its great emotional force subsided; however, his impact upon the religion of health, happiness and prosperity and his attacks upon creeds, dogmas, and ecclesiasticism remain as one of the outstanding landmarks in New Thought and even in American history.

X. JOEL GOLDSMITH

1. *General Characteristics.* Joel Goldsmith (1882-1964) who began his career as an independent healer at the age of thirty-six and who devoted himself exclusively to therapy, is a unique personality in New Thought. Although his ideology is largely in accord with the general principles of the movement, it exudes a flavor all its own. Without affiliation to any church or organization, his books attained wide and continuing popularity. In addition to a dozen pamphlets, DeVorss offers no less than twenty-four of his titles in hardback, most of which were produced after he was sixty years old. After 1949, he made his home in Hawaii; but he traveled and lectured all over the world.

He delineated his teaching or philosophy in a series of widely distributed volumes called *The Infinite Way*, issued between 1954 and 1959. Other well-known titles are *The Art of Meditation, God the Substance of All Form, Conscious Union with God, Living the Infinite Way, Contemplative Meditation, The Art of Spiritual Healing, The Spiritual Interpretation of Scripture*, and *Attitude of Prayer*. In all of these, similar ideas are reiterated over and over. He also wrote pamphlets with such names as *Business and Salesmanship*.

Since he had been for sixteen years a Christian Science practitioner before he struck out on his own, we need not be surprised that he uses many terms characteristic of this Church. When he abandoned institutionalized religion in 1928, he widened his message so that it might appeal, not only to the followers of Unity, Divine Science, the Science of Mind, etc., but also to many of those still in the conventional churches.[1] He made no attempt to establish a new organization, or to align himself with one already existing.[2] Instead, he sought and found his audience through lectures and books throughout the field of New Thought.

2. *Oriental Influence.* He must have studied Eastern religions, for we find a strong admixture of orientalism, particularly the lore of India, in Goldsmith.[3] Like Fox and others, he believed in Karma, pre-existence, and reincarnation;[4] but since, in the Western world, no large religious following was possible except on the basis of the Christian Scriptures, he made these his principal authority, which, of course, he interpreted "spiritually."[5]

Goldsmith relied heavily on a number of Biblical passages, among which the following are frequent:

"Of myself I can do nothing."
"I and the Father are one."

"Before Abraham was, I am."
"My grace is sufficient for thee."[6]
"The Kingdom of God is within me."
"I am come that you might have life and have it more abundantly."
"Except the Lord build the house, they labor in vain that built it."
"I will never leave nor forsake thee."

3. *Technique*. Goldsmith's healing differs from that of most metaphysicians, especially those of the Hopkins-Troward-Holmes school. We read again and again that affirmations are useless.[7] It is totally wrong, he declares, to tell Jane Smith that, since she is a child of God, she cannot be sick or sinful.[8] Repetition and "mental work" are likewise rejected[9] in favor of spiritual healing. We should never pray for anything specific, such as healing or wealth.[10] The practitioner should never give what is known as a "treatment."[11] Thought, as such, is not a power or a thing, but only an avenue of awareness;[12] and disease is never caused by thinking or "mortal mind."[13]

4. *Contradictions*. There seems to be a basic difference in his system. On the one hand, he admits that the medical profession does cure or alleviate many diseases; at the same time, however, he makes the most extreme claims for The Infinite Way—his individual contribution to New Thought theory and therapy. We should understand, therefore, that when he speaks of those healed by *materia medica*, he refers to those who have not achieved God-Consciousness through his gospel; the seemingly miraculous cures he proclaims, on the other hand, are achieved only on the higher plane of existence which he postulates as a possibility available to those who will attain The Infinite Way.

5. *The Infinite Way*. Goldsmith says that this reveals the nature of God as a single infinite power, intelligence, and love; the nature of every individual as one with God in quality and character, but expressed in a multiplicity of forms, and the nature of discord as a misconception of God's manifestation in the universe.[14] It is a God-Experience, a realization of the Christ within.[15] This definition and description are elaborated in numerous passages,[16] and constitutes the core of Goldsmith's philosophy.

As in all metaphysical systems, the Swedenborgian concept of God is central here also, and is the foundation for the Infinite Way of Life and Healing. The Father-Mother God[17] is inscrutable, unknowable, indefinable: no one can name him, know what he is, or describe him.[18] At best, we can only comprehend some of his attributes: he is Immutable and Infinite Law;[19] the substance of all form;[20] the spiritual, creative principle of the universe;[21] the source of all being;[22] the One Life and Universal Consciousness.[23] He is Light and Life;[24] that which is manifest in creation;[25] the Central Office of the solar system;[26] the infinite ocean in which we all exist.[27] "God is a state of Being, a state of infinite Intelligence, and ever-present love."[28] He is the Infinite

Invisible,[29] the Creative Principle,[30] the universal soul,[31] the power which is poured into every natural form.[32] He is the divine essence or presence.[33] Above all, God is One, and all dualist concepts can only create suffering wherever they are accepted.[34] God is the omnipresent and Infinite Father.[35] He is goodness and health;[36] he is All-Action;[37] he is the universal Intelligence, equally distributed among all members of the human race.[38] He is the spirit of Christ within you.[39]

Since God is in every individual form and is the source of all existence, we can understand that I and the Father are one. We are individualizations of everything that God is;[40] we are not merely human, but spiritual, beings[41]— everything that God is.[42] Christ is not a person or an historical entity,[43] but the universal mind manifested in Jesus[44] and a divine activity operative in all of us.[45] Christ is simply the human *self*,[46] that *I* which is something quite different from the body.[47] The coming of the Christ in the world signifies only the acceptance of the Christ-spirit among humanity.[48] The mission of Jesus was to introduce to mankind the divine ideas of spiritual freedom.[49] The *I*, the self, being eternal, has no beginning and can have no end.[50] Death is a transition,[51] a momentary lapse of consciousness,[52] which will quickly be restored on the next plane and continue as before.[53] Dying is no greater adventure than traveling to California or Europe.[54] Where the right belief exists, the body becomes immortal during the present life and on the present plane.[55]

In his discussion of sin, sickness, and error, Goldsmith declares on the one hand that they are akin to a mirage or a dream;[56] people are victimized by them because they are subject to the hypnosis or mesmerism of false belief.[57] Aging is such an illusion, and there is no reason why we cannot be as vital at ninety as at nineteen.[58] Disease is man-created;[59] evil, sickness, and deformity are the result of suggestion.[60] No one dies except by his own consent.[61] Error is never a reality.[62] There are cripples in the world because people are subject to inherited race belief.[63] No person is actually sick, sinful, or impaired.[64] Since belief in cancer[65] or arthritis is a mere superstition, cancer or arthritis may easily be cured.[66] Every disease is merely a misinterpretation of some activity of God,[67] and may, therefore, be overcome.[68] Goldsmith declared that he cured many patients in a single hour;[69] he described people with terminal cancer who became completely well,[70] and with tuberculosis whom he had healed.[71]

6. *Matter, Disease, and Medicine.* There are, however, passages in which Goldsmith seems conventional enough. Some people, he declares, are good, some bad, others intolerable.[72] The world has made all men mutual enemies.[73] Material things are the gods of this world,[74] and men worship fame, fortune, and position.[75] Matter, he declares, not only exists, but is indestructible.[76] Sin and disease are certainly indisputable facts of life.[77] He respects the doctors[78]

and admits that they have been so successful finding remedies for diseases that these may disappear within the next half century;[79] but this is because God now operates more effectively through this method than was once the case.[80] The body can be improved through exercises at a gymnasium.[81] If patients desire medical aid, they should be encouraged to seek it;[82] and no attempt should ever be made to administer spiritual healing to those who disbelieve in its efficacy."[83]

7. *Healing.* Health is achieved through contact with God;[84] God's understanding heals us, when we become receptive; spiritual wisdom is health.[85] "Health is the realization of God as the source of all activity and the substance of all form...."[86] "The healing agency is the consciousness that is developed through" rapport or attunement with "the Christ-consciousness of the practitioner...."[87] A perfect spiritualization results when the inner consciousness flows out to form the completely healthy body.[88] Health, happiness, prosperity all flow into the outer life from within.[89] But if we cut ourselves off from the source of life, we soon wither away.[90]

"Health is of God," we read, and the universal recognition of this fact would make it available to everyone.[91] It can be realized by anyone who understands that "whatever is necessary in the government of the body is performed as an activity of God."[92] Healing takes place when we arrive "at a state of consciousness in which sin, disease, and death have no reality" and no longer need rid ourselves of these forms of discord.[93] The secret of healing consists in understanding that God *is* and that he is good, that his nature is Love and Wisdom.[94] The patient must close his eyes and fill himself with God.[95] Health is achieved by the process of spiritualization,[96] which is attained through the reading of spiritual literature, the hearing of spiritual wisdom, and the association with those already on the spiritual path.[97]

Health, we read, is an eternal state of spiritual being,[98] attained or attainable when the individual realizes a true God-consciousness,[99] and depends on a personal realization of the divine presence.[100] When the consciousness is filled with the spirit of truth, one need say nothing, for the healing Christ then becomes operative.[100] It is not the body which is, or needs to be, healed;[102] rather, it is the real I, the eternal I AM, which is the individual deity, thus transforming the body into the image of itself.

Goldsmith's principal thesis is that since God is infinite, nothing else and no other supply can exist. As soon as we realize the infinity of God and that he is closer than breathing, the result is infinite abundance.[103]

Healing follows the spiritualizing influx, of which we read again and again.[104] It is not something that one person does for another,[105] but rather something which everyone can and must do for himself.[106] It is achieved through meditation, an exercise reminiscent of the Hindu swami, whose methods are described in detail.[107] A consciousness of truth is thus established.[108] Goldsmith declares that he pursued this technique 9 or 10 hours daily,[109] handled as many as 135 calls a day, and worked 7 days a week.[110] "This is the way—constant, constant meditation, a constant turning within so that this inner impulse is kept fresh."[111] "Spiritual healing is accomplished through divine silence...."[112] It is the highway to the Kingdom of God.[113]

Healing is accomplished by mutual meditation on the part of healer and patient, which leads to spiritualization, or the realization of God-consciousness. "Our object," says the author, "is to attain a measure of that mind which was in Christ Jesus, and then let It do with us what It will."[114]

Goldsmith rejects the orthodox doctrine of Atonement as a matter of course;[115] and, as we have seen, his Christ is not a person but a universal power.

9. *Health and Success.* According to Goldsmith, "supply" and success do not consist of money or fame.[116] And we are admonished to relinquish material things.[117] Money and property, he declares, do not constitute "supply."[118] We should never work to make a living merely, but for the joy of the work itself,[119] and then let the livelihood be the by-product of the activity. We should never think of personal gain;[120] we should never pray for "things."[121] Health and wealth are not added to our lives, but are included in them as part of God-realization.[122] Sin, sickness, and poverty are simply the penalty for trying to live entirely on the material plane.[123] We should never attempt to heal or enrich, *per se*;[124] we do not demonstrate health or wealth— only the God-Presence, of which all other good is a by-product.[125] We should never worry over "supply;"[126] for, once spiritualized, we will receive everything we need. We do not need dollars, nor need we be concerned over them; they should be regarded like streetcar transfers.[127] As we overcome the world, we no longer sweat and stew, for we understand that we do not live by bread alone. As for the body, keep it clean, and then have no further concern over it; as for all outward necessities, take no thought of them either, for we are in God's eternal keeping.[128]

XI. EMMETT FOX

1. *Biographical.* Emmett Fox (1886-1951) was a layman who became a great exponent of New Thought. And, like Drummond, Troward, and others, he was an Englishman who had already made his mark in another field— electrical engineering. Soon after entering the movement, he lectured to growing audiences at Higher Thought Centers in England; his real career, however, began when he arrived in the United States in 1930.

Dr. W. John Murray had founded the Church of the Healing Christ in New York in 1906, and had spoken to large crowds in the ballroom of the Hotel Waldorf-Astoria; when he died, his place was assumed for a while by Dr. A.C.

Grier, who shortly resigned. Emmett Fox, already launched on an independent career, was called to the ministry of this church, and occupied its pulpit for nearly twenty years. After he was ordained to the ministry by Nona Brooks, the Church was renamed The First Church of Divine Science of New York.

2. *Success.* The success of this church was simply fantastic. The congregation grew into the thousands. As an exponent of New Thought, Fox remains almost without peer in America or the world. At first, meetings were held in the Hippodrome; when this was demolished, services were held in the Manhattan Opera House, and finally in Carnegie Hall, where overflow audiences filled auxiliary rooms twice a week.

For more than forty years, books and pamphlets by Fox have been best sellers; only Trine and Norman Vincent Peale have been more popular through the written word. DeVorss offers nine full-length books and fifty booklets by Fox. Such titles as *Alter Your Life*, 1931, *Power through Constructive Thinking*, 1932, *The Sermon on the Mount*, 1934, and *Sparks of Truth*, 1937, have sold in the hundreds of thousands; they are found on the book tables of most New Thought churches, are dispensed in hundreds of religious bookstores, and are used by ministers of many denominations. What is even more extraordinary is the fact that their luster has not faded with the years—a fate which has overtaken so many others.

Having read seven of his books, we are amazed at the power of Emmett Fox. There is nothing even remotely original in his thought; his appeal, we believe, lies in its simplicity and forthrightness. He stated that he would never use a three-syllable word if one or two would express his idea, and he declared that he would write nothing beyond the understanding of a ten-year-old. While the esoteric creator may find a fit audience which is small, only the popularizer can reach the masses of millions. Charles Braden says[1] that when he attended a service in Carnegie Hall in 1947, Dr. Fox impressed him as one who spoke with authority, not one who theorized; not as one who merely believed but as one who *knew*.

Furthermore, Fox was limited in his range of thought. His themes were few, but direct and filled with conviction. His sermon, says Dr. Braden, lasted only twenty minutes; he spoke without oratorical flourish or elaboration. But the audience was intent, almost spellbound. And when the service was over, hundreds clustered around the literature tables, where four people were kept extremely busy selling the books and pamphlets authored by the speaker.

Most of his volumes consist of essays or sermons previously composed. *Power through Constructive Thinking* and *The Sermon on the Mount* seem to be his only complete and original works. Pamphlets and booklets are reprints of chapters or sections taken from works already published. Such volumes as *Sparks of Truth* and *Make Your Life Worth While*, 1942, consist of short compositions, many taken from earlier books. *Around the Year with*

Emmett Fox, published in 1952, contains 365 short pieces, never more than a page, to be read as devotional exercises on each day of the year. The fact that such a book remains popular after more than 30 years indicates that Fox has become, for countless devotees, a source of profound inspiration.

3. *Message and Method.* Fox was a master of New Thought ideology. God, he declares, is Infinite Mind.[2] He is the Great Source, Substance Itself.[3] The universe is instinct with this impersonal deity, who has Seven Main Aspects: Life, Truth, Love, Intelligence, Soul, Spirit, and Principle.[4] Fox often uses the Swedenborgian methods of exegesis to interpret the Scriptures: the Lord's Prayer[5] and the story of Daniel in the Lion's Den[6] are given extensive expositions in this manner, as are The Four Horsemen of the Apocalypse, where we learn that more than ninety-nine per cent of all humanity are riding the Pale Horse.[7] Genesis and the Seven Days of Creation[8] as well as Adam and Eve[9] are treated in a similar manner. In fact, what is perhaps the author's principal work, *The Sermon on the Mount*, is simply a scriptural interpretation of chapters 5, 6, and 7 of the gospel of Matthew.

Without the spiritual interpretation of Scriptures, we do not see how New Thought—at least as a religion founded primarily on actual Christian documents—could have been established. Fox tells us again and again that the letter killeth and the spirit giveth life and light.[10] "The Bible is not like any other book," he observes; "it is a spiritual vortex through which spiritual power pours from heaven to earth, and the reason why most people derive comparatively little profit from its study is that they lack the spiritual key."[11]

Employing this Swedenborgian method, every expression becomes a wonderful revelation of supreme and living truth. Such terms as Lebanon, Carmel, Sharon signify "certain spiritual faculties" which gradually develop as man awakens spiritually.[12] When we read of the heathen, the wicked, or the enemies within our own households, the reference is always to our own evil thoughts.[13] Jerusalem means the awakened spiritual consciousness.[14] *Heart* in the Bible means the subconscious mind.[15] Since Daniel is Everyman, being assailed with trouble is being thrown into the lion's den.[16] When we are told to turn the other cheek, this means only that we should change our thoughts when faced with error.[17] The Four Horsemen of the Apocalypse symbolize the four elements found in human nature.[18] The fish, fowl, and beasts of Genesis represent the qualities which belong to the spiritual man.[19] Adam symbolizes body and Eve soul.[20] Eating of the forbidden fruit means belief in limitation.[21]

As a whole, Fox is an orthodox exponent of New Thought. Again and again, he proclaims the potency of spiritual influx;[22] the universe is governed by Cosmic Law,[23] and there is no such thing as luck or chance.[24] God works through us by means of scientific prayer,[25] and sickness is treated successfully by positive affirmation.[26] Belief in the reality of evil is the cause of sickness.[27]

Old Age and even death are only beliefs.[28] Worry creates our hell,[29] and evil emotions, especially fear, are the cause of evil.[30] We attract and gravitate toward whatever is similar to ourselves.[31]

There is no fiery hell hereafter; nor is there any fate except that which we create for ourselves. There will be no idleness or harp-playing in the next dispensation.[32]

Organized religion is always in danger of becoming an industry to provide a good living for numerous officials.[33] And first and most of all, each and every one of us should understand that health, prosperity, and happiness constitute God's will and plan for all mankind.[34]

7. *Eschatology.* Although the concept of a spiritual body and the painless transition at death to the spiritual plane or realm is found throughout New Thought, it is nowhere proclaimed with greater simplicity or detail than in Emmett Fox. The Swedish seer presented this as a revelation based on personal knowledge: he declared, as we have seen, that he had conversed with a hundred thousand departed spirits, and had observed millions of them in the Spirit World. Fox, however, never tells us how he knew all this: he merely states it as a fact.

He delineates what happens at death[35]—where the spirit goes and what it does—what kind of body it possesses, a celestial one, which slips from the physical but continues as the seat of all feeling or sensation.[36] Even in normal life, this etheric entity (as with Swedenborg) can slip away at will, but remains attached to the physical like a kite soaring away on a Silver Cord, the severing of which is known as death. Following this transition, we wake up very much as one rising from sleep; and with this, the new life begins.[37] On the spiritual plane, we will all be young again, like a four-dimensional life, and communicate through extrasensory perception.[38] Hypocrisy will therefore be impossible.[39]

Although, on this new plane, there are different localities,[40] the transition will effect no positive change at all,[41] for "you will go to the sort of place and be among the sort of people for whom you have prepared yourself by your habitual thinking and your mode of living while on this earth."[42] However, we do not pass at once into heaven, which is "the conscious Presence of God."[43] As with Swedenborg we must progress further before ultimate union with the divine may be achieved. There is no "hell," but there are places which will be without pleasure of constructive fulfillment, because they will be in accord with those who have been activated by selfishness in this life and so continue into the beyond.[44]

There will be no childbirth on the next plane, and we will meet and associate only with those who are like ourselves.[45] The intellectual and artistic opportunities will be without limit; and we will at last be able to solve all the age-old problems of religion and philosophy which have heretofore proved insoluble.[46]

When the Silver Cord is severed, the physical body is discarded; and, since it has no further use or value, it should simply be cremated.[47] The body passes again into the earth, but the person lives on forever. "A thousand years from now," says Fox, "I shall still be alive and active somewhere else; and so the events of today have only the importance that pertains to today."[48]

Fox proclaims with equal simplicity and assurance another age-old doctrine rarely found in New Thought: that of reincarnation, modeled closely upon ancient Brahmanism, Buddhism, and Platonic sources, except that the intervals of torture in hell are omitted. Like the Hindus, Fox can imagine no adequate means of explaining the facts of life—people born crippled, blind, diseased, mentally retarded, poverty-stricken—except as punishment for sins committed in previous existences. "The answer is," he declares, "that you have lived before, not once, but many, many times, and that in the course of those many lives you have *thought* and *said* and *done* all sorts of things, good and bad, and the circumstances into which you were born are but the natural outcome of the way in which you have lived and comported yourself in your former lives."[49]

Our Karma will rule one existence after another until, at last, we may be able to escape what the Buddhists call The Wheel of Life. "You need not come back if you will consecrate your whole heart upon God, seek His Presence until you realize it *vividly*, and live to do His Holy Will.... If you can really do this...you will leave this earth planet to enter full communion with God, and you need never come back."[50] Thus, at last, it will be possible to achieve Nirvana, but it will, unlike the Buddhist, be a divinely conscious state.

In the meantime, millions of etheric-body-souls hover in the earth's atmosphere, while awaiting their next incarnation, or union with a human embryo. "It should be understood," declared Fox, "that incarnation takes place at the moment of conception."[51] And thus, into the world again the human being "arrives a newborn body with no conscious memory of the past."[52] Once more, he grows into childhood, then into manhood, and finally passes into the etheric state when the Silver Cord is broken again.

XII. HORATIO W. DRESSER

1. *History*. Few names in New Thought are more illustrious than that of Horatio W. Dresser (1866-1954). And surely no one could have been more amply endowed for the work he was to do: his parents, Julius and Annetta Gertrude Dresser, had, as we have seen, been patients and devotees of Phineas Quimby. Born in the year Quimby died, Horatio continued throughout a long career as one of the most prolific and popular New Thought writers. Although neither an organizer nor an original scholar or thinker, he was the herald of a new religious psychotherapy which recognized that its true field lay in minis-

tering to the mentally disturbed. In volume after volume, he proclaimed this gospel: Charles S. Braden lists thirty-two books credited to him,[1] all of which present various facets of developing New Thought. In addition to other activities, he became editor of *Arena* in 1898, and from this position of authority, exercised great direct influence upon the movement.

2. *Studies.* Dresser never identified himself with any group, but remained for several decades the outstanding spokesman for the movement in general. His first book, *The Power of Silence*, published in 1895, had gone through fifteen editions by 1903;[2] and it was during the years immediately preceding and following the latter date that he wrote most of his popular expositions of Quimbyesque-Swedenborgianism. In 1905, he undertook advanced studies at Harvard under the tutelage of William James and Josiah Royce, where he was awarded a Ph.D. in 1907—at the age of forty-one. We may well believe that these men interacted intellectually, and that the Swedenborgian echoes in *The Varieties of Religious Experience* stem as much from contacts with Dresser as from the influence of the Elder James.

For a time, Dresser served as a lecturer at the Theological Seminary of the New Church in Cambridge and in 1919 he was ordained a Swedenborgian minister. In 1925, however, he retired from clerical life; his books, written between 1923 and 1930, deal with ethics, psychology, history, and comparative religion. His last work, *Knowing and Helping People*, 1933, was written from the Unitarian rather than the specifically New Thought or Swedenborgian point of view.

We note again that it was Horatio Dresser who published the *Quimby Manuscripts* in 1921.

3. *Evaluation: the Psychic Scientist.* With unflagging interest the present writer has perused eight of Dresser's books, all preceding 1920. They are precise, intellectual, and carefully worded: although they lack the fire and intensity of R.W. Trine, each is a milestone in the development of New Thought. In his second book, *In Search of a Soul*, 1897, we find a pre-Freudian exposition of the three-level construction of the human psyche which the author must have absorbed from Evans and Swedenborg. "First we have," he declares, "the plane of acute consciousness, of passing sensations, of thoughts about them, of all sorts of moods, selves, ideas, emotions, fears, hopes and desires. Then we have the plane of subconscious action, governed by the suggestions given it by the conscious self; and, finally, the higher or reflective self, the self of illumination or superconsciousness, of guidance, reason."[3]

The Higher Self of Dresser is similar to the Freudian conscience and the Lower Self to the Freudian Id. However, we find that this is a moral division rather than one depending on inherited characteristics and social indoctrination. "The term 'higher self' I...use to denote the revelation of God in the finite soul...."[4] "The first evidence, then, that there really is a higher self is its contrast with the lower—the self of doubts, distrusts, temptations, and selfish motives...looking upward with longing to the higher."[5] "The lower self urges one to follow its dictates, holding out inducements and rewards. The conscience simply presents its 'ought' for one's consideration: ours is the choice to turn aside or to obey."[6] "One knows that there is a higher self because one is thrown into discord with the lower. And one knows there is a lower self, because one would at all times be like the higher, and cannot; for the lower asserts its sway...."[7]

4. *Theology.* The Higher Self is God immanent, or "Mind," which, when acting "according to the laws...better understood, will be our salvation from error, sin, and disease."[8] We have, therefore, within us, for our use or misuse, *"the greatest power in the universe."*[9] This is true because the Swedenborgian deity is omnipresent: "there is only one ultimate force, of which heat, light, electricity, etc. are manifestations.... All events, as well as all particular manifestations of the one force, therefore belong together."[10] "Physical man seems to be the only creature who is open to all these interpenetrating forces.... your body or mine...may at the same time be open to all the physical forces resident in the ether...spiritually open to the soul-life which more intimately connects us with the mind and heart of God."[11]

This leads to Dresser's persuasion of immortality: "the individual soul is really never separate nor apart from the divine self-hood.... you and I are instruments...of the divine nature, embodiments of its life, wisdom, and power...not limited by time, without beginning and without ending, and therefore not subject to birth and dissolution...."[12]

The doctrine of influx is often reiterated: "again and again one turns to the fountain-head of life's stream, to become re-created and strengthened.... The incarnation of the Spirit in the forms of worlds, rocks, plants, men—this is the miracle of the universe."[13] "Starting with the coarser grades of manifestation—the rocks, the vegetable world, and the lower forms of animal life—we find them less highly organized, and consequently revealing less of what we term the higher nature, or soul of the universe.... The higher we ascend, the more closely we approach the very heart and beauty of life...."[14]

5. *Theory of Healing.* Dresser's next treatise, *Methods and Problems of Spiritual Healing*, was published in 1899. In the preface, he declares that he is not in the business of mental healing nor does he give advice concerning specific application of mental cure. He is not a follower of any sect and does not subscribe to the full creed of those who advocate mental remedies in the cure of disease. He is simply a truth-seeker.[15] He declares that not only pain, but physical disease also, is real. "Moreover," he continues, "one has good reason to doubt if the 'cures'" of Christian Science "really are cures, for actual facts are almost never procurable from a Christian Scientist."[16] It should be

noted that they "have permitted people to die rather than call a regular physician" and have thus "harmed the cause of mental healing more than they have helped it by their fanatical zeal."[17] And therefore, "the time must come when every Christian Scientist shall...be 'brought low'; and, if some fall so far from the throne of abstract grace as to require the help of a regular physician, out of this severe lesson they will probably learn more wisdom than is contained in their entire philosophy of idealistic abstraction."[18]

The secret of health and mental healing is inseparable from a true theology and the reality of divine influx. When the higher self is in control and when the mind-body entity of man is in full communication with deity, then the physical is far less likely to be contaminated by disease: "you may make the changed state.... permanent by opening the mind and receiving new life and power directly from the fountain-head.... If you have entered the silence and communed with God, you will know what I mean."[19]

In one of the more elaborate passages, Dresser declares: "There is no need for an external creator, only the existence of a resident, progressive Power, moving within us, and carrying onward to remoter ends that which already exists.... It is perpetual flux, except so far as law and the sum total of force are concerned. Its power is universal, owning matter and consciousness, things and ideas alike. It is the great becoming, achieving life of the universe, the progressive revelation of God.

"Thus broadly understood, there is not an atom, not a star, not an accident, nor a purpose, that lies outside of its sphere. It is the greatest revelation the human mind has ever made; and, from the time of the general discovery and proclamation of the law, every branch of knowledge has gradually been falling into line.... It is incontestably the only hypothesis which in any way accounts for the development of life...."[20]

One of Dresser's most important theoretical works is *Health and the Inner Life* (1906). Chapter I describes the methods and contributions of Quimby; Chapter II is a Personal Testimony written by his mother, Annetta Dresser, in tribute to her healer. Among the First Teachers, priority is given to Warren Felt Evans, whose "acquaintance with the writings of Swedenborg...enabled him so readily to grasp and develop the ideas he gained from Mr. Quimby.... But in books like.... *The Divine Love and Wisdom*, there are teachings which lead very directly to the practical method for which Mr. Quimby stood. Dr. Evans only needed to find a man who was actually proving what he had theoretically anticipated in order to accept the entire therapeutic doctrine."[21] In another passage, we read: "Mr. Quimby and his followers point out, agreeing with Swedenborg, that man has no life and power of his own, no good quality apart from God: for God alone is the source of life."[22]

6. *Psycho-Therapy.* The idea of Influx is here, as throughout New Thought, repeated again and again. "This First Cause, or God, or Father, is,

therefore, the great generative source of all that exists.... this first Cause...is literally the omnipresent life and mover of every living thing...."[23] Now "this wisdom, being omnipresent, is not limited to any one person. All can have it whether they now possess it or not."[24] As "healer and patient advance together...they are filled with the divine influx."[25]

Here we find Dresser deeply concerned over the physical effects of morbid fears. He recalls the young Calvinist whom Quimby told that his religion was killing him.[26] He "found that the fears, emotions, and beliefs which were factors in producing the patient's disease were intimately connected with religious creeds and experiences."[27] And now we find Dresser emphasizing that New Thought is the key, not only to health, but also to "happiness and success" in every aspect of life.[28]

In *A Physician to the Soul* (1908), Dresser has advanced significantly in the direction of religious psychoanalytic therapy. Throughout, he implies not only the actuality of matter, but also of physical diseases which are beyond the reach of mental cure. He praises the work of the "Emmanuel Church, Boston," which has "spread to other churches. Wisely conservative, the founders of this movement first won the cooperation of the medical profession, then limited the practice of psychotherapy to the cases of functional and nervous diseases which were pronounced eligible by competent physicians."[29]

Thus a specific, yet grandiose, vista for mind-cure beckoned the mental practitioner. Since the psychosomatic ailments of mankind may outnumber the purely physical, and since the body is unquestionably and profoundly influenced by psychic states, mental healers should candidly admit the reality of matter and physical diseases and leave the treatment of such maladies to the regular physicians. The mental healers can still pre-empt a rich harvest from their own beneficent activity. Although Quimby had not fully realized this great truth, he was actually a precurser of the psychoanalysts; his patients were beyond the reach of ordinary medicine for the simple reason that their maladies were not of physical, but of mental, origin.

Perhaps the most distinctive contribution of Dresser consists in the fact that he may have been the first who fully realized, well before the Freudian psychology was known in America, the relationship between ill-health and neurosis. "There are people of a neurotic type," he wrote, "who wear upon us, not merely because of their nervous 'atmosphere'; but because of the underlying mental attitude, usually one of self-centeredness.... Then there are vampires, neurological parasites, who cling like vines and send out psychophysical tentacles much more tenacious than a vine. There are imperious, dominating personalities of power sufficient to rule an entire household...."[30]

Dresser understood that the mentally ill "need patient analysis, together with gentle advice...."[31] The healer "should know, (1) the actual state of the patient, mentally, physically, socially; (2) the chief causes of the most central of these states, in the light of the inner history, and, (3) the underlying moral or religious attitude." When this is changed, "moral regeneration will begin; there will be an altered mental tone and accompanying physical responses."[32]

To many people, observes Dresser, "it is still an entirely new idea that mental states bear any relation to bodily health.... little is known about mental influences in general...." However, "it is well known that religious emotions produce powerful effects, and nearly everybody knows something about the power of imagination; but here acquaintance with the subject usually ceases."[33] "To know how and why mental influences affect the body for good or evil, we must understand these disturbing influences and learn the ways in which mental life may be shaped anew."[34]

Dresser cites many cases of neurasthenic disease and cure. For example, there was the ex-Christian Scientist who literally believed that there is no matter. She dwelt in an artificial world and, attempting to break with her "scientist" teacher, induced a profoundly traumatic experience. Only through gradual and sympathetic analysis was this woman enabled to escape her prison into a world of freedom and reality, where she could finally accept the actual existence of trees and flowers.[35]

He describes "the daughter whose mother is out of sympathy with her, whose sisters despise her, while a whimsical father rules over all and defeats every plan for a change in home life. Or, it is a wife in distress who has grown morbid because she pines for the attention her husband might give her...."[36] Again, "here is a young woman...bound to a selfish mother, less intelligent than herself, whom she vainly tries to please. The more she does for her mother, the more is expected and the less her efforts are appreciated. Opportunities to change her occupation or to travel have come to her, which she has been obliged to decline because her mother refused to change her abode. She has repeatedly overworked, become nervously prostrated, and been compelled to go to a sanitarium or hospital. Health partially regained, she has" gone "through the same round again, not a whit wiser, mystified by her repeated illnesses, unable to get light from specialists in nervous diseases."[37]

The world is filled with similar tragedies, and very often the mental-moral dislocation assumes a purely physical appearance. To help such people, then, becomes the role of the counselor, the mental healer, the ministers in the churches of New Thought.

7. *A Literary Colossus.* One of Dresser's most ambitious works is *The Philosophy of the Spirit* (1908), which includes his Ph.D. thesis, *The Element of Irrationality in the Hegelian Dialectic.* This is much too elaborate for summary here: suffice it to say that it adds nothing philosophically to what was published in previous works; it may, however, be called the author's most extensive exposition of Swedenborgianism. Its central message is its theology, which envisions "God as the central reality, the eternal basis of all that lives

and thinks.... the abiding essence within and behind both the inner world of states and the world of things."[38]

In 1917, Dresser published *The Spirit of the New Thought*, consisting of twenty-two essays by himself and other leaders in the movement written between 1887 and 1916. Swedenborgian ideology is present, to a greater or lesser extent, throughout.

In 1919, Dresser published *A History of the New Thought Movement*, which remained the classic work on the subject until Charles S. Braden's *Spirits in Rebellion* appeared in 1963. In 1921, however, as we have noted, Dresser gave the world his crowning literary labor, *The Quimby Manuscripts*, carefully edited by him; thus, once and for all, was settled the precise contribution of that extraordinary innovator who ministered to the victims of psychosomatic ailments.

XIII. CHRISTIAN DAA LARSON

1. *Rise and Decline.* Christian Daa Larson (1874-1945?) is unique in the history of American letters. He flourished for more than twenty years following 1907; he conducted correspondence courses in which great numbers, including Ernest Holmes, were enrolled; his books, published by Thomas Y. Crowell, sold in the hundreds of thousands. But his meteoric career fell into obscurity under the Great Depression of the Thirties. The *Cumulative Book Index* for 1912 lists twelve of his titles; that for 1928, twenty-seven; but in 1933, only three were still in print, and thereafter, none at all. The Library of Congress lists forty-two in its master catalog. But now his name is rarely found in biographical dictionaries; his books are gradually vanishing from the libraries, and now only one or two of his titles can be obtained from DeVorss.

Neither his popularity nor his decline is too difficult to comprehend: he was a product of and the spokesman for the current Zeitgeist. There is nothing original in his writings; they reflect little scholarship or scientific knowledge. His pages abound with echoes from Troward, whom he must have studied assiduously. He had his own spiritual interpretations of Scriptures, as do so many other New Thought writers. Although his pages are filled with Swedenborgian ideology, this was probably derived from intermediate sources. His books, filled with joy and unlimited optimism, are lacking in practical solutions; they are simplistic, their style runs to repetition and redundancy. We believe that his personal magnetism must have been the secret of his success; but we must recognize that he had a powerful message, not only for his generation, but for all time.

He wrote books with such titles as *Brains, and How to Get Them*, *The Pathway of Roses*, *Business Psychology*, *How to Stay Young*, *Perfect Health*, *What is Truth?*, *The Ideal Made Real*, *How Great Men Succeed*, *Mind Cure*,

Nothing Succeeds like Success, Your Forces and How to Use Them; and *Poise and Power*. These inspirational messages were extremely popular in the business community, where his gospel of health, happiness, and prosperity was received enthusiastically, especially during the halcyon years following World War I.

2. *Literary Style*. Passages in *The Pathway of Roses*, which are paralleled in Troward, illustrate his style. "There is only one will in the universe just as there is only one mind. The one mind is the mind of God, the one will is the will of God. The mind of individual man is an individual or differentiated expression of the Infinite Mind, and the largeness of this human mind depends upon how much of the one mind man may decide to appropriate. Man has the freedom to incorporate in his own individual consciousness as much of the Infinite Mind as he may desire; and as the mind of the Infinite is limitless, the mind of man may continue to become larger and larger without any end."

And again: "the path of the divine will is upward and onward forever, and its power is employed exclusively in building more lofty mansions for the soul. Therefore, the will of God does not produce sickness, adversity, or death; on the contrary, the will of God eternally wills to produce wholeness, harmony, and life."[1]

3. *Philosophy*. The concept of Influx is often implied and the Laws of Correspondence are stated repeatedly.[2] The universe is necessarily good. Evil is simply emptiness, resulting "from lack of life."[3] It is an inherited race-belief;[4] it is created when we go away from God,[5] and when we express a material belief, we create disease.[6] The cosmos is governed by immutable law,[7] and if we observe it, all ills must disappear.[8] Caring properly for the body, which is the temple of the living spirit,[9] constitutes simply obedience to the cosmic law.[10] "Whoever discerns clearly the spiritual essence or divine substance, which is the basis or soul of all reality, will manifest...not only purity, but absolute immunity from all disease...."[11]

We read a great deal about "cosmic consciousness";[12] this is the supreme good which flows into our minds and bodies when we open up the channel to receive it.[13] "Open the heart to the Influx of Infinite Love, and all that God can give will come with His love."[14]

Larson is a firm exponent of Trowardian Affirmation, which plays so large a role in the healing technique of Ernest Holmes also. "Give positive expression, in thought, word, action, and life, to that which we know to be real.... Make your life a living affirmation of the great things that are before...."[15]

The world which God desires for us "is not a future state of existence, but an eternal state.... It is therefore at hand, here and now. To enter the 'Pearly Gates' is to enter that better world—God's own true world, where all is well."[16] In this immediately attainable heaven, we are to think nothing but opulence, whether this be in the form of "life, health, power, wisdom, spirituality, or greater abundance in external things...."[17] Christ came that we might have life and have it more abundantly.[18] This being true, the very idea of self-sacrifice must be eliminated. Being filled with the Christ-Spirit means that we are able to enjoy all that is good in this life, spiritual, emotional, material.[19]

The author emphasizes the Trowardian theory of evolution: "To enter into the cosmic world, therefore, is to enter into freedom, health, harmony, and wholeness.... everything that promotes the highest good for body, mind, and soul. The cosmic life is the apex of all ascending life.... the realization of everything that is ideal.... the attainment of the one supreme goal in the living of divine life."[20] And thus, we become the "Sons of God."[21]

Although an impersonal God is postulated, his concept is reconciled with the idea of personalness in the Trowardian tradition.[22] Through the individualization in the human soul, the cosmic power assumes personality. All souls are therefore one: "God is not a personality, but he is personal to every personality in existence."[23] He is the "limitless sea of divinity in which we live and move and have our being."[24] And when this Christ-power enters and takes possession of us, we are filled with the same essence which was in Christ-Jesus to the degree that made him unique in the history of mankind.[25]

4. *Redemption.* This occurs on entering "the cosmic state," where "the entire world is clothed with the sun; the waters of the deep reflect the radiant glory of celestial kingdoms, and the mountains proclaim the majesty and the power of the life that is lived on the heights. Nature sings the everlasting praises of Him who is closer than breathing, nearer than hands and feet, and every human countenance beams with the beautiful smile of God. The flowers declare the thoughts of the Infinite; the forest chants the silent prelude to worship, while the birds inspire the soul to ascend to the vast empyrean blue. We are speechless with ecstasy...."[26]

As the preceding illustrates the florid style of the writer, so the following reflects his simplistic theory: "The righteous man is never weak, never sick, and is never in a state of discord or disorder.... Sickness, weakness, discord, and all other adverse conditions come from the violation of law somewhere in human life, but the righteous man violates no law."[27] Again, "no person could become sick that is always filled and protected with the power of right thought."[28]

There are passages, however, in which the author seems somewhat more realistic. "Worry," he declares, "has crippled thousands of fine minds and brought millions to an early grave. We simply cannot afford to worry and must never do so under any condition whatever."[29] We must not be critical or hostile toward others, for to be so is self-destructive;[30] if we would have peace of mind, we must show love and kindness and practice justice.[31]

5. *Health, Happiness, and Prosperity.* This is the message of Christian Daa Larson; and it is emphasized particularly in a chapter entitled "Talk Health,

Happiness, and Prosperity."[32] We are to think and affirm these benefits at all times, on all occasions, to all people, and in all places. "Talk happiness. When things look dark, talk happiness. When things look bright, talk more happiness. When others are sad, insist on being glad."[33]

Again, "Talk Health. It is the best medicine. When people stop talking sickness, they will stop getting sick. Talk health and stay well. Talk health to the person who is sick and you will cause him to think health. He who thinks health will live health, and he who lives health will produce health."[34]

Finally, "Talk prosperity. When times are not good, man himself must make them better, and he can make them better by doing his best and having faith in that power that produces prosperity. When men have faith in prosperity, they will think prosperity...and you can give men faith in prosperity by constantly talking prosperity, and then men will live prosperity and thus do that which produces prosperity. They may not listen at first, but perseverance always wins. Prosperity is extremely attractive.... Think prosperity, talk prosperity, and live prosperity.... You can remove fear by talking prosperity."[35]

6. *The Psyche.* The only Larson book now printed by DeVorss is *Your Forces and How to Use Them*, first published in 1912. In this, the author reflects the New Psychology of Evans and Freud as a solution for human problems; here we find detailed discussions of the conscious, the subconscious, and the superconscious levels of the human psyche.[36] However, his concepts are quite different from the Freudian Id and Superego. We find virtually no reference to Christian or religious sources: the Christ is mentioned only in a single paragraph,[37] and the only allusion to God is found in a sentence where we are told never to kneel before him.[38] In short, the entire approach is secular.

Larson is chiefly interested in the conscious and the subconscious aspects of the mind. His thesis is that the latter constitutes a vast reservoir of potential power and accomplishment, into which we can channel positive and constructive thought; by so doing, we develop the capacity to achieve whatever goal we may desire. "The subconscious," he says, "may be defined as a vast mental field permeating the entire objective personality...or as a great mental sea of life, energy, and power, the force and capacity of which has never been measured."[39] The human system is a living, creative dynamo,[40] which can produce surplus energy,[41] but which, unless utilized, simply lies dormant and useless.[42]

7. *Success.* The "I AM," or the Ego, is the center of each individual life. It is the Supreme You.[43] It is the Great Within, and when it comes into contact with the source of all things, we reach the borderland of cosmic consciousness.[44]

The *sine qua non* of success and greatness is to be an individual[45] and to make every desire, feeling, and thought positive.[46] To succeed in life, a man must be thinking "all the time of what he wishes to obtain and achieve."[47] Since the majority do not know what they really want, they accomplish little, and usually fail.[48] They do not continue long enough or concentrate sufficiently[49] on a single objective, and thus they scatter their energies.[50]

To achieve success and greatness, we must avoid all the evil and destructive passions, such as anger, hatred, malice, envy, jealousy, revenge, worry, and fear.[51] If, on the other hand, you think constructively, you "accumulate volume, capacity, and power in your mental world, until you finally become a mental giant."[52]

We become whatever we channel into the subconscious mind. We can train our bodies "to possess the same virile youth at one hundred as the healthiest man or woman of twenty may possess." The only reason we grow old is "the result of what the subconscious mind has been directed to do during past generations."[53] Present "possibilities indicate that improvement along any line, whether it be in working capacity, ability, health, happiness, or character, can be secured without fail if the subconscious is properly directed."[54] "It is when we combine mental action in the conscious, subconscious, and superconscious that we get the results we desire."[55] You can do whatever you are determined to do;[56] you can realize any ambition.[57] If you think success, you will achieve it.[58] Men become mental giants because they have great thoughts.[59]

The Law of Success is this: "Know what you mean, and then want it with all the power that is in you."[60] As you channel this energy into your subconscious, it becomes a source of unlimited power.

Larson has no illusions concerning humanity as a whole. Most people are only driftwood;[61] although Nature gives everyone the power to achieve greatness, few do so because they fail to utilize their latent forces.[62] One reason for this failure is that they are mentally dependent.[63] It "is positively wrong for any individual...to follow any one man...or any group of men...under any circumstances whatever."[64] The world is filled with capable men and women who have made little of their lives "because they have not the will to apply all their ability."[65]

Success comes only to those who have the character to press on to higher attainments and greater achievements year after year.[66] Greatness is a life-long undertaking and superior men and women are the result of constant endeavor. To date, humanity has achieved greatness only among a few distinguished individuals; but what they have done, all can do—and if they were to do so, we would have a race of supermen.[67]

8. *The Setting Star.* Christian Daa Larson made an immense impact during the decades of his influence and glory. But when the stock market crashed in 1929 and the fearful clutches of the Great Depression seized upon

the hearts and minds of men in the following years, his optimistic gospel fell upon unheeding ears; and his books soon disappeared from the *Cumulative Index* and his myriads of readers were reduced to an elite few.

XIV. ERNEST S. HOLMES AND FENWICKE L. HOLMES

1. *Outward History.* Ernest Shurtleff Holmes (1877-1960), who was the founder of the Church of Religious Science and author of *Science of Mind*, is one of the most redoubtable figures in the history of New Thought. Poor during his boyhood, he received little formal education and no theological instruction.[1] As we explain in a later chapter, the brothers worked closely together for several years in California; later they collaborated in a series of free lectures delivered in various important cities and attended by immense crowds, at which as many as a thousand would sign up for classes at $25 each.

In 1925, the brothers dissolved partnership: Fenwicke continued as a brilliant and successful author and lecturer, while Ernest devoted himself to teaching, healing, and the building of a church—actually a denomination. In 1926, Ernest published *The Science of Mind*, which he called HIS revelation and which remains the basic textbook of the Church of Religious Science. As the years brought greater maturity to the author, the work was revised and expanded. By 1938, it attained its final format in 667 pages. In 1954, this edition had gone through twenty-three printings, and there have been many more since then.

Ernest wrote a small library, among which the more popular volumes are *This Thing Called Life, How to Use Science of Mind,* and *Creative Mind and Success,* which explain and particularize the philosophy of *Science of Mind.*

How the magnificent Mother Church of Religious Science was built on Wilshire Boulevard in Los Angeles and how an important denomination developed is another story: suffice it here to say that Ernest S. Holmes continued unceasingly in his labors until his death in 1960 and that his elder brother, Fenwicke, outlived him and wrote his biography.[2]

2. *The Teachings of Fenwicke L. Holmes.* The philosophic systems and the ideologies of the brothers are nearly identical, and we find that of Fenwicke fully set forth in *The Law of the Mind in Action* and in *The Faith that Heals,* 1921. Although he does not say precisely that God is the Central Sun of the Universe, his theological concept is based on this premise. God is the "Creative Spirit, everywhere present, eternally here. In Him is all life.... He is unlimited."[3] He is the original stuff of the cosmos, the source of light, heat, vitality. He is the impersonal source of power, the infinite law and principle which governs the universe and every manifestation that exists: the stars, the planets, the earth, the animals, and all vegetation. Most of all, Man, child of

God, is divine spirit," and, as such, "shares His resources, lives, moves, and has his being in God as an infinite sea."[4] He declares that "the same substance is in the flaming sunrise, the flying bird, and the flowering bush. The one substance composes your body, your environment, and your wealth."[5] God is "All of Life, Love, and Wisdom, and not as a person..."[6] "To conceive of God *as a person* is to recognize *two* powers in the universe," which would reduce the cosmos to chaos and zero.[7] God is Life, Love, and Wisdom.[8]

This living, pulsating, creative, and ever-active force or power, which Fenwicke Holmes usually calls Cosmic Consciousness, constantly and universally streams forth as a life-giving influx which sustains and heals every sentient thing and conscious creature. It is the impartial, impersonal spirit with universal powers and limitless resources from which man may draw substance and energy "*at his own will*."[9] It is "*the Thinker that conceives things, the substance of which things are composed, and the power that sustains them.*"[10]

Nothing in the universe or in human life is static, for the "Cosmic Consciousness is continuously creative."[11] This is, of course, a simple restatement of the Swedenborgian Doctrine of Influx, which Holmes emphasizes again and again. We must place ourselves in alliance with the Unseen, the supernal forces which will then possess us.[12] When a man enters the secret places of the Most High, he draws from the springs of Life, peace, and plenty, and there the Lord will renew his strength because his mind and soul are receptive and his body will be healed.[13]

This influx is always available, but the "Creative Spirit enters only the door that is open," and benefits only that person who is receptive.[14] When this is the case, "the pure, clear stream of love divine" flows through his body and carries away all impure and selfish thoughts, and cleanses mind and body of all sin.[15] There are "certain brain-centers and nerve-systems especially adapted to the influx of pure ideas from the universal" creative force.[16] As the "Creative Mind becomes to us what we become to It," there is no limit except our own capacities to receive the beneficence available.[17] We are like electric bulbs which, according to their capacity, draw light from the central power system.[18]

The Swedenborgian Law of Correspondences lies at the base of Fenwicke's theory concerning disease and its cure. Since God is the Universal All, there can be no duality, or evil, in the universe. In his finite scope, Man is microcosm filled with macrocosmic deity; and since there is no sin, evil, or disease in God, these can have no reality in Man. For every material existence, there is a spiritual prototype or correspondence. The universal law of the cosmos must be obeyed if we are to "create our own heaven" and avoid "our own hell."[19] The universal mind, which is God, corresponds exactly to that of a human individual.[20] Under "the Law of Correspondences, you manifest or externalize...just what you think within."[21]

Since God is universal and Man is the microcosm, and since there is no evil force in the universe, neither organic nor functional disease can be endowed with reality.[22] However, since thoughts are potent things, wrong thinking attracts disease and right thinking casts it out.[23] We are all subject to, or influenced by, the contagious thought-atmosphere which surrounds us.[24] Whenever we permit a negative thought to rule, we become the victims of its suggestion; and we can be cured only by positive thinking.[25]

Since God is the Positive All-Good, negations are non-entities: "as darkness is legislated out of existence by.... light, so evil is reduced to zero by the presence of a contrary thought."[26] Sin is not willful sickness, only ignorance, which never calls for moral judgment or condemnation.[27] To cast out evil, therefore, one declares: I am spirit, life, and Divine Mind. No evil can befall the spiritual mind."[28] To achieve the happy life, we need only "Bring Up the Aggregate of Our Thinking for Health, Wealth, and Love So That It Shall Outbalance Any Possible Amount of Negative Thinking."[29]

Such, according to Fenwicke L. Holmes, is the foundation for the religion of health, happiness, and prosperity.

3. *The Swedenborgianism of Ernest Shurtleff Holmes.* As was the case with his brother, the metaphysical base for Ernest S. Holmes's philosophy and practical work is found in the Swedenborgian concepts of deity, influx, correspondence, and Christ-Power. "The physical universe," we read, "is the Body of God—the invisible Principle of All Life. Our physical being is the body of the unseen man."[30] This "First Cause, Spirit, Mind" or "invisible Essence" is "The Thing Itself";[31] it is the "origin of everything"[32] and "the Universal Energy."[33] It is the "One Central Life, from Whose Self-Existence all draw their livingness...."[34] God is the unmade, co-eternal substance of the universe which is governed by immutable law.[35] He is the Creative Intelligence,[36] which exists in everything.[37] There is one Mind which is God and is in me, and there is one spiritual body, which is also mine. Within me is the mind of Christ and my body is the Body of God.[38] We live, as it were, surrounded by a sea, which is God,[39] our substance and supply.[40] In virtually Swedenborgian terminology, we learn that, since we are made of the same stuff as the Central Fire of the Universe, we are the offspring of the Supreme Spirit.[41] We read that "the *sun* stands for the inner Spiritual Principle," which always shines when we remove the obstructions of unbelief.[42] The Creator is the immutable, inexorable, and impersonal manifestation of the Mother-Father God.[43]

God is a triune principle;[44] he is the physical universe manifested as body;[45] he is also the "invisible Life Essence of all that is, the intelligent Energy running through all."[46] Being infinite, God is indeed greater than man,[47] who is a finite form; but the mind of man is part of the mind of God,[48] man is God objectified.[49] Actually, the divinity which constitutes man's inner life is the only knowable God.[50] Man is the microcosmic image of the macrocosmic deity.[51]

The Christ-concept of Holmes is scarcely less central than his theology. Since we are the offspring of the Supreme Spirit, mankind enjoys a universal sonship, which is the Christ within,[52] the Christ-Mind,[53] the immanent savior.[54] This Power is always present, to a lesser or greater degree, in every human being.[55]

The man "Jesus became the Christ through a complete realization of the Unity of Spirit...."[56] He "became the embodiment of the Christ, as the human gave way to the Divine Idea of Sonship."[57] We must comprehend that "Christ is God in the soul of man."[58] "As the external Jesus gave way to the Divine, the human took on the Christ Spirit and became the Voice of God to humanity."[59] Christ is the manifestation of God as universal idea.[60] The indwelling Christ is generic man, "The Real Man."[61]

Christ, then, is not a person or an individual; he is, rather, an omnipresent power, available to everyone without measure and existent in each of us to whatever degree we can absorb and assimilate this energy and illumination.

Holmes's theology and Christology lead directly to his concepts of death and immortality, which, again, are distinctly Swedenborgian. The soul is the true human entity, which controls the body, "its legitimate effect."[62] Thus, our true bodies are eternal for they are "not made with hands."[63] No man will ever die, for the Spirit of God is within and cannot change; therefore each life is forever.[64] The soul needs a physical body temporarily, but when this is no longer adequate, it is discarded and the soul continues to function, but more subtly.[65] Actually, we are spirits now, as much as we ever shall be.

This Swedenborgian doctrine is repeated over and over: if the soul can project a body here, there is no reason to doubt that it will create another for the eternal life.[66] The future body will resemble the present one, but will be free from disease, old age, or any other undesirable condition.[67] Once we become unconscious of death, we will easily pass "from this life to the next" without even being aware of the transition.[68] Thus, we prepare, not for death, but for eternal life, a passage which will be a "glorious experience."[69] Like the eagle, free from his cage, the soul will soar from its home of heavy flesh to its native heights, in the Father's house.[70] Resurrection is nothing more or less than rising from a belief in death.[71] "The physical disappearance of Jesus after his resurrection was the result of the spiritualization of his consciousness."[72]

Since the immortal soul exists, there can be no doubt of spirit communication.[73]

Another Swedenborgian concept which animates Holmes's thinking is the Doctrine of Correspondence. "In the subjective world," he writes, "there must be a correspondent of everything in the objective...."[74] And again: "The spiritual world contains an image of the physical; the physical is a counterpart of the spiritual."[75]

One of the most pervasive ideas found in Holmes is the Swedenborgian Doctrine of Influx. The great creative force or power which is and sustains the universe is constantly and universally sending forth its beneficent stress of energy; and every vegetative, sentient, or intelligent entity draws upon this for life, illumination, and well-being. The creative mind of God flows through the universe.[76] The Divine Spirit fills me with perfect life, exclaims the author: "*I am bathed in pure spirit...*"[77] and "receptive...to the influx of perfect life...."[78] It is essential that we "open up our own ever-widening channel for this Divine Influx,"[79] a "Power which flows through you without effort...."[80]

Our spirits are part of the Universal Spirit[81] and "when we open our minds to the influx of Divine Wisdom we are allowing our lives to be guided by the Infinite."[82]

4. *Evil.* In Holmes's system, sin and evil are mere negatives and must never be regarded as entities. There can be no duality in the universe since God is All in All; the devil has no existence except in negative thought,[83] and sin is only a mistake,[84] for which punishment "is an inevitable consequence."[85] Actually, there is neither sin nor sinner;[86] since there is no God-ordained evil, it can have no existence of its own.[87]

Evil is a problem only because we believe in it; it is neither person, place, nor thing, and it will disappear as we discard destructive methods.[88] Heaven and hell are states of consciousness, and the latter is the abode of a morbid imagination.[89] Heaven is a kingdom which can exist within us; hell is a discordant state, a belief in cosmic duality, a sense of separation from God.[90] Since there is no evil in the universe, such things as hell or a devil can exist nowhere except in our own delusions.[91]

5. *The Theory and Technique of Healing.* The preceding leads directly to the often-expressed Holmes theory of disease and healing, which is simply applied Christianity.[92] However, we should note that the metaphysician is not yet sufficiently advanced to set bones or to walk on water;[93] nor does he reject *materia medica*, pills, drugs, or the ministrations of a medical doctor whenever these will be of help.[94]

There is no doubt that the medical profession would agree with Holmes that there are many self-induced diseases and that extreme worry,[95] suppressed desire,[96] or unexpected grief may eventuate in death;[97] and that metaphysical and psychological methods have an important field of their own,[98] especially in the treatment of emotional disturbances.[99]

Holmes, however, does not hesitate to venture into areas where the more conventional healers may not follow. He declares categorically that "since the Law of God is Infinite, from the spiritual viewpoint, there is no *incurable disease*...."[100] And he declares "that man is a spiritual being now as much as he ever shall become" and "the spiritual man has no disease."[101] "Sickness is not a spiritual reality; it is an experience—an effect and not a cause."[102]

What, then, is disease? It is "an impersonal thought-force operating through people which does not belong to them at all."[103] "*Disease is not an entity.*"[104] It is "the mesmeric effect of race-thought.... a heritage of the ages believed in by so many persons that it seems to be true."[105] It is "human experience...operating from the subconscious reaction of the whole race."[106] Since there is no material body to be healed, there can be no material disease.[107]

Only by discrediting all valid testimony can we deny that bodily healing by mental and spiritual means is a fact.[108] This treatment "is a consciousness of the Unity of all Life and the spiritual nature of all being. Man's life is rooted in the Universal and the Eternal...."[109]

Holmes does not say categorically but certainly implies that resurrection from death will one day be possible and that even cancer will one day yield to one sufficiently endowed with spiritual power.[110] Since colds have no part in life, we can rid ourselves of them by simply declaring our disbelief in them.[111] Nor is there any need to grow old.[112]

The practitioner heals through the operation of impersonal, immutable, and universal law.[113] He employs the Law of Life, which is simply to affirm its truth[114] and to accept its operation for himself and his patient.[115] His treatment consists in declarations to the effect that the patient is a spiritual being who lives and moves in the Divine Wisdom and who is receptive to the inexhaustible energy of the universe, the influx of perfect life.[116] Or, again, "there is no thought of failure that can operate through this person's mind. He is open to the influx of new ideas.... He is sure of himself, because he is sure of God."[117]

The certainty that God is everything and omnipresent is the basis for all spiritual treatment.[118] Since thoughts are things,[119] the healing mentality of the practitioner is transferred to the patient and removes negation and error. This treatment is equally effective whether present or absent.[120] In order to heal, it is only necessary for the practitioner to convince himself.[121] Weariness, like sickness, is only an error of mind.[122]

Over and over, Holmes explains that the "practitioner consciously removes the apparent obstruction, and leaves the field open to a new influx of Spirit."[123] He permits the "stream of Creative Energy to take definite form."[124] He heals because he believes that there is but one·Creative Intelligence in the universe and that this flows in unlimited supply through every individual.[125] The patient must cooperate by permitting the Life Essence to flow freely through him.[126] If the victim of asthma will declare his body to be a receptive channel for the operation of the God-Life, the obstruction will pass away.[127]

This beneficent flow and influx is as effective to create success as it is to restore health. The practitioner declares that "there is no thought of failure that can operate through this person's mind."[128] Again, "he allows the Divine Wholeness to flow through him...There is a new influx of inspiration into his thought."[129] As this mental affirmation opens the consciousness to a new influx of Life, success is certain to ensue.[130] Even one who has missed his golden opportunities can still enjoy an open, rich, full, abundant life.[131] The Universal Mind can be tapped, not only to secure health, but to change and control surrounding conditions so that they will grow into affluence.[132]

6. *Christian Science Influence.* Undoubtedly, Christian Science helped to shape Ernest's early thinking, for at eighteen he studied *Science and Health* and his mature works reflect its influence. Several times he uses the term *mortal mind* in Mrs. Eddy's sense.[133] Like her, he frequently calls Jesus the Wayshower[134] and he calls mental healing a demonstration.[135] He often refers to the Mother-Father God.[136] Like her, he prescribes absent treatment;[137] and declares that evils and diseases are errors of false belief,[138] which can be removed by correct ones.[139] Against false conditions, the practitioner must use mental argument.[140] Holmes, like Mrs. Eddy, believed in clairvoyance,[141] and declared that Love is God or God is Love.[142] Interestingly enough, he agreed with her also in stating that glasses will no longer be necessary for anyone who reaches a subjective realization that there is One Perfect Vision which sees through him[143] and that we are not dependent upon them.[144] It should also be noted that, as in *Science and Health*, we find an elaborate glossary at the end of *Science of Mind* which, as the author explains, does not always "keep faith with regular dictionary definitions."[145] In the tradition of Swedenborg, Mrs. Eddy, and others, Holmes interprets Scriptural passages spiritually so that they might mean whatever he should desire.[146]

Even though "God plays no favorites, and the Law of the Universe cannot reverse its own nature," Holmes places great value in fasting and prayer "because they open up great fields of receptivity in our minds."[147] Prayer is a mental act which must accept its own answer in order to set into operation the energy of divine influx.[148]

7. *Psychoanalysis.* Holmes often approaches the Freudian method or techniques of psychoanalysis. Just as the surgeon sets a broken bone with no ethical opinion about his patient,[149] so must the practitioner refrain from any moral judgment concerning his patient's emotional disturbances.[150] He may not agree, but he must never be unsympathetic. "The slightest sense of condemnation or judgment about the patient" makes healing impossible.[151] He discusses at length the case of an eminent architect who was on the verge of insanity because of his subconscious hatred for a brother and who was healed when the cause of his distress was revealed to him.[152] As in Freud, the explanation is the cure. Holmes describes the treatment and healing of alcoholics;[153] that of a woman who was going mad with imagined abdominal pains resulting from emotional stress;[154] of a child who had traumatic experiences because of parental conflicts;[155] of a cultured woman of sixty who was tormented by voices.[156] Holmes declares that psychoanalysis "is making a splendid contribution in teaching us how to rebuild consciousness. But it will

remain incomplete unless spiritual values are added."[157] And this was precisely what the Church of Religious Science was designed to accomplish: a marriage between religion and the Freudian technique.

8. *Health, Happiness, and Prosperity.* This carries us to the culminating aspect of New Thought, which is, above all, a religion of Health, Happiness, and Prosperity. It is intended to redeem us from sickness, hate, morbidity, and poverty, all defined as an impoverishment of thought, a failure to comprehend that substance and supply are spiritual and therefore limitless.[158] "Supply is the general term used to govern every conceivable need. It awaits demand and is available to all who believe."[159]

To be happy, well, and prosperous, we need only trust the universe.[160] When there is peace and harmony in thought, health, happiness, and prosperity will follow.[161]

"Spirit is Substance and Substance is supply. This is the keynote to a realization of the more abundant life, to the demonstration of success in financial matters. It is right that we should be successful, for otherwise the Spirit is not expressed."[162] Money is the symbol for God's substance.[163] All acquisition of material things that give happiness or joy is in accord with nature and belongs to the Divine Kingdom.[164] A businessman will become more successful by imagining his place filled with customers who are delighted with his service and buying his merchandise.[165] The Law of Power enables us "to bring health, happiness, and prosperity into our lives or into the lives of others."[166] We gain success by seeing through poverty into abundance.[167] By becoming "conscious of Divine Guidance," we gain "complete happiness, abundant health, and increasing prosperity."[168]

The tribute and monument to Ernest Shurtleff Holmes is found and expressed in the many churches he has founded and the tens of thousands who have found peace and surcease from sorrow in his reviving gospel.

Chapter 7

THE SCOPE OF NEW THOUGHT

I. LITERATURE AND PUBLICATIONS

There are two principal publishers of New Thought literature: the first is the Rare Book Company, P.O. Box 957, Freehold, New Jersey 07728, which for many years has supplied scholars and students with copies of rare books long out of print. Many of these were necessary for the preparation of this work, and from them we obtained the extremely rare books by Warren F. Evans, John V. Dittemore, Georgine Milmine, Adam Dickey, and Edward Kimball, together with various early editions of *Science and Health* and other early writings by Mary Baker Eddy; and also works by Augusta Stetson, Emma Curtis Hopkins, Edwin Franden Dakin, as well as those of early severe critics of Christian Science whose books are now rarely found either in libraries or in bookstores anywhere.

The second great source of New Thought material is DeVorss & Company of Marina del Ray, California, which calls itself the Metaphysical Capital of the World. Its 1980 catalog lists no less than 1,240 authors and nearly 2,500 titles dealing with a great variety of subjects and written by authors from many countries and different periods of time. New Thought literature is very well represented; it covers also a broad spectrum of psychoanalytical material; among all this, we find, for example, several books by Carl G. Jung, Karen Horney, Kahlil Gibran, and H.P. Blavatsky. The *Aquarian Gospel of Jesus*

Christ is featured as best seller; and many titles by such New Thought exponents as Joel Goldsmith, Emmett Fox, Ernest Holmes, and Joseph Murphy are given special prominence.

In a volume called *Who's Who in New Thought*, published in 1977 by Tom Beebe, who moved to Sun City, Arizona a few years ago, we find 171 listings of authors in the New Thought movement, together with the titles of 774 books. Of the authors, 84 were still living and 284 books are credited to them. Among the historical figures are Horatio W. Dresser, Emmett Fox, Ernest and Fenwicke Holmes, Emma Curtis Hopkins, Ralph Waldo Trine, Ella Wheeler Wilcox, and Emanuel Swedenborg, all of whom are featured. Considerable space is also devoted to Susy Smith, Frederick Rawson, Walter Clemson Lanyan, Ursula Gestefeld, and Joseph Murphy.

Swedenborg's works are included in full: not only those on religion, but also those dealing with science and philosophy.

Every New Thought organization publishes voluminous materials of its own; and most churches have their book rooms or libraries which offer a vast amount of reading materials in great variety. The International New Thought Alliance (INTA) publishes a slick quarterly called *New Thought*. This organization, however, has no relationship with Christian Science, which operates in complete separation from all others. In addition to *The Christian Science Journal*, the *Sentinel*, the *Monitor*, the *Quarterly*, and the *Herald of Christian Science*, it offers for sale, not only the works of Mary Baker Eddy, but also the writings of such authors as Wilbur, Beasley, Tomlinson, and the second biography by Powell. It discourages contacts with other organizations and urges its members to read nothing except literature authorized by the Mother Church.

Every New Thought denomination has, of course, its own current publications and means of reaching its members and the public. The Unity School of Christianity, for example, with its multi-million dollar complex in Lees Summit, Missouri, utilizes both radio and TV programs, which are heard and/or seen by large numbers of people; it also features its most popular work, the twelve *Lessons in Truth*, by Emilie Cady, and it publishes a great variety of small pamphlets which sell for small sums or are given away free. There are also many medium-sized volumes in hardback, especially those by Charles Fillmore, and several current periodicals: *Wee Wisdom*, *Daily Word*, and the magazine *Unity*, all of which are printed and distributed in large quantities.

The Church of Religious Science, in addition to featuring the works of Ernest S. and Fenwicke L. Holmes, publishes a local newsletter and a monthly magazine, *Science of Mind*, which includes a complete roster of churches, ministers, and practitioners.

The International Church of Religious Science also publishes a monthly called *Creative Thought*, which lists its churches and personnel.

The Church of Divine Science, with headquarters in Denver, features a variety of books by Nona Brooks, Fannie B. James, and Malinda E. Cramer. Its principal textbook is called *Divine Science: Its Principles and Practices*. It, too, publishes a monthly which lists its churches, pastors, and practitioners and which is called *Aspire*.

We go into considerable detail concerning the publications of each group in the chapters dealing specifically with them. For a partial list of New Thought publications—especially those studied or consulted in the preparation of this work—the reader should note the titles listed after some of the chapters, and especially the bibliography at the close of this book.

We should point out that there is a sense of profound freedom throughout the New Thought movement. The churches and their ministers have nothing to hide; they seek information and dialogue on all questions. Their articles of faith are founded on sincere and basic concepts which, even though not always demonstrable as if they were mathematical equations, are nevertheless impregnable to the attacks or doubts of agnostics or rationalists.

This helps to create an outlook and a spirit to be found in no other religious or philosophical organization which has a definite body of beliefs and principles.

II. THE NEW THOUGHT MINISTRY

The most ambitious attempt to compile a complete roster of New Thought churches and personnel is contained in Tom Beebe's book, already mentioned. This lists the names of 818 churches and organizations, of which 764 are in the United States, as follows: United Churches of Religious Science, 139; Unity, 386; Divine Science, 21; International Churches of Religious Science, 66; Independents, 152; and foreign, 54.

Mr. Beebe states that he sent requests for information to 1,400 individuals and churches, but he received information from only 75 per cent of these. We know, therefore, that his totals probably include less than three quarters of those existing. Actually, his listings give only 21 for Divine Science, whereas the correct number is 33; for Religious Science, his total falls short by 217, and there is no doubt that he missed a great many which may be captioned under Independents or miscellaneous. There is no doubt that there are now well over one thousand New Thought churches and organizations, of which some eighty or ninety per cent are in the United States.

The largest portion of Beebe's book lists in alphabetical order the names of 1,360 individuals who are prominent and active in the movement; their addresses are given, their congregations are described, and details are included concerning their ministers.

It may be interesting to note that the volume entitled *Yearbook of American and Canadian Churches*, published by the National Council of Churches, 475 Riverside Drive, New York City, completely ignores all New Thought churches, including those of Christian Science, their schools and periodicals, as if they did not exist. However, it lists a number of denominations which have less than 500 members and only from 2 to 5 pastors or clergymen. We find, for example, the Evangelical Lutheran Church of America, which has only three clergymen; we find several others with less than ten congregations and ministers. However, it includes Jehovah's Witnesses and the Church of Jesus Christ of Latter-Day Saints, as well as others which certainly do not belong among the conventional religious bodies.

Now, then, are the New Thought churches non-existent, or are they simply non-religious? A good question, indeed!

It is impossible to estimate accurately the total membership of New Thought churches or organizations, nor yet the influence of their philosophy beyond their own specific boundaries. However, including Christian Science, we know that there are at least 3,000 such entities, of which perhaps 85 per cent are in the United States. If congregational membership averages 100, there will be about 300,000; if 200, double that number, which means, in any event, that the movement is a quite substantial one in the religious sphere. We have visited churches which conduct two services every Sunday morning, each of which is attended by 300 or more. There are magnificent sanctuaries in many cities where hundreds attend every service.

Even within its own confines, therefore, New Thought has become a significant phenomenon; and the outreach of its ideology—the influence of its basic philosophy—has penetrated tens of thousands of "conventional" church congregations—although they will not admit it—to such an extent that they have become definitely different from the predecessors whose names they still bear; in fact, many of them now resemble New Thought in their ideology more than they do that of John Calvin, Jonathan Edwards, Martin Luther, or even John Wesley.

This, in fact, is the true measure of its role, and that of Swedenborg, Emerson, Parker, Warren Felt Evans, Ralph Waldo Trine, and a host of others who beckon to us from the realms of the departed.

Mr. Beebe lists seventeen New Thought schools and seminaries, together with their addresses and the names of their executives:

ACADEMY OF UNIVERSAL TRUTH
Seattle, Washington

COLLEGE OF DIVINE METAPHYSICS
Indianapolis, Indiana

COLLEGE OF UNIVERSAL TRUTH
Madrid, Nebraska

DIVINE SCIENCE FEDERATION INTERNATIONAL
Denver, Colorado

DR. CORRINNE'S PRAYER CLINIC AND SCHOOL OF
METAPHYSICS
East St. Louis, Illinois

INSTITUTE OF APPLIED METAPHYSICS
Punta Gorda, Florida

INSTITUTE OF APPLIED METAPHYSICS
Centerville, Ohio

INSTITUTE OF RELIGIOUS SCIENCE
Los Angeles, California

INSTITUTE OF RELIGIOUS SCIENCE
San Francisco, California

METAPHYSICAL BIBLE INSTITUTE OF PRACTICAL CHRISTIANITY
Los Angeles, California

THE PHOENIX INSTITUTE
Chula Vista, California

SCHOOL OF ABSOLUTE RELIGIOUS SCIENCE
Los Angeles, California

SCHOOL OF CHRISTIAN PHILOSOPHY
Phoenix, Arizona

SCHOOL OF CHRISTIAN PHILOSOPHY
Atlantic City, New Jersey

UNITED CHURCH OF RELIGIOUS SCIENCE: SCHOOL OF MINISTRY
Los Angeles, California

UNITY SCHOOL OF CHRISTIANITY
Unity Village, Missouri

UNIVERSITY OF METAPHYSICS
Portland, Oregon

III. THE INTERNATIONAL NEW THOUGHT ALLIANCE (INTA)

A. *History, Organization, and Membership*

The International New Thought Alliance was established at a convention held in St. Louis in 1916. It was preceded by the International Divine Science Association of 1892 and the International Metaphysical League of 1900. These two had come into existence under the leadership of several outstanding exponents, among whom were Horatio W. Dresser and Charles Brodie Paterson. Its first regular congress was held in San Francisco in 1915 and such an INTA convocation has been held every year—with only two exceptions—since that time.

Presently, INTA has its national headquarters in Scottsdale, Arizona. Its president is Blaine C. Mays, pastor of the Phoenix Unity Church of Christianity. He is also the editor of the quarterly magazine, *New Thought.*

The most important attempt to establish all New Thought groups under a single umbrella is INTA, which lists all its members in its quarterly. Here we find in the Summer 1983 issue the names, addresses, and ministers of 316 entities, of which 289 are in the United States. Of these, 66 belong to the Unity School of Christianity, 125 to Religious Science and Science of Mind, 16 to Divine Science, and 109 are what may be called miscellaneous or Independents. Of these forty-six became members in the year preceding August, 1983.

These, however, constitute only a fraction of all New Thought congregations: for example, *Aspire* lists 33 Divine Science churches; *Science of Mind* lists 347 churches and Study Groups; *Creative Thought*, published by the International Church of Religious Science, lists 85 churches and 485 practitioners, and Unity now has more than 400 churches. Furthermore, we know that there are several hundred independent New Thought congregations of which that of Robert Schuler is one of the larger and more important.

B. *Declarations*

There are, of course, specific differences among New Thought organizations, both in statements of faith and in techniques of operation. However, there are certain basic principles on which they all agree; and these are concerned primarily with the nature of God and the Christ-Spirit, both of which are universal entities. They are also united in the conviction that the purpose of religion should be to achieve the good life in the here and now; in short, that our highest objective ought to be the attainment of health, happiness, success, prosperity, and freedom from guilt and worry, all of which is intended to place the communicant in profound rapport with all living creatures, especially his fellow-men.

In subsequent chapters, we will attempt to delineate and particularize the teachings and practices of the most important New Thought groups or denominations. Here we simply summarize what INTA says concerning its history, its goals, its purposes, and its faith. We quote the following verbatim from one of its brochures:

1. *Its History*

The term "New Thought" has been applied to the metaphysical movement which began with P.P. Quimby more than a century ago. The meaning of the words in this context was given by Judge Thomas Troward, one of the great leaders in the movement. It comes from the creative law of mind or Spirit and refers to the fact that a new thought embodied in consciousness produces a new condition. New Thought was taken as the name of an alliance which held its first conference in 1915. On January 20, 1917, the Alliance was incorporated as the International New Thought Alliance, familiarly known as INTA.

Through its service, the Alliance has proven its spiritual integrity. It does not depend on personalities, but demonstrates the truth. Many people want to take steps to insure the continuance of this ministry, not only through their financial support while here, but through bequests which will insure that their financial help will continue to assist this divine ministry.

The International New Thought Alliance is incorporated under the laws of the District of Columbia as a religious, educational, non-profit organization.

2. *Its Goals*

To unify all churches, centers, and schools in the New Thought field in a spiritual framework that provides for, and encourages, full freedom of expression and function.

To marshall the potential strength of the many groups, and focus it into coordinated power directed for the whole individual.

The healing of all nations.

3. *What It Can Do*

It can enlarge and enrich your way of life. It can universalize your vision and consciousness and increase your wealth of fellowship with kindred souls.

It can make you aware that you are a part of a great spiritual movement and a tremendous power for good.

It will reveal to you that the greatest secret in living life with blessings abundant is in serving with wisdom and understanding.

4. *What It Is*

INTA is a free and open alliance of truth-motivated individuals and organizations who desire to unfold and practice a positive life-style of spiritual maturity and who are dedicated to the universal propagation of these principles as described in the Declaration of Principles. INTA is an alliance uniting the individuals and organizations with common determination to bring out the best in individuals through an understanding of these eternal verities.

The International New Thought Alliance is a year-round working organization, democratic in structure, and serves as the means through which metaphysical schools, churches, and centers of like mind can work together.

INTA does not function as a church, school, policy-making organization, publishing house, promoter of certain doctrines, sectarian creeds or dogmas. INTA does not promote or engage in spiritualism or other occult phenomena. INTA is not a political, social, or economic group, nor does it authorize such groups. It does not ordain or train individuals to become authorized or New Thought ministers, practitioners, teachers, or counselors. It does not engage in denominational practices, favor any particular group, or recognize any hierarchy.

New Thought is a synonym for growth, development, perpetual progress. It deals not with limitations; it sets no bounds to the soul's progress, for it sees in each soul transcendental faculties as limitless as infinity itself.

New Thought may be said to possess a fixed ideal, that of an eternal search for Truth. The adherents of New Thought worship the omnipotent God, the indwelling God, in whom we live, and move, and have our being.

5. *Its Purpose*

To teach people to come into a conscious realization of the divinity within, and the unity of God and man, so that out of the sublimity of our souls we can say, "I and the Father are one," is the supreme purpose and meaning of New Thought....

Because no church or school, regardless of its strength, can lift the world consciousness alone, the INTA is to serve as the spearhead combining the united strength of all units to move forward dynamically in the discharge of its great mission. It is not absorbing but expressing the good of all groups that each will remain autonomous and make its individual contribution....

To encourage newly formed centers with interest and attention and assist whenever and wherever possible.

To invite and encourage the training of leaders and ministers and to raise all teaching to an accredited academic level.

To encourage the teaching of New Thought at all levels, paying more attention to the children, youth, and adult groups.

To maintain a flow of materials into the archives of the New Thought movement.

6. *Statement of Principles, Adopted in 1954*

We affirm the inseparable oneness of God and man, the realization of which comes through spiritual intuition, the implications of which are that one can reproduce the Divine perfection in his body, emotions, and in all his external affairs.

We affirm the freedom of each person in matters of belief.

We affirm the Good to be supreme, universal, and eternal.

We affirm that the Kingdom of Heaven is within us, that we are one with the Father, that we should love one another, and return good for evil.

We affirm that we should heal the sick through prayer, and that we should endeavor to manifest perfection "even as our Father in Heaven is perfect."

We affirm our belief in God as the Universal Wisdom, Love, Life, Truth, Power, Peace, Beauty, and Joy, "in whom we live, move, and have our being."

We affirm that our mental states are carried forward into manifestation and become our experience through the Creative Law of Cause and Effect.

We affirm that the Divine Nature expressing itself through us manifests itself as health, supply, wisdom, love, life, truth, power, peace, beauty, and joy.

We affirm that the universe is the body of God, spiritual in essence, governed by God through laws which are spiritual in reality, even when material in appearance.

These statements may be considered the bases for INTA activity. In 1553, in Geneva, Michael Servetus Villanovanus was burned at the stake by John Calvin for having declared in his book, *De Erroribis Trinitatis*, that God, instead of being a Trinity of persons, is, instead, one of manifestation, in which, as Father, he constitutes the substance of the universe, as Word or Son, its energizing force, and as Holy Spirit or Christ, its vitalizing and illuminating element. This concept crept into the theology of John Milton and was basic in Swedenborg's reconstruction of Christian doctrine. And here we see that it constitutes the base on which New Thought ideology is constructed.

C. *The Congresses*

The 67th Congress of INTA was held in San Diego, California, July 25-30, 1982, where, as usual, it convened at one of the very best hotels. The charge for attending all meetings was $100 for members and $125 for others. Presiding over it was the Reverend Blaine C. Mays and Robert Stevens, Executive Director of the Decanso, California Unity Retreat. The theme of the convention was "Anchoring in the Sea of Life," with different portions of the program dedicated to doing so in Prosperity, Wholism, Meditation, Love, and Happiness. There were about 60 sessions, including workshops and general meetings, and at least a thousand were in attendance. The second day was devoted to the memory of Joseph Murphy, the ex-Catholic priest who died in 1980 and whose books and cassettes are among the most popular in New Thought. We should note that at least sixty individuals exercised key parts of one kind or another in the programs, which were certainly far more elaborate than most conventional churches could duplicate.

One remarkable feature at all INTA congresses is the vast array of books offered for sale and written by a variety of authors. Table after table is loaded down with this literature, which is transferred into the hand of readers avid for information and inspiration.

The 68th Congress, at which Blaine C. Mays again presided, was held at the Hyatt-Regency in Phoenix from July 31st to August 5th, 1983. There were about 500 full-time registrations, mostly from out of town, with people in attendance from some foreign countries and from practically every state in the Union. At some of the general evening meetings, there were 800 or 900 in attendance; and it is certain that well over 1,000 individuals took some part in the proceedings. The theme of the Congress was "Let Your Son Shine"—which was a cryptic reference to the Son-Christ which permeates universal essence. Pictures and brief biographies of ninety principal participants were printed in the General Announcement.

The six-day program was filled practically from early morning until late in the evening. Each day began with a Hatha Yoga exercise. On each day except Sunday, there was an Intensive Dialogue from 9 to 11 A.M.; there was a business meeting for INTA members only from 11:30 to 12:30. Every day, except Sunday and Wednesday, there were three workshops from 1 to 2 and from 2:30 to 3:30 P.M., followed by two workshops and a general meeting in the Ballroom from 4 to 5. From 7 to 8, there were two workshops and a Demonstration in the Ballroom, followed by a final general session from 8:30 to 9:30. Not counting the INTA business sessions or the Hatha Yoga exercises, there were about sixty workshops and general meetings. Admission was free—with a love offering—at the general meetings; but there was a fee for participation in any of the workshops—to which all were admitted who had paid the registration fee of $100.

There was a great banquet in the Ballroom on Wednesday evening with more than 500 present; at this, awards were presented, a great many persons were introduced, and a roll-call of the states showed how many had come from all parts of the country.

It would be impossible here to summarize what was said at the many meetings. However, we might note that the first speaker was Marcus Bach, who appeared on the afternoon program of July 31st. The evening session was addressed by the actress Anne Francis and by the Futurist Barbara Marx Hubbard.

At the afternoon program in the Ballroom, outstanding speakers discussed such New Thought progenitors as Quimby, Emerson, Troward, Emma Curtis Hopkins, Ernest Holmes, Charles Fillmore, Nona Brooks, and Modern-Day Mystics.

As in past years, the literature tables were loaded with educational material; in a cursory examination, we counted about 900 different items. We found, however, very few hardback books—those which may be described as books were for the most part in soft cover. And we noted a marked development since the 62nd Congress held in the same place in 1977: the enormous number of cassettes now being offered. Dozens of prominent ministers have prepared single tapes or albums containing anywhere from two to eight in a collection. Thus people can go home and listen to New Thought expositions in the comfort and leisure of their own living rooms.

I conversed with several individuals—mostly women—who said they would not miss the experience of attending the Congress for anything in the world. And consider this: if forty or fifty new churches join INTA every year, who can envision the size and the quality of the Congress in the year 2000?

The 69th Congress was held at the Riviera Hotel in Las Vegas, July 22-27, 1984; there were ninety-two featured speakers and President Blaine Mays presided again.

Chapter 8

THE CHURCH OF DIVINE SCIENCE

I. HISTORY

The early history of the Church of Divine Science is related in the volume *Divine Science: Its Principles and Practice*, "As told by Nona Brooks, Cofounder" (1861-1945). She states that in 1886, she was living with her sister in Pueblo, Colorado and was a close friend of Mrs. Frank Bingham, who had been seriously ill for months. Since local physicians were unable to do anything for her, she sought the aid of specialists in Chicago, who informed her that her case was extremely critical, that they could not promise a cure, and that she would have to remain there for a year under special treatment.

A friend then suggested that she seek the aid of Emma Curtis Hopkins. Three weeks with her brought a marvelous restoration of radiant health. She returned to Pueblo filled with the new gospel, and she soon began holding classes of her own to reveal her discovery and impart her knowledge to others.

Nona Brooks had herself been in very poor physical condition for several months, able to eat only soft food. Although she at first placed little faith in Mrs. Bingham's teaching, she nevertheless attended her classes, during the fourth of which she was healed, "flooded," she says, "with a great light...It filled me! It surrounded me! I discovered that I had been instantly and completely healed.... I love to tell of the blessed change in outlook that came to me, the remarkable healing, of the quick improvement in the financial situation" of our family. "In fact, our entire lives were transformed."

However, Nona Brooks and her sister, Fannie B. James, rejected the concept of a nonexisting universe because it was visible; instead, they decided that form was the product of God's creative activity and that the visible world was something not to be denied, but to be interpreted correctly and understood. They concluded early that they must emphasize God and his action in human life and focus attention on his presence rather than on the false concepts entertained in the community.

They had no thought at this time (1887) of establishing a church or a movement. However, they soon formulated a metaphysical system in which creation is the expression of God and partakes of the same substance. This is the concept most frequently expressed in Divine Science literature and is called Omnipresence.

Now the three sisters, including Alethea, began working together "earnestly studying our basis, the Omnipresence of God, in order to discover ever deeper meanings to this fundamental truth of our philosophy and to learn to apply it more definitely to the welfare of ourselves and others...."

It so happened that for several years before these women began their work in Colorado, another lady, Malinda E. Cramer, had come to almost identical conclusions. "She burned," we read, "with the desire to show others that...they could be freed from disease, poverty, and inharmonies of all kinds." She held meetings and taught classes in her home in San Francisco. She also did effective healing. She had incorporated a Home College of Divine Science in 1887, and two years later came to Denver, where she met Nona and her two married sisters. When they came face to face, they knew at once that they belonged together, and there was the closest feeling of unity. "Mrs. Cramer's healings," says Nona, "were the most remarkable I have ever seen." When she died in 1907, Denver became the headquarters for Divine Science, as it has been ever since.

Soon more and more people began asking for help, and classes were started. In 1896, Nona resigned as a school teacher to devote her entire efforts to healing and teaching. As the work expanded, headquarters were established in a downtown building, in which an office and a classroom were located.

The Divine Science College was incorporated in 1898, where teachers were trained, from which churches were organized, and whence ministers and practitioners were developed. In 1899, the First Divine Science Church was established, in which Nona served as minister for thirty years. Sister Fannie was president of the College for fifteen years.

Charles Braden supplies additional historical data (*Spirits in Rebellion* 264-284). As a denomination, the Church developed slowly. In 1916, there were still only three congregations; in 1925, fifteen; in 1984, as we have noted, there are thirty-three. The Denver Church—costing $90,000—was dedicated in 1922 and its debt was liquidated three years later. This, and its Educational Center, is located on East 14th Street.

In 1922, Nona Brooks took her movement into INTA, which now lists sixteen of its thirty-three congregations, placing it fourth in the number of churches to be found in any New Thought denomination at this time.

In 1902, Nona began the publication of a small monthly called *Fulfillment*, which was superseded in 1906 by the *Divine Science Quarterly*. This, in turn, gave way to *Power Magazine* in 1912, which continued until 1915 when the publication *Daily Studies in Divine Science* began. This was incorporated with the *Divine Science Monthly* in 1930, which became *Aspire* in 1951, the most important current publication of the Church.

The Divine Science Federation was established in 1957. This is located in the Denver Educational Center and is responsible for the publication and distribution of all Divine Science literature.

II. DIVINE SCIENCE THEOLOGY AND CHRISTOLOGY

The omnipresence of God is the basic principle of Divine Science (*Mysteries* 6). This oft-stated concept is all-pervasive. "God," we read, is "everywhere. We know the Universe as the One Substance in action. A universal God must be present in his creation;" (*Ibid.* 17); and further: "God is His universe" (*Ibid.* 19). "God is Creator and Creation" (*Ibid.* 39); and God is "substance in manifestation" (*Ibid.* 31). "He is the life, intelligence, love, and power of all that is" (*Divine Science: Its Principles and Practice* 203); "He is the substance of all that is created" (*Ibid.* 136). We learn, furthermore, that since God is all and everywhere, Man also must be divine and partake of His nature: "as we know that that which is true of God's nature is also true of our own—for we are the image and likeness of God—we enter into a state of mind which accepts the truth that God has provided for us all that we can possibly need. This is the first step in meditation. It is called *Recognition of Omnipresence*" (*Ibid.* 86).

The concept of Jesus and of the Christ in Divine Science is basically the same as in all New Thought. As manifested in the flesh, Jesus "became the personification of Christ. By his resurrection, he revealed that life is greater than death..." (*Ibid.* 126). "The same Christ-principle which evolved in Jesus is in each of us and is wholly capable of guiding our unfoldment to its destined goal" (*Ibid.* 127). "Jesus attained the highest concept of sonship...He was a *conscious* Son of God. He accepted the Christ; He lived as the Christ" (*Ibid.* 139-140). "Jesus is our Wayshower because his clear realization of the Fatherhood of God and the Sonship of man demonstrated how the Christ manifests in the flesh...until the man, *the effect*, becomes the true embodiment of the Christ, *the indwelling cause*" (*Ibid.* 127). Thus "Jesus attained his Christhood by recognizing...the divine nature of the Christ...the impersonal idea of MAN in and of the infinite Mind before any individual existence, and is the substance of all individual existence" (*Ibid.* 143).

There is, therefore, a Universal Christ-Spirit which permeates and vivifies all creation and from which we can draw for our own unfoldment and fulfillment without limitation. Jesus was simply *conscious* of this fact and was therefore able to absorb so much of it that he could perform his divine mission.

III. STATEMENTS OF FAITH

If Divine Science can be said to have a creed, it is contained in its Statement of Being and Belief:

STATEMENT OF BEING (*Ibid.* 46)

God is All, both invisible and visible.
One Presence, One Mind, One Power is all.
This One that is all is perfect life, perfect love, and perfect substance.
Man is the individualized expression of God and is ever one with this
    perfect life, perfect love, and perfect substance.

STATEMENT OF BELIEF (*M* 22)

God is Life.
What God is comes forth in Divine activity.
We live, move, and have our Being in God-Life.
By Divine Power we are alive now.
I know that Life is perfect, for God is All.
Man is Living Soul, brought forth perfect in nature.
Man is divine, because he is one with God.
Man has the power to realize the truth of Being, and to accomplish the
    best in every relation and activity.
Consciousness of God is the light of the world.

WHAT DIVINE SCIENCE TEACHES (*P&P* 192)

The Fatherhood of God and the brotherhood of man.
The incarnation of the Spirit of God in mankind.
The spiritual source of all substance.
The unity of life in all its phases.

The immortality of the individual soul.

The transcendence and immanence of God.

God, the Uncreate and the Create, the Invisible and the Visible, the Absolute and the Relative, the Universal and the Individual.

The power of right thinking to release into expression man's divine inheritance.

IV. RELIGION AS SCIENCE

As we know, the word *Science* is used constantly in New Thought; Quimby practiced *science*, and most New Thought churches feature the term. This is reminiscent of the ancient Gnostics, who declared that their teaching was a *gnosis*, or certain knowledge. It is therefore perhaps no mere coincidence that these early Christians held that the Christ was simply a divine emanation or Spirit which endowed Jesus with unique power which enabled him to be the Great Examplar.

Divine Science constantly stresses the close relationship between science and the Christ-religion. It is a divine science because it is based on the omnipresence of God and proves by the law of expression that innately man can be only what God is (*P&P* 190). Since we know that the universe is a unity and is governed by unchangeable law, and since God is the substance thereof in manifestation, there can be no doubt that whatever applies to God applies likewise to the human race. Since all this is true, the system is one of *gnosis*; it depends, not on faith or speculation, but on demonstrable fact.

Thus, there is no possible conflict between the discoveries of the great scientists and the basis of true religion; actually, they complement and reinforce each other in a unity of dichotomy which creates a single whole.

V. THE CONCEPT OF EVIL

Evil in Divine Science is and must of necessity be unreal; for, since God is All and He is All-Good, there is no room for duality (*M* 72) and only a conceptual—not an actual—existence can be postulated for evil. There is no such thing as Mortal Mind as set forth in Christian Science (*P&P* 172). "There is," we read, "no evil to the one who lives with the vision of God before him. Evil is the result of a mental condition caused by fear, ignorance, doubt, unbelief. As fear is the cause of suffering, so is it the cause of evil" (*M* 48). Again and again the power of thought is emphasized: evil and suffering are the result of wrong thinking (*Ibid.* 48-49). "Gradually," we learn, "during the progress of man's slow growth through the ages, individuals have discovered that thought is of great importance, that it is a determining factor in making man's outer world, that it is a ready tool for improving his affairs" (*P&P* 48). Illness, to a considerable degree, is the result of race-mind or consciousness, which weighs heavily upon the masses; people have believed that sickness is a reality; most people accept this error and are therefore "susceptible to race experiences" (*Ibid.* 99-100). Thus, since God is omnipresent and "infinite, there is no evil" (*Ibid.* 105).

If it is difficult for an outsider to grasp or agree with this, we must understand that it is basic in Divine Science. Ignorance alone is the cause of evil in the form of ill-health (*Ibid.* 102). Since Man and God are identical (*Ibid.* 62, 70) in essence, "we are alive in God. Can God," asks Nona Brooks, "suffer and be sick? Since the good is eternal, what about evil? Has it any place in the plan of existence? Could it really exist? Like suffering, evil is in the thought-realm" (*M* 46). Thus, "evil is a temporary condition of the mentality, which can be banished when we choose to live aright.... Evil is being overcome by the setting of a higher thought standard for the race" (*Ibid.* 47).

VI. INTERPRETATION OF ORTHODOX DOCTRINES

Divine Science, like New Thought in general, denies that Jesus died as a sacrifice to atone for human sin; instead, there is an At-one-ment by which "the Christ consciousness within is the redeemer of world thought, and is 'the way, and the truth' that brings each into *conscious* at-one-ment, or agreement, with his Source, and this way Jesus revealed" (*P&P* 145-146).

By the Immaculate Conception, we are simply to understand the truth of all birth as revealed in Jesus which makes us all the children of God. "It is the realization that man's source is in the Perfect...God" (*Ibid.* 417-448).

There is no such thing as original or inherited sin, for every individual is born in purity as a son of God.

Baptism, instead of being in water, is "the immersion of every thought in divine consciousness (the Holy Spirit), in love that seeketh not its own, in parity of purpose, of thought, and of deed. 'Fire' is the light of understanding which consumes darkness and ignorance" (*Ibid.* 150-151).

Since Divine Science is in complete accord with modern scientific discovery, "evolution is" simply "man's coming to know. 'Evolution...is the outshining of divinity in man' " (*Ibid.* 51-52). Evolution in Divine Science means the attainment of completeness and perfection by following the light of the Holy Ghost (*Ibid.* 152).

Divine Science rejects the ritual of communion in which the bread and blood of Jesus are ingested, either sacramentally or symbolically. We drink his blood as we receive a true consciousness of life and we eat his flesh when we realize that our own bodies are divine portions of the Omnipresence. "In a

Divine Science communion service, we come together to learn how to commune every moment" (*Ibid.* 154).

Millions of individuals have awaited and still expect a literal return of Jesus at the head of a great host of angels to establish the Kingdom of Heaven. However, the Second Coming is simply the "redemption" which "comes by revelation of what always is.... The second appearing or coming is seeing omnipresent life, love, intelligence, and substance.... When man discovers that he is the Truth, God manifest in flesh, he knows he is the Christ, and Christ has come the second time" (*Ibid.* 154-155).

"Resurrection," we read, "is the culmination of life process in the one who lives in the resurrection consciousness: it is the end of one process and the beginning of another" (*M* 143).

Divine Science has definite teachings concerning death. In one respect, it is what happens to an individual when he becomes the victim of sin or ignorance, which is the opposite of freedom. "He who frees himself from these limitations—sin, sickness, and fear—shall not taste of death" (*Ibid.* 60). In another respect, however, it is simply a transition of the immortal entity from this plane of existence to another and higher one (*Ibid.* 61). "Why then," asks the author, "should we dread journeying from one plane of activity to another" when "we are promoted to the next higher; so it is when we have learned the lessons in one stage of development in the process of education..." (*Ibid.* 67). And further: "Do you believe in God? If you do, you must see that death is only a name for an event in Life Eternal" (*Ibid.* 69).

Interesting also is the teaching in regard to True Prayer which, we read, "is acknowledging, approving, and acting according to the true nature of Being. Prayer is a state of receptivity in which Truth is accepted. It is communion with God and realization of the Divine Presence" (*P&P* 235). We pray during Meditation.

We enter into prayer during meditation in which "we make our definite affirmative statement of the truth we wish to dwell upon in order to attain a deeper realization of it as an actuality in our own experience. We repeat this affirmation several times until we feel its truth and think of nothing else. As we dwell upon it with all our attention, feel it in the core of our hearts, we lift our consciousness into a state of true prayer. This is the second step in meditation and is called *affirmation*" (*Ibid.* 86-97).

And again, "to pray and depend upon God as the source of life and strength is to worship in Spirit and in Truth...This is consciousness of life Eternal" (*Ibid.* 92).

Prayer consists basically in addressing the subconscious self in order to impress upon it the highest aspirations of the conscious intellect. It does not consist in requests to any external power or entity for gifts, help, or favors: quite the reverse—it consists in statements of truth which will enable the individual to advance into higher planes of living, enable him to achieve success in all endeavors, and accomplish the best possible aims and objectives. It is, in short, the means of spiritual realization—of attaining identity with the Creative Force of the Universe.

Six steps are prescribed for Meditation (*Ibid.* 88-92) during which Affirmative Prayer creates the inner consciousness which leads to victory over all conceptions of evil. "Meditation and practice are the two phases of strong living" (*Ibid.* 91). "Regular, persistent practice of affirmative Prayer will bring us eventually to the place where we will establish a strong, unwavering belief in the Christ Mind, which is the eternal Self of each one" (*Ibid.* 92).

VII. THE THEORY OF HEALING AND WELL-BEING

In Divine Science, we have not only ordained ministers, but also practitioners, or healers, whose role may be even more significant. There is no feeling of antipathy or resentment toward the regular medical profession. One with a broken bone is told to seek help there; if one has an aching or abscessed tooth, he should go to a dentist. However, Divine Science declares that even illnesses which present all the symptoms of organic disease can often be healed—such as arthritis or carcinoma. However, not everyone is healed. And this is indeed a mysterious field which perhaps no one fully understands.

There is no doubt that millions of people suffer from psychosomatic illness of various kinds. For example, I know a woman who developed an elaborate hypochondria at an early age; she could and did project into her body various acute symptoms diagnosed by medical experts as a serious heart condition or some other ailment. When one symptom no longer met her subconscious needs, it disappeared and she promptly developed another. The point is that she *wanted* these ailments; had she desired to be free of them, there is no doubt that a wise practitioner could have guided her to success.

The Divine Scientist does not tell his "student" what to do or not to do but, instead, conveys his own spirit of wholeness or health, which completely changes the attitude and thinking of the one who is suffering. Thus, one who is addicted to alcohol, tobacco, or drugs is not told to abstain; his thought processes are so altered that he no longer needs or desires them. This is the cure.

The same holds true of that vast horde of corrosive emotions which fill the minds of countless victims as they swell up from the subconscious and create destructive desires and often culminate in fears, deceit, violence, or a guilt-complex. When all levels of the psyche are cleansed, there is healing—a resurrection into a new and better life.

Nona Brooks declares that health is the natural condition (*M* 73). "Mental healing does not differ much from the old conception of healing the body by external means, for the mental power of one person [the practitioner] is supposed to restore another to health. Spiritual healing is realization; it does not bring about anything, but realizes what is already there" (*Ibid.*). Thus "healing is not a physical process, but a spiritual realization; and...health is not a condition of physical well-being only, but the realization of a state of wholeness in the individual" (*Ibid.* 71).

"Healing," we read, "goes much deeper than the getting rid of a particular illness or complaint. It is a process of whole-making, a process which is always at work within us if we will but recognize it and cooperate with it" (*P&P* 98). Again, "healing consists of getting back into the right relation to Life, the original creative order" (*Ibid.* 100). "The Infinite created us out of its own health; healing is the awareness of that health as our own nature" (*Ibid.* 102). Thus, you must "think and speak health only, if you wish to realize it" (*Ibid.* 103).

"A practitioner is one who is skilled in ignoring appearances and seeing only the perfection of real Being. Consequently, he is able to assist a student in knowing the truth more clearly...A practitioner understands that unfoldment into knowledge precedes the desired unfoldment into a health conscious-ness.... he trains us to come to a realization of our unity with the Infinite, and when this is accepted, we recognize our consequent wholeness and permanent healing results" (*Ibid.* 104-105).

Significant are the teachings in regard to aging—the later years of life. Old age is simply a belief about the body (*M* 53). There is no need to go downhill simply because of advancing years. Not to live fully is the only real death (*Ibid.*). Age is simply a mental, not a physical, condition (*Ibid.* 54). "There is neither youth nor age to the one who knows God as his life; there is increas-ingly powerful living. The use of our faculties should not be affected by the addition of years. What are years in themselves? How shall we keep young? How shall we overcome the belief in years? It is all worked within. The mentality must be kept active and powerful by identifying it with the one Mind which knows neither youth nor age. Let us keep alert; inertia is a sign that we are forgetting to keep close to God" (*Ibid.* 55).

Thus, the Divine Scientist exclaims with Browning:

Grow old along with me! The best is yet to be,
The last of life, for which the first was made.

VIII. THE DIVINE SCIENCE OPERATION

Dr. Donald Perry, Executive-Secretary of the Divine Science Federation

International for twenty-five years, explained that the Church has three closely related corporations, all organized under the laws of Colorado. In addition to the Federation, there is the First Divine Science Church of Denver and the Divine Science Educational Center, all of which are situated in a complex of fine buildings located at the corner of 1819 East 14th Avenue and Williams Street. The Church itself is an impressive structure with a triple-arch entrance, rows of Ionic columns, and a seating capacity of about 800. The Educational Center and Federation have offices in wings which extend on both sides of the sanctuary. Some twenty-five or thirty persons work in the headquarters.

The Federation, which was established in 1957, produces and distributes all Divine Science literature, including a number of books and the monthly periodical, *Aspire*. It also ordains ministers and licenses Practitioners and Teachers. It also serves as the center for all Divine Science churches.

All local churches are completely autonomous and financed by their own membership. However, in order to use the name Divine Science, or be a member of the Federation International, they must have a minister prepared by the Educational Center and ordained by the Federation. Qualified Practitioners and Teachers must be licensed by the Federation and their certificates must be renewed annually. The property of local churches is wholly under the control of their own boards of trustees; and should the congregation dissolve or terminate its activity, the disposal of its assets is subject only to Federal law.

Considerable latitude may exist among ministers, teachers, and practitioners; however, since they must give evidence of substantial adherence to the teachings of the Church, especially as set forth in the textbook, *Divine Science: Its Principle and Practice*, and since teachers and practitioners must renew their certificates every year, it is not likely that any of these will deviate very far from the basic teachings of the Church. Should any minister, church, or congregation go off on an extreme tangent—which, it seems, has never happened—its affiliation could and would be terminated and it would not be permitted to use the name. This provision in the bylaws of every local congregation is a prerequisite for membership in the Federation International.

The Federation is an integral part of INTA; however, the membership of individual churches is left entirely to their own decision. As we have noted, of the 33 Divine Science churches, 16 maintain membership in INTA.

One of the most important activities at the headquarters is the preparation of practitioners, teachers, and ministers by the Educational Center. This is directed by a seven-member Board of Trustees; in addition to a full-time Director and Secretary, it has a faculty of seven members. The Center has two departments: Field Services and Ministry. It does not grant degrees or function as a traditional academic institution, but sponsors study courses which lead to Certificates of Recognition and to ordination for the Ministry. It offers residence and correspondence courses to those who wish merely to learn more about the teachings of Divine Science; those who wish to take the more advanced graduate program will, upon satisfactory completion of the work, receive the Divine Science Certificate of Recognition and be entitled to use the designation DSG.

The satisfactory completion of the graduate program is a prerequisite for those wishing to become Practitioners, Teachers, or Ministers. Basic Courses are offered by correspondence or field instruction and consist of twenty lessons which should be completed within a year from the date of enrollment.

In order to enroll in any of these courses, students must give evidence of sufficient understanding of the basic principles of Divine Science before proceeding in any advanced study.

Teachers sometimes serve as assistants to ministers in local churches, but their principal function is to teach lay individuals the basic principles of Divine Science and to train Practitioners in the areas where they work and reside. The work of Practitioners consists in counseling and healing according to the teachings of the Church; and they treat every kind of malady—physical, emotional, mental, organic, and psychosomatic.

All candidates for the ministry must spend at least one summer session in intense study at the Educational Center.

In correspondence or field instruction, the Basic Course leading to a Certificate of Recognition are (1) The Fundamentals of Divine Science, (2) The Bible I, (3) Spiritual Psychology, (4) Consecration, and (5) The Life and Teachings of Jesus I. The last is a prerequisite for admission to Advanced Studies, but an elective for others.

The Practitioner Training Program requires resident training of about six months, but this is usually conducted by ministers or licensed practitioners or teachers in local churches. When this work is finished, the student's record must be submitted to the Educational Center, and he must pass an examination before receiving certification to practice.

The Teacher Training Program is designed to develop the student's proficiency as a teacher of one or more of the Basic Courses available for field instruction. Applicants are encouraged to attend a summer session offering an advanced course. The remainder of this program is of about six months duration at local churches under the guidance of their ministers.

Teachers must be licensed by the Federation before they may teach and they must renew their certifications annually. Prerequisites are satisfactory completion of the Divine Science Graduate Program plus The Life and Teachings of Jesus I.

The most advanced work is that required for ministerial ordination, for which applicants often come from other denominations and already have a great deal of previous training and experience in the ministry. Prerequisites for ordination, in addition to satisfactory completion of the Basic Course, are The Life and Teachings of Jesus I and at least two other courses taken in residence: (1) Communications, and (2) Church Administration (unless the applicant can show sufficient expertise in these fields). Several other courses are also offered in residence: (1) Bible II, (2) Spiritual Psychology II, (3) The Life and Teachings of Jesus II, and (4) The Interrelationship of Science and Religion. Other advanced courses may be taken by correspondence: (1) The Unfoldment of Christianity, (2) The Essence of New Thought, and (3) Significant Facets of Living World Religions.

Before ordination by the Federation, a minister is required to spend not less than two years as a minister of a local Divine Science congregation.

IX. THE WRITINGS AND TEACHINGS OF JOSEPH MURPHY

Dr. Joseph Murphy, educated as a Jesuit priest in early life—who was for many years the minister of the Divine Science Church in Los Angeles—is perhaps the most popular writer in New Thought. The Autumn 1982 issue of the magazine of that name carries a full-page ad featuring forty-one of his publications and fifty-four of his cassettes. DeVorss offers 34 of his books and pamphlets. At the time of his death in 1980, he had "retired" to accept the ministry of the Divine Science Church of El Toro, California, near Leisure World. During his career, he lectured and conducted classes not only in many parts of the United States, but also abroad.

First, we will briefly summarize some of the ideas expressed in his most popular book, *The Power of the Subconscious Mind*, published in 1963, which has sold nearly a million copies.

It seems that the author was attracted to New Thought shortly after 1920 when he was healed of a cancerous growth called sarcoma "by using the power of the subconscious mind, which created me and still governs all my vital functions." Since he found himself in close agreement with Divine Science, he devoted the remainder of his long life to its ministry.

Although he does not mention Nona Brooks or her church in this book, its entire outlook and focus is identical with theirs. He has long discussions concerning the efficacy of Affirmative Prayer, which is addressed by the conscious to the mysterious and all-powerful Subconscious Mind; he declares that health is the normal and sickness the abnormal condition of humanity; right thinking, transmitted by the conscious to the subconscious, creates health in mind and body; this process can, and frequently does, accomplish miraculous healings, as evidenced at Lourdes and elsewhere; he cites instances where lung cancer and tuberculosis have been healed by this method; poverty, he says, is simply an unnecessary condition of mind; material riches are highly desirable and within the reach of everyone by the technique of Affirmative and Positive Prayer.

However, there is much of a practical nature acceptable to vast numbers of afflicted individuals. He declares, for example, that for a student to succeed in a chosen profession, he must work hard and long; and this effort must arise from a profound love for the work itself. In order to get along with others, we must regard them with respect and empathy; for marriage to bestow happiness, the pair must love and cherish each other and never try to make each other over in their own images. Fear, he declares, is perhaps man's greatest enemy, and he prescribes steps by which it can be overcome. *Success* should be the lot of everyone and, for its attainment, it is only necessary that the Subconscious Mind be imbued with the correct desires and convictions; for in its operation, this aspect of the human psyche is supreme in potential achievement.

Although Dr. Murphy does claim healings of organic diseases by the power of the Subconscious, the principal thrust of his work deals with the passions, which lurk in the depths of the human Id, which he calls the subconscious mind. Thus, it is directed toward problems which belong specifically in the field of psychoanalysis—no doubt of primary importance throughout New Thought. He explains how we can become well-liked among colleagues and fellow-workers; how to attract the best marriage partner; how to overcome the desire for tobacco, alcohol, and drugs, as well as other stimulants; how to free oneself from a guilt-complex; how to make advancing years the best and most fruitful of life. "Age," he says, "is not the flight of years, but the dawn of wisdom."

Since Murphy's books are written in a simple and direct idiom, we are not surprised that they have sold in the millions and continue among the best sellers of all time, not only specifically in New Thought, but in the general religious and devotional literature of the modern world, and even outside the churches or their followings themselves. All in all, we would say that his impact on the movement may have exceeded that of any other minister or author, at least since the death of Ernest Holmes.

In preparation for the following analysis, we have studied the following works:

Riches Are Your Right, 1952 (RAYR)
How to Attract Money, 1955 (HTAM)
Peace within Yourself, 1956 (PWY)
Quiet Moments with God, 1958 (QMWG)
The Miracle of Mind Dynamics, 1962 (MMD)
The Amazing Laws of Cosmic Mind Power, 1965 (ALCMP)
Telepsychics, 1973 (T)

The Cosmic Energizer, 1974 (TCE)
Within You Is the Power, 1977 (WYIP)

There are many other popular New Thought writers; but Murphy's books are featured so widely and given such prominence, that we feel this special attention should be accorded him.

1. *The Author's Claims.* Murphy states that thousands who had followed the techniques he advocated had declared to him that they had achieved "miraculous results" in their lives, and that they had found healing from so-called incurable diseases; complete freedom from guilt; success and prosperity in business; the way to become and stay well all the time; how to obtain good fortune; how to enjoy peace of mind, fulfillment of desire, and marital happiness, and how to create harmony at home or in places of work, where previously there had been nothing but discord and suffering (MMD 6).

The key to all this was the great discovery that their destiny was in their own hands and that they could obtain finer, happier, and richer lives—or, as he calls it, Triumphant Living—by placing the right input into their subconscious and bringing this in tune with the Infinite (*Ibid.* 7).

2. *The Basic Thesis.* The means by which all this is to be accomplished is expressed in many passages and particularly in *The Amazing Laws of Cosmic Mind Power*, wherein he declared (97-98) that when you see clearly that what you think, feel, believe, and give mental consent to, either consciously or subconsciously, will determine all happenings, events, and circumstances of your life, you will thus be able to banish fear, resentments, or condemnation of yourself and others. Since individuals can influence their subconscious minds either positively or negatively and since the latter is amoral and impersonal, everyone, through his freedom of choice, can create the kind of inner psychic life in which he will enjoy health, happiness, and prosperity (*Ibid.* 92). By purifying your inner emotions, you can transform yourself (*Ibid.* 149, WYIP 57) by impregnating your subconscious mind with high and pure thoughts and ideals (MMD 192).

3. *The Concept of God.* God, declares Murphy, is the Universal Presence and Power which is available to everyone, whether atheist, agnostic, or holy man (WYIP 9). God is the Cosmic Energizer (TCE 141); the Living Spirit which animates all things (*Ibid.*); the Life Principle expressed in all human beings (*Ibid.* 168); the mighty psychic power which exists within them (*Ibid.* 197). He is *not* anthropomorphic in any sense (*Ibid.* 42, T 83). The greatest secret and discovery of the age is that God is indivisible, the only Presence and Power, Cause and Substance in the Universe (*Ibid.* 36). He is the Power which exists in all men (*Ibid.* 75); the Omnipresent Spirit (*Ibid.* 82); the Infinite and Creative Intelligence (MMD 156, 193). He is the One Mind, the One Life, the One Law, that exists in the Universe, Our Father (QMWG 15). He is the

Higher Self in Man, which makes him a child of God (*Ibid.* 22); He is the only Presence and Power which exists—he is Life and this is the Life of Man (*Ibid.* 24); all things are One—the Substance of God (*Ibid.* 45); He is the creative Law in man's subconscious mind (*Ibid.* 46); He is everywhere—omnipresent (*Ibid.* 50, RAYR 56). Man's spiritual power is the God within him (QMWG 11). He is the Power of Life flowing into man's subconscious mind (MMD 52, QMWG 13, 27), the sense of oneness with God, with all there is, with Life, the Universe, and all men (QMWG 33). He is the truth which manifests itself in humanity (*Ibid.* 35).

4. *God and Man.* Perhaps no concept in Murphy is more pervasive than that which expresses the unity of Man with God. You and all men are the children of God, or the Sons of the Living God (WYIP 33, TCE 61, MMD 143). Your mind is God's mind; since God is all there is, I am one with God, who is my Father (QMWG 26, 41, 48). Since all there is is a manifestation of Spirit or God, I am a perfect reflection of God (*Ibid.* 29); my body is God's body (*Ibid.* 30, 32) and my source (*Ibid.* 44). Man is God in human form (*Ibid.* 69). God speaks through me (*Ibid.* 30). I am the temple of the Living God— God is the life within me (*Ibid.* 39) and that Life is my Life (*Ibid.*24). God is my companion (*Ibid.* 40) and my partner (*Ibid.* 52) God prospers me in mind, body, and affairs (*Ibid.* 51); His spirit makes me whole, radiant, healthy, happy, and more youthful (*Ibid.*54).

The God in me is limitless (RAYR 11). Since God is personified in all human beings (*Ibid.* 16), I am divine and fearless (*Ibid.* 19). God is the very essence within me (*Ibid.* 20); He is my inner voice, my identity with an infinite source of supply (*Ibid.* 25). The Life of God vitalizes every action of my being (*Ibid.* 26). I am a channel for the divinity which is the God in everything—the river of peace which flows through me (*Ibid.* 32). Since we are all the children of God, we are also brethren (*Ibid.* 35). God indwells in everyone (*Ibid.* 43). He is the invisible source from which all things flow (HTAM 50, 55).

5. *The Concept of Jesus and the Christ.* When Jesus, who was illumined conscious mind, put on the wisdom of the subconscious, he became Jesus Christ—the ideal man (WYIP 159) and is called the Wayshower (PWY 18). The same Christ-Power which was in Jesus exists in all of us (*Ibid.* 19). He was a man born like all others, but he attained great heights through discipline, meditation, prayer, and communion with God. There is really no reason why any man may not excel him in wisdom and power, for there is no limit to the potential glory of man, since God is infinite and all men share the same power (*Ibid.* 205). Thus, you are Jesus Christ or the Spiritual Man in action and you represent the illumined reason and the Christ-Power in your subjective or subconscious self (*Ibid.* 238-239).

6. *Spiritual Interpretation of Scripture.* In this regard, we find that Murphy follows the examples of Swedenborg, Quimby, Mary Baker Eddy,

Charles Fillmore, and many others, who could not accept all of the Bible as statements of ordinary fact. We must not, he warns, use this sacred volume in the traditional way (HTAM 44).

Spiritual interpretations abound in Murphy's writings; however, the volume entitled *Peace Within Yourself*, which is an analysis of the Fourth Gospel, consists of a line-by-line symbolic interpretation of the entire book. We must understand, he declares, that the Bible has a meaning wholly apart from its literal sense. John, for example, means Intellect (PWY 25); water means Truth (*Ibid.* 28); as with Fillmore, the twelve faculties of man are symbolized by the twelve disciples of Jesus (*Ibid.* 33, HTAM 48). Wine means the objectification of your ideals (PWY 40); born again means to think in a new way (*Ibid.* 57); Philip means perseverance and Peter faith (*Ibid.* 101); entering a ship means adopting a new mental attitude (*Ibid.* 103); the brethren of Jesus symbolize Life, Faith, Trust, Desire, and Ideals (*Ibid.* 117). Jesus' going up on the Mount of Olives means ascending into spiritual understanding (*Ibid.* 126); adultery means idolatry, or spiritual immorality (*Ibid.* 128). A Pharisee is anyone who lives merely in the senses and adheres to dead rites or rituals (*Ibid.* 148); Mary and Martha represent the conscious and the subconscious minds (*Ibid.* 165); Judas symbolizes our problems or difficulties (*Ibid.* 175, 194); the New Heaven is our new state of consciousness (*Ibid.* 179); the Son means your mind (*Ibid.* 184); the mansions in Heaven are new states of consciousness (*Ibid.* 200); Barabbas indicates a state of mind which robs us of peace, harmony, and prosperity (*Ibid.* 266). The treasures which we are to lay up in Heaven are the truths of God which we can possess in our own souls (HTAM 31). The bread of the Holy Communion represents the bread of life, such as thoughts of peace, joy, love, good will, courage, faith, and confidence (WYIP 248-249).

7. *Money and Success*. Again and again, Murphy emphasizes the goodness of money, wealth, and *supply*. Poverty, he declares, is a mental disease (HTAM 9); it is certainly no virtue, for God wants us all to have abundance (*Ibid.* 10). There is no good in asceticism (TCE 88). We are all born to succeed (HTAM 11). Money is simply the symbol of God's opulence (*Ibid.* 15).

However, this does not mean that we may injure others in obtaining an ample supply for ourselves. We can be wealthy and prosperous without doing harm to anyone (*Ibid.* 27). If we cheat others, we are robbing ourselves (*Ibid.* 26). To get money, as such, should never be our goal (*Ibid.* 14). It is the excessive desire for it which is evil (*Ibid.* 13). We should claim for ourselves only what we claim for all others (*Ibid.* 30). This, in essence, is the practice of the Golden Rule. Finally, the willingness to contribute to the good of mankind will make you wealthy—riches are primarily a state of mind (*Ibid.* 16, 43). To be happy and prosperous it is only necessary that we *feel* happy and prosperous (*Ibid.* 39).

8. *Rejection of Orthodox Dogmas and Concepts.* Like other proponents of New Thought, Murphy completely denies the conventional religious concepts. In one passage, he specifically rejects the doctrines of the Immaculate Conception, the fall of man, the judgment day, the blood of the lamb, salvation, hell, and damnation—all of which, he declares, must be regarded as old myths exemplifying inner psychological and spiritual truths (MMD 58). There is no devil or evil (*Ibid.* 50); difficulties and problems are our devils (*Ibid.* 185); nor is there any such thing as original sin (*Ibid.* 144); God condemns no one (*Ibid.* 148), and by at-one-ment is simply meant the union of two souls seeking their way back to the heart of reality (*Ibid.* 147).

However unorthodox Murphy's concept of the hereafter might be, he never doubted the continuation of the human entity; there is no death, he declares, for you will always be alive somewhere (WYTP 47, 199); the so-called dead are only people who have gone to another dimension (T 53); they have departed onward and upward into a higher form of existence (*Ibid.* 212, 217).

9. *The Power of Thought and Faith.* Like Charles Fillmore, Ernest Holmes, and other leaders in New Thought, Murphy constantly stresses the crucial importance of conscious thought and its power in shaping and transforming life by a proper input into the subconscious. The entire volume, *Quiet Moments with God,* consists of affirmative prayers in which the former implants into the latter the concepts which will reshape the individual's life and create a firm foundation for a realizing faith, which confers the power to attain whatever goal or objective the person may desire. Man has this power to change and transform his subconscious (WYIP 132). This is accomplished by a spiritual treatment which can remake all the cells in the body and thus create a health that will reject all manner of disease (QMWG 75) and, in addition, confer wealth and prosperity (*Ibid.* 72). This thought is creative, for you have domination; your subconscious mind obeys you, since it is in tune with the Infinite (*Ibid.* 68); it is the same power within you which moves the world (*Ibid.* 67); man is whatever he thinks all day long (*Ibid.* 59).

However, it must be understood that for the subconscious mind to become effective, it must believe completely that it will achieve what it desires; once this faith is established, it will always attain its objective.

When this is accomplished, the Amazing Laws of Cosmic Mind Power come into play; and Mark 11:23 serves as the Biblical authority for this concept and declaration, since it states:

> For verily I say unto you, That whosoever shall say unto this mountain (your problem, difficulty), Be thou removed (that is eradicated, dissolved), and be thou cast into the sea (that means the "sea" of your subconscious, where the healing, or solution, takes place and problems disappear); and shall not doubt in his heart (the heart means your

subconscious mind, i.e., your conscious thought and your subjective feeling must agree), but shall believe that these things which he saith shall come to pass; he shall have whatsoever he saith (ALCMP 30).

Thus, whenever our conscious thought has implanted in the subconscious a total belief or faith that whatever is desired will come to pass, then it is certain that success will follow. When such faith and belief is expressed in affirmative prayer, it cannot fail to achieve the envisioned results (T 95).

The power of thought can therefore accomplish miracles in every aspect of life; can create a heaven within, can transform us into images of perfection, and can confer, among other blessings, health, happiness, and prosperity.

However, evil or negative thoughts are gangsters, thieves, and assassins that maim and kill (HTAM 60). And a sense of guilt is a common mental disease (MMD 149).

In *Telepsychics*, the author goes into detail concerning this operation. When the right mental image is created in the subconscious (T 21), this becomes its Law (*Ibid.* 39); it can produce a hell or a heaven in the state of our consciousness, depending on the kind of thought we have placed therein (ALCMP 31).

10. *The Power to Heal.* The union of the subconscious mind with the Universal Power which is God confers upon the former a miraculous capacity for healing and well-being. Sometimes this is called the Cosmic Energizer, Telepsychics, the Power within You, the Cosmic Mind Power, or the Dynamics of Mind; but all mean essentially the same—the unique influence of the human subconscious, working with the Universal Mind, to create the kind of life the individual desires for himself; and when wedded to faith, desire in the mind is like a seed planted in the ground (RAYR 23).

Although most of the many cases cited deal with psychosomatic ailments and problems, there are various others in which organic diseases are said to have been healed. Most of them whatever their nature, are caused by disturbances which accompany the emotions of fear, hatred, hostility, jealousy, guilt or inferiority complexes, or the condemnation of self or others (ALCMP 91, 192). Accidents are caused by mental or emotional disorders (MMD 191). Millions are literally sick from worry (ALCMP 171-172). And alcoholism—as well as other destructive habits—have psychosomatic causes which can be overcome (MMD 107). When the mind is cleansed of these evils and discords, marvelous healings can result.

Fear and wrong beliefs will materialize in dire developments. A pipe can cause cancer of the skin if we believe that smoking will do so, even if there is no tobacco in it (WYIP 65). A shopkeeper was robbed because he expected to be (*Ibid.* 173). One man became allergic to roses because he believed this might happen (*Ibid.* 211). One man got a stiff neck because he believed the draft from a fan would cause it (MMD 100).

Murphy describes case after case in which evil emotions cause physical ailments. One woman developed colitis because her dominating mother prevented her from marrying; but when she freed herself, this inflammation disappeared (*Ibid*. 46). An educated, wealthy, and virtuous woman, possessing all the luxuries of life, developed a corrosive guilt-complex because years before she had been a call-girl. When she was relieved of this guilt, she became well and happy, at peace with herself (*Ibid*. 103). One woman became overweight because she hated her husband; but when she forgave him and herself, her problem was solved (RCE 51). One man, now happily married, had a fearful guilt-complex because many years before, he had deserted a pregnant wife; he made a habit of finding fault with everyone at the office where he worked and thus became very unpopular. When he sent his ex-wife $30,000, he forgave himself, was promoted in his office, and established rapport with his twenty-year-old daughter (*Ibid*. 56-58). When a former harlot forgave herself, she conquered her feelings of guilt and worthlessness, and achieved a happy marriage (150-151). One woman had suffered an illness for years because of suppressed hatred for her mother-in-law; but when she forgave herself for doing so and ceased harboring negative and destructive thoughts about her, and instead, blessed her in affirmative prayer, she was completely healed (*Ibid*. 136-137). One young woman, who had already gone through four divorces, discovered that her troubles were caused by resentment and jealousy—emotions which debilitated her entire organism. When she blessed her former husband and overcame her negations, she achieved perfect happiness and peace of mind (T 163). One woman who had ulcers and was totally miserable was filled with resentment toward others; when she overcame this, her troubles disappeared (*Ibid*. 150-151). One man, who blamed his blindness on the malefic stars, found that the real cause of his trouble was his jealousy of a business associate and his resentment toward his mother-in-law. When he blessed his associate and persuaded his mother-in-law to move, he regained perfect vision (WYTP 36-37). In another case, a woman developed arthritis because of a festering hatred for an ex-husband and mother-in-law. When she overcame this hostility, the malady disappeared (*Ibid*. 112-113).

Murphy declares that he had personally observed psychosomatic healings of this kind thousands of times. However, he relates other instances in which destructive emotions caused serious organic malfunctions. One woman was cured of both cancer and arthritis when she stopped hating her ex-husband (*Ibid*. 128). One woman developed cancer by hating her daughter-in-law, but was cured of this when she ceased to do so (ALCMP 61). One man developed asthma and high blood pressure because of hatred for a sister who had received all of an inheritance in which *he* thought he should have shared; this had driven him into a guilt-complex which made life almost intolerable, but when he overcame his resentment toward his sister, both maladies disappeared (*Ibid*. 90-91).

On the other hand, marvelous results can be attained through the power of the subconscious mind. He tells, for example, the story of a young man who believed he was denied the opportunity to obtain an education because of his race and religion and that because of this he could never go to medical school; but when he imagined that he saw a medical diploma with his name inscribed thereon and hanging on the wall in front of him, doors opened for him and in due course he became a physician (*Ibid.* 24-25). By similar technique, a shy girl, who never had any dates, obtained an engagement ring and a wonderful husband (*Ibid.* 64). An actress who had been unable to obtain any parts because she was filled with fear and a low estimate of herself became a great performer (*Ibid.* 130). The reason for these achievements was that consciousness of anything produces it (HTAM 24), and thought is the road to opulence (*Ibid.* 40).

However, Murphy found many instances in which desires were not fulfilled, even though the people involved believed they had used the correct techniques for achievement. The Law of Life, he declares, is the Law of Belief; we demonstrate what we believe, and whatever we sow into our subconscious, that shall we also reap. There are no incurable diseases—only incurable people. Thus, those who pray for health, happiness, and prosperity, but do not believe they are truly worthy of them, or have doubts that they will eventuate, will have no success (MMD 47). One man declared that, while his wife's prayers were always answered, his were not; but the reason was that, while *she* really believed, he did *not* (T 92-93).

The healing that any one achieves is strictly according to his faith and belief (TCE 69). For example, one woman who said that she believed in the Commandments and practiced the Golden Rule, was ever unhappy, unsuccessful, and frustrated. Her problem was due to the fact that subconsciously she expected failure and reverses (*Ibid.* 65-66). A businessman who affirmed mentally that he possessed opulence failed to get anywhere because in his subconscious he had, all his life, imagined a lack of this (*Ibid.* 158-159).

There are differing degrees of faith and belief, and consequently only comparable success in achievement. To each will be given according to his faith. The subconscious can heal an ulcer in one individual; but another with a greater degree of belief will overcome cancer or tuberculoisis, for this is as easily done by God as it is for the body to heal a cut on a finger (ALCMP 45-46).

The road to success in healing consists in quiet meditation during which the individual addresses his subconscious with affirmative prayer. The mind removes all tension from the body by talking to it—as Myrtle Fillmore did—telling it to relax, and then it must obey. In that quiet, receptive, peaceful condition, attention is focused on whatever is desired; and the results can be amazing success and triumph (*Ibid.* 35).

In the practice of spiritual or mind-healing, we should follow these four steps:

(1) Turn away from the ugly picture and acknowledge the Infinite Healing Power.

(2) Contemplate God and declare that Divine Love and Harmony fill your entire being.

(3) Decree that the Infinite Healing Presence is silently permeating your entire being and producing wholeness, beauty, and perfection there.

(4) Continue to give thanks for the action of the Healing Presence, and then wonders will happen to you (TCE 125).

Chapter 9

THE CHURCH AND SCHOOL OF
CHRISTIAN PHILOSOPHY

The Church and School of Christian Philosophy, one of many independents in the New Thought movement, was founded by Dr. Raymond N. Holliwell in Atlantic City, New Jersey. A few years ago, they came to Phoenix, Arizona, where they are housed in a fine center at 6017 East Hollyhock. Services are held there every Sunday; and the founder has been active in New Thought for about sixty years. We understand there is an extension of the Church in South Africa; although there are no other congregations in the United States, his voluminous writings have reached a great many people and many of his students are active in the movement. At one time, he was president of INTA.

He has published a great many small pamphlets containing sermons; he has also prepared three manuals used in class instruction which set forth his philosophy, called Scientific Christianity. Perhaps his most important work is a volume entitled *Working with the Law*, which sets forth in clear and concise language the general principles and specific techniques which he proclaims.

Dr. Holliwell quotes a great deal from the Scriptures, but, like others in New Thought, he rejects the dogmas of the traditional churches—such as the doctrine of original sin, the trinity of persons, the sacrifice of Jesus-Christ as an atonement for sinners, and the communion of bread and wine as an actual or symbolic sacrament. He declares that heaven is not a place, but a state of mind; that the promised land is the here and now; that God intends that

318

health, happiness, and prosperity should be the lot of everyone, and that it is an error to believe that bliss hereafter will be a reward for poverty in this life. He seeks health, happiness, and prosperity for his followers *in this life*; and these are to be attained by obeying the basic Law of Life, or God, by which the individual creates in his outward existence the excellence which arises from the subconscious when this is placed in total attunement or at-one-ment with God, who is the spiritual totality of existence.

The following is a concise statement of the belief held by the School of Christian Philosophy:

The most important thing about any individual is his philosophy, his plan of life, the central theme of his daily and his ideal existence. Man's philosophy is his life. We feel that an aimless life is worthless. Unless we have a goal sufficiently momentous to accord with our human ability and aspirations, we don't experience a full rich life. Thus we approach philosophy with a spirit of friendliness, with a spirit of cooperation, with a sincere and ardent wish to be enlightened. With this spirit we are convinced that metaphysics (the Science of Being), is a most essential and indispensable element in life.

Idealistic metaphysics is desired because it explains body as the expression of the mind. It adds dignity to our souls by endowing us with Infinite possibilities for realization. It explains God and offers an explanation for immortality. It attributes to us free will and choice. It adds significance to us as rational beings in a rational world. It does not oppose science but yields to science that which belongs to it. It teaches the study of man and his being.

Regarding metaphysics as a real factor in our lives, we consider an explanation of the Cosmos, God, as something vital, as a central thread which may appreciably help us to mold our careers. We choose a philosophy which, not only intellectually but also practically, yields the greatest benefit.

Christian Philosophy is the idealism of Christ Jesus. It is an arrangement of both ethical and spiritual principles. We believe the Christ teachings to be superior to other teachings in that they are unlimited in scope and can become real and factual in daily living. These teachings are the study of ideals which incorporate the theory of knowledge, logic, ethics, and metaphysics.

The School of Christian Philosophy teaches the Truth of God and His Creation, man and his oneness with God, unity as the basic law of the universe, and consciousness as the determining power in the life of each one of us. We acknowledge every advance in the world of natural science, art and religion as the futher expansion of man's understanding of God. We proclaim the right of man through positive thinking and harmonious living to a wealth of goodness and satisfaction, to a prosperous, healthy, happy life. We believe that much of the distress in human life is due to a lack of wisdom and proper training and is unnecessary. We know that life is intended to be and can be a joy and a continual blessing.

These ideas and principles are repeated with prolific illustrations in Dr. Holliwell's class Manuals and in his other publications.

In the Manual *Mechanics of the Mind* (Lesson 9), he describes the three levels on which the human psyche operates; although these are called by different names, they are equivalent to those set forth by Warren Felt Evans. Here they are called Conscious Mind (the rational), the metaphysical (the subconscious), and the Spiritual (the Freudian Superego). The conscious speaks to the metaphysical, and therein is then embodied the great unseen power which each individual possesses and which is always at work, and can be the force to propel him to higher levels of success in endless progression. It enables him to achieve health, happiness, and prosperity. This latent power lies dormant within us unless it is developed, but its capacity for achievement is without limit; the power is the Christ which is God and exists in every human being awaiting fruition (*Ibid.* Lesson 8).

In *Working with the Law* we find the most detailed exposition of the hidden power and the techniques by which it may be utilized. Although Holliwell, like Joseph Murphy, believes that physical healings which seem miraculous do occur, his principal thrust is accomplishment by quite practical methods. We must work to succeed; we must have a deep love for what we are doing; we must be profoundly devoted and dedicated to the end we seek. The drive to reach the heights of achievement must be motivated from the inner psyche and directed into day-to-day activity.

At the base of his teaching is the thesis that *God is Law* (pp. 7 and 96), not only in the universe as a whole, but also in each individual. A violation of this law consists in having wrong beliefs or erring thoughts, which are the evils of this world, but which man can control and correct (*Ibid.* 12). Obedience to this Law is the key to success (*Ibid.* 14, 24); it is the creative process which can lead in any direction (*Ibid.* 17). Prayer is the method by which the conscious mind imbues the subconscious with the aims it will seek to accomplish (*Ibid.* 19). Mind and thoughts are powerful instruments (*Ibid.* 29); they form the outer world of each person (*Ibid.* 30). Thoughts of failure bring failure (*Ibid.*); but thoughts of success, preceded by a practical plan or idea (*Ibid.* 15), will bring the desired results. Since like seeks like, the Law of Attraction decrees that we shall become what we think (*Ibid.* 64). If we *think* harmony, satisfaction, and plenty, they will come to us (*Ibid.* 66). Thus everyone can start his journey toward health, success, happiness, and riches (*Ibid.* 94). We attract whatever we seek or expect (*Ibid.* 104).

However, he emphasizes again and again that, in order to attain a worth-while objective, we must have it clearly in mind and be dedicated to its attainment; such, for example, was the young man who, when asked what his religion was replied that it was Sears, Roebuck & Company. In due course, he was promoted to an executive position in the firm (*Ibid.* 53). Such is the law of success in business (*Ibid.* 72, 74, 112).

Thus, the secret of health, happiness, and prosperity lies in ourselves, in right thinking, which results in a subconscious propulsion toward the All-Good. If you think poverty and disease, you will be poor and sick. (*Ibid.* 109, 172), but man is born to be rich (*Ibid.* 178); and if you will use your time constructively (*Ibid.* 193) and think aright, you can, since your resources are unlimited (*Ibid.* 171), achieve your ambition, whatever it may be (*Ibid.* 181).

This, in brief, is the gospel and the technique offered by Dr. Raymond N. Holliwell.

Chapter 10

THE UNITY SCHOOL OF CHRISTIANITY

I. HISTORY

1. *Sources.* The Unity School of Christianity was founded by Charles and Myrtle Fillmore in 1889; their story and that of their organization is told by James Dillet Freeman in *The Household of Faith*, published in 1951, and more fully in the same work, expanded as *The Story of Unity*, 1978. Additional sources are Hugh D'Andrade's *Charles Fillmore*, published in 1974; Thomas E. Witherspoon's *Myrtle Fillmore: Mother of Unity*, 1977, and *The Unity Way*, by Marcus Bach, 1982.

2. *Early Background.* Charles Fillmore, 1854-1948, and Myrtle Page, 1845-1931, who became his wife in 1881, first met in Dennison, Texas, when he was a clerk in a railroad office and she was a school teacher. She was reared in a Methodist-Episcopal family with nine children; and it seems that from girlhood she had been taught, or had developed, the tendency to think of herself as an invalid or subject to physical incapacities or diseases. Charles had a very different childhood. Born in what were then the wilds of Minnesota, he lived in a log cabin in a climate so cold that often the thermometer hovered around forty below zero. At the age of ten, he had a serious accident when skating in which his leg was severely injured; as Freeman notes, this was probably the determining incident of his life (*The Story of Unity* 24).

Although his dislocated leg and the terrible infections which followed were treated by a series of physicians, it grew steadily worse. Charles later declared that he "was bled, leached, cupped, seasoned, lanced, blistered, and raveled. Six running sores were artificially produced on my leg to drain out the diseased condition that was presumed to be within" (*Ibid.*). He hobbled around on crutches, and sometimes it seemed that he would be unable to survive. When the infection finally healed after two years, it left a withered leg. For years, he wore a metal brace and walked only with the aid of a cane.

After the meeting in Texas, Myrtle returned to Clinton, Missouri, while Charles went to Colorado, where he entered the real-estate business. In the meantime, they carried on a lively correspondence, through which their attraction ripened into love. They were married on March 29, 1881, in her home town. They left at once for Colorado, where he again undertook the real-estate business, this time in Pueblo. There he prospered and there their son Lowell was born in 1882, and Rickert in 1884. However, they soon left for Kansas City, Missouri, which was then in the midst of a tremendous boom in which property prices were reaching unprecedented levels. Again, he entered the real-estate business and was soon earning a substantial income. However, since Myrtle's health was failing, they made a brief trip to Colorado, but soon returned to Kansas City, where Myrtle was struck with tuberculosis. Her health deteriorated to a point at which the future seemed almost hopeless. According to an unverified legend, she had, at that time, considerable faith in medicine and drugs, and had a cabinet full of bottles containing pills and medications of various kinds. For a time, they toyed with the idea of going again to the clear mountain air of the West, but decided against it. So the couple, with their growing boys, later joined by a third, Royal, born in 1889, remained in Kansas City. As a result, the Great Illumination of their lives was soon to occur there.

3. *Rebirth and Healing.* By 1886, Myrtle had become so ill and discouraged that she was ready to try almost anything, no matter how absurd or irrational it might seem. Everything had been tried and had failed; she was now almost ready to die. And so it was that when Emma Curtis Hopkins sent one of her representatives from her Metaphysical College of Chicago, Dr. E.B. Weeks, to lecture in Kansas City, Myrtle decided to attend. Charles accompanied her.

Although the lecture did not impress *him* very much, to *her* it was a revelation of infinite magnitude. She was totally transformed. She obtained a new and different conviction which blazed in her mind. One statement made by the speaker was, she believed, directed especially to her, and she felt a great wave of healing power surge through and engulf her in ecstasy. "I am a child of God and therefore I do not inherit sickness," she repeated over and over; and, as she did so, her malady began to recede. In two years she could exult in the possession of a vibrant, permanent, and infectious condition of perfect health. Thus, at the age of forty-one, she experienced, as it were, a resurrection into a new and glorious life. She stated in a letter published in *Unity* that, as she talked to the various parts of her body, they were gradually cleansed of all impurities and became completely sound and well.

The Fillmores later visited Emma Curtis Hopkins in Chicago, and in future years she was often a speaker at Unity headquarters in Kansas City. They also studied at the Metaphysical College.

With Charles, things proceeded in a different tempo. As he observed his beloved wife rise from deathly illness into glorious health and happiness, he could not deny the evidence of his senses. He therefore began an extensive study of metaphysics. Gradually, he was convinced, and in due course he became not only a convert to the new faith, but one of the most important and effective apostles of New Thought. This development resulted not so much from his wife's miraculous cure as from the fact that, as his own convictions solidified, a marvelous healing occurred; his hip healed completely and, in time, he discarded the steel extension on his leg and walked without a cane, an experience which he described in his *Atom Smashing Power of Mind* (132-133):

I can testify to my own healing of tuberculosis of the hip. When a boy of ten, I was taken with what was at first diagnosed as rheumatism but developed into a very serious case of hip disease. I was in bed over a year, and from that time an invalid in constant pain for twenty-five years, or until I began the application of the divine law. Two very large tubercular abscesses developed at the head of the hip bone, which the doctors said would finally drain away my life. But I managed to get about on crutches, with a four-inch cork-and-steel extension on the right leg. The hip bone was out of the socket and stiff. The leg shriveled and ceased to grow. The whole right side became involved; my right ear was deaf and my right eye weak. From hip to knee the flesh was a glassy adhesion with but little sensation.

When I began applying the spiritual treatment, there was for a long time slight response in the leg, but I felt better, and I found that I began to hear with the right ear. Then gradually I noticed that I had more feeling in the leg. Then, as the years went by, the ossified joint began to get limber, and the shrunken flesh filled out until the right leg was almost equal to the other. Then I discarded the cork-and-steel extension and wore an ordinary shoe with a double heel about an inch in height. Now the leg is almost as large as the other; the muscles are restored, and although the hip bone is not yet in the socket, I am certain that it soon will be and that I shall be made perfectly whole.

4. *The Beginning of Unity.* As the fame of these healings spread, more and more people came to the Fillmores for help and counsel. For a time, Charles continued in real estate, giving part time to spreading the new faith. In order to reach a growing audience, he brought out the first issue of *Modern Thought* in April 1889, devoted, as it said, to the Spiritualization of Humanity from an independent standpoint. At first, the magazine had no distinctive orientation or point of view; however, it was not long before Charles began the formulation of his convictions in his own mind. Thus, in a few months, he wrote an editorial divorcing himself from all forms of occultism, hypnotism, spiritualism, palmistry, astrology, and other popular forms of metaphysics, and dedicated his efforts to Pure Mind Healing as demonstrated by Jesus Christ (*Ibid.* 57). However, he made it clear that his were not the orthodox ideas espoused by Christian Science (*Ibid.*). In April 1890, the name of the magazine was changed to *Christian Science Thought*; in June 1891, it appeared in a format of eight pages with its permanent name of *Unity*.

In 1889, there were only a few subscribers to *Modern Thought*; however, by the next year, three rooms were being rented in the Deardorff Building in downtown Kansas City, where the organization carried on the work with the help of one hired printer. For a few years, *Thought* and *Unity* were both published; however, in 1895, they were consolidated as *Unity*, which before long became a forty-page publication. In 1893, *Wee Wisdom* was established, a magazine for children, under the editorship and direction of Myrtle Fillmore. The *Daily Word* was established in 1924.

A number of other magazines were started and discontinued over the years. Today, the School publishes only three, all monthlies; *Unity*, with 430,000 subscribers; *Wee Wisdom* with 100,000, and *Daily Word*, of which 2,500,000 copies are printed every month.

5. *Unity under Way.* As soon as Unity had publications of its own, it became a going concern. Although it had not yet assumed any wealth or developed a substantial labor force, it so happened that H. Emilie Cady, a homeopathic physician in New York City had—with a book entitled *Finding the Christ in Ourselves*—so impressed the Fillmores that they went to great lengths to induce her to write a series of articles stating the Principles of Practical Christianity. In September 1894, the first of twelve appeared in *Unity*. When these were completed, they were published in book form under the title *Lessons in Truth*. This little volume of less than 200 pages has been of remarkable influence, not only in Unity, but in the entire New Thought movement. By 1983, almost two million copies had been printed; it probably constitutes the most complete and rounded statement of Unity principles and techniques available in a brief exposition. Although Dr. Cady never visited the Unity complex in Missouri, she soon began to devote her entire time and efforts to the movement and her words have reached into the hearts and minds of people to the ends of the earth.

6. *Silent Unity*. Almost from the beginning Unity embarked on additional and unusual services. Of these, one of the first was The Society of Silent Help. In the April 1893 issue of *Thought*, Myrtle wrote that "all over the land are persons yearning for Truth, yet so dominated by the surrounding error that they find it almost impossible, without a helping hand, to come into harmony with the divine Spirit" (*Ibid.* 81). Unity set out to supply aid, comfort, courage, and healing to anyone anywhere who asked for it. A group at headquarters met every evening at 10 P.M. for at least fifteen minutes in silent thought, prayer, and meditation to repeat the following words:

> God is all goodness and everywhere present. He is the loving Father, and I am His child and have all His attributes of life, love, truth, and intelligence. In Him is all health, strength, wisdom, and harmony; and as His child, all these become mine by a recognition of the truth that *God is all* (*Ibiḍ.* 82).

All those who asked for help were told to commune with God at the same time and with the same words, wherever they might be. In time, great numbers were conducting this ritual of spiritual unity over wide areas. Letters asking for help soon streamed into headquarters in ever-increasing numbers from people who were sick, confused, or unhappy. As the circle of participants widened, it was found that it would be better to change the hour to 9; and the name was changed to Silent Unity.

At the beginning, all requests came in the form of letters; then, in due course, a twenty-four-hour, seven-days-a-week telephone service was instituted, and those grieved in mind, body, or spirit could call at any time and pour out their souls to a deeply sympathetic counselor. There is a toll-free line intended for those in urgent need or who cannot afford to pay for a long-distance call.

The extent to which Silent Unity has grown is one of the marvels among modern religious phenomena. In 1903, it had 10,000 correspondents; in 1978, there were more than a million. In 1900, half a dozen workers manned the project; in 1982, it required more than 200. There are more than 2,000 telephone calls and 5,000 letters every day, each and everyone of which receives individual attention, even though no compensation is demanded or, in many cases, given. In 1982, Silent Unity received more than 2,500,000 letters from people seeking help.

Many healings may, of course, have been purely psychosomatic; but countless beneficiaries have declared that they have been healed of such physical ailments as cancer, tuberculosis, blindness, deafness, and arthritis. And this does not include the hosts who were relieved of mental stress and various neuroses or psychoses, even insanity. No wonder that the number of Unity churches and classes and their membership have proliferated.

7. *Expansion.* In 1890, the Fillmores moved their operation from the Deardorff to the Hall Building; in that year, they visited Chicago, as we have noted, and established a close working relationship with Emma Curtis Hopkins. They also attended the Columbia Exposition in 1893; in 1896, they were hosts to the International Divine Science Association in Kansas City. Although Unity joined INTA when it was organized, Charles was disappointed with its heterogeneity and Unity withdrew. It rejoined in 1919, but remained only until 1922. Today many of its churches belong to the Alliance and one of its ministers is its president, but the organization as a whole is not a member.

The Unity Society of Practical Christianity was incorporated in 1903, not as a church, but "for scientific and educational purposes, viz.: the study and demonstration of universal law" (*Ibid.* 105). In this, it has never changed.

In 1898, the Fillmores obtained a house which had rooms large enough to serve for offices and headquarters and also for their meetings. By 1900, however, these accommodations were too small, and a hall was rented in which to conduct the Sunday services. Here and to the house came the lame, the halt, the blind, the sick, and the neurotic, who sometimes demanded and were given the floor to tell their stories and air their grievances.

Charles now determined that Unity must have a permanent headquarters of its own; he therefore initiated a Building Fund, which, however, even by 1905, contained only $601. The future did not seem very promising. Since publications were mailed out at less than cost and since no fees were placed upon the services of Silent Unity, funds during the early years were scarce indeed. However, as healings occurred, grateful people began giving voluntarily; and the $601 increased rapidly. But had it not been for a businessman who mortgaged all his properties in order to lend $40,000 to the organization, the new headquarters at 913 Tracy Street could not have been completed at an early date. Here the cornerstone for a three-story building, forty by seventy, was laid in 1906. This included a chapel seating 200 people, a library, reception rooms, and offices; it also had accommodations for Silent Unity, a printing shop, and the distribution of the Unity publications.

In due course, other buildings were erected on or near the same site; thus, after seventeen years, the organization had a substantial and commodious home and center of its own, and it remained at this location until 1948. At the end of 34 years, when it had 400 workers, the operation was removed to Unity Village at Lees Summit, Missouri, where it now has 1,650 acres of land and a complex of buildings and facilities possibly worth at least $50,000,000.

8. *Further Growth and Development.* Financing in Unity differed sharply from that in most religious organizations. Since it never pressed people for donations or conducted high-pressure fund-raising campaigns, many doubted that sufficient money would ever be available. However, as the outreach of Silent Unity became more widespread, and as Unity literature penetrated

farther and more deeply, people who had been raised from despair or had been healed of maladies responded with gifts, sometimes generous or even munificent. Thus it was that a gradual but vast expansion became possible; and in due course, a beautiful and debt-free headquarters in peaceful surroundings was completed—a phenomenon without parallel elsewhere in the Free New Thought movement.

In 1918, Unity bought a large lot on the Country Club Plaza in Kansas City, where the magnificent Unity Temple now stands. Begun in 1940, it was completed in 1948 at a cost of more than a million dollars.

The Fillmores had concluded that their future home should be away from the dirt, noise, and bustle of a great and growing metropolis. Thus it was that in 1920, Unity purchased fifty-eight acres about fifteen miles southwest of the city. This was the beginning of Unity Village, which has been expanded to its present size. The first buildings were constructed in the English Cotswold style and included a home for the Fillmores called The Arches, completed in 1925. At last, Myrtle had her dream house (*Ibid.* 131). There were, of course, various other structures, including a 165-foot tower, which dominates the landscape, completed in 1929.

However, when the Great Depression struck in the fall of 1929, all work at Unity Village ceased and could not be resumed until the close of World War II. In 1947, the development had proceeded to a point where the printing plant could be moved to the new center. In 1949, the whole complex was sufficiently advanced to house all departments. Facilities of all kinds have now for years been in place at Unity Village, including a motel, cafeteria, housing for students, etc. When the change occurred, the 400 workers moved from 913 Tracy Street in Kansas City to Unity Village.

Charles Braden states that in 1962 the replacement value of the plant was estimated at $5,000,000. Since then many new buildings and other facilities have been added, and the program still continues as the work of Unity goes on expanding. In 1982, there were 500 permanent workers there, including the 200 who man Silent Unity.

Tens of thousands of people visit Unity Village every year; it has a building completed in 1975 which includes a chapel seating 1,100, a cafeteria with dining space for 300 persons, and several additional banquet rooms and others for workshops.

From this center issue letters, pamphlets, periodicals, and other publications every year totalling tens of millions of pieces of mail; its outreach encompasses the globe.

Myrtle Fillmore died in 1931 at the age of eighty-six; Charles died in 1948 at the age of ninety-four. Lowell died in 1975, at the age of ninety-three.

Their sons carried on the work of Unity. The youngest, Royal, died in 1923; but Lowell and Rickert took up the mantle and continued in the footsteps of their parents. Rickert, who died in 1965, was the architect who superintended the early construction at Unity Village. Lowell undertook major responsibility for the organization, especially after the death of his father. Thus, even though many others have become deeply involved, Unity has been and remains substantially a Fillmore project. Charles Rickert Fillmore is now the president of Unity.

9. *Other Activities*. Unity publishes, in addition to scores of small pamphlets, the three monthly periodicals we have mentioned. The *Daily Word* appears in fourteen languages. Silent-70 sends its literature free to 8,000 public institutions in the United States and abroad.

In the early twenties, Unity purchased radio station WOQ in Kansas City, where it broadcast regular programs until 1934. Then it was sold, because better results could be obtained by supplying commercial outlets with prepared materials. In the 1950s, Unity began a somewhat similar service for TV outlets, some of which carry the programs as a public service.

As James Dillet Freeman remarks (*Ibid.* 218), the influence of Unity extends far beyond the parameters of its own churches or membership—a statement applicable to New Thought in general. Its teachings have ameliorated the doctrines of the old-line denominations to a point where, compared to their predecessors, they are scarcely recognizable. Thousands of people, distressed in body, mind, or emotions, and finding neither solace nor healing in the old churches, have found homes in Unity or other New Thought organizations.

10. *The Present Scope of Unity*. There is no doubt that among those who have pioneered and contributed to the growth and influence of New Thought, the Fillmores rank among the foremost. During the early years, *Unity* magazine did not even mention churches or ministers—only places where its literature could be obtained. Even in 1940, it listed only 160 conference members, of whom 72 were Licensed Teachers. In 1960, there were 203 Ministers and Teachers; the April 1970 issue of the publication lists 264 churches and study classes, without indicating how many there were of each. The October 1982 *Directory* lists 407 ministers with churches and 206 Affiliated Study Classes or Groups.

If the expansion of Unity continues at the present rate, it is not unreasonable to expect that within a few years its churches and classes will increase from 613 to a thousand.

II. A VISIT TO UNITY VILLAGE

1. *The Complex*. As the visitor approaches the Village, he passes between two large pillars and soon faces the 165-foot tower, which dominates the whole

scene and in which 100,000 gallons of water are stored. Just behind this stands the spacious two-story building, completed in 1929, which houses Silent Unity. Beyond and behind this looms the immense and magnificent Administration Building, completed in 1950, with its red-tile roof, which combines beauty with massive utility. This stands as a permanent monument to the architectural genius of Rickert Fillmore. It is 765 feet long, has 3 floors, and includes a 6-story tower-like structure. It is about eighty feet wide overall, but has large wings extending in both directions. About half of the first floor is underground, where the tremendous task of preparing and mailing some 85,000,000 pieces of literature is accomplished annually. On the second and third floors are great numbers of offices; one wing of the third floor houses rooms containing archives of Unity and New Thought literature and a library with 46,000 volumes, including 6,000 by New Thought authors. The Visitor's Center and Book Store are at the east end; just to the right is the new Activities Center, with its splendid chapel seating 1,100; and to *its* right we find the Inn and Cafeteria. These two buildings, completed in 1975, cost between $3 and $3.5 million.

The power plant is located south of the Administration Building.

In addition to the motel and student cottages, we find many single homes scattered about the spacious premises; there is also a nine-hole golf course; there are tennis courts and other recreational facilities.

Mr. Otto Arni, long-time trustee, stated in an interview that the land may be worth about $10,000 an acre—or $16,500,000. He was very reluctant in making an estimate of the possible replacement value of the property—which is debt-free, but he agreed that $50,000,000 has been mentioned as a conservative amount.

He explained that the Unity School of Christianity is incorporated as a church-school facility under Missouri law, that it is governed by an eight-member, self-perpetuating Board of Trustees, who serve for life. He added that at one time the lay employees were not enrolled in Social Security but that now they are. Since he stated that the average wage or salary of all Unity employees would probably approximate $10,000 a year, I concluded that the payroll, the Social Security contributions, the cost of paper, printing (press work is now performed by commercial contractors in the city), postage, heating, repairs, and other expenses could not be less than $12 or $14 million a year—all of which is derived from subscriptions for periodicals, the sale of books, and, probably most of all, from contributions or "love offerings." Unity has never pressed anyone for money, has never conducted a money-raising campaign, and depends heavily on gifts, bequests, donations, etc., which flow annually into headquarters in a multi-million-dollar stream.

To survey the beautifully, well-kept grounds and talk to the friendly people at Unity—as I did in December 1982—is indeed an inspirational experience.

2. *The Editor of Unity Magazine.* Mr. Thomas Witherspoon, editor of *Unity* magazine, perched high in his office in the Administration Building, proved a rich source of information. He received from thirty to fifty letters every day, all of which were carefully considered. Before him lay one from a woman who sent in eight subscriptions, but no money—all of which would be filled in the hope that some of them might become Unity supporters. One correspondent wanted extra copies to give to friends—the request would be honored. One ordered the magazine, saying she would pay later when she could afford to do so. One woman wrote a long letter and sent one dollar; another enclosed forty-two dollars with a short note of appreciation. And so on and on.

Mr. Witherspoon said that of Emilie Cady's *Lessons in Truth*, 1,800,000 have now been printed, that all the books written by Charles Fillmore have surpassed the million mark. Unity publishes hundreds of small pamphlets dealing with a great variety of subjects—many of which are given away free.

He stated that 2,500,000 copies of *Daily Word* are printed monthly, and that it appears in 14 languages. Its subscription price is two dollars a year, but many copies are given away or sent for one dollar. *Unity* magazine has 430,000 subscribers at $4.00 a year; *Wee Wisdom*, at $5.00, has 100,000.

He said that the Church Ministry is a secondary element in total Unity activity. For example, on a given Sunday, there might, perhaps, be 50,000 people in attendance; but Silent Unity alone handles at least 2,500,000 letters and hundreds of thousands of telephone calls annually from people of every description who ask for counsel or prayer. The churches, he said, came into existence almost as an accident, and had undergone considerable development only in recent years.

He stated that Unity, as an organization, has not joined INTA because it refused to include in its declaration of belief or principles a statement concerning Jesus Christ. However, individual churches and ministers are free to join the Alliance, and many have done so. He added that Unity has no relationship at all with Christian Science and only an indirect one with other New Thought organizations, which often ask for help or advice. Unity differs from these in that it has no practitioners as such, but emphasizes the work of Silent Unity and Silent-70, of which there are no comparable counterparts in any other organization.

Mr. Witherspoon noted that Unity has an enormous outreach among people of every religious persuasion, or none at all. Its literature is read by Jews, Catholics, rationalists, every shade of Protestant opinion or belief. Unity never asks anyone what his religion or opinions may be: it merely seeks to help those in need of spiritual assurance, personal confidence, or help in some emotional problem. Most of those who receive Unity literature are unchurched or belong to some other church.

Unity literature reaches millions of people who have no affiliation or contact with its churches. It has, for example, a Book Club of 60,000 members and a Cassette Club with 40,000, all of whom order the material emanating from Unity and help distribute it among their friends and acquaintances.

For the most part, Unity promotes its own publications, but it handles some by other authors, such as Emmett Fox, whose writings are very popular in Unity circles.

3. *Silent-70.* In 1910, a project called Silent-70 was launched by the Fillmores, the purpose of which was to provide free literature to people who asked for it or who could not afford to pay for it. Publications such as *Lessons in Truth, Daily Word,* and *Unity* are sent to thousands of hospitals, convalescent homes, children's nurseries, public libraries, etc. Subscriptions are entered free for individuals in all branches of the armed services, as well as for chaplains, military hospitals, libraries, reading rooms, service centers, or clubs on military bases in the United States and abroad. Any member of the services who requests it receives free literature.

One special project of Silent-70 is the distribution of Unity literature to inmates in prisons and other penal institutions, where it is said to have transformed the lives of thousands. Any response from a prisoner or an ex-convict is given priority attention and he will receive a special packet of free literature.

Such material is also sent world-wide, especially to the peoples of emerging nations. Foreign institutions which care for orphans will be sent copies of *Wee Wisdom*; and displaced persons receive free Unity literature on six continents.

Nor are the needs of needy individuals forgotten or ignored, especially those who are visually or otherwise handicapped. Literature in Braille and in the form of cassettes is sent to countless thousands throughout the world, particularly the *Daily Word* which, as we have noted, is printed in fourteen languages.

Thousands too poor to renew their subscriptions ask for and receive *Unity* and other literature without charge.

We do not know precisely how many pieces of literature are sent annually by Silent-70; however, we understand that millions belong in this category— with a volume that continues to increase every year.

Like all Unity projects, Silent-70 is financed by "love offerings" received from those able and willing to contribute to this cause.

We know of no other church or organization that operates or offers a similar service to the public. It is therefore unique.

4. *Silent Unity.* The interview with James Dillet Freeman, Director of Silent Unity, was one of the highlights of my visit to Unity Village. He is the author of many books, including *The Story of Unity*, which we have quoted. I met him in the office in the Silent Unity Building where Charles Fillmore once spent most of his working hours.

As I walked across the spacious first and second floors, I observed many of the 200 people who man this project. Theirs is indeed a tremendous task, handling an enormous number of letters and the telephone calls that come in hour after hour, around the clock without ceasing, every day of the year. As I had passed the building the previous evening, I had noted the light in the fifth window from the left in the second story where the twelve neon bars— symbolizing the twelve powers of man—radiate from a central fixture and can be seen during all the hours of darkness.

Mr. Freeman stated that more than 2.5 million letters arrive annually from nuns, priests, executives, workers and businessmen, rich and poor, people with or without religions of their own, but all seeking help for some illness, for emotional turmoil, or for a friend or relative in need. Every letter is answered without delay and includes an affirmative prayer.

In 1969, there were 63,000 telephone calls; in 1982, 750,000, of which 13,000 came on the 800 toll-free line from people in a state of severe crisis who either could not pay for the call or were in a state of emergency. If, for example, someone calls who says he is on the verge of committing suicide, an effort is made to obtain his telephone number, which will be called in perhaps ten minutes to discover what has happened to the individual and whether he can be saved or helped. If his address is known, a letter will be addressed to him or an attempt made to reach some local agency which may intercede in his or her behalf.

Of the 200 employees of Silent Unity, about three-fourths answer letters and the others man the telephones. They try to keep calls at not more than five, or at most, ten minutes, for there are always others waiting. There are fourteen lines in full operation between 7 A.M. and 11 P.M.—and five or six during the deep hours of the night.

No fees are charged or asked for any of this service. There is no income except the "love offerings" from those who appreciate the work of Silent Unity. Since the payroll alone must be at least $2 million a year, in addition to the cost of mailing millions of letters and operating an immense telephone service, etc., we believe that the voluntary contributions must total at least $4 or $5 million a year.

Mr. Freeman stated that Silent Unity has never during its ninety-year history put on a campaign to raise money. Once only he put a short article in the *Daily Word* explaining the needs and the cost of service; the response was extremely generous.

Mr. Witherspoon declared—and Mr. Freeman agreed—that hundreds, perhaps thousands, have written that they have been healed of organic diseases of every description; and, although there is no way to verify most of these statements, it is hard to doubt the actual authenticity of some of them. And then there are the grateful multitudes who, with the help of Unity, have overcome addiction to alcohol, tobacco, and other destructive habits, most of whom, even though they do not join Unity churches or become integral in the movement, take its literature and show their appreciation by making gifts, large or small, totalling altogether, millions every year.

At this point, we should point out that Unity has no quarrel with the medical profession; no one is told to abstain from such help or the use of prescriptive medicines. Unity seeks simply to supplement the aid given by other means, especially when all of these have failed: for example, it will give a person who has suffered broken bones and terrible bodily injury in an accident the courage and hope without which recovery might be impossible. Unity would never think of telling such a victim to rely on Affirmative Prayer alone, but rather to seek and use this to obtain the strength necessary to emerge victorious from tragedy.

We should add that Unity looks upon the beneficent ministrations of the good physician as simply another illustration of the Law of God or Good always operative in the Universe and in Man.

5. *The Unity School of Religious Studies.* We learned in an interview with Connie Fillmore Strickland—great-granddaughter of Charles Fillmore—who is head of the Unity School of Religious Studies, that this is an integral part of Unity itself, and that it operates two principal programs—one for lay students and the other for the preparation and ordination of ministers. There are usually between sixty and seventy students enrolled in the School at any one time; it is manned by a staff of eight or nine "professors." Plans for expansion are underway.

The program for lay students has two divisions: one for individuals who wish merely to learn more about Unity teachings and practices. These come to Unity Village for two-week courses or seminars, and repeat these for several years. When a person has accumulated 130 hours, he/she is given a Certificate of Recognition, which confers no particular authority but serves chiefly as a milestone of progress in Unity realization and understanding.

More important is the course of study leading to the status of Licensed Teacher, a position which is granted by the Association of Unity Churches on condition that the student-applicant:

(1) receive a diploma upon the completion of at least 150 hours of credit;

(2) pass a written test or examination;

(3) teach twenty-four adult classroom hours from a selected list of Unity books or material, available from AUC;

(4) apply for and receive credentials as a Licensed Teacher from AUC after being recommended by the minister with whom the applicant is working; and

(5) attend a Skills Development Seminar at Unity Village.

The Licensed Teacher must demonstrate qualifications to teach, lead, speak in public, operate a class, etc. Sometimes LTs serve as Assistant Ministers; often they act as leaders of Study Classes or Groups, and in many instances, they proceed with additional study leading to ministerial ordination.

The other principal program of the School prepares ministers for ordination. They are required to spend at least two years in residence study, where the emphasis is on Bible history and Fillmore's Fundamental Unity teachings. In order to qualify for the ministry, the advanced student must receive the following number of credits in the five departments of the School:

(1) Biblical Studies and Skills (40 credits),
(2) Metaphysical Studies and Skills (30 credits),
(3) Historical Studies and Skills (22 credits),
(4) Interpersonal Studies (18 credits), and
(5) Communication Studies and Skills (10 credits).

No one can serve as the minister of a Unity church without first meeting these requirements.

When asked about the range of freedom and variation to be found among Unity ministers, Connie Strickland stated that they must accept and teach the basic principles of Unity; however, a considerable degree of difference is to be found in what she called "fine tuning," such as opinions in regard to reincarnation and whether God is a Mother-Father deity.

6. *The Association of Unity Churches (AUC)*. Mr. Charles Neal, Director of Ministry Services in AUC, explained that this organization replaced the former Field Department in 1966, which had monitored the LTs and directed the ministers with the issuance of BULLETIN IV. In effect, it relinquished central control over them and conferred substantially complete autonomy upon AUC, which is an independent corporation organized under the laws of the State of Georgia; it rents office space in the Administration Building, and is controlled by a twenty-one-member Board of Trustees, of whom seven are elected by the churches in seven areas, seven at the Annual Conference, and the remainder by the other fourteen. Presidents are elected for one-year terms.

AUC issues a Newsletter called *Contact* ten times a year; this discusses various matters of interest to ministers and local churches.

Like other Unity activities, AUC operates almost entirely on the basis of "love offerings"; some churches give substantially, others perhaps little or nothing. The November 1982 issue states that the income for the five months ended August 31 was $255,956.93, and the expenses $260,517.43—a shortfall of $4,450.40.

In order to use the Unity name and be a Unity Church, a local congregation—organized under the laws of its own state and completely independent and self-reliant financially—must include a provision in its articles of incorporation and bylaws that, should it dissolve and terminate its existence, its assets will revert to the AUC, which will then use them to establish a new Unity church in the same area.

Mr. Neal agreed with Connie Strickland and Mr. Witherspoon that considerable freedom and variation are to be found among individual ministries; however, if a Unity church is to go by that name it must conform substantially to Unity teachings as promulgated by the Unity School of Religious Studies and to be found in the writings of Charles Fillmore. Mr. Neal stated, for example, that a minister could accept or reject a belief in reincarnation, but that he could not imagine a Unity minister who doubted the immortality of the soul in some form.

He stated that although the financing is done on the local level, AUC now has an Expansion Program under which some form of assistance may be provided for beginners—such as a Study Class—attempting to become a regular church.

He stated that the AUC had 396 churches, 421 active and 150 inactive or retired ministers, and that there were about 300 Study Classes and 150 Licensed Teachers. He added that there are no formal requirements for the establishment of a Study Class. It can meet in a home and can consist of any number of persons. Sometimes it may be organized and led by a lay person who has received a Certificate of Recognition, sometimes by a Licensed Teacher, sometimes by no one in particular. But every now and then, these embryonic originals become flourishing congregations.

Mr. Neal stated that he estimated the active church membership at about 75,000; that there are individual sanctuaries, such as the Temple in Kansas City, which could not be replaced for less than several million dollars; that he himself was for years the minister of a Detroit congregation which had more than 2,000 attendees each Sunday, and that another, in Grosse Pointe nearby, was even larger.

Finally, I asked him where Unity ministers, for the most part, come from. And he declared, without hesitation, that they *all* come from other faiths—as he himself emerged from the English High Episcopal Church—because they, like him, find the old creeds lacking in power to supply vital human needs, and that Unity meets this yearning for union with something greater than ourselves emanating from the Divine Reality of All-Embracing Existence.

III. STATEMENTS OF FAITH

Although Charles Fillmore is said to have stated that an explicit Statement of Faith would be inappropriate because Unity might change its opinion or belief at any time, we have found such declarations in Cady's *Lessons in Truth* and inside the front covers of *Daily Word.* The former contains the following Affirmations (43-45):

First: God is Life, love, intelligence, substance, omnipotence, omniscience, omnipresence.

Second: I am a child or manifestation of God, and every moment His life, love, wisdom, power flow into and through me. I am one with God, and am governed by his laws.

Third: I am Spirit, perfect, holy, harmonious. Nothing can hurt me or make me sick or afraid, for Spirit is God, and cannot be hurt or made sick or afraid. I manifest my real self through the body now.

Fourth: God works in me to will and to do whatever He wishes me to do, and He cannot fail.

In the *Daily Word*, we find similar affirmations, which are usually continued unchanged in a series of issues. The following was printed under date of February 1967, but it was almost identical to the statements of previous years.

PEACE: Let liberty, justice, peace, love, and understanding be established in me and throughout the world, in the name of Jesus Christ.

WORLD LEADERS: Through the Christ-Mind, you are unified in thought, purpose, and understanding, and inspired to right action for the security and freedom of all mankind.

ILLUMINATION: The love of Christ fills my heart, and shines through me, making me a radiant center of light.

PROSPERITY: The love of Christ fills my heart, and prepares the way for my success and prosperity.

HEALING: The love of Christ fills my heart, and quickens the life forces within me. I am healed and restored.

Unity also publishes a small pamphlet called *Unity's Statement of Faith*, which contains some elements not accepted by many of its ministers and members, and which reads, in part, as follows:

1. We believe in God, the one and only omnipotent, omniscient, and omnipresent Spirit-mind.

2. We believe in Christ, the Son of God, in whom is imaged the ideal creation, with perfect man on the throne of dominion.

3. We believe in Christ-Jesus, the Son of God made manifest in Jesus of Nazareth, who overcame death, and who is now with us in His perfect body as the Way-Shower in regeneration for all men.

4. We believe in the Holy Spirit, which baptizes the universe and man

with the thoughts of God and perpetually establishes the divine law in all manifestation.

5. We believe in the supremacy and the eternity of the good, as the one and only objective of man and of all things visible and invisible.

6. We believe in the twelve disciples, the twelve powers of man, going forth into mind and body with power and authority to teach, preach, heal, and wholly save man and the world from sin, sickness, and death.

7. We believe that "God is spirit," as Jesus taught, and that all of His Spirit is with us at all times, supplying every need.

8. We believe that divine intelligence is present in every atom of man and matter, and that the more abundant life, which Jesus promised, is flooding the world and quickening the minds and the bodies of men everywhere.

9. We believe that the original authority and dominion given to man was over his own thoughts, emotions, feelings, and passions, and that, in the lawful exercise of this authority, he will harmonize all discords within and without and restore the kingdom of God on the earth.

10. We believe in the creative power of thoughts and words....

11. We believe that the "kingdom of God" can be attained here and now by overcoming the world, the flesh, and the Adversary through Jesus Christ.

12. We believe in the at-one-ment that Jesus reestablished between God and man, and that through Jesus we can regain our original estate as sons of God.

13. We believe that the prayer of faith will save the sick, resurrect the body from "trespasses and sins," and finally overcome the last enemy, death.

14. We believe that the more abundant life, which Jesus promised, is poured into the race stream as a vitalizing energy, and that, when accepted in faith, it purifies the life-flow in our bodies and makes us immune to all diseased thoughts and germs.

15. We believe that sense consciousness may be lifted up...and that all men may be again restored to paradise through faith, understanding, and practice of the divine law, as Jesus Christ taught and demonstrated.

16. We believe that creative Mind, God, is masculine and feminine, and that these attributes of Being are fundamental in both natural and spiritual man....

17. We believe that we live, move, and have our being in God-Mind; also that God-Mind lives, moves, and has being in us, to the extent of our consciousness.

18. We believe that the body of man is the highest-formed manifestation of creative Mind and that it is capable of unlimited expression of that Mind....

19. We believe that...man can transform his body and make it perpetually healthy, therefore immortal, and that he can attain eternal life in this way and in no other way.

20. We believe that the blood of Jesus represents eternal life; that the body of Jesus represents incorruptible substance....

21. We believe that spirit, soul, and body are a unity, and that any separation of these three is transgression of the divine law....

22. We believe that the dissolution of spirit, soul, and body, caused by death, is annulled by rebirth of the same spirit and soul of man to be a merciful provision of our loving Father....

23. We believe that the kingdom of heaven or harmony is within man and that through man the law and order existing in Divine Mind are to be established on the earth.

24. We believe that the "second coming" of Jesus Christ is now being fulfilled, that His Spirit is quickening the whole world.

25. We believe that the Golden Rule...should be the standard of action among men.

26. We believe that Jehovah God is incarnate in Jesus Christ and that all men may attain the Christ perfection by living the righteous life.

27. We believe that the Word of God is the thought of God expressed in creative ideas and that these ideas are the primal attributes of all enduring entities in the universe, visible and invisible.

28. We believe in the final resurrection of the body, through Christ. We believe that we do free our minds and resurrect our bodies by true thoughts and words and that this resurrection is being carried forward daily and will ultimate in a final purification of the body from all earthly errors....

29. We believe all the doctrines of Christianity spiritually interpreted.

30. Almighty Father-Mother, we thank Thee for this vision of Thine omnipotence, omniscience, and omnipresence in us and in all that we think and do, in the name of Jesus Christ, Amen!

We should note that this Statement follows the teachings of Charles Fillmore closely and literally; but that various Unity ministers now doubt, deny, or merely ignore such tenets as incarnation, the Mother-Father God, the immortality of the human body, the incarnation of Jehovah-God in Christ-Jesus, and, to a lesser extent, some of the other declarations.

Some fear that this Statement could harden into a dogmatic creed. A statement called General Information reads in part:

Unity School of Christianity is a non-denominational religious organization of worldwide scope.... It has no strict creed or dogma and attempts to lead all people, regardless of organizational barriers or theological differences, to a new personal experience of spiritual unity with God and with one another. Unity emphasizes that God is in each individual, and through prayer and meditation each person can find God for himself.

In the words...of Charles Fillmore, "Unity is a link in the great educational movement inaugurated by Jesus Christ.... the Truth we teach is not new, neither do we claim special revelations or discovery of new religious principles.... Our purpose is to help and teach mankind to use and prove the eternal Truths...."

Today, under the direction of Charles R. Fillmore, president (and grandson of the founders), Unity School offers a wide variety of services to aid individuals in their spiritual quests. Through its prayer ministry, worship services, and educational classes, as well as literature, cassette tapes, and radio and television programs, the Unity movement has attracted people of many ages, creeds, races, and nationalities....

Unity School has retreat facilities for persons seeking inspiration and spiritual growth. Each year, the retreat staff plans a number of week-long retreats attended by persons of various faiths from many parts of the world. Retreats feature meditations, lectures, workshops, and Bible study, as well as times for relaxation, recreation, and music.

Unity School operates one of the largest religious publishing houses in the Midwest.... Unity literature is printed in twelve languages and in Grade 2 Braille....

Unity Village Chapel offers a wide variety of services, classes, and lectures for individuals who are seeking spiritual growth and greater self-understanding. Each event is designed to present spiritual principles in a way that encourages individual application....

Free guided tours of Unity School are offered daily.... Formal gardens, fountains, fields, woodlands, and lakes accent the serene setting and provide an appropriate atmosphere for Unity's prayer, education, and publishing activities.

IV. THE CURRENT PUBLICATIONS

1. *Wee Wisdom.* This periodical, begun by Myrtle Fillmore in 1893 as an eight-page magazine, is the oldest religious publication for children in the world. It is issued ten times a year, has forty-eight pages, five and a half by eight and a half inches in size, is printed in large, bold-face type, and includes pictures, drawings, and illustrations. For November 1982 it had six stories or articles, A Prayer of Faith, a variety of cartoons, and a dozen short poems

written by children in the third to the seventh grades in their schools. The text is gauged for children from nine to twelve or thirteen years of age.

Of course, it is written from the Unity point of view, but not obtrusively. It could be, and probably is, received by many of other faiths or of no particular creed. Everything is intended to entertain, give pleasure, and inculcate happiness and good conduct.

A story called "The Hopi Way" is probably indicative of a general approach. A boy named Mark was constantly making himself obnoxious to the other children in his school. After he had broken the Kachina doll belonging to one of the girls, she went out of her way to show him kindness and consideration; and when she discovered that his parents were dead and that his grandparents, with whom he lived, had no interest in his school work, she offered him transportation to an evening party. He responded by making a belt for the doll—which had been mended—and from then on showed an entirely different and happier attitude toward everyone.

In the "Action Corner with Pete and Polly," the publishers take an opportunity to convey some Unity teaching and ideology. Here children are told that they become heroes if they return kindness for abuse; doing so constitutes greatness and makes one a hero. And we read: "Grandma says that a truly great hero, Jesus Christ, came to Earth to teach us about this greatness, this power within. It is our own Christ power. It is the Best Self in each of us that we can call upon at any time. It is our own special *braveness* that shows us how to be heroes in our own hearts."

2. *Unity*. This is its oldest publication; originally founded in 1889, it has been issued under different names, sizes, and formats. In 1962, it contained thirty-six pages, seven and a quarter by ten and a half inches in size, printed in two columns. In 1982, the format was similar to *Wee Wisdom*, but there were sixty-four pages. The November 1982 issue contains six major articles entitled "The Magnetic Power of Thanksgiving," "Nourishing the Life Force," "To Give Is to Receive," "A Unity Look at Fixed Incomes," "The Monster in the Closet," and "Thank God for Prayer." There are a variety of shorter pieces, such as "A View from Unity Village," "Questions on the Quest," "The Football Game," "Magical, Mystical Days," "A Message from Silent Unity," and a number of poems, prayers, and devotional items.

Over the years, most of the material later published in book form has appeared as a series of articles in *Unity*; this is true of most of the books written by Charles or Myrtle Fillmore.

3. *Daily Word*. More than 2,500,000 copies of this, begun in 1924, are printed monthly with 48 pages. It appears in two formats: one, in heavy type, is five and a half by eight and a half inches; the other, much larger edition, is four by five and a half inches and can be carried in a purse or vest pocket. On the back of each one, as we have seen, there is a short verse by James Dillet

Freeman. Each includes, in addition to the Affirmation of Faith, one or two poems and two or three inspirational articles with such titles as "Four Solid Rules to Bring Happiness," "The God in You Is Coming Through," "Trust: Our Weapon against Worry," and "Wonderful Words of Life."

However, the principal portion of the little magazine consists of as many one-page devotionals as there are days in the month—each one being a Daily Word. There is an almost endless variety of subjects; at the bottom of the page, we find an appropriate verse from Scripture. In the November 1982 issue, we found such subjects as Healing, Forgiveness, Prosperity, Home, Science, Order, Rest, Love, Light, Comfort, Strength, Thanksgiving, Truth, and Courage. Each day, the Unity disciples read the given passage in silent communion, hoping for health, peace, happiness, and prosperity (a subject which seems to occur more often than any other). Success is another favorite topic; and for July 13, 1982, we find the following:

I Am a Sucess-Oriented, Spiritual Being

Success and achievement are much desired goals, whether it be in business matters or career, or in our own soul growth and emotional unfoldment. We yearn to feel that we are progressing in life and making an important contribution to the world.

We are spiritual beings, on the pathway of progress and fulfillment, possessing the keys that open doors to outer success. Prayer helps us to recognize our true nature and also activates the inner urge to use more of our talents and abilities and to give expression to the God-potential within us. Prayer benefits us in another important way—it give us peace of mind which enables us to enjoy the small successes of every day as we work toward the larger achievements.

Whatever our dreams and goals, we can know that we are success-oriented, achievement-oriented spiritual beings.

"Then you shall make your way prosperous, and then you shall have good success."—Josh. 1:8

V. THE SYSTEM OF EMILIE CADY

Since Emilie Cady's *Lessons in Truth* is the most popular and widely used textbook in Unity, we believe it desirable that we summarize its teachings. It was first published in 1894, and our page references are to the 1936 edition.

"God," declares the author, "is Spirit, or the creative energy which is the cause of all visible things" (6). He is not a "stern, angry judge only awaiting an opportunity somewhere to punish bad people who have failed to live a perfect life here" (*Ibid.*). Nor is he a person having life, intelligence, love, power. He is, instead, the total of all good, manifested or unexpressed (7). He is "the substance" of each "rock, tree, animal, everything visible...differing only in degree of manifestation..." (8). God is the Father-Mother deity, an impersonal principle (11). The "real substance within everything we see is God..." (13). He is the Great Reservoir, of which every human being is a radiation (23). All joy and power are of God, all good that becomes visible is God (34).

Again: "God is the substance of all things"—the invisible out of which all visible things are formed (56-57) and which is unlimited in supply (57). He is infinite substance as well as tender Father (133), the unifying substance of all things (134); as Mother-Father, he is an ever-present help in trouble.

The concept of Christ is likewise Servetian and in consonance with New Thought in general; "the Christ at the center of your being and your consciousness" is a hidden "place into which no outside person can either induct you or enter himself" (89). There is "a definite inner revealing of the reality of our indwelling Christ through whom and by whom come life, peace, power, all things—aye, who is all things..." (90). This Christ is the means by which the Father reveals himself (92); this is the Son of God—the Christ who lives in you (90).

Thus it is that we may have the mind of Christ in all things (97). In truth, Christ is the life, the quickening force, within us (104); he is the master of spiritual knowledge (111). Desired results will accrue to us when our thoughts turn to spiritual things "embodying the indwelling Christ in our entire being" (122). "It is through the indwelling Christ that we are to receive all that God has and is, as much or as little as we can or dare to claim" (142). Christ—the Spirit of God—speaking in Jesus, the Nazarene, its human embodiment, declared, " 'I am the way, the truth, and the life' " (149).

Christ, then, is a universal power, an aspect or manifestation of God, and is available to everyone in whatever measure he is able or desires to receive or partake of it.

Dr. Cady's concept of evil or Mortal Mind is simply "the consciousness of error" (10). Since man has free will, it is possible for Mortal Mind—the opposite of the divine or indwelling Christ—to control our thinking and our actions. Since God is universal spirit and substance, the only form of what we call evil consists in false beliefs, errors of thought. Thus "the mortal mind may make false reports" (18). "Our minds," we read, "have been tuned toward the external of our being, and nearly all our information has been gotten through our five senses." Thus "we have thought wrong, because misinformed by these senses, and our troubles and sorrows are the result..." (20).

We know that grief can turn the hair white in a few hours, fear makes the heart beat wildly. Thoughts can turn the blood to acid, and the belief that we are miserable sinners can paralyze both mind and body. All this is error, wrong thinking; and these maladies are simply psychosomatic, as are a large portion of all human ailments.

The Real Self within us is never sick or afraid, or selfish (30); we need only deny the existence of such conditions in order to banish or render them harmless (31). The road to health and happiness consists in the denial of mistaken beliefs (33).

Since God is the Universal All, including man (34), there can be no duality. Evil has no actual existence; it is only the absence of Good, of God, even as darkness is nothing but the absence of light, as cold is the absence of warmth— and both vanish when the sun appears (35).

There is, therefore, no evil (or devil) (36).

There is no reality or life or intelligence apart from Spirit (36).

Pain, sickness, poverty, old age, and death are not real, and they have no power over me (36).

There is nothing in all the universe for me to fear (36).

Since evils are mere appearances, they need not, must not, disturb you (44).

All suffering results from a bondage to the flesh (138), which is the failure to recognize our spiritual nature and the fact that we are part and parcel of the Universal God.

These were the Affirmations of Dr. Emilie Cady.

In her system, it is our right and even our *duty* to enjoy life. No religious concept can be more erroneous than the belief that we must suffer want or pain here in order to be eligible for a joyous existence hereafter in another realm (27). We need not go or do without the good things of life here and now. Did not Jesus say that he came that we might have life, and have it more abundantly? Did he not promise that if we ask, we shall receive? Did he not say that all things would be added unto us (29)? It is a false belief that sickness and poverty here are means of serving God (32) To believe that we serve God by renunciation is a totally false concept (145). We are to make our heaven in the here and now and enjoy life to the fullest degree.

Dr. Cady's doctrine of health and Influx are definitely Swedenborgian. Again and again, she speaks of the inflow of power and energy from the divine source, which is God, who continues to pour into us unlimited wisdom, life, power, all good, because to give is the law of His being (24). Again: "All your happiness, all your health and power, come from God. They flow in an unbroken stream from the fountainhead into the very center of your being and radiate from center to circumference, or to the senses. When you acknowledge this constantly and deny that outside things can hinder your happiness or health or power, it helps the sense-nature to realize health and power and happiness" (38, 48).

When we talk to God in Affirmative Prayer, "new life, new inspiration, new supplies from the Fountainhead may flow in," and we achieve peace and harmony within ourselves and with all our surroundings (146).

All this leads directly to the author's doctrine and teaching concerning healing, mental and physical. "When first the Truth was taught," she declares, "that divine presence ever lives in man as perfect life, and can be drawn on by our recognition and faith to come forth into full and abundant life and abounding health, it attracted widespread attention, and justly so" (115). Teachers and students devoted their entire efforts to these ends. However, the time has now arrived when we should seek and achieve more than mere healing of body or emotional distress, for God wants to give us a great deal more than this, desirable and beautiful as it is.

In addition, therefore, to simple healing, the grand objective of New Thought should be to achieve the better and fuller life which comes with the consciousness of the Indwelling Christ in our entire beings (122). Thus, we will achieve a life in union with God and the Christ-Spirit who came and who constantly comes into the world that we might have life and have it more abundantly in all its forms and aspects.

VI. THE TEACHINGS OF CHARLES FILLMORE

1. *The Sources.* The following volumes have been studied in preparation for this section, and symbols for citations and references are shown in the text:

> *Atom-Smashing Power of Mind* (ASPM)
> *Christian Healing* (CH)
> *Jesus Christ Heals* (JCH)
> *Keep a True Lent* (KTL)
> *Metaphysical Bible Dictionary* (MBD)
> *Mysteries of Genesis* (MG)
> *Mysteries of John* (MJ)
> *Prosperity* (P)
> *Talks on Truth* (TT)
> *Twelve Powers of Man* (TPM)

2. *Theology.* At the base of Fillmore's thought lies, of course, his concept of God or deity; and this resembles closely the Servetian Modal Trinity. It is not likely that anyone in American New Thought had studied Servetus, but we know that his concepts had been adopted by many who knew nothing of him *per se.* Since Swedenborg had a similar concept, he may have been the proximate source. At all events, it is certain that the theology of Unity is basically one of aspect or manifestation, although expressed under a variety of symbols.

The Father, we read, is Mind and Living Principle (MJ 18); he is the source of all existence (TT 99); he is the unlimited reservoir of power (JCH 25); he is the Primal Cause (CH 10) and the living formless Substance (JCH 29); he is the only reality (TPM 35); he is the Creative Mind (JCH 18); he is the Universal Substance (*Ibid.* 60); he is the Omnipresence which pervades all things (*Ibid.* 24).

In such a universal power or substance, there can be no such entity as a personal God (JCH 34, KTL 25). God, instead, the living power, is omnipotent in the universe (MJ 59, TPM 18), the only reality (TPM 34), the source of life and health (JCH 23-27) and the stream of energy which flows throughout the Universe (P 24). This deity is the all-nurturing Mother-Father God (MG 23, MJ 74, TT 99, P 36), the All-in-All, which makes duality in creation impossible (TT 149).

This Servetian concept is expressed or implied in many passages. "When we say that there is one being with three attitudes of mind, we have stated in plain terms all that is involved in the intricate theological doctrine of the Trinity. The priesthood has always found it profitable to make complex that which is simple" (CH 19). "The Father is Principle. The Son is Principle revealed in the creative plan. The Holy Spirit is the executive power of both Father and Son, carrying out the creative plan" (TT 134, MJ 136).

God is thus a unity manifested in three forms: "God [and] Holy Spirit...are one fundamental Mind in its three creative aspects" (JCH 63). "This is a metaphysical statement of the divine Trinity, Father, Son, and Holy Spirit" (*Ibid.* 121-122).

God, we read, is the universal, visible substance of the Universe, the only " 'substantial' substance." Second in the Godhead is "the word of God...the revelation to man...of his own being.... the Word is the working power of God." The "Holy Spirit, third in the Trinity," is an outpouring of spiritual quickening, which "speaks, searches, selects, reveals, reproves, testifies, leads, comforts, distributes to every man...the 'deep things of God' " (KTL 14-17).

This Servetian Trinity, then, consists of the Father, who is the substance of the universe; the Son or Word, who is its energizing force or power, and the Holy Spirit, which is the quickening illumination which ministers to all men.

3. *Jesus and the Christ.* With Fillmore, as generally in New Thought, Jesus and the Christ are entirely different entities. The former was a human being, basically similar to all others; but the Christ with which he was so richly endowed pre-existed (JCH 10-11, ASPM 100), and was that aspect of the Trinity known as the Word, the energizing force and power which pervades all existence, a divine emanation available to man, which can be appropriated in whatever degree his capacity enables him to do so.

What, then, was Jesus? Again and again he is called the Wayshower, the Great Exemplar, the Teacher of Truth (TPM 4, 35, 70, 136). It was his consciousness of the indwelling Christ which gave him the power to accomplish his divine mission (P 36, TT 167, KTL 197) and enabled him to purify his body so that it could become immortal (TPM 158). By restoring the broken life-current between God and man, he became the "savior" for those who follow him (MG 39).

What, then, was the Christ? He is the light of God in the world (TT 17), the great and eternal I AM (MJ 87, 128), the perfect God-Idea (*Ibid.* 64), the God-Mind imaged in everyone (JCH 178, ASPM 100), the Power that spoke through Jesus (MJ 92).

The churches have taught entirely false doctrines concerning Christ and Jesus. For one thing, the Christ has appeared in many incarnations over the ages (KTL 131) and will be made manifest again. No error could be greater than to believe that Jesus will return to this earth in physical form (JHC 54, KTL 26). By the first coming of Christ is meant simply receiving the Truth into the conscious mind; and the second is the awakening and regeneration of the subconscious mind through the superconscious or Christ-Mind in the human psyche (TPM 15).

The church-doctrine that Jesus died as an atoning sacrifice for the sins of humanity is a total perversion of truth. All men are born as Sons of God and have no contamination except their own errors and misconceptions; they need only be taught the true and proper pathway to salvation. When men cease to believe in the personality of God and Christ, they may, in their consciousness, achieve unity with the God-Mind. "This is the at-one-ment with the Father" which "dissolves forever that inner monitor called accusing conscience" (KTL 53). "Atonement," we read, "means the reconciliation between God and man through Christ. Jesus became the way by which all who accept Him may 'pass over' to the higher consciousness" (*Ibid.* 185).

Again: "We have been taught by the church that Jesus died for us—as an atonement for our sins. By human sense, this belief has been materialized into a flesh-and-blood process in which the death of the body on the cross played an important part. Herein has the sense of consciousness led the church astray" (TT 164). The at-one-ment consisted in uniting our state of consciousness with the more, interior one of the Father. What died upon the cross was the consciousness of all mortal beliefs that hold us in bondage—such as sin, evil, sickness, fleshly lusts, and death—which he overcame (*Ibid.* 166).

4. *Spiritual Interpretation of Scripture.* Like other proponents of New Thought, Fillmore could accept only portions of Scripture in its literal sense. The Bible, he says, is absolute truth, but veiled in symbols (ASPM 162). They have an inner and outer meaning (MG 8), which must be understood. In fact, the entire Bible is an allegory (CH 29-30). Its every passage has a spiritual, as well as a literal, meaning (MG 26). In reading it, "we should go back to the letter and see the spiritual sense of the parables and symbols used to teach the truth..." (KTL 97).

Three of Fillmore's books are devoted to the spiritual interpretation of Scripture. The *Mysteries of John* quotes every verse of the Fourth Gospel and then gives their spiritual interpretation; the *Mysteries of Genesis* accomplishes a similar purpose. The *Metaphysical Dictionary* is an immense work which, in alphabetical sequence, interprets several thousand Biblical terms, together with their commonly accepted and then their hidden meaning. For example, we learn that Gethsemane was, according to popular understanding, merely a garden near Jerusalem; but spiritually, it is "the struggle that takes place within the consciousness when Truth is realized as the one reality...This is often the agony—the suffering—that the soul undergoes in giving up its cherished idols or in letting go of human consciousness." We are also told that the "devil" we are to overcome is the adverse will, which makes you believe you are a son of the flesh. There is no basis for a belief in hell or eternal punishment (CH 112). Hell is only a figure of speech, a state of mind (*Ibid.* 113, KTL 116). The Holy City, the New Jerusalem, symbolizes the resurrected body (TT 112) as well as the heaven to be consummated in new conditions on earth (*Ibid.* 129). The twelve sons of Jacob represent twelve foundation faculties in man (JCH 151-153) and the twelve disciples of Jesus indicate a higher expression of these faculties (MG 69). The crucifixion means the giving up of the whole personality (MJ 145).

The conventional concept concerning the sacrament assumes an entirely different meaning in Unity. "When we appropriate words of truth, 'eat them,' so to speak, we partake of the substance and life of Spirit and build the Christ body. This is partaking of the body and blood of Jesus Christ, the true sacrament that vitalizes the body by renewing the mind. Every student of Truth builds the Christ body as he constantly abides in the Christ Mind through daily meditation upon the words of Truth" (ASPM 78).

The heaven of which people dream is only something that can exist within us (TT 31). The serpent of the Old Testament is merely sense consciousness (MG 48). Satan is sensation (*Ibid.* 45). There is no such thing as evil (devil) unless your thought permits it to enter (P 59); and to do so, it must be invited (*Ibid.* 96).

5. *The Power of Thought.* Fillmore was certainly a pioneer and amazingly perceptive in the field of psychic philosophy; and, with him, it became the basis of his religion—as well as his healing technique in Practical Christianity. He recognized and understood the three-level operation of the human psyche. "Volumes," he declared, "might be written about faith in relation to the conscious, subconscious, and superconscious departments of mind; or about its centers of action in the body" (MG 77). Sometimes he calls them "spirit, soul, and body," by which "we come into the perfect expression of Godlikeness—one man, one Christ, one God (*Ibid.* 104).

Again and again he refers to these: briefly, the conscious mind is the reason or understanding by which we live in the world of sense; the subconscious is deeply buried in the psyche, but constitutes the driving and emotional force which shapes our lives; the superconscious is that higher faculty which some call conscience (CH 23), and which is also the human aspect by which we live during sleep (MG 159).

"The subconscious mind is the vast, silent realm that lies back of the conscious mind and between it and the superconscious" (KTL 87). The average thinker knows nothing about the subconscious mind and very little about the superconscious; this book presupposes a knowledge of both (TPM 3).

It is of the utmost importance, declares Fillmore, that we understand the relationship between the conscious and the subconscious, which "is the realm that contains all past thoughts. First, we think consciously and this thought becomes subconscious, carrying on the work of building up or tearing down, according to its character. The subconscious mind cannot take the initiative, but depends on the conscious mind for direction. When one is quickened of Spirit, one's true thoughts are set to work and the subconscious states of error are broken up and dissolved" (ASPM 76).

Thus, the conscious mind or reason thinks thoughts, good or bad, and relays them into the subconscious, where they become operative in directing the human organism—physical, mental, emotional, and spiritual—into the condition which will result. Since this process also controls the cells of the body, it will determine whether it will be healthy or diseased.

This analysis leads directly to the nature and crucial importance of THOUGHT (TPM 144). The body is simply the instrument thereof (ASPM 20). The moving powers in life are men's thoughts and words (CH 62). Every organ of the body is affected by the action of the will (*Ibid.* 101). The body obeys the mind, which is the secret of metaphysical healing (TT 118). Thus, the power of thought can produce health (*Ibid.* 149). Man has the power to dissolve all discord and diseases by the power of words (CH 64). We develop diseases and we create perfection by imagining either of them (*Ibid.* 96-97).

The effects of thought are all-pervasive, which is the reason that placebos can heal (JCH 108). If we think evil exists, we make it an active force (CH 52). To achieve health, we must will it (P 112). We can change the body by changing our attitude toward it (MG 135). Right desire will achieve its wish (P 102), but negative thought brings destruction (*Ibid.* 103). We must not carry a grudge against anyone (CH 126). Worry is a thief and a robber (P 110). Therefore, we must cleanse our minds (ASPM 72); we should entertain only worthy thoughts (P 123).

Thought can create old age (TT 49), and the belief in death is killing thousands (*Ibid.* 45), but a disbelief in sickness can drive it away (*Ibid.* 56).

This power of thought becomes effective by Affirmative Prayer in which the conscious mind fills the subconscious with Truth and health (ASPM). Affirmation will create and establish peace, prosperity, and health (JCH 37-38, 44).

In prayer, we should never ask for gifts or special favors. We should, instead, ask that the will of God enter into us and become a moving factor in our lives (CH 72). Thus, prayer draws true ideas from the Universal Mind and man accumulates spiritual substance, life, and intelligence (*Ibid.*); prayer should never be a supplication, but a jubilant thanksgiving (*Ibid.* 70), an affirmation of what is awaiting us from the Father (JCH 67). By this exercise of spiritual power, all things are possible (*Ibid.* 72).

Because most people are influenced by Race Mind—that is, beliefs and opinions which have come down to us from our ancestors—man today has a diseased and dying body (MJ 181) which can be reformed and healed only by developing right thought through the affirmation of Truth.

6. *Sin and Sickness vs. Health.* In the Unity system, sin, hell, sickness, the devil, and ignorance are largely equated with one another; they are caused by, or consist of, hate, fear, and other negative or corrosive thoughts and emotions (ASPM 148). "A short definition of sin," we read, "is ignorance" (MJ 90); but this has no power or reality of its own (JCH 59). We are to be saved, not from hell, but from the delusions of sense (TT 140). Health is the normal human condition (*Ibid.* 143) and the divine heritage of everyone (JCH 136). The body is the temple of God and healing is a divine process (TT 120). Sickness, therefore, cannot be of God (*Ibid.* 56); and we make our own heaven (health) or hell (sickness) within ourselves (MJ 76).

The relationship of man to God is the basis of healing and happiness. Our life in the Universal Divine Mind is unlimited (CH 41); we can heal ourselves from every illness by conforming to it (*Ibid.* 39). We can pick up the universal life-current and thereby vitalize our bodies. These mental impulses start currents of energy that form and also stimulate molecules and cells already formed, producing life, strength, and animation where lethargy and impotence existed before (JCH 4-5).

Fillmore declares that marvelous healings have occurred (*Ibid.* 14). Many considered incurable by the medical profession have experienced incredible cures (ASPM 131-132). Even the dying have been restored to health (*Ibid.* 89). The fact is that every organ in the body can thus be renewed (*Ibid.* 142). By talking to the various parts of your body as if to a patient (CH Preface), you can create new cells therein (TT 153); and by this treatment, you simply affirm their health and soundness (CH 48); you affirm the perfection of your body and deny the existence of sickness (*Ibid.* 49). The power of your thought and your subconscious mind accomplish the cure.

7. *Distinctive Positions of Unity.* Fillmore had studied extensively and was himself a penetrating thinker who clothed his New Thought in a distinctive garb. He declared that the Christianity of Jesus was killed less than 300 years after the crucifixion and that its true adherents were stoned, quartered, and

burned by an aristocracy which ruled through a union of church and state (*Ibid.* 101-102). Creeds were established by a privileged clergy which paganized its teachings to a point where they became unrecognizable (*Ibid.* 132-133). The Church developed a tyrannical priesthood; and the Protestant Reformation accepted most of the doctrines and turned the literal meaning of the Scriptures into another idol. Creeds and dogmas, which subvert the religion of Christ-Jesus, elevated the clergy into a highly privileged class (*Ibid.* 132), which has kept the masses in ignorance for centuries (ASPM 84).

Thus, the churches have prevented the progress of the human mind (TT 124); and a new and necessary reformation is now dawning upon mankind (ASPM 129).

The Swedenborgian doctrine of Influx appears often in Fillmore's writings, and is called by that name. However, in order to receive this divine emanation, we must open our minds to it and thus draw this spiritual substance into ourselves (MG 66). It is a universal stream of spiritual healing (JCH 157). It is the expression of God's love (*Ibid.* 25). It is the river of life flowing from its divine source (TT 148). When you affirm that "divine substance flows in all its fullness through me," you will be healed and you will enjoy prosperity (KTL 84).

Like the ancient Gnostics—and for a similar reason—Fillmore declared that Christianity is based on certain knowledge. "Christianity," like mathematics, "is a science because it is governed by scientific principles of mind action" (CH 40). "The only real science," he declares, "is the science of Spirit. It never changes.... So let it be understood that we are teaching the science of Spirit.... Understanding of the laws governing the realm of Spirit will make it possible to attain this consciousness and to receive the inspiration whenever requirements are met" (*Ibid.* 7-8).

7. *Practical Advice.* In addition to his metaphysics, Fillmore offered many practical suggestions for the attainment of successful living. For example, don't buy on the easy-payment plan (P 125); don't live beyond your means (*Ibid.* 129); conserve your energy (TT 50); in all your endeavors, you must help yourself if you are to succeed (*Ibid.* 95). Prosperity is the reward of effort (P 64).

For a full and satisfying life, you must focus on something more than, and beyond, the mere making of money (TT 57). However, the evil here lies not in the money itself—which is a necessary means of exchange—but in the danger of becoming a slave to it (CH 124-125).

Again and again, he emphasizes the evils and dangers of sex-abuse (TPM 23, 37, 56-57, 145, 165, 166, 167, 168, 169, MG 47). Evil sex habits now dominate a great many (MG 124); and the sex-relation must be submitted to the rule of right reason. To indulge in bodily sensation for its own sake is a sin (P 19); and the passions should always be kept under strict control.

However, asceticism has no place in Fillmore's plan (MG 52). A simple life neither should nor need be ascetic (P 107). To condemn or repress our natural needs and instincts is completely contrary to God's commands (TPM 152-155).

Every person should seek, and has a right to own, property—a sufficiency of goods and supply, but this means something more than piling up possessions (KTL 101). We should not accumulate riches for their own sake (P 89). But there is no virtue in poverty (*Ibid.* 90); every home should be prosperous (*Ibid.* 107), and it is God's will that it should be so (*Ibid.* 113). Jesus never taught that poverty is a virtue in itself (*Ibid.* 186); the universe contains plenty of Substance for everyone (*Ibid.* 21). We certainly need not be poor to be righteous (*Ibid.* 80).

One of the most successful methods of achieving true prosperity is by giving to the Lord (*Ibid.* 138); by so doing, the soul becomes godlike (*Ibid.* 133); we should put God first in our finances (*Ibid.* 141). "True riches and real prosperity are in the understanding that there is an omnipotent substance from which all things come and that by the action of our mind we can supply ourselves with that substance..." (*Ibid.* 167).

We get more and more of God's gifts by the affirmation of prosperity (*Ibid.* 74), and as an illustration of this, Fillmore revised the twenty-third Psalm (*Ibid.* 69):

The Lord is my banker; my credit is good.
He maketh me to lie down in the consciousness of omnipresent
     abundance;
He giveth me the key to His strongbox.
He guideth me in the paths of prosperity for His name's sake.
Yes, though I walk in the very shadow of debt,
I shall fear no evil, for Thou art with me;
Thy silver and Thy gold, they secure me.
Thou preparest a way for me in the presence of the collector;
Thou fillest my wallet with plenty; my measure runneth over.
Surely goodness and plenty will follow me all the days of my life;
And I shall do business in the name of the Lord forever.

8. *Men, Regenerated and Divine.* Perhaps the copestone of Fillmore's teaching is found in the attainment of health, which is a regeneration that makes a man, in a sense, divine. He emphasizes that Man, Christ, and God are integrally related entities (TPM 118, 119). Man is created in the likeness of God (KTL 32, 56; TT 167, 143). Since man also gets his existence from God (KTL 24), he is the offspring of God (MG 11) and resembles Him (CH 8). God resides within us (CH 8, 10). Since man is a free agent, he has the power to do

as he wishes; God never forces anyone to do anything (*Ibid.* 99); all things are within man's grasp. The spirit and body are a unit (TPM 40). "But the real man is not flesh and blood.... These are but his outer garments,.... You are just as fully the son of God as was Jesus, or any other Christlike man who ever existed. The I AM is the same in all men and women" (KTL 56). Man is the inlet and outlet of Divine Mind (CH 24), which is the only reality (P 9), and which is the universal, eternal substance of God (*Ibid.* 83). Man, therefore, is all that God is (CH 33).

There is a process by which man can become a Son of God. When he "becomes conscious of himself as a spiritual being, knowing himself to be the Christ of God, he is I AM, and ready to recreate his world" (MG 42). It was this consciousness which enabled Jesus to become Christ (ASPM 37), and the same process "makes each of us the 'only begotten Son,' a particular and special creation" (CH 15, TT 169).

As we rise by affirmation, this results in regeneration, "a permanent trans-mutation of physical vitality into higher consciousness" (MJ 27). This "New Birth is simply the realization by man of his spiritual identity with the fullness of power and glory that follows" (*Ibid.* 37-38). This may also be called the Second Birth, "a process of mental adjustment and body transmutation that takes place right here on earth" (CH 24).

The body of man is by nature immortal (KTL 98); and there is good reason to believe every atom therein is a center of intelligence which could, by the control of the will, live forever (*Ibid.* 60). The "body will be so transformed within and without that it will never go through the change called death. It will be a resurrected body, becoming more and more refined...until it will literally disappear from the sight of those who see with the eye of sense" (TT 111-112). Thus, man may at last achieve a new and spiritual body (*Ibid.* 159).

Death, says Mr. Fillmore, is only a negation (*Ibid.* 40) and is without reality (MJ 63). It came into the world through the ignorant use of life, and death can be put out only by the wise use of life. Sin and ignorance are the cause of death (ASPM 147, MJ 62). It is the "result of a wrong concept of life and its use" (TT 45). We can, therefore, be rescued from it (KTL 21) by rising into life (*Ibid.* 98, 99).

Fillmore believed that reincarnation occurs in the continuous cycle of life and death. After what is called death, those who have lived honestly and purely find peace and happiness for a time; and, in due course, reappear on earth in human form (TT 158-159). He declared this to be a logical process (JCH 13, 49); and a belief in it has been accepted by all scriptural writers who were spiritually wise (MJ 96). As the mind receives the Christ-quickening, "it will continue to grow in grace, incarnation after incarnation, until the rejuv-enating life has overcome death and reincarnation is no longer necessary" (KTL 28). "Every man inhabiting this earth and the psychic realms immediately surrounding it," declares Mr. Fillmore, "has gone through this process of dying and being reincarnated many times. You who read these lines have had experience as a thinking, free-acting soul for millions of years..." (TPM 138).

This, in brief, is the religious system and teaching of Charles Fillmore.

VII. LOWELL FILLMORE

1. *Leading Personality in Unity.* Many books, written by various individuals, have been published by Unity, setting forth its teachings and practices; and its periodicals over the years have contained thousands of articles on a multiplicity of subjects. However, even though considerable freedom is exercised in these, there is never any rejection or serious deviation from the principles laid down by the founder, and there are no substantial additions. It is therefore unnecessary to examine or analyze this vast lode of material in order to understand what Unity now represents in the field of New Thought.

We therefore conclude this examination with a review of one of the most important volumes we have found in addition to those written by Emilie Cady and Charles Fillmore. This is *The Prayer Way to Health, Wealth, and Happiness* by Lowell Fillmore, the eldest son in his family, who became president of Unity when his father died in 1948 and who was the editor of *Unity* from 1909 almost to the time of his death in 1975. He wrote thousands of contributions to *Unity* magazine and was probably its principal contributor.

Although, in the main, he follows his father's ideology closely, there is a subtle and pervasive difference; his approach is more practical and less likely to provoke doubt or controversy. For example, he never speaks of the Mother-Father God; nor does he mention reincarnation or the possibility of human immortality; nor does he suggest that man has the attributes of God. He does not discuss the sacrament or attack the regular churches. We believe that his purpose was to popularize and simplify the appeal of Unity. However, in most areas, he is in complete agreement with his predecessors; and we note that he emphasizes the importance of thought and the power of the subconscious mind even more than previous authors.

2. *Arrangement of the Book.* The book is divided into fourteen sections, each preceded by a Prayer Drill, which consists of a model Affirmation, one for each of seven days. For example, in Section 4, called The Magnetism of Love, we find the following:

First Day. Divine love is now working through me, adjusting all the details of my life.
Second Day. Divine love fills me with joy and health.
Third Day. Divine love helps me to solve all my problems.

Fourth Day. Divine love is the fulfillment of the law in my affairs.

Fifth Day. Divine love draws prosperity to me.

Sixth Day. Divine love protects me from all harm.

Seventh Day. Divine love abides with me continually and satisfies my soul.

The Prayer Drill for Section 12 deals with health:

First Day. Because my body is the temple of the living God, I am keeping it holy in His name.

Second Day. I am thankful because God's life, substance, and intelligence sustain and glorify my body.

Third Day. My heart is right with God.

Fourth Day. Every day I rededicate my body to God's service.

Fifth Day. God is my life, and because His life is abundant, my life is abundant.

Sixth Day. The substance of my body is not subject to sin and disease, because it is an expression of divine substance.

Seventh Day. I bless my body and lift it up in my esteem because it is a temple of the living God.

The author offers his readers what he called his Metaphysical Gadgets, which have become very popular in Unity.

I go to meet my good.

My heart is right with God.

Divine love through me blesses and multiplies this money (received or paid out).

I am a radiant center of divine love.

There is nothing lost in spirit.

I greet the presence and power of God here.

No man cometh unto me save the Father send him.

There is but one presence and power here.

Life. Peace.

The spirit of the Lord goes before me making safe, happy, and satisfactory my way.

I am spirit and spirit cannot be sick.

The Christ in me greets the Christ in you.

The whole volume, we may say, is an exposition of the all-pervading principles by which health, happiness, and prosperity may be achieved, and the pathways to be pursued in their attainment.

3. *Religious and Metaphysical Teachings.* Since Lowell Fillmore's basic

teachings are in complete agreement with those of Dr. Cady and his father, we need merely note that in most areas he simply gives explanations, elaborations, or practical applications of the Unity system. This is true of his concept concerning the Unal Deity, who is the All-God and the substance of the universe; of the relationship between Jesus and the Christ, and especially of the power of words and thought and how these operate through the conscious into the subconscious mind. He declares that even though many illnesses are psychosomatic, organic diseases also may be healed; that evil thoughts—such as those of fear, hatred, worry—emanating from the conscious mind can cause degeneration in all the cells of the body and work havoc there.

The Kingdom of Heaven can exist only within us and, like hell, is simply a condition of mind. By placing himself in complete harmony with God, man can achieve health, wealth, and happiness through a process of Affirmative Prayer.

Like his father, Lowell offers practical suggestions to his readers. Always follow the Golden Rule; praise others and yourself; always speak constructively—never negatively; don't worry, criticize, or condemn; never try to get revenge on others for real or fancied affronts or injuries.

If you ask for more, you will receive it; you will generally, or always, find in anything you examine whatever you expect or for which you are seeking.

VIII. FINALE

A visit at Unity Village—with its high Water Tower, spacious grounds, magnificent Administration Building, beautiful chapel, Silent Unity Center, and various other installations—is certainly an exhilarating experience, and the general warmth and friendliness of the people who operate the complex will be long remembered. We know of nothing else distantly comparable in the United States or, for that matter, in the world.

Charles Fillmore once stated that he did not wish to declare his beliefs in the form of a creed since he might change his mind at any time; and we must understand that the teachings of Unity are, to a certain degree, flexible and may undergo definite change and development. We have noted that Lowell Fillmore did not assert or restate a number of beliefs emphasized in the writings of his father; and we know, for example, that many Unity ministers do not accept the doctrine of reincarnation or believe that the human body may become immortal.

In a letter to this writer, Mr. Thomas E. Witherspoon, author of *Myrtle Fillmore: Mother of Unity* and editor of *Unity* magazine, stated that the organization now is not what it was in the beginning. "We are not discarding the foundation he [Charles Fillmore] built, but we are constantly changing.

The one constant is the *one, good God* idea.... You would get a better idea of what Unity is now by studying our current magazines and books—than by delving into what Mr. Fillmore wrote in 1910.... Some of those ideas are given short shrift today in Unity."

(However, all the works of the Founder are still featured and sell in great numbers in new editions, and the ideas expressed there are repeated in Unity's *Statement of Faith*.)

We should note that the organization now publishes, in addition to its three periodicals, 94 books, most of which are priced at $4.95. It also issues a great number of booklets, pamphlets, cassettes, and other materials.

A visitor in the Administration Building may be surprised to discover that, at 11:00 A.M., all work ceases for a few moments while a sonorous voice intones the Lord's Prayer over the intercom system, as the entire personnel assumes a prayerful position.

The following Affirmation is on display in the lobby of the Administration Building; it was a favorite of Charles Fillmore:

The joy of the Lord is your strength.
God in me is infinite wisdom. He shows me what to do.
In all thy ways acknowledge him, and he will direct thy path.
I can do all things through Christ, which strengthened me.
Naught can disturb me, for Christ is my peace and my poise.
All things work together for good.
In quietness and in confidence shall be your strength.
Faith is the strength of the soul inside, and lost is the man without it.
The greatest teaching ever given us is—Christ in you, the hope and the
   glory.
God is my help in every need.

The following PRAYER FOR PROTECTION is on display at the Visitor's Center:

The Light of God surrounds me;
The love of God enfolds me;
The power of God protects me;
The presence of God watches over me;
Wherever I am, God is!

Chapter 11

THE CHURCHES OF RELIGIOUS SCIENCE

I. HISTORY THROUGH 1954

1. *The Two Churches.* We speak of two, because, since 1953-4, the denomination has been split into two divisions: (1) The United Church of Religious Science and (2) The Church of Religious Science International. However, we cover both under a single heading because they regard Ernest Shurtleff Holmes (1887-1960) and, to a lesser extent, his brother Fenwicke as their founders and they use *The Science of Mind* as their textbook and principal guide. Now, however, they have different headquarters, entirely separate organizations, and no interrelationship except what might be found in respect to other New Thought groups. Both participate in INTA in very much the same manner; membership in the Alliance is determined by individual churches, as is the case in Unity. However, both divisions of Religious Science are officially members of INTA, which Unity is not.

2. *Early Life and Education.* Ernest Holmes was born in Lincoln, Maine, on January 21, 1887, a rural section of the state, the youngest of nine children. He entered the public school at Grafton Notch, at the age of five. In 1894, the family moved to Bethel, where, at the age of seventeen, he enrolled at Gould's Academy, which he left shortly thereafter. This seems to have terminated his formal or regular schooling. However, he was an avid reader and, together

358

with his parents, absorbed the contents of the Bible, a book called *The Story of the Bible*, and *The Natural Law in the Spiritual World* by Henry Drummond.

Ernest had an extremely active and inquisitive mind. From earliest boyhood, he was constantly seeking answers to the profound questions and problems of life. He absorbed the writings of one challenging author after another. One of the first of these, after Drummond and the Bible, to exercise a deep formative influence on his thinking was Ralph Waldo Emerson, whom he "discovered" in 1907. Then came Thomas Troward (author of *The Doré* and *The Edinburgh Lectures*), and shortly, Walt Whitman and Robert Browning. Holmes often quotes Emerson; and there is little doubt that Troward influenced him profoundly and that *he* did a great deal to bring the works of this English thinker to the attention of the New Thought movement in America.

In 1908, he enrolled in the Leland Powers School of Expression in Boston, where he also attended Christian Science services. In 1909, he began an intensive study of the writings of Christian Daa Larson, with whom, in later years, he established a close working relationship.

We believe, however, that the single most decisive catalyst in the development of Holmes' mature thought was that Grand Lady, Emma Curtis Hopkins, who, though well advanced in years, was still active when he studied under her in 1924. It was probably she who introduced to him the concept of cosmic consciousness, an idea which permeates much of his thought.

Fenwicke graduated from the Hartford Theological Seminary and became a very successful Congregational minister in Venice, California in 1912, where he continued in this capacity for six years.

At twenty-five, Ernest visited his brother and decided to remain in California, where he obtained employment as a playground director at a public school. In 1915, he attempted to fuse metaphysics, psychology, and philosophy.

Thus, we find that Ernest's intellectual and religious development proceeded on the basis of his own personal investigation and convictions; and his knowledge was derived from individual and eclectic sources—a fact common among the great creative and religious thinkers and innovators of all ages.

3. *The First Activity and Publications.* The brothers published their first magazine, *Uplift*, in 1916, and secured their first practitioner. In 1917, Fenwicke resigned from his pulpit and joined Ernest in a full-time endeavor. Their first action was to open a sanitarium in Los Angeles. In 1918, Ernest began a successful series of lectures at the Strand Theatre. In 1919, they published their first books: Ernest's was *Creative Mind* and Fenwicke's *The Law of the Mind in Action*, which we have already summarized and which is still widely used in Religious Science study classes and churches. Beginning in 1920, the brothers teamed up in lecture tours in various cities, especially in the East,

where they held free meetings in large theaters, filled to capacity. These were followed by classes, often attended by a thousand students who paid $25.00 each for a series of lessons.

In 1923, Ernest began lecturing in the Philharmonic Theater in Los Angeles to steadily growing audiences. He also conducted study classes, which were extremely popular. However, in 1925, the brothers decided to go separate ways. Fenwicke went East, where he was very successful as a lecturer. Ernest remained in the West, where he continued to study, attain greater depth of understanding, and influence an ever-increasing circle of students and followers.

4. *The Textbook, Science of Mind, is Published.* In 1926, Ernest began holding Sunday services in the Ambassador Hotel Theater; and he brought out the first edition of his classic, *Science of Mind.* Ironically enough, since this was published by Dodd, Mead, and Company, the copyright of this best seller still belongs to this corporation. The Introduction to this 667-page opus consists of twenty-five pages in four parts (The Thing Itself, The Way It Works, What It Does, and How to Use It), which, in brief, set forth the underlying principles of Religious Science.

5. *No Desire for Religious Organization.* Like other leaders and writers in New Thought, Ernest Holmes—at least for many years—really had no desire to establish churches or a religious organization; he wanted simply to lecture, teach, train practitioners, and publish his materials. Had nothing more than this ever been done, in due course, he would probably have taken his place as another historic figure, along with Quimby, Dresser, Troward, Larson, Fox, and others. As in the case of Unity, churches developed largely as an accident and outside the personal volition or encouragement of the Founder.

6. *A Magazine and an Institute!* In 1927, two important events took place. The Institute of Religious Science and School of Philosophy was founded and chartered under the laws of the state of California; the Ebell Club was rented, where lectures and classes were conducted. The purpose of this was to train an ever-increasing number of practitioners who would minister to those troubled in mind or body with spiritual mind-healing and affirmative prayer. The second great step was the publication of the magazine, *The Religious Science Monthly,* the name of which was changed to *Science of Mind* in 1929. It has been the principal current literary organ of the movement ever since. Its purpose, it declared, was to

promote the universal consciousness of life which binds together all in one great whole and to show that there is such a thing as Truth, and that it may be known in a degree sufficient to enable the one knowing it to live a happy, useful life, wholesome, healthful, and constructive....

In accordance with Holmes's objectives, the Institute did not sponsor any churches or subdivisions for years. The sixty-four-page issue of *Science of Mind* for December 1930 lists twenty-two practitioners, all in California; one of its principal portions, comparable to the *Daily Word* of Unity, had a Meditation for each day of the month, a feature which has been continued ever since. The name of this section was changed in 1950 to Inspiration for Today; and in 1955 to Daily Guide for Richer Living, which has been its heading ever since.

In 1935, the eighty-page magazine included a picture of the building at 3251 West Sixth Street which had just been purchased and which still serves as the headquarters of the corporation, the name of which was changed to The Institute of Religious Science and Philosophy in the same year. That issue of the magazine listed thirty-six practitioners, all in California, as well as sixty-one locations in various parts of the country where Religious Science literature could be obtained. One 1940 ninety-six page issue names seventy-nine practitioners, of whom forty operated out of the headquarters, and it lists seventy-three locations where literature was sold. It also names various places in California where meetings were being held currently, in addition to those at headquarters.

The eighty-page issue of December 1945 has a list of Chartered Religious Science Activities. In addition to meetings at headquarters, there were seventeen other locations in California, three in other states, and one in Canada—a total of twenty-two. It also listed 140 practitioners, of whom 128 were in California. Interestingly enough, Christian Daa Larson is among these.

7. The Developing Organization. After 1930, one important event followed another. In 1932, Robert H. Bitzer, whom Holmes had invited to come from Boston to California, proposed that his congregation be incorporated as the Hollywood Institute of Religious Science. However, this was not done until 1940. In 1934, the auditorium at the Biltmore had become too small to accommodate the growing attendance at Holmes's Sunday lectures; as a result, the Wiltern Theater was leased, where he continued to lecture—as well as later at the Beverly—until 1956.

In March 1938, daily radio broadcasts were begun; and in September, the policy was initiated of establishing chapters of the Institute wherever groups with at least a hundred members applied for such status. The same month chapter status was granted to the Glendale Association, and in October to one in Huntington Park.

In November, the Institute adopted definite rules for the ordination ritual of ministers. In February 1939, a chapter was established in Ventura, and in May another in West Los Angeles. At the same time charter organization plans and bylaws were adopted; and in July, requirements for ministerial ordination were established. In 1941, a qualification policy for practitioners was adopted. In December 1942, Science of Mind Study Groups were authorized under the direction of qualified practitioners. In 1944, the Department of Education, operating under a full-time dean, replaced the Committee on Education.

8. *A Church Organization at Last!* Thus it was becoming obvious that a church-movement was underway, perhaps spontaneously, whether Ernest Holmes wanted it or not. A number of his students had established centers of worship and teaching where his ideas were emphasized and whose following continued to increase. Robert Bitzer, for example, conducted services for a large congregation at 7677 Sunset Boulevard, Hollywood. Other outstanding leaders were Carmelita Trowbridge in Alhambra, Charlotte Garrick-Cook in San Francisco, and Raymond C. Barker in New York. The June 1946 *Science of Mind* listed a Directory of Chartered Religious Science Activities, which operated twenty branches or chapters of the Institute in California, eight in other states, and one in Montreal, Canada—a total of twenty-nine. These were not, we should note, called churches, and their ministers were called leaders; actually, they were teachers who gave lessons every Sunday morning, which is what the sermons in all Religious Science churches are still called. However, in all but the name, these branches of the Institute of Religious Science and Philosophy had by this time become a denomination or association of churches. This development had taken nearly twenty years and, as we have noted, was really spontaneous, if not accidental.

After 1945, the growth was rapid. The December 1946 issue of *Science of Mind* lists forty-five branches, of which sixteen were outside California. It also lists 249 practitioners, of whom 192 were in California, 53 in other states, and 4 in foreign countries. Obviously, Science of Mind was spreading far and wide. The 1949 issue also lists nineteen Study Groups, of which fourteen were in California and one in South Africa; it also lists twenty-four branches with leaders in California, eleven in other states, in addition to the Founders Institute at 3251 West Sixth Street in Los Angeles.

However, the pressure had been increasing for the creation of an official denomination or association of churches with all the financial and other advantages available to such an organization. Thus it was that in June 1949 the International Association of Religious Science Churches was established, and its Articles of Incorporation and Bylaws approved, for the purpose of transforming the chapters or branches of the Institute of Religious Science and Philosophy into a regular church incorporated under the laws of California. Chapter status was abolished; the branches became members of the IARSC. Holmes became a charter member and the honorary president of its Board of Trustees.

The new association was authorized to grant memberships to local groups; but any minister would have to be trained and ordained by the Institute, which continued as a separate entity, and the IARSC had no control over its policies or requirements. The Institute was governed by a self-perpetuating Board of Trustees and on this the individual churches had no representation. This created some friction among the members. A slight compromise was effected when they were allowed to name two representatives to the Board of the Institute; however, the control remained in the hands of the self-perpetuating Board.

In 1953, the Institute proposed a new form of organization under which the IARSC would be replaced by the Church of Religious Science; the old bylaws were repealed and new ones approved. However, substantial control, the educational work, and the preparation and ordination of ministers would still remain with the Institute.

9. *Rejection and Withdrawal.* Since the IARSC was by this time a functioning organization with its own bylaws and elected officials, this program met with refusal from some of the churches, which perhaps regarded this arrangement as one similar to that existing in the Christian Science Church, with its central and authoritarian control.

Thus it was that nineteen members of the IARSC simply withdrew and severed all ties with the Institute; and, according to their historians, simply remained intact as an organization with complete autonomy and no integral relation with the headquarters on West Sixth Street in Los Angeles.

Of the sixty-six churches listed in *Science of Mind* just preceding the rupture, forty-seven accepted the proposal and remained with the Founders Church and the Institute.

10. *An Identical Statement of Faith.* However, since both divisions looked upon Ernest Holmes as their Teacher and source of Truth and inspiration and both continued to use *Science of Mind* as their principal textbook, both to this day proclaim an identical Statement of Faith, which was formulated by Ernest Holmes and reads as follows:

We believe in God, the Living Spirit Almighty; one, indestructible, absolute, and self-existent Cause. This One manifests itself in and through all creation but is not absorbed by its creation. The manifest universe is the body of God; it is the logical and necessary outcome of the infinite all-knowingness of God....

We believe in the incarnation of the Spirit in man and that all men are incarnations of the One Spirit....

We believe in the eternity, the immortality, and the continuity of the individual soul, forever and ever expanding....

We believe that the Kingdom of Heaven is within man and that we experience this Kingdom to the degree that we become conscious of it....

We believe the ultimate goal of life to be a complete emancipation from all discord of every nature, and that this goal is sure to be attained by all....

We believe in the unity of all life, and that the highest God and the innermost God is one God....

We believe that God is personal to all those who feel this indwelling Presence....

We believe in the direct revelation of Truth through the intuitive and spiritual nature of man, and that any man may become a revealer of Truth who lives in close contact with the indwelling God....

We believe that the Universal Spirit, which is God, operates through a Universal Mind, which is the Law of God; and that we are surrounded by this Creative Mind which receives the direct impress of our thought and acts upon it....

We believe in the healing of the sick through the power of the Mind....

We believe in the control of conditions through the power of this Mind....

We believe in the eternal Goodness, the eternal Loving-kindness, and the eternal Givingness of Life to all....

We believe in our own soul, our own spirit, and our own destiny; for we understand that the life of man is God.

In one statement, which is a favorite in the churches he founded, Ernest Holmes stated: "Religious Science is a correlation of the laws of science, the opinions of philosophy, and the revelations of religion, applied to human needs and the aspirations of man."

Could anything be more direct, succinct, and all-encompassing?

The following are some favorite citations from Holmes:

We all look forward to the day when science and religion shall walk hand in hand through the visible to the invisible.

Science knows nothing of opinion, but recognizes a government of law whose principles are universal.

Revelation must keep faith with reason and religion with law—while intuition is ever spreading its wings, for greater flights—and science must justify faith in the invisible.

In each of us there exists the Divine Image of ultimate perfection, for God indwells everything which He creates.

God is Power—the only Power. Center yourself in this God-Power, and you have every right to expect all the good which you desire.

Through an inherent law of Mind, we increase whatever we praise. Praise yourself from weakness into strength, from ignorance into intelligence, from poverty into abundance.

The Law of Reciprocity—of giving of your time, talent, and material possessions—should precede the asking and receiving of abundance.

The perfect body is the fulfillment of the Divine Ideal and is the real man which all of us hope to manifest.

II. THE CHURCH OF RELIGIOUS SCIENCE INTERNATIONAL

1. *Name and Headquarters.* Although the name International Association of Religious Science Churches (IARSC) is still a trademark designating it, this was changed officially to the Church of Religious Science International in 1972. Its headquarters is housed in a handsome and spacious building at 3130 5th Avenue in San Diego, where its monthly periodical, *Creative Thought*, is published and which serves as the center of its activities.

2. *Growth.* The IARSC was, as we have noted, created in 1949; and in 1953, with nineteen member churches, it began operation as a separate entity from the Religious Science Institute. In an official statement the International declares that the IARSC went on as before, but that a number of churches withdrew from it—meaning those which became the Church of Religious Science with headquarters on West Sixth Street in Los Angeles.

Since then, the growth of the IARSC has been steady and rapid, especially in recent years, as shown in the following table:

Year	Churches	In U.S.	In Calif.	Foreign
1954	19	18	13	1
1960	30	29	14	1
1965	42	40	19	2
1970	47	44	21	3
1975	65	61	34	4
1982	86	81	40	5

We note, therefore, that, although California remains as the stronghold of the Church, its members have spread to other areas in the United States and even abroad to a degree and in a proportion quite beyond what existed at the beginning, when thirteen of the nineteen churches were in the area of origin. In 1982, in addition to the eighty-six churches, which had ordained ministers, there were nine societies headed by Leaders, three of them located in foreign countries.

3. *The Magazine Creative Thought.* This has been issued monthly since

1953; it consists of forty-eight pages in a rather small format, four by six inches, comparable in size to the *Daily Word* of Unity, which it resembles in other ways as well. The present editor, Catherine Hubbell, has a statement called Thoughts printed on the inside of the front cover. Then follow several short articles by well-known Religious Science writers, usually occupying eight pages; then comes the reading or meditation for each day of the month— also by well-known New Thought authors—which have such titles as I Am Inspired; I Use Time Effectively; I Am Health; I Learn Quickly; I Am At Peace with Myself; I Have Spiritual Authority; I Listen to My Inner Self; I Am Opportunity Conscious; My Inner World Perfects the Outer; I Dwell in the Wisdom of Spirit; I Am Well, Strong, and Happy; My God Is My Self-Expression; My Business World Is the Dominion of God; I Am Prosperity and I Prosper; I Am Rich; I Live a Healthy Life; Life Is Complete; I Am Free and Mighty; I Am Rooted in Divine Power. These are affirmative prayers of almost infinite variety, all dedicated to a life of health, happiness, and prosperity. In the centerfold of every issue is a Lesson numbered by the month of issue. For example, in that for September 1982, we find Lesson Nine, by Carl Ray Ambrose. The subject is Intuition, which is regarded as a form of divine guidance and which, in everyday living, "reveals to you what you need to know in order to keep your life peaceful." Each number also includes a complete roster of all churches, societies, and practitioners. On the back cover we find a quotation from such men as Raymond Barker, Robert Bitzer, Kahlil Gibran, Ralph Waldo Emerson, and Walt Whitman.

4. *Three Aspects of Approach.* The Church publishes a brochure which states that anyone may approach Religious Science through any one of three aspects and thus discover a new dynamic and creative way of thinking:

> As a *philosophy* Religious Science presents a practical, down-to-earth way of thinking about the nature of the universe and man's relationship to it. It considers man's place in the scheme of things and how he can better live up to and express the potentialities within him. Such an increased understanding broadens his scope of activity and releases him from limitation and fear. As a creation of God expressing His nature, he discovers his rightful position as a co-creator with God.

> As a *religion* Religious Science is something to believe and have faith in. Not in an abstract manner, but as a belief and a faith that have significance and value in every aspect of life. As a religion it brings to your understanding truths which have been announced by prophets of the world's religions. It presents a sound way of thinking and not questionable concepts subject to doubt and speculation.

> As a *science* Religious Science presents specific and definite ideas which each can demonstrate for himself in his own life and experience.

No formula is involved, but there are offered certain methods, techniques, and procedures which, if properly used, enable a person to discover and experience a better way of life. The procedure is called spiritual mind treatment—the elevation of prayer out of a routine ritual to its highest and most effective point. Spiritual mind treatment brings together and uses basic religious ideas and scientific knowledge of mind-body relationships.

5. *Democracy in Organization.* During a visit to the headquarters in San Diego, we received important help and information from the Assistant to the President. The Church has an elaborate set of bylaws which spell out the details of its organization and operation. One element stressed therein is the spiritual necessity for democratic procedures, individual responsibility, the autonomy of the member churches, and the control over the national organization by representatives duly elected by them. The Preamble of the Bylaws declares:

> We hold that spiritual unity among men can most effectively be manifested under a democracy, wherein the inherent freedom and divine individuality of all members may express for the good of all in understanding, brotherly love, justice, and equality....
> We declare that the future good of Religious Science can best be maintained in the consecrated hands of the many, under a spiritual democracy, rather than in the hands of even the most capable few.

6. *Membership.* The Bylaws provide that membership may consist of churches, Societies, and Centers, which shall be required to meet certain qualifications to be established by the Board of Directors. Societies have no voting power; churches must have duly qualified and ordained ministers; every church must use Articles of Incorporation and a set of bylaws approved by the International. Any church, society, or center has the right to withdraw from membership at any time; but if it does so, it may no longer use a name or trademark belonging to the Corporation.

7. *Government.* All legislative power is vested in a Congress which consists of accredited representatives of the member churches and centers and of all pastors or leaders of these. This Congress, which meets at least once annually, has the power to determine its membership and to admit or expel, by a two-thirds vote. It elects the Board of Directors and levies and collects contributions for the support of the International.

The Board of Directors, which acts as the executive and judicial body of the organization, consists of nineteen members, of whom thirteen are ordained ministers and six are lay members in good standing who have completed basic courses of study in Religious Science. All Directors are elected by Australian ballot for a period of three years. Any such Director may be removed by a two-thirds vote of the Board, but he has a right to appeal such action to the entire Congress at its next annual convocation. The Board, which elects its own officers, meets at least twice between congresses; and it is their duty and function to carry on and manage the business of the Corporation.

When any vacancy occurs on the Board, except by expiration of term in office, this is filled for the interim period by the Board itself.

The Board has broad powers to establish general standards of procedure for the International, its churches, centers, and societies. It determines the qualifications for approval and licensing of ministers, teachers, leaders, and practitioners; and can expel any such individual for just cause by certain procedures which entail provisions for appeal.

The Board can also grant or rescind charters for any church, center, or society; it establishes salaries for personnel, administers all funds necessary for the welfare of the International, controls all publications, manages its finances, and appoints or creates any committee or department deemed necessary to carry on its work.

The President of the Congress also presides over all meetings of the Board of Directors and performs such other functions as normally pertain to such executive office.

All churches and centers select and send voting representatives to the annual congresses; each sends one for every fifty active members, in addition to the pastor; however, no church may have more than twenty delegates.

At the Annual Congress, a Nominating Committee prepares a slate of candidates for office; however, any number of additional nominations may be made from the floor; election is by Australian ballot.

8. *The Board of Education.* One of the most important bodies in the International is the Board of Education, which consists of five members appointed by the Board of Directors for a term of five years, with one expiring annually. The President serves as an ex-officio member of the Board of Education.

This Board establishes the curriculum to be followed for all Religious Science International class instruction, the conditions under which credit will be granted for the successful completion of the accredited class-instruction, and the criteria for granting transfer credits from other organizations. It also recommends to the Board of Directors minimum tuition charges for instruction, additional requirements for the qualification of practitioners and ministers, and the requirements for the accreditation of teachers.

All instruction is given in the local churches by accredited teachers under the general supervision of the local ordained pastor; however, there are occasional seminars held in San Diego or elsewhere under the general sponsorship of the International in which ministers and leaders can deepen their understanding of Religious Science.

For licensing a minister, four-year courses of study are prescribed; in addition to this, after receiving a license, the minister serves at least two years in a local congregation before ordination.

Practitioners must take three years of instruction before receiving licenses, and these must be renewed annually.

All licenses and ordinations are determined and issued at the headquarters by the Board of Directors.

10. *The Operation of the Churches.* As noted, the local organizations enjoy a great degree of autonomy. The headquarters has prepared a model for Articles of Incorporation which are to be used as the basis in whatever state the branch may be located. This provides that should a church dissolve—that is, terminate all activity—its assets must revert to the International. This is a requirement for membership in the association.

In the model bylaws prepared for the member-churches, a similar provision is mandatory; however, should a going congregation decide to disaffiliate, it can do so and take its property with it, but it may not thereafter use any name or trademark which would indicate membership in the International. And before taking such action, it must discuss the issue with a representative from headquarters, who will meet with the Board of Trustees and the membership for a full discussion of the reasons for the proposed separation.

Churches are administered by a Board of Trustees with a suggested membership of seven but not more than nine, elected to staggered three-year terms.

No person can serve as the pastor of an International church unless he has been licensed and ordained by the Board of Directors.

Regular procedures are set·forth by which the congregation can expel undesirable members, and even for the removal of the minister.

11. *Practitioners.* While the United Church of Religious Science has twice as many churches as the International, it lists an average of less than 4 practitioners, while the December 1982 issue of *Creative Thought* lists 498, or an average of more than 11 per church. The Reverend Lola Mays, minister of the Mesa Church, stated that she trains more of these than any other church in the denomination except that in New York. We do not know the precise reason for·this disparity unless it is that the International emphasizes the need and importance of this service and activity more than the other denomination.

We learned from one minister that practitioners generally devote their efforts more or less equally to three kinds of counseling: (1) those with physical ailments; (2) those with emotional problems, such as alcoholism or neuroses, and (3) those who need help in achieving proper adjustments with others in family or other personal relationships, or in achieving desirable economic objectives.

One brochure states that the practitioner is a person of high spiritual consciousness, skilled in mind-treatment, dedicated to the cause of helping others, and licensed to practice professionally. Such treatment, it declares, consists in healing the mind, body, and affairs through the use of Scientific Prayer, which can change the individual's consciousness and thereby accomplish an improvement in body and outward relationships—a change not done *for* you, but *through* you. The practitioner is simply a teacher and the patient is a student.

You need a practitioner, we read, if you are too close to your problem to see the situation clearly; if you lack the experience and understanding necessary to remove your difficulty, and if you feel a real need for help and instruction.

Most of the practitioners operate out of their own homes, although some list office numbers and addresses. Thus, some engage in this as a part-time, others as a full-time profession or career.

The brochure quotes the following fees for treatments: $20.00 for a single lesson; $50.00 for a week; and $150.00 for a month.

III. *PSYCHO-CYBERNETICS* BY MAXWELL MALTZ

Although an analysis of the teachings of Ernest Holmes would be just as pertinent here as in our discussion of the United Church of Religious Science, we will defer it for that division of this chapter since the documents we summarize are all published by that denomination. We have already analyzed the works of Joseph Murphy, Thomas Troward, Emma Curtis Hopkins, Emmett Fox and others whose writings are so popular in New Thought. However, since *Psycho-Cybernetics* by Maxwell Maltz is used perhaps more intensively by teachers and ministers in the International than elsewhere in the preparation and instruction of practitioners, we will here devote a few pages to a summary of this very important work.

This book, first published in 1960, has been so popular that it has sold more than a million copies. It does not belong strictly in the New Thought cycle, because it advances no opinions concerning the deity or other specifically metaphysical concepts, although it refers sometimes to Jesus and passages in the Bible; nor does it advance beliefs in immortality or miraculous healings for organic diseases. However, in other areas its ideology is so similar to that found in Quimby, Emma Curtis Hopkins, Charles Fillmore, Ernest Holmes, and many others as to make the author a favorite among their adherents, as well as with a great many who belong to other denominations or to none at all. The fact is that his analysis of human beings and their problems, as well as the solution for success and happiness, differs more in semantics than in the basis upon which it is founded.

The dictionary defines cybernetics as a science dealing with the comparative study of the operation of complex electronic computers and the human nervous system. Maltz refers to the subconscious mind simply as the unconscious. This, he declares, is a vast storehouse in which records are kept of all experiences (20, 228); although individuals have no conscious memory of these, they are ever present and exercise a dominating influence. The brain, therefore, and the nervous system constitute a computer-like machine which directs the conscious organism into the pathways it will seek and traverse (19-23).

Man, we are told, is not a machine, but he uses one—the creative, impersonal servo-mechanism, which is the brain and the nervous system, the computer in which all past experience is stored, as in a tape-recorder (xx, 12, 14, 17, 20, 37, 71, 226). However, this mechanism has no imagination of its own, and it can only receive, retain, and direct (22); and it cannot tell the difference between real and imagined failure (206).

Maltz agrees with Fillmore and other New Thought writers in so many details that he appears as one of their disciples. He declares, for example, that you should never condemn or criticize yourself (61, 62, 170); you must accept yourself as you are (114, 116); never carry a grudge or a grievance (130, 147, 152); you ought to forgive others as well as yourself (146, 149); never take counsel from your fears (216); overcome evil with good (219); think positive thoughts only (70); treat other people well (112, 170); and compliment at least three persons every day (171).

The most important thing in the world is for a person to create the best possible self-image through self-esteem (xix, i, 91). In order to improve, we must create this self-image through the constructive use of our subconscious servo-mechanism (38, 45).

Among all the areas in which Maltz finds himself in complete agreement with other writers, none is more pervasive than the influence of thought upon a person's behavior, health, success, and happiness, which are normally the great objectives in life. In order to achieve these, it is necessary to program the servo-mechanism—i.e., the subconscious—into the proper basis for accomplishment. When a proper self-image has been created, the battle for all these is half won. Every person, says the author, is engineered for success (25). Our bodies are equipped to maintain health, cure diseases, and remain youthful (228). In other words, health is the normal and disease the abnormal state of man. He tells the story of a comparatively young man who, because of discouragement, aged twenty years in a few weeks; but when the cause of this was revealed to him and removed, he regained his former appearance and zest in an equally short time (47-49). Negative ideas will cause inferiority complexes which, in turn, cause any number of dire results (50, 54). Your imagination can make you fail or succeed, according to its influence (51). In order to succeed, we must think success (113); we must also have a feeling and desire for it (68); it is necessary that a goal be set (70); if we picture ourselves as failures, we will become failures (206). It is possible to make an old man of one who is only thirty by the power of thought (238); on the other hand, it is possible to maintain a youthful capacity and appearance well beyond the seventies (237-239). Placebos have proved effective because the patient thinks he has received an effective curative substance—which exists solely within his own organism (237). Conscience can make us into cowards even when we have nothing to fear (164). By thinking pleasant thoughts, we can achieve happiness (91); fear and negative thoughts must therefore be avoided and banished (97). A person's hand can be burned by a cold poker if he believes it is hot (29); a man will be terribly frightened of a stuffed image if he thinks it is a wild bear (31).

On the other hand, the power of thought can help you overcome bad habits such as alcoholism (28). In order to achieve health and happiness, there are certain things you must do. "The method consists in learning, practicing, and experiencing new habits in thinking, imagining, remembering, and acting, in order to (a) develop an adequate and realistic self-image, and (b) use your creative mechanism in achieving particular goals" (13). That is to say, as Fillmore and Murphy also declared, that your conscious mind must pour into your subconscious the elements which will transform the latter into a creative force for the achievement of your objectives. Maltz declares that he was propelled into this realm of constructive thought as a result of his experiences as a plastic surgeon; he found that cosmetic surgery helped some to reshape and glorify their lives; but for others, no matter how successful the facial operation, there was no regeneration or improvement. The secret lay within the patient; with or without the surgery, if he developed self-confidence and a good self-image, his problems were solved; but if this did not happen, nothing else availed (10-11).

From his long experience and observation, Maltz found that some people have a Failure Mechanism in the subconscious and are, therefore, constant failures. The formula for this consists of (1) frustration, hopelessness, futility; (2) misdirected aggressiveness; (3) insecurity; (4) loneliness, which is lack of "oneness"; (5) resentment against others and onself, and (6) emptiness—a feeling of worthlessness (119). On the other hand, he had also observed the formula for success and happiness: (1) a sense of direction, (2) understanding, (3) courage and faith, (4) charity toward others and oneself, (5) self-confidence, and (6) self-acceptance—the development of the best possible self-image (104).

Although Maltz does not refer to God as Universal Spirit or Intelligence, there are a few passages which hint at something similar. He says, for example, "I believe there is ONE LIFE, one ultimate source, but that this ONE LIFE has many channels of expression and manifests itself in many forms" (245). "Life and power," he declares, "is not so much contained in us, *as it courses through us*" (227). And he concludes his treatise with these words:

> Finally, let us not limit our acceptance of Life by our own feelings of unworthiness. God has offered us forgiveness and the peace of mind and happiness that come from self-acceptance. It is an insult to our Creator to turn our backs upon these gifts and to say that his creation—man—is so "unclean" that he is not worthy, or important, or capable. The most adequate and realistic self-image of all is to conceive of yourself as "made in the image of God." "You cannot believe yourself the image of God, deeply and sincerely, with full conviction, and not receive a new source of strength and power."

IV. THE UNITED CHURCH OF RELIGIOUS SCIENCE

A. *The Headquarters Complex*

1. *A Visit There.* In February 1983, this writer spent some time at the headquarters of the Church located on West Sixth Street, Los Angeles. Mr. William Lynn and Mr. Mark H. Shaw, the Chief Executive Officers, were most gracious in supplying information and documents, enabling me to give a correct description of the Church operation. Other officials were also very helpful.

The headquarters occupies almost an entire block with 310 feet of frontage on Sixth Street and extending 600 feet back on New Hampshire to Fifth Street. Buildings include the Church offices with 21,155 square feet at 3251 West Sixth, the Magazine Building at 3257, the World Ministry of Prayer at 3261-5, and, on the corner of Berendo, the magnificent Founder's Church, begun in 1958 and dedicated January 3, 1960, with 1,487 luxurious seats, where two services are held each Sunday morning. This Church has 8,000 members.

On land facing Berendo, the Church owns 370 feet of frontage, on which several apartments are located. At the southwest corner of Fifth and New Hampshire are facilities housing the Department of Education, the Library, and the Youth Center. With entry from New Hampshire, there is a large parking lot in almost constant use, in addition to which a garage across the street is leased to accommodate the throngs who attend Sunday services. The land area totals 155,350 square feet, or about 3.5 acres.

All this, of course, is near the heart of downtown Los Angeles, where land values run into fantastic sums for a few square feet. The visitor cannot help contrasting this location with that of Unity, which has nearly three square miles of land in an open countryside. One has a rural atmosphere, the other the hustle and bustle of a great metropolis. Which is preferable?

In a document, *Request for Proposal*, the Church expresses a willingness to consider the sale or other use or disposition of the property. The sanctuary cost $1.5 million; the complex now has an official appraisal of $839,105, but its replacement value is estimated at more than $12 million. The Church budget for 1980-81 exceeded $4 million. Its net "book" worth was then $7,700,000, in addition to which the assets of its clergy and employee retirement fund exceeded $2.5 million.

The Library has one of the largest collections of New Thought literature in the world—some eight or ten thousand volumes and constantly growing—available for use especially by ministerial students or candidates.

There are at least one hundred full-time employees at the complex, in addition to others who work part-time or on a contract basis, such as the teachers who constitute the faculty in the Department of Education.

More than 300,000 people pass through the doors of the complex annually for ongoing activities or to obtain help of some kind.

2. *History.* As already noted, the Founder's Church and the Institute of Religious Science broke with the International Association of Religious Science Churches in 1953-4 and new bylaws were prepared for the Church of Religious Science; and in 1968, it was decided to establish a single corporation as an umbrella or association of churches, of which all individual congregations could be members with all the advantages accruing to religious associations without the necessity of individual incorporation. This system was finally approved in 1972. In 1982, it was decided to emphasize the term *Science of Mind* and gradually de-emphasize the name Religious Science as a marketing strategy. In October 1982, Articles of Incorporation were filed with the Secretary of State in California to establish Science of Mind International, controlled by the United Church of Religious Science.

The growth of the Church, especially in recent years, has been spectacular. Consulting back issues of *Science of Mind,* we found the information set forth in the following table:

Year	Listed Practitioners		Church Organizations		Churches		Study Groups	Foreign Organizations
	In California	Outside	Total	Domestic	In California	Total		
1955	155	95	50	50	40	50	None	None
1958	187	33	59	57	45	58	1	2
1960	199	31	76	74	51	71	5	2
1965	122	29	82	76	55	76	6	6
1970	119	32	103	96	58	79	24	7

Year	Listed Practitioners		Church Organizations		Churches		Study Groups	Foreign Organizations
	In California	Outside	Total	Domestic	In California	Total		
1978	60	19	147	139	79	125	22	8
1983	45	36	355	319	89	175	180	36
1984	46	43	394	353	98	189	205	41

The number of churches since 1955 has increased from 50 to 189, the study groups from none to 205. Whereas forty of the churches were in California in 1955, only about half of them—ninety-eight—were there in 1984. Strangely enough, the number of listed practitioners declined from 230 in 1960 to 81 in 1983; however, Mr. Lynn explained that one reason for this is that a charge is made for listing in the magazine. Actually, there were 555 in 1980 and 603 in 1983.

He stated that the active membership is now between 35,000 and 40,000. A document called *Profile: United Church of Religious Science* contains the following statistics for March 1, 1981: membership, 36,025; chartered churches, 146, of which 38 were established during the two previous years, and 8 fellowship churches. There were at that time 150 study groups, of which 89 had been in existence less than a year; 603 active and 33 retired practitioners; 147 active and 117 retired or inactive clergy, and 47 candidates.

3. *Study Groups.* Marjorie Staum, Assistant Director of Member Churches, in charge of Study Group Development, explained that every such listed organization has a leader called a Director, but that there is no formal requirement for its establishment or operation. A group can come into existence wherever individuals interested in Science of Mind meet, but not in sufficient numbers to form a church or hire a minister. Any individual can organize it; and it usually meets in a private home for the purpose of studying the principles of Science of Mind. All such classes or groups receive materials for study, which consist of a variety of cassettes, pamphlets, and texts. Each group, to maintain its status, makes two Progress Reports a year.

Most of the groups are small and Ms. Staum estimated the average number at seven or eight persons. However, many of these have grown rapidly, and most of the fifty churches established since 1978 developed from these groups.

4. *Science of Mind Publications.* On the second floor of a building owned by the Church at 600 New Hampshire are the offices of the Science of Mind Publications, which includes the monthly magazine of the same name, with a circulation of 100,000. Although some of the books available from this office are issued by other publishers, it prepares, prints, and distributes an enormous quantity of literature. Its 1983 catalog listed thirty-nine titles under its own copyright, in addition to about thirty under that of others.

5. *The Ministry of Prayer.* This is an operation basically similar to that of Silent Unity—but on a smaller scale. It has nine full-time practitioners who operate several phone lines on a twenty-four-hour basis. It sends out about 9,000 letters monthly, answers 1,800 telephone calls from people in distress, answers 1,200 requests received by mail for personal help or counsel. It has about 900 contributors and its monthly income is about $18,000. When computers are installed, it is expected that its capacity for service will double without increasing the personnel. As in Unity, this Ministry is supported entirely by voluntary contributions from those who have been helped.

6. *The Holmes Center for Holistic Healing.* On the third floor of the building on New Hampshire is located the office of the Holmes Center for Holistic Research and Healing. Barbara Waldron, Executive Director, explained its purpose and operation.

It holds annual one-day symposiums attended by about a thousand people in Los Angeles; the ninth was held on April 27, 1982, at which several speakers with national reputations presented the results of their research. For example, at the last convocation—titled Pathways to Healing Body, Mind, and Soul— Dr. Lawrence Le Shan spoke on "The Mechanic and the Gardener: Making the Most of the Holistic Revolution in Medicine"; Dr. Tassilo Albus on "The Spa: Water and Herbs, A Faith in Healing"; Dr. Beverley Rubik and Dr. Elizabeth Rauscher on "The Validity of One Healer's Power"; Dr. E. Douglas Dean on "A Review of Healing in Europe," and finally there was Round Table with several scientists and physicians who answered questions from the audience.

Ms. Waldron emphasized that the Center itself does not engage in healing; its purpose is to encourage, and, so far as possible, help to finance research projects by qualified scholars in medical schools and universities. In an average year, it operates on a budget of about $150,000; and grants will total from $40,000 to $100,000, depending on available funds—all of which derive from interested and philanthropic donors.

During a recent period, grants were made to Dr. William C. Dement of the Stanford University School of Medicine for research in "The Healing Potential of a Dream State"; to Dr..Gary Schwartz of Yale University for investigating "Good Humor and Good Health"; to Dr. Joseph Kamiya and Dr. Jean Millay of the Langley-Porter Neuropsychiatric Institute for research in "Physiological Synchronization in Healing"; to Dr. William H. Redd, of UCLA and the University of Illinois for investigating "Behavioral Approaches to Reduce Pain and Nausea of Cancer Treatments"; to Dr. Kouki Nakata of UCLA for research in "A Self-Help Program for Persons with Catastrophic Illness"; to Dr. Daniel J. Benor of the Albert Einstein Medical Center for research in "Suggestion and Psychic Healing in Human Surgical Patients"; to Dr. Ray Rosenthal of the American Medical Student Association and Foundation for research in "Alternative Designs for Medical Education," and to Dr. Dean Ornish for research in "A Randomized, Controlled Trial of Stress Reduction and Dietary Changes in Treating Ischemic Heart Disease."

This is a sample of the kind of work which is sponsored by the Holmes Center for Research in Holistic Healing.

We should note that the basic objective of the Center is to establish a scientific validation for the phenomena of healing by methods outside the world of traditional medicine—in short, to correlate the spiritual or mental process with the physical. It seeks this result through scientific investigation and evaluation; it has no quarrel with the regular medical profession, but wishes simply to supplement its operation by proving the close interrelationship existing between the mind and the body of man.

The fact that literally scores of leading medical doctors and university scholars now endorse and cooperate with the Holmes Center indicates the extent to which it has penetrated thinking in the highest intellectual circles; in fact, it has risen to a position and status which elevates it quite beyond any need to fear attacks from any source, such as those which were hurled at Christian Science, especially during its early years.

B. *The Church Structure*

1. *The Bylaws.* These are the rules and regulations enacted by the delegates from the autonomous member churches, which are granted affiliation and charters after meeting certain qualifications.

The country is divided into four districts, each of which has approximately an equal number of churches and active members. Each district elects a Steering Committee consisting of six persons who serve three-year staggered terms, of whom at least three must be laymen, one an ordained minister, and one a licensed practitioner who is not also a minister. Each district holds a convention in odd years, while the United Church holds one in every even-numbered year. The same delegates meet in both the district and the general conventions. All ordained ministers are automatically delegates to the conventions at both levels. Each church elects one delegate for each fifty enrolled members, but no more than ten may be elected from any one congregation.

All lay delegates are elected by the Board of Trustees in the churches they represent.

Each member of the Board of Trustees of the United Church and its President as well as the Chief Executive Officer serve as delegates to the general convention.

A Board of Trustees consisting of sixteen members elected by the general convention constitutes the Executive Agency of the Church. The delegates at this convention are entrusted with supreme power in Church affairs. It hears and considers the reports of the Board of Trustees; conducts workshops for the betterment of the movement; makes recommendations to the Board of Trustees; considers resolutions to amend the Bylaws; can recall and remove any elected official, after conducting an investigation, as set forth in the Bylaws.

Retired and inactive ministers and representatives from study groups may attend the general conventions, but have neither voice nor vote.

The sixteen-member Board of Trustees—four elected from each district—is probably the most important governing entity in the Church. It consists of eight ordained ministers and eight qualifying lay members of congregations; they serve four-year terms, but may not immediately succeed themselves. No employee or any Vice-President may be a Trustee.

The Board of Trustees determines the requirements for ministerial and practitioner training, licensing, and ordination; it elects and can remove any and all officers of the Church; it appoints committees and prescribes the powers and duties of all officers, practitioners, and ministers; it can borrow money and determine Church financing; it serves as the Trustee for all Church assets—tangible and intangible; it can establish such subsidiary corporations as it may deem advisable; and establish or alter the boundaries of the districts as may from time to time be desirable. This Board shall meet at least once a year or as often as it may deem necessary.

The Board appoints an Executive Committee consisting of five of its own members, which shall meet for the transaction of routine business. It may establish or designate other committees for specific purposes, of which one is the Standing Advisory Committee on Education and Ecclesiastics, consisting of nine members—seven of whom shall be ordained ministers and two licensed practitioners—which shall make recommendations on policy matters relative to educational and ecclesiastical questions. It shall also establish a Standing Committee on Practitioner Policy, consisting of nine members, of whom two are ordained ministers and the others licensed practitioners.

The officers of the corporation shall be the Chairman and Vice-Chairman of the Board, a Secretary, and a Treasurer, empowered to exercise the duties and functions usually appertaining to such positions.

By a three-fifths vote, the Board of Trustees may change, repeal, or amend any provision in the Bylaws, provided two-thirds of the delegates present at a general convention approve such action. However, all district conventions, by a three-fourths majority, may override the action of the Board of Trustees and even that of the general convention, and such determination is final.

Up to 1983, the Founder's Church, operating as an integral part of the Institute of Religious Science, had been a separate entity. Now, however, plans have been completed to enroll it as a member church, with only the same rights and privileges which belong to all others.

Since the member churches elect the delegates to both the district and the general conventions, and since these have power to amend, revise, or repeal any provision in the Bylaws, it is obvious that the principle of democratic control is well established. However, since the Institute, which is an independent corporation organized in 1927 and reincorporated in 1935, exercises a very significant central control, the United Church in this respect differs sharply from the IARSC. However, the individual churches could, we suppose, if they so wished, sever this relationship; we can only conclude that they not only accept this authority in wholehearted agreement, but that this is one of the principal reasons why they adhere to, and are loyal members of, an organization which, to a large extent, is directed by and from the headquarters. Others might prefer to place greater authority and responsibility in the individual churches; however, the much greater growth of the United Church would indicate that the majority prefer a central source of educational authority.

2. *Member Churches and Study Groups.* A 120-page document called *Church Code* describes the operation of member churches and study groups. This contains the Church Code, first prepared in 1974, later amended and ratified in its present form in 1980. Included are sections dealing with Charter Requirements; Federal and Income Tax Laws; A Clergy and Employees' Retirement Plan; Study Groups; Annual Reports to the Department of Member Churches; and Miscellaneous Exhibits, including Models of Agreement of Affiliation; Bylaws, and several others.

Under Charter Requirements, we find that twenty-five persons may qualify to obtain a charter—however, this has now been increased to fifty. In order to obtain membership, a congregation must submit an Affiliation Agreement, copies of its proposed bylaws, a filing fee of $200, Resolutions for tax-exemption, an Insignia Agreement, articles of incorporation (where necessary), and certain other formal documents. However, in most cases this is not necessary since the general exemption from the IRS of the United Church covers also all its affiliated members.

The Agreement of Affiliation becomes valid and binding only upon approval by the Commision on Church Affairs—located in Los Angeles—and by the Board of Trustees, and when executed by the officers of the United Church.

One section describes the generous retirement plan established for the clergy and lay employees of the Church.

Study groups may be established in any locality where there is no other opportunity to study the principles of Religious Science. The Directors of these may perform christenings and conduct funeral services, but may not perform wedding ceremonies.

Under Miscellaneous Information, we find Suggested Rules of Procedure to be followed by a group wishing to obtain a charter. This is followed by the Agreement of Affiliation in which the applicant agrees that it, its Board of

Trustees, and its officers "shall be unqualifiedly subject to the ecclesiastical law and authority of the United Church, which shall have absolute control in all matters of ecclesiastical jurisdiction." The member church agrees to incorporate as a tax-exempt entity under the laws of its own state in order to obtain property tax-exemption—not necessarily to avoid income taxation.

The Agreement also provides that a Board of Trustees shall be elected in conformity with guidelines set forth in the model bylaws, shall establish a standard for membership, and shall maintain proper records at all times. It must have a minister duly licensed and/or ordained by the United Church, and it must adopt retirement plans and insignia in accordance with instructions as set forth by the central authority.

The Agreement provides that it can be terminated only by special procedures set forth therein.

Under its terms, the member church is entitled to teach accredited courses in Religious Science prescribed by the Commission on Education. Students shall receive appropriate recognition—diplomas and certificates—upon the satisfactory completion of such study.

It is specifically stated that neither the member church nor the United Church shall have any claim whatever upon the assets of the other, nor shall either become responsible for the liabilities or obligations of the other. Member churches are autonomous and self-reliant financially.

The member church agrees that it may not license or ordain a minister, or license any teacher or practitioner, and will not establish a branch church— since all such functions belong to the central authority.

Exhibit D of the Church Code is a model of suggested Bylaws. This states that the member church will be subject to the authority of the United Church, that its purpose is to serve the spiritual needs of its community by teaching the principles promulgated by Ernest Holmes. It prescribes conditions for membership and the form of organization to be adopted, how records shall be kept and voting done, how and when business meetings shall occur, what constitutes a quorum, how trustees—from five to eleven in number—shall be elected, who shall be eligible to serve in this capacity and what their term of office shall be—three years; that no trustee can succeed himself; how vacancies may be filled; the officers and how they are to be elected; how finances shall be handled, and how audits must be conducted.

The member church agrees to engage the services only of a minister and practitioners duly licensed and/or ordained by the United Church; it agrees not to support, encourage, promote, or endorse any teaching or practice of such things as astrology, spiritualism, hypnotism, hypnotherapy, fortune-telling, or any other philosophy not in accord with the teachings of the United Church.

The suggested Bylaws contain provisions which no congregation in the

IARSC would accept: namely, that upon dissolution, termination, or disaffiliation, all the assets of the church shall revert to the United Church. However, Mr. Lynn assured me that this—especially the provision in regard to disaffiliation—is purely voluntary, and is not included in most Agreements or Bylaws; he declared that not only can member churches take their property with them upon disaffiliation, but that several have done so. However, the member church must agree that if it wishes to separate, it must arrange a conference with a representative from headquarters; and such action can be taken only if two-thirds of the voting membership of the church determine upon such a course.

Finally, the Bylaws provide that should a member church violate its Agreement of Affiliation in such a manner as to place the church in jeopardy or bring it into disrepute, the Commission on Church Affairs may forfeit its charter and terminate its affiliation with and membership in the United Church of Religious Science.

C. *The Department of Education*

The educational department operates under two divisions: the Institute of Religious Science and the School of Ministry, which are cognate but separate organizations.

1. *The Institute.* Since its establishment in 1927, this had by 1983 trained or educated more than 160,000 persons in the principles of Science of Mind in Extension Courses. A brochure describing this work states that it has been teaching leaders in the fields of religion and philosophy and that it is now known throughout the world as the foremost institution of its kind; that it has enabled people from all walks of life "to experience more happiness, better health, and greater success.... The testimony of thousands demonstrates that the principles of the Science of Mind are not theoretical, but very practical ...and have proved their worth and are opening the doorway to new and wonderful experiences for those who use them daily."

The classes, which are conducted entirely at the local level, present a "synthesis and summation of basic religious thought, and modern metaphysical, philosophical, and scientific concepts."

Each person who enrolls in the Basic Science of Mind course receives a copy of the textbook, *Science of Mind*; a metaphysical dictionary; forty-eight weekly lessons in four separate mailings of twelve each, and weekly letters to supplement, explain, and clarify the studies being pursued. At the conclusion of each twelve-lesson course, the student takes a written examination; upon the satisfactory completion of all lessons, the graduate is given a Certificate of Completion.

The 48 segments are based on pages 63 to 307 of the official textbook. Each week, the students study very carefully several pages; at the weekly class session, this material is discussed and explained.

Completing this Extension Course is a prerequisite for most advanced work both in the Institute and the School of Ministry.

In 1980-1, 4,000 students graduated from the two-year Basic Course in The Science of Mind. Classes were conducted in 113 churches; and there were 50 offering study leading to certificates of recognition as practitioners in the Church—an activity also under the direction of the Institute.

2. *The School of Ministry*. The School of Ministry is one of the most important activities in the Church complex. Its resident enrollment rose from 32 in 1976 to 114 in 1980; in 1981, it was 110; in the spring quarter alone it was 93. The enrollment varies during different parts of the year; in February 1983 it was 55. In 1976, it graduated sixteen ministerial candidates, who received the Religious Science Fellowship Recognition (RScF). The number of graduates during recent years has averaged about twenty-eight.

The School offers two principal courses of study; in addition to that leading to the ministry, there is a General Studies program intended for practitioners and others who wish to develop their understanding and expertise "in metaphysics, communication, and leadership for the New Age...."

In addition to the RScF recognition, the School also offers a doctorate degree; however, this is not undertaken unless there are at least ten candidates.

The Dean is the only full-time staff employee; generally, there are eight or nine other members who serve on the faculty at any given time; however, the total number of faculty and consultants listed in the 1981-2 catalog total thirty-three. These include religious authorities, such as Marcus Bach, who is a former professor in the School of Religion at the University of Iowa. Several are prominent ministers in the Church of Religious Science; others hold positions in colleges or universities, chiefly in the Los Angeles area.

A full three-year course of study is required for the RScF recognition. The course consists of a Freshman, Intermediate, and Senior year, of which most of the first only "can be taken in the field." In order to qualify for such advanced study—that is, to become a candidate for the ministry in the United Church of Religious Science—certain prerequisites, such as the completion of the two-year Basic Course in the Science of Mind, will suffice. Other prerequisites include the possession of a previously earned degree; amassing a sufficient number of credits in relevant fields from colleges, seminaries, or universities; having a current practitioner's license in the United Church, or the completion of relevant professional training or experience.

The program leading to the doctorate requires two additional years—eight quarters—of study and the satisfactory completion of a dissertation which must be "an original work; be a contribution to the field of metaphysics with an obvious relationship to cosmology, ontology, and/or epistemology, and be of suitable quality for publication." In short, it should be an actual contribution to the sum-total of religious knowledge.

Each year of study consists of at least three ten-week quarters, in each of which not less than fifteen hours of credit are to be earned. This involves 135 hours of credit, each of which requires one hour in class plus two hours spent in study or other exercises outside the classroom. Thus, during one quarter 150 hours will be spent in classes and 300 in outside work, during the year a total of 1,350 hours, and for the completion of the ministerial course 4,050 hours, at the satisfactory completion of which the Religious Science Fellowship Recognition is awarded.

The 1981-82 catalog includes a typical course which would be pursued. Seven courses are offered in administration; eight in communication and homiletics; six in general and five in Science of Mind metaphysics; six in psychology; eight in religion; seven in science; six in workshops; and six more in Directed Independent and Advanced Study.

Most courses confer 3 hours of credit; quite a few, 2.3; and some only 1 or 1.2.

The tuition fee is $180 for each three-hour course; a year's tuition—for forty-five credits—is $2,700, or $8,100 for the three years of study leading to the ministerial status.

D. *The Practitioners and Their Code*

The training and education of practitioners is carried on entirely by teachers—usually ministers—on the local level under the direction of the School of Continuing Education, which is a division of The Institute of Religious Science. The prerequisite for the two years of Professional Practitioner Studies—leading to certification as a licensed practitioner in Spiritual Mind Healing—is the basic two-year course in Science of Mind metaphysics, already described.

A leaflet called "You and Your Practitioner" states:

> Spiritual Mind Treatment is based upon the belief that we are surrounded by a Universal Mind, which reacts to our thoughts according to Law. Through the use of scientific technique, Spiritual Mind Treatment (which is really scientific prayer) the individual's consciousness (his belief about himself) is changed, thereby causing a change in his body and affairs.... As an individual's faith in his ability to use this Law of Mind grows stronger, his capacity to know the Truth of his being develops, bringing happier self-expression.

The leaflet continues:

A licensed Religious Science Practitioner is one who has been trained to help people use the art and skill of Spiritual Mind Treatment to solve problems and to correct conditions. He has the understanding to impersonally assist clients to handle their personal problems. A Practitioner lives, demonstrates, and practices Spiritual Truth.

The Professional Practitioner Studies cover two years, each consisting of three ten-week terms. These classes, which meet for three hours weekly, are taught by ministers or accredited instructors. Thus, there are 30 sessions each year, totalling 180 hours before the completion of the studies. I have gone through the special textbook for Term I of each year, written by Reverend Marsha Mendizza and Mary M. Jaeger and supplied by Dean Kouji Nakata of the School of Continuing Education. There are elaborate explanations covering several hundred pages of the curriculum to be followed in developing practitioner candidates into full-fledged professionals. Term I begins the process of changing consciousness, which is the goal of this term. The first year then goes on with two more terms, or twenty sessions, in which the practitioner-candidate develops his capacity to understand the Science of Spiritual Mind Healing.

The second year of these Professional Studies is an Accredited Course, also of thirty three-hour sessions, in which the candidates become practitioners-in-training. In other words, during this advanced curriculum, each student learns to make practical application of what he/she has learned or is learning. The goals of Year II are set forth as follows:

(1) to have students actually experience life as a licensed practitioner;

(2) to make them proficient in communication skills;

(3) to improve their skills in written and oral mind treatment;

(4) to have them learn how to write and deliver meditations;

(5) to provide them with opportunities to enunciate spiritual principles with ease;

(6) to deepen their spiritual consciousness;

(7) to move their awareness from the relative to the absolute;

(8) to assist them in knowing that a practitioner's responsibility is to maintain an active awareness that THE SPIRITUAL MAN IS PERFECT;

(9) to have them develop a personal Practitioner's Manual, and

(10) to enable them to understand the role of the Practitioner, his privileges, duties, obligations, Code of Ethics, and his many spiritual and ecclesiastical relationships.

For each of the six terms covering these studies, there is a large manual, consisting altogether of about 1,500 pages. We can only conclude that when all of this has been fully understood and digested, the student-candidate has absorbed an education which is probably without parallel in the religious field.

Mr. Lynn stated that a great many testimonials have been received attesting that help has been given and that cures have occurred even in cases of organic disease. Even if these cannot be verified by medical proof, it is certain that clients *believe* they have been aided or cured—which, in a sense, amounts to the same thing. Practitioners treat every kind of personal difficulty, whether emotional, physical, neurotic, spiritual, financial, or involving family dissensions or troubles at places of work. Many of these, of course, are psychosomatic.

Some practitioners have business offices where they pursue full-time work and where clients with appointments are treated; however, most of their work is part-time, out of their own homes.

The Church publishes a pamphlet called *Practitioner's Code*, which sets forth their functions and the nature of their work, which is under the supervision of the Commission on Church Affairs, which establishes the policies for granting Recognition Certificates and grants licenses for the practice of Spiritual Mind Healing according to the principles enumerated in the textbook *Science of Mind*. Candidates must be members of the United Church of Religious Science; they must complete satisfactory interviews, oral and written examinations, and must pass psychological tests and meet proficiency standards, as prescribed by the Commission. They must agree to practice faithfully and exclusively the principles and techniques taught in the Science of Mind textbook; to abide by the Practitioner's Code; to devote a definite portion of their time to professional practice, and to maintain a telephone and suitable quarters for their work.

Licenses must be renewed annually and renewals must be approved by the minister of the church to which the practitioner belongs. Licenses can be terminated for anyone found not in compliance with the Code.

The Code of Ethics under which the practitioner operates stipulates that he must not give advice in matters of law, finance, or the use of drugs or medicines; he must not prescribe diets or vitamins or employ or advise any therapy except Spiritual Mind Treatment. It is considered unethical for him to criticize anyone or speak in a derogatory manner to a client or about his work. He is expected to cooperate fully with the Religious Science activity of the church of which he is a member.

The relationship between the practitioner and his client must be completely confidential, as is that of a medical doctor or psychiatrist with his patient. Nor may he offer any guarantee of success to his client as a result of treatment.

The practitioner is expected to support his church financially in an identifiable manner; he is also expected to help in the preparation of a newsletter, in the Dial-a-Prayer ministry, by calling on the aged and infirm, by attending and working in healing workshops, and in other areas of church activity. Whenever his minister asks him to do so, he should agree to perform any service which will be of benefit to the church and the congregation.

The practitioner must never criticize or attack any other branch of the healing profession; on the contrary, he must hold the regular medical doctors in the highest esteem by recognizing them as representatives of the healing power in the Universe. He must also at all times cooperate with the legal authorities in such matters as reporting communicable diseases and any accidental death which comes to his attention.

The practitioner may conduct funeral or christening services, but may not perform wedding ceremonies.

He must at all times conduct himself with dignity so as to bring respect to his profession and his church.

He must realize that he represents its healing arm, that he is an important ecclesiastical representative, and that his work is crucial in accomplishing the objectives of the United Church of Religious Science. "The eyes of his fellow church members, as well as the public at large, are on" him. "The future growth of the Church...to a great extent, depends upon the manner in which the Practitioner performs his professional activities and...his work with the United Church of Religious Science and the Member Church to which he belongs."

The suggested minimum rates for treatment given in the aforementioned leaflet are as follows: Single treatment, $15.00; for one week, $35.00; or by the month, $100.00.

E. *The Ministerial Code*

The Commission on Church Affairs—an agency of the Ministerial Senate—formulates and recommends the specific policies governing the conditons prerequisite for licensing and ordaining ministers in the Church, who are established in three categories: Novitiate, Licentiate, and Ordained.

Any person, upon payment of Application and Examining fees, who meets the requirements of the Code and who has received a call from a member church, may apply for ministerial status to the Department of Member Churches and file a formal application with the Director of that Department.

A graduate of the School of Ministry who has received his RScF recognition shall have the right to make such application to the Department, which will review the applicant's qualifications; in addition to meeting established requirements, he must show evidence of moral and emotional fitness; upon the successful completion of all requirements, he will receive a license which places him on the eligibility list of approved ministerial candidates.

A minister from another denomination who desires to apply for a license as a minister in the United Church of Religious Science may do so by taking and passing the Ministerial Licensing Examinations and Motivational Tests required by the Commission on Church Affairs; the results of this will determine the category of licensing to which he may be eligible.

Whenever the Commission deems it in the best interests of the Church, it may grant Novitiate status for a period of one year to any applicant who passes all examinations successfully. Such ministers must make quarterly reports to the Department of Member Churches, and the license must be renewed before the expiration of the year.

A Novitiate Minister may become a Licentiate applicant provided he is a Licensed Practitioner and has satisfactorily completed all interviews, written and oral examinations, motivational tests, and met the proficiency standards prescribed by the Commission on Church Affairs.

In order to become an Ordained Minister, the Licentiate must first serve at least two years in a member church or in some other ecclesiastical capacity. Once ordained, he cannot lose this status; however, his privileges, affiliations, and associations may be revoked if he is found to be in flagrant violation of the Ministerial Code.

Any applicant for ministerial status in any category must show that he holds an exclusive membership in the United Church of Religious Science, must make the principles and techniques presented in the Science of Mind textbook the basis of his teaching and practice, and must declare that he is willing to abide by the Ministerial Code and be governed by the laws of the United Church of Religious Science.

Articles VIII and IX of the Ministerial Code provide elaborate procedures by which a minister may be removed from his pulpit and have his license suspended or revoked.

The Code declares that the every minister in the Church is in a unique profession; he is a teacher, a counsellor, a Practitioner; he should exercise a healing influence on all who come into contact with him; he is a spiritual therapist of the highest order, and he commits himself to the following ideals:

(1) to lead those who seek guidance into an assurance and acceptance of wholeness and well-being;

(2) to reflect an image and a breadth of heart which expresses a great desire to serve;

(3) to abide by the Truth that the Kingdom of Heaven is within us;

(4) to love mankind, be generous and unselfish with all others, and to be free from fear and superstition;

(5) to use warmth and compassion in relation to all members of his congregation;

(6) to engage in no activities involving moral turpitude;

(7) to remain true always to the principles and ideals of Religious Science;

(8) to know always that God is over all, through all, and in all, and that the mind in each of us is that which was in Christ Jesus;

(9) to center his thought upon the Universal Divine Presence;

(10) to let the peace of God abide in his heart, through love forever;

(11) to vow allegiance to the Church of Religious Science;

(12) to give unqualified support to the Church;

(13) to dedicate himself to the spiritual needs of those who call upon him for help;

(14) to continue in faithful meditation and diligent study in order to expand his consciousness and ministry;

(15) to dedicate himself to the Truth of word and action, and

(16) to abide by the policies and regulations set forth by the Board of Trustees of the United Church of Religious Science and by the local Church of which he is the Minister.

V. ADDITIONAL TEACHINGS OF ERNEST S. HOLMES

Since we have already analyzed Ernest Holmes's basic classic, *Science of Mind*, together with two more of his works, as well as two of those by his brother, Fenwicke, we will, at this point, only summarize the basic contents of several shorter and later publications:

> *Words That Heal Today* (WTHT)
> *Freedom from Stress* ((FFS)
> *It's Up to You* (IUY)
> *Ideas for Living* (IFL)
> *Freedom to Live* (FTL)
> *Practical Application of Science of Mind* (PASM)
> *Discover a Richer Life* (DRL)
> *Know Yourself* (KY)
> *It Can Happen to You* (ICHY)

1. *The Concept of Deity.* This is all-pervasive in all of Holmes's thinking. Spirit, Mind, and Substance, he wrote, are universal—"pure energy becoming tangible through Law in the form provided for it by thought and idea, and whether we think of law as being spiritual, mental, or physical, it makes no difference, providing we realize that the three work together in perfect unity, being but different functions of the great Law of God" (DRL 17).

Again and again, he stressed the unity and divinity of all existence: God is one and all there is (*Ibid.* 26). All creation exists as the expression of God (*Ibid.* 42); in fact, the universe itself is God (*Ibid.* 47) and constitutes unlimited abundance (*Ibid.* 81). Thus "intelligence is manifest in everything from the blade of grass to our own theoretical speculations about the nature of the universe" (FTL 11). God is a law written in the vegetable, animal, and human kingdoms (*Ibid.* 12). God is Good or harmony (*Ibid.* 30). He is the divine presence which fills all space and form *(Ibid.* 40). He is an impersonal life Principle which animates the universe (PASM 58). Since this is true, He is available to all persons at all times (IUY 87). He is a unitary wholeness (IFL 61). He is the Great Director who knows where everything belongs in the universe (*Ibid.* 88). Since God is energy, He is also everything that exists as an expression or manifestation of Himself (FFS 76). He is the universal Intelligence, Spirit, Absolute Cause, Existence, or Reality which fills and constitutes the universe (KY 92). The Trinity, we read, is the Spirit that directs, the Law which executes, and the creation which results (*Ibid.* 24-25).

2. *God and Man.* Since God is everything and since man is the highest manifestation in creation, their interrelation is highly significant. God is an inner light in man (*Ibid.* 22), which is the essence of his being, the Eternal God, the everlasting Spirit or Father (*Ibid.* 25). Humanity is cradled in the Infinite and all men are the offspring of the Most High (FTL 94). There is a divine unity binding us all together (FFS 23). We are all children of God (*Ibid.* 70); and therefore we are God in the germ (*Ibid.* 95). Man is the center of all self-conscious life and God is the Principle which animates him (KY 28). Since God individualizes Himself in man (*Ibid.* 62), he has and cannot lose his divinity (DRL 42). Over and over, Holmes emphasizes that every human being is an incarnation and individualization of God (*Ibid.* 43, 51, IUY 37, KY 92). The realization of this fact should remove from everyone any sense of inferiority he may have, every inferiority complex, and the need for psychological adjustment—and would probably heal all the physical diseases in the world (KY 93). From this it follows that every man is his own savior because he has a direct approach to Reality. Daily, we should learn and believe our Oneness with God (IUY 79). This momentous discovery is the greatest ever made by man (FTL 22). The universal livingness which permeates all things in infinite variations and individualizations (KY 27) is the reality within us which knows no difference between itself and the Great Self, or God. It is the indwelling "I" (*Ibid.*)

The concept of divine Influx, perhaps derived from Swedenborg, is found almost everywhere in Holmes. There is, he declares, an influx of divine ideas which stimulates the human will to a divine purposefulness (*Ibid.* 21). This is a universal mind which flows through every individual (*Ibid.* 61). There is a river of life flowing from the mind of God which renews our vigor, remakes our strength, and enables us to heal our bodies and our fortunes and bring peace into our hearts (*Ibid.* 91).

3. *Jesus and the Christ.* It is interesting to note that in addition to calling Jesus the *Wayshower*, as was first done in Christian Science, he also uses other appellations very similar to those used by the ancient Essenes in regard to their leader and by the early Christian Ebionites in regard to Jesus. Again and again, especially in *Words That Heal Today*, he is called the Master, the Exemplar, The Teacher, the Enlightened One, the Great Revelator, the Man of Wisdom, the Great Physician, a Spiritual Genius. Elsewhere he is called the Cosmic Man (KY 94).

However, there is a sharp differentiation between Jesus and the Christ, who is not a historic Jesus, but simply that which lives and moves and breathes in every human being (DRL 41). Jesus is designated the Christ only because he realized a belief in the universal spirit which he called God or the Heavenly Father (IUY 33). He was a man like all other men, both as to his humanity and his divinity (*Ibid.* 36); what distinguished him was the fact that he had laid hold on the power of spirit (FTL 27). By at-one-ment we mean merely that, if we misuse the Law of God, we must suffer until justice has been done (IFL 52).

4. *Hell, the Devil, Etc.* As in New Thought generally, Holmes denies all such concepts with scorn. Hell, the devil, etc. are only myths (DRL 12); since God is all, there can be no fundamental evil or duality in the universe (*Ibid.* 24). Since the Kingdom of Heaven is within us, no condition, no place, no person except oneself can expel it (IUY 78). Heaven and hell are simply states of mind (*Ibid.* IFL 52). No punishment has been prepared for us—all such ideas are fabricated only out of the morbidity of man's imagination (FTL 15). To believe in hell is to be tied to ignorant superstitions (*Ibid.* 18). Sin is only a mistake (IUY 55, PASM 31); and we are not sinners or on our way to hell (FTL 68). We are not punished because of our sins, but by them (PASM 34).

However, let there be no error about this: since we create our own hell, it is certainly real enough for those who believe in it; but when we transpose our thought to heaven, its supposed flames are at once extinguished (*Ibid.* 13).

5. *The Power of Mind and Thought.* Again and again, Holmes explains the intimate relationship which exists between our conscious thinking and our deep, unconscious, or subjective motivations (KY 45). Since the former acts as a feeder to the latter and since we have free will or choice, we can change our negative mental states to positive (PASM 9, 20, 21); our subjective state of thought produces our psychosomatic ailments and problems (KY 46). Almost all accidents, for example, are unconsciously motivated (*Ibid.* 45). Thus our conscious thought can make the body ill or well (*Ibid.* 89); and changing the conscious thought-pattern can transform our lives (DRL 47). Thoughts are tools with which we can work (PASM 51); we get what we desire or regard as normal (*Ibid.* 61), and it is done to us according to our belief (*Ibid.* 63).

Thought is creative, for both good and ill (FTL 34); negative thought is the most terrible of all our troubles (*Ibid.* 35). Evil and lack will disappear when we cease to contemplate them or give them power (*Ibid.* 37). We can banish evil simply by denying it (*Ibid.* 38).

Mind exists on four levels: (1) the unconscious intelligence of the atom, (2) the simple state exhibited in the animal kingdom, (3) the self-conscious rational life of human beings, and (4) the cosmic consciousness which is also defined as our sense of unity with the whole creation (KY 31-32).

In this realm, what is called Race Thought—the collective ideology of humanity (PASM 56)—is of the greatest importance, "for it depresses the whole human race with fear and morbidity and creates a field of psychic confusion, affecting all of us" (FTL 83).

6. *The Conscious and Subconscious Mind.* Holmes often discusses the complex nature of psychic operations. The mind, he declares, operates on three planes: (1) the material, (2) the mental, and (3) the spiritual (KY 9). Spirit is the subtle power that *thinks* (*Ibid.* 15). Man, consisting of mind, soul, and body, has an inner life which transcends the psyche (*Ibid.* 19). "The subjective [subconscious] state of our thoughts constitutes ninety per cent of our total thought-content.... All these unconscious thoughts and thought-patterns— motivations, conflicts, impressions, whatever you want to call them—are beneath our conscious threshold, but they also help to constitute our entire thought" (DRL 33). Only the conscious mind has the power to change the subconscious mind (PASM 15).

7. *Spiritual Mind-Healing.* The intimate relations between the conscious and subconscious mind exerts profound influence upon the latter, a fact which leads directly to the efficacy of Spiritual Mind-Healing. Holmes describes, for example, the case of a woman who has been blind for some time but who recovered her sight simply by declaring that she was glad that she could see (KY 42). People are sick, poor, and unhappy because their conscious minds are choked with wrong words and concepts (*Ibid.*). Science of Mind means simply that we are to use the conscious mind to build into the subconscious functions that will operate beneficently; and for this reason, psychosomatic medicine is effective (*Ibid.* 44). When the right ideas are poured into the subconscious by the conscious mind, they will eliminate negative ideas of discord, disease, and limitation (*Ibid.* 85).

A mental treatment becomes a reality in the spiritual world just as a kernel of corn becomes a physical reality through the creative power existing in matter (IUY 56). In order to accomplish spiritual healing, it is necessary for a practitioner to accept with a realizing belief that there is a Power which responds to human thought; that this Power does, directly and specifically, respond to his word, and that he is an active league with the only real Power that exists (*Ibid.* 58).

However, the healer deals with the concept of disease, not as an unreality of experience, but as a wrong arrangement resulting from wrong thoughts (DRL 53). To an ever-increasing degree, psychosomatic medicine is demonstrating that the power of thought can make us sick or can heal us (*Ibid.* 56). This is based on certain and scientific knowledge. In successful treatment, we first determine the good we desire, declare it specifically, accept it as our own actual experience, and *know* that it will be manifested in accordance with Law (PASM 84).

Science of Mind never denies that people really *are* sick. Furthermore, it is right and good to use drugs, surgery, sanitation, and proper exercise. Hospitals are necessary (DRL 89); the sick should by all means seek regular medical assistance when it will help or is needed (ICHY 23). "Science of Mind holds no dogmas, has no superstitions, but believes in the good in everything" (PASM 35). God speaks every time a scientist discovers a new invention (KY 23). Science of Mind simply offers a bridge from all such things to the achievement of perfect and permanent health. Its treatment includes psychosomatic medicine as well as that of the regular physician. It proclaims the unity of all things; and, as a result, many leading physicians have now adopted its principles (DRL 85).

Spiritual mind treatment begins with a recognition that there is one Life, which is God; that this Life is perfect and that every person being treated is a divine being (KY 70). In so doing, the process by which people are relieved of guilt is scientific, for the cause of neuroses, buried deep in the subconscious, is removed (*Ibid.* 71). Healing cannot ensue unless the practitioner believes that universal Intelligence exists as God; that this is in us because we exist, and that we are individualizations thereof (*Ibid.* 94-95).

The great majority of all diseases are invoked unconsciously by mental or emotional action (DRL 86). Thus, all such disease is unnatural and does not belong to the real person at all—if it did, no one could heal it. Any doctor will tell you that the body has great power to heal and fight off disease (*Ibid.* 87). Thus we are scientifically correct when we say that, if we change our mental state, we can alter our outward form (FTL 24).

However, although all psychosomatic illness is peculiarly susceptible to mind-healing, many of those bedridden by organic ailments have been fully cured by this method. The records of the Church abound with testimonials to this effect.

8. *The Nature and Efficacy of Prayer*. There is a true science of prayer, which can be followed by anyone (ICHY 90). However, mere supplication is contradiction (*Ibid.* 91). It never consists of pleading for anything (PASM 86-87). Effective prayer consists of affirmations, expressed in four steps: (1) recognition, (2) identification, (3) declaration, and (4) acceptance of those facts and conditions which we desire and already know to exist (ICHY 93-94).

Thus prayer becomes a creative process (KY 75), as is the Lord's Prayer found in the Gospel of Matthew. The words *Our Father which art in heaven* mean merely that we possess an inner and accessible divine power (DRL 63).

Holmes provides many model prayers, one of which reads as follows:

> I now accept my divine birthright. I now consciously enter into my partnership with love, with peace, with joy, with God. I feel the infinite Presence close around me. I feel the warmth, the color, and the radiance of this Presence like a living thing in which I am enveloped.
>
> I am no longer afraid of life. A deep and abiding sense of calm and of poise flows through me. I have faith to believe that the Kingdom of God is at hand. It is right where I am, here, now, today, at this moment.
>
> I feel that there is a Law of God which can, will, and does govern everything. Therefore, I feel that everything in my life is constructive, everything in my thought that is life-giving is blessed and prospered. It blesses everyone I meet. It makes glad everyone I contact. I am united with everything in life, in love, in peace, and in joy. And I know that the Presence of Love and Life gently leads me and all others, guiding, guarding, sustaining, upholding, now and forever (*Ibid.* 71).

Thus, "affirmative prayer, or spiritual mind-treatment, is the recognition of this universal creative Presence and Power which surrounds us and is responsive to us" (IUY 76).

9. *The Successful Life.* In order to achieve true success in life, we must banish all feelings of hatred, bitterness, and fear (PASM 32, IFL 54); we must hold no grudge (PASM 33); only love, which also brings happiness, can make us attractive (IUY 47).

Although poverty is no virtue (FFS 42), success does not necessarily consist in making money (IUY 19). We are not struggling for wealth as such (*Ibid.* 22); prosperity is a state of mind (*Ibid.* 21). In order to achieve a successful life, ten steps are essential:

(1) overcome all negative mental attitudes,
(2) stop worrying,
(3) overcome a sense of inferiority,
(4) think about your own personality,
(5) make your work as easy as possible,
(6) count your blessings,
(7) forgive yourself and others—do not carry grudges,
(8) learn how to get along with others,
(9) use prayer and affirmative meditation in personal achievement,
(10) get the most out of your religion (IUY 89-94).

An important ingredient for success consists in not growing old merely because of advancing years. Holmes describes a woman well past seventy who played a very energetic game of tennis (ICHY 59-60). And he gives a list of great men whose achievements came largely during a very ripe age.

There are, he declares, three general periods in the lives of most people: (1) preparation—up to about twenty-five; (2) work and family obligations—about twenty-five to fifty or sixty, and (3) the age of retirement and frustration (IUY 10-11). And this is where the problem of aging often arises: instead of feeling worn out and useless in the third period, we should make this the Golden Era for humanity. We can forget old age and remain young all our lives (FFS 58-63); since the mind of God cannot grow old (DRL 94), there is no reason why ours should ever become senile or inactive.

10. *Specific Religious Concepts.* Religion, declares Holmes, is a belief in an invisible, superhuman power or powers—in a God or gods—any system of faith, doctrine, or worship (DRL 11).

The new religion now dawning on mankind will be a spiritual psychology, an idealist philosophy, and a system of metaphysics designed consciously to create in the mind a recognition and realization that the eternal is one with man, that this creative intelligence is available to all humanity, that the dynamic and purposive Power which urges everything forward is latent in man, who can discover the Divine Presence within himself (*Ibid.* 12-13).

Holmes had no doubt concerning the continuity of the human entity. We shall go on, he declared, into eternity (IUY 9). We have always existed and we always will exist (FFS 44) in another world which will be like this one (*Ibid.* 63). He considered it impossible for anyone to be truly happy in this life unless he could believe in the continuation of his own existence (IUY 10).

"Death," he declares, "is but the gateway to a larger life" (IFL 93). And "personally, I consider that the immortality of the individual life has been conclusively proved; and I am convinced that you and I and everyone else are destined to live forever, because the life which we now experience is the Life of God in us. It is the Life of God in us that is eternal, not the external form of flesh" (IFL 89).

Chapter 12

A NEW THOUGHT RELIGIOUS SERVICE AND MESSAGE

Attending a service in a New Thought church is usually an inspirational experience; and, at least for a stranger, very different from one in an old-line church, an evangelical denomination, or even in Christian Science. There is a pervasive sense of affection and camaraderie; the newcomer is welcomed, sometimes with a hug or a warm, vigorous handclasp, and sometimes, either at the beginning or during the meeting, everyone stands and turns to those in front of, behind, or beside him or her and introduces himself with an expression of good-will.

The stranger is impressed with the prevailing sense of joy and happiness which exudes from everyone. It is obvious that these people intend to enjoy life to the utmost and make the most of every moment.

If one asks those in attendance how or why they happen to be here, the reply usually involves some experience which created a special interest in New Thought. They were disappointed with the religious organizations in which they were reared; their questions were never resolved satisfactorily; they received no help for personal problems; they suffered intensely from condemnation or a sense of guilt or from frustration, or they felt useless, worthless, or rejected. Some may explain that they received help and healing from emotional distress or physical malfunctions in New Thought. Others declare that it helped them overcome and eliminate such addictions as smoking or alcoholism. Some say they have been cured of organic diseases.

One cannot spend a couple of hours listening to New Thought services and mingling with the congregation without imbibing a sense of pleasure at simply being there, breathing the fresh air, and experiencing a vibrant vitality.

At most services I have attended, there is a soloist—and a good one—who sings a lilting and happy melody. The congregation, which is completely uninhibited, sometimes breaks into applause in response to anything which it believes merits such appreciation. There is a sense of freedom, totally absent in the ordinary church service anywhere else.

At some services, the Lord's Prayer is sung by the congregation. As the organ orchestrates its accompaniment, the voices of the people roll forth in powerful consonance; and, as the climax approaches, the words *For thine is the Kingdom, and the Power, and the Glory forever* rise in such a crescendo that one can literally feel the auditorium vibrate. As the anthem concludes with its *Amen*, peace and calm descend upon the congregation.

Although most New Thought churches have hymnals of their own, selections from these are not used as often in the old-line churches.

These people, who say that heaven and hell are simply conditions of mind instead of specific places, are not worried about condemnation for sin by some unseen power. They regard the universe as beneficent, and they intend to make the best possible use of it. Instead of looking for trouble, they are seeking success, harmony, happiness; and they mean to do whatever they can or is necessary to achieve them. This does not mean, however, that their moral standards are lower or less strict than those of people who belong to the conventional churches. Quite the reverse, for they believe that they will be punished for any wrong-doing or act of aggression committed against others. There is no such thing as forgiveness or atonement for our sins by an external agency. Any "sin" against another will be eradicated only by complete restitution and forgiveness. And is there any higher possible form of morality?

Ministers in New Thought churches are usually well educated and capable speakers. Many of them have come from other denominations where they are prepared in conventional seminaries; their sincerity can scarcely be questioned for, in most cases, they left more lucrative positions because of conscience or intellectual convictions. When the old faith proved inadequate to meet their spiritual needs or their intense craving for personal integrity, they came into New Thought; and, since they were already versed and exercised in pulpit techniques and parish ministry, the transition was not very difficult or lengthy. Actually, they did not need any substantial re-education, for they had already adopted a New Thought attitude and orientation; it was only necessary to train them in certain specific techniques and for them to study the basic texts in their new affiliations.

The sermon—usually called the lesson or message—will be an inspirational discourse on any one of a multitude of topics, as varied as are the articles to be found in *Aspire, Creative Thought, Science of Mind, Daily Word,* or *Unity* magazine. This is always intended as a help or an explanation of personal problems, which are to be solved, or at least reduced in intensity. It may be a discussion of the relation of the conscious to the subconscious mind and the way in which the individual can gain mastery over his own life by the proper use of these. I have never heard any discussion of orthodox dogmas in a New Thought church. One minister remarked that his people rarely mention sin—they merely enjoy it, at which there was an uproarious laughter.

The talk usually lasts about thirty minutes—rarely more than thirty-five. For those who desire further study, most churches provide lessons during the week, in some cases several between one Sunday and the next.

The minister may use a theme as a text taken from Holmes' *Science of Mind*; in the Church of Divine Science, some passages from the writings of Nona Brooks or Emma Curtis Hopkins may be combined with some quotation from the Bible. In Unity, there is a vast storehouse consisting of literature emanating not only from headquarters but from the world of New Thought writers, all of which can supply material. The possibilities are limitless, and a minister could go on for years with a variety of themes without ever repeating himself. For example, in one series of "lessons," Reverend Blaine C. Mays of the Phoenix Unity Church spoke on the following subjects: "How to Enjoy Your Trip to the Top," "Your Right to Peace of Mind," "How to Love Your Neighbor," "How to Get Results through Prayer," "How to Move up in Life," "Self-Esteem Is God-Intended," "Life's Greatest Benefits Are Yours," "A Spectacular You," "Your Place in the Success Plan," "Heavenly Flavor," "Your Uniqueness," "Get Involved with Life," "How to Add New Zip to Living," and "Overcoming Fear of Criticism." We could go on and on for pages.

Reverend Tom Johnson of the Church of Religious Science in Canoga Park, California offers a great number of tapes from sermon-lessons, of which the following are typical: "Love Is Always There," "You Are the Doctor," "The Law and the Word," "Feeling Good," and "Does Success Mean Happiness?" Also "The Power within Us," "The Gold Mine of You," "Our Business Is to Create," "Prosperity/Love," "Peace of Mind/Health," "How to Get Loose," "The Search for Significance," "The Power of Guilt," "Be Free of Envy," and "Think Big." There are dozens or hundreds of others. Every minister creates a series of his own.

New Thought groups and organizations express their beliefs in somewhat differing terms. But, after interviewing many New Thought ministers and studying all the available Statements of Faith published by New Thought groups or churches, I have concluded that the following sets forth in simple language what all accept as the basis of their thought and action:

Statement of New Thought Principles

That such dogmas as original sin, Predestination, the Tripersonal Trinity, and salvation through the sacrificial death of Jesus, should be discarded.

That God is Universal Essence or Existence, the substance of all things, tangible and intangible, material or spiritual.

That this God-Essence is impersonal, yet beneficent, and works for the good of all who realize this and utilize the blessings offered.

That man is an individualized expression of the divine essence in an inseparable oneness; and therefore has unlimited potential for perfection in his body, his emotions, and in all his activities.

That, since all human beings are parts of this divine essence, they constitute a universal brotherhood and should and can learn to live in peace and harmony with each other.

That this divine essence expresses itself in humanity as health, wisdom, life, truth, peace, beauty, joy, well-being, and prosperity.

That, since every human being is an embodiment of the divine essence, each one should look upon himself or herself as a being of great worth.

That we should banish all thoughts of guilt or self-condemnation.

That we should likewise refrain from the condemnation of others.

That the Christ is a universal Power available to everyone and all can partake of this to whatever extent they apply themselves to do so.

That Jesus was the Great Wayshower or Exemplar who had absorbed greatly of this Christ-Spirit and was therefore empowered to perform his mission, which was to show humanity the way to the abundant life.

That, since this was the mission of Jesus, each person should seek his Great God in the attainment of health, happiness, and prosperity in the here and now.

That we should seek truth wherever it may be found; that we should examine and analyze the various "truths" offered, and accept for ourselves that only which meets our personal needs and can serve as our own guide.

That hell and heaven are conditions of mind and not physical places to which souls may be at some future time consigned.

That a personal heaven and salvation are attainable through a consciously self-directed process of moral regeneration.

That there is a divine influx from the divine essence into man and throughout all creation, which serves as the basis of universal well-being.

That this divine influx or Intelligence is present in every material or spiritual manifestation throughout every portion of the universe.

That the Bible is the Word of God, but that it can be understood correctly only through spiritual interpretation.

That the mind has power to heal or cause physical ailments.

That human thought has creative power over the physical body.

That there is a subconscious as well as a conscious mind; and that the latter transmits ideas and motivations into the subconscious, which then exercises control over our emotional lives, and, to a large extent, determines the health or degeneration of the physical body.

That the mind and the body are so interrelated that a host of illnesses are psychosomatic; that the way to physical health is through a healthy mind, which will be reflected in a healthy body.

That healing can be accomplished through Affirmative Prayer.

That advancing age should retain vigor and vitality and should not bring mental or physical senility or debility.

That the great objective of religion should be the achievement of a personally happy, healthy, and prosperous life.

In many New Thought churches the following song and hymn is sung by the congregation at the conclusion of the service:

Let there be peace on earth, and let it begin with me,
Let there be peace on earth, the peace that was meant to be.
With God as our Father, brothers all are we,
Let me walk with my brother in perfect harmony.

Let peace begin with me, let this be the moment now,
With every step I take, let this be my solemn vow;
To take each moment, and live each moment, in peace eternally;
Let there be peace on earth, and let it begin with me.

At the beginning of the song, all the members of the congregation rise and clasp hands; as their voices rise in unison, there is a sense of good-will and affection; as the last line approaches its end, all raise their arms above their heads in token of triumphant and pervading peace, which is to include all mankind.

Those who have never attended a New Thought service should do so, if merely for its healing and elevating experience. And this applies, not only to those in need of comfort and solace, but to persons of any religious persuasion or orientation as well as to those who have no such commitment at all.

BIBLIOGRAPHIES AND CITATIONS

CHAPTER 1: SWEDENBORG, THE FOUNTAINHEAD

BIBLIOGRAPHY

The symbols at the left are used in the citations, where numbers refer to sections in Swedenborg's writings, or to pages in those of other authors. Where other works are cited, their names are given. The works of Swedenborg are published by the Swedenborg Foundation of New York.

SELECTED WORKS ABOUT SWEDENBORG

Noyes   *History of American Socialisms*, John Humphrey Noyes, 1962

Park.   *Collected Works*, Theodore Parker, 2 Vol., 1979

Emer.   *Swedenborg, the Mystic*, An Essay, Ralph Waldo Emerson

Dufty   *Swedenborg, the Scientist*, J.G. Dufty, 1938

Grat.   *The Three Jameses*, G. Hartley Grattan, 1962

Sig.   *The Swedenborg Epic*, Cyriel Odhner Sigstedt, 1952

USE   *Emanuel Swedenborg, the Spiritual Columbus*, U.S.E. (Undated)

Yng.   *The Philosophy of Henry James, Sr.*, Frederic H. Young, 1951

Tro.   *Swedenborg: Life and Teaching*, George Trobridge, 1938

SWEDENBORG'S PRINCIPAL WORKS

JD	*Journal of Dreams*, 1744
WLG	*The Worship and the Love of God*, 1745
SP	*The Spiritual Diary*, 5 Vol. 1749-65
AC	*Arcana Coelestia*, 12 Vol. 1749-56
AE	*The Apocalypse Explained*, 6 Vol., 1756-59
H&H	*Heaven and Its Wonders and Hell*, 1758
DNJL	*Doctrine of the New Jerusalem concerning the Lord*, 1763
DNJHS	*Doctrine of the New Jerusalem concerning the Holy Scriptures*, 1763
DLNJ	*Doctrine of Life for the New Jerusalem*, 1763
DNJF	*Doctrine of the New Jerusalem concerning Faith*, 1763
DLW	*The Divine Love and Wisdom,* `1763
DP	*The Divine Providence*, 1764
AR	*The Apocalypse Revealed*, 2 Vol., 1766
CL	*Conjugal Love*, 1768
TTCR	*The True Christian Religion*, 2 Vol., 1771
MATC	*The Messiah about to Come*, Bryn Athyn, 1949
MTW	MISCELLANEOUS THEOLOGICAL WORKS, New York, 1959
NJHD	*The New Jerusalem and Its Heavenly Doctrine*, 3-205
BE	*Brief Exposition of the Doctrine of the New Church*, 207-313
WH	*The White Horse Mentioned in the Apocalypse*, 354-384
LJBD	*The Last Judgment and Babylon Destroyed*, 507-588
CCLJ	*Continuation concerning the Last Judgment*, 58-608
CCSW	*Continuation concerning the Spiritual World*, 609-634
PTW I	POSTHUMOUS THEOLOGICAL WORKS, Vol. I, New York, 1956
DeCor	*Coronis: or the Appendix to the True Christian Religion*, 17-97
INC	*Invitation to the New Church*, 115-143
CNC	*Canons of the New Church*, 165-226
DNJCC	*Doctrines of the New Jerusalem concerning Charity*, 227-281
LJ	*The Last Judgment*, 379-477

CSW	*Concerning the Spiritual World*, 478-514
5 MR	*Five Memorable Relations*, 521-532
JGW	*Justification and Good Works*, 537-546
CWC	*Conversations with Calvin*, 554-574
INC	*The Doctrine of the New Church*, 555-560
PTW II	*Marriage*, 433-466

CITATIONS

1. Tro. 1955, 287
2. Noyes 531
3. Park. II 8, I 222
4. Emer.
5. Republished by Swed. Press of Chicago
6. Tro. 224-225
7. Emer.
8. Sig. 8
9. PTW I 9
10. Sig. 19 ff.
11. Dufty 17-18
12. Sig. 26-27
13. *Ibid.* 33
14. *Ibid.*
15. *Ibid.* 117, 490
16. *Ibid.* 107-117
17. *Ibid.* 133-140
18. Tro. 227-241, Sig. 133-164
19. Sig. 5
20. *Ibid.* 321-324
21. *Ibid.* 408
22. *Ibid.* 401-403
23. *Ibid.* 389
24. *Ibid.* 390
25. *Ibid.* 393
26. *Ibid.* 395
27. *Ibid.* 395, 398, 404-405
28. *Ibid.* 404-405
29. *Ibid.* 405
30. *Ibid.*
31. *Ibid.* 405-407

32. *Ibid.* 408
33. *Ibid.*
34. *Ibid.* 44-46
35. *Ibid.* 42-43
36. *Ibid.* 57-58
37. *Ibid.* 86-91
38. *Ibid.* 124-125
39. Pp. 9-25
40. INC 55
41. Sig. 184
42. JD 25, Sig. 184
43. JD 22 ff., Sig. 185
44. JD 33, Sig. 186
45. PTW I 590-591
46. JD 88, Sig. 191
47. JD 83, Sig. 191
48. Sig. 188
49. *Ibid.* 183
50. JD 100, Sig. 192-193
51. Sig. 198
52. *Ibid.* 199
53. MATC 18
54. Sig. 210
55. *Ibid.* 203, 207
56. *Ibid.* 209
57. Sig. *179, 181, 308, PTW I 591*
58. *PTW I 591*
59. *Ibid.* 571
60. Tro. 108
61. Sig. 427, 379-380
62. *Ibid.* 340-341
63. *Ibid.* 342-343
64. *Ibid.* 269-270
65. *Ibid.* 278-281, Tro.

195-197
66. Sig. 339
67. *Ibid.* 419
68. *Ibid.* 301-302, 419-422
69. *Ibid.* 419
70. AR 531, Sig. 318
71. USE 166
72. SD 1092-1101
73. *Ibid.* 1934, 2922, 3653, 4530, AC 59, 816, 968, 5180
74. BE 98
75. AC 7502
76. *Ibid.* 3833
77. *Ibid.* 10, 137
78. *Ibid.* 2310
79. MTWT 62, DNJHS 94, SD 5179
80. AC 563, 404
81. *Ibid.* 599, 600
82. AE 861
83. *Ibid.* 544
84. *Ibid.* 445
85. *Ibid.* 447, SD 6096
86. SD 434
87. CL 494
88. SD 4842
89. *Ibid.* 4321, 4412
90. *Ibid.* 4842
91. WH 16, NJHD 266
92. AC 4766
93. *Ibid.* 3993, AR 959
94. AC 1032
95. *Ibid.* 4747, 4190, 2986

96. AE 1179
97. *Ibid.* 1180
98. AC 4818
99. *Ibid.* 4751
100. LJ 259, AC 5057
101. AC 4847
102. CCSW 81, 82
103. AR 759
104. DNC 3
105. AR 537
106. *Ibid.* 605
107. *Ibid.* 634
108. *Ibid.* 749
109. AE 1079-1080
110. *Ibid.* 713
111. *Ibid.* 714
112. LJBD 58
113. Tro. 44-45
114. INC 46
115. Tro. 52
116. AC 9020
117. AR 802
118. TTCR 94
119. AC 9410
120. LJBD 57
121. H&H 508, AE 1035
122. AE 1065
123. *Ibid.* 1091
124. *Ibid.* 1071
125. *Ibid.* 1049
126. AR 802
127. *Ibid.* 796
128. INC 24
129. AR 836
130. LJBD 64
131. AR 784
132. *Ibid.* 759
133. LJBD 62
134. AR 759
135. *Ibid.* 770
136. *Ibid.* 784
137. *Ibid.* 786
138. *Ibid.* 787
139. LJBD 55
140. AR 802
141. H&H 321, 417
142. LJBD 10
143. AC 9440, 9441, 6695, 10, 837
144. *Ibid.* 9582
145. *Ibid.* 3636
146. DLW 300
147. *Ibid.* 157
148. DP 1
149. TTCR 70
150. *Ibid.*
151. AE 349 a
152. *Ibid.* 349 b
153. Sig. 134
154. Ff. *De Erroribus Trinitatis* II 5
155. CNC V iii 5
156. *Ibid.* V III 2
157. AE Vol. VI 513, 520
158. BE 64
159. CNC V ii 1
160. TTCR 81, AR 962
161. AC 9866
162. TTCR 26
163. DNJL 32
164. *Ibid.* 46
165. AC 2083
166. *Ibid.* 1124
167. TTCR 364
168. DLW 353
169. *Ibid.* 355
170. AC 3884
171. DLW 337
172. AC 5937
173. *Ibid.* 8175
174. *Ibid.* 5982
175. AE 573 b
176. *Ibid.* 936
177. DeCor. 19
178. AE Vol. VI, 421
179. AC 3634
180. AE 969
181. DP 328
182. AC 313, DP 328
183. AC 2308
184. *Ibid.* 6495, 6488
185. WLG 78, 189
186. CNC III viii
187. DLW 221
188. AE 805 b (7)
189. *Ibid.* 800
190. AC 10, 026
191. AE 806
192. AC 3061
193. *Ibid.* 1573
194. TTCR 4, 102, 827, LJ 68, CCSW 66
195. AE 726
196. TRCR 489
197. AC 3854
198. AR 875
199. AE 585 a
200. *Ibid.*
201. *JGW 7*
202. *INC 6*
203. *DP 129 (1) (6)*
204. *AC 2881*
205. *TTCR 356*
206. *BE 65*
207. *AE 948*
208. *Ibid.*
209. *Ibid.* 427 a
210. DLNJ 63
211. H&H 533
212. AC 4063
213. AE 940
214. TTCR 580
215. AC 248
216. TRCR 412
217. DNJCC 72
218. *Ibid.* 126
219. DLNJ 1
220. AC 3776
221. TTCR 425
222. AE 932
223. H&H 364
224. *Ibid.*
225. TTCR 746
226. AC 6934
227. *Ibid.* 7038
228. AE VI 379
229. DNJCC 167
230. *Ibid.* 164

231. *Ibid.* 158
232. AE 236 b
233. DLNJ 66
234. AC 945, 995
235. H&H 528
236. AC 7318
237. *Ibid.* 1877
238. H&H 357
239. *Ibid.* 360, 361
240. AC 1673
241. *Ibid.* 2027
242. TTCR 788
243. LJBD 6
244. *Ibid.* 73
245. AC 5852
246. CNC III ii 6
247. CSW 316
248. *Ibid.*
249. DP 27
250. LJBD 15
251. AE 537 a
252. CCSW 37
253. 5 MR II 4
254. DLW 390
255. CCSW 32
256. AC 2481, 2483
257. SD 662, 804-805, 808, 2347
258. AE 920
259. DNJHS 93, 94
260. AC 154
261. TTCR 795
262. CL 44
263. H&H 414
264. TTCR 738 (2)
265. CL 1-26, TTCR 728-752
266. TTCR 746
267. CL 207
268. H&H 489
269. CL 17
270. *Ibid.* 207
271. *Ibid.*
272. *Ibid.* 416
273. CL 37
274. *Ibid.* 45 (3) (4) (5) (7)
275. MAR 55, 68
276. *Ibid.* 5
277. CL 355
278. MAR 55
279. H&H 489
280. *Memorabilia,* "Potency"
281. CL 355
282. AE 992
283. *Ibid.* 888
284. AC 8232
285. *Ibid.* 6559
286. *Ibid.* 695
287. AC 4533, 4798, 5566, 5573, AE 554, 866
288. Published 1875, p. 540
289. SD 4494
290. *Ibid.* 6107, 6108
291. AR 531, SD 6107
292. PTW I 589-590
293. AC 6221
294. AE 322, 447
295. AC 4227
296. AC 5713, SD 4585
297. USE 131, SD 4348
298. AC 5711, 5712
299. SD 4592, 2439, 2716
300. *Ibid.* 2299
301. AC 5726
302. Sig. 375
303. TTCR 4
304. CL 1, TTCR 4
305. TTCR 779, DP 135
306. TTCR 768
307. Revelation 12:1
308. AR "Spiritual Sense" Ch. XII
309. *Ibid.* 533
310. *Ibid.* 534
311. *Ibid.* 479
312. AE 707
313. *Ibid.* 758
314. *Ibid.* 762, AC 10249
315. BE 1, AR 914, DNJL 63, 65, AE 431 b, TTCR 107
316. CNC V x 4
317. TTCR 788
318. DeCor. Sum. LII
319. *Ibid.* 24
320. *Ibid.* Sum. LV, AE 948
321. AE 865
322. *Ibid.* 730 a
323. PTW I 587

CHAPTER 2: THE SHAKERS

BIBLIOGRAPHY

The author spent weeks taking notes from original Shaker documents and from the Primary Sources listed below in a reserve section of the Library of Congress. These range from small pamphlets to massive tomes, so fragile that they must be handled with the greatest care. All of these were written by

Shakers, ex-Shakers, or by persons who had direct and personal experience with the cult. For citations, we use symbols on left.

SECONDARY SOURCES

Andrews	Andrews, Edward Deming, *The People Called Shakers*, 1963
Nordhoff	Nordhoff, Charles, *The Communistic Societies of the United States*, 1961
Noyes	Noyes, John Humphrey, *History of American Socialisms*, 1872

PRIMARY SOURCES

Bates	Bates, Paulina, *The Divine Book of Holy and Eternal Wisdom Revealing the Word of God*, 616 pp., 1849
Advent	Blinn, Henry, *Advent of Christ in Man and Woman*, 1906
Manifest.	*Manifestation of Spiritualism among the Shakers*, 1899
Brown	Brown, Thomas, *An Account of the People Called Shakers*, 372 pp., 1812
Account	Chapman, Eunice, *An Account of the Conduct of the Shakers in the Case of Eunice Hawley Chapman and Her Children*, 1818
Constit.	*Constitution of the United Society of Believers*, 1833
Christ's	Duncan, Meacham, and Youngs, *Testimony of Christ's Second Appearing*, 602 pp., 1808
Dunlavy	Dunlavy, John, *The Manifesto, or a Declaration of the Doctrines and Practices of the Church of Christ*, 520 pp., 1818
Plain	*Plain Evidences by Which the Nature and Character of the True Church of Christ May Be Known and Distinguished from All Others*
Dyer	Dyer, Mary, *A Portraiture of Shakerism*, 446 pp., 1822
Narrative	Dyer, Thomas, *A Compendious Narrative Elucidating the Character, Dispositon, and Conduct of Mary Dyer, by Her Husband*, 88 pp., 1819
Eads	Eads, Hervery L., *An Expression of Faith*, 1875
Elkins	Elkins, Hervey, *Fifteen Years in the Senior Order of Shakers*, 136 pp., 1853
Auto.	Evans, Frederick Williams, *Autobiography of a Shaker and Revelation of the Apocalypse*, 162 pp., 1869
Ann Lee	*Ann Lee, A Biography*, 187 pp., 1858
Tests of	*Shaker Communion, or Tests of Divine Inspiration*, 1871

Treatise	*Treatise on Shaker Theology* (No Date)
Shakerism	*Shakerism, Its Meaning and Message,* 1859
Who Is	*Who Is Ann Lee? What Evidence Is There She Is the Second Messiah?* 1889
General	*General Rules of the United Society and Summary Articles of Mutual Agreement and Release,* 1833
Green	Green, Clavin, *Summary View of the Millennial Church,* 1823
Holy	*Holy Mother Wisdom, The Youth's Guide in Zion and Holy Mother's Promises, Given by Revelation,* 1842
Hymns	*Hymns and Poems for the Use of Believers,* 1833
Discourse	Leonard, William, *A Discourse on the Order and Propriety of Divine Inspiration and Revelation and the Second Appearing of Christ,* 1853
Mace	Mace, Fayette, *Familiar Dialogues on Shakerism; in Which the Principles of the United Society are Illustrated,* 1837
Kentucky	McNemar, Richard, *The Kentucky Revival, or A Short History of Shakerism,* 1807
Detected	*"Shakerism Detected," Examined and Refuted,* 1833
Answer	*A Concise Answer to the General Inquiry, Who or What Are the Shakers?* 1825
Series	*A Series of Lectures on Orthodoxy and Heterodoxy,* 1832
Selection	*A Selection of Hymns and Poems for the Use of Believers,* 1833
Meacham	Meacham, Joseph, *A Concise Statement of the Principles of the Only True Church,* 1790
Covenant	*The First Covenant of the Church of Christ,* 1781, Published 1935
Laws	*The Millennial Laws,* first printed by E.D. Andrews in 1963, in *The People Called Shakers*
Praises	*Millennial Praises,* 1813
Reuben	Rathbon, Reuben, *Reasons Offered for Leaving the Shakers,* 1800
Rathbun	Rathbun, Valentine, *An Account of the Matter, Form, and Manner of a New and Strange Religion Taught and Propagated by a Number of Europeans Living in a Place Called Niskeyuna,* 1781
Remonstrance	*A Remonstrance against the Testimony and Application of Mary Dyer, Requesting Legislative Interference against the United Society, Commonly Called Shakers,* 1818
Revelation	*Revelation of the Extraordinary Visitation of Departed*

Spirits of Distinguished Men and Women of All Nations and Their Manifestation through Living Bodies of Shakers, 1845

Sacred   *Sacred Hymns*, 1845

Examination   *Shaker Examination before the New Hampshire Legislature*, 1849

Stewart   Stewart, Philemon, *The Holy, Sacred, and Divine Roll and Book: From the Lord God of Heaven to the Inhabitants of the Earth*, 402 pp. 1843

Testimonies   *Testimonies concerning Mother Lee*, 1827

Summary   Wells, Seth, and Green, Calvin, *Summary View of the Millennial Church or United Society of Believers*, Published by Order of the Ministry, 320 pp., 1823

Meaning   White, Anna, and Taylor, Leila S., *Shakerism, Meaning, and Message*, 1904

Woods   Woods, John, *Shakerism Unmasked*, 1826

Youngs   Youngs, Benjamin Seth, *Testimony of Christ's Coming*, 1808

Promises   *Millennial Promises*, 1813

CITATIONS

1. *Auto.* 54
2. *Ibid.*
3. Andrews 8
4. *Auto.*, 56-57
5. Andrews 8-11
6. *Ibid.*
7. *Ann Lee* 221
8. Andrews 4
9. *Ibid.*
10. *Ibid.* 11-12
11. *Ibid.* 12
12. *Manifest.* 12
13. *Tests of* 86-87
14. Andrews 15
15. *Ann Lee* 26-27
16. Andrews 20
17. *Ibid.* 22
18. *Ibid.*
19. *Testimonies* 41
20. Andrews 22
21. Rathbun 3
22. *Ibid.* 4
23. *Ibid.* 10
24. *Ibid.* 5
25. *Ibid.*
26. *Ibid.*
27. *Ibid.*
28. *Ibid.*
29. *Ibid.* 6-7
30. *Ibid.* 12
31. *Ibid.*
32. *Ibid.* 10
33. *Ibid.* 11
34. *Ibid.* 12
35. *Ibid.* 8
36. *Ibid.* 9
37. *Ibid.* 8
38. *Ibid.*
39. *Ibid.* 9
40. *Ibid.*
41. *Ibid.* 13, 17
42. *Ibid.* 12
43. Andrews 33
44. *Ibid.* 35
45. *Ibid.* 39
46. *Ibid.* 40
47. *Ibid.* 41-44
48. *Ibid.* 45-47
49. *Ibid.* 54-55
50. *Ibid.* 290
51. *Ibid.* 64
52. *Ibid.* 65
53. *Kentucky* 19
54. *Ibid.* 20
55. *Ibid.*
56. *Ibid.* 21
57. *Ibid.* 22-23
58. *Ibid.* 23
59. *Ibid.* 23-24
60. *Ibid.* 24

61. *Ibid.* 26
62. *Ibid.* 28
63. *Ibid.* 61-62
64. *Ibid.* 62
65. Woods 18
66. Andrews 223
67. *Ibid.* 292
68. Nordhoff 256
69. *Ann Lee* 35-36
70. Nordhoff 256
71. U.S. Census
72. *Hastings* III 783
73. Andrews 292
74. Nordhoff 256
75. Andrews 80
76. Nordhoff 256
77. *Covenant* V
78. Chapman 35
79. *Ibid.* 76-77
80. *Account* 170-171
81. *Ibid.*
82. *Ibid.*
83. *Ibid.* 290
84. Dyer 42
85. *Christ's* 2
86. *Testimonies* 22
87. *Account* 93-94
88. *Examination* 38
89. Dyer 96-97
90. *Ibid.* 106
91. *Ibid.* 139
92. *Ibid.* 266, 161, 55
93. Woods 13
94. *Ibid.* 37
95. *Remonstrance* 4
96. *Ibid.* 5
97. Elkins 102
98. *Ibid.* 105
99. *Ibid.* 104
100. *Remonstrance* 5-6
101. Woods 36
102. *Auto.* 60
103. *Manifest.* 8
104. *Ibid.* 15-16
105. *Ibid.* 16
106. *Ibid.* 18

107. *Ibid.*
108. *Ibid.* 28
109. *Ibid.*
110. Elkins 42
111. *Manifest.* 32
112. *Ibid.* 55
113. *Ibid.*
114. *Ibid.* 89-92
115. Elkins 102
116. *Manifest.* 60
117. Elkins *cf.* Nordhoff, 240-242
118. Andrews 155
119. Elkins 34
120. *Ibid.* 45
121. Philadelphia 1869
122. *Revelation* 8-9
123. *Ibid.* 9-10
124. *Ibid.* 11-12
125. *Ibid.* 13
126. *Ibid.* 14-27
127. *Manifest.* 35
128. Stewart 5
129. *Ibid.* 11
130. *Ibid.* 107
131. *Ibid.* 111
132. *Ibid.* 118
133. *Ibid.* 180 ff.
134. *Ibid.*
135. Bates 658
136. *Ibid.* 418-493
137. *Ibid.* 501-567
138. *Ibid.* 587-650
139. *Auto.* 16-17
140. *Ibid.* 25-26
141. *Ibid.* 18-20
142. *Ibid.* 26
143. *Ibid.* 32-33
144. *Ibid.* 33
145. *Ibid.* 34
146. *Ibid.* 60
147. *Ibid.*
148. *Account* 101
149. *Sacred* 121
150. *Discourse* 52
151. *Ibid.*

152. *Ibid.*
153. *Ibid.* 55
154. *Ibid.* 155
155. *Ann Lee* 103
156. *Ibid.* 106
157. Dyer 32
158. *Ibid.* 37-38
159. *Ibid.* 38
160. *Ibid.* 39
161. *Ibid.* 40
162. *Ibid.* 98-99
163. *Ibid.* 99
164. *Ibid.* 309
165. *Account* 217
166. Dunlavy 519
167. *Ann Lee* 55
168. *Ibid.* 65, 67
169. *Ibid.* 82
170. *Ibid.* 108
171. *Ibid.* 119
172. *Who Is* 4
173. *Ibid.* 9
174. *Treaties* 2-5
175. *Who Is* 11
176. *Summary* 202
177. *Ibid.* 207
178. *Ibid.* 215
179. *Ibid.* 216
180. *Ibid.* 216-219
181. *Ibid.* 257
182. Stewart 107
183. Bates 239
184. *Ibid.* 249, 330
185. *Ibid.* 339
186. Eads 3
187. *Ibid.* 7
188. *Ibid.* 8
189. *Auto.* 48
190. *Ibid.* 50
191. *Sacred* 24
192. *Ibid.* 69
193. *Ibid.* 62-63
194. *Ibid.* 132
195. *Auto.* 7
196. *Summary* 130-131
197. *Sacred* 92

198. Luke 14:26
199. Dyer 126
200. *Ibid.* 161
201. *Ibid.* 207
202. *Ibid.* 208
203. *Ibid.* 269
204. Woods 18
205. *Ibid.* 37
206. *Ibid.*
207. Elkins 105 ff.
208. Chapman 12
209. *Account* 41
210. *Discourse* 78
211. *Ibid.* 86
212. *Tests of* 50
213. *Auto.* 7
214. *Ann Lee* 59
215. *Ibid.* 69
216. *Ibid.* 60
217. *Ibid.* 58
218. *Examination* 86
219. *Discourse* 86
220. *Ibid.* 78
221. Bates 60
222. *Ibid.* 393
223. *Ann Lee* 69
224. *Ibid.* 70
225. *Who Is* 7-8
226. *Ibid.* 10
227. *Auto.* 152
228. *Ibid.* 59
229. *Tests of* viii
230. *Ibid.* 60
231. *Ibid.* 75
232. *Ibid.* 80
233. *Ann Lee* 61
234. *Sacred* A
235. *Shakerism* 342
236. *Tests of* 3
237. *Ibid.* 22
238. *Ibid.* 24
239. *Ibid.* 27
240. *Ibid.* 30
241. *Discourse* 49
242. *Ann Lee* 13
243. *Test of* 6

244. *Ibid.* 49
245. *Ibid.* 6
246. *Ibid.* 7
247. *Ibid.* 36
248. *Ibid.*
249. *Ibid.* 37
250. *Ann Lee* 16
251. *Tests of* 49
252. *Ann Lee* 71
253. *Ibid.* 72
254. *Ibid.* 73
255. Rev. 13:1, 11-12
256. *Auto.* 62-63
257. *Tests of* 50
258. *Ibid.*
259. *Ibid.* 99
260. *Ann Lee* 79
261. Christ's 169 ff.
262. *Ibid.* 185
263. *Ibid.* 202
264. *Ibid.*
265. *Ibid.* 261
266. *Ibid.* 277
267. *Ibid.* 278 ff.
268. *Ibid.* 300-336
269. *Ibid.* 348
270. *Ibid.* 350 ff.
271. Dyer 161
272. Stewart 118
273. Woods 13
274. *Christ's* 461-491
275. *Account* 40
276. *Tests of* 22
277. Dyer 38
278. *Summary* 315
279. *Ibid.* 315-316
280. Dyer 40
281. *Tests of* 100
282. Summary 302 ff.
283. *Ibid.* 309 ff.
284. *Disourse* 49
285. *Auto.* 181
286. *Tests of* 89
287. *Ibid.* 88
288. *Sacred* B
289. *Ibid.* E

290. *Tests of* 2
291. *Summary* 115
292. Dyer 138
293. *Ibid.* 190
294. *Ibid.* 197
295. *Ibid.* 278
296. *Summary* 257-258
297. *Discourse* 1
298. Elkins 44
299. *Sacred* 26-27
300. *Ibid.* 30
301. *Ibid.* 153, 154
302. *Ibid.* 126
303. *Sacred* 18
304. *Ibid.* 17
305. Dyer 39
306. *Ibid.* 66
307. Woods 35
308. *Ann Lee* 114
309. Bates 41
310. *Sacred* M, P
311. *Ibid.* 10-11
312. *Summary* 259
313. *Ibid.* 260
314. *Ibid.*
315. *Ibid.* 262
316. *Ibid.* 266
317. *Ibid.* 268
318. *Ibid.* 272
319. *Ibid.* 284 ff.
320. *Ibid.* 290 ff.
321. Elkins 20
322. *Sacred* 22
323. *Ann Lee* 44
324. *Ibid.* 45-46
325. *Ibid.* 49-50, 51
326. *Ibid.* 51, 52
327. *Ibid.* 54
328. Covenant 7-9
329. *General* 1-2
330. *Ibid.* 3
331. *Ibid.*
332. *Ibid.* 4
333. *Sacred* 8
334. *Ibid.* 106
335. *Ibid.* 78

336. *Wars* II viii 2-13   338. Andrews 197-198   340. *Historical* 45
337. Nordhoff-211   339. *Ibid.* 198   341. Andrews 113-115

CHAPTER 3: PHINEAS PARKHURST QUIMBY

BIBLIOGRAPHY

FAM   Goldsmith, Margaret, *Franz Anton Mesmer*, Doubleday, 1934

PoPPQ   Dresser, Annetta Gertrude, *The Philosophy of P.P. Quimby*, 1895

THMS   Dresser, Julius A., *The True History of Mental Science*, 1887

QMSS   Quimby, P.P., *The Quimby Manuscripts*, edited by Horatio W. Dresser, 1921 (includes the letters of Mary Baker Patterson to Quimby)

QMSS   Quimby, P.P., *The Quimby Manuscripts*, edited by Horatio W. Dresser, 1961

MH   Zweig, Stephen, *Mental Healers*, New York, 1932

CITATIONS

1. QMSS 269
2. Published in Boston
3. THMS 10-11
4. *Ibid.* 12-13
5. QMSS 40
6. *Ibid.* 54, 38
7. *Ibid.* 43
8. *Ibid.* 47
9. *Ibid.* 47-48
10. *Ibid.* 48
11. *Ibid.* 38
12. *Ibid.* 67
13. *Ibid.* 53, 57
14. *Ibid.* 57
15. *Ibid.* 150-151
16. *Ibid.* 277
17. *Ibid.* 70
18. *Ibid.* 324
19. *Ibid.*
20. *Ibid.* 323
21. *Ibid.* 330
22. *Ibid.* 408
23. *Ibid.* 409
24. *Ibid.* 422
25. *Ibid.* 128
26. *Ibid.* 389
27. PoPPQ 109
28. *Ibid.*
29. *Ibid.* 110, QMSS 324
30. QMSS 323, 337
31. *Ibid.* 324
32. PoPPQ 91
33. QMSS 327
34. *Ibid.* 185
35. *Ibid.* 196
36. *Ibid.* 243
37. *Ibid.* 403
38. *Ibid.* 422
39. *Ibid.* 340
40. *Ibid.* 122
41. *Ibid.* 320
42. *Ibid.* 344
43. *Ibid.* 346
44. *Ibid.* 185
45. *Ibid.* 215
46. *Ibid.* 217
47. *Ibid.* 210
48. *Ibid.* 214
49. *Ibid.* 150
50. *Ibid.* 120
51. *Ibid.* 208
52. *Ibid.* 228
53. *Ibid.* 178
54. *Ibid.* 126-127
55. *Ibid.* 283
56. *Ibid.* 312
57. *Ibid.* 143, 170
58. *Ibid.* 228
59. *Ibid.* 242
60. *Ibid.* 388

61. *Ibid.* 143
62. *Ibid.* 176, 369, 407
63. *Ibid.* 201, 370
64. *Ibid.* 346-347
65. *Ibid.* 422
66. *Ibid.* 189
67. PoPPQ 112, 113
68. QMSS 209
69. *Ibid.* 216, 246
70. *Ibid.* 353
71. *Ibid.* 369, 273
72. *Ibid.* 273
73. *Ibid.* 340
74. *Ibid.* 326
75. *Ibid.* 283
76. *Ibid.* 224
77. *Ibid.* 355-356
78. *Ibid.* 339
79. *Ibid.* 369-370
80. *Ibid.* 398
81. *Ibid.* 379
82. *Ibid.* 408
83. *Ibid.* 379
84. *Ibid.* 255-256
85. *Ibid.* 345
86. *Ibid.* 338, 271
87. *Ibid.* 294, 269
88. *Ibid.* 295
89. *Ibid.* 299
90. *Ibid.* 336-337
91. *Ibid.* 289
92. *Ibid.* 332, 261
93. *Ibid.* 329, 242
94. *Ibid.* 384
95. *Ibid.* 378
96. *Ibid.* 169
97. *Ibid.* 270, 241
98. *Ibid.* 230, 241
99. *Ibid.* 276, 287
100. *Ibid.* 278
101. *Ibid.* 288
102. *Ibid.* 205, 142
103. *Ibid.* 318
104. *Ibid.* 232, 271, 277
105. *Ibid.* 215
106. *Ibid.* 210, 259

107. *Ibid.* 271
108. *Ibid.* 231-232
109. *Ibid.* 325
110. *Ibid.* 338
111. *Ibid.* 276
112. *Ibid.* 277, 262
113. *Ibid.* 331
114. *Ibid.* 267
115. *Ibid.* 328
116. *Ibid.* 262-263
117. *Ibid.* 334
118. *Ibid.* 277
119. *Ibid.* 259
120. *Ibid.* 231-232, 173, 328, 416
121. *Ibid.* 306
122. *Ibid.* 76
123. PoPPQ 100
124. QMSS 204
125. *Ibid.* 259
126. *Ibid.* 78-79
127. *Ibid.* 55
128. *Ibid.* 277
129. *Ibid.* 337, 123
130. *Ibid.* 362
131. *Ibid.* 352
132. *Ibid.* 360
133. *Ibid.* 105-106
134. *Ibid.* 106
135. *Ibid.* 346
136. *Ibid.* 347
137. *Ibid.* 398
138. *Ibid.* 396
139. *Ibid.* 350
140. *Ibid.* 287
141. *Ibid.* 277, 283
142. *Ibid.* 360
143. *Ibid.* 363
144. *Ibid.* 190
145. *Ibid.* 387, 388, 393, 394
146. *Ibid.* 394
147. *Ibid.* 395
148. *Ibid.* 72
149. *Ibid.* 71
150. *Ibid.* 351

151. *Ibid.* 353-354
152. *Ibid.* 284
153. *Ibid.* 288
154. *Ibid.* 260
155. *Ibid.* 277
156. *Ibid.* 15
157. *Ibid.* 43
158. *Ibid.* 418
159. PoPPQ 33
160. QMSS 179, 180, 222, 227, 421
161. *Ibid.* 61
162. *Ibid.* 334
163. *Ibid.* 167, 275
164. *Ibid.* 118, 141, 167
165. *Ibid.* 194
166. *Ibid.* 222-223
167. *Ibid.* 413
168. *Ibid.* 257
169. *Ibid.* 50-51
170. *Ibid.* 278
171. *Ibid.* 73, 327
172. *Ibid.* 336, PoPPQ 107
173. QMSS 397
174. *Ibid.* 246
175. *Ibid.* 403, cf. PoPPQ 70
176. QMSS 213
177. PoPPQ 23
178. *Ibid.* 24
179. QMSS 270, 271
180. *Ibid.* 285
181. *Ibid.* 134, 214
182. *Ibid.* 234, 368
183. *Ibid.* 61, 367
184. *Ibid.* 269
185. *Ibid.* 300
186. *Ibid.* 118
187. *Ibid.* 311
188. *Ibid.* 220
189. *Ibid.* 174
190. *Ibid.* 280
191. *Ibid.* 80
192. *Ibid.* 296-297
193. *Ibid.* 180

194. *Ibid.* 182
195. *Ibid.* 177
196. *Ibid.* 179
197. *Ibid.* 194
198. *Ibid.* 223
199. *Ibid.* 402
200. *Ibid.* 80
201. *Ibid.* 270
202. *Ibid.* 52-53
203. *Ibid.* 253-254
204. *Ibid.* 277
205. *Ibid.* 154
206. *Ibid.* 63
207. *Ibid.* 104-105, 110
208. *Ibid.* 117
209. *Ibid.* 129
210. *Ibid.* 139-140

211. *Ibid.* 217-218
212. *Ibid.* 376
213. PoPPQ 86
214. QMSS 169
215. *Ibid.* 319
216. *Ibid.* 204
217. *Ibid.* 286
218. PoPPQ 20-21
219. QMSS 143
220. *Ibid.* 369
221. *Ibid.* 370
222. *Ibid.* 407
223. *Ibid.* 372
224. *Ibid.* 327
225. *Ibid.* 406
226. *Ibid.* 227
227. *Ibid.* 177

228. *Ibid.* 171-172
229. *Ibid.* 412-413
230. *Ibid.* 379-380
231. *Ibid.* 344-345
232. *Ibid.* 369-370
233. *Ibid.* 400
234. *Ibid.* 405
235. *Ibid.* 375
236. *Ibid.* 203
237. *Ibid.* 200-201
238. *Ibid.* 215
239. *Ibid.* 250
240. *Ibid.* 344
241. *Ibid.* 327
242. *Ibid.*
243. *Ibid.* 202
244. PoPPQ 48

CHAPTER 4: WARREN FELT EVANS

BIBLIOGRAPHY

CD — *The Celestial Dawn*
HI — *The Happy Islands*
HIL — *Health and the Inner Life*
NA — *The New Age and Its Messenger*
MC — *The Mental Cure*, 1869
MM — *Mental Medicine*, 1872
SB — *Soul and Body*, 1876
DLC — *The Divine Law of Cure*, 1881
PMC — *The Primitive Mind-Cure*, 1884
EC — *Esoteric Christianity*, 1886

CITATIONS

1. HI 119
2. CD, HI
3. PMC 77
4. NA 7
5. *Ibid.* 8
6. SB 97
7. *Ibid.* 16
8. DLC 120
9. EC 134
10. *Schaff-Herzog Ency. of Religious Knowledge* IX 354
11. MC 20
12. DLC 22-23
13. *Ibid.* 26

14. MC 238
15. DLC 223
16. PMC 148
17. EC 24
18. DLC 63
19. *Ibid.* 260
20. *Ibid.* 190
21. EC 17
22. MC 21, MM 93, PMC 123
23. EC 87, 92, 96, 102-103
24. MC 22
25. MM 170
26. PMC 170
27. DLC 72
28. EC 74
29. MC 349
30. EC 66-67
31. DLC 53
32. EC 70
33. SB 58
34. MC 240
35. DLC 237, 238
36. *Ibid.* 134
37. *Ibid.* 137
38. *Ibid.* 79, 108
39. PMC 175
40.. DLC 80
41. PMC 35
42. DLC 125, PMC 158
43. *Ibid.* 238
44. EC 32
45. MM v
46. DLC 43
47. MC 76-77
48. EC 95
49. SB 42-43
50. MC 237-238
51. *Ibid.* 216-217, 224
52. DLC 59
53. *Ibid.* 167
54. EC 103
55. MC 36
56. *Ibid.* 29
57. MM 18-19
58. *Ibid.* 25

59. EC 171
60. MC 228
61. *Ibid.* 65
62. DLC 245
63. *Ibid.* 163-165
64. SB 67, 68
65. MC 27
66. EC 28
67. DLC 168
68. *Ibid.* 168-169
69. MC 108
70. EC 64
71. SB 96
72. *Ibid.* 9
73. PMC 12-15
74. EC 69
75. PMC 87, 119
76. MC 58
77. EC 53
78. DLC 229-230
79. MC 196
80. *Ibid.* 54
81. *Ibid.* 153
82. *Ibid.* 284
83. DLC 51
84. MC 175
85. EC 31
86. MM 14
87. *Ibid.* 13-14
88. DLC 78
89. *Ibid.*
90. MM 92
91. DLC 253
92. *Ibid.* 217
93. MC 104-105; MM 102-104
94. SB 41
95. PMC 22-27
96. *Ibid.* 28
97. *Ibid.* 35
98. MM 174
99. MC 163
100. *Ibid.* 113
101. SB 140-141
102. MM 97-104
103. DLC 159

104. *Ibid.* 147
105. *Ibid.* 160-161
106. SB 10
107. MM iv
108. PMC iv
109. *Ibid.*
110. MM 12
111. EC 170
112. MM 60
113. EC 69
114. MC 143
115. MM 39
116. MC 167
117. DLC 55
118. EC 63
119. PMC 121
120. *Ibid.* 38
121. EC 43
122. DLC 236
123. MM 85
124. *Ibid.* 140
125. *Ibid.* 137
126. MC 246
127. DLC 186, MC 246
128. *Ibid.* 188
129. PMC 97
130. MM 23
131. *Ibid.* 26
132. *Ibid.* 135
133. EC 132
134. MM 148
135. SB 118
136. *Ibid.* 128
137. DLC 44
138. *Ibid.* 56
139. SB 56
140. DLC 126-127, 42, MM 12
141. SB 3-4
142. PMC 98
143. EC 5
144. DLC 167
145. *Ibid.* 177, 268
146. PMC 84
147. MM 21-24
148. SB 52-53

149. PMC 85
150. EC 149
151. *Ibid.* 150
152. *Ibid.* 58-59
153. MM 17
154. MC 318
155. EC 55
156. PMC 86
157. MM 16
158. PMC 60
159. *Ibid.* 104
160. EC 170
161. *Ibid.* 4
162. DLC 210
163. *Ibid.* 296
164. MM 185
165. DLC 294
166. MC 220
167. *Ibid.* 245
168. PMC 58
169. *Ibid.* 59
170. *Ibid.* 74
171. *Ibid.* 60
172. *Ibid.* 57

173. DLC 298, PMC 65
174. MC 276
175. MM 80
176. PMC 198
177. MC 259
178. PMC 113-114
179. *Ibid.* 51
180. MC 71
181. EC 120-121
182. PMC 51, 59
183. *Ibid.* 199
184. *Ibid.* 202
185. MC 268
186. PMC 200
187. DLC 274
188. EC 123-124
189. *Ibid.* 124
190. PMC 158
191. MC 261
192. MM 152
193. MC iii, 63, 98, 153, 155, 168, 215, 350, etc.
194. *Ibid.* 107

195. *Ibid.* 63
196. MM 163-164, etc.
197. *Ibid.* 42
198. *Ibid.* 47-49
199. *Ibid.* 45, 44
200. *Ibid.* 90-91, 113-114
201. *Ibid.* 99
202. *Ibid.* 109-110
203. *Ibid.* 102-103
204. *Ibid.* 49-51
205. *Ibid.* 50
206. *Ibid.* 52-53
207. *Ibid.* 148
208. DLC 58
209. *Ibid.* 282
210. *Ibid.* 83
211. *Ibid.* 99
212. *Ibid.* 103
213. PMC 102
214. EC 131
215. DLC 268
216. MM 142
217. PMC 98

CHAPTER 5: CHRISTIAN SCIENCE
BIBLIOGRAPHY

(Since there are many hundreds of citations in this chapter, we have saved space by placing them in the text, using the symbols given below.)

THE WORKS OF MARY BAKER EDDY

S&H *Science and Health*
Citations from first and second editions, shown as follows: (I *S&H* 213); those for the third to the fifteenth, which are two-volume editions, citations shown thus: (III *S&H* I, 167).
Science and Health with Key to the Scriptures includes all later editions, through the 226th, shown thus: (16 *S&H* 497); and citations for the definitive edition (F 459). Successive citations from the same work are indicated only by page numbers in the text.

SofM 1876	*Science of Man*, 1876 edition
SofM 1883	*Science of Man*, 1883 edition
CM	Church *Manual*
C&C	*Christ and Christmas*
CSH	*Christian Science Hymnal*
JCS	*Journal of Christian Science*
CSJ	*The Christian Science Journal*

THE PROSE WORKS, INCLUDING THE FOLLOWING

Mis.	*Miscellaneous Writings*
Ret.	*Retrospection and Introspection* (the autobiography)
Un.	*Unity of Good*
Pul.	*Pulpit and Press*
Rud.	*Rudimental Divine Science*
No	*No and Yes*
Pan.	*Christian Science vs. Pantheism*
'00	*Message to the Mother Church, 1900*
'01	*Message to the Mother Church, 1901*
'02	*Message to the Mother Church, 1902*
Heal.	*Christian Healing*
Peo.	*The People's Idea of God*
My.	*The First Church of Christ, Scientist, and Miscellany*

OTHER IMPORTANT SOURCES

Beasley	Beasley, Norman, *The Cross and the Crown*, Duel, Sloan, and Pearce, 1952
Dak.	Dakin, Edwin Franden, *Mrs. Eddy, the Biography of a Virginal Mind*, Scribner's, New York, 1930
Dickey	Dickey, Adam H., *The Memoirs of Mary Baker Eddy*, Merrymount Press, 1927
Ditt.	Dittemore, John V., and Bates, Ernest Sutherland, *Mary Baker Eddy*, Alfred Knopf, New York, 1932
Kimball	Kimball, Edward A., *Lectures and Articles on Christian Science*, Watt, 1921
Mil.	Milmine, Georgine, *The Life of Mary Baker Eddy, and the History of Christian Science*, Doubleday, 1909
Olston	Olston, Albert E., *The Facts and Fables of Christian Science*, Author, Chicago, 1912
Peabody	Peabody, Frederick W., *The Religio-Medical Masque-*

rade, Fleming H. Revell Co., New York, 1910

—— *The Faith, Falsity, and Failure of Christian Science*, Fleming H. Revell Co., New York, 1925

Powell   Powell, Lyman P., *Christian Science, the Faith and Its Founder*, G.P. Putnam's Sons, New York, 1908

—— *Mary Baker Eddy*, The Macmillan Co., New York, 1930

Studdert   Studdert-Kennedy, Hugh A., *Christian Science and Organized Religion*, The Farallon Foundation, Los Gatos, Calif., 1930

—— *Mrs. Eddy*, The Farallon Foundation, Los Gatos, Calif., 1947

Tomlinson   Tomlinson, Irving C., *The Revelations of St. John an Open Book*, The Open Book, Dorchester, Mass., 1922

—— *Twelve Years with Mary Baker Eddy*, CSPS, 1945

CS   Twain, Mark, *Christian Science*, Harper and Brothers, New York, 1900

Wilbur   Wilbur, Sibyl, *The Life of Mary Baker Eddy*, CSPS, 1907

SELECTED GENERAL BIBLIOGRAPHY

Anonymous, *The Faith and Works of Christian Science*, Macmillan Co., New York, 1909

Bancroft, Samuel Putnam, *Mrs. Eddy As I Knew Her in 1870*, The Rare Book Co.

Bill, Annie Co., *Christian Science vs. Plagiarism*, Beauchamp, 1921

Braden, Charles Samuel, *Christian Science Today: Power, Policy, and Practice*, SMU Press, Dallas, Texas, 1958

Brown, W. Gordon, *The Evolution of the Christian Science Organization*, Foundational Book Co., 1970

Brown, William Lear, *Christian Science, Falsely So-Called*, Fleming H. Revell Co., New York, 1921

Buckley, J.M., *Faith Healing, Christian Science, and Kindred Phenomena*, Century Co., New York, 1892

Buskirk, James Dale, *Religion, Healing, and Life*, Macmillan Co., New York, 1952

Chester, John, *Ruth, the Christian Scientist*, H.H. Carter & Karrick, Boston, 1888

Christian Science Hymnal, The, CSPS, 1909

Coppage, L.J., *Christian Science in the Light of Reason*, Standard Publishing Co., Cincinnati, Ohio, 1914

Corey, Arthur E., *Christian Science Class Instruction*, The Farallon Foundation, Los Gatos, Calif., 1950

—— *Class Notes*, The Farallon Foundation, Los Gatos, Calif., 1950, 1956, 1962

—— (With Robert E. Merritt) *Christian Science and Liberty*, De Vorss & Co., Los Angeles, 1970

Directors, Christian Science Publishing Society, *Christian Science Wartime Activities*, CSPS, 1947

Doorly, J.W., *God and Science*, Frederick Miller, Ltd., London, 1949

—— *The Pure Science of Christian Science*, Foundational Book Co., London, 1946

Dresser, Annetta Gertrude, *The Philosophy of P.P. Quimby*, The Church of the Truth, Boston, 1895

Dresser, Horatio W., *Christ or Science*, Willing Publishing Co., San Gabriel, Calif.

Dresser, Julius, *The True History of Mental Science*, Alfred Midge & Sons, Boston, 1887

Eddy, Mary G. Baker, *Historical Sketch of Metaphysical Healing*, Author, Boston, 1885

Fisher, H.A.L., *Our New Religion*, Jonathan Cape and Harrison Smith, New York, 1930

Flynn, W. Earl, *Christian Health Science vs. Christian Science*, W.F. Black & Co., Minneapolis, 1910

Gestefeld, Ursula, *How to Control Circumstances*, The Exodus Publishing Co., Chicago, 1908

—— *Jesuitism in Christian Science*, The Exodus Publishing Co., Chicago, 1888

—— *The Joyous Birth*, The Exodus Publishing Co., Chicago, 1910

—— *The Science of the Larger Life*, William Rider & Son, London, 1909

Gifford, M.W., *Christian Science against Itself*, Jennings & Page, Cincinnati, Ohio, 1902

Gray, James M., *The Antidote to Christian Science*, Fleming H. Revell Co., New York, 1907

Haldeman, I.M., *Christian Science in the Light of the Scriptures*, Fleming H. Revell Co., New York, 1909

Hanna, Septimus J., *Christian Science History*, CSPS, 1890

Hopkins, Emma Curtis, *Christian Medical Practice*, High Watch Fellowship, Cornwell Bridge, Conn., 1958

Humiston, Charles E., *The Faith, Falsity, and Failure of Christian Science*, Fleming H. Revell Co., New York, 1925

Huse, Sibyl Marvin, *Twelve Baskets Full*, G.P. Putnam's Sons, New York, 1922

Kimball, Edward A., *Teaching and Addresses*, Kratzer Publishing Co., 1917

Laird, Margaret, *All Is One*, Laird Foundation, Los Angeles, 1957

—— *Government is Self-Government*, The Portal Press, Evanston, Ill., 1952

Larson, Christian Daa, *The Good Side of Christian Science*, E.J. Clode, New York, 1916

Lord, Frances, *Christian Science Healing*, Lily Publishing Co., Chicago, 1888

McCabe, Joseph, *The Absurdities of Christian Science*, E. Haldeman Julius, Girard, Kansas

Mangasarian, M.M., *What Is Christian Science?* Author, Chicago, 1921

Merritt, Robert E. and Corey, Arthur E., *Christian Science and Liberty*, DeVorss & Co., Los Angeles, Calif. 1970

New York City Christian Science Institute, *Vital Issues in Christian Science*, G.P. Putnam's Sons, New York, 1914

Orgain, Alice L., *Distinguishing Characteristics of Mary Baker Eddy's Progressive Revisions of Science and Health*, Rare Book Co., 1933

—— *The Story of the Christian Science Church Manual*, Rare Book Co., 1934

Peabody, Frederick W., *The Complete Exposure of Christian Science*, Fleming H. Revell Co., New York, 1901

—— *The Religio-Medical Masquerade*, Fleming H. Revell Co., 1913

Peel, Robert, *Christian Science: Its Encounter with American Culture*, 1964

—— *Mary Baker Eddy: The Year of Discovery*, 1966

Quimby, P.P., *Christ or Science*, Willing Publishing Co., San Gabriel, Cal.

—— *Manuscripts*, Thomas Y. Crowell Co., New York, 1921

—— *Manuscripts*, The Julian Press, New York, 1961

Ramsay, E. Mary, *Christian Science and Its Discoverer*, CSPS, 1935

Riley, Woodbridge, Peabody, Frederick W., and Humiston, Charles E., *The Faith, the Falsity, and the Failure of Christian Science*, Fleming H. Revell Co., New York, 1925

Searle, George M., *The Truth about Christian Science*, Paulist Press, New York, 1916

Sheldon, Henry C., *Christian Science So-Called*, Eaton & Mains, New York, 1913

Smith, Hanover P., *Writings and Genius of the Founder of Christian Science*, 1886

Snowden, James H., *The Truth about Christian Science*, Westminster Press, Philadelphia, 1921

Springer, Fleta Campbell, *According to the Flesh*, Coward-McCann, New York, 1930

Stetson, Augusta E., *My Spiritual Aeroplane*, G.P. Putnam's Son, New York, 1919

—— *Reminiscences, Sermons, and Correspondence*, G.P. Putnam's Sons, New York, 1917

—— *Vital Issues in Christian Science*, G.P. Putnam's Sons, New York, 1914

Sturge, M. Carta, *The Truth and Error of Christian Science*, E.P. Dutton & Co., New York, 1903

Zweig, Stephen, *Mental Healers*, The Viking Press, New York, 1932

CHAPTER 6: THE GREAT POPULARIZERS
I. INTRODUCTION
II. THE UNITARIAN SWEDENBORGIANS

CITATIONS

1. *Representative Men*, Caldwell Co., p. 125, 132
2. The Divinity School Address, Am. Unitarian Association, 3-4
3. *Ibid*. 4-5
4. *Ibid*. 19
5. *Ibid*. 20
6. *Representative Men*, 96
7. *Ibid*. 99
8. *Ibid*. 118-119
9. *Ibid*. 128, 137-138
10. Noyes, *History of American Socialisms*, 531
11. *Works*, Trubner & Co., 1879, Vol. II 73
12. *Ibid*. 191
13. *Ibid*. 51, 119, 156
14. *Ibid*. 88
15. *Ibid*. 195
16. *Prayers*, Trubner & Co. 15, 21, 39, 45, 51, 61, 77, 88, 92, 98, 102, 109, 125, etc.
17. *Works*, *Ibid*. 72
18. *Prayers* 8; 35
19. *Works*, 215
20. *Ibid*. 217
21. *Ibid*. 222
22. *Prayers* 98
23. *Ibid*. 122

III. HENRY JAMES, SR.

CITATIONS

1. C. Hartley Grattan, *The Three Jameses*, 47-48
2. *Ibid*. 52-53
3. *Christianity, the Logic of Creation*, 81-83
4. *The Three Jameses* 53
5. *Moralism and Christianity* 92-93
6. Cf. Frederic Young, *The Philosophy of Henry James, Sr.* 318-319
7. *The Church of Christ Not an Ecclesiastism* 81-82; 87-88; 122-123
8. *Christianity, the Logic* 172-173
9. *Tracts for the Times* 17
10. *Christianity, the Logic* 208-210
11. *Substance and Shadow* 230
12. *Moralism and Chris-tianity* 81-82
13. *Ibid*.
14. *The Nature of Evil* 259-261
15. *Substance and Shadow* 230
16. *Young* 319
17. *Ibid*. Chapter Four, pp. 29-69
18. *The Three Jameses* 106-107
19. *Literary Remains* 388-390

IV. HENRY DRUMMOND

CITATIONS

1. *Natural Law in the Spiritual World* 19
2. *Ibid.* 20
3. *Ibid.*
4. *Ibid.* 21
5. *Ibid.* 56-57
6. *Ibid.* 5
7. *Ibid.* 28
8. *Ibid.* 29
9. *Ibid.* 32, Cf. 59-60
10. *Ibid.* 32, cf. 55
11. *Ibid.* 69, 70
12. *Ibid.* 33-34
13. *Ibid.* 40
14. *Ibid.* 41
15. *Ibid.* 43
16. *Ibid.* 45
17. *Ibid.* 47
18. *Ibid.* 50
19. *Ibid.* 51
20. *Ibid.* 68
21. *Ibid.* 72
22. *Ibid.* 78 f.
23. *Ibid.* 81
24. *Ibid.* 82
25. *Ibid.* 83
26. *Ibid.* 87
27. *Ibid.* 88
28. *Ibid.* 89-90
29. *Ibid.* 93
30. *Ibid.* 94
31. *Ibid.* 95
32. *Ibid.* 96
33. *Ibid.* 99
34. *Ibid.* 103
35. *Ibid.* 126
36. *Ibid.* 109 ff.
37. *Ibid.* 122
38. *Ibid.* 126
39. *Ibid.* 127
40. *Ibid.* 138
41. *Ibid.* 139
42. *Ibid.* 143
43. *Ibid.* 146
44. *Ibid.* 147
45. *Ibid.* 148
46. *Ibid.* 151-178
47. *Ibid.* 164, 181
48. *Ibid.* 168
49. *Ibid.* 173
50. *Ibid.* 259
51. *Ibid.* 284
52. *Ibid.* 191
53. *Ibid.* 196
54. *Ibid.* 215
55. *Ibid.* 246
56. *Ibid.* 252
57. *Ibid.*
58. *Ibid.*
59. *Ibid.* 285
60. *Ibid.* 307 ff.
61. *Ibid.* 314-315
62. *Ibid.* 320-322
63. *Ibid.* 323
64. *Ibid.* 324
65. *Ibid.* 336-337
66. *Ibid.* 345
67. *Ibid.* 346
68. *Ibid.* 347
69. *Ibid.* 348
70. *Ibid.* 362
71. *Ibid.* 373
72. *Ibid.* 377
73. *Ibid.* 379-382
74. *Ibid.* 389-391

V. EMMA CURTIS HOPKINS

CITATIONS

1. *Spirits in Rebellion* 143
2. *Mary Baker Eddy* 265
3. *Ibid.* 272
4. *Spirits in Rebellion* 144
5. *Scientific Christian Mental Practice*, Lesson Three, pp. 69-70
6. Lesson Two 46
7. *Ibid.*
8. Lesson Five 107; Lesson Seven 138
9. *Ibid.* 110
10. Lesson Seven 148
11. Lesson Nine 182
12. *Understanding the Scriptures* 11-12
13. Lesson Ten 200
14. Lesson Eleven 231
15. Lesson Five 112-113
16. *Ibid.* 114
17. *Ibid.* 112
18. Lesson Twelve 261-262

VI. THOMAS TROWARD

CITATIONS

1. For example, in his acceptance of the Law of Biogenesis
2. *The Hidden Power*, Robert McBride & Co. 9
3. *Edinburgh Lectures*, Dodd, Mead & Co. 55
4. *The Doré Lectures*, Dodd, Mead & Co. 1
5. *Ibid.* 3
6. *Ibid.* 6
7. *Ibid.* 7
8. *Ibid.* 10
9. *Ibid.*
10. *Ibid.* 15
11. *Ibid.* 16-17
12. *Ibid.* 16
13. *Ibid.* 20
14. *Ibid.*
15. *Ibid.* 23
16. *Ibid.* 26
17. *Ibid.* 27
18. *Ibid.* 29
19. *Ibid.* 35
20. *Ibid.* 38
21. *Ibid.* 44
22. *Ibid.* 45
23. *Ibid.* 50
24. *Ibid.* 51
25. *Ibid.* 53
26. *Ibid.* 55
27. *Ibid.* 57
28. *Ibid.* 65
29. El 9; cf. *The Law and the Word* 52-53
30. *Ibid.* 20
31. *The Creative Process in the Individual* 55
32. EL 15
33. *Ibid.* 17
34. *Ibid.* 18
35. *Ibid.* 19
36. CP 67
37. LW 50
38. EL 45
39. HP 7
40. CP 6
41. EL 46
42. *Ibid.* 59
43. *Ibid.* 14
44. *Ibid.* 15
45. *Ibid.* 47
46. *Ibid.* 9
47. *Ibid.* 13
48. HP 52
49. EL 42
50. *Ibid.* 48-49
51. *Ibid.* 42
52. LW 109
53. EL 48
54. *Ibid.* 50
55. CR 38
56. *Ibid.* 80
57. EL 11
58. *Ibid.* 8
59. LW 68
60. CP 79
61. *Ibid.* 52-53; EL 4
62. CP 136
63. EL 37
64. CP 30
65. *Ibid.* 31
66. *Ibid.* 36
67. EL 53
68. *Ibid.* 52
69. HP 174
70. *Ibid.* 177
71. *Ibid.* 51
72. CP 141
73. EL 35
74. CP 10
75. *Ibid.* 39
76. *Ibid.* 167
77. HP 182
78. EL 100
79. HP 188
80. EL 91
81. CP 45
82. HP 207
83. EL 128
84. *Ibid.* 22
85. *Ibid.* 23
86. *Ibid.* 24
87. *Ibid.* 25
88. *Ibid.* 30
89. *Ibid.* 26
90. *Ibid.*
91. *Ibid.* 28
92. *Ibid.* 27
93. *Ibid.* 74
94. *Ibid.* 75
95. *Ibid.*
96. *Ibid.* 69
97. *Ibid.* 79
98. *Ibid.* 77
99. *Ibid.* 78
100. *Ibid.* 32
101. LW 154

102. *Ibid.* 1
103. CP 91, 18
104. HP 83
105. EL 44
106. *Ibid.* 42
107. *Ibid.* 65-66
108. *Ibid.* 58
109. *Ibid.* 105
110. *Ibid.* 16
111. *Ibid.* 15
112. LW 73
113. EL 12
114. *Ibid.* 49
115. *Ibid.* 50
116. CP 131
117. LW 87-88
118. *Ibid.* 87
119. EL 67

120. CP 58-59
121. LW 100
122. EL 80
123. LW 97
124. HP 36
125. *Ibid.* 145
126. CP 38, 41
127. *Ibid.* 132
128. HP 42
129. EL 36
130. HP 65-66
131. CP 37
132. HP 142
133. EL 96
134. *Ibid.* 105
135. *Ibid.* 78
136. HP 167
137. LW 113, 139

138. CP 86
139. *Ibid.* 86, 88
140. EL 9
141. CP 95; LW 164
142. LW 162; CP 110
143. LW 179
144. *Ibid.* 133
145. CP 176
146. *Ibid.* 95
147. LW 195
148. *Ibid.* 204
149. CP 145
150. *Ibid.*
151. HP 119
152. LW 110
153. CP 157
154. EL 70

VII. CHARLES BRODIE PATTERSON

CITATIONS

1. *What is New Thought* 35-36
2. *Ibid.* 7
3. *Ibid.* 11; 14, 84, 220, 235
4. *The Will to Be Well* 41, 53
5. *What Is* 56; *The Will* 12
6. *The Will* 24
7. *Ibid.* 117
8. *Ibid.* 118; 12, 23
9. *Ibid.* 166; 22
10. *Ibid.* 52; *What Is* 3
11. *What Is* 22
12. *Ibid.* 35
13. *The Will* 101
14. *Ibid.* 166
15. *Ibid.* 187
16. *Ibid.* 246-247

17. *Ibid.* 37
18. *What Is* 43
19. *Ibid.* 43
20. *Ibid.* 93
21. *Ibid.* 151
22. *The Will* 124
23. *What Is* 37
24. *Ibid.* 58
25. *Ibid.* 91
26. *Ibid.* 94
27. *Ibid.* 119
28. *The Will* 35
29. *Ibid.* 131
30. *Ibid.* 122
31. *Ibid.* 13
32. *Ibid.* 123
33. *Ibid.* 108
34. *Ibid.* 243
35. *Ibid.* 244
36. *What Is* 13

37. *Ibid.* 33
38. *The Will* 204
39. *What Is* 148
40. *Ibid.* 149
41. *The Will* 101
42. *What Is* 131
43. *The Will* 202
44. *What Is* 15
45. *The Will* 217
46. *Ibid.* 219
47. *What Is* 130
48. *Ibid.* 156
49. *Ibid.* 161
50. *Ibid.* 61
51. *The Will* 182
52. *Ibid.* 101-102
53. *What Is* 84
54. *The Will* 86
55. *What Is* 223
56. *Ibid.* 224

57. *Ibid.* 225
58. *The Will* 87
59. *Ibid.* 91
60. *Ibid.* 92
61. *Ibid.*
62. *Ibid.* 90
63. *Ibid.* 97
64. *What Is* 163
65. *Ibid.* 165
66. *Ibid.* 14
67. *The Will* 146
68. *Ibid.* 85

69. *Ibid.* 253
70. *Ibid.* 70
71. *What Is* 48
72. *Ibid.* 74
73. *The Will* 14
74. *Ibid.* 20
75. *Ibid.*
76. *What Is* 15
77. *Ibid.* 16
78. *Ibid.* 223
79. *Ibid.* 226
80. *Ibid.* 228

81. *Ibid.* 200
82. *Ibid.* 134
83. *The Will* 55
84. *What Is* 155
85. *Ibid.* 15
86. *Ibid.* 53
87. *The Will* 199
88. *Ibid.* 126
89. *Ibid.* 123
90. *Ibid.* 27
91. *What Is* 152

VIII. THE NEW THOUGHT POETS

CITATIONS

1. *The Heart of New Thought* 6
2. *Ibid.* 36
3. *Ibid.* 11-12
4. *Ibid.* 16
5. *Ibid.* 79
6. *Ibid.* 76
7. *Ibid.* 20
8. *Ibid.* 51
9. *Ibid.* 25
10. *Ibid.* 49

11. *Ibid.* 28
12. *Ibid.* 39
13. *Ibid.* 79
14. *Ibid.* 76
15. *Ibid.* 33
16. *Ibid.* 34
17. *Ibid.* 60
18. *Ibid.* 51
19. *Ibid.* 54
20. *Ibid.* 40-41
21. *Ibid.* 41

22. *Ibid.* 44
23. *Ibid.* 63-65
24. *Ibid.* 66
25. *Ibid.*
26. *Ibid.* 69
27. *Ibid.*
28. *Ibid.* 70
29. *Ibid.* 71
30. *Ibid.* 91
31. *Ibid.* 92

IX. RALPH WALDO TRINE

CITATIONS

1. *What All the World's A-Seeking* 16
2. *Ibid.* 20, 30, 34, 162
3. *Ibid.* 50
4. *Ibid.* 58-59
5. *Ibid.* 87
6. *Ibid.* 95
7. *Ibid.* 111
8. *Ibid.* 112-113
9. *Ibid.* 116-117

10. *Ibid.* 146, 150-152
11. *Ibid.* 154-155; 160-161
12. *Ibid.* 185
13. *In Tune with the Infinite* 199
14. *Ibid.* 11-12
15. *Ibid.* 17
16. *Ibid.* 38-39
17. *Ibid.* 142-143

18. *Ibid.* 54
19. *Ibid.* 57
20. *Ibid.* 58
21. *Ibid.* 61
22. *Ibid.* 82-83
23. *Ibid.* 83
24. *Ibid.* 121
25. *Ibid.* 122
26. *Ibid.* 95
27. *Ibid.* 137

28. *Ibid.* 146
29. *New Alignment* 197
30. *In Tune* 205-209
31. *Ibid.* 204-205
32. *Ibid.* 29
33. *Ibid.* 198
34. *Ibid.* 176-177
35. *Ibid.* 192
36. *Ibid.* 178
37. *Ibid.* 181
38. *Ibid.* 187
39. *Ibid.* 190
40. *Ibid.* 30
41. *Ibid.* 140
42. *The New Alignment of Life* 18

43. *Ibid.* 39
44. *Ibid.* 45
45. *Ibid.*
46. *Ibid.* 55
47. *Ibid.* 58-59
48. *Ibid.* 135-141
49. *Ibid.* 61
50. *Ibid.* 62-63
51. *Ibid.* 63
52. *Ibid.* 64
53. *Ibid.* 66-67
54. *Ibid.* 69
55. *Ibid.* 74
56. *Ibid.* 75-80
57. *Ibid.* 80-85
58. *Ibid.* 95-100

59. *Ibid.* 102-103
60. *Ibid.* 105
61. *Ibid.* 119
62. *Ibid.* 122
63. *Ibid.* 125
64. *Ibid.* 126-127
65. *Ibid.* 129-134
66. *Ibid.* 160
67. *Ibid.* 72
68. *Ibid.* 191
69. *Ibid.* 193
70. *Ibid.*
71. *Ibid.* 195
72. *Ibid.* 201
73. *Ibid.* 212
74. *Ibid.* 224-225

X. JOEL GOLDSMITH

CITATIONS

1. *Conscious Union with God* 243
2. *God, the Substance of All Form* 19
3. Cf. discussion of Buddha's Illumination in *God, the Substance* 95-99
4. *The Art of Spiritual Healing* 123, 137; also *Conscious* 251
5. Cf. *Spiritual Interpretations of Scripture*
6. Cf. Bunyan's *Grace Abounding*
7. *The Art of SH* 27
8. *Ibid.* 63; *Conscious* 158
9. *Conscious* 79
10. *The Art of SH* 25, 141, 185
11. *Conscious* 48
12. *Ibid.* 65

13. *God, the Substance* 15
14. *The Art of SH* 40
15. *Living the Infinite Way* 33
16. *The Art of SH* 149, 184; *Conscious* 125, 126, 148
17. *Art of Meditation* 152; *The Art of SH* 12
18. *Conscious* 187; *Living* 47, 64; *God, the Substance* 108
19. *The Art of SH* 76, 110; *Living* 38
20. *God, the Substance* 53-54; *Conscious* 12; *Art of Meditation* 84
21. *Art of SH* 26; *Living* 81
22. *Art of SH* 28; *Living* 47

23. *Conscious* 12, 15; *God, the Substance* 12, 17, 116, 125, 126, 158
24. *Conscious* 21; *Living* 83-84; 85, 87; *God, the Substance* 42, 73
25. *Art of SH* 28, 41
26. *Conscious* 181
27. *Ibid.* 192
28. *Art of Med* 37
29. *Ibid.* 39
30. *Ibid.* 76
31. *Ibid.* 84
32. *Ibid.* 127; *God, the Substance* 53-54
33. *Conscious* 41
34. *Ibid.* 16
35. *Living* 93, 103
36. *God, the Substance* 68
37. *Ibid.* 72
38. *Ibid.* 62

39. *Living* 110
40. *Conscious* 37; *Art of Med* 77
41. *Art of Med* 19
42. *Conscious* 127
43. *Ibid.* 185, 186
44. *Ibid.* 191
45. *Living* 40, 110
46. *Conscious* 112
47. *Art of SH* 112-113
48. *Conscious* 78
49. *Ibid.* 17
50. *Art of SH* 118, 119; *Conscious* 45, 203
51. *Conscious* 76
52. *Ibid.* 202; *God the Substance* 82, 84
53. *Art of SH* 122
54. *God, the Substance* 86
55. *Living* 75
56. *Art of SH* 59
57. *Ibid.* 61, 63; *Conscious* 85
58. *God, the Substance* 75
59. *Art of SH* 33; *Conscious* 92
60. *Ibid.* 94; *Conscious* 84
61. *God, the Substance* 83
62. *Conscious* 43
63. *Ibid.* 63, 146, 163
64. *Ibid.* 138, 162
65. *Ibid.* 143
66. *Ibid.* 44

67. *Ibid.* 213
68. *Ibid.* 136
69. *Art of SH* 102
70. *God, the Substance* 61, 121
71. *Art of SH* 54
72. *Art of Med* 96
73. *Ibid.* 94
74. *Ibid.* 134
75. *Ibid.* 116
76. *Art of SH* 48
77. *Ibid.* 51
78. *God, the Substance* 15
79. *Art of SH* 11
80. *Ibid.* 32
81. *God, the Substance* 129
82. *Conscious* 143
83. *Ibid.* 135
84. *Art of SH* 13
85. *Art of Med* 118
86. *Ibid.*
87. *God, the Substance* 71, 172, 173
88. *Ibid.* 56
89. *Living* 32
90. *Ibid.* 22
91. *Art of Med* 137
92. *Ibid.* 138
93. *Art of SH* 54
94. *Ibid.* 19
95. *Ibid.* 136
96. *Art of Med* 54
97. *Ibid.*
98. *Conscious* 18
99. *Ibid.* 19

100. *Ibid.* 29
101. *Ibid.* 25
102. *Ibid.* 23
103. *Art of SH* 147
104. *Ibid.* 171; *Art of Med* 20, 92; *Conscious* 105; *God, the Substance* 15
105. *God, the Substance* 15
106. *Ibid.* 37
107. *Conscious* 227
108. *God, the Substance* 26
109. *Art of Med* 52-53
110. *Art of SH* 98
111. *Art of Med* 53
112. *God, the Substance* 39
113. *Living* 116, 120, 135
114. *Art of Med* 8
115. *God, the Substance* 93
116. *Living* 19
117. *Ibid.* 12-13
118. *Art of SH* 145
119. *Ibid.* 137-138
120. *God, the Substance* 64
121. *Ibid.* 37
122. *Living* 66
123. *Ibid.* 51
124. *Ibid.* 44
125. *Ibid.* 41
126. *Conscious* 151
127. *Ibid.* 121
128. *Ibid.*

XI. EMMETT FOX

CITATIONS

1. *Spirits in Rebellion* 353-355
2. *Power Through Con-*structive Thinking 123, 170
3. *Ibid.* 92
4. *Alter Your Life* 119-148; reprinted in *Around the Year*

11-19
5. *Power* 13-40
6. *Ibid.* 101-109
7. *Alter* 7-30
8. *Ibid.* 34-61
9. *Ibid.* 62-83
10. *Power* 100
11. *Ibid.* ix. Cf. *Sermon on the Mount* 12
12. *Ibid.* 118
13. *Ibid.* 75, 84, 105
14. *Ibid.* 10
15. *Ibid.* 96
16. *Ibid.* 102-103
17. *Sermon* 82-83
18. *Alter* 8
19. *Ibid.* 55

20. *Ibid.* 64
21. *Ibid.* 71
22. *Ibid.* 153; *Power* 2, 110, 173, 174
23. *Power* 259
24. *Ibid.* 265
25. *Ibid.* 137
26. *Ibid.* 113, 140
27. *Alter* 70
28. *Ibid.* 123
29. *Power* 178
30. *Ibid.* 131, 163
31. *Ibid.* 250
32. *Alter* 64
33. *Power* 143
34. *Ibid.* 91
35. *Ibid.* 201-230

36. *Ibid.* 203
37. *Ibid.* 205
38. *Ibid.* 207
39. *Ibid.* 208
40. *Ibid.*
41. *Ibid.* 209
42. *Ibid.*
43. *Ibid.* 211
44. *Ibid.* 212
45. *Ibid.* 214
46. *Ibid.* 216
47. *Ibid.* 223
48. *Ibid.* 230
49. *Ibid.* 234
50. *Ibid.* 238
51. *Ibid.* 247-248
52. *Ibid.* 241

XII. HORATIO W. DRESSER

CITATIONS

1. *Spirits in Rebellion*; 530-532
2. *Ibid.* 160
3. *In Search of a Soul* 36
4. *Ibid.* 90
5. *Ibid.* 108
6. *Ibid.* 113
7. *Ibid.* 120-121
8. *Ibid.* 21
9. *Ibid.*
10. *Ibid.* 192
11. *Ibid.* 196
12. *Ibid.* 168
13. *Ibid.* 187-188

14. *Ibid.* 213-214
15. *Methods and Problems of Spiritual Healing*
16. *Ibid.* 37
17. *Ibid.* 34
18. *Ibid.* 39
19. *Ibid.* 24-25
20. *Ibid.* 75-76
21. *Health and the Inner Life* 118-119
22. *Ibid.* 244
23. *Ibid.* 135
24. *Ibid.* 137
25. *Ibid.* 223

26. *Ibid.* 87
27. *Ibid.* 226
28. *Ibid.* 142
29. *A Physician of the Soul* 99
30. *Ibid.* 39
31. *Ibid.* 19
32. *Ibid.* 20-21
33. *Ibid.* 25
34. *Ibid.* 34
35. *Ibid.* 22-23
36. *Ibid.* 12-13
37. *Ibid.* 48-49
38. *The Philosophy of the Spirit* 114

XIII. CHRISTIAN DAA LARSON

CITATIONS

1. *Pathway of Roses* 17-18
2. *The Ideal Made Real* 251
3. *Pathway* 300
4. *Ibid.* 312

5. *Ibid.* 326
6. *Ibid.* 178
7. *Ibid.* 25
8. *Ibid.* 28
9. *Ibid.* 87
10. *Ibid.* 29
11. *Ibid.* 35
12. *Ibid.* 42
13. *Ibid.* 49
14. *Ibid.* 83
15. *Ibid.* 129
16. *Ibid.* 141
17. *Ibid.* 154
18. *Ibid.* 165
19. *Ibid.* 169
20. *Ibid.* 186
21. *Ibid.* 188
22. *Ibid.* 213 ff.
23. *Ibid.* 217
24. *Ibid.* 225
25. *Ibid.* 240, 242, 287
26. *Ibid.* 354
27. *The Ideal Made Real* 66
28. *Ibid.* 35
29. *Ibid.* 25
30. *Ibid.* 26
31. *Ibid.* 27-28
32. *Ibid.* 160-69
33. *Ibid.* 160
34. *Ibid.* 162
35. *Ibid.* 161-162
36. *Your Forces and How to Use Them* 23-34
37. *Ibid.* 170-171
38. *Ibid.* 171
39. *Ibid.* 58
40. *Ibid.* 219
41. *Ibid.* 220
42. *Ibid.* 229
43. *Ibid.* 18
44. *Ibid.* 20
45. *Ibid.* 24
46. *Ibid.* 26
47. *Ibid.* 39
48. *Ibid.*
49. *Ibid.*
50. *Ibid.* 41-42
51. *Ibid.* 49
52. *Ibid.* 53
53. *Ibid.* 61
54. *Ibid.* 67
55. *Ibid.* 31
56. *Ibid.* 74
57. *Ibid.* 75
58. *Ibid.* 89
59. *Ibid.* 94
60. *Ibid.* 139
61. *Ibid.* 164
62. *Ibid.* 165
63. *Ibid.* 170
64. *Ibid.*
65. *Ibid.* 172
66. *Ibid.* 63
67. *Ibid.* 62

XIV. ERNEST HOLMES AND FENWICKE L. HOLMES

CITATIONS

1. *Spirits in Rebellion* 286
2. Cf. above work
3. *The Law of the Mind in Action* 1
4. *Ibid.*
5. *The Faith That Heals* 69
6. *The Law* 166
7. *Ibid.* 167
8. *Ibid.* 20, 22, 46, 74, 86, 166
9. *The Faith* 18
10. *Ibid.* 17
11. *Ibid.* 25
12. *The Law* 93
13. *Ibid.* 124
14. *Ibid.* 139
15. *Ibid.* 170
16. *Ibid.* 174
17. *Ibid.* 188
18. *Ibid.* 195
19. *Ibid.* 15
20. *Ibid.* 40
21. *Ibid.* 76
22. *Ibid.* 206, 100
23. *Ibid.* 150
24. *Ibid.* 159
25. *Ibid.*
26. *Ibid.* 104
27. *Ibid.* 105
28. *Ibid.* 152
29. *Ibid.* 115
30. *Sc. of Mind* 98-99
31. *Ibid.* 26
32. *Ibid.* 35
33. *Ibid.* 48
34. *Ibid.* 67
35. *Ibid.* 70
36. *Ibid.* 611
37. *Ibid.* 77
38. *How to Use the Science of Mind* 87; *This Thing Called Life* 139
39. *This Thing* 60; *Science of Mind* 246, 98
40. *Sc. of Mind* 405
41. *Ibid.* 484-485
42. *This Thing* 121
43. *Sc. of Mind* 583
44. *Ibid.* 80, 81
45. *Ibid.* 373
46. *Ibid.* 480

47. *Ibid.* 392
48. *Ibid.* 390
49. *Ibid.* 608
50. *Ibid.* 599
51. *Ibid.* 106, 113, 134
52. *This Thing* 61
53. *Ibid.* 107
54. *How to Use* 76
55. *Sc. of Mind* 366
56. *Ibid.* 337
57. *Ibid.* 603
58. *Ibid.* 413
59. *Ibid.* 422
60. *Ibid.* 578-579
61. *Ibid.* 601
62. *Ibid.* 100
63. *Ibid.* 491
64. *Ibid.* 546-547
65. *Ibid.* 375
66. *Ibid.*
67. *Ibid.* 376
68. *Ibid.* 492
69. *Ibid.* 388
70. *Ibid.*
71. *Ibid.* 630
72. *Ibid.* 104
73. *Ibid.* 377, 379, 385
74. *Ibid.* 105
75. *Ibid.* 483, 581
76. *How to Use* 1, 4
77. *Ibid.* 35
78. *Ibid.* 45; *Sc. of Mind* 363
79. *This Thing* 112
80. *Ibid.* 129, 135
81. *Sc. of Mind* 11
82. *Ibid.* 585
83. *Ibid.* 584
84. *Ibid.* 383
85. *Ibid.* 623, 633
86. *Ibid.* 516
87. *Ibid.* 337
88. *Ibid.* 590
89. *Ibid.* 124
90. *Ibid.* 598
91. *This Thing* 28, 30
92. *How to Use* v
93. *Sc. of Mind* 219
94. *Ibid.* 320
95. *Ibid.* 145
96. *Ibid.* 237
97. *Ibid.* 240
98. *How to Use* 115
99. *Ibid.* 141
100. *Sc. of Mind* 215-216
101. *How to Use* 88-89
102. *Sc. of Mind* 177
103. *Ibid.* 585
104. *Ibid.* 589
105. *How to Use* 102; *Sc. of Mind* 624
106. *How to Use* 103
107. *Sc. of Mind* 409
108. *Ibid.* 137-138
109. *Ibid.* 163-164
110. *Ibid.* 365, 175
111. *Sc. of Mind* 252
112. *This Thing* 68
113. *Ibid.* 143
114. *Ibid.* 42
115. *How to Use* 11
116. *Ibid.* 44-45
117. *Ibid.* 97-98
118. *Ibid.* 69-70, 119
119. *Sc. of Mind* 183; *How to Use* 65
120. *Sc. of Mind* 178; *This Thing* 47
121. *This Thing* 130
122. *Sc. of Mind* 226
123. *Ibid.* 59
124. *Ibid.* 194
125. *Ibid.* 228
126. *Ibid.* 233, 443
127. *Ibid.* 243-244
128. *How to Use* 97
129. *Ibid.* 107
130. *Ibid.* 110
131. *Sc. of Mind* 305
132. *Ibid.* 394
133. *How to Use* 101
134. *Sc. of Mind* 631
135. *How to Use* 127, 128, 134; *Sc. of Mind* 279, 314, 287, 583; *This Thing* 44
136. *Ibid.* 449, 583
137. *Ibid.* 178
138. *Ibid.* 189, 412, 589, 590
139. *Ibid.* 228
140. *Ibid.* 233
141. *Ibid.* 382
142. *Ibid.* 504
143. *Ibid.* 220
144. *Ibid.* 231
145. *Ibid.* 575-646
146. *Ibid.* 441, 449, 463, 473-476
147. *Ibid.* 455
148. *Ibid.* 458
149. *How to Use* 140
150. *Ibid.* 141
151. *Ibid.*
152. *This Thing* 78-80
153. *Ibid.* 82-86
154. *Ibid.* 132-135
155. *Ibid.* 99-100
156. *Ibid.* 102-105
157. *Ibid.* 105
158. *Sc. of Mind* 620
159. *Ibid.* 635-636
160. *Ibid.* 33
161. *Ibid.* 604
162. *Ibid.* 262
163. *Ibid.* 613
164. *How to Use* 65
165. *Sc. of Mind* 300
166. *This Thing* 42
167. *Ibid.* 28
168. *Ibid.* 91

ADDITIONAL BIBLIOGRAPHY

The following books and authors, in addition to those listed in connection with the chapters on Swedenborg, the Shakers, and Christian Science, have been studied or consulted in the preparation of this work.

Addington, Jack Ensign, *Introduction to the Science of Mind*, 1954

Allen, James, *Eight Pillars of Prosperity*, Thomas Y. Crowell Co., New York, 1911

Anderson, Wing, *Health, Wealth, and Happiness While You Sleep*, The Kosmon Press, Los Angeles, 1948

Andrews, Edward Deming, *The People Called Shakers*, The Dover Publications, New York, 1963

Atkinson, W.W., *The Inner Consciousness*, Advanced Thought Publishing Co., Chicago, 1908

——*The Law of New Thought*, Psychic Research Co., Chicago, 1902

——*Reincarnation and the Law of Karma*, Yogi Publication Society

——*Mind Power: The Secret of Mental Magic*, Yogi Publication Society, Chicago, 1912

Bach, Marcus, *They Have Found a Faith*, Bobbs, Merrill Co., Indianapolis, 1946

——*The Unity Way of Life*, Prentice-Hall, New York, 1962

Bailes, Dr. Frederick, *The Secret of Healing*, Scrivener & Co., Los Angeles, 1962

——*The Spiritual Foundation of Freedom*, 1951

——*What Is This Power That Heals?* 1950

Barker, Raymond Charles, *How to Change Other People*, Author, New York, 1947

——*Money Is God in Action*, New York, 1960

Barney, Laura Clifford, *Some Questions Answered of Abdu'L—Baha*, Bahai Publishing Committee, Wilmette, Illinois, 1930

Baxter, Betty, *The Betty Baxter Story*, Published by Rev. Don Heidt, 1951

Beebe, Tom, *Who's Who in New Thought*, CSA Press, Lakemont, Georgia, 1977

Besant, Annie, *Esoteric Christianity*, Theosophical Publishing Home, Los Angeles, 1901

Blavatsky, H.P., *Isis Unveiled*, The Theosophy Co., Los Angeles, 1931
—— *The Secret Doctrine*, The Theosophical Publishing Co., London, 1888

Braden, Charles S., *Spirits in Rebellion*, SMU Press, Dallas, Texas, 1963
—— *These Also Believe*, Macmillan Co., New York, 1960
—— *Varieties of American Religion*, Willett, Clark and Co., 1949
—— *War, Communism, and World Religions*, Harper & Brothers, New York, 1953
—— *The World's Religions*, Abingdon Press, New York, 1954

Brooks, Nona L., *Mysteries*, Divine Science Federation International, Denver, 1924

Buskirk, J. Dale, *Religion, Healing, and Health*, Macmillan, New York, 1952

Butterworth, Eric, *Unity: A Quest for Truth*, Robert Speller & Sons, New York, 1965

Cady, Emilie, *God a Present Help*, Unity School of Christianity
—— *How I Used Truth*, Unity School of Christianity
—— *Lessons in Truth*, Unity School of Christianity

Carnegie, Dale, *How to Stop Worrying and Start Living*, Simon and Schuster, New York, 1951
—— *How to Win Friends and Influence People*, Simon and Schuster, New York, 1936

Clark, Glenn, *How I Found Health through Prayer*, Harper and Brothers, New York, 1940

Collier, Robert J., *The Secret of the Ages*, 7 vol., R. Collier, New York, 1926

Collins, Mabel, *Light on the Path of Karma*, The Theosophical Press, Wheaton, Illinois, 1944

Cramer, Malinda E., and James, Fannie B., *Divine Science: Its Principles and Practice*, Divine Science Federation International, Denver, 1957

Curtis, Donald, *How to Be Happy and Successful*, The Science of Mind Church of Religious Science, Los Angeles, 1960

D'Andrade, Hugh, *Charles Fillmore, Herald of a New Age*, Unity School of Christianity, 1974

Delme, Corinne, *Healing Miracles of Jesus Christ*, The New Age Press, Los Angeles, 1950

DeWaters, Lillian, *How to Have Health*, Stamford, Conn., 1919
—— *The Time Is at Hand*, Stamford, Conn. 1930

Dinnet, Ernest, *What We Live By*, Simon and Schuster, New York, 1932

Douglas, Lloyd, *Magnificent Obsession*, Willet Clark & Co., Chicago, 1933

Dresser, Annetta Gertrude, *The Philosophy of P.P. Quimby*, The Church of Truth, Boston, 1895

Dresser, Horatio W., *Health and the Inner Life*, G.P. Putnam's Sons, 1906

——*A History of New Thought*, Thomas Y. Crowell Co., New York, 1919

——*In Search of a Soul*, G.P. Putnam's Sons, New York, 1907

——*Methods and Problems of Spiritual Healing*, G.P Putnam's Sons, 1899

——*The Philosophy of the Spirit*, G.P. Putnam's Sons, New York, 1908

——*A Physician of the Soul*, G.P. Putnam's Sons, New York, 1908

——*The Spirit of New Thought*, George G. Harrap and Co., Ltd., London, 1917

Dresser, Julius A., *The True History of Mental Science*, Alfred Midge and Son, Boston, 1887

Drummond, Henry, *The Greatest Thing in the World*, Collins, London

——*Natural Law in the Spiritual World*, H.M. Caldwell Co., New York

Eddy, Mary Baker, *Concordance to Miscellaneous Writings*, Trustees under the Will of Mary Baker Eddy, Boston, 1915

——*Historical Sketch of Metaphysical Healing*, Author, Boston, 1885

Esslemont, J.E., *Baha-U'Llah and The New Era*, Bahai Publishing Trust, Wilmette, Illinois, 1950

Evans, Warren Felt, *The Divine Law of Cure*, H.H. Carter, Boston, 1881

——*Esoteric Christianity and Mental Therapeutics*, H.H. Carter and Karrick, Boston, 1886

——*Mental Cure: Illustrating the Influences of the Mind on the Body*, H.H. Carter, Boston, 1872

——*Mental Medicine: A Theoretical Treatise on Medical Psychology*, H.H. Carter, Boston, 1872

——*The Primitive Mind-Cure*, H.H. Carter, Boston, 1884

——*Soul and Body; Or The Spiritual Science of Health and Disease*, Colby & Rich, Boston, 1876

Favorite Radio Talks, A Compilation, Unity School of Christianity, 1950

Fillmore, Charles, *Atom-Smashing Power of Mind*, Unity School of Christianity, 1949

——*Christian Healing*, Unity, 1941

——*Jesus Christ Heals*, Unity, 1939

——*Keep a True Lent*, Unity, 1953

——*Mysteries of Genesis*, Unity, 1936

——*Mysteries of John*, Unity, 1965

——*New Ways to Solve Problems*, Unity, 1947

——*Prosperity*, Unity, 1960

——*Talks on Truth*, Unity, 1965

——*The Twelve Powers of Man*, Unity, 1964

——*You Can Be Healed*, Unity, 1937

Fillmore, Charles, and Cora, *Teach Us to Pray*, Unity
——*Christ Enshrined in Man*, Unity
Fillmore, Lowell, *Things To Be Remembered*, Unity
——*The Prayer Way to Health, Wealth, and Happiness*, Unity, 1964
Fillmore, Myrtle, *How to Let God Help You*, Unity, 1956
——*Letters*, Unity, 1936
Fosdick, Harry Emerson, *Adventurous Religion*, Grosset and Dunlap, New York, 1946
——*Living under Tension*, Harper and Brothers, New York, 1941
——*The Man from Nazareth*, Harper and Brothers, New York, 1949
——*The Meaning of Service*, Association Press, New York, 1920
——*The Modern Use of the Bible*, Macmillan Co., New York, 1924
——*On Being Fit to Live With*, Harper and Brothers, New York, 1914
——*What is Vital in Religion?* Harper and Brothers, New York, 1931
Fox, Emmet, *Alter Your Life*, Harper and Brothers, New York, 1931
——*Around the Year with Emmet Fox*, Harper and Brothers, New York, 1952
——*The Four Horsemen of the Apocalypse*, Harper and Brothers, New York, 1942
——*The Golden Key*, Harper and Brothers, New York, 1931
——*Life As Consciousness*, Unity School of Christianity, 1955
——*Make Your Life Worth While*, Harper and Brothers, New York, 1942
——*Power through Constructive Thinking*, Harper and Brothers, New York, 1932
——*Reincarnation*, Harper and Brothers, New York, 1939
——*The Sermon on the Mount*, Harper and Brothers, New York, 1934
——*The Seven Days of Creation*, Harper and Brothers, New York, 1945
——*The Seven Main Aspects of God*, Harper and Brothers, New York, 1942
——*Sparks of Truth*, Grosset and Dunlap, New York, 1937
Freeman, James Dillet, *The Household of Faith*, Unity School, 1951
——*The Story of Unity*, Unity School, 1951
——*The Story of Unity*, Unity School, 1978
Gatlin, Dana, *Prayer Changes Things*, Unity School
Gestefeld, Ursula, *How to Control Circumstances*, Exodus Publishing Co., Chicago 1908
——*The Joyous Birth*, Exodus Publishing Co., Chicago, 1910
——*The Science of the Larger Life*, William Rider & Son, London, 1909
Goldsmith, Margaret, *Franz Anton Mesmer*, Doubleday, Doran, & Co., Garden City, New York, 1934
Goldsmith, Joel, *The Art of Meditation*, Harper and Brothers, New York, 1956
——*The Art of Spiritual Healing*, Harper and Brothers, New York, 1959

———*Business and Salesmanship*, Willing Publishing Co., San Gabriel, Calif., 1947

———*Conscious Union with God*, The Julian Press, New York, 1962

———*God, the Substance of All Form*, University Books, New York, 1962

Grattan, C. Hartley, *The Three Jameses*, New York University Press, New York, 1962

Green, Arthur Jay, *Not Anything Happens by Chance*, Church of Divine Truth and College of Mental Science, Seattle, Wash.

Hall, Manly Palmer, *The Adepts: The Arhats of Buddhism*, Philosophical Research Society, Los Angeles, 1957

Hamblin, Henry Thomas, *Divine Adjustment*, Science of Thought Press, Chichester, 1937

Harrison, John F.C., *Quest for the New World: Robert Owen and the Owenites*, Charles Scribner's Sons, New York, 1969

Hart, H. Martyn, D.D., *A Way That Seemeth Right*, James Ratt & Co., New York, 1897

Hawkins, Ann Ballew, *Phineas Parkhurst Quimby, Revealer of Spiritual Healing to This Age*, DeVorss, Los Angeles, 1951

Holley, Horace, *Bahai Scriptures*, Brentano's, New York, 1923

Holliwell, Raymond, *Working with the Law*, Author, 1939

Holloway, Mark, *Heavens on Earth: Utopian Communities in America*, Dover Publications, New York, 1966

Holmes, Ernest, *Alcoholism, Its Cause and Cure*, Institute of Religious Science, Los Angeles, 1941

———*The Bible in the Light of Religious Science*, Robert M. McBride Co., New York, 1929

———*Creative Mind*, Dodd, Mead & Co., New York, 1957

———*Discover the Richer Life*, Science of Mind Publications, Los Angeles, 1978

———*Freedom from Stress*, Science of Mind Publications, Los Angeles, 1964

———*Freedom to Live*, Science of Mind Publications, Los Angeles, 1969

———*How to Develop the Faith That Heals*, Robert M. McBride Co., New York, 1925

———*How to Use Science of Mind*, Dodd, Mead & Co., New York, 1948

———*Ideas for Living*, Science of Mind Publications, Los Angeles, 1979

———*It's Up to You*, Science of Mind Publications, Los Angeles, 1980

———*Know Yourself*, Science of Mind Publications, Los Angeles, 1982

———*Science of Mind*, Dodd, Mead & Co., New York, 1961

———*This Thing Called Life*, Dodd, Mead & Co., New York, 1953

———*This Thing Called You*, Dodd, Mead & Co., New York, 1948

———*What Religious Science Teaches*, Institute of Religious Science, 1944

—— *Words That Heal Today*, Dodd, Mead & Co., New York, 1949

—— *Your Invisible Power*, Church of Religious Science, 1940

Holmes, Ernest, and Kinnear, Willis, *A New Design for Living*, Prentice-Hall, Englewood Cliffs, N.J., 1959

—— *Practical Application of Science of Mind*, Science of Mind Publications, Los Angeles, 1958

—— *It Can Happen to You*, Science of Mind Publications, Los Angeles, 1959

Holmes, Fenwicke L., *The Law of the Mind in Action*, Robert M. McBride, New York, 1930

—— *Twenty Secrets of Success*, Robert M. McBride, New York, 1927

—— *Ernest Holmes: His Life and Times*, Dodd, Mead & Co., New York, 1970

Hopkins, Emma Curtis, *Esoteric Philosophy in Spiritual Science*, High Watch Fellowship, Cornwall Bridge, Conn.

—— *High Mysticism*, High Watch Fellowship

—— *Scientific Christian Mental Practice*, High Watch Fellowship

—— *Understanding the Scriptures*, High Watch Fellowship, 1940

Hornaday, William H.D., *Life Everlasting*, DeVorss & Co.

—— *Success Unlimited*, DeVorss, Santa Monica, Calif., 1952

Hyde, Lawrence, *Isis and Osiris*, E.P. Dutton & Co., New York, 1948

Ingraham, E.V., *Meditation in the Silences*, Unity School of Christianity

James, William, *Human Immortality*, Houghton, Mifflin & Co., New York, 1898

—— *The Meaning of Truth*, Longmans, Green & Co., New York, 1909

—— *Pragmatism*, Longmans, Green & Co., 1948

—— *Selected Papers on Philosophy*, E.P. Dutton, New York, 1917

—— *Varieties of Religious Experience*, Longmans, Green & Co., 1908

—— *The Will to Believe*, Longmans, Green & Co., 1907

Jones, E. Stanley, *Abundant Living*, Abingdon-Cokesbury, New York, 1922

—— *The Way to Power and Poise*, Abingdon-Cokesbury, New York, 1926

Keller, Helen, *My Religion*, Bard Books, Avon Book Division, New York, 1927

Kinnear, Willis, and Holmes, Ernest, *A New Design for Living*, 1982

—— *The Creative Power of Mind*, Prentice-Hall, New York, 1957

Krishnamurti, Jedda, *The Kingdom of Happiness*, Boni and Liverwright, New York, 1927

Laird, Margaret, *All Is One*, Laird Foundation, Los Angeles, 1957

—— *Government Is Self-Government*, Portal Press, Chicago, 1952

Larson, Christian Daa, *The Creative Power of Mind*, L.N. Fowler Co., London

—— *The Great Within*, L.N. Fowler, London

——*The Ideal Made Real*, Thomas Y. Crowell Co., New York, 1912

——*Leave It to God*, DeVorss & Co., Marina del Rey, Calif., 1968

——*The Pathway of Roses*, Thomas Y. Crowell Co., New York

——*Your Forces and How to Use Them*, L.N. Fowler, London, 1906

Levi, *The Aquarian Gospel of Jesus Christ*, DeVorss & Co., Marina del Rey, Calif. 1981

Lewis, Edwin, *The Revival Pulpit*, Nashville, Tenn., 1944

Lichtenstein, Rabbi Morris, *Jewish Science and Health*, Jewish Science Publishing Co., New York, 1925

Liebman, Joshua Loth, *Peace of Mind*, Simon and Schuster, New York, 1946

McKenzie, John, *Two Religions: Hinduism and Christianity*, The Beacon Press, Boston, 1952

Maltz, Maxwell, *Psycho-Cybernetics*, Wilshire Book Co., North Hollywood, Calif., 1960

Marden, Orison Swett, *How to Get What You Want*, Thomas Y. Crowell Co., New York, 1917

Metaphysical Bible Dictionary, Unity School of Christianity, 1960

Militz, Annie Rix, *Both Riches and Honor*, Unity School

Miller, R. DeWitt, *You DO Take It with You*, Citadel Press, New York, 1955

Muller, Herbert J., *Religion and Freedom in the Modern World*, University of Chicago Press, Chicago, 1963

Murphy, Joseph, *The Amazing Laws of Cosmic Mind-Power*, Parker Publishing Co., West Nyack, New York, 1973

——*The Cosmic Energizer: the Miracle Power of the Universe*, Parker Publishing Co., 1974

——*How to Attract Money*, Willing Publishing Co., San Gabriel, Calif., 1955

——*The Miracle of Mind Dynamics*, Prentice-Hall, Englewood Cliffs, N.J. 1964

——*Peace within Yourself*, DeVorss & Co., Marina del Rey, Calif.

——*The Power of Your Subconscious Mind*, Prentice-Hall, Englewood Cliffs, N.J., 1963

——*Quiet Moments with God*, DeVorss & Co., Marina del Rey, Calif., 1958

——*Riches Are Your Right*, Willing Publishing Co., San Gabriel, Calif., 1952

——*Telepsychics, the Magic Power of Perfect Living*, Parker Publishing Co., West Nyack, New York, 1973

——*Within You Is the Power*, DeVorss & Co., Marina del Rey, Calif., 1977

Newhouse, Flower A., *Natives of Eternity*, Lawrence G. Newhouse, Vista, Calif., 1950

Nordhoff, Charles, *The Communistic Societies in the United States*, Hillary House Publishers, New York, 1961

Noyes, John Humphrey, *History of American Socialisms*, Hillary House Publishers, Ltd., New York, 1962

Ouseley, S.G.J., *Science of the Aura*, L.N. Fowler Co., London, 1949

Page, Kirby, *How Does God Deal with Evildoers?*, Author, LaHabra, Calif.

———*Living Abundantly*, Farrar & Rinehart, New York, 1944

———*Living Joyously*, Rinehart & Co., New York, 1950

———*The Meek Shall Inherit the Earth*, Author, LaHabra, Calif., 1948

———*Power from the Bible*, Author, LaHabra, Calif.

Palmer, Clara, *You Can Be Healed*, Unity School of Christianity, 1937

Parker, Theodore, *Collected Works*, 2 vol., Trubner & Co., London, 1879

Patterson, Charles Brodie, *The Will to Be Well*, The Alliance Publishing Co., New York, 1902

———*What Is New Thought?*, Thomas Y. Crowell Co., New York, 1913

Peale, Norman Vincent, *The Art of Living*, Doubleday & Co., New York, 1938

———*A Guide to Confident Living*, Prentice-Hall, New York, 1948

———*Not Death to All*, Prentice-Hall, Englewood Cliffs, N.J., 1948

———*The Power of Positive Thinking*, Prentice-Hall, 1952

———*Sin, Sex, and Self-Control*, Doubleday & Co., Garden City, New York, 1965

———*Stay Alive All Your Life*, Prentice-Hall, Englewood Cliffs, 1957

———*The Tough-Minded Optimist*, Prentice-Hall, Englewood Cliffs, 1961

Pratt, George K., M.D., *Your Mind and You*, Funk & Wagnalls Co., New York, 1924

Quimby (From) to Christ Truth, The Christ Truth Foundation, Portland, Oregon

Quimby, P.P., *The Philosophy of P.P. Quimby*, Edited by Annetta Gertrude Dresser, The Builder's Press, Boston, 1895

———*The Quimby Manuscripts*, Thomas Y. Crowell Co., New York, 1921

———*The Quimby Manuscripts*, The Julian Press, New York, 1961

Rabani, Ruthyyth, *Prescription for Living*, Bahái Publishing Committee, Oxford, England

Ramacharaka, Yogi, *Hatha Yoga, Or the Philosophy of Well-Being*, Yogi Publication Co., Chicago, 1932

———*Gnani Yoga*, The Yogi Publication Society, Chicago, 1906

Rawson, F.L., *Healing by the Realization of God*, Society for Spreading the Knowledge of True Prayer, 1918

———*Life Understood from a Religious and Scientific Point of View*, Crystal Press, London, 1912

———*Man's Concept of God*, London, 1935

———*The Nature of Prayer*, London, 1930

———*Plea for the Open Door*, Crystal Press, London, 1915

———*True Prayer in Business*, Crystal Press, London, 1917

Regardie, Israel, *The Romance of Metaphysics*, The Aries Press, Chicago, 1946

Rix, Harriet Hale, *Christian Mind Healing*, Master Mind Publishing Co., Los Angeles, 1914

Royce, Josiah, *The Religious Aspect of Philosophy*, Harper and Brothers, New York, 1958

Russell, Robert Alfred, *The Creative Silence*, Denver, 1961

Salisbury, Mary E., *From Day to Day with the Faithful*, Barse and Hopkins, New York, 1912

——*From Day to Day with New Thought*, Barse and Hopkins, New York, 1912

Scott, Ernest F., *The Ethical Teachings of Jesus*, Macmillan Co., New York, 1960

Seabury, David, *Help Yourself to Happiness*, Garden City Publishing Co., Garden City, New York, 1942

——*How Jesus Heals Our Minds Today*, Little, Brown & Co., Boston, 1940

——*How to Get Things Done*, Little, Brown & Co., New York, 1949

Seale, Ervin, *Learn to Live: The Meaning of the Parables*, Science of Mind Publications, Los Angeles, 1965

——*Ten Words That Will Change Your Life*, William Morrow & Co., New York, 1954

Sears, William, *Thief in the Night*, George Ronald, London, 1961

——*The Wine of Astonishment*, George Ronald, Garden City Press, Great Britain, 1965

Seton, Julia, *Concentration: The Secret of Success*, E.J. Clode, New York, 1912

——*The Key to Health, Wealth, and Life*, E.J. Clode, New York, 1917

Shanklin, Imelda, *Selected Studies*, Unity School of Christianity, 1926

Shenck, Ruthane, *Being Prospered*, Unity School of Christianity, 1928

Simpson, James Y., *The Spiritual Interpretation of Nature*, Hodder and Stoughton, London, 1912

Spaulding, Baird T., *Life and Teachings of the Masters of the Far East*, 2 vol., California Press, San Francisco, 1924

Swananda, Swami, *Divine Life*, Swanada Publication League, Himalaya, 1950

Swedenborg, Emanuel, *Heavenly Doctrine*, The Swedenborg Society of London, 1911

——*Religion and Life*, The Swedenborg Society, London, 1961

Sykes, John, *The Quakers*, J.B. Lippincott, Co., New York, 1959

Tonge, Mildred, *A Sense of Living*, Pendle Hall, Penna., 1954

Towne, Elizabeth, *Practical Methods for Self-Development*, The Elizabeth Towne Co., Holyoke, Mass., 1904

Townshend, George, *Christ and Baha'U'llah*, George Ronald, London, 1957

Trine, Ralph Waldo, *The Higher Powers of the Mind and Spirit*, Dodge, 1913

——*In Tune with the Infinite*, Thomas Y. Crowell & Co., New York, 1897

——*The New Alignment of Life*, Dodge Publishing Co., New York, 1913

——*What All the World's A-Seeking*, Thomas Y. Crowell & Co., New York, 1896

Trobridge, George, *Swedenborg: Life and Teaching*, The Swedenborg Foundation, New York, 1955

Troward, Judge Thomas, *The Creative Process in the Individual*, Robert McBride & Co., New York, 1932

——*The Doré Lectures*, Dodd, Mead & Co., New York, 1909

——*The Edinburgh Lectures on Mental Science*, Dodd, Mead & Co., New York, 1909

——*The Hidden Power*, Robert McBride & Co., New York, 1921

——*The Law and the Word*, Robert M. McBride & Co., New York, 1925

Tweedle, Violet, *The Cosmic Christ*, Rider & Co., London, 1930

Vining, Elizabeth Gray, *The World in Tune*, Pendle Hall, 1952

We Knew Mary Baker Eddy, Series of Three Volumes by Admirers, Christian Science Publishing Society, Boston, 1943, 1950, 1953

Wilcox, Ella Wheeler, *The Heart of New Thought*, Psychic Research Co., Chicago, 1902

——*New Thought and Common Sense*, W.B. Conkey, Chicago, 1908

Wilson, Ernest C., *The Great Physician*, Unity School of Christianity, 1935

——*Have We Lived Before?* Unity School

Wilson, Margary, *Believe in Yourself*, J.B. Lippincott, Philadelphia, 1948

Witherspoon, Thomas E., *Myrtle Fillmore: Mother of Unity*, The Unity School of Christianity

Wood, Henry, *The New Thought Simplified: How to Gain Harmony and Health*, Lee Shepherd, Boston, 1904

——*The Symphony of Life*, Lee Shepherd, Boston, 1904

Young, Frederick Harold, *The Philosophy of Henry James, Sr.*, College and University Press, New Haven, Conn. 1951

Zweig, Stefan, *Mental Healers*, The Viking Press, New York, 1932

INDEX